Police Behavior, Hiring, and Crime Fighting

This edited collection by internationally recognized authors provides essays on police behavior in the categories of police administration, police operations, and combating specific crimes. Individual chapters strike at critical issues for police today, such as maintaining the well-being of officers, handling stress, hiring practices, child sexual exploitation, gunrunning, crime prevention strategies, police legitimacy, and much more.

Understanding how police are hired and behave is a way of understanding different governments around the world. The book will cover the practices of countries as diverse as China, Germany, India, Japan, Turkey, South Africa, the United States, and others. Readers will be exposed to aspects of police that are rarely, if ever, explored.

The book is intended for a wide range of audiences, including law enforcement and community leaders and students of criminal justice.

John A. Eterno received his Ph.D. from the State University of New York at Albany. He is a professor, associate dean, and director of graduate studies in criminal justice at Molloy College and a retired captain from the New York Police Department. Molloy College has recognized his accomplishments with specific awards in various areas, including research/publication, teaching, and service. He has penned numerous books, book chapters, articles, and editorials on various topics in policing. Some examples of his most recent publications: an op-ed in the *New York Times* titled "Policing by the Numbers"; peer-reviewed articles in outlets such as *Justice Quarterly*, *Public Administration Review*, and *Police Practice and Research*; and books including *The Crime Numbers Game: Management by Manipulation* (with Eli B. Silverman), *The New York City Police Department: The Impact of Its Policies and Practices*, and *The Detective's Handbook* (with Cliff Roberson).

Ben Stickle, Ph.D., is an associate professor of criminal justice administration at Middle Tennessee State University and has been teaching criminal justice courses since 2010. He holds a Bachelor of Arts in sociology from Cedarville University and a Master's of Science and Doctor of Philosophy in justice administration from the University of Louisville. His research interests include policing, property crime, and emerging crime types (package theft and metal theft), focusing on crime prevention, environmental crime, rational choice, and qualitative methods. Stickle has published in peer-reviewed journals such as the *American Journal of Criminal Justice*, *Police Practice and Research*, *Criminal Justice Policy Review*, and *Policing: An International Journal*, and is the author of *Metal Scrappers and Thieves: Scavenging for Survival and Profit*. He frequently engages in practitioner partnerships with over 20 years' experience in the criminal justice field and currently serves as a program evaluator for several Bureau of Justice Assistance grants focused on justice-mental health responses, offender reentry, and human trafficking.

Diana Scharff Peterson, Ph.D., has nearly 20 years of experience in higher education, teaching in the areas of research methods; comparative criminal justice systems; race, gender, class, and crime; statistics; criminology; sociology; and drugs and behavior at seven different institutions of higher education. Scharff Peterson has been the chairperson of three different criminal justice programs over the past 15 years and has published in the areas of criminal justice, social work, higher education, sociology, business, and management. Her research interests include issues in policing (training and education) and community policing, assessment and leadership in higher education, family violence, and evaluation research and program development. She was Professor of Criminology and Graduate Program Director at the University of Texas of the Permian Basin. She has published more than 30 articles in areas of criminal justice, sociology, social work, business management, and higher education and is the liaison and representative for the International Police Executive Symposium (consultative status) for quarterly annual meetings at the United Nations in New York City, Geneva, and Vienna, including the Commission on the Status of Women in New York City. She formerly served as the managing editor of *Police Practice and Research: An International Journal*.

Dilip K. Das, Ph.D., is the president, International Police Executive Symposium (IPES), and editor-in-chief, *Police Practice and Research: An International Journal*. After receiving his Master's degree in English literature, Das joined the Indian Police Service, an elite national service. After 14 years in the service as a police executive, including chief of police, he moved to the USA in 1979, where he achieved another Master's degree in criminal justice, as well as a doctorate in the same discipline. Das has authored, edited, and co-edited more than 40 books and numerous articles. He is the series editor of *Advances in Police Theory and Practice* and *International Police Executive Symposium Co-Publications*. He has traveled extensively throughout the world in comparative police research; as a visiting professor at various universities, including organizing annual conferences of the IPES; and as a human rights consultant to the United Nations. Das has received several faculty excellence awards and was a distinguished faculty lecturer.

Advances in Police Theory and Practice Series

Series Editor: Dilip K. Das

Cold Cases: Evaluation Models with Follow-Up Strategies for Investigators, Second Edition
James M. Adcock and Sarah L. Stein

Crime Linkage: Theory, Research, and Practice
Jessica Woodhams and Craig Bennell

Police Investigative Interviews and Interpreting: Context, Challenges, and Strategies
Sedat Mulayim, Miranda Lai, and Caroline Norma

Policing White-Collar Crime: Characteristics of White-Collar Criminals
Petter Gottschalk

Honor-Based Violence: Policing and Prevention
Karl Anton Roberts, Gerry Campbell, and Glen Lloyd

Policing and the Mentally Ill: International Perspectives
Duncan Chappell

Security Governance, Policing, and Local Capacity
Jan Froestad and Clifford Shearing

Police Performance Appraisals: A Comparative Perspective
Serdar Kenan Gul and Paul O'Connell

Policing in France
Jacques de Maillard and Wesley G. Skogan

Women in Policing around the World: Doing Gender and Policing in a Gendered Organization
Venessa Garcia

Police Behavior, Hiring, and Crime Fighting: An International View
Edited by John A. Eterno, Ben Stickle, Diana Scharff Peterson, and Dilip K. Das

Police Behavior, Hiring, and Crime Fighting

An International View

Edited by
John A. Eterno, Ben Stickle,
Diana Scharff Peterson, and Dilip K. Das

NEW YORK AND LONDON

First published 2022
by Routledge
605 Third Avenue, New York, NY 10158

and by Routledge
2 Park Square, Milton Park, Abingdon, Oxon, OX14 4RN

Routledge is an imprint of the Taylor & Francis Group, an informa business

© 2022 Taylor & Francis

The right of John A. Eterno, Ben Stickle, Diana Scharff Peterson, and Dilip K. Das to be identified as the authors of the editorial material, and of the authors for their individual chapters, has been asserted in accordance with sections 77 and 78 of the Copyright, Designs and Patents Act 1988.

All rights reserved. No part of this book may be reprinted or reproduced or utilised in any form or by any electronic, mechanical, or other means, now known or hereafter invented, including photocopying and recording, or in any information storage or retrieval system, without permission in writing from the publishers.

Trademark notice: Product or corporate names may be trademarks or registered trademarks, and are used only for identification and explanation without intent to infringe.

Library of Congress Cataloging-in-Publication Data
Names: Eterno, John, 1959– editor.
Title: Police behavior, hiring and crime fighting : an international view /
   edited by John A. Eterno, Ben Stickle, Diana Peterson, and Dilip K. Das.
Description: New York, NY : Routledge, 2022. | Series: Advances in police
   theory and practice | Includes bibliographical references.
Identifiers: LCCN 2021013400 (print) | LCCN 2021013401 (ebook) | ISBN
   9780367497156 (hardback) | ISBN 9780367491000 (paperback) | ISBN
   9781003047117 (ebook)
Subjects: LCSH: Police—Cross-cultural studies. | Crime
   prevention—Cross-cultural studies. | Law enforcement—Cross-cultural
   studies.
Classification: LCC HV7921 .P554 2022 (print) | LCC HV7921 (ebook) | DDC
   363.2—dc23
LC record available at https://lccn.loc.gov/2021013400
LC ebook record available at https://lccn.loc.gov/2021013401

ISBN: 978-0-367-49715-6 (hbk)
ISBN: 978-0-367-49100-0 (pbk)
ISBN: 978-1-003-04711-7 (ebk)

DOI: 10.4324/9781003047117

Typeset in Bembo
by Apex CoVantage, LLC

Access the Support Material: www.routledge.com/9780367491000

Contents

Acknowledgments	x
Editors' Introduction	xi
Series Editor's Preface	xiii
List of Contributor Biographies	xvi

PART I
Police Behavior
1

1 **Cultivating Well-Being Among Police Officers: Examining Challenges in the Workplace**
3

PHILIP BIRCH, MARGARET H. VICKERS, SALLY GALOVIC, AND MICHAEL KENNEDY

2 **An Interdisciplinary Perspective on the Tragedy of Police-Citizen Encounters: From Social Dilemma via Fairness to Coordination**
22

KATHARINA FRIEDERIKE STRÄTER AND RENÉ HORNUNG

3 **The Doctrine of Minimum Force in Policing: Origins, Uncertainties, and Implications**
39

RICHARD EVANS AND CLARE FARMER

4 **Perceptions of Police Officers of the Floating Population: A Pilot Study of Community Justice Initiatives in China**
56

JURG GERBER AND DI JIA

5 **Municipal Police Department's Use of Facebook: Exploring the Potential for Differences Across Size Classifications**
66

BRADLEY D. EDWARDS, DUSTIN L. OSBORNE, RYCHELLE MOSES, LOGAN S. LEDFORD, AND GABRIELA SMITH

6 **Consent Decrees on Police Organizations: Policies and Practices**
83

ALLAN Y. JIAO

7 **Police Discretion: An Issue of Untestable Reasonability in a Law Enforcement Process**
97

JEAN CLAUDE GEOFREY MAHORO

viii Contents

8 The Role of Legitimacy in Police Reform and Effectiveness:
A Case Study on the Bangladesh National Police   111
HEATH GRANT, SHANNA O'REILLY, AND STACI STROBL

9 Police Behavior and Public Understanding: Insights and Innovations   128
JOHN A. ETERNO

PART II
Hiring and Training   141

10 Hired With Competence: An Examination of Police Hiring
Standards in Canada   143
SCOTT E. BLANDFORD

11 An Examination of Police Corruption Utilizing the Theory
of Planned Behavior   161
BEN STICKLE

12 Relationship of Police Stress With Coping, Moral Reasoning,
and Burnout   174
PRIYA XAVIER

13 An Evaluation of Safety and Security: A South African Perspective   191
DORAVAL GOVENDER

14 The Effects of Medical and Recreational Marijuana Policies on
Hiring in US Municipal Police Departments: A Case Study of
Mesa Police Department, Mesa, AZ   204
DIANA SCHARFF PETERSON AND CARLOS AVALOS

PART III
Crime Control   215

15 Policing Cybercrime: Is There a Role for the Private Sector?   217
RICK SARRE

16 Gunrunning 101: A How-To Guide About What to Look For   228
GREGG W. ETTER SR. AND JEFFERY M. JOHNSON

17 United We Stand: Collaborations to Combat Human Trafficking in
Central Florida   242
KETTY FERNÁNDEZ, MADELYN DIAZ, JOLENE VINCENT, LIN HUFF-CORZINE, JAY
CORZINE, AND TOMAS J. LARES

Contents ix

18 Are Attacks Against Abortion Providers Acts of Domestic Terrorism?: A Three-Box Operational Sub-Theory of Merton's Anomie 253

GREGG W. ETTER SR. AND HANNAH COLLISON (*NEE SOCHA*)

19 Freedom Versus Safety on the Roadways in Mesa, AZ: Analysis of Distracted Driving Incidents 270

DIANA SCHARFF PETERSON

20 An Overview of Wildlife Enforcement Cooperation in Canada and North America 287

SAMANTHA DE VRIES

21 A National Perspective on Retail Theft 301

MELODY HICKS AND BEN STICKLE

22 Sustained Footwear Characteristics Across Athletic Footwear Over Several Years: A Case Study of Impression Wear Patterns for Investigative Value 311

LEE M. WADE

Index 319

Acknowledgments

A collective work like this cannot happen without a tremendous effort by many people. We want to thank Dr. Dilip K. Das for his work in founding the International Police Executive Symposium. Without his forward thinking, this book would not be possible. We also want to thank our families for putting up with all the work and time we have dedicated to this compendium. In addition, we want to thank four graduate assistants—Patrick Ruland, Katherine McCabe, Elizanne Warren-Russell, and Garrett Jeanes—whose tireless work and dedication to this project cannot be overstated.

Editors' Introduction

Police Behavior, Hiring, and Crime Fighting is the culmination of years of work. Internationally renowned scholars and practitioners author the 24 chapters. The editors have woven a tapestry of countries and current issues facing modern policing. Chapters range from police stress, social media use, police legitimacy, and police discretion to discussions on fighting human trafficking, wildlife crime, and retail theft. This volume brings together research and practices worldwide, contributing to an understanding of policing to help scholars, leaders, experts, and students address the volatile situation with law enforcement today.

The editors laboriously selected authors for their expertise, region, and topic. Then, we carefully vetted these chapters and meticulously determined where the chapters fit and had authors write and rewrite until we were satisfied that the authors' meanings were clear to the reader. Additionally, we added discussion questions to each chapter's end as a unique feature to spur discussion and as a springboard for future research. Beyond all this, most of these chapters were presented at major international conferences by scholars and practitioners who provided first-hand insights into the issues. This volume will be an excellent text or reader for various classes in criminal justice and related programs. Disciplines such as cross-cultural studies, policing, law enforcement, homeland security, controlling deviance, police hiring, and training are only a few of the many subject areas covered in this compendium. As the authors are scholars and leaders in the field, no other single volume touches on the wide variety of topics covered. Whether one is interested in cybersecurity or the police culture, this volume succinctly covers nearly any topic of interest in the areas of police behavior, hiring, and crime fighting. Police leaders will also find this book full of innovative ideas to help guide them through current policing issues.

The first section on police behavior contains a wide variety of information. Notably, it covers countries such as Bangladesh and China, which are welcomed additions to our book as discussions on policing in these countries are rarely found in scholarly books on police. Further, the variety of topics in this section will help nearly every person interested in police behavior. Consent decrees, for example, are currently a typical way of handling negative behaviors by police agencies. Indeed, they are so commonplace in handling such issues as racist or illegal behavior by agencies that nearly all experts are now citing them as a best practice for dealing with difficult agencies. Understanding the doctrine of minimum force and the use of discretion is undoubtedly key to comprehending police behavior.

The second section covers hiring and training, including chapters on hiring practices, police stress, and corruption, addressing some of the most hotly contested and critical issues facing law enforcement worldwide. Also, society's evolving standards are critically important to understand as the police are, to some degree, a reflection of society. The chapter on medical marijuana is essential to comprehending how society evolves morally over time and how that influences police hiring.

The last section is on crime fighting. Indeed, this is a crucial aspect of the policing role. Rick Sarre's chapter on cybersecurity is particularly noteworthy since its focus is on fairly new challenges that law enforcement faces in our modern world. Human trafficking and gunrunning are also critical areas covered in this section, among others.

Overall, this collection of works develops an understanding of police and police work that spans many countries and issues. This compendium's contribution to the field of policing in these difficult times is not only important but necessary. We must learn from experts how to handle various situations in the best way possible. This work will help our police and police agencies understand best practices, and leaders/scholars can adopt those practices and policies that make sense to them. In conclusion, policing is an ever-evolving field; we must be vigilant in staying up to date and knowledgeable of trends in other counties. With its diversity of experts, ideas, and countries, this book is well equipped to do just that.

John A. Eterno, Ben Stickle, and Diana Scharff Peterson

Series Editor's Preface

While the literature on police and allied subjects is growing exponentially, its impact on day-to-day policing remains small. The two worlds of research and practice of policing remain disconnected, even though cooperation between the two is growing. A major reason is that the two groups speak in different languages. The research work is published in hard-to-access journals and presented in a manner that is difficult for a lay person to comprehend. On the other hand, the police practitioners tend not to mix with researchers and remain secretive about their work. Consequently, there is little dialogue between the two and almost no attempt to learn from one another. Dialogue across the globe among researchers and practitioners situated in different continents is, of course, even more limited.

I attempted to address this problem by starting the IPES, www.ipes.info, where a common platform has brought the two together. IPES is now in its 27th year. The annual meetings that constitute most of the major annual events of the organization have been hosted in all parts of the world. Several very impressive publications have come out of these deliberations, and a new collaborative community of scholars and police officers has been created whose membership runs into several thousands.

The International Police Executive Symposium (IPES) has annual meetings throughout the world. All the editors have attended these meetings. They involve a collaboration of practitioners, scholars, and other experts in law enforcement. Ideas are exchanged in a unique way as all at the meeting not only share their research but also collaborate during social events. In this volume, the best ideas are brought forth from several of these meetings. Individuals and groups from a cornucopia of countries were selected to write these chapters. Over a period of years and several meetings, the editors have chosen the best ideas and present them in this volume.

An account of the IPES meetings in included on the next page.

The global influence and service of IPES was recognized by the United Nations and, as a result, IPES is in special consultative status with the United Nations.

Dilip K. Das, Ph.D., Professor
Founding President, International Police Executive Symposium, IPES,
www.ipes.info
Founding Editor-in-Chief, Police Practice and Research: An International
Journal, PPR, www.tandfonline.com/gppr (2000–2020)
Series Editor, Advances in Police Theory and Practice; Interviews with Global
Leaders in Policing, Courts and Prisons and Routledge IPES Co-publication
Professor of Criminal Justice, Coppin State University, Baltimore, Maryland

Series Editor's Preface

The International Police Executive Symposium was founded in 1994. The aims and objectives of the IPES are to provide a forum to foster closer relationships among police researchers and practitioners globally; to facilitate cross-cultural, international, and interdisciplinary exchanges for the enrichment of the law enforcement profession; and to encourage discussion and published research on challenging and contemporary topics related to the profession. One of the most important activities of the IPES is the organization of an annual meeting under the auspices of a police agency or an educational institution. Every year since 1994 annual meetings have been hosted by such agencies and institutions all over the world.

Past hosts have included

Year	Country	Theme	Host
1994	Switzerland	Police Challenges and Strategies	Canton Police, Geneva, Switzerland
1995	Spain	Challenges of Policing Democracies	International Institute of the Sociology of Law, Basque Country, Spain
1996	Japan	Organized Crime	Kanagawa University
1997	Austria	International Police Cooperation	Federal Police in Vienna, Austria
1998	The Netherlands	Crime Prevention	Dutch Police, Europol
1999	India	Policing of Public Order	Andhra Pradesh Police, Hyderabad, India
2000	USA, Illinois	Traffic Policing	Northwestern University, Center for Public Safety
2001	Poland	Corruption: A Threat to World Order	Police of Poland
2002	Turkey	Police Education and Training	Turkish National Police
2003	Bahrain	Police and Community	Kingdom of Bahrain
2004	Canada	Criminal Exploitation of Women and Children	Abbotsford Police Department Canadian Police College Royal Canadian Mounted Police University College of the Fraser Valley Vancouver Police Department
2005	The Czech Republic	Challenges of Policing in the 21st Century: A Global Assessment	The Czech Police Academy, The Ministry of the Interior, The Czech Republic
2006	Turkey	Local Linkages to Global Security and Crime: Thinking Locally and Acting Globally	Turkish National Police

Year	Country	Theme	Host
2007	Dubai	Urbanization and Security	Dubai Police
2008	USA, Ohio	Police Without Borders: The Fading Distinction Between Local & Global	Cincinnati Police Department & Ohio Association of Chiefs of Police
2009	FYR Macedonia	Policing, the Private Sector, Economic Development & Social Change: Contemporary Global Trends	Ministry of Interior, Republic of Macedonia
2010	Malta	Tourism, Strategic Locations & Major Events: Policing in an Age of Mobility, Mass Movement and Migration	Commissioner John Rizzo and Malta Police
2010	India	Community Policing: Theoretical Problems and Operational Issues	Government of Kerala and the Kerala Police Department
2011	Argentina	Policing Violence, Crime, Disorder, & Discontent: International Perspectives	IPES
2011	Sweden	Contemporary Issues in Public Safety & Security	The Blekinge Technological Institute and the Swedish Police
2012	USA, New York	Economic Development, Armed Violence and Public Safety	In Cooperation with United Nations Dept of Economic & Social Affairs NGO Branch
2013	Hungary	Global Issues in Contemporary Policing	The Ministry of Interior and The Hungarian National Police
2014	India	Policing by Consent: Theoretical Challenges and Operational Issues	Kerala Police Department
2014	Bulgaria	Crime Prevention & Community Resilience: Police Role with Victims, Youth, Ethnic Minorities and Other Partners	IPES and the Bulgarian Ministry of Interior
2015	Thailand	Police Governance and Human Trafficking: Promoting Preventative and Comprehensive Strategies	The Royal Thai Police Association, The Royal Thai Police and Shinawatra University
2016	USA, Washington DC	Urban Security: Challenges for 21st Century Global Cities	The George Washington University
2017	England	Organized Crime & Terrorism: Policing Challenges for Local to International level	Liverpool John Moores University
2018	Austria	International Police Cooperation	United Nations Office on Drugs and Crime
2019	Serbia	Contemporary Police Challenges in Light of a New World and New Knowledge	IPES

The executive summary of each meeting is distributed to participants as well as to a wide range of other interested police professionals and scholars. In addition, a book of selected papers from each annual meeting is published through Taylor & Francis. A special issue of *Police Practice and Research: An International Journal* (PPR) is also published, with the most thematically relevant papers after the usual blind review process.

Dilip K. Das, Ph.D., Founding President, IPES and Founding Editor-in-Chief, PPR

Contributor Biographies

Carlos Avalos is a law student at the University of Loyola at New Orleans, College of Law. For the past decade, he has written and reported on government and police transparency, police conduct, and racism in policing in Southern California. He received his MPA (Master of Public Affairs) at Arizona State University in 2019. After law school, Avalos plans on working as a prosecuting attorney, focusing on governmental corruption. He served as a state delegate for the 47th District in South California for five years, two terms. After law school, he will begin work on a Ph.D., in criminology, focusing on government corruption and police transparency.

Philip Birch, B. Soc. Sci. (Honors); P.G. Cert. (HEP); P.G. Cert. (SSRM); P.G. Dip. (Soc. Sci.); MSc.; Ph.D., is an associate professor of criminology and policing in the Centre for Law and Justice at Charles Sturt University, Australia. He has previously held posts at the University of Western Sydney; the University of New South Wales, Sydney, Australia; and the University of Huddersfield, in the United Kingdom. Prior to entering academia. Birch worked as a criminologist in the field, holding posts in the UK prison service as well as in the crime and disorder field, which involved managing a specialist crime unit. He has published internationally, including books, book chapters, peer-reviewed articles and government reports in his main areas of research—offender management and rehabilitation; police, prisons, and probation practices; and gender-inclusive violence, with a particular focus on domestic family violence and sex work. In 2019, Birch was invited to present his research at the United Nations. He has secured over $860,000 in research funding and support grants, which has addressed a variety of themes within his areas of expertise. Birch holds an honorary research fellowship in the School of Psychology, University of Central Lancashire, UK, as well as a Professoriate Associate at the Ashworth Research Centre, Mersey Health Care, National Health Services, UK. He is also a fellow of the Higher Education Academy. Birch was the co-founder and inaugural editor in chief of the *Journal of Criminological Research, Policy and Practice* (JCRPP, 2014–2017) and *Abuse: An International Impact Journal* (2020–present). He is also the editor in chief of *Salus: An International Journal for Law Enforcement and Public Safety* (2018–present). He also sits on the editorial board of the *Journal of Aggression, Conflict and Peace Research*.

Scott E. Blandford, Ph.D., During Blandford's 30-year policing career with a major police service, he served in a number of operational and supervisory positions, including developing a competency-based performance management system and career development process, as well as re-engineering the promotional process. Blandford also has over 25 years of experience in developing and teaching courses at the college and university level and is currently the program coordinator (undergraduate) and graduate coordinator for all public safety programs at Wilfrid Laurier University. As a life-long learner, Blandford has completed a

Fanshawe College Management Studies Certificate and a Dalhousie University Certificate in Police Leadership, is a graduate of the Bachelor of Professional Arts (criminal justice major) program at Athabasca University, and has completed a diploma in public administration and Master of Public Administration degree at the University of Western Ontario. Blandford completed his Doctor of Business Administration (DBA) degree at Columbia Southern University, with a research focus on organizational development within police organizations.

Hannah Collison (nee Socha), MS, works for the Missouri Department of Social Services. She was formerly employed by the Raymore, Missouri, Police Department. Ms. Collison earned her bachelor's and Master's degrees from the University of Central Missouri.

Jay Corzine is a professor of sociology at the University of Central Florida. His research specializations include substance use, urban problems, and policy issues related to law enforcement and crime control. Publications have appeared in several journals, including *Social Forces, American Journal of Sociology, Criminology,* the *Journal of Contemporary Criminal Justice, Deviant Behavior, Justice Research and Policy,* and other refereed journals and non-refereed sources targeted to law enforcement. In addition to being active in scholarly associations, he was an invited member of the Futures Working Group sponsored by the FBI and Police Futures International and a guest lecturer for the Behavioral Science Unit of the FBI. Prior research has been funded by the National Science Foundation, the Center for Substance Abuse Treatment, the Distilled Spirits Council of America, and state and local agencies.

Dilip K. Das, Ph.D., is the president, International Police Executive Symposium (IPES), and editor-in-chief, *Police Practice and Research: An International Journal.* After receiving his Master's degree in English literature, Das joined the Indian Police Service, an elite national service. After 14 years in the service as a police executive, including chief of police, he moved to the USA in 1979, where he achieved another Master's degree in criminal justice, as well as a doctorate in the same discipline. Das has authored, edited, and co-edited more than 40 books and numerous articles. He is the series editor of *Advances in Police Theory and Practice* and *International Police Executive Symposium Co-Publications.* He has traveled extensively throughout the world in comparative police research; as a visiting professor at various universities, including organizing annual conferences of the IPES; and as a human rights consultant to the United Nations. Das has received several faculty excellence awards and was a distinguished faculty lecturer.

Samantha de Vries is currently a Ph.D. student in the School of Criminology at Simon Fraser University in British Columbia, Canada. Current research is on international cooperation and challenges and opportunities faced in combating the illicit wildlife trade, with a focus on Canada (and North America) and Kenya (and Eastern Africa). Conducted field research over a six-month period in Kenya during a research internship with the United Nations Office on Drugs and Crime Global Programme for Combating Wildlife and Forest Crime and attended the Interpol Wildlife Crime Working Group meeting in 2019 in Singapore. Previously worked for the Correctional Service of Canada for approximately eight years as a correctional officer (level one and two), first aid instructor, and crisis and hostage negotiator for the Pacific region.

Madelyn Diaz is a Ph.D. student in the department of sociology, studying within the crime and deviance track at the University of Central Florida, where she also received her MA in applied sociology and BA in criminal justice. She is a former Department of Homeland Security and US Marshals intern and recently served as managing editor for *Homicide Studies.* She is an active member of UCF's Social Theory Relationships and Interpersonal Violence Exposure (STRIVE) research lab and holds professional memberships with the xviii Contributor Biographies

Homicide Research Working Group, American Society of Criminology, American Sociological Society, and Southern Sociology Society. Her research interests include human trafficking, the criminology of place, interpersonal violence, and quantitative methodologies.

Bradley D. Edwards, Ph.D., is an assistant professor in the department of criminal justice and criminology at East Tennessee State University. His research interests include the impact of the media on crime and justice, attitudes toward the police, policy analysis, and criminal justice education.

John A. Eterno, Ph.D., is a professor and associate dean of graduate studies in criminal justice at Molloy College in Rockville Centre, New York. Dr. Eterno is a retired captain in the New York City Police Department. He serves on the board of directors for the American Academy of Law Enforcement Professionals-Long Island. Dr. Eterno is recognized by the federal courts as an expert witness on police, is regularly quoted in various media outlets, and speaks internationally on police-related topics. Dr. Eterno is widely published, and examples of his works can be seen in *Justice Quarterly*, *Public Administration Review*, *The International Journal of Police Science and Management*, *The Criminal Law Bulletin*, and many others. His recent books include *The Crime Numbers Game: Management by Manipulation* (with Eli B. Silverman), *The Detective's Handbook* (with Cliff Roberson) and *The New York City Police Department: The Impact of Its Policies and Practices*.

Gregg W. Etter Sr., Ed.D., is a professor of criminal justice at the University of Central Missouri. Dr. Etter earned his bachelor's and Master's degrees from Wichita State University and his doctorate from Oklahoma State University. He retired as a lieutenant with the Sedgwick County Sheriff's Office after serving from 1977 to 2006. He is rated as a gang expert by the National Gang Crime Research Center.

Richard Evans, Ph.D., is a criminologist, historian, and writer. He was lecturer in criminology at Deakin University in Australia from 2011–2020 and is now an honorary research fellow. In addition to criminology, he has taught and published in fields as diverse as disaster studies, crime history, and media ethics.

Clare Farmer, Ph.D., is a senior lecturer in criminology at Deakin University in Australia. She has published widely with respect to procedural justice, due process, and sentencing. Her current research interests include discretionary police powers, policing and firearms, and responding to sexual offending from the perspective of victims.

Ketty Fernández, MA, is a Ph.D. candidate (ABD) in sociology at the University of Central Florida (UCF), where she is currently a graduate research assistant in the Violence Against Women cluster. She is a former SSA Distinguished Paper Award recipient, a Delores A. Auzenne Fellowship and Summer Mentoring Fellowship recipient, and served as managing editor for *Homicide Studies*. She holds an MA in applied sociology from UCF and a BA in psychology from Caldwell University. Her research interests include violence against women, with an emphasis on sexual assault and rape; human trafficking; and racial/ethnic inequalities.

Sally Galovic, Ph.D., (Cand.), is a researcher and qualified teacher who has been working with young people and Indigenous communities in Australia for nearly two decades. Her expertise and experience led her into research with young Arrentre and Pitjinjarra people and the Northern Territory Intervention in 2007 and subsequent research in ethnography, criminal justice, and policing. She has worked as a research assistant on a number of projects funded by the Australian Research Council at Western Sydney University and Charles Sturt University since 2006. Galovic teaches in secondary and tertiary institutions in the areas of criminology and justice studies and is a Ph.D., student at Charles Sturt University while concurrently completing her qualifications in law. Her Ph.D., research interests are procedural justice, community-driven design, and the use of disruptive technology in ADR in policing Indigenous communities in Australia.

Jurg Gerber is a professor in the department of criminal justice and criminology and director of international initiatives in the College of Criminal Justice at Sam Houston State University. For the last 20 years, he has also served as *Professor Invité* at the University of Lausanne (Lausanne, Switzerland), and he spent a year as a Fulbright Scholar at Kaliningrad State University in Kaliningrad, Russia. Research interests include white-collar crime, criminology, drug control policy, and international criminal justice issues. He has co-edited two books on drug policy and one on white-collar crime and has published extensively in all the aforementioned areas.

Burak M. Gönültaş earned his Ph.D. from Istanbul University Forensic Science Institute and is assistant professor in the Social Work Unit of Cumhuriyet University, Sivas. His research focuses on criminal investigation, child abuse and sexual abuse, criminal profiling, and forensic social work. His recent work has appeared in *Child Abuse and Neglect* and *International Journal of Offender Therapy and Comparative Criminology*.

Doraval Govender, Ph.D., is a professor in the security management program in the department of criminology and security science in the School of Criminal Justice in the College of Law at the University of South Africa, Pretoria.

Heath Grant. Prior to returning to the full-time faculty of John Jay College of Criminal Justice in 2013, Dr. Grant was most recently the director of research of the Police Executive Research Forum, a leading Washington, DC, organization dedicated to advancing law enforcement and crime prevention internationally. Formerly, as CEO of Success for Kids (SFK), he oversaw the planning, implementation, curriculum development, partnerships, and strategic program alliances and evaluation of the organization's international programs and services. A 15-year program executive, his experience and innovative style has positioned SFK's unique approach to social emotional learning as one of the most sought-after program partnership opportunities throughout Africa, the Middle East, Europe, and the Americas. On behalf of the Asia Foundation, he also recently developed training curricula for the Bangladesh Police on community policing. He subsequently conducted an assessment there related to the status of community policing in the country. He recently led a research effort for the State Department to assess youth violence issues in the Caribbean and make recommendations for systems-wide change. Since 2019, Dr. Grant has served as the director of the Master's program in criminal justice at John Jay College.

Melody Hicks, BS, MCJ, is a criminal justice practitioner, as well as an adjunct professor in the criminal justice administration department at Middle Tennessee State University. Her areas of expertise include crime data analysis, situational crime prevention, emerging crime types, and ethics in policing. Hicks has been published in the *American Journal of Criminal Justice*, as well as the *Journal of Criminal Justice Studies* for her contributions to the study of porch pirates and package theft.

René Hornung, MA PR (police superintendent) is the head of the department for police training and subject-related education at the Police Academy Saxony-Anhalt, Germany. He is responsible for the training of self- and social competencies, sports training, practical training, firearms training, and the training of operationally related self-protection skills.

Besides, he holds a Master's degree in educational sciences. In addition to his work at the police academy, he is an external doctoral student at the educational science department of the Martin-Luther-University Halle-Wittenberg. His thesis deals with the area of tension between pedagogical communication and police communication.

Lin Huff-Corzine, Ph.D., is a professor of sociology at the University of Central Florida. Her research focuses on violent crime, with articles published on topics such as mass murder, the effects of drug transportation routes on homicide and robbery, firearm lethality, risk factors associated with assaults on police officers, the spatial distribution of sexual assaults, and the impact of medical resources on lethal violence rates in cities. More recently, she has begun publishing on human trafficking and is a contributor along with her co-authors to the 2017 book *Human Trafficking*, edited by Hugh Potter, Jeff Goltz, and Mike Gibson, which outlines how human trafficking is being combatted in the Central Florida area, and an article in *Police Practice and Research* that addresses human trafficking as well. Professor Huff-Corzine co-authored *The Currents of Lethal Violence*, a monograph, and has published in numerous journals, including *Criminology*, *Homicide Studies*, *Violence and Victims*, *Justice Quarterly*, *Victims and Offenders*, the *Journal of Child Sexual Assault*, *Deviant Behavior*, the *Journal of Research on Crime and Delinquency*, *Justice Research and Policy*, and the *Journal of Contemporary Criminal Justice*.

Di Jia is an assistant professor in the department of criminal justice and criminology at Metropolitan State University of Denver, CO, USA. She worked as a police officer in China before earning her doctorate at Sam Houston State University. Her research interests include policing, community justice and neighborhood quality of life, homeland security and counterterrorism.

Allan Y. Jiao received his Ph.D. in criminal justice from Rutgers University and Master's in Public Administration from Lewis and Clark College. Dr. Jiao served as a member of the Regional Gun Violence Research Consortium and was a Senior Fulbright Research Scholar in Hong Kong and a research consultant for the National Development and Research Institute. He has engaged in research with and provided professional services to many police organizations in the world. Currently a professor of law and justice studies at Rowan University, he has published extensively in policing, including refereed journal articles, books, and book chapters. His teaching and research interests include primarily policing in the United States and comparative criminal justice issues.

Jeffery M. Johnson, Ed.D. is a lecturer of legal studies at the University of Mississippi. Dr. Johnson earned his bachelor's and Master's degrees from Washburn University and his doctorate from Delta State University. He served with the Kansas Highway Patrol from 1996 to 2000. He is rated as a gang expert by the National Gang Crime Research Center.

Michael Kennedy, B. Soc. Sci. (Hons), Ph.D., has been a senior lecturer in the Western Sydney University Bachelor of Policing program since 2004. Between 1978 and 1996, Dr. Kennedy was a detective in the New South Wales Police, and he specialized in organized and major crime investigation. Dr. Kennedy has also worked with the Brigade de répression du Proxénétisme and the Brigade du protection des Mineurs in Paris. Dr. Kennedy worked extensively with the Arabic-speaking community and also specialized in child protection and sexual assault investigations. Between 2013 to 2017, Dr. Kennedy was head of the ISLES (Security and Law Enforcement) program on behalf of Western Sydney University in the Islamic Republic of Maldives. All the enrolled students were from Maldives police service, Maldives immigration, Maldives customs and the private security sector.

Contributor Biographies **xxi**

Tomas J. Lares is the founder/president of United Abolitionists, formerly Florida Abolitionist, Inc., and the co-founder/chairman of the Greater Orlando Human Trafficking Task Force, Inc. Lares has 28 years of human services experience at the local, state, and national level, managing and starting nonprofit and public advocacy initiatives. In 2004, Lares was made aware of the crime of human trafficking by US Senator Sam Brownback of Kansas. In 2005, he was instrumental in facilitating one of the first human trafficking seminars in Central Florida, which over 100 individuals and stakeholders attended (www.unitedaboli tionists.com/tomas-lares/).

Logan S. Ledford is a Ph.D. student in criminal justice and criminology at Georgia State University. His research interests include police stress, police legitimacy, and crime and justice in ruralized contexts. In the past, he has explored stress among state-level conservation officers, furthering understanding on how crime problems are affecting those who patrol recreational areas. In the future, he hopes to continue examining the impact of stress and related concepts in the policing profession.

Jean Claude Geofrey Mahoro is a Rwandan holding a Master of laws degree (LL.M) and bachelor of law (LL.B), respectively, from Universitas Diponegoro in and University of Rwanda. Previously, he served as a civil registrar and notary officer in Muhanga District, Rwanda. In 2014, he got an award with honorable mention after winning an international contest on fiscal law by Lex-led Group, a Washington-based group of economic lawyers. He served as a teacher of tax law in E.S. Kageyo, Gicumbi District, Rwanda. In the same year, he interned with Forzley & Associates, Global Health Legal Advisors, for six months, conducting research on East African Community (EAC) Health legal issues and got an awarded of excellence. In 2011, he taught English at G.S. Rwamiko, Gicumbi District.

Geofrey has carried out research on various topics in international law, human rights, environmental law, and law enforcement published in different journals. Among others, his works include *Patenting Deal in Indonesia, Article 20 of the Patent Law in the Political Perspective of International Trade Law* (2020); *ICAO's Role in Environmental Protection and Its Shortcomings Under Rapid Growth of Aviation Industry* (2019); and *Regulation of Radio Frequency Spectrum and Its Implementation Challenges in the Perspective of International Law* (2019). Geofrey has broadened his knowledge by undertaking numerous training and courses on human rights, arbitration of international trade disputes, and conflict resolution and management offered by reputable universities.

Through internship and volunteering, Geofrey worked with multiple institutions, including the National Commission for Human Rights of Rwanda (NCHR), AEGIS Trust, Never Again Rwanda, and Peace One Day, in which he gained diverse skills in international law and sustainable peace and development. In this light, Geofrey initiated and managed the "Walk for Peace" on April 24, 2015. The walk gathered 5,000 participants in commemoration of the genocide against the Tutsi of 1994 in Rwanda. Geofrey is currently working on different research topics in law-related fields.

Rychelle Moses is currently pursuing her Ph.D. in criminal justice at the University of Louisville. Her research interests include domestic violence, sexual assault, and rural criminology. Her previous research has included examining perceptions of campus sexual assault resources, specifically among Appalachian students.

Shanna Tova O'Reilly is an international development and humanitarian affairs practitioner with broad experience in the areas of good governance, security, the rule of law, migration, economic growth, and service provision. She has worked with funding to design, implement, and evaluate programs for a variety of US and multilateral donor efforts, including the US Agency for International Development (USAID); Department of Justice (DOJ); State Department; and the Interamerican Development (IDB) Bank across Latin America, South and Southeast Asia, North Africa, and the Middle East. Specifically, from 2011 to 2013, She served as the senior director for the Asia Foundation's community-based policing program in Bangladesh. This was part of a larger police reform initiative built around developing new ideas and approaches to policing meant to enhance institutional capacity for citizen engagement.

Dustin L. Osborne, Ph.D., is an assistant professor in the department of criminal justice and criminology at East Tennessee State University. His research interests revolve around rural crime and culture. His most recent works appear in *Police Practice and Research* and the *International Journal of Rural Criminology*.

Diana Scharff Peterson, Ph.D., has nearly 20 years of experience in higher education, teaching in the areas of research methods; public policy analysis; comparative criminal justice systems; race, gender, class, and crime; statistics; criminology; sociology, and drugs and behavior at seven different institutions of higher education. Scharff Peterson has been the chairperson of three different criminal justice programs and has published in the areas of criminal justice, social work, higher education, sociology, business, and management. Her research interests include issues in policing (training and education), community resilience and community policing, distracted driving legislation, assessment and leadership in higher education, and family violence. Currently, Scharff Peterson is finishing two concurrent Master's degrees at Arizona State University: Social Justice and Human Rights and Public Affairs (Emergency Management) in May 2021, while teaching undergraduate and graduate classes in the department of public affairs in the Watts College of Public Service and Community Solutions. She is trained in GIS, geographic information systems software. Scharff Peterson has been the NGO liaison for the International Police Executive Symposium in New York, New York; Geneva, Switzerland; and Vienna, Austria since 2011, serving as a human rights consultant to the United Nations.

Özgür Sarı, Ph.D., is an associate professor, earned his Ph.D. from the Middle East Technical University department of sociology, and worked at the Public Administration Institute for Turkey and the Middle East. His research focuses on development, modernization, social transformation, urbanization, criminology, and social movements.

Rick Sarre, Ph.D., is emeritus professor of law and criminal justice and an adjunct professor with the University of South Australia: Justice and Society. He is a fellow of the Australian and New Zealand Society of Criminology and currently the president of the South Australian Council for Civil Liberties.

Gabriela Smith works for the Community Coalition Against Human Trafficking, a nonprofit agency that serves trafficked individuals in East Tennessee. She graduated from East Tennessee State University in 2018 with a bachelor's degree in psychology, then again in 2019 with a Master's degree in criminal justice and criminology. Her interest in the criminal justice system has led to her passion for working with at-risk youth in her community.

Ben Stickle, Ph.D., is an associate professor of criminal justice administration at Middle Tennessee State University. He holds a Ph.D., in justice administration from the University of Louisville. Stickle has nearly 20 years of law enforcement and private security experience. He has published several scholarly journal articles, book chapters, and a book. His research interests include policing, crime prevention, and property crime (metal theft and package theft) (www.benstickle.com).

Katharina Friederike Sträter, Ph.D., is a research assistant at the department of law and economics and chair of management accounting at Martin-Luther-University Halle-Wittenberg, Germany. She is interested in microeconomics, bargaining and game theory, and further theoretical approaches dealing with the broader topic of conflict resolution as well as theories of bounded rationality. Besides her theoretical research, she is engaged in qualitative empirical research and analyzes determinants of the quality of police-citizen encounters, among others.

Staci Strobl, Ph.D., is a professor of criminal justice at UW-Platteville and researches policing and minority communities around the world, having been published in a wide variety of academic journals, such as *Policing & Society*, the *International Journal for Crime, Justice & Social Democracy*, and the *British Journal of Criminology*. She is the author of *Sectarian Order in Bahrain: The Social and Colonial Origins of Criminal Justice* (2018). In 2019, she and two colleague received the Outstanding Article Award for the Division of White Collar and Corporate Crime of the American Society of Criminology (ASC) for a publication entitled "Getting into Deep Water: Coastal Land Loss and State-Corporate Crime in the Louisiana Bayou," which appeared in the *British Journal of Criminology*.

Margaret H. Vickers, Ph.D., held the position of professor of management with the School of Management at the University of Western Sydney until 2017, when she retired. Professor Vickers has significant expertise in qualitative research, especially related to illness and disability, and its impact at work. She has researched many aspects of workplace adversity: bullying in the workplace, resilience in workers, being made redundant, living and working with unseen chronic illness, caring for a child with disability while working full time, emotions in the workplace, and living with mental illness. Professor Vickers served as chair of the board of directors (2008) of the Independent Living Centre (ILC) New South Wales and served on the board from 2007 to 2009. Professor Vickers has authored over 120 international refereed publications in addition to two international research books exposing the lives of people dealing with disability who work: *Work and Unseen Chronic Illness: Silent Voices* (Routledge, New York and London, 2001) and *Working and Caring for a Child with Chronic Illness: Disconnected and Doing it All* (Palgrave MacMillan, London, 2006). Professor Vickers was editor-in-chief of the international *Employee Responsibilities and Rights Journal* (Springer, New York) and an editorial/international advisory board member of the *Journal of Management and Organisation; Review of Disability Studies: An International Journal; Qualitative Research in Organizations and Management: An International Journal; Administrative Theory & Praxis; International Journal of Action Research; First Person*, a Subsection of *the Organizational Management Journal;* and the *Asia Pacific Journal of Business Administration*. Professor Vickers has successfully supervised a higher Doctorate, numerous Doctorates, Master's Honours, and bachelor's Honours to completion, and she has been awarded several prestigious Australian Research Council (ARC) grants, as well as attracting significant external funds from external industry partners.

Jolene Vincent, Ph.D., is currently a lecturer of criminology in the department of sociology at the College of William and Mary in Williamsburg, Virginia. She received her Ph.D., in sociology with a concentration in crime and deviance in 2018 from the University of Central Florida (UCF) in Orlando, Florida, USA. As a sociological criminologist, her research interests include lethal and non-lethal violence using quantitative and qualitative methods. Dr. Vincent's research on human trafficking appears in a refereed book titled *Human Trafficking: A Systemwide Public Safety and Community Approach*, Goltz et al. (Eds.) (West Academic Publishing, 2017). Her peer-reviewed manuscripts on serial homicide are published in *Deviant Behavior* and the *Journal of Forensic Sciences*. Dr. Vincent's findings on gender differences in prescription opioid misuse among US black adults are reported in *Substance Use & Misuse*. Her more recent research is featured in *Leisure Sciences*, as well as a piece on Homeland Security investigations included in *Criminal Justice in America: The Encyclopedia of Crime, Law Enforcement, Courts, and Corrections*. In addition to her teaching and research, Dr. Vincent has served as the assistant director and senior data analyst of the UCF department of sociology's crime lab for three years and was the managing editor of *Homicide Studies*. As a first-generation college student, she enjoys mentoring students throughout their academic careers. Dr. Vincent has received several awards, including the Graduate Student Teaching Award, the Love of Learning Award, and the Best Graduate Student Paper Award. Her discipline-related memberships include the Homicide Research Working Group, the American Society of Criminology, the Southern Sociological Society, the Southwestern Social Science Association, and numerous honor societies.

Lee M. Wade, Ph.D., holds a BS in criminology and Master of Public Administration from the University of West Georgia, and he earned his doctorate in criminal justice from the University of Southern Mississippi. Dr. Wade currently teaches law enforcement courses and criminal investigation courses to both forensic science and criminal justice students. His research interests involve crime scene investigation methods, police use of technology in operations, and perceptions of use of force. Dr. Wade has over 15 years' experience in the criminal justice system. He was a police officer for over 10 years in the state of Georgia, where he worked as a patrol supervisor, DUI task force officer, and investigator and supervised the office of professional standards and training.

Priya Xavier, Ph.D., is a social science researcher and assistant professor teaching management science subjects for post-graduates and undergraduates. She is a faculty advisor in Enactus in the university in which she works and is associated with many projects undertaken by the Enactus team. Her recent project is the Ford-funded Fly Life project, which is making automatic drones for helping drug delivery during the COVID period. She is MBA, MA HRM, Ph.D., qualified with 11 years of teaching experience.

Part I

Police Behavior

Chapter 1

Cultivating Well-Being Among Police Officers

Examining Challenges in the Workplace

Philip Birch, Margaret H. Vickers, Sally Galovic, and Michael Kennedy

Introduction

This chapter presents qualitative data gathered through an interview process as part of a small-scale exploratory study within New South Wales Police Force (NSWPF), Australia. The exploratory study aimed to support the cultivation of well-being among police officers through examining aspects of the policing environment and workplace. The study on which this chapter is based used a non-probability sample made up of 14 police officers (see Table 1.1), selected from two local area commands (LACs), one command being in a city location, the other command being in a regional location. This approach to sampling was adopted in order to considered differences between police practice in city and regional locations.

The data collected was analyzed using a thematic analysis, resulting in a rich description of the dataset. By using an inductive approach to analyzing the data, according to Braun and Clarke (2006), themes are allowed to emerge from within the data and are not imposed from existing theoretical frameworks. The themes emerging from the dataset centered on three broad themes: *Policing and Trust, Surveillance of Police Officers, and Workplace Support Dualities.* This chapter considers each of these themes before concluding with a series of recommendations to address the challenges police officers face within their workplace that can enhance and promote well-being.

Policing and Trust

The importance of trust in workplaces, including police organizations (Schafer, 2013), has been discussed at length by previous researchers (Ellwart, Wittek, & Wielers, 2012; Innocenti, Pilati, & Peluso, 2011; Kannan-Narasimhan & Lawrence, 2012; Spector & Jones, 2004; Thomas, Zolin, & Hartman, 2009; Vickers, 2008). The New Public Management's (NPM) view of organizations has been described as a chain of low-trust, principal/agent relationships, rather than fiduciary or trustee-beneficiary ones (Perry, Engbers, & Jun, 2009) concurrent to NPM being lauded as a reform framework proposed to reverse declining trust in organizations (Yang & Holzer, 2006). While a lack of appreciation for affective responses to workplace events has been found to produce productivity and morale problems (Kiel & Watson, 2009), effective managers know that motivating people, keeping people, and creating productive work environments require positive affect (Kiel & Watson, 2009)—including the presence of trust. The best police leaders have been noted to communicate effectively and promote trust within their work groups: Chief Burtell Jefferson of the Metropolitan Police Department, Washington, DC, USA, would be a relevant case in point (Williams & Kellough, 2006). Based on those interviewed, trust is not only desired by members of the NSWPF, but as also an occupational requirement. Trust was reportedly required in many domains and roles of police work: trust between officers doing operational aspects of their job; trust between operational

DOI: 10.4324/9781003047117-2

Table 1.1 Sample by Gender and Service Length

Gender	Service length
Male	11–20 yrs.
Male	11–20 yrs.
Male	11–20 yrs.
Male	11–20 yrs.
Male	21–30 yrs.
Male	21–30 yrs.
Female	0–10 yrs.
Male	0–10 yrs.
Male	0–10 yrs.
Female	0–10 yrs.
Female	11–20 yrs.
Male	11–20 yrs.
Male	21–30 yrs.
Female	0–10 yrs.

officers and management; officers trusting that the organization would support officers when they needed it; and trust that the organization's structures, polices, and processes were appropriate and adequate to provide the support that officers felt they needed. The interview data revealed that if trust was absent or doubted, problems would arise. Past research has noted that in all organizations, trust and mutual trust are integral elements of high-performance teams and require close attention by management to maintain (e.g., Kannan-Narasimhan & Lawrence, 2012; Thomas et al., 2009; Vickers, 2008). Trust has also been identified as being fragile and reciprocal in nature: building trust among team members can take a long time but, if betrayed, can take even longer to repair.

Needing to Trust

Officers spoke frequently and frankly about the need for trust:

> But it's just a matter of knowing who you can trust. As I said, trust is a massive thing.

Officers spoke often of the need for trust but that sometimes it was not present, and needed to be:

> When you feel as though you haven't got the support of those, that you can't trust them, to be quite honest, they stab you in the back. The cops talk; we're terrible gossipers. I hate gossip. Rumour, gossip and innuendo just doesn't wash with me. If someone hasn't got the balls to say it to your face, my honest opinion is they should just shut their mouth and move on. I've got no time for it; I don't like it. It's negative.

Trust between operational officers and management has been noted by past researchers as a strong constituent element in what is termed "the psychological contract" (Dick, 2006; Noblet, Rodwell, & Allisey, 2009). The psychological contract is a term used to describe what management expect from its employees, and vice versa. While the contract itself can be dynamic and organic in nature and is usually formed without a specific formula or model, it frequently has a very strong influence on determining behavior within organizations by individuals. Researchers confirm that staff perceptions that the psychological contract had been breached would also be seen as a significant breach of trust.

Trust was a binding factor within many of the workplace relationships for those interviewed for this research. The reading of situations, scenarios, and relationships (with other police and with the community) was reported to be a constituent element that informed the psychological contract that officers believed they had entered into with each other, and with management, on a day-to-day basis. Officers spoke about not just needing their colleagues to be trustworthy individuals, but of their being able to be trusted to do their job competently:

> I think people have to earn your trust just as I have to earn other people's trust. I probably, especially at the upper levels of the police, I understand why some bosses used certain staff, because you trust them. . . . I'm not talking about the inherent trust is the ethical one and all that sort of stuff. But the trust about, ideally, about whether they can get the job done needs to be built up with me. They have to show that they can actually do it and that sort of thing. I get disappointed if people let you down, especially if you communicated on X, Y, Z being done, and it doesn't get done at once.

The data also revealed a need for trust that can manifest either consciously or unconsciously and in numerous areas. This need for trust was in several areas: between police officers working together, between police officers and the senior hierarchy of the organization, and with the broader community. Given the inherent risk of police work, trust was seen to be essential to the role and process of police work so that officers might execute their professional responsibilities adequately, but also with a sense of security and confidence, feeling that the organization and its management would be behind them if they faltered or struck trouble:

> Being able to trust the people you work with, having confidence in the people you work with. At the end of the day, if I'm working with you, my life is in your hands and my partner. So, I've got to be able to trust you knowing full well that I've got the utmost confidence in my work colleagues; that they've got my back, I've got their back.

Researchers such as Dick (2006) have confirmed that when trust is precarious, or absent, the entire psychological contract, whatever it might comprise, can be called into question. This, in turn, can be very detrimental to working individuals, especially their ability to function effectively and remain motivated. If officers felt their psychological contract with management had been breached or not fulfilled by the other party, the sense of betrayal accompanying this could undermine existing trust even further. This has been confirmed in the literature and can potentially harm the organization in a number of ways: through lowered morale; reduced motivation; and increased leave-taking, absenteeism, and resignations. There was evidence of this in our data. For example, one officer reported that they had been bullied at work, but they did not trust the organization or senior colleagues enough to share the difficulties they were experiencing on the job. This officer's reported view was that if they had reported the bullying to a senior colleague, this would have made matters worse for them. At the time of interview, the bullying had, fortunately, ceased, and this officer confirmed that they were very relieved they had told no one:

> Upon reflection, I'm glad I didn't go to a sergeant. I'm glad I didn't go to anybody in the police force and tell them what I was going through. Because of course, you've got that kind of trust or whatever. But ultimately, he's going to have to go to that [other officer] and say, "What's going on?" And they're going to talk and everything else comes from that and it happens again.

The importance of trust in a positive workplace culture and in supporting officer well-being cannot be overstated. While requiring further evidence to confirm the substance of possible difficulties around trust between officers and within the organization, it is the case that if officers could not trust the organization, its processes, and its management to support them, this would be highly likely to have a negative impact on their well-being, performance, motivation, desire to return to work after stressful events, and their intention to remain with the organization.

Staff Turnover

Staff turnover was also recognized as a clear problem by NSWPF management (NSWPF, 2013), but also by police officers interviewed. Evidence of their concern and some of the possible reasons for it emerged in some of the respondent stories. NSWPF research (NSWPF, 2013) has already confirmed that many officers are still leaving the organization on stress-based medical discharge and that between January 1, 2009, and May 18, 2011, 66% of officers leaving the organization had received a medical discharge. The peak age of discharge (post 1988, with claims) was 36 to 40 years (44%). The majority (82%) of medical discharges were between the ages of 31 and 45 years. The length of service (post 1988 discharge, with claims) was mostly around 16 to 20 years. However, 26% of medical discharges were in service for between 11 and 15 years, and 24% were between 6 and 10 years. Of the post-1988 discharges with claims group, 79% were discharged with only psychological injuries while 14% had both physical and psychological injuries. Very disturbing is that 93% of all medical discharges from NSWPF had a psychological component (NSWPF, 2013). Understandably, the problem of staff turnover is of concern and clearly having an adverse effect on well-being.

Participants also spoke about there being a certain "type" of person who can succeed in policing. This so-called "ideal officer" varied among participants' reports but included commonalities in relation to attitude; ability to deal with pressure; and, importantly, what the ideal officer's beliefs might be about the job and it what it should entail:

> You've got to love cops and robbers. You've got to love chasing criminals. . . . There seem to be people who join this job and it's almost for a social life or something, some of the younger people. I don't begrudge them that, but it'd be nice if they also had a passion for actually arresting people, the right people, that is.
>
> There are a couple of cases here at the moment and I understand why they want to stay in this job: because of the pay. But they should not be here; they should never have joined this job. They're stressful people. They worry about everything and this isn't the job where you can worry about things. If you worry about minor things, don't join this job.
>
> You've just got to be hard working. I mean 90% of all jobs are just the same. You've just got to have a go really. You've just got to be a hard worker. If you get out there and have a go, you're going to build up your skills. The icing on the cake would be if they love to arrest criminals and if they treat people well on top of that. I mean I don't know what else you've got to do.
>
> Only a certain type of person, I think, could do it. . . . It just makes me want to prove that I'm strong enough. If you don't want to be here, this can be hell on earth. I think some people who don't want to be here, and possibly never wanted to be here, but struggled to get out, would be very unhappy in their job.

High staff turnover has been noted as being very harmful to many organizations, but also in police organizations (e.g., see Johnson, 2012). One study compared the impact of voluntary and involuntary turnover on organizational performance among police departments and found that voluntary turnover had a more negative impact. It was also suggested in that study that managers needed to address the concerns of strong performers in police organizations in order to reduce their dissatisfaction and their incentive to leave. In addition to this, while it would normally be expected that the turnover of poor police performers might be beneficial to the organization, this same study claimed that the departure of poor performers could also become detrimental to organizational performance if their vacancies were not filled quickly.

Officers interviewed in this study were also reportedly concerned about how the high levels of staff turnover and how this might have been negatively impacting the NSWPF organization and their ability to do their jobs:

> We do a very bad job of replacing staff after they've transferred out. . . . Because someone will transfer out, and we don't advertise their position until after they've transferred out. Which means that there has been no real induction or handover from the person going out, to the person coming in. . . . Regardless of whether the person on their way out a great operator or a raving lunatic is, regardless of that, they've still got all that local knowledge and history that they've built up over two, three, four or five years, whatever it might be. And that just disappears overnight. It's gone on the back of a removals truck. Then you get someone else who comes in and will be keen, and then they've got to start all over again.

If management were believed to have not offered support to staff who needed it, or were seen to have deliberately undermined staff, this was considered by interviewees to be a likely cause of turnover and absenteeism. The outcome for remaining officers was also reported: that they then needed to be reliant on less experienced, less effective, less knowledgeable replacements, compared to those who had left the organization:

> [On the previous commander] Dysfunctional. He didn't have balls. He made it so much worse, giving into all the underlings and no senior management support whatsoever. It was piss-poor management, it really was. Well, we had inspectors going off on stress leave and refusing to work with him and it was not good. Then I'd lose them, and I'd have no support because the ones that replaced them, like the sergeants that acted up, were piss poor.

Respondents in this research believed that the way officers were managed could have been responsible, at least in part, for the high staff turnover. This would be something the NSWPF could look toward improving in the future, especially if such a concern is confirmed during later research:

> They talk to some of the constables like they're kids. . . . That's why half the people leave the police, I think. It's because they're sick of being treated like a kid, because it's just embarrassing.

This research also exposed participant perceptions that it was very difficult to advance within the NSWPF. There was a perception that getting promoted was very onerous and, worse, that it was perceived to be unpredictable and exclusive. If it is widely reported during interviews that internal promotions are very difficult—next to impossible, even—to achieve, such beliefs, whether true or not, can also negatively impact staff motivation and intention to remain with the organization:

> When I was going through the promotions process that was probably the biggest anxiety that I had.
>
> The promotion system, instead of police, this is way out there. Police should be paid on seniority and not on what rank they obtain. Because now we just have people who, all they want to do is sit around and study for the next exam or boost their CV or make connections on how to get promoted. . . . That all changed when they brought in merit-based promotion. I used to just see guys just sitting around studying. While I was doing police work, I'd just watch guys sit around and study so they could pass the test so they can get promoted. I don't see how that's of benefit.
>
> It's not as bad anymore but there's still that degree that people are more interested in getting promoted more than helping the public. That's organisation wide. I'm sure every station's exactly the same. Their concerns are to get promoted and it's got nothing to do with helping someone on the street.

Police officers at all levels of NSWPF showed evidence of concern with the problem of staff turnover in the organization. Some of the early messages presented here suggest that attention to some management practices may offer one means to address the problem of staff leaving the organization prematurely.

Surveillance of Police Officers

The issue of surveillance was the second theme to emerge from the dataset of this exploratory study. Police officers reported that they were routinely observed, even scrutinized and judged, as part of their daily routine when doing their job. This was perceived by them to be a particular challenge; police officers interviewed frequently spoke of how they were challenged both personally and professionally by surveillance processes and individuals, from numerous quarters, that pervaded their lives and the conduct of their job. The sources of surveillance they spoke of were also expanding and changing and existed simultaneously with ongoing changes taking place within NSWPF as an organization. The sources of surveillance specifically commented on by officers in this study are explored next; however, one of the main issues that was reported on in this study was how surveillance takes place, how it was constructed, and what its impact is on police officers as individuals and as a collective.

Other Police Officers and Surveillance

While surveillance of police officers has been shown to inhibit their discretionary behavior (such as inviting leniency when dealing with offenders), the increased potential for litigation facing police was also reported to have risen dramatically over the last three decades. From this increasingly litigious context has grown the term *litigaphobia*, which describes a deep-seated anxiety around the legal action that threatens a person who is executing their role.

As police officers are able to make complaints through the same legislation as the public, one aspect of concern raised during interviews was the potential conflict that could arise for an officer, especially with regard to their role in complaints that have been made. They could either be involved as a complainant or as an officer defending a claim.

Officers involved in this research consistently reported the pressure and effects of the "complaint system" that surrounded this police legislation, suggesting that this could impact them daily. Research suggests that almost 30% of complaint reports made against police officers are made by fellow officers, with the remainder of complaints being made by the public (NSW Ombudsman, 2014). The impact of this system is enforced not only by statute in law, but also by other factors discussed by interviewees.

For example, the question of the integrity of the process and the officers making complaints about other officers arose. Interviewees shared their perceptions of the complaint system and spoke about their experiences with it. While agreeing that individual officers should have the right to complain about other officers if the genuine need arose, officers interviewed also felt that the evidence used to support such complaints needed to be verified in some way to ensure its validity at the outset, to ensure the avoidance of purely vexatious complaints going forward that could potentially damage the reputation of an officer and yet still be without reasonable cause:

> Now I've had numerous made against me over the years, which I know were done for no other reason than to try and affect the way that I was doing business against those people. . . . I was taking on one particular person who was breaching his conditions all the time. He started making allegations against me, you know, taking bribes and stuff like that, which is just totally untrue. But the police department, wanting to be open and honest and transparent, did an investigation, one to showed him that, "No, this hadn't occurred." . . . Because unless they offer some actual evidence and something reasonable and decent about the complainant, we shouldn't even have to touch it.

When speaking of having the right to complain via the Police Service Act, officers also spoke of the fact that, once a complaint had been made, those handling the complaints (also from within the police) needed to follow protocols to ensure the protection of the NSWPF as an organization. The stated concern by interviewees lay not with the need to protect NSWPF, but that in doing so, there could arise a conflict of interest in which the interests of the officers, either as complainants or those being complained about, were not necessarily remaining highlighted against the backdrop of NSWPF needing to protect itself. Here, again, the question of officers needing to trust in the organization to support police officers doing their work arose through discussion of the administrative processes used to respond to this constant community and police scrutiny:

> The person who's doing the investigation has no rights; he can't say anything at all. He can't talk to anyone about it, he can't defend himself and he can't defend anyone else. I've been caught in this situation many a time, where you know what's being said about you is bullshit. But because you're being investigated, you're tied by the Police Service Act, the bloody complaints management system, that you can't disclose anything. You can't defend yourself. That's really bad. That is really damaging for the police because all they're hearing is gossip, rumour and innuendo that's being spread in the meal room and they're not hearing the full side of it.

Ombudsman

The NSW Ombudsman is viewed as a further set of eyes gazing on police along with other police, the general public, and the media. While the Ombudsman may not have powers to prosecute and may exercise discretion in regard to what is recommended for further review or inquiry, the Ombudsman is still considered an "external agency" by police officers and one that represents the community, rather than only serving as an investigating, independent body.

> I've had to do quite a few recently where it's just, unfortunately, these ones were encouraged by the Ombudsman. To put it bluntly, they were crap, absolute crap. There were police officers doing their job and it was legitimate and they were doing it. But they were just listening to the community who were having a whinge.

The Ombudsman, again, rather than being an independent investigator and having a legal representative force of its own, was viewed as another "organization" with extraneous powers to directly determine or direct police activity, rather than investigate and recommend actions to remediate. While the Ombudsman's function in reality may be to handle complaints, it was the process of investigation that was the cause of much disruption to the lives of officers interviewed:

> I'd love to change the complaint management system in the cops. I'd love to be able to just get rid of all the bullshit that we're faced with and, honestly, the encouragement of complaints from other organisations outside the cops, such as the Ombudsman. If we could get that so they can really feel the confidence that they can go out and do it and not be scrutinised for everything they do. That would help them a lot. . . . All you hear them say is, "It's fucked. It's absolute bullshit. And why are we having to answer these questions? Especially when we're dealing with complaints where there's no substance behind it." There's no quality behind it but somebody's decided to make a complaint, so we've got to go through the process.

The Ombudsman investigations could be framed as an additional external organizational stressor for police officers, one that may be necessary but that was perceived as being potentially adversarial and prosecutorial in its purpose. The Ombudsman's Office was considered by some in the interviews to be open to potential exploitation by those in the general public (or within the service) whose claim could be vexatious and without basis.

> Probably one of our biggest frustrations is external agencies, especially government orientated.
> I know we can triage complaints; we can get rid of them. But even the triage process still takes a bit of effort. For me to triage a complaint and get rid of it, it could take me two hours. That's two hours of my time that could much be better spent, rather than sitting there dealing with need to be or have a whinge or a gripe at the police force. People are going to be unhappy when we deal with them because we deal with people that are at their lowest of their lives.

The potential fallout from public complaints and the perceptions of an unbridled process raised the question of whether the NSWPF was also at the mercy of other external agencies such as insurance companies during such processes. This served to compound a sense of police feeling like machines that were sometimes "damaged" but could be fixed up easily and cheaply:

> I really don't want to see us go down the path of having our organisation when it comes to staff who are suffering or who are off duty, on return-to-work plans or whatever,

I don't want to see it get to the point where the decisions are being made and reigns are being pulled by insurance companies. Because we're not motorcars. We're not trying to get out of fixing up something that's been damaged in a motor vehicle accident for the cheapest quote.

General Public

Further concerns with surveillance and complaints were also discussed, especially about the NSWPF's handling of both internal and externally initiated complaints concurrently. One officer spoke at length about the Police Services Act (2003), a legislative imperative that places responsibility for processing and resolving complaints, both internal and external, with NSWPF itself—a situation some would describe as "police policing the police." As noted earlier, internal complaints are certainly an issue of concern for many officers in NSWPF, but so are complaints from the public. Both were reported to take a lot of resources to respond to. The NSWPF's response and how it was handled were also seen to be potential areas for undermining trust in the organization:

> We probably get one out of every 20 or 30 complaints gets substantiated, and the other 29 are crap. There's no value in it and there's nothing there to justify why it was made in the first place.

The general public, as an external stakeholder in the NSWPF, was also described as another source of surveillance by several officers interviewed. Public perceptions of police officers and how they conducted themselves as individuals and as an organization were part of the reported experience of "feeling watched." There was also a strong perception by interviewees that police officers—how they conduct themselves and the job they are required to do—were always in the public eye:

> It's hard not to switch off, especially when you sign up for a job where you're never not a police officer. On a day off you're still expected to step in sometimes. . . . So, you can't really turn off. The pressures through judicial system and public expectations.

But even with this scrutiny, there remained a strong sense from those interviewed that police as individuals, and as an organization, worked for the community. It was believed to be important that the community felt confidence in the police:

> I think to a degree . . . people pretty much think of you as their own personal resource. They want to be able to know that they can stop you in the street. They want to be able to talk to you while you're standing at the bar having a beer on a Friday night at the meat raffles or wherever it is. They want to know that you won't bullshit to them, because they can just see through that. So, having a complete, both feet, jump straight in, is what they want.

While the constant scrutiny and surveillance by the general public was viewed with concern, police officers interviewed also suggested that frequently they enjoyed and were proud of being noticed by members of the public. Certainly, though, the constant scrutiny, if not well managed, could also become a source of significant stress for officers, especially in regional areas where they were "closer" and better known personally to the members of the communities they served.

The impact of constant surveillance cannot be underestimated; police reported feeling "watched," and losing confidence, knowing they were constantly on show. They were afraid a mistake would be harshly judged by the general public and others who had a role in the surveillance of the police. They also feared that such mistakes could have negative consequences for them as individuals and for the organization. Officers need to believe NSWPF will support them, even when they make mistakes that might reflect badly on NSWPF for a short period, so they can trust the organization, and themselves, to carry out their duties with confidence.

Workplace Support Dualities

Dualisms and dualities in the workplace happen where there is a coexistence of two opposing states or parts, which may be physical and organizational (e.g., NSWPF offering psychological support for officers to support their well-being but processes within that same organization leaving officers feeling vulnerable, traumatized, or humiliated) or personal and individual. Several such organizational dualities were exposed during interviews, especially around police officers experiencing anxiety and confusion when doing their jobs. Such confusion, tension, and anxiety often resulted, as noted earlier, from the wide array of both operational and organizational stressors, as well as dichotomies that were believed to exist between job expectations and realities. These also combined with perceptions of ongoing scrutiny and surveillance from so many sources internal and external to the organization. Officers spoke, possibly as a result of all this, about their constant comparisons between what "is" and what "ought to be" when doing their work.

Accessing and Perceptions of Support

It was apparent that NSWPF was concerned with offering support to officers at all levels in the organization who were undertaking police work. There was little argument against notions that police needed support—physically, psychologically, emotionally, managerially, and structurally—from the NSWPF organization. Evidence of needing and wanting this has been reconfirmed in the stories quoted here. NSWPF have also done considerable work in reviewing the status of these support needs within the organization, and it is noted that many initiatives have been undertaken and remain in place intended to remedy this critical officer and organizational concern. The NSWPF Review of Injury Management Practices (2011), for instance, emphasizes the need of the organization to focus on the abilities and strengths of returning officers to work, as well as underscoring the need to step away from a previously adversarial system that has served to undermine trust and open communication in the workplace. It would appear that most of those interviewed for this report would agree with this desired objective.

Officers interviewed all had a general sense of the systems in place within the organization to support their well-being. Depending on the issue for the individual officer, they spoke of being aware of various options available to support their physical, mental, and emotional well-being. However, it did not appear that there was always a full and thorough understanding of what was available, nor was it clear that officers believed that such support procedures and policies were fully supported by management. Support that was reportedly used was often considered by officers to be something much broader and less formal than many of the current formal programs and services within the organization. Support was regarded as something that ideally should be given, offered, or shared between people and in a myriad of situations in the workplace.

Officers were reportedly grateful that NSWPF had recognized the need for such support and developed a strong recognition of mental health injury. However, they believed a gap still remained in terms of the ability of officers to access the formal support programs that had been made available by the organization to assist. Interviews revealed that, while officers still often preferred to talk to peers or mentors informally, they also recognized that there was a strong need for a personal and professional rapport and trust to exist in order for such informal processes to be workable. There was also recognition that there needed to be more than just the informal sharing mechanisms because suicides happened, now and in the past. One officer spoke of how well the informal processes could work but noted their inadequacy, nevertheless:

> The only support was the old, "sit around on a Thursday night cut-out" . . . . Back then, we're talking a long time ago, pre–Royal Commission, you'd have a couple of beers at work on the Thursday night in the meal room and have a chinwag. That, still to this day, I still believe is one of the best support mechanisms you have, because although we didn't have the [EAP] and all that sort of stuff, we had each other. People would talk to each other. But on the same token, we also had a lot of police back then commit suicide. Because they didn't feel that they could talk openly and honestly.
>
> We've become a lot better now in identifying that people need to have support for these things. Everyone's different too. Like some people enjoy the EAP; enjoy counsellors. I never have. I've enjoyed talking to people that I trust and dealing with it that way.

It would appear that the stigma felt by those interviewed around acknowledging stress remains strong in NSWPF and is working against the organization's best efforts to provide emotional, physical, and psychological support to officers. And while stress triggers might be different for sworn officers, reported responses to stress by sworn and unsworn interviewees was fairly consistent and included an acknowledgment that organizational support was required for stress and strain:

> I suppose doing child protection was the trigger. It was the thing that finally wore me down and had the breaking point. There I was working long hours doing plenty of miles, pretty much working on my own without support and carrying a lot, everyone else's emotional baggage. Which meant that I was full. . . . [W]hen you're stuck in it, in that dark place, yeah, it's difficult.

Unfortunately, and despite a clear need, it became clear that the Employment Assistance Program (EAP) and other NSWPF support services were still rarely accessed as a result of the perceived stigma surrounding doing so.

> I was diagnosed with the dreaded PTSD back in 2003. So, that's a roller coaster ride where you not only ride it on your own but the collateral damage of your family that ride along with you. . . . I was offered an opportunity to come back when I came back to work, in my return-to-work plan, after three months, transferring into the command . . . [w]hich was a positive for me, because as far as I was concerned, I was adamant that my time was done. I thought I was pretty well unemployable, and this is back in 2003. So, we're 10 years down the track now. That was a steppingstone to get back into the workplace.

Return to work after injury and organizational support for this was greatly valued by this officer. It was felt that there was additional pressure of having a PTSD diagnosis. While expressing extreme gratitude for a safe return to work, which enabled officers to continue their work and career into the future, extreme anxiety was reported around the diagnosis and treatment of PTSD, presenting a two-pronged choice for those who suffered this particular mental health injury. First, they reported needing to decide if they should risk reporting it to the organization and taking the risk (that they perceived to be high) that a corollary of shame would follow. Second, officers also spoke about what they perceived as danger for them in returning to a place of work that they felt would not necessarily support them adequately and preserve their dignity upon their return.

Support was also discussed in relation to informal mentoring and support programs needing to directly include involvement from management. Respondents felt that support in the job of policing did not necessarily need to come from formalized programs or extensive training, but rather from senior staff and peers sharing real-life experiences that may mirror those currently experienced by injured officers. This would serve to assist injured officers in feeling that they were not alone in their experiences and trauma and not feel that they were "less of a police officer" because of having experienced and acknowledged some very traumatic events and their responses to them.

Experienced officers who had shared their traumatic experiences were seen as very helpful to those less experienced and enabled a less stigmatizing avenue of support for those in need. Many officers recognized that they had difficulty discussing their emotional pain or accessing formal support services to do so. They also reported not knowing how to openly express their inner turmoil and seek help and not wanting to because it might impact their work life negatively in the future. Those discussing the value of such informal support, perceived comradeship, and open dialogue within the workplace felt that this was an ideal platform to enable them to seek the support that they recognized was needed to cope.

> So, I know early on when I was probably 20, I saw an incident . . . where basically this guy had run from an RBT site. He'd rolled the car on [a main] Road. I turned up and he was still hanging in the car upside down. I went, "No worries." Next thing I looked down and his brain was right beside my foot. I went, "Oh, that's a bit ordinary." But what was more gross, was across on the arm-guard railing on the other side, his face had actually been cut off. Peeled off like a mask, sitting on the ground. It was looking up at you.

The description from this officer is a vivid recollection of what was, clearly, a very traumatic experience. But also evident in his description were euphemisms used to describe appalling events, possibly used to cover, or at least to understate, how he was really feeling. Finding a person's brain next to his foot was described as "ordinary"; that same person's face peeled off like a mask on the ground was described merely as "gross." Here was an example of a traumatic episode from years earlier being shared and remembered in excruciating detail. And no help had been sought by this officer at all to deal with any of it. He had spoken of his ordeal with no one: just carried it around in his head until a senior colleague shared a similar experience, and the officer finally felt able to share his trauma without feeling stigmatized:

> That took me, I reckon, six months to deal with because I couldn't, being young and inexperienced, I couldn't talk about it. I couldn't explain it and I was having numerous sleepless nights. It wasn't until we were actually sitting around the meal room one night at work. . . . We were having a chinwag and one of the senior constables was just talking about different things. He talked about something he saw and how it affected him and gave him sleepless nights. I went, "That's affected you?" He went "Yeah, yeah." I went,

"Oh." Then I told my story and once I realised that it was normal for us to experience that, it really helped me. I wasn't different to anyone else.

This kind of support from senior officers was considered paramount to successfully managing stress in policing. It was believed that, regardless of an individual's levels of resilience, without this kind of support from senior officers and colleagues, it would be very challenging, even impossible, for any of them to cope:

To do this job for a lengthy period of time you need to have resilience. You've got to have resilience. . . . I am pretty resilient too, whatever. But what I did learn is I cannot do my job and operate at this level without the supporting commander.

If there was a perception of an absence of what officers thought was *accessible* support within the NSWPF, some officers (mostly new recruits) indicated that they would seek support outside the organization. But not all said they would do this. It is recognized that if there was a supportive network for them to access, such as family and friends, that could be invaluable. However, efficacious external support networks cannot be relied upon to always be available for new recruits (or more experienced officers) to access, and if they aren't, the well-being and potential longevity of that those officers could be jeopardized. And it remains the case that some officers choose not to speak to anyone about the events in their working day.

More experienced officers discussed the informal support processes that had existed within the workplace and how, over time, this had changed because of the introduction of more formal support policies and processes. It was felt that, while more formal systems should remain in place, they may not be accessible to all equally because of personal or situational circumstances that may prevent access. Evidence presented here confirms that accessing such formal services was perceived as stigmatizing by many, deterring their access to them. Officers sometimes made it clear that, in this more contemporary setting, the opportunity or likelihood for a dialogue to exist to offer peer support that they would have enjoyed was not present.

One officer spoke of having been moved away from support networks when they were transferred to a different location; this is a factor that might need to be carefully considered in the future when transferring officers to different LACs:

To begin with, you try to stay in contact. But then it gets a bit hard because you're hearing about people's lives. . . . Because I'm the only one in my class that got [to a different location] and a lot of my friends were stationed, it not together, within a 20-k radius. So, you kind of feel like everyone's getting on with their life and your kind of stuck, to an extent.

Regarding use of formal return-to-work support mechanisms and their ability to support returning officers, some espoused the multiple benefits of positive involvement from management in offering support to their colleagues. This, from a senior officer who felt they had contributed to the well-being of a junior officer in need of support:

I went and spoke to this young officer. She's a good kid but I could see that she was jaded. She just was virtually dragging her feet into the door. I asked her if she was interested. The six-week rotations turned into almost three months. She finishes up later on this month. She's taken on board two high-risk juvenile offenders to intensely case manage them. In the time that she's been doing that, so probably for the last six to eight weeks, neither of these kids have been locked up. Neither of them has been identified for committing a crime. I'm, just thinking, "You know, how easy is it?" She's loving it. Talking to her only this morning on the phone, she's totally reinvigorated. She's coming back to work, back to her substantive role in uniform which she's part of a proactive team which concentrates on addressing crime and locking up crooks. You can just; you can see the change in her face and hear the change in her voice.

Support that was visibly offered and received by and between all ranks of the NSWPF was thought to be very valuable. Support was also felt to be valuable just by the presence of very senior officers; it was considered valuable that very senior staff would make the time and effort to be among staff at all levels, and in all locations, in the NSWPF:

> I do like our leadership at the top at the moment. I think Mr. Scippione[1] to me is show-ing really strong character as a Commissioner for Police for Newcastle, Sydney, Wol-longong, North Coast and South Coast. But he needs to spread his view and needs to encompass the fact that he is the Commissioner for the whole state. I haven't seen the man, in five years, come out to the Western Region.

Communication in Distress

Officers discussed their perceptions of support and levels of communication within the organ-ization, specifically as these were perceived under stressful circumstances. Most officers under-stood, acknowledged, and respected the need for the chain of command and rank. However, there were also reported frustrations with the operation of some lines of communication, particularly if there had been an expectation of support from management around a traumatic event, and it had not been received. Indeed, some officers described a lack of support when they had expected support to be forthcoming; many went further, describing their experience of being criticized and attacked, rather than receiving collegial or managerial support when they needed it:

> I know this has been dragging on. In actual fact, we'd got emails recently from manage-ment at this facility here telling us that this matter's been dragging on and on and on, for way too long, and "What the fuck is going on with this?" "It's got nothing to do with us. What the fuck are you talking to us for?" It really upset us. It really did. We were fucking ropable and if it wasn't for the fact that he is an Inspector of Police I would have been up there and I would have punched his lights out because of the way he spoke to us in this email. It was disgraceful.

Some respondents indicated they wanted to do what the NSWPF Review of Injury and Management Practices (2011) report recommended but felt they had not been furnished with sufficient information to do what was expected of them as managers, and that when infor-mation regarding mental health support initiatives came to them from NSWPF, it had been passed to them through unexpected channels. It was suggested that when this happened, their positions were undermined, as was the organization's, and confusion emerged regarding lines of authority:

> I would question why we were doing this. And "Where does this tie into what we were already doing?" He didn't directly reply. . . . "Can you consult with me so we can—?" You know, "We'll drive this but, like, how about a bit of consultation?" I didn't get a

reply. No reply. There was another example of a similar thing where they . . . questioned but in courteous way. It was never, no. They just got no reply. . . . We have a chain of command in the police force, of course. And he could email and/or talk to anyone he wants to. He's a Commander. But at the moment he goes around his Inspectors and his senior management team straight to the sergeants for something that should be done in consultation with the Inspectors, and the management team to then drive. You then get the "Well, who's running the show?" Or "Who do I report to?" Or "What's going on here?" from your subordinates.

You've got my subordinates going, "What the hell's going on? Why are we doing this?" Or "Did you know about this?" And I'll say, "I don't know. I've got no idea. I'm going to work it out."

Other managers have reported having to withhold information from others and have done so deliberately to try and get their staff to focus on what can be done, rather than what cannot. Some officers reported their belief that they were under no obligation to explain further to those reporting to them what was going on. However, the response from staff reporting to them who were left with insufficient information (in their view, was to become disengaged and demotivated and to feel belittled:

I think a lot of people get upset and disgruntled or that sort of thing with management if you don't communicate things. Because you're not telling them; you don't have to tell them what you're doing. You just [tell somebody] when you can do something.

Another issue is that those believing they were not receiving sufficient information felt ill prepared to do their jobs. Some officers expressed confusion when they didn't understand the lack of information they were receiving, feeling that they had been left to read situations themselves to try and understand them, rather than having a person they could defer to for support; seek reassurance from; and possibly, with guidance, initiate a resolution if need be.

Longer-serving officers in particular spoke at length about interpersonal conflict being an issue. For some, their response was simply to stop communicating about something, or to that person, altogether—not really an ideal outcome from the organization's point of view:

But as I said to him at the end, "Regardless of what happens, at the end of this conversation, when I get up and open that door, we will never ever fucking discuss this again. Because I'm over it. You think you're over it? I'm over it." . . . I'm a bit of a venter, I admit to that. But I like to vent and when I do, then I'll move on.

Other managers spoke of their intolerance of workplace gossip and rumor, suggesting that not only did they not encourage it, but they were also fearful of its effects on staff. However, they remained concerned with the ongoing need for transparency in communication.

Chinese whispers won't come into play, variances won't come into play. It's just got to be very clear and very transparent.

Unfortunately for officers who were the subject of rumors, their reported response was often to withdraw from the organization as a mode of self-protection. However, the unfortunate and serendipitous consequence of this was that they were then without the support of colleagues, formally or informally, at a time when they needed it most:

> I've had rumours spread about me recently but at the end of the day . . . they're rumours. I really don't care. But apart from that I don't really socialise with police officers outside of work therefore I wouldn't say that I know everything that goes on.

Discussion and Conclusion

The chapter has presented empirical findings to consider the challenges faced by police officers in their workplace, challenges that can have an adverse effect on an individual's well-being. Through the exploration of three key themes—*Policing and Trust, Surveillance of Police Officers, and Workplace Support Dualities*—a number of issues have been raised that negatively impact police officers as individuals, as a group, and as an organization. Whilst the dataset presented in this chapter is from a small-scale study, it is not without its merits in terms of making recommendations and having implications for further study that can facilitate the cultivating of well-being among police officers. It is both important and necessary in the first instance to outline the key findings presented in this chapter and how they adversely affect well-being.

The dataset, first, reported on the need for trust in doing police work, with trust being of significance and frequently needing to be very high, in numerous directions, and among numerous stakeholders. Police officers reported needing and desiring high levels of trust: between officers and senior managers, between colleagues at similar levels working in teams, between police officers and the public they serve, and between police officers at all levels and the organization itself. Trust was identified as crucially needed and, when absent, as contributing to a host of problems for individuals and throughout the operation of the organization. The dataset then reported on surveillance and how the police officers who were interviewed felt this impacted their work.

The type and level of surveillance by many stakeholders within and outside the organization placed great pressure on those interviewed when doing their duties as such they felt they were always being "watched" and "judged." The police officers interviewed also felt that, given this high level of surveillance from many quarters, making a mistake that could result in a trouble for themselves and for the organization was highly likely and of concern. This surveillance was reported by those interviewed as coming from other police officers, the NSWPF organization, the community, and the NSW Ombudsman. There are possibly other sources of surveillance not reported on in this chapter that may further contribute to officer concerns (e.g., the role of the media). Questions of trusting the organization to support them given their perception of exposure and vulnerability also arose in connection with these high levels of surveillance. Finally, the dataset revealed problems with workplace support, with officers noting that while NSWPF had put in place numerous measures intended to support officers with psychological injury and to assist officers' return to work after extended medical or stress leave, that many of these procedures and processes were having unintended negative effects and outcomes for all involved (managers administering them and officers accessing them).

It was frequently reported that officers knew of the various support avenues available to them through NSWPF, especially those pertinent to psychological injury and recovery, but deliberately avoided using them. Reasons cited for this seemed to point to the organizational culture of NSWPF, including the unhelpful operationalization of some of its formal and informal procedures, as well as officers reporting being shamed and humiliated if they showed weakness and/or accessed any of the formal services available to help them. Reports of feeling shamed and humiliated were also found to have exacerbated and extended any experiences of individual trauma through dealing with the internal procedures (or their aftermath) that were intended to assist. Significantly, concerns were raised by officers who felt that any involvement with these processes could also have a deleterious impact on their continuing career and future trajectory in the organization. These unintended outcomes may well go toward explaining why, when officers go on any kind of stress- or psychological injury–related leave, they rarely returned to active (or any other) duties with NSWPF but exited the organization permanently, taking their skills and experience with them.

The exodus of junior staff from NSWPF, as well as the high numbers of staff on medical, disability, or stress leave at any given time (including those leaving the organization after extended medical or stress leave or who may have left due to misaligned expectations as to what the job entailed), especially the more experienced officers, was also regarded as a significant loss by officers throughout the organization at all levels, not just management. The loss of skills and experience at all levels was considered a problem by many of the officers interviewed, one that was placing a considerable burden on those who remained in the NSWPF having to continue their work and deal with serious operational issues as required by the job but with insufficient or inexperienced staff to support them. While the NSWPF management knows of the loss of staff and the high numbers on disability and stress leave, what NSWPF management may not be aware of is how seriously officers at all levels of the organization view the situation. They may also not have realized how much staff speak of avoiding the support processes that are currently being made available to them.

Officers interviewed found it extremely beneficial to be able to share their experiences, especially those traumatic ones they had encountered, with a supportive, trusted colleague. Several officers spoke directly of problems that pointed to their having a psychological injury that was very helpfully responded to through such conversations with peers and mentor figures they trusted in the organization. While it is not being suggested that the formal processes currently in place to support officers be reduced, perhaps some kind of informal or formal mentoring or discussion program be commenced that would facilitate opportunities for sharing between peers and colleagues. This could be especially helpful between very experienced, longer-tenured officers and less experienced ones and, in a trusting and confidential environment, supplement the current role of formal counseling and other EAP services now offered by the organization. Some officers simply did not wish to access formal counseling services, and a more informal approach being encouraged and made available internally, perhaps in an informal setting outside the walls of NSWPF LACs, would assist.

The findings presented in this chapter point toward areas that NSWPF and other policing organizations facing similar issues can reasonably respond to, both in the short and longer term. This can be facilitated by the following initial recommendations. First, police organizations such as NSWPF consider doing a cultural audit of the organization on a regular basis (perhaps annually, or every second year) to measure and identify areas of concern within the culture and climate of the workplace. This would enable the organization to respond to problematic organizational cultural characteristics, including what seems to be emerging as a key issue in this study: officers needing formalized support for their psychological injuries choosing not to access those services currently on offer by NSWPF due to fear of being shamed, humiliated, or otherwise stigmatized and their future careers being negatively affected as a result.

A review of police management communication and other managerial styles and processes should be carefully considered by police organizations such as NSWPF. Research involving observational work, including "shadowing" senior officers, is recommended as it might assist in pinpointing problem areas, people, LACs, and disrespectful behavior. It might also enable the highlighting and recording of what excellent senior managers are doing that is different from those who are less well respected by staff.

Police research is also needed targeting possible and prospective new recruits, as well as school children and their parents, to learn how a police organization like NSWPF is currently perceived and, especially, what community members and aspiring recruits believe police work entails. If there is a major mismatch between community expectations and the reality of modern police work, perhaps some advertising or other informational work might be carried out to remedy these misaligned expectations. This would also enable a realignment of the expectations of new recruits entering the organization so they could have a more realistic appraisal of what police operational work and working in a police organization like NSWPF might entail. This reported mismatch of expectations arose in a number of interviews and seemed to point to a major reason why shorter-tenure officers might be leaving the organization prematurely.

The existence of negative workplace behaviors by officers at all levels in police organizations, as reported on in the study presented in this chapter, needs to be responded to by the respective police organizations. Seminars and training are needed to inform officers not just of what negative behaviors are and what they may look like, but also the significant and deleterious outcomes that manifest from them if they are left to continue in a workplace unchecked. Bullying, for instance, is a widely misunderstood term, with serious consequences for all those caught up in it, but few understand its serious nature or the misconceptions and flawed assumptions that exist pertaining to it. Evidence of the existence of continuing negative workplace behaviors, as presented in this chapter, would suggest that there remains potential for psychological injury to officers within an organization such as NSWPF as they go about their working day. Seminars addressing the nature of bullying, harassment, and incivility are recommended to inform officers of the nature of these behaviors and to dispel the many myths surrounding them.

Finally, senior officers in an organization such as NSWPF should be encouraged to find ways and means to speak informally with other officers at all ranks to share their past traumatic experiences in ways that show other officers their experiences with them and their understanding. These could be via small internal organizational talks, seminars, facilitated focus group meetings, or one-on-one meetings with junior officers present. In such sessions, officers at all levels (especially new recruits and junior officers) could hear senior staff speak of such events so they might feel less alone. It would be useful for staff in police organizations to hear senior officers acknowledge and speak publicly of the trauma, shock, sleeplessness, anxiety, loss, pain, grief, and other mental health injuries that senior officers may have sustained—and recovered from—earlier in their long and successful careers.

The empirical findings presented in this chapter underpin a number of implications and recommendations. Consequently, it would appear that while there are many challenges faced by those working in a police organization, there is also a range of responses that can be implemented that could make a significant difference to those in that workplace. The effect of these responses is wide ranging and can include building and establishing trust as well as improving communication among those in the organization, which ultimately contributes to the cultivation of well-being among police officers.

Discussion Questions

1. What risk factors can impede police officer well-being?
2. How can these risk factors be mitigated?
3. What protective factors can support police officer well-being?
4. In what ways can the police organization support police officer well-being?
5. Consider the role of family members and close friends in providing support to police officers. What impact can this have on police officer well-being?

Note

1. Former NSW police commissioner, August 2007 to March 2017.

References

Braun, V., & Clarke, V. (2006). Using thematic analysis in psychology. *Qualitative Research in Psychology, 3*(2), 77–101.

Dick, G. P. (2006). The psychological contract and the transition from full to part-time police work. *Journal of Organizational Behavior, 27*(1), 37–58.

Ellwart, L., Wittek, R., & Wielers, R. (2012). Talking about the boss: Effects of generalized and interpersonal trust in workplace gossip. *Group & Organization Management, 37*(4), 521–549.

Innocenti, L., Pilati, M., & Peluso, A. M. (2011). Trust as moderator in the relationship between HRM practises and employee attitudes. *Human Resource Management Journal, 21*(3), 303–317.

Johnson, R. R. (2012). Police officer job satisfaction: A multidimensional analysis. *Police Quarterly, 15*(2), 157–176.

Kannan-Narasimhan, R., & Lawrence, B. S. (2012). Behavioral integrity: How leader referents and trust matter to workplace outcomes. *Journal of Business Ethics, 111*, 165–178.

Kiel, L. D., & Watson, D. J. (2009). Affective leadership and emotional labor: A view from the local level. *Public Administration Review, 69*(1), 21–24. https://doi.org/10.1111/j.1540-6210.2008.01936.x

Noblet, A. J., Rodwell, J. J., & Allisey, A. F. (2009). Police stress: The role of the psychological contract and perceptions of fairness. *Policing: An International Journal of Police Strategies & Management, 32*(4), 613–630.

NSW (New South Wales) Ombudsman. (2014). *NSW Ombudsman annual report 2015–16.* Retrieved April 5, 2017, from www.ombo.nsw.gov.au/__data/assets/pdf_file/0007/19798/NSWOmbudsman-Annual-report-2013-2014.pdf

NSW Police Force. (2011). *Review of injury management practices.* Retrieved April 5, 2017, from www.police.nsw.gov.au/__data/assets/pdf_file/0013/213070/Injury_Management_Review.pdf

NSW (New South Wales) Police Force. (2013). *Annual report 2012–2013.* Retrieved April 5, 2017, from www.opengov.nsw.gov.au/download/13662

Perry, J. L., Engbers, T. A., & Jun, S. Y. (2009). Back to the future? Performance-related pay, empirical research, and the perils of persistence. *Public Administration Review, 69*(1), 39–51.

Police Services Act. (2003). *An act to provide for the establishment and regulation of the police service.* Retrieved April 14, 2017, from www.austlii.edu.au/au

Schafer, J. A. (2013). The role of trust and transparency in the pursuit of procedural and organisational justice. *Journal of Policing, Intelligence and Counter Terrorism, 8*(2), 131–143.

Spector, M. D., & Jones, G. E. (2004). Trust in the workplace: Factors affecting trust formation between team members. *The Journal of Social Psychology, 144*(3), 311–321.

Thomas, G. F., Zolin, R., & Hartman, L. (2009). The central role of communication in developing trust and its effect on employee involvement. *Journal of Business Communication, 46*(3), 287–310.

Vickers, M. H. (2008, December). From the editor-in-chief's desk: Employers and employees thinking about trust. *Employee Responsibilities and Rights Journal, 20*(4), 223–226.

Williams, B. N., & Kellough, J. E. (2006). Leadership with an enduring impact: The legacy of chief Burtell Jefferson of the metropolitan police department of Washington, DC. *Public Administration Review, 66*(6), 813–822.

Yang, K., & Holzer, M. (2006). The performance-trust link: Implications for performance measurement. *Public Administration Review, 66*(1), 114–126.

Chapter 2

An Interdisciplinary Perspective on the Tragedy of Police-Citizen Encounters

From Social Dilemma via Fairness to Coordination

Katharina Friederike Sträter and René Hornung

Introduction

On Christmas Eve, 2015, a policeman in Herborn (Germany) was stabbed to death while performing a simple identity and train ticket inspection. The 27-year-old attacker was shot several times but survived, although badly injured (FAZ, 2015). A couple of months before, in Halle (Saale) (Germany), while attempting to stop a speeding motorcyclist, a policeman was run over and died. The motorcycle rider then lost control of his bike, collided with a streetlight, and died as well (MZ, 2015). Considering the continuing violence between particular groups of citizens and police in the United States, the two German incidents might appear to be of subordinate importance. Nevertheless, these few examples indicate that routine daily encounters such as providing security for sport events and rallies, simply checking someone's identity, and conducting traffic controls may escalate into enormously dangerous situations for both citizens and the police. Whereas these more violent events are in the media spotlight, the general increased aggressiveness of people as shown by gestures, mime, and verbal communication are also equally problematic in everyday interactions (e.g., Behr, 2011, 2014).

In response to the increase in aggression, the police are taking more intensive steps to protect themselves. The discussion about the appropriateness of means of self-protection has, accordingly, also intensified over the last decades as it often obstructs the endeavor to consolidate service-oriented policing. As one of the less publicly visible actions, the intensified schooling in self-protection skills and the sensitization for potentially dangerous situations has become a stronger focus during job training (Füllgrabe, 2013, 2014). Having "one hand on the gun" during traffic control situations (Zeit Online, 2014; Der Tagesspiegel, 2001), as well as the use of body cams in routine situations to record interactions with the public for mutual advantage (Ziems, 2006; Weigel, 2015) are far more obvious. Even though many individuals accept[1] the more militarized appearance of police and an increased willingness to draw their weapons, the tactical change does lead to a more aggressive and impersonal police force.[2,3] The ubiquitous situations of danger, especially against of the backdrop of terror, may aggravate this overall tension.

In summary, it seems that potentially aggressive parts of police and citizens are stuck in vicious cycles of mutual armament. To give a fresh impetus to this debate, this chapter opens an interdisciplinary dialogue between game theory and police practice. Within this dialogue, the authors—one of whom is a practitioner and the other an economist—abstract from the real-word problem and, thus, transfer the situation into the world of models. This transformation allows us to find theoretical solutions for simplified real-world problems that, in turn, can be discussed from a practical point of view. Such a proceeding is common neither for a theorist nor for a practitioner. Consequently, this interdisciplinary collaboration unquestionably

DOI: 10.4324/9781003047117-3

requires lots of translational efforts, indulgence, and the willingness to change viewpoints. However, it allows us to obtain fresh and fruitful perspectives both on the problem in practice and the existing theories.

Accordingly, the chapter is structured as follows: First, the special nature of meetings between citizens and the police is introduced in more detail. On this basis, the circumscribed situations are (re-)constructed and analyzed game theoretically. In the following, the assumption of purely self-interested actors is dropped in favor of the consideration of reciprocal fairness. It is demonstrated that, from a theoretical perspective, mutual cooperation can be implemented on the basis of positive first- and second-order expectations. Subsequently, necessary preconditions for the implementation of bilateral cooperation are discussed with regard to their practical relevance.

The Special Nature of Police-Citizen Encounters

Before transferring the situation into the world of models, the considered types of meetings between citizens and the police, their characteristics, and specialties are introduced. Analyzing get-togethers of citizens and the police as well as the respective parties' interrelation has a long tradition, especially in the fields of social, psychological, and political sciences. Sykes and Clark (1975) categorize these meetings as *encounters*. An encounter is characterized as a "natural unit of social interaction in which focused interaction occurs" (Goffman, 1961, pp. 7–8). Individuals participating in an encounter disperse after completing their temporary joint activity and do not share common endeavors in the long run (Sykes & Clark, 1975). However, during focused interactions, the parties tacitly agree to pay at least as much cognitive and visual attention to their respective counterpart as in normal conversation (Goffman, 1961).

According to Skogan (2006), police-citizen encounters can be differentiated into contacts that are initiated by citizens and those that are initiated by the police. In the first type of situation, civilians seek police assistance (sought contacts), whereas in the second one, citizen are approached by the police for different reasons (e.g., traffic control) (unsought contacts) (Clancy, Hough, Aust, & Kershaw, 2001).

Contacts between citizens and the police are distinct from ordinary citizen-citizen encounters. The citizens enter such situations involuntarily or out of an exceptional situation in which they need help. The police enter the situations as part of their job. In accordance with their mandate, the police are equipped with appropriate authority as well as the right to use violence if necessary. For this reason, a natural imbalance of power characterizes the encounter (Sykes & Clark, 1975). The degree to which the police generally display their authority and, in contrast, the degree to which the authority of the police is accepted by civilians have changed over the recent decades, as the following paragraphs summarize.

Considering the period of the 1970s, Sykes and Clark (1975) state that police-citizen encounters must revolve around the "exchange of deference and maintenance of proper demeanor" (p. 588). The police officer as a symbol of the law and an authority who must be respected (regardless of the situation) can show less regard toward the citizens. In contrast, the citizens must always be deferential toward the police. Such an expectation about the other party's behavior reflects the prevailing imbalance of power. On the one hand, the given rules of conduct can be seen as obligations for one party. On the other hand, they set up the basis for the respective other party's expectations. Thus, the subordinate group (citizens) is consequently supposed to exhibit appropriate deference toward the police. The police, in turn, expect to be treated respectfully while acting in a commanding manner. Refusing deference to an officer and not accepting his decreed authority were interpreted as the beginning of a public rebellion (Goffman, 1956; Sykes & Clark, 1975).

Substantial clashes between civilians and the police in the past have shown that aggressive policing does not increase citizens' support.[4] Realizing that the police are dependent on citizens' cooperation and support to solve and prevent crime effectively, to maintain the social order, and to be successful in performing all their other duties (Rosenbaum, Schuck, Costello, Hawkins, & Ring, 2005), a change from an authoritative toward a more cooperative basic attitude occurred. To maintain cooperation, the "most reasonable course of action for police agencies would have been to earn the trust of the public by working with citizens in a respectful fashion" (Brown & Benedict, 2002, p. 544). Within the course of the implementation of different interpretations of community policing, the imbalance of power between civilians and the police has become at least less visible. The police generally seek to appear as a friendly service provider rather than an aggressive authority.[5] However, as practical experiences and recent events clearly show, a positive interaction at eye level and, thus, bilateral cooperation are far from being fully implemented. To analyze police-citizen encounters on a rather abstract level, the respective situations can be translated into the world of game-theoretical models as is shown in the next section.

Police-Citizen Encounters—A Dilemma?

In the following, the situation is constructed game theoretically. Therefore, it is necessary to reduce the complexity of the real world by focusing on a handful of aspects as defined subsequently. The model considers unsought police-citizen encounters only. Ignoring the actual process of interaction, a strategic game is considered where two players, the police P and the citizens C simultaneously[6] decide whether they would prefer to engage in rebellious and aggressive conduct $(A_m, m \in \{P,C\})$ or to exhibit cooperative behavior $(C_m, m \in \{P,C\})$. Different levels of escalation in aggressive behavior will not yet be incorporated. Thus, staying with the example of a traffic control situation and adopting the perspective of an officer in practice, the modeled situation is best comparable to the situation just before he stops a car.

The consideration of police and citizens is made on an aggregated level so that players are representatives of their respective groups. Since both the group of citizens and the group of police consist of several subgroups that exhibit different predispositions for escalation, the respective relevant groups have to be chosen and specified in more detail.

According to Van Maanen (1978), the group (originally) termed *assholes* can be defined to be of most importance to the considered escalations. Encounters with this group are the most critical ones since those people are assumed to challenge the legitimacy and the authority of the police. By, for example, not accepting a fine for speeding, questioning the necessity of being stopped, or physical resistance, they run the risk of being treated harshly (Van Maanen, 1978; Kääriäinen & Sirén, 2012).[7] In the following, it will be assumed that this group of citizens is torn between cooperative and aggressive conduct. They choose one of the two strategies according to their anti-authoritarian "personality" and the given incentive structure. The following analysis is restricted to encounters between police and such "problematic" citizens as characterized earlier. In turn, for the group of the police, only those who internally make this decision are considered. From a practical perspective, this group seems to be the rather professional one. Those who are always cooperative or always aggressive, regardless of the situation, either have a missing awareness of risk or a missing willingness to cooperate generally.

In the following, the players' strategies and the resulting game are specified in more detail. Additionally, the resulting combinations of strategies are evaluated from both players' perspective. The availability of two pure strategies (A_m, C_m) that constitute the set of strategies S_m for the players $m \in \{P,C\}$ results in a total of four different strategy combinations as illustrated

The Tragedy of Police-Citizen Encounters   25

in Figure 2.1. The individual preferences regarding the situations are expressed using a payoff structure that provides information about the preferability of one situation to another. Thereby, higher payoffs are assigned to preferred situations and vice versa. With regard to the following model, it is assumed that payoffs are cardinal utilities. Consequently, small letters w to z are defined as positive real numbers that represent the ordering of the four different situations with regard to the general preferability as well as its strength. The coefficient X explicitly accounts for the possibility of scaling. With regard to the resulting payoff structure the following holds: $w_m X_m > x_m X_m > y_m X_m > z_m X_m$ for $m \in \{P,C\}$; $w_m,\ldots,z_m \in R^+$; $X_m \in R^+$, meaning that a situation with payoff $w_m X_m$ is strictly preferred to the situation with payoff $x_m X_m$, etc.[8]

An intense discourse between the authors results in the following evaluation of the four different situations, starting with the police's perspective: The worst situation for the police is one in which a cooperative strategy, implying a weak focus on self-protection and a friendly demeanor, coincides with an aggressive strategy chosen by the citizen. On the one hand, the inadequately friendly behavior on the part of the police might result in physical or psychological injuries. On the other hand, every police-citizen encounter can be seen as a "moral contest in which the authority of the state is either confirmed, denied, or left in doubt" (Van Maanen, 1978, p. 316). The denial of the state's order without an appropriate answer can be assumed to yield disutility for the institution of the police as a whole (payoff $z_P X_P$).

On the other hand, if well protected, aggressive police meet with non-aggressive citizens, the risk of potential injury is minimized for the police even though the high degree of protection was unnecessary. The high level of self-protection and harshness can be assumed to enhance self-confidence. The preference to choose a harsh approach toward citizens in general can also be motivated by the inner socialization of the police group. In the light of defensive solidarity within the group, the police seal themselves off from the "rest of the world" and prefer to approach citizens authoritatively (Ohlemacher, 2000) (payoff $w_P X_P$).

A lower level of self-protection in combination with cooperative citizen behavior would not lead to what can roughly be called injuries, but the potential vulnerability makes this situation less preferable to the former one. Also, the effort that has to be spent in order to overcome the natural distance between police and citizens has to be taken into account (payoff $x_P X_P$).

Although an aggressive stance from the police perspective implies that the officers are optimally prepared and ready to (re-)establish their authority in case of aggressive citizen behavior, they must deal with all the inconveniences that such a confrontation might bring (payoff $y_P X_P$).

The worst situation from the considered social group of citizens' perspectives is the one in which they exhibit cooperative behavior even if they don't like to, whereas the police act aggressively and show a lack of appreciation of the citizen's endeavor. In addition to the disutility that playing the nice guy brings along, they experience disutility from the police "failure" to recognize their attempts (payoff $z_C X_C$). By contrast, if aggressive citizens can catch the police unawares, they can act out their pent-up tension without worrying about the police reaction. Whether a criminal prosecution will follow remains undetermined at this moment (payoff $w_C X_C$). Mutually aggressive behavior protects the citizens from their experience of disutility of cooperation in contrast to the former situation; the risk of being injured or punished must be considered at once (payoff $y_C X_C$). Bilateral cooperation would, on the one hand, lead to disutility from behaving cooperatively, but, on the other hand, the credit stemming from recognizing the given behavior must be considered (payoff $x_C X_C$).

The overall situation can be represented as a normal form game (Figure 2.1):

		Citizen (C)	
		$\mathcal{A}_C$	$\mathcal{C}_C$
Police (P)	$\mathcal{A}_P$	$y_P X_P$; $y_C X_C$	$w_P X_P$; $z_C X_C$
	$\mathcal{C}_P$	$z_P X_P$; $w_C X_C$	$x_P X_P$; $x_C X_C$

$$w_m X_m > x_m X_m > y_m X_m > z_m X_m \text{ for } m \in \{P, C\}; w_m, \ldots, z_m \in \mathbb{R}^+; X_m \in \mathbb{R}^+$$

Figure 2.1 The Initial Situation

(Source: The authors)

As is common in economic theory, the further analysis of the game starts from the assumption of purely self-interested actors. Within the framework of economic theory, this assumption is often heavily criticized. Interestingly, it does fit the situation between potentially problematic citizens and the police quite well. Potentially problematic citizens and the police are often opposed to each other with hardened fronts. This leads to situations in which citizens deny the police all human individuality and act as if the other party is a non-human and abstract entity. The same holds vice versa. Such a way of thinking leads to the ignorance of the respective other party's interests—and a purely self-interested orientation finds its way into the situations.

Analyzing the game assuming purely self-interested actors shows that both police and citizens have dominant strategies[9] constituting a Nash equilibrium,[10] in which both parties plan to play aggressive strategies. Given the players' characters as assumed in the model, it is always beneficial for the police to utilize a high level of self-protection and a harsh approach. It is convenient for the group of potentially aggressive citizens to exhibit aggressive behavior as well. However, this Nash equilibrium is not Pareto-efficient since both parties would be mutually better off in the bilateral cooperative situation. In summary, the individual incentive structure leads to an overall situation that has the structure of a (prisoner's) dilemma and that results in an equilibrium situation, which—from an outside perspective—is not desirable at all. Both parties could be better off simultaneously realizing a situation of cooperation. Unfortunately, cooperation is not equilibrated since both parties always have an incentive to deviate from it.

From a theoretical perspective, numerous components and mechanisms could be introduced into the model to overcome the dilemmatic situation, ranging from punishing non-cooperative behavior to the consideration of finitely or infinitely repeated interactions, among others. However, no considerations mentioned so far break with the assumption of purely self-interested actors as discussed in the previous section. From a theoretical as well as a practical perspective, it is of high interest to incorporate social goals into the model and to analyze the respective changes and implications since, from a practical perspective, this would presume that parties do consider each other as social entities rather than impersonal groups or forces. The adoption of Rabin's (1993) theoretical concept of fairness equilibria allows the consideration of pro- as well as anti-social behavior in simultaneous games based on reciprocity as demonstrated in the next section.

Incorporating Fairness

Observed deviations from the assumption of exclusively self-motivated actors and the resulting rise of behavioral economics have led to the implementation of altruism and other social goals into theoretical concepts (e.g., Fehr & Schmidt, 2003).[11] One of the most prominent approaches incorporating fairness concerns into game theory might be Rabin's (1993) concept of a fairness equilibrium[12] since he was the first who "made the notion precise and explored the consequences of reciprocal behavior" within the framework of game theoretical models (Fehr & Schmidt, 2003, p. 226). Within the context of this enrichment of theory, experimentally observed human behavior constitutes the basis for modifications in most cases, so also in the case of Rabin. Rabin (1993) grounds his modification of existing theory on the (experimental) observation that the same people who aim to help those people who helped them are also willing to hurt those who hurt them. Such behavior is also called reciprocal behavior: Humans are willing to sacrifice their own well-being (in theory: individual amounts of ordinary payoffs) to reciprocate their opponents' behavior.

Considering reciprocity in games with simultaneous moves requires the inclusion of players' expectations regarding the intentions of other players. Thus, the formalization of intentions takes into account not only what the parties actually do "but also what they could have chosen to do and did not" (Gui & Sugden, 2005, p. 112). Because of the simultaneousness, it is not possible to observe the opponent's behavior in a first step and reply to it in a second. Consequently, the actors must build expectations about the behavior of their opponents. The model, therefore, considers two kinds of intended fairness: 1) fairness that is expected to be shown toward the opponent by choosing a particular (individual) strategy, given the expectations about the strategy the opponent will choose, and 2) fairness a player expects to receive from the other, given the expectation about the other's strategy choice as well as the expectation about the other's expectation about the individual strategy choice.

The incorporation of fairness, thus, implicitly assumes that the players have perspective-taking abilities and can employ at least two levels of strategic reasoning (Grosskopf & Nagel, 2007; Nagel, 1995). Even if it might seem to be a bit confusing to form expectations about other people's expectations, experimental results show that humans are very well able to think through at least two iterated steps of a strategic situation—if they want to.

Incorporating beliefs into the model thus requires not only that the strategy a_m (from the set of strategies S_m) that is actually chosen by player $m, m \in \{P,C\}$, is taken into account, but also m's expectations e_n^1 about the strategy that $n, n \in \{P,C\}, n \neq m$, will play as well as m's expectation e_m^2 about n's expectation about m's strategy choice.[13] Technically, the incorporation of a fairness–corrective term into the utility function allows the transformation of the initial, *material* game into a *psychological* one.[14] Therefore, player m's *material payoff*[15] is supplemented with two expressions: 1) There is a functional expression $f_m\left(a_m, e_n^1\right)$ that displays the kindness that m exhibits towards $n, m \neq n$; and 2) There is an analogous expression $\widetilde{f}_n\left(e_n^1, e_m^2\right)$ that captures the kindness that m expects n will muster up toward him. Through the multiplicative connection of the two terms, advantages and disadvantages of reciprocity can be integrated (formula 1).

$$U_m\left(a_m, e_n^1, e_m^2\right) \equiv \pi_m\left(a_m, e_n^1\right) + \widetilde{f}_n\left(e_n^1, e_m^2\right) \cdot \left[1 + f_m\left(a_m, e_n^1\right)\right] \tag{1}$$

Consequently, the overall utility (U_m) with which a situation is evaluated depends on the players' expectations $\left(e_n^1, e_m^2\right)$ and the actual strategy choice $\left(a_m\right)$. It incorporates the material payoff as stated in the initial game $\left(\pi_m\left(a_m, e_n^1\right)\right)$ as well as additional utility or disutility from fairness ($\widetilde{f}_n\left(e_n^1, e_m^2\right) \cdot \left[1 + f_m\left(a_m, e_n^1\right)\right]$).

Emergence and composition of utility stemming from fairness are as follows:

Whether player m appears to act kindly or unkindly toward n is measured in comparison to the equitable payoff

$$\pi_n^c\left(e_n^1\right) = \frac{\pi_n^h\left(e_n^1\right) + \pi_n^l\left(e_n^1\right)}{2}$$, where $\pi_n^h\left(e_n^1\right)$ is the highest payoff from the set of Pareto-efficient

payoff pairs $\Pi\left(e_n^1\right)$ that player n could achieve and $\pi_n^l\left(e_n^1\right)$ the corresponding lowest one. Without consideration of the Pareto criterion, $\pi_n^{min}\left(e_n^1\right)$ denotes the worst possible payoff player n could realize. Thereby, $\Pi\left(e_n^1\right)$ represents the set of all feasible payoffs for player n after restricting the payoff space with player m's belief about player n's strategy choice.[16] The kindness function

$$f_m\left(a_m, e_n^1\right) \equiv \frac{\pi_n\left(e_n^1, a_m\right) - \pi_n^c\left(e_n^1\right)}{\pi_n^h\left(e_n^1\right) - \pi_n^{min}\left(e_n^1\right)}$$ finally measures how nice player m is being to his oppo-

nent. Kind behavior causes the kindness function to be positive, unkind to be negative, and neutral behavior to be equal to zero. The function expressing player m's expectations about player n's kindness,

$$\widetilde{f}_n\left(e_n^1, e_m^2\right) \equiv \frac{\pi_m\left(e_m^2, e_n^1\right) - \pi_m^c\left(e_m^2\right)}{\pi_m^h\left(e_m^2\right) - \pi_m^{min}\left(e_m^2\right)}$$, is analogously structured on the basis of the first- and

second-order beliefs and is not influenced by the action that is taken by the respective player. It is important to note that both fairness functions have no dimension and are normalized to the interval $\left[-1; \frac{1}{2}\right]$. Thus, the additively connected fairness part of the overall utility function generally becomes less and less influential as the material payoffs rise.[17]

On the basis of the modified utility function, it is possible to apply the fairness equilibrium concept that defines an equilibrium as a pair of best response strategies $\left(a_P, a_C\right) \in \left(S_P, S_C\right)$, such that for $m \in \{P, C\}, n \neq m$, $a_m \in argarg\, U_m\left(a, e_n^1, e_m^2\right)$ and $e_m^2 = e_m^1 = a_m$ holds.[18] Applied to the initial (prisoner's) dilemma situation, it is now possible to analyze particular circumstances, under which the Pareto efficient and mutually cooperative strategy combination is equilibrated given that the players' beliefs are congruent and correct ($e_m^2 = e_m^1 = a_m = C$ for $m = P, C$).[19] In the modified game, the utility, for example, of the police[20] playing the (equilibrium) strategy C yields utility

$$U_P = x_P X_P + \frac{1}{2} \cdot \left(1 + \frac{1}{2}\right) = x_P X_P + 0.75,$$ whereas unilateral deviation would lead to an

overall utility of

$$U_P' = w_P X_P + \frac{1}{2} \cdot \left(1 - \frac{1}{2}\right) = w_P X_P + 0.25,$$ given that cooperation is common knowl-

edge. This implies that deviating from the equilibrium would only be profitable if $w_P X_P + 0.25 > x_P X_P + 0.75$ or $0.5 < \left(w_P - x_P\right) X_P$ (Figure 2.2).

Obviously, the stability requirement to establish the cooperative fairness equilibrium is influenced by two different factors: the scaling of the problem $\left(X_P\right)$ as well as the payoff difference between cooperation and aggression $\left(w_P - x_P\right)$ (assuming that the citizens cooperate). The larger the scales in general, the more difficulties arise establishing the bilateral cooperative situation. This result arises due to the problem that the dimensionless "fairness part" is additively linked with the utility that is expressed via material payoffs.[21] Likewise, the larger the difference between w and x (i.e., the more preferable one situation is compared to the other measured in purely material payoffs), the less easy it is to establish cooperation. Unquestionably, it is not possible to interpret the stability requirement $0.5 < \left(w_m - x_m\right) X_m, m \in \{P, C\}$ as a numeric requirement since it, of course, depends on the actual numbers chosen for the construction of the model. Nevertheless, interpreting simply the idea that cooperation and mutual collaboration can be implemented based on expectations regarding fairness and reciprocity gives a helpful insight as discussed in the subsequent section.

		Citizen (C)	
		$\mathcal{A}_C$	$\mathcal{C}_C$
Police (P)	$\mathcal{A}_P$	... ; ...	$w_P X_P + 0.25$; ...
	$\mathcal{C}_P$	... ; $w_C X_C + 0.25$	$x_P X_P + 0.75$; $x_C X_C + 0.75$

Figure 2.2 The Cooperative Fairness Equilibrium
(Source: The authors)

		Citizen (C)	
		$\mathcal{A}_C$	$\mathcal{C}_C$
Police (P)	$\mathcal{A}_P$	$y_P X_P - 0.25$; $y_C X_C - 0.25$	... ; $z_C X_C - 0.75$
	$\mathcal{C}_P$	$z_P X_P - 0.75$; ...	... ; ...

Figure 2.3 The Aggressive Fairness Equilibrium
(Source: The authors)

Besides the problem arising from the general vulnerability of the fairness equilibrium based on easily dominating material payoffs, another characteristic of the overall concept has to be discussed. Whereas the mutually cooperative fairness equilibrium is dependent on expectations and the configuration of material payoffs, the conventional Nash equilibrium, consisting of mutually defective strategies, is a fairness equilibrium for any value of material payoffs and mutually malevolent expectations as well (Figure 2.3).

Whereas the bilateral benevolent situation can only be an equilibrium, if the material payoffs are sufficiently small, the mutual malevolent or purely self-interested one additionally exists for all scales of payoffs. In this hostile situation, both players pursue their ambition to maximize their own material payoff as well as their desire to harm each other. This plurality of potential equilibria (which might constitute a sub- or superset of common Nash equilibria) (Rabin, 1993) is a quite realistic feature of Rabin's (1993) concept (Fehr & Schmidt, 2003) that reflects the vulnerability of stable reciprocal cooperation.

Having two potential fairness equilibria instead of one Nash equilibrium causes the problem to change from being a (social) dilemma to being a special kind of coordination game—a situation in which it is no longer possible to clearly predict which of the two equilibria will be constituted. The question of whether the good or the bad fairness equilibrium will be established is generally difficult to answer. The answer depends in large part on the kind of self-fulfilling prophecy that is inherent in the second part of the equilibrium definition: the convergence or coordination of expectations $\left(e_m^2 = e_m^1 = a_m \right)$. The actual strategy choice and first- and second-order expectations all have to converge to either cooperation or aggression.

Aside from the fact that the mutually cooperative fairness equilibrium is, in any case, the more vulnerable one as it can be destroyed by sufficiently large material payoffs, it must be common knowledge on which of the situations the players' expectations do actually converge. The plurality of equilibria is occasionally deemed to be a shortcoming of Rabin's (1993) concept (e.g., Fehr & Schmidt, 2003). However, for the considered case of police-citizen encounters, the given plurality perfectly catches important characteristics of the real-life situation, as the following section will demonstrate.

Police-Citizen Encounters—A Question of Coordination of Expectations

As shown in the previous section, incorporating reciprocity based on expectations about fairness intentions converts the initial dilemma situation into a (quasi-)coordination game in which the mutually cooperative as well as the mutually uncooperative situation might be equilibrated. In the presence of several potential equilibria, the players' strategy choices must "somehow be coordinated to achieve the preferred equilibrium as the outcome" (Dixit, Skeath, & Reiley, 2009, p. 760).[22] However, coordination is not (always) easy to realize. Schelling (e.g., 1960, 2005) explicitly analyzes the resolution of coordination problems incorporating strategic reasoning. In his groundbreaking book *The Strategy of Conflict*, he states that solving tacit coordination problems requires one to "coordinate predictions, to read the same message in the common situation, to identify the one course of action that their (the players') expectations of each other can converge on" (Schelling, 2005, p. 54). According to Schelling (2005), people "*can* often concert their intentions or expectations with others if each knows that the other is trying to do the same" (p. 57). The key to solving coordination problems tacitly is to find a key that is somewhat salient—or focal—so that every player can identify this strategy to be the key strategy. A focal point, thus, can abstractly be defined as "a point for convergence of expectations" (Sugden & Zamarrón, 2006, p. 610). Possible reasons that empower a strategy to be of salience vary greatly with the nature of the problem. For physical coordination problems, a strategy can be salient for optical or geometrical reasons, whereas for other problems, the background of a common history, a common culture, or common experiences might cause conspicuity.[23]

However, a game with two fairness equilibria differs slightly from ordinary coordination games. The latter games are theoretically characterized by the fact that, based on material payoffs, several situations are Nash equilibria in any way. In this respect, the resulting problem is a problem of equilibrium selection. In reality, this selection problem might be resolved under consideration of converging expectations. Considering the modeled situation of police-citizen encounters, the material payoff structure yields the constitution of a single Nash equilibrium, which also is a fairness equilibrium according to Rabin (1993). Only expectations that deviate from the (Nash-)equilibrated situation might have the power to constitute the cooperative situation as a fairness equilibrium. The resulting problem, thus, is a problem not of equilibrium selection, but of equilibrium constitution. The mutually cooperative equilibrium does not exist as long as expectations do not diverge from the Nash equilibrium and converge toward fairness. This, in turn, makes the importance of expectation management even more salient and gives rise to lots of further research, as the following section points out.

Implications

Even if the game-theoretical analysis of police-citizen encounters might appear quite abstract from the practitioner's point of view, it is possible to extract many fruitful ideas about how the quality of police-citizen encounters can be improved.

Ascertaining the dilemma. The intense interdisciplinary discussion about the (perceived) individual preferability of the different situations within the initial model points to the fact that the overall situation exhibits, indeed, a dilemmatic character resulting from the individual preferability of one situation to another. This coming together of individually incentivized strategies is driven by, among other things, the pure self-interest that is assumed in theory and exhibited in practice. The assumption of purely self-interested actors, which fits the real-life situation quite well, causes the parties to follow strictly dominant, aggressive strategies. On the one hand, this implies that the parties are stuck in a devil's circle of mutual armament. On the other hand, it points to the fact that an implementation of reciprocal cooperation is not possible if both the citizens and the police are not bent on switching perspectives generally.

Within the interdisciplinary dialogue, this is quite interesting for the following reason: From an economist's perspective, the self-interest assumption was brought into question and modified in *theory* since real-life human behavior does often deviate from it. By contrast, within the frame of police-citizen encounters, the assumption of purely self-interested entities seems to hold in practice too well so that a modification of practice must be targeted. A purely self-interested orientation of the police and/or the citizens keeps them imprisoned in the structure of the (prisoner's) dilemma. This is a stumbling block for any kinds of cooperation and implies that, in practice, the dialogue between citizens and the police must be intensified—or, since it is often practically nonexistent, it has to be initiated.

Recognizing the coordinative character. The missing awareness of the potentially coordinative character of the situation might be the most basic problem when talking about police-initiated police-citizen encounters in the light of the game-theoretical model as introduced here. Exclusively self-interested parties are trapped in the original situation of a (prisoner's) dilemma and do not realize that 1) the situation might rather be a coordination situation, and 2) mutual coordination of positive beliefs might be beneficial. In a nutshell: If the situation is (perceived to be) a dilemma, then it really is a problem. If it is (perceived to be) a problem of coordination, talking about it might help. Thus, in a second step, the parties have to be aware of the necessity to coordinate their predictions. As Sugden and Zamarrón (2006, p. 614) summarize with a downright virtuous simplicity, each party has to have in mind the idea of "*We* need to coordinate *our* predictions." Moreover, the term *cooperation* in his function, as the crux of the parties' common need, is "irreducible plural: it takes two to coordinate" (Sugden & Zamarrón, 2006, p. 614). Consequently, if the endeavor is to overcome the dilemma of mutually aggressive behavior, both parties have to be aware of the fact that—in case they break with their purely self-interested orientation—they are confronted with a coordination problem, in which coordination—either on the good or the bad equilibrium—is only possible if the parties' beliefs are coordinated.

Management of expectations. According to Rabin's (1993) concept of a fairness equilibrium, first-order expectations, second-order expectations, and the actual strategy choice must be congruent in order to constitute an equilibrium. To implement the cooperative situation as an equilibrium, it is necessary to manage expectations in a way that bilateral cooperative behavior is common knowledge and, thus, focal. This means that cooperation has to be what the parties actually *do* (a_m), what they expect the other party will do $\left(e_m^1\right)$, and what they expect the other party expects oneself to do $\left(e_m^2\right)$.[24] In a very first step, this implies that the parties have to be aware of the fact that not only actions but also expectations—their own as well as the opponent's—matter. The individual consideration of expectations requires the schooling of perspective-taking abilities and self-reflection skills.

Hand in hand with selected empirical research regarding the perception of fairness in police-citizen interactions (e.g., Brown & Benedict, 2002; Tyler, 1988), as well as Schelling's concept of focal points, the definition of Rabin's fairness equilibrium also indicates that a common history—the history of police-citizen encounters—influences the salience of a particular situation. If the police behavior has been perceived to be procedurally fair (which, in this special case, means that the police have acted in a transparent, friendly, and cooperative manner in the past), then the citizens might expect the police to act cooperatively in the future. Thus, e_p^1 (the citizen's expectations about the police's strategy choice) can be a priori shaped by (positive or negative) past encounters. But this is only one parameter influencing mutual cooperation according to the theoretical model. Thus, the prevailing focus on research regarding the perception of procedural fairness might fall short.

Considering the group of citizens, it is also important to influence and manage the expectations they have about the expectations the police might have regarding their own strategy choice $\left(e_C^2\right)$. Referring to van Maanen (1978), this second-order belief, in particular, seems to be one of the main forces driving potential conflicts. Problematic citizens often seem to assume that the police expect them to cause trouble in whatever way—just because the police pick them, for example, for a traffic control stop. Just by looking at a group of potentially problematic citizens, or just by being "the police," the police might create the impression that they expect that the citizens might be aggressive.

A successful management of citizens' second-order beliefs seems to be very difficult. One possible way to shape citizens' expectations might be to make the reasons behind the aims, targets, means, and the police's appearance more transparent. Explaining why police do things in the particular way might do away with prejudices.[25] For the German case, some "guidelines" explaining proceedings and bilateral behavior in traffic control situations can be found on police websites. However, because so few people avail themselves of the police home page in order to gather information about traffic controls, this attempt seems to be futile.

In addition, the police perspective has to be considered. Again, the police expectation about the strategy the citizens might choose is shaped by experiences—and bad experiences steer expectations toward aggression. As in the citizens' case, police expectations about the citizen's expectations about the police's behavior is difficult to manage. Even if surveys frequently show that the police are highly esteemed by a large number of citizens, in general, the police struggle with accepting this appreciation. On the one hand, direct negative experiences and the overall difficult and increasingly dangerous situation diminish the impression that the police are well regarded. On the other hand, a strongly manifested differentiation into "the police" on the one hand and "all the others" on the other hand going hand in hand with the socialization within the group of police influences police behavior toward general mistrust of what citizens say, think, and do. Following a "self-perception" that feeds on citizens' expectation that the police generally are an aggressive authority, the actual behavior will be aggressive following a vicious cycle of self-fulfilling prophecies (Behr, 2013a, 2013b).

Limitations

Considering the parties as groups and restricting the modeling to the group of problematic citizens is unquestionably debatable: It might not always be possible to clearly distinguish between generally cooperative citizens and the weak-minded ones. Consideration of signaling problems might give further insights at this point. Via trustworthy signaling, citizens could be able to provide an indication of whether they plan to be coordinative or aggressive even in one-shot games. However, any kind of signaling would be closely linked to the debate of stereotyped thinking on the part of the police. Citizens could try to signal their belonging to a particular predefined group—either a cooperative or an aggressive one. Besides the fact that it is highly debatable how to ascertain the signals' trustworthiness, individuals typically dislike being stereotyped. Consequently, it is, of course, highly interesting to analyze (theoretical) consequences of signaling. However, the practical relevance of signaling is debatable.

Recalling the technicalities, Rabin (1993) states the modified utility function in his original paper, as given in the theory section of this chapter. Unfortunately, in the original model, it seems not to be entirely clear what "material payoffs" really are. Given the use of equitable payoffs, the material payoffs have to be cardinal utilities implying that the considered entities are very well able to deal with probabilities in the required rational way.[26] In this light, it is highly debatable to model the fairness "add on" as a dimensionless additive normalized to the interval of $\left[-1;\frac{1}{2}\right]$. Recalling that the concept of cardinal utilities allows different numerical representations of a single preference structure as long as the representatives are positive affine transformations of each other, the fairness additive can by overridden by the chosen scaling itself. The other way around, it is technically possible to downscale the material payoffs so that the fairness concerns dominate. It is difficult to argue that the scale variable X really accounts for the "stakes" of the game and not only for the "scale" of the game. Nelson (2001), arguing on the basis of "stakes," suggests an alternative formulation of the utility function that leaves the particular kind of interaction between material payoff and fairness open. In contrast to Rabin's (1993) original version, this formulation allows the modeling of overall utility in a way that mutual aggression might positively contribute to the overall utility (formula 2). However, such a modification would not alter the model's implications.

$$V_m\left(a_m,e_n^1,e_m^2\right) \equiv v_m\left[\pi_m\left(a_m,e_n^1\right),\tilde{f}_n\left(e_n^1,e_m^2\right)\cdot f_m\left(a_m,e_n^1\right)\right] \tag{2}$$

However, since every modeling is an (occasionally extreme) abstraction from real-world problems, these deficiencies should not hide the fact that it is very well possible to gain valuable implications about how dilemma situations could be overcome—even if a broader interpretation is needed.

Conclusion

After taking a closer look at the special nature of police-citizen encounters, interactions of the police and a potentially aggressive sub-population of citizens were game-theoretically reconstructed. Adopting Rabin's (1993) idea of fairness equilibria, a possible mean of establishing the mutual cooperative situation as a fairness equilibrium on the basis of respective expectations was developed. The fact that not only the mutually cooperative situation but also the mutually aggressive situation has the potential to be equilibrated alters the situation from being dilemmatic to being coordinative. Possible methods of establishing mutual expectations of fairness were discussed with the aim of overcoming the initial dilemma and to implement a positive and cooperative climate during encounters. The modeling underlines the fact that mutually cooperative situations are highly vulnerable. On the one hand, the fairness incentives can be easily overridden by other concerns. On the other hand, it seems to be difficult to make expectations of fair behavior focal. Besides some critical aspects discussed in the previous sections, Rabin's (1993) concept generates valuable insights and gives a push to further ways of research. As pointed to earlier, especially the citizens' second-order expectations as well as the police's expectation are insufficiently studied. Using qualitative methods starting from interviews might give enormously interesting insights into possible reasons behind (mis) cooperation.

An additional issue, which can be discussed in the light of Rabin's (1993) concept, is the impact of legislation on cooperation. Within the scope of the model, it can be argued that legal regulations might be able to influence the situation in a positive way as long as they only "help" people form the "right" expectation. As soon as they definitely "force" a party—say, the citizens—to cooperate, then the strategy of being aggressive seems not to be available any longer, and all fairness concerns are nullified. As soon as one party is (legally) forced to cooperate, it becomes impossible to prove whether cooperation grows out of fairness intentions or coercion—thus, the incentive to reciprocate the fair behavior cannot be perpetuated any longer. Staying with the example introduced earlier, applying Rabin's argument would imply that the police have no incentive to care about fairness at all and focus solely on material well-being. This leads to an equilibrium outcome in which the citizens cooperate, and the police appear to be aggressive due to their focus on self-protection. Thus, on the basis of Rabin's (1993) concept, the endeavor to strengthen the legal regulations punishing aggressive citizen behavior, as currently discussed in Germany, can be discussed from different perspectives. If the overriding aim is to eradicate aggressive citizen behavior, then harsher penalties might be an appropriate means. But if fairness is considered, forcing the citizens to cooperate might not be a suitable means to implement the mutually cooperative situation on the basis of reciprocity.

Moreover, on a meta level, the chapter reveals that the somewhat unorthodox way to systematically and abstractly develop a model for a real-life problem and, secondly, apply a quite formal game-theoretical solution-concept can be very insightful. This might be surprising since, in the case of Rabin's (1993) concept, the initial modeling was done on the basis of rather simple experimental results and, presumably, a certain amount of gut feeling and introspection so that, at a first glance, the practical usefulness seems to be debatable. Conclusively, this points to the fact that all the tools that are available should be used to gain at least a partial understanding of the conflicts with which we are confronted. Furthermore, the insights raise implications for further research. Therefore, particularly with respect to the first- and second-order expectations of police, it would be desirable to collect data to sketch the current situation in more detail and to verify the models' implications. In addition, experiments might be conducted to test the models' implication in the field as well as in an abstract manner in the lab.

Discussion Questions

1. What do you think of the idea that police and citizens are stuck in a vicious circle of mutual armament? Does that match your personal experience?
2. In economic theory, it is often assumed that actors are purely self-interested in a sense that they only consider their "material payoffs" (although it is not always entirely clear what exactly "material payoffs" are). This assumption is often considered to be far from reality: Critics argue that social preferences related to altruism, fairness, and reciprocity play an important role in interactive and interdependent decision situations. What do you think about the balance between self-interest and social preferences in the case of police-citizen interactions? Consider the perspectives of both police and citizens.
3. To be able to consider first- and second-order expectations regarding possible behavior, individuals must have "perspective-taking abilities": i.e., they must be able to put themselves into the other party's shoes. Do you think that (and/or to what extent) the parties (police and citizens) do switch perspectives in the real world?
4. To help people understand why the police do things the way they do, it might be beneficial to improve transparency regarding police procedures. Discuss this topic in light of the fact that police procedural guidelines are often internal matters.
5. Police expectations regarding citizen behavior are closely related to the question of police *trust* in citizens. Police trust in citizens, however, seems to be generally underexplored. Discuss the pros and cons of police trust in citizens.

Notes

1. For the German case, see, for example, Lorei (2001).
2. Note that this introduction mainly focuses on the current situation in Germany. The situation in the US, for example, seems to have escalated even more. See, for example, Terrill (2016).
3. This subsumption of means especially holds for the German case. The focus on self-protection, the usage of weapons, and the overall aggressive appearance is even more common in other countries.
4. Some of the most influential clashes within the US are, for example, summarized in Brown and Benedict (2002).
5. For the German case, see, for example, Posiege and Steinschulte-Leidig (1999), who note that the police, in order to maintain closeness to citizens, should act in a distinct customer-oriented manner. See also, for example, Behr (2013a, 2013b), who, in the course of several interviews, states that the German police have established a customer-oriented image that is beneficial for encounters with middle-class citizens. But it is important to note that the distinct service orientation, as Behr (2013a, 2013b) argues, might foster problems with civilians belonging to the fringes of society.
6. At this point, the discussion about the appropriateness of a simultaneous-moves representation might pop up. Since the game-theoretical construction done so far deals with unsought contacts, it is beyond dispute that, on the individual level, the police officers initiate the encounter by approaching the targeted individual, then the particular citizen (re-)acts and so on and so forth. However, on the aggregate level, the simultaneous character of the interaction can be well motivated. With regard to the general orientation toward the civilians, the police have to make an overall decision about how to approach citizens, whereas, it seems indeed appropriate to assume that the group of citizens, which is further differentiated later on, developed a general attitude toward the police and acts accordingly.
7. Assuming that it is not possible for the police to differentiate whether people belong to the group of problematic citizens or not would include a signaling problem. But this line of thought will not be considered in the following.
8. Note that, in this case, payoffs are cardinal utilities. At first glance, it might seem unnecessary to express the payoffs in such an abstract way. But, in the light of cardinality requirements that must be considered within Rabin's (1993) framework, it is necessary to assume that the players considered are able to deal with probabilities adequately. The coefficients XP and XC represent the permitted scaling. The usage of the scale variable is in accordance with Rabin (1993). He used a scale variable to increase and decrease the "stakes" of the game, not to scale the preference representation. This issue is discussed in more detail in the section "Implications."
9. A strategy is called dominant if it leads to higher payoffs than all the other strategies that are available—whatever strategy the opponent might choose (e.g., Dixit et al., 2009).
10. A Nash equilibrium denotes a combination of strategies in which none of the players has an incentive to deviate from the situation unilaterally. Thus, the situation is stable (e.g., Dixit et al., 2009).
11. As it is the case in the simple (prisoner's) dilemma constructed earlier, the assumption of actors who are exclusively motivated by their material well-being, the self-interest hypothesis, is deeply rooted in economic and classically game-theoretical concepts. Even if a variety of experimental studies attack these assumptions, altruism, fairness, reciprocity, and other social goals did not find explicit entrance into the respective models for a long time.
12. For a classification and discussion of Rabin's (1993) work, see, e.g., Camerer (1997), Fehr and Schmidt (2003, 2006), or Sobel (2005).
13. Rabin's (1993) groundbreaking idea has been further developed by, for example, Nelson (2001) and Dufwenberg and Kirchsteiger (2004) (sequential reciprocity). Rabin (1997) also developed a fairness framework for repeated games.
14. The underlying framework of psychological games traces back to Geanakoplos, Pearce, and Stacchetti (1989).
15. The material payoff refers to the cardinal utility values in the initial matrix.
16. So player m chooses the payoff pair $\left(\pi_m\left(a_m, e_n^1\right); \pi_n\left(e_n^1, a_m\right)\right)$ from the set $\left(e_n^1\right) \equiv \left\{\left(\pi_m\left(a, e_n^1\right); \pi_n\left(e_n^1, a\right)\right) \mid a \in S_m\right\}$ where S_m denotes player m's set of strategies.
17. For criticism on that issue and an alternative approach, see Nelson (2001).
18. This issue will be discussed in more detail in the chapter that deals with coordination of expectations.
19. This part of the equilibrium definition will be discussed in more detail later on.
20. Since the game is symmetric, it suffices to analyze one perspective—the other perspective can be derived analogously.
21. This criticism will be discussed in more detail in the section on limitations.
22. The well-known "Battle of the Sexes" game, as well as the reconstruction of the tricky situation in which two people strive to meet in New York, but only agreed on a particular date and time and forgot

36   Katharina Friederike Sträter and René Hornung

to fix a meeting place are prominent examples of coordination games (e.g., Schelling, 1960, 2005). For further explanations regarding coordination games, see, for example, Osborne (2004) or Dixit et al. (2009).

23. As several studies indicate, a common history, in particular, seems to be important to resolving tacit police-citizen coordination problems as past meetings, both positive and negative, have an impact on the prospective behavior (see, e.g., Tyler & Folger, 1980; Tyler, 1988; Brown & Benedict, 2002; Mazerolle, Antrobus, Bennett, & Tyler, 2012).

24. This discussion provides several connecting factors with Bicchieri's concept of the social norms that can be defined as a function of the beliefs and preferences that members of a population have (e.g., Bicchieri, 1990, 2006).

25. This means, for example, clarifying that a traffic control stop is not meant to hold citizens up to ridicule but to improve the safety of all citizens.

26. Of course, in the case of the original prisoner's dilemma, it might be reasonable to assume that utilities are linear in "years of prison," but as soon as no issues are on the table that are easy to measure with a "real-world" quantitative measure, cardinal utilities have to be assumed. Camerer (2003) refers to the "material payoffs" as "monetary payoffs." This might be reasonable for some of Rabin's examples—but, considering, for example, the "Battle of the Sexes" game, it seems to be difficult to monetize gains and losses of going (together) to the opera or attending a boxing match.

References

Behr, R. (2011, Oktober 27). *Wenn der Schutzmann jammert: Werden Polizisten öfter Opfer von Gewalt? Nein—trotzdem müssen sie lernen, professioneller mit Aggressivität umzugehen.* Retrieved from www.zeit.de/2011/44/P-Polizei

Behr, R. (2013a, March 6). *1315 Straftaten: Gewalt gegen Polizei nimmt zu.* Retrieved from www.shz.de/regionales/schleswig-holstein/panorama/gewalt-gegen-polizisten-nimmt-zu-id21306.html

Behr, R. (2013b, February 13). *Die Sprache der Straße verstehen.* Retrieved from www.maz-online.de/Brandenburg/Die-Sprache-der-Strasse-verstehen

Behr, R. (2014). *Über Polizei und Gewalt.* Retrieved from www.b-republik.de/archiv/ueber-polizei-und-gewalt?aut=1104

Bicchieri, C. (1990). Norms of cooperation. *Ethics, 100*(4), 838–861.

Bicchieri, C. (2006). *The grammar of society: The nature and dynamics of social norms.* New York, NY: Cambridge University Press.

Brown, B., & Benedict, W. R. (2002). Perception of the police: Past findings, methodological issues, conceptual issues, and policy implications. *Policing: An International Journal of Police Strategies & Management, 25*(3), 543–580.

Camerer, C. F. (1997). Progress in behavioral game theory. *The Journal of Economic Perspectives, 11*(4), 167–188.

Camerer, C. F. (2003). *Behavioral game theory: Experiments in strategic interaction.* New York, NY: Russell Sage Foundation.

Clancy, A., Hough, M., Aust, R., & Kershaw, C. (2001). *Crime, policing and justice: The experience of ethnic minorities. Findings from the 2000 British crime survey* (Report No. 223). London: Home Office Research, Development and Statistics Directorate.

Der Tagesspiegel. (2001, February 20). *Mehr Eigensicherheit für Polizei: Verkehrskontrollen mit gezogener Waffe.* Retrieved from www.tagesspiegel.de/berlin/mehr-eigensicherheit-fuer-polizei-verkehrskontrolle-mit-gezogener-waffe/204862.html

Dixit, A. K., Skeath, S., & Reiley, D. H. (2009). *Games of strategy* (3rd ed.). New York, NY: Norton & Co.

Dufwenberg, M., & Kirchsteiger, G. (2004). A theory of sequential reciprocity. *Games and Economic Behavior, 47*(2), 268–298.

FAZ Frankfurter Allgemeine Zeitung. (2015, December 24). *Haftbefehl wegen Mordes nach Messerattacke erlassen.* Retrieved from www.faz.net/aktuell/gesellschaft/kriminalitaet/polizist-in-herborn-getoetet-haftbefehl-wegen-mordes-nach-messerattacke-erlassen-13983733.html

Fehr, E., & Schmidt, K. M. (2003). Theories of fairness and reciprocity—evidence and economic applications. In M. Dewatripont, L. P. Hansen, & J. T. Stephen (Eds.), *Advances in economics and econometrics* (pp. 208–257). Cambridge: Cambridge University Press.

Fehr, E., & Schmidt, K. M. (2006). The economics of fairness, reciprocity, and altruism—experimental evidence and new theory. In S. C. Kolm & J. M. Ythier (Eds.), *Handbook of the economics of giving, altruism and reciprocity vol. 1 foundations* (pp. 615–653). Amsterdam, Netherlands: Elsevier B. V.

Füllgrabe, U. (2013). Eigensicherung: Psychologische Grundlagen polizeilicher Eigensicherung. *Deutsche Polizei, 8*, 11–16.

Füllgrabe, U. (2014). *Psychologie der Eigensicherung: Überleben ist kein Zufall.* Stuttgart, Germany: Boorberg.

Geanakoplos, J., Pearce, D., & Stacchetti, E. (1989). Psychological games and sequential rationality. *Games and Economic Behavior, 1*(1), 60–79.

Goffman, E. (1956). The nature of deference and demeanor. *American Anthropologist, 58*(3), 473–502.

Goffman, E. (1961). *Encounters: Two studies in the sociology of interaction.* Indianapolis, IN: Bobbs-Merrill Company Inc.

Grosskopf, B., & Nagel, N. (2007). The two-person beauty contest. *Games and Economic Behavior, 62*, 93–99.

Gui, B., & Sugden, R. (2005). *Economics and social interaction: Accounting for interpersonal relations.* Cambridge: Cambridge University Press.

Kääriäinen, J., & Sirén, R. (2012). Do the police trust in citizens? *European Comparison: European Journal of Criminology, 9*(3), 276–289.

Lorei, C. (2001). *Ergebnisse einer Bürgerbefragung zur Akzeptanz von polizeilichen Kontroll-und Eigensicherungsmaßnahmen.* Retrieved from www.gdp.de/gdp/gdp.nsf/id/DE_Ergebnisse_einer_Buergerbefragung_zur_Akzeptanz_von_polizeilichen_Kontroll-_und_Eigensicherungsma

Mazerolle, L., Antrobus, E., Bennett, S., & Tyler, T. R. (2012). Shaping citizen perception of police legitimacy: A randomized field trial of procedural justice. *Criminology, 51*(1), 33–63.

MZ Mitteldeutsche Zeitung. (2014, April 24). *Das Drama auf der Europachaussee.* Retrieved from www.mz-web.de/halle-saalekreis/toter-polizist-und-motorradfahrer-in-halle-das-drama-auf-der-europachaussee,20640778,30520610.html

Nagel, R. (1995). Unraveling in guessing games: An experimental study. *The American Economic Review, 85*(5), 1313–1326.

Nelson, W. R. (2001). Incorporating fairness into game theory and economics: Comment. *The American Economic Review, 91*(4), 1180–1183.

Ohlemacher, T. (2000). Mit dem Rücken gegen die Wand: Die Polizei in der Sackgasse einer defensiven Solidarität? *Deutsches Polizeiblatt, 1*, 10–14.

Osborne, M. J. (2004). *An introduction to game theory.* New York, NY: Oxford University Press.

Posiege, P., & Steinschulte-Leidig, B. (1999). *Bürgernahe Polizeiarbeit in Deutschland: Darstellung von Konzepten und Modellen.* BKA Forschung, Kriminalistisch-kriminologische Forschergruppe, BKA Wiesbaden, Germany: BKA.

Rabin, M. (1993). Incorporating fairness into game theory and economics. *The American Economic Review, 83*(5), 1281–1302.

Rabin, M. (1997). *Fairness in repeated games* (Working Paper No. 97–252). Berkeley, CA: University of California.

Rosenbaum, D. P., Schuck, A. M., Costello, S. K., Hawkins, D. F., & Ring, M. K. (2005). Attitudes toward the police: The effect of direct and vicarious experience. *Police Quarterly, 8*(3), 343–365.

Schelling, T. C. (1960). *The strategy of conflict.* Cambridge, MA: Harvard University Press.

Schelling, T. C. (2005). *The strategy of conflict* (Reprint of the 1980 version). Cambridge, MA: Harvard University Press.

Sobel, J. (2005). Interdependent preferences and reciprocity. *Journal of Economic Literature, 43*(2), 392–436.

Skogan, W. G. (2006). Asymmetry in the impact of encounters with police. *Policing and Society, 16*(2), 99–126.

Sugden, R., & Zamarrón, I. Z. (2006). Finding the key: The riddle of focal points. *Journal of Economic Psychology, 27*(5), 609–621.

Sykes, R. E., & Clark, J. P. (1975). A theory of deference exchange in police-civilian encounters. *American Journal of Sociology, 81*(3), 584–600.

Terrill, W. (2016). Deadly force: To shoot or not to shoot. *Criminology and Public Policy, 15*(2), 491–496.

Tyler, T. R. (1988). What is procedural justice? Criteria used by citizens to assess the fairness of legal procedures. *Law & Society Review, 22*(1), 103–135.

Tyler, T. R., & Folger, R. (1980). Distributional and procedural aspects of satisfaction with citizen-police encounters. *Basic and Applied Social Psychology, 1*(4), 281–292.

Van Maanen, J. (1978). The asshole. In P. K. Manning & J. Van Maanen (Eds.), *Policing: A view from the street* (pp. 221–238). Santa Monica, CA: Goodyear Publishing Company. Reprint Retrieved from http://64.6.252.14/class/377a/Readings/vanmaanen-1978.pdf (pp. 307–328).

Weigel, C. (2015). Alles im Blick? Polizeiliche Bodycams in Deutschland und den. *Forum Recht, 2,* 57–59.

Zeit Online. (2017, September 3). *Die gezückte Waffe soll Routine werden.* Retrieved from www.zeit.de/gesellschaft/zeitgeschehen/2014-08/polizei-schiessen-offensive-waffenhaltung

Ziems, C. (2006). *Videoüberwachung bei Anhalte-und Kontrollvorgängen zur Eigensicherung der Polizeibeamten: Eine Analyse der Rechtslage in Brandenburg, Bremen, Hamburg, Hessen, Niedersachsen, Nordrhein-Westfalen und Rheinland-Pfalz.* Berlin, Germany: Logos.

Chapter 3

The Doctrine of Minimum Force in Policing
Origins, Uncertainties, and Implications

Richard Evans and Clare Farmer

Author Note: This chapter sets out key issues regarding the doctrine of minimum force. It draws from and synthesizes key arguments from a book by the same authors. Evans and Farmer (2020) examines the use of force by police and presents the results of a comparative analysis of four jurisdictions, which explores the effect on community and police officer safety of routinely arming police.

Introduction

There is strange sense of vertigo when, as a scholar, you set out to research an unproblematic, basic aspect of your discipline and discover that it is not nearly as simple as you had imagined. This is particularly true for a criminologist. Ours is a discipline accustomed to challenging received wisdom, to probing conventional explanations. When we began exploring the theory and practice of policing and the use of force, we expected some confounding results. But not in relation to one of the core tenets of modern policing: the doctrine of minimum force. We had known and believed in this basic aspect of policing for all our professional lives, had read about it in numerous secondary texts, and routinely taught it to students: police are able to use force, but only when necessary, only to achieve legitimate objectives, and only employing the minimum level required (see, for example, Palmer, 2017, p. 386; Edwards, 1999, p. 171; Buttle, 2010, p. 35). The same principle is formalized in police codes of conduct and human rights laws (for example, United Nations, 1979, Article 3; Equality and Human Rights Commission, 2019; Victoria Police, 2003). But probing the origins and theory of minimum-force policing has been both difficult in execution and challenging in its results. Like an orthodox Christian looking to the Bible to confirm the idea of the Holy Trinity (Marius, 1973, p. 42), we have discovered that behind an apparently solid doctrinal façade is a building site, empty apart from a few piles of bricks.

In this chapter, we explore the doctrine of minimum-force policing. We first set out the uncertain and fluid framework upon and within which minimum force has been constructed and draw attention to interconnected notions of policing by consent, de-escalation, excessive force, police discretion, and legitimacy. The relationship between the embedded doctrine of minimum-force policing and the normalization of routinely armed police is then examined—emphasizing a disconnect between the conceptualization and operationalization of minimum force. We draw from and synthesize key arguments from our recently published book, which examines whether the routine arming of police officers correlates with an increased level of safety (Evans & Farmer, 2020). Through a comparative analysis of four jurisdictions, two of which deploy routinely armed police and two that do not, we found little evidence to support the presumed safety effects of routinely arming police officers. In conclusion, we argue

DOI: 10.4324/9781003047117-4

Minimum Force and "Peel's Principles"

for robust empirical research to test the efficacy of the doctrine of minimum force and, in particular, to ensure an ongoing examination of the effects (for police officers themselves and the community more broadly) of routinely armed policing.

Minimum Force and "Peel's Principles"

In his celebratory history of British policing, published in 1948, Charles Reith waxes lyrical about how, despite deeply entrenched hostility, Sir Robert Peel's New Police won over public opinion:

> They [police officers] were told that they must cultivate good relations with the public by combining modesty and firmness. And dignity of manner and address, with good humour and kindly friendliness, and by showing infinite patience under provocation. They were taught to behave in a manner that would induce the public to regard them as friends and servants, and to see the exercise of their authority as policemen was neither bullying nor tyrannical, but simply and solemnly a service to the public. By quiet and unobtrusive fulfilment of these instructions, the police eventually conquered public hostility.
>
> (Reith, 1948, p. 63)

Note the use of the passive voice. "They *were told*. . . . They *were taught*." Where did this advice come from? Reith admired Charles Rowan and Richard Mayne, the joint commissioners of London's Metropolitan Police at its founding in 1829, and gives them much of the credit for the new style adopted and for its success. Rowan and Mayne, Reith argues, had a vision of "the close and friendly relationship between the police and the public" that eventuated. Reith describes this development as a "miracle," especially given initial public hostility (1948, p. 44).

Toward the end of his book, Reith lists "nine police principles," which include the use of force (1948, p. 94). Police are instructed (Principle 6) "to use physical force only when the exercise of persuasion, advice and warning is found to be insufficient . . . and to use only the minimum degree of physical force which is necessary on any particular occasion." Crucially (according to Principle 2), "the power of the police to fulfil their functions and duties is dependent on public approval of their existence, actions and behavior and on their ability to secure and maintain public respect." Without securing such respect (Principle 1), "crime and disorder" would require "repression by military force and severity of legal punishment." There are at least four different versions of the principles (often referred to as "Peel's Principles") in circulation: two with twelve principles, one with ten, and one (that originating with Reith) with nine (Lentz & Chaires, 2007). While there is overlap, only the nine-principle list specifically enjoins minimum force.

In their study of the origins of the various published versions of the principles, Lentz and Chaires (2007, p. 73) note how, in policing textbooks, the principles are usually reproduced with minimal analysis, and there is no evidence that Sir Robert Peel had anything to do with their drafting. The principles do not appear as part of the legislation that created the New Police nor in the general instructions that were issued to every new police officer from 1829. The earliest known presentation of the principles as a list is in Reith's 1948 book. Consequently, they appear to be "an invention of twentieth-century policing textbooks" (Lentz & Chaires, 2007, p. 69). Reith had access to original documents held in the Scotland Yard library, but he does not claim the principles are associated with Peel, nor does he cite his sources. The list is presented by Reith in a chapter titled "British Police Today" as an evolving set of dicta that helps the reader understand what he views as contemporary best practice (Reith, 1948, p. 94).

However, "[t]hat Peel's principles were invented . . . does not necessarily make them a fiction" (Lentz & Chaires, 2007, p. 70). Regardless of their origins, they remain enormously influential across policing jurisdictions. The UK Home Office still has them displayed on its website, where they are intended to provide a "definition of policing by consent" (Home Office (U.K.), 2012). Similarly, in a document outlining a strategy for policing to 2025, Australia's Victoria Police declare: "The principles established by Sir Robert Peel in 1829 when he created the London Metropolitan Police, remain relevant today and inform many aspects of the Vision [for Victoria Police]" and reproduce a slightly modified nine-point list (Victoria Police, 2014, p. 9).

Any attempt to find sources for the doctrine of minimum-force policing seems to loop back to Reith and the policing principles he published in 1948. Their origins are obscure, but the principles articulate an approach to the use of force that has been hugely influential. William Bratton, who from the mid-1990s served as police commissioner in New York and Boston, and as chief of the Los Angeles Police Department, referred to the principles as "my bible" (*New York Times*, 2014).

However, what underpins the doctrine of minimum-force policing? Despite almost two centuries of the practice, the theory remains thin.

The Framing and Development of Minimum Force

Reith presents the idea of policing by consent and the embedded doctrine of minimum force as a lucky accident (Reith, 1948, 1952). Rowan and Mayne, the two men who, with London's Metropolitan Police, created the first modern police service, had a hunch that minimum force was the best approach, and it happened to work. Rowan and Mayne's approach to policing derived power from public cooperation rather than fear. Reith argues that previous conventional thinking had been that police must be "wholly repressive" (Reith, 1948, p. 61) in order to be effective. What he calls the "discovery" (p. 94) that this was not the case unlocked the path to "miracles in the science and art of policing" (p. 63). The New Police proved a success in London, and the model of an unarmed civilian police who were themselves subject to the law was rapidly taken up in other, though not all, parts of Britain and the British Empire (Critchley, 1977). It is unclear whether this was a unique event, dependent on the insights and personalities of two reforming public servants, or the challenges associated with industrialization would have led inexorably to the New Police.

Perhaps the most insightful examination of the evolution of the use of force by police is the work of Egon Bittner (Bittner, 1975). He argues that the emergence of modern policing is part of a gradual reduction of personal violence in society, a broad social movement both facilitated by and necessary to a modern world of advanced economies and large cities in which strangers must peacefully coexist. The use of force has been removed from almost every aspect of life in modern society: "paper, not the sword, is the instrument of coercion of our day" (Bittner, 2005, p. 166). The gradual move toward a less violent society has little to do with high motives, such as political conviction or religious faith. Rather, driving the change is "the lackluster ethic of utilitarianism" (Bittner, 1975, p. 20). The common good (greater peace) happens to coincide with the personal good:

> Our desire to abolish violence is fundamentally based not on the belief that it is spiritually reprehensible, but on the realization that it is foolish. Forceful attack and the defense it provokes have an unfavorable input/output ratio; they are a waste of energy. A simple, hardheaded, business-like calculus dictates that coercive force, especially of a physical nature, is at best an occasionally unavoidable evil.

(p. 20)

But no matter how thoroughly force is removed from the routine business of life, in the end, the capacity to use force must exist:

> [T]he only practical way of banishing the use of force from life generally is to assign its residual exercise—where according to circumstances it appears unavoidable—to a specially deputized corps of officials, that is, to the police as we know it.
>
> (Bittner, 2005, p. 166)

Bittner argues that the potential for the use of force is the defining characteristic of modern policing. There is an astonishing variety of situations to which police might be called, but there is a common thread:

> The policeman, and the policeman alone, is equipped, entitled, and required to deal with every exigency in which force may have to used, to meet it. Moreover, the authorization to use force is conferred upon the policeman with the mere proviso that force will be used in amounts measured not to exceed the necessary minimum, as determined by an intuitive grasp of the situation.
>
> (Bittner, 2005, p. 165)

In his development of Bittner's theory on policing, Brodeur (2010) draws a distinction between military force, which will often be maximized to ensure the annihilation of enemies, and police force, which must be limited to the minimum necessary. The reason for this limitation is as follows:

> [A] great deal of police crisis intervention involves protecting all parties involved [including criminal offenders]. . . . Since it would be self-defeating to use more force than is necessary to protect people from themselves, managing a crisis is not equivalent to clamping down on it. Using minimum force is not merely incidental to the police mandate, but constitutive of it.
>
> (Brodeur, 2010, p. 108)

By this view, the minimum-force doctrine is merely pragmatic. To be effective, the police need public support, and that is endangered if police use force which is seen to be "excessive." However, that assessment—what is "excessive" force in any given situation—is a cultural and situational construct. It can and does vary and so can be the object of political struggle. Minimum force may well be the product of "the lackluster ethic of utilitarianism" (Bittner, 1975, p. 20), but political actors need to perceive that utility and articulate and push for it. That, according to Reith, was the achievement of Rowan and Mayne (Reith, 1948, 1952). By listing his principles of policing, hoping to demonstrate what he regarded as the singular genius of "British Police Today," Reith was in effect doing the same thing (Reith, 1948).

The contest over what philosophy should underpin policing is long running. In his seminal 1969 study of policing in India, Bayley notes the poles of opinion.

> Does the readiness of police to use force call forth hostility and violence in the general public, and particularly among suspects, or is readiness to use force essential to prevent a greater amount of violence from the public and suspects? . . . [P]olice authorities in the United States and Great Britain proceed on the basis of diametrically opposed theories in this matter, for the British policeman does not carry a firearm, the American policeman

always does. Police authorities in Britain believe that to go armed, to prepare visibly for war, would trigger a greater amount of violence among those they contact; American police, on the other hand, believe that their sidearm is an essential deterrent, and without it they would be helpless in enforcing the law.

(Bayley, 1969, p. 24)

He observes that, at the time of writing, there was little evidence to support either position—both were matters of faith and custom. Writing decades later, Bayley (2002) further explores whether there is a tension between observing due process, such as respect for human rights, and police effectiveness. He concludes that there is not:

[T]he choice between hard (deterrent) and soft (rule-of-law) policing is false. In order to become effective at preventing crime, police need to be protective of human rights so that they can enlist the willing cooperation of the public. Policing by consent, to use the British slogan, is more effective at crime prevention and control than is hard-nosed law enforcement by socially isolated police.

(Bayley, 2002, pp. 142–143)

In contrast with his 1969 writings, Bayley (2002) draws on a great deal of published research that supports the importance to police effectiveness of public support and cooperation. This work includes Bayley's own discussions of policing by consent (1985) and democratic policing (1999) and Skolnick and Fyfe's investigation of policing and excessive force (1993). More recent comparative studies emphasize the great variations that exist internationally around police use of force, in terms of formal legal rules and normative community standards (Knutsson & Kuhns, 2010). Interwoven with the acknowledgment of variations in expectations of police is the complex area of police discretion. In their discussion of police discretion, Bronitt and Stenning (2011) acknowledge the topic's semi-mythological origins with the New Police and Peel's Principles (they refer to Reith's nine-point version): "These principles do not address the issue of discretion directly, but the idea of discretion underscores several of them" (Bronitt & Stenning, 2011, p. 323).

Others have explored the issue under the rubric of "legitimacy," arguing that a broad public perception of legitimacy is a prerequisite for effective policing (Tyler, 2006; Tyler & Wakslak, 2004). Legitimacy can be engendered by and manifested through a range of contexts, such as police effectiveness and procedural justice, as viewed by the policed community (Bradford & Jackson, 2016; Huq, Jackson, & Trinkner, 2017; Tyler & Jackson, 2014). A key element in the perceived legitimacy of the police is community acceptance that officers use force appropriately and in accordance with public expectations—both of which are embodied within the doctrine of minimum force. In the end, however, the argument becomes circular. There are aphoristic statements, such as "When police act beyond the law, they lose their moral authority" (Bayley, 2002, p. 143). Research studies of public attitudes support these, but it is acknowledged that such attitudes differ depending on the place and time (Bayley, 1995). In their study of media discourse surrounding police use of lethal force in the United States, Hirschfield and Simon (2010) demonstrate that police violence is usually framed in such a way that police actions are justified and legitimized while victims are often demonized. In their initial response to the death of George Floyd, on May 25, 2020, Minneapolis police asserted that Mr. Floyd had resisted officers and "appeared to be under the influence" (Minneapolis Police, 2020). The official police statement was headed "Man Dies After Medical Incident During Police Interaction," and the facts provided regarding his death were minimal. Mobile phone footage of the incident itself led to community outrage and was a catalyst for the reinvigorated Black Lives Matter movement. The officers concerned were subsequently dismissed and are facing criminal charges (*New York Times*, 2020).

Police legitimacy requires that officers meet public expectations about the use of force, but public expectations are influenced by many factors, including media perspectives, notable events, the views expressed by authority figures, and the words and actions of the police themselves. One of Bayley's key insights is that a society's police are not just reflective of that society and its institutions; rather, police are important political actors. How police act and how they choose to use their special privileges in relation to violence have a significant role in shaping the policed community (Heslop, 2015). To examine this contention, we look again at the story of the New Police.

Does Minimum Force Require Peace or Create It?

As a model of policing, minimum force represented a significant break with convention (Palmer, 1988). The New Police were unarmed and were not overtly ruthless or oppressive in their behavior toward the policed community (Palmer, 1988). As an approach to policing, perhaps to the surprise of many, it worked. Reith claims the New Police

> eliminated the need of repression of disorder by military force and the infliction of civilian casualties. They created liberty and personal security for individuals which initiated an immense expansion of social intercourse and amenities. They eliminated the need of carrying arms.
>
> (Reith, 1952, p. 171)

The reality cannot have been so clear cut or so rapid. Later police historians have problematized the "march of progress" narrative, questioning both the reputed ineptitude of traditional policing prior to 1829 and the rapid success of the New Police afterward (Devereaux, 2001). Taylor's (1997) study of early English policing agrees that progress toward public acceptance of the New Police was slow and uneven but concludes that by the end of the nineteenth century, the English police officer had become a broadly accepted figure among the community. Ackroyd's (2000) history of London explores the competing historical views and the evidence of contemporary sources on the issue and concludes, "[A]gainst the records of the violence and energy of the London crowd [before 1829], we must place this evidence of almost instinctive obedience' to the police observed by the end of the nineteenth century" (Ackroyd, 2000, p. 289).

Inevitably, "the close and friendly relationship between the police and the public" of which Reith boasted in 1948 (p. 44) endured many strains and shocks in subsequent decades. Writing in the early 1970s, Reith's fellow police historian T.A. Critchley expresses the worry that the social changes of his day—increased individualism, breakdown of traditional communities, and the like—place the tradition of minimum force and policing by consent under threat (Critchley, 1973). He argues that only stable and homogenous societies with broadly accepted laws can hope to develop policing by consent in this way and attributes the success of the English police model in the nineteenth and early twentieth centuries to just such a broad social consensus. This argument seems obviously false. The New Police were started in large part because of serious and worsening social divisions, and they were not warmly or immediately welcomed (Storch, 1975). Support for the police was at first both sectoral and fragile, and police officers had a difficult task in negotiating their role in urban neighborhoods (Ignatieff, 1979).

Reith (1948) emphasizes the violence and rejection the New Police faced. He argues that it was precisely the unarmed, minimum-force character of the new organization that allowed it to succeed and, over time, to act in its own right as a stabilizing factor in the community. Reith reports American visitors to Britain in the 1940s, expressing the view that the British policing style was "soft" and was only possible because the British people were even softer: indeed, "sheep":

> If he had the opportunity of seeing a baton charge, or the police in action . . . [when it was needed] to make use of their own force . . . he would have found reason to change his mind. The degree of physical force which is sometimes the minimum that is necessary for the achievement of a police objective can be extremely formidable.
>
> (Reith, 1948, p. 111)

That such force rarely needed to be used was, Reith argues, a consequence of the minimum-force doctrine. Reith's writings on the excellence of British policing seem complacent to the modern reader, but still, he has a point. This is illustrated by another historical example of the creation of an unarmed police service. Though less well known—it is absent from any policing textbook the present authors have found—the An Garda Siochana in the Republic of Ireland is perhaps a more compelling operationalization of the minimum-force doctrine even than that of the New Police.

Prior to 1922, Ireland was policed by the Royal Irish Constabulary (RIC), which was armed, centralized, and operated from barracks. As the struggle for Irish independence intensified in the early twentieth century, the RIC came to be seen as an agent of oppression, a tool of the British hegemony (Brewer, Guelke, Hume, & Moxon-Browne, 1996, p. 86). In 1922, Ireland won partial independence through armed struggle. The Anglo-Irish Treaty created the Irish Free State (later the Republic of Ireland) but at the expense of accepting partition and the creation of Northern Ireland. Hard-line Republicans denied the legitimacy of the Free State and took up arms against its government, leading to civil war. In the midst of this chaos, the new Irish state had to establish a police service (Brady, 1974). As is common in the post-colonial experience, existing institutions were adopted. The police were given a new name, An Garda Siochana ("guardians of the peace"), but most of its officers were veterans of the RIC, and existing structures and ranks were adopted (Mulroe, 2016). It was, however, transformed into an unarmed force. McNiffe (1997, p. 26) argues, "Disarming the emerging force was perhaps the most significant contribution to ensuring it became a civilian rather than a semi-military body." McNiffe makes the case that it was precisely the unarmed character of the new force, which was the key to its success.

> The decision . . . to send out unarmed policemen was both courageous and ambitious. In many respects the new force had modelled itself very closely on its predecessor, the RIC, but this was a clear break with tradition. This decision influenced the public perception of the force and greatly facilitated its acceptance by all sides of the community.
>
> (McNiffe, 1997, p. 96)

Like many police services, since the 1980s, the An Garda Siochana has faced major scandals over corruption and malpractice, including accusations of excessive use of force (Manning, 2012; O'Sullivan, 2015). What is notable, though, is that the question of arming the Garda is nowhere raised as part of a reform program. In recent years, specialist armed-response units have been deployed, but regular operational police remain unarmed. Indeed, the Garda has recently reduced the number of officers who carry firearms, from 27% to 19%, by withdrawing weapons from police who did not genuinely need them (Gallagher, 2020).

The Operationalization of Minimum Force

Although its origins lack certainty, the overriding expectation of the doctrine of minimum force is clear and conceptually consistent. By contrast, the operationalization of minimum force in the particular context of policing interactions is more ambiguous. There is an absence of objective or sufficiently quantifiable language with which to determine or assess what constitutes acceptable "minimum" force in a given situation. Interpretation of the term *minimum* is subjective; any incident in which risk is evident will inevitably be perceived and responded to differently by individual officers. An assessment of minimum force will depend on a range of variables, each of which is subject to individual interpretations within particular situational, jurisdictional, organizational, and operational contexts. Despite a robust body of research examining police decision-making (such as Bolger, 2015; Miller, 2015; Terrill & Paoline, 2013; White, 2002), there is no algorithm or objective model through which to determine a required policing response or the appropriate level force to be deployed.

In practical terms, the operationalization of minimum force relies on police discretion, sometimes exercised alone and, often, in situations that are unstable, unpredictable, and evolving rapidly (Bronitt & Stenning, 2011; Klockars, 1985; Mastrofski, 2004; Nowacki, 2015). A core aspect of any discretionary decision to use force is the choice to deploy one or more of a range of verbal and physical responses. The decision will not only reflect the nature and perceived seriousness of the incident, relevant operational guidelines, and individual officer characteristics; it will also be determined by the equipment available and at hand. Options may include verbal commands; the use of restraints (such as handcuffs); physical containment; and/or the deployment of various agents designed to incapacitate, such as CS gas, batons, conducted energy devices (tasers), or firearms. It is self-evident that an officer with no or limited equipment will have fewer discretionary options than an officer in possession of a comprehensive set of offensive and defensive resources. When the role played by discretion in any police decision to use force is combined with potentially immediate and lethal use of firearms, the specific risk of harm to individuals intersects with procedural justice and wider notions of legitimacy (Bradford, Milani, & Jackson, 2017).

Despite the consensus underpinning the concept of minimum force, the use of force by police is a contentious and much-discussed topic (see, for example, Bradford & Jackson, 2016; Kuhns, Knutsson, & Bayley, 2010; Squires & Kennison, 2010; Waddington, 2007; Waddington & Wright, 2010). As the ultimate expression of police power, incidents culminating in the fatal police shooting of civilians garner varying degrees of attention, both with respect to formal investigation and legal oversight and in terms of media and other public scrutiny. Some individual police shooting incidents may generate national and even global interest. Examples include the June 2017 murder of Justine Damond by police officer Mohammed Noor in Minneapolis, Minnesota (B.B.C., 2019; Walker, 2018), and the fatal shootings in 2005 of Jean Charles de Menezes by armed officers from London's Metropolitan Police and, in 2008, of 15-year-old Tyler Cassidy by officers from Australia's Victoria Police (Human Rights Law Centre, 2011; McCulloch & Sentas, 2006; Walker, 2018). In the past, less attention was usually given to the quantum of police shootings (fatal or non-fatal) and other expressions of force within and between individual jurisdictions or what this reveals about the use of force. In 2020, however, this pattern has been challenged by Black Lives Matter and similar protest movements across a number of jurisdictions. In the US, protests have been sparked by individual incidents of police violence, such as the shooting death of Breonna Taylor in Louisville,

Kentucky, on March 13; the May 25 killing of George Floyd in Wisconsin, and the August 23 shooting of Jacob Blake by police in Kenosha, Wisconsin, which left Mr. Blake paralyzed (McFadden, 2020). As well as highlighting individual injustices and excess force, these events have drawn attention to both quanta and trends in the use of force by police. Whether this heightened public awareness of broader issues of police use of force will be sustained remains to be seen (Yanique, 2020).

The facility for police officers to use force (which may be lethal in some situations) and the doctrine of minimum force are both embedded within operational policing. But to what extent is the broad acceptance of the routine arming of police officers compatible with the universal expectation of minimum-force policing?

The Pressure to Arm and the Paradox of Armed Police

The Irish example lends support to Reith's thesis that the very fact of a police service being unarmed is a de-escalating factor in terms of levels of violence in society more generally, and against police in particular. However, this suggestion runs counter to contemporary trends. In almost every jurisdiction, police are becoming increasingly militarized in their uniforms and equipment, to be armed if they are not already so, or to carry more and more powerful weapons if they are (Mummolo, 2018).

That police should and must be armed with powerful and visible weaponry is a view that is entrenched across multiple jurisdictions but that finds its ultimate expression in American policing. George Fletcher Chandler, an influential police reformer in the 1920s, epitomized this perspective:

> [A]ny arm that has been used under the rules of warfare may be used by the police. This includes revolvers, pistols, rifles of every description, tanks, machine guns, Gatling guns, gas, and even artillery . . . the revolver . . . should be carried on the outside of the uniform in the place where it can be most easily drawn.
>
> (Chandler, 1930, pp. 44–45)

Chandler's philosophy endures in practice across America. Armed police and other law enforcement officers are ubiquitous; firearms are worn prominently and drawn readily. Fatal shootings of civilians are far from uncommon. According to a recent analysis, approximately one in every 1,000 black American men will be killed by a police officer (Edwards, Lee, & Esposito, 2019). This statistic sits in stark contrast to the doctrine of minimum force. The US is, arguably, not an exemplar of minimum-force policing. There are, however, some indicators of change, as thought is given to consideration of ways in which common policing interactions, such as traffic stops, could be dealt with and managed more safely. For example, in November 2020, the city of San Francisco commenced a trial in which health professionals rather than police officers are dispatched to respond to emergency calls from non-violent people managing mental health or substance abuse issues (Westervelt, 2020). Given the link between fatal shootings of civilians by police officers and mental illness (Evans, Farmer, & Saligari, 2016), this initiative strives to reduce such harms. Routine traffic stops are the most common reason for civilian contact with police officers, and what start out as minor infringements can escalate and lead to fatal outcomes for civilians (Bureau of Justice Statistics, 2021; O'Connor, 2021). Woods (2020) has developed a framework through which traffic enforcement can be assigned away from police officers to non-armed traffic agencies. These examples are small steps and are a long way from general implementation. However, they do acknowledge and are a response to the often fatal reality of minimum-force policing in the United States.

Existing research has typically examined the police use of force in relation to individual events; situational, organizational, and other factors influencing decision-making processes; or within specific jurisdictions, whether at the local or national level. Comparative jurisdictional approaches are more limited. Knutsson and Strype (2010) and Hendy (2014) examined police officer experiences of and attitudes toward carrying and using firearms in Norway (routinely unarmed) and Sweden (routinely armed). Knutsson and Strype (2010) found that the routinely armed Swedish police discharge firearms more frequently than those in Norway and that more police and community members are injured by police firearms. Despite the increased risk of harm, Hendy (2014) concluded that Swedish police officers feel safer and more protected as a direct result of being armed. Evans et al. (2016, p. 150) examined gun violence in the US, Great Britain, and Australia and concluded that "the fewer people (including police officers) who have access to firearms, the safer that community is." Osse and Cano (2017) collected data from 11 countries and compared the number of deaths caused by police use of firearms with national homicide rates (in only one of the 11 jurisdictions were the police not routinely armed). Their research found that the overall rate of killings by police using firearms correlates strongly with overall homicide rates. The current authors drew from Osse and Cano's study to examine the nexus between routinely armed policing and safety. Farmer and Evans (2020) compared homicide rates in routinely armed and unarmed jurisdictions and found insufficient evidence that routinely arming police officers increases or ensures community safety. Hendy (2019) analyzed police conflict resolution in New Zealand (routinely unarmed) and South Australia (routinely armed). He found that police in South Australia were more likely to use verbal and physical control behaviors than police in New Zealand. With a focus on gun control, Sarre (2018) compared gun violence, associated operational and legislative responses, and their effects in Australia and the US. The current authors are continuing a four-way cross-jurisdictional analysis of routinely armed and unarmed jurisdictions (Farmer & Evans, 2019; Evans & Farmer, 2020). The research has found no evidence that routinely arming police officers increases the safety of the officers themselves or the community.

The doctrine of minimum force does not require that police be unarmed. Where police are routinely armed, they almost always have a formal commitment to use no more force than is necessary. For example, the routinely armed police in Victoria, Australia, are guided by ten operational safety principles, of which three are avoid confrontation; avoid force; and, where the use of force cannot be avoided, use only the minimum amount reasonably necessary (Victoria Police, 2003). In Belgium, where police are also routinely armed:

> [O]fficers are only allowed to use coercion (including the use of firearms) under certain conditions prescribed by law. Police officers may use force when they are pursuing a legal goal which cannot be achieved in another, non-violent way. The use of force must be reasonable and in proportion to the legal objective.
>
> (Noppe, 2015, p. 119)

Use of force policy is commonly expressed as a continuum, a pyramid, or a wheel—beginning with the mere presence of police officers through verbal interventions, bodily force, and use of non-lethal weapons to the use of lethal force (Hess, Orthmann, & Cho, 2015, pp. 431–433; Ombudsman Ontario, 2016, pp. 24–30). These models usually include a commitment to de-escalation, the principle that while police can use force if necessary, police are not "locked in" to a pattern of escalating force (Ombudsman Ontario, 2016, pp. 46–51). Police in a crisis situation should always be alive to the possibility that options other than force, especially communication, remain possible and that the level of threat can be reduced by such means (Buttle, 2010).

However, there is increasing pressure on the tradition of unarmed policing. In both New Zealand and Great Britain, two jurisdictions where police have eschewed the routine carriage of firearms, there has been considerable recent pressure for police to be armed. In 2010, following a survey of NZ Police Association (NZPA) members, 72% supported the routine arming of officers, and the NZPA promoted this change as a way to increase the safety of police officers (Police News, 2010). Opinion fluctuated in the years that followed but intensified again following the terror attack in Christchurch in 2019. New Zealand police are trialing the use of "armed response teams," intended to support regular operational police, who will continue not to carry firearms (Guardian, 2019). This decision has been met with protest and unease among some New Zealanders, and the police commissioner has conceded that opinion within the police service is divided on the issue (Bhatia, 2019; Bond, 2019a, 2019b). In Great Britain, several high-profile incidents and perceived changes in criminal behavior, such as a rise in random knife crime, have caused the routine arming of police to be questioned more openly (Dodd, 2018; Eustachewich, 2018).

Something that is striking by its absence is a theoretical or evidentiary basis for the expectation that police and the community are safer when police routinely carry firearms than when they do not. That carrying firearm increases safety is simply asserted, presented as an unchallenged and unchallengeable truth. There has been some questioning of the nature and form of police firearms training and its utility to police in practice (Morrison & Vila, 1998) and some concern about the effects of police militarization (Delehanty, Mewhirter, Welch, & Wilks, 2017; Goldsworthy, 2014; Mummolo, 2018). However, there is little evidence to support the basic effectiveness of a routinely carried police firearm in improving officer or community safety.

Studies of the evolution of police firearms policy in Britain show that it is largely reactive (Rogers, 2003). Incidents in which unarmed police have failed to prevent a tragedy lead to pressure for increased police access to and deployment of firearms, whereas incidents in which armed police kill or seriously wound a non-offender increase concern about armed police and the need for non-lethal alternatives to firearms (Rogers, 2003). Waldren (2007) presents part of the reason for arming police as a matter of morale: in the wake of violence, especially lethal violence directed at police, officers feel exposed and unsafe without weapons of their own. However, he notes the essentially symbolic nature of the routine arming of police:

> [T]he chances of an armed confrontation when on routine foot patrol, are remote. The reality is that the officers are there to be seen—a clear signal that the police are taking a particular problem seriously, that they have guns and that they are prepared to use them.
>
> (Waldren, 2007, p. 261)

Hendy (2014), drawing on Squires and Kennison (2010), also refers to morale but adds a complicating factor. Officers who are armed "feel safer," but this is not necessarily the case. Indeed, the greater confidence resulting from the possession of a firearm may make officers more likely to expose themselves to dangerous situations and actually increase their risk of harm (Hendy, 2014).

Discussing the more militarized appearance adopted by a (not routinely armed) police service in Great Britain, De Camargo (2016) demonstrates that there is self-awareness among police of the implications of the "military look." She quotes an officer:

> At least part of the rationale for a military trickle-down is emotional. When we wear these details, we are wearing safety; we wrap ourselves in a little bit of military security and feel more protected somehow.
>
> (De Camargo, 2016, p. 120)

Hendy (2014) reveals similar feelings of protection and safety in his study of Norwegian (unarmed) and Swedish (armed) police. One Swedish officer is quoted saying, "I would feel naked to go out [on patrol] without a gun. I could not do it now because I started with a gun" (Hendy, 2014, p. 188).

Hendy, Mummolo, and others are steadily building and developing our understanding of policing and weapons. However, without a coherent body of theory and/or a robust evidence base, the debate over the routine arming of police officers remains largely rhetorical.

Concluding Comments: The Need for Evidence

There is an inherent tension between the normalization of routinely armed police and the doctrine of minimum-force policing. The arming of police represents, both practically and symbolically, a shift from one rhetorical position to another. On one side are Peel's Principles and Charles Reith: "The success of the British police lies in the fact that they represent the discovery of a process for transmuting crude, physical force" (Reith, 1952, p. 162). On the other side, police armament is presented as a matter of common sense. However, rhetorical or presumption-driven justifications are not sufficient for such an important aspect of policing and society. Police legitimacy, the broad acceptance of police authority by the community, is vital to successful policing. While the particular expectations of the community vary and are subject to change, researchers have consistently found that an essential component of that legitimacy is the belief that police will use force within limits set by law and, more broadly, by community standards. Even at less critical levels of policing—routine interactions such as traffic stops—research has highlighted the importance of perceptions of procedural and operational fairness (Mazerolle, Antrobus, Bennett, & Tyler, 2013; Tankebe & Liebling, 2014; Tyler, 2006; Tyler & Wakslak, 2004). Where police routinely carry firearms, they are, in effect, empowered to exercise potentially lethal levels of force at any time and in any place. In such circumstances, the need for and expectations of legitimacy are even greater (Reiner & O'Connor, 2015; Yesberg & Bradford, 2019).

There is, therefore, a need to quantify and monitor the effects upon the doctrine of minimum force, and with respect to police and community safety, of how police carry and use firearms. Specifically, researchers must probe beyond the rhetorical positions that have traditionally shaped discussion. What is the actual effect, in the real world, of routinely arming police officers? Are the police safer? Is the community safer? These basic questions need to be explored with an open mind and with reference to evidence. In the book from which this chapter draws, the current authors are continuing their research. They demonstrate that meaningful comparative real-world studies can be made, which can start to provide evidence-based answers to these questions (Evans & Farmer, 2020).

Of course, the operationalization of minimum force is determined by more than the presence or absence of a firearm. It is influenced by a complex set of drivers, including procedural, cultural, situational, political, demographic, and individual officer characteristics. Nevertheless, at a macro level, meaningful comparisons can be made: to establish the quantum of risk associated with routinely armed police, to examine correlations between key measures of safety and the presence or absence of firearms, and to offer an empirical rather than rhetorical assessment of the effect of routinely armed police on the application of the doctrine of minimum force. Is the principle of minimum force merely an aphorism, a rhetorical position vulnerable to challenge? Or can the efficacy of minimum-force policing, for both the community and police themselves, be demonstrated with tested evidence?

Discussion Questions

1. In your own words, explain what you understand to be the doctrine of minimum-force policing. Does your understanding differ from what is discussed in this chapter?
2. In 1969, David Bayley raised the question, "Does the readiness of police to use force call forth hostility and violence in the general public, and particularly among suspects, or is readiness to use force essential to prevent a greater amount of violence from the public and suspects?" Which approach to using force best describes policing in your own community?
3. Black Lives Matter and similar protest movements are drawing public attention to patterns and quanta of police use of force, not just specific instances of misconduct. In what ways does this shift present an opportunity for police services to reform?
4. Imagine that there is a change of government in a jurisdiction with high rates of crime and that you are given the opportunity to create a new police service there. What model of use of force would you adopt and why? What aspects of the local culture and society would influence your decision?
5. Think about policing in your own community. If your police are routinely armed, are there duties you believe that they could carry out safely without the need for firearms? If your police are not routinely armed, what duties do you think most clearly justify carrying firearms?

References

Ackroyd, P. (2000). *London: The biography*. London: Chatto & Windus.

Bayley, D. H. (1969). *Police and political development in India*. Princeton, NJ: Princeton University Press.

Bayley, D. H. (1985). *Effectiveness of police response, Denver 1982*. Ann Arbor, MI: Inter-university Consortium for Political and Social Research.

Bayley, D. H. (1995). Police brutality abroad. In W. Geller & H. Toch (Eds.), *And justice for all: Understanding and controlling police abuse of force* (pp. 261–276). Washington, DC: Police Executive Research Forum.

Bayley, D. H. (1999). *Capacity-building in law enforcement* (pp. 1–4). Canberra: Australian Institute of Criminology.

Bayley, D. H. (2002). Law enforcement and the rule of law: Is there a tradeoff? *Criminology & Public Policy, 2*, 133–154.

BBC (2019). Justine Damond: U.S. policeman jailed for Australian's murder. *BBC News Online*. Retrieved December 9, 2019, from www.bbc.com/news/world-us-canada-48562834

Bhatia, R. (2019, November 2). Strong opposition to planned armed police units. *Stuff.co.nz*.

Bittner, E. (1975). *The functions of the police in modern society: A review of background factors, current practices, and possible role models*. New York, NY: Jason Aronson.

Bittner, E. (2005). Florence Nightingale in pursuit of Willie Sutton: A theory of the police. In T. Newburn (Ed.), *Policing: Key readings*. Cullompton, Devon: Willan.

Bolger, P. C. (2015). Just following orders: A meta-analysis of the correlates of American police officer use of force decisions. *American Journal of Criminal Justice, 40*(3), 466–492.

Bond, J. (2019a, November 3). Auckland residents protest as number of armed police officers grows. *New Zealand Herald*.

Bond, J. (2019b, November 11). Police armed response team arrest in suburban area raises concerns. *New Zealand Herald*.

Bradford, B., & Jackson, J. (2016). Enabling and constraining police power: On the moral regulation of policing. In J. Jacobs & J. Jackson (Eds.), *Routledge handbook of criminal justice ethics*. Oxon: Routledge.

Bradford, B., Milani, J., & Jackson, J. (2017). Identity, legitimacy and "making sense" of police use of force. *Policing: An International Journal, 40*(3), 614–627.

Brady, C. (1974). *Guardians of the peace*. Dublin: Gill and Macmillan.

Brewer, J. D., Guelke, A., Hume, I., & Moxon-Browne, E. (1996). *The police, public order and the state: Policing in Great Britain, Northern Ireland, the Irish Republic, the USA, Israel, South Africa and China.* Houndsmill: Macmillan.

Brodeur, J. P. (2010). *Elements of a theory of policing.* Oxford: Oxford University Press.

Bronitt, S., & Stenning, P. (2011). Understanding discretion in modern policing. *Criminal Law Journal, 35*(6).

Bureau of Justice Statistics. (2021). *Traffic stops.* Retrieved from www.bjs.gov/index.cfm?tid=702&ty=tp

Buttle, J. (2010). Officer safety and public safety: Training the police to use force in the United Kingdom. In J. Knutsson & J. B. Kuhns (Eds.), *Police use of force: A global perspective.* Santa Barbara, CA: Praeger.

Chandler, G. F. (1930). *The policeman's manual: A standard guide to the latest methods and duties of American police.* New York, NY: Funk & Wagnall.

Critchley, T. A. (1973). The idea of policing in Britain: Success or failure? In J. C. Alderson & P. J. Stead (Eds.), *The police we deserve.* London: Wolfe.

Critchley, T. A. (1977). Peel, Rowan and Mayne: The British model of urban police. In P. J. Stead (Ed.), *Pioneers in policing.* Maidenhead: McGraw Hill.

De Camargo, C. R. (2016). *A uniform not "uniform": An ethnography of police clothing, performance, gender and subculture in neighbourhood policing* (Ph.D., thesis). University of Salford, Manchester.

Delehanty, C., Mewhirter, J., Welch, R., & Wilks, J. (2017). Militarization and police violence: The case of the 1033 program. *Research & Politics, 4*(2), 1–7. Retrieved from https://journals.sagepub.com/doi/pdf/10.1177/2053168017712885

Devereaux, S. (2001). Before the bobbies: The night watch and police reform in metropolitan London, 1720–1830. *Journal of British Studies, 1*, 146.

Dodd, V. (2018, May 17). UK police chiefs discuss officers routinely carrying guns. *Guardian.*

Edwards, C. J. (1999). *Changing policing theories: For 21st century societies.* Leichhardt: Federation Press.

Edwards, F., Lee, H., & Esposito, M. (2019). Risk of being killed by police use of force in the United States by age, race—ethnicity, and sex. *Proceedings of the National Academy of Sciences, 116*(34), 16793–16798.

Equality and Human Rights Commission. (2019). *Article 2: Right to life.* Retrieved from www.equalityhumanrights.com/en/human-rights-act/article-2-right-life

Eustachewich, L. (2018, July 19). Knife attacks and murders spike in the UK. *New York Post.*

Evans, R., & Farmer, C. (2020). *Do police need guns? Policing and firearms: Past, present and future.* Singapore: Springer Publishing.

Evans, R., Farmer, C., & Saligari, J. (2016). Mental illness and gun violence: Lessons for the United States from Australia and Britain. *Violence & Gender, 3*(3), 150–156. doi:10.1089/vio.2015.0049

Farmer, C., & Evans, R. (2019). Primed and ready: Does arming police increase safety? Preliminary findings. *Violence & Gender, 7*(2), 47–56 [Special Issue on Gun Violence]. doi:10.1089/vio.2019.0020.

Farmer, C., & Evans, R. (2020). Do police need guns? The nexus between routinely armed police and safety. *The International Journal of Human Rights.* Retrieved from www.tandfonline.com/doi/full/10.1080/13642987.2020.1811694

Gallagher, C. (2020, September 28). Large sections of Garda to be disarmed following review. *Irish Times.* Retrieved from www.irishtimes.com/news/crime-and-law/large-sections-of-garda-to-be-disarmed-following-review-1.4365987#

Goldsworthy, T. (2014, August 19). Urban combat: Ferguson and the militarisation of police. *The Conversation.* Retrieved from https://theconversation.com/urban-combat-ferguson-and-the-militarisation-of-police-30568

Guardian. (2019, October 18). New Zealand police to start armed patrols after Christchurch massacre. *Guardian.*

Hendy, R. (2014). Routinely armed and unarmed police: What can the Scandinavian experience teach us? *Policing: A Journal of Policy and Practice, 8*, 183–192.

Hendy, R. (2019). *Procedural conflict and conflict resolution: A cross-national study of police officers from New Zealand and South Australia* (Ph.D., thesis). University of Cambridge. Retrieved November 28, 2019, from www.repository.cam.ac.uk/bitstream/handle/1810/291692/PhD%20R%20Hendy%20Thesis%20-%20Screen.pdf?sequence=1

Heslop, R. (2015). The contribution of David H. Bayley, policing research pioneer. *Police Practice & Research, 16*, 512–526.

Hess, K. M., Orthmann, C. H., & Cho, H. L. (2015). *Introduction to law enforcement and criminal justice* (11th ed.) New York, NY: Thomas.

Hirschfield, P. J., & Simon, D. (2010). Legitimating police violence: Newspaper narratives of deadly force. *Theoretical Criminology, 14*, 155–182.

Home Office (U.K.) (2012). *Definition of policing by consent.* Retrieved from www.gov.uk/government/publications/policing-by-consent/definition-of-policing-by-consent

Human Rights Law Centre. (2011). *Police shooting: Coroner's findings highlight urgent need for reform of police training on use of force.* Retrieved from www.hrlc.org.au/news/2017/5/10/police-shooting-coroners-findings-highlight-urgent-need-for-reform-of-police-training-on-use-of-force

Huq, A. Z., Jackson, J., & Trinkner, R. (2017). Legitimating practices: Revisiting the predicates of police legitimacy. *British Journal of Criminology, 57*(5), 1101–1122.

Ignatieff, M. (1979). The police and the people: The birth of Mr. Peel's blue locusts. *New Society, 3*, 443–445.

Klockars, C. B. (1985). *The idea of police.* Beverly Hills, CA: Sage Publications.

Knutsson, J., & Kuhns, J. B. (2010). *Police use of force: A global perspective.* Santa Barbara, CA: Praeger.

Knutsson, J., & Strype, J. (2010). Police use of firearms in Norway and Sweden: The significance of gun availability. *Policing & Society, 13*(4), 429–439.

Kuhns, J., Knutsson, J., & Bayley, D. (2010). *Police use of force: A global perspective.* Santa Barbara, CA: Praeger.

Lentz, S. A., & Chaires, R. H. (2007). The invention of Peel's Principles: A study of policing "textbook" history. *Journal of Criminal Justice, 35*, 69–79.

Manning, P. (2012). Trust and accountability in Ireland: The case of An Garda Síochána. *Policing & Society, 22*, 346–361.

Marius, R. (1973). *Luther.* Philadelphia, PA: Lippincott.

Mastrofski, S. D. (2004). Controlling street-level police discretion. *American Academy of Political and Social Science, 593*(1), 100–118.

Mazerolle, L., Antrobus, E., Bennett, S., & Tyler, T. R. (2013). Shaping citizen perceptions of police legitimacy: A randomized field trial of procedural justice. *Criminology, 51*, 33–64.

McCulloch, J., & Sentas, V. (2006). The killing of Jean Charles de Menezes. *Social Justice, 33*(4), 92–106.

McFadden, S. (2020, September 3). Black Lives Matter just entered its next phase. *The Atlantic.* Retrieved from www.theatlantic.com/culture/archive/2020/09/black-lives-matter-just-entered-its-next-phase/615952/

McNiffe, L. (1997). *A history of the Garda Síochána: Asocial history of the force 1922–52, with an overview of the years 1952–97.* Dublin: Wolfhound Press.

Miller, L. (2015, May–June). Why cops kill: The psychology of police deadly force encounters. *Aggression and Violent Behaviour, 22*, 97–111.

Minneapolis Police. (2020). *Minneapolis police statement: 26 May 2020.* Retrieved November 2, 2020, from www.insidempd.com/2020/05/26/man-dies-after-medical-incident-during-police-interaction/

Morrison, G. B., & Vila, B. J. (1998). Police handgun qualification: Practical measure or aimless activity? *Policing, 21*(3), 510.

Mulroe, P. (2016). Policing twentieth century Ireland: A history of An Garda Siochana. *Irish Political Studies, 31*, 336–339.

Mummolo, J. (2018). Militarization fails to enhance police safety or reduce crime but may harm police reputation. *Proceedings of the National Academy of Sciences, 115*(37), 9181–9186. Retrieved February 24, 2019, from www.pnas.org/content/115/37/9181

New York Times. (2014, April 16). Sir Robert Peel's nine principles of policing. *New York Times.* Retrieved from www.nytimes.com/2014/04/16/nyregion/sir-robert-peels-nine-principles-of-policing.html

New York Times. (2020, October 23). What we know about the death of George Floyd in Minneapolis. *New York Times.* Retrieved from www.nytimes.com/article/george-floyd.html

Noppe, J. (2015). Studying police use of force: Definitional challenges and methodological considerations. *Criminology, Security and Justice: Methodological and Epistemological Issues, 3*, 105–132.

Nowacki, J. S. (2015). Organizational-level police discretion: An application for police use of lethal force. *Crime & Delinquency, 61*(5), 643–668.

O'Connor, M. (2021, January 13). What traffic enforcement without police could look like. *The Appeal.* Retrieved from https://theappeal.org/traffic-enforcement-without-police/

Ombudsman Ontario (Canada) (2016). *A matter of life and death: Investigation into the direction provided by the ministry of community safety and correctional services to Ontario's police services for de-escalation of conflict situations.* Toronto: Ombudsman Ontario.

Osse, A., & Cano, I. (2017). Police deadly use of firearms: An international comparison. *The International Journal of Human Rights, 21*(5), 629–649.

O'Sullivan, N. (2015). Building trust and confidence—challenges and opportunities for the Garda Síochána. *Irish Probation Journal, 12,* 7–21.

Palmer, D. (2017). Police and policing. In D. Dalton, W. De Lint, & D. Palmer (Eds.), *Crime and justice: A guide to criminology* (5th ed., pp. 377–404). Pyrmont: Thomson Reuters.

Palmer, S. H. (1988). *Police and protest in England and Ireland, 1780–1850.* Cambridge: Cambridge University Press.

Police News (New Zealand) (2010). Police association conference calls for general arming of police. *Police News, 43,* 272.

Reiner, R., & O'Connor, D. (2015). Politics and policing: The terrible twins. In J. Fleming (Ed.), *Police leadership: Rising to the top* (pp. 42–70). Oxford: Oxford University Press.

Reith, C. (1948). *A short history of the British police.* Oxford: Oxford University Press.

Reith, C. (1952). *The blind eye of history: A study of the origins of the present police era.* London: Faber & Faber.

Rogers, M. D. (2003). Police force—an examination of the use of force, firearms and less-lethal weapons by British police. *Police Journal, 3,* 189–203.

Sarre, R. (2018). Gun control: An Australian perspective. In *Gun Studies* (pp. 177–195). England, UK: Routledge.

Skolnick, J. H., & Fyfe, J. J. (1993). *Above the law: Police and the excessive use of force* (p. 242). New York: Free Press.

Squires, P., & Kennison, P. (2010). *Shooting to kill? Policing, firearms and armed response.* Chichester: John Wiley & Sons.

Storch, R. D. (1975). The plague of the blue locusts: Police reform and popular resistance in northern England, 1840–57. *International Review of Social History, 20*(1), 61–90.

Tankebe, J., & Liebling, A. (2014). *Legitimacy and criminal justice: An international exploration.* Oxford: Oxford University Press.

Taylor, D. N. (1997). *The new police in nineteenth-century England: Crime, conflict and control.* Manchester: Manchester University Press.

Terrill, W., & Paoline, E. A. (2013). Less lethal force policy and police officer perceptions: A multisite examination. *Criminal Justice and Behaviour, 40*(10), 1109–1130.

Tyler, T. R. (2006). *Why people obey the law.* Princeton, NJ: Princeton University Press.

Tyler, T. R., & Jackson, J. (2014). Popular legitimacy and the exercise of legal authority: Motivating compliance, cooperation, and engagement. *Psychology, Public Policy, and Law, 20*(1), 78–95.

Tyler, T. R., & Wakslak, C. J. (2004). Profiling and police legitimacy: Procedural justice, attributions of motive, and acceptance of police authority. *Criminology, 2,* 253.

United Nations. (1979). *Code of conduct for law enforcement officials.* New York, NY: United Nations.

Victoria Police. (2003). *Victoria police manual.* Melbourne: Victoria Police.

Victoria Police. (2014). *Victoria police blue paper: A vision for Victoria police in 2025.* Melbourne: Victoria Police.

Waddington, P. A. J. (2007). Use of force. *Policing: A Journal of Policy and Practice, 1*(3), 249–251.

Waddington, P. A. J., & Wright, M. (2010). Police use of guns in unarmed countries: The United Kingdom. In J. B. Kuhns & J. Knutsson (Eds.), *Police use of force: A global perspective.* Santa Barbara, CA: Praeger.

Waldren, M. (2007). The arming of police officers. *Policing: A Journal of Policy and Practice, 1*(3), 255–264.

Walker, D. (2018). *Fatal force: A conversation with journalists who cover deadly, highly-publicized police shootings* (Master's thesis). Retrieved November 30, 2019, from https://scholarcommons.sc.edu/etd/4755

Westervelt, E. (2020, October 19). Removing cops from behavioral crisis calls: "We need to change the model." *NPR.* Retrieved from www.npr.org/2020/10/19/924146486/removing-cops-from-behavioral-crisis-calls-we-need-to-change-the-model

White, M. D. (2002). Identifying situational predictors of police shootings using multivariate analysis. *Policing: An International Journal of Police Strategies & Management, 25*(4), 726–751.

Woods, J. B. (2020). Traffic without the police. *Stanford Law Review*, *73*. Retrieved from https://papers.ssrn.com/sol3/papers.cfm?abstract_id=3702680

Yanique, T. (2020). Learning experiences: The Black Lives Matter protests in Atlanta, Georgia. *Times Literary Supplement*, *6124*, 9.

Yesberg, J. A., & Bradford, B. (2019). Affect and trust as predictors of public support for armed police: Evidence from London. *Policing and Society*, *29*, 1058–1076.

Chapter 4

Perceptions of Police Officers of the Floating Population

A Pilot Study of Community Justice Initiatives in China[1]

Jurg Gerber and Di Jia

Community justice is a relatively recent concept (Clear, Hamilton, & Cadora, 2011). Definitions vary on the meaning of this concept, but at its core are the ideas of community policing, community courts, and community corrections. More importantly, whereas the traditional criminal justice model deals with cases, community justice has the following foci: 1) places, not just cases; 2) a proactive, rather than reactive approach; 3) problem solving, not simply allocating blame; 4) decentralization, not hierarchy; and 5) fluid organizational boundaries (Clear et al., 2011). These focal concerns represent the starting point for this chapter. However, particular emphasis will be placed on being proactive and problem-solving oriented and having fluid organizational boundaries.

Kim, Gerber, and Beto (2012) examined the potential of partnerships between police and community corrections agencies in Asia, through the lens of community justice. As they argued, the criminal justice system in the US is in many ways three loosely related subsystems. These three relatively independent subsystems are expected to keep communities safe and to control crime to the extent possible. However, this is exceptionally difficult because the system usually becomes involved only after crimes have been committed. In other words, the failure of social control has already occurred when representatives of criminal justice become active. Furthermore, the task of officers is complicated by the fact that the various agencies are involved at different times. Whereas police agencies are involved with offenders in the early stages of the criminal justice processes, community corrections agencies may become involved years later in the lives of these same offenders. To complicate matters further, police and community corrections see their roles very differently. Police define their function primarily in terms of law enforcement, but parole and probation agents think of themselves as agents of corrections as the term *community corrections* implies (Corbett, 1998).

In the current chapter, we examine the role the police play in Chinese society in terms of community justice. In particular, we examine the Chinese police and their relationship with the floating population in China. As we explain in more detail later in this chapter, while this term has been historically used to denote the relatively unskilled rural migrant laborers in urban areas, more recently it has also been used to describe young urban professionals who are geographically mobile. The term, in other words, is used to describe part of the underclass and what in the US have been called yuppies (young urban professionals).

Proponents of community justice argue that criminal justice agencies must tailor their interaction with the various "communities" and community groups to the latter's unique characteristics. What constitutes good police practices with one "community" or community group may not be effective at all with another one. This fact will undoubtedly pose a challenge for Chinese police in dealing with their floating population(s). At the same time, in a discussion of the relative successes of community policing, Brogden and Nijhar (2005, p. 85) argued that criminal justice in Japan, Singapore, and China is characterized by "close cooperation between police, state, prosecution, and the penal system," that "citizens are encouraged

DOI: 10.4324/9781003047117-5

to assist in maintaining public order," that "the police are granted considerable discretion in dealing with offenders," and that "the community police have wider functions than in the West." It remains to be seen if these characteristics of Chinese society assist the police in dealing with the floating population.

The Floating Population in China and Criminal Justice

As we explained in more detail elsewhere (Gerber & Jia, 2019), the term *floating population* (or *people*) is a special term in population regulation legislation in China. A general definition of floating people is the legal definition (*Liudongrenkou*), based on the Chinese household (*Hukou*) registration system. According to the "Regulations on Household Registration in the People's Republic of China (PRC)" in 1958, the floating people (they are also called "recurrent people" in foreign literature) are individuals and families who leave the place where they registered as residents for more than six months (Shen & Huang, 2003). They are then registered in a new place as the floating population (*Liudongrenkou*) by the local registration system (Li, 2006). This category of people includes two sub-categories: those who migrated from rural areas to urban areas and those who migrated from the underdeveloped cities to developed cities (Lo & Jiang, 2006).

Compared with other types of floating people in China, such as laid-off workers or young graduates from universities, peasants who have freed themselves from the land and have moved to urban areas in order to earn higher wages face more challenges when transitioning to living in the city. According to the Chinese *Hukou* system, they are not classified as urban residents and thus are not qualified to receive city welfare benefits (Lo & Jiang, 2006). They lack a sense of belonging to the urban environment and feel they are floating in the city like duckweed without roots (*bdue*); consequently, they have been named floating people in China (Crang & Zhang, 2012; Fan, 2002; Woronov, 2004). When reviewing the previous literature on Chinese floating people, many studies focus on the first group of the migrants, mostly peasants, from rural areas to the urban areas (Bakken, 2004; Liu, Messner, Zhang, & Zhuo, 2009; Zhang & Song, 2003) and referred to as *nongmingong* (Wang, 2009). The "peasants" are the largest population sector, and they are bound to the place where they were born by the rigid Chinese household registration system (Lo & Jiang, 2006). Except for limited opportunities for them to get urban residential registrations (*Hukou*), peasants have historically lacked social mobility in China (Lo & Jiang, 2006).

However, this stability of household residency was completely challenged by China's "open-up" policy in the 1980s (Zhang & Song, 2003). On one hand, a "new agricultural policy allowed rural peasants to participate in sideline production and open market activities, which stimulated the peasants' enthusiasm to produce" (Lo & Jiang, 2006, p. 109). On the other hand, the market-oriented economy created huge demands for a labor market in the urban areas. Crang and Zhang (2012) explained,

> [S]ince the 1980s, huge industrial and commercial development has occurred, especially concentrated in China's special economic zones such as Shenzhen and in the coastal cities of Guangzhou creating an acute labor shortage in those industrializing regions. As a result, a large number of rural dwellers from poor provinces like Sichuan, Jiangxi, Hunan, Guangxi, Guizhou have moved to these development areas.
>
> (p. 497)

Rural migrant workers (*nongmingong*) became the earliest generation of floating people in China. According to Wei (1999), *nongmingong* are the main component of the Chinese floating population, accounting for as much as two-thirds of the total in 1990s.

The relationship between the floating people and criminal justice is a topic that attracts interest from sociologists and criminologists both in China and overseas based on their impact on China's contemporary society. The floating people have been able to find work because of an expanding labor market and thus have made significant contributions to Chinese society. However, they have also been seen as one of the causes of the rise of urban crimes and social problems, phenomena that many other countries experienced in the early stages of industrialization and urban growth (Zhang & Song, 2003). Some scholars have tried to examine the floating people and their impact on Chinese crime rates and social changes. According to previous studies, the floating people have some characteristics that make them more likely to be involved in the criminal activities or victimization than those in other social sectors in China (Bingwen, 2008; Curran, 1998; Deng & Cordilia, 1999; Lo & Jiang, 2006; Shi & Wu, 2010, Zhang & Song, 2003).

First, inadequate income and inequality of resource allocation resulting from the traditional household registration system (*Hukou*) are the primary causes for high crime rates among floating people (Gerber & Jia, 2019). Second, the weakness of their social bonds to the original household registration (*Hukou*) makes the floating people in China suffer from social marginalization and low external control, which increases their likelihood of committing crimes in urban areas (Lo & Jiang, 2006, p. 106). Since 1978, China has been experiencing rapid economic growth and urbanization created by "the history's largest flow of rural urban migration in the world" (Zhang & Song, 2003, p. 386). As a result, "the old social order and a new social order coexist" (Liu et al., 2009, p. 96). This social environment has a negative influence on floating people's mobility, which is a "potentially dangerous detachment from the moral order that in China has always been associated with strong connections to localities" (Crang & Zhang, 2012, p. 902).

The geographic concentration of their settlement in the large cities is the last cause of their criminal involvement. Most migrants have to live in the "villages in cities" (*chengzhongcun*) that have emerged as big cities, swallowing up peripheral rural settlements (Zhang, 2005). These settlements are officially classified as non-urban areas and can provide the migrants with basic living conditions at relatively low cost (Zhang, 2016). For instance, there were 867 of these urban villages in the Beijing Municipal Area that accounted for 49.5% of the total residential land (Zheng, Long, Fan, & Gu, 2009, p. 428) in 2008. Zhang (2001) explained the underlying reason that accounts for the shape of those "non-stat-socioeconomic spaces"— *Chengzhongcun*. Based on a study of Zhejiang Village, some of the members of the unofficial community of floating people in Beijing were

> too far away from their places of origin to be reached by rural authorities but at the same time are not integrated into the urban control system. For many years, local urban officials were unwilling to extend their jurisdiction to rural migrants because they were considered "outsiders" in the cities and thus were not seen as subject to urban regulation. It was this lack of official control that created opportunities for migrants to develop their own social and economic niches in the cities. Later, migrant leaders gained local control through patronage and clientele list networks within these newly emerged migrant enclaves.
>
> (Zhang, 2001, p. 182)

An empirical study conducted by Zhang et al. in 2003 has also suggested that income gaps and geographic distance are related significantly to the mobility of the rural population and are the critical causal factors of their criminal behaviors (Zhang & Song, 2003).

Although rural migrants suffer from the systemic disadvantages of China's persisting *Hukou* system (Sun & Fan, 2011, as cited by Crang & Zhang, 2012, p. 896), the social and economic conditions of floating (migrant) populations have improved due to recent changes in Chinese politics and public services. Li (2006) argued that Chinese local governments took different measures to

> dismantle the barriers blocking migrants from the urban labor market by setting up job centres, free legal services for migrant workers to collect delayed salary payment, and labor protection. More recently, rural-urban migrants in some cities have started to gain access to various urban social provisions, such as minimum wage, pensions and health insurances.
>
> (p. 176)

However, at the same time, some scholars also pointed out that, besides the *Hukou* system, there were other reasons accounting for the isolation and social stigma of Chinese floating people, such as "market competition" (Huang, Guo, & Tang, 2010) and "social exclusion and market" (Zhang, 2011).

In short, the rapid economic growth in China has weakened the stability of the rural population maintained by the Chinese household registration system and has generated floating people in China. The social disadvantages of floating people, such as inadequacy of education, low incomes, and the breakdown of both geographical and social bonds, make the floating people susceptible to criminal behavior. Previous studies and their findings have indicated that the floating people phenomenon is a valuable research topic in criminological studies. Until now, their social characteristics, social mechanisms, and social impact have been studied and accepted only to a limited extent. There are still critical issues and new trends that have not been touched upon by criminologists from either China or overseas. The rapid social and economic development of China has constantly added new research elements to the study of floating people, which increases the academic and practical value of these studies.

Methods

We had an opportunity to interview police officers in three large metropolitan areas in Eastern, Central, and Northern China. We relied on personal contacts to identify officers who either work in police stations that routinely deal with members of the floating population or who themselves expressed a strong interest in the topic. In accordance with the approval obtained from the Institutional Review Board of Sam Houston State University, all interviewees were assured of complete anonymity, and thus the areas where we conducted the interviews are not identified further. Interviews included three group interviews lasting about two hours each and involved a total of 12 officers. Each officer had several years of experience working with members of the floating population. Responses from officers are identified by the interview groups (Interview Group A, B, or C) in which they participated.

Interviews were semi-structured in format. We had a checklist of topics that guided us in general, but it became apparent fairly quickly that the interviewees tended to have interests and experiences that led them to be able to address certain topics easily, but they were unable, or more reticent, to address others. Consistent with qualitative in-depth interviewing guidelines, we let the interviewees determine the nature and direction of the interviews.

In addition to the interviews, we were able to gather some printed materials that are of relevance. Also, the junior author, being a former police officer and native Mandarin speaker, was able to rely on her experiences but, because of her background, could also serve as liaison and interpreter. The senior author does not speak Mandarin and thus had to rely on interpreters during interviews that the junior author did not attend.

Results

We began the research process without any preconceived notions other than a general goal of ascertaining whether or not Chinese police follow theoretical community justice concepts when interacting with members of the floating population. A preliminary assessment shows that this the case in some instances, but the daily reality of police work in these communities is more complex than what a simple yes or no would imply. It is these complexities that we will now examine by focusing on several issues that the police officers raised.

It is also noteworthy that we do not claim to possess overall answers to our research questions. We simply have obtained an image of the floating population from a police perspective. Furthermore, given that we base our conclusions on the opinions of 12 police officers, it is accurate to say that we have conducted a pilot study that should be followed by a more elaborate research project.

Composition of the Floating Population as Perceived by Police Officers

Consistent with our expectations, police officers expressed that the term *floating population* entails several population groups. One demarcation involves the interaction between education and the presence or absence of professional skills. Some members of the floating population, also sometimes referred to as "New Citizens" by some of the officers, are highly educated, possess professional skills, and have migrated to Chinese cities in search of professional employment. They tend to come from urban backgrounds and blend in well with the local population of the destination cities. In fact, they are indistinguishable from the local population in terms of appearance, language, and mannerisms but do not necessarily have identical residential rights (Interview Groups A, B, and C).

The other major category consists of relatively uneducated migrants with a low level of job skills. They tend to have moved to their destination cities from rural areas or from Western China. They do not blend in well with the local population. The dialects they use identify them as migrants, and their appearance and mannerisms identify them even to a casual observer as being most likely uneducated manual workers or their family members (Interview Groups A, B, and C).

Police Officers' Assessment of Community Perception of the Floating Population

Community perception—that is, the perception of the members of the local residential population—is more complex than what an outside observer might expect. One would expect the relatively well-educated segment to be well accepted, but not the relatively uneducated segment. We found some limited support for this expectation; specifically, the well-educated group was always seen as accepted by the community (Interview Groups A, B, and C). However, the situation with respect to the less educated members of the floating population was not as straightforward as expected. Some officers saw them as well accepted. They argued that community members see all member of the floating population, regardless of educational level, as making a significant contribution to the communities in which they live (Interview Group C). Other officers disagreed with this perspective. They argued that local residents do not like the low-skilled members of the floating population. They see them as troublemakers who are responsible for the rise in crime rates. At the same time, they sometimes benefit economically from their presence by renting out apartments or rooms to them (Interview Group B). This finding to some degree verified the conclusion of Liu and colleagues in 2009, which revealed that "rural migrant concentration affects fear of crime indirectly through its impact on perceived disorder" (Liu et al., 2009, p. 102).

Police Perception of the Floating Population

According to our interviewees, police perception of the floating population mirrors the perception of the local residents. The well-educated segment is seen as similar to the local population, whereas the other segment was seen as more problematic than the local population by some officers, but the exact opposite was perceived by other officers (Interview Groups A, B, and C). One of the officers in Interview Group B saw the residential population in their area as lazy and believed that it was the floating population that was responsible for the economic well-being of the region, not the residential population. This officer also perceived the members of the floating population to have more favorable attitudes about the police than the local population. They perceived this to be the case because members of the floating population don't have as much of a support network as the locals and thus rely more on the police for services.

Crimes Committed by and Against Members of the Floating Population

We expected that the floating population, at least the uneducated segment, to be seen as responsible for a large percentage of predatory crimes. However, while we found some support for this interpretation (Interview Groups A, B, and C), the reality is once again more complex. For instance, officers in Interview Group A stated that members of the floating population "commit a disproportionate number of thefts, fighting, and burglaries." This interpretation was challenged by other officers, who believed that the floating population was underrepresented among offenders and that most crimes were committed by members of the local population.

However, there was almost universal agreement that members of the floating population are overrepresented among crime victims (Interview Groups A, B, and C). The relatively uneducated of the floating population are believed to lack awareness of crime prevention and are therefore more likely to be victimized (Interview Group C).

Public Order Offenses and the Floating Population

Several officers in Group B addressed the issue of public order offenses and the floating population. Its members are believed to be more likely to drink alcohol excessively. This fact is seen as leading to money shortages, which leads to their committing a disproportionate share of property crimes. This was especially the case around holidays. Because they spent their money soon after earning it, they had no money for train tickets to visit their families for the holidays and thus committed property crimes (Interview Group B). This tendency has led to an innovative program in that locality, described later in this chapter, aimed at preventing that form of crime.

Members of the floating population are overrepresented in prostitution according to our police officers. This is the case for the prostitutes as well as their customers. At least half of each are not part of the local population, according to the police officers. Similarly, gambling and low-level drug offenses are disproportionately committed by members of the floating population (Interview Groups A and B).

Police Programs for Members of the Floating Population

One of the major premises of community justice theory is that communities that have the highest crime rates and thus are subject to the most repressive criminal justice system attention should be the focus of preventive criminal justice system activities. Thus, if police in China engage in community justice activities, they should have programs that assist the floating population, particularly the segment with low levels of educational attainment. Indeed, we identified numerous programs of such a nature. Some are programs that are exclusively designed for the floating population while others are designed for the general population but made available to the floating population.

Mediation services are an example of the latter. Most local police stations in China have mediation offices. Citizens who are in a civil dispute with each other can use the mediation offices for conflict resolution. It is not infrequent that a dispute that involves a local resident and a member of the floating population is settled by the mediation office. While some officers see little differences between the two population groups' use of these offices, others see local residents as having to make compromises in order to resolve conflicts with the migrants (Interview Group B).

Chinese police run various activities aimed at making the citizens aware of new forms of criminal victimization. While these campaigns are intended for both local and migrant populations, a special emphasis is often put on educating the latter. Reasons given for this special emphasis include their high rates of victimization and the perceived lack of education among some segments of the migrant population (Interview Groups A and C).

Some programs are designed mostly for the migrant population and, consistent with community justice guidelines, are joint programs with other governmental agencies. The aim is not to deal with crime directly, but to improve social conditions for the most vulnerable and, thus, to ameliorate criminogenic conditions and lower crime rates indirectly. Some programs that officers mentioned include the following:

- Migrants can earn certificates in work skills training programs that will help them get jobs.
- Medical services for pregnant women and new mothers and medical care for small children are free for migrants.
- People with mental problems are taken to mental hospitals. Residents have to pay for the stay in the hospitals; migrants receive the services for free because the government pays for them (Interview Group B).
- Finally, two officers in one of the interviews mentioned a local program that involves community justice principles. Because migrant workers tended to spend their earnings quickly, a local policy has been instituted that employers must withhold 60% of workers' wages until the end of the year. In the past, there was a spike in crime around that time; workers had spent their money and were unable to buy train tickets to go home for the holidays. They then committed crimes to get money; now there has been a sharp decline in property crimes around the holidays. This program was suggested by the police and implemented by local government (Interview Group B).

Discussion

The premise of community justice theory is that repressive criminal justice intervention has adverse consequences for vulnerable communities and populations (Clear, Hamilton, & Cadora, 2011). At the same time, it is in the very communities that are plagued by high crime rates that community justice initiatives can have the greatest impact. In China, the floating population is one such community. While it is not a homogenous category of people, the poorly educated members who tend to be from rural backgrounds play economic roles that blacks and Hispanics play in the US, North Africans in France and Italy, and Eastern and Central Europeans in North-Western Europe (Gerber & Jia, 2019). They tend to be economically weak, perform jobs that the local residential population is unwilling to do, and are quite often subject to prejudiced attitudes. Furthermore, they sometimes are singled out for differential and unfair treatment by the criminal justice system. Conversely, if agents of social control follow community justice practices, they can ameliorate problematic conditions from which the floating population in China, or any of the other marginalized groups in the other countries, suffer.

The methodology of the current study does not let us conclusively state if the police in China achieve these goals. We only interviewed 12 officers in three cities about their perceptions of community justice initiatives that police pursue in their interactions with members of the floating population. Nevertheless, we feel confident in concluding tentatively that they at least attempt to pursue goals that are consistent with community justice initiatives. In the preceding pages, we described programs and attitudes that displayed aspects of community justice principles. It is clear that at least some segments of the general population and agents of social control believe that the floating population is responsible for a disproportionate share of predatory crime. Thus, we have found support for the claims made in the literature (Bingwen, 2008; Curran, 1998; Deng & Cordilia, 1999; Lo & Jiang, 2006; Shi & Wu, 2010; Zhang & Song, 2003). However, it is equally clear that the police attempt to counteract these tendencies with programs that are at least partially consistent with community justice principles. Program initiatives that let officials deal with members of the floating population in a preferential manner, designed to offset past problems and inequities, include job skills training, medical care for pregnant women, and wage withholding for migrants. While none of these programs deal directly with crime or the criminal justice system, if they are successful, there will be less need for criminal justice intervention in the future. In general terms, these programs are consistent with Clear et al.'s (2011) principles of community justice.

There is a need for a formal evaluation of these programs and Chinese police commitment to principles of community justice. As a result of this pilot study, we can provide only tentative support. We see a need for future research along three lines: 1) Researchers need to draw a more representative sample of Chinese police officers. We propose to draw a random sample of Chinese police officers from several cities and replicate this study with such a sample. 2) Conversely, it might be possible to do a case study of a successful program or local police department/station. Whereas the proposed research will provide quantitative support for our conclusions, a case study would provide qualitative documentation for proponents of community justice initiatives. 3) Finally, researchers should also study the perception of the members of the floating population. In order to understand the effectiveness of such programs, the perceptions of those affected most directly must be studied. Community justice initiatives are designed to make criminal justice procedures better for a community. There is a need to assess whether or not the programs we identified achieve this goal.

Discussion Questions

1. What are the key characteristics of community justice? How is this concept different from criminal justice?
2. What is the nature of the floating population in China?
3. How do police officers in this pilot study view the floating population in China?
4. To what extent did the authors find support for community justice principles among Chinese police officers?

5. The authors acknowledge that they can only provide tentative support for their findings as a result of their research design. How can the researchers improve the generalizability of their findings?

Note

1. Revised version of a paper presented at the annual meetings of the International Police Executive Symposium, in Belgrade, Serbia, 2019.

References

Bakken, B. (2004). Moral panics, crime rates and harsh punishment in China. *Australian & New Zealand Journal of Criminology*, *37*(1 suppl.), 67–89.

Bingwen, Z. (2008). 30 years of reform and openness in China: Development and challenges of social security system for floating population. *Chinese Journal of Population Science*, *128*(5), 2–17.

Brogden, M., & Nijhar, P. (2005). *Community policing: National and international models and approaches*. Portland, OR: Willan Publishing.

Clear, T. R., Hamilton, J. R., & Cadora, E. (2011). *Community Justice* (2nd ed.). London: Routledge.

Corbett, R. P., Jr. (1998, Summer). Probation blue? The promise (and perils) of probation-police partnerships. *Corrections Management Quarterly*, *2*(3).

Crang, M. A., & Zhang, J. (2012). Transient dwelling: Trains as places of identification for the floating population of China. *Social and Cultural Geography*, *13*(8), 895–914.

Curran, D. J. (1998). Economic reform, the floating population, and crime: The transformation of social control in China. *Journal of Contemporary Criminal Justice*, *14*(3), 262–280.

Deng, X., & Cordilia, A. (1999). To get rich is glorious: Rising expectations, declining control, and escalating crime in contemporary China. *International Journal of Offender Therapy and Comparative Criminology*, *43*(2), 211–229.

Fan, C. C. (2002). The elite, the natives, and the outsiders: Migration and labor market segmentation in urban China. *Annals of the Association of American Geographers*, *92*(1), 103–124.

Gerber, J., & Jia, D. (2019). Community policing and community justice: Studying a marginalized population segment in the people's Republic of China. In E. W. Plywaczewski (Ed.), *Current problems of penal law and criminology* (8th ed., pp. 451–461). Bialystok, Poland: Beck.

Huang, Y., Guo, F., & Tang, Y. (2010). Hukou status and social exclusion of rural—urban migrants in transitional China. *Journal of Asian Public Policy*, *3*(2), 172–185.

Kim, B., Gerber, J., & Beto, D. R. (2012). An empirical assessment of police-community corrections partnerships in Texas: A model for Asian societies. *Asia Pacific Journal of Police & Criminal Justice*, *9*, 1–16.

Li, B. (2006). Floating population or urban citizens? Status, social provision and circumstances or rural-urban migrants in China. *Social Policy & Administration*, *40*(2), 174–195.

Liu, J., Messner, S. F., Zhang, L., & Zhuo, Y. (2009). Socio-demographic correlates of fear of crime and the social context of contemporary urban China. *American Journal of Community Psychology*, *44*(1–2), 93–108.

Lo, T. W., & Jiang, G. (2006). Inequality, crime and the floating population in China. *Asian Journal of Criminology*, *1*(2), 103–116.

Shen, J., & Huang, Y. (2003). The working and living space of the "floating population" in China. *Asia Pacific Viewpoint*, *44*(1), 51–62.

Shi, X., & Wu, J. (2010). Floating population, income inequality and crime. *Journal of Shandong University (Philosophy and Social Sciences)*, *2*, 003.

Sun, M., & Fan, C. C. (2011). China's permanent and temporary migrants: Differentials and changes, 1990–2000. *Professional Geographer, 63*(1): 92–112.

Wang, Z. (2009). A discourse on creating and rendering educational and cultural enrichment services to rural migrant workers by public libraries. *National Science Library, Chinese Academy of Sciences*, *2*(2), 14–31.

Wei Jinsheng. (1999). Chinese urban recurrent population definition, situation and problems. *Renkou and Jihuashengyu*, *6*, 7–13.

Woronov, T. E. (2004). In the eye of the chicken: Hierarchy and marginality among Beijing's migrant school-children. *Ethnography*, *5*(3), 289–313.

Zhang, K. H., & Song, S. (2003). Rural-urban migration and urbanization in China: Evidence from time-series and cross-section analyses. *China Economic Review*, *14*, 386–400.

Zhang, L. (2001). Migration and privatization of space and power in late socialist China. *American Ethnologist*, *28*(1), 179–205.

Zhang, L. (2005). Migrant enclaves and impacts of redevelopment policy in Chinese cities. *Restructuring the Chinese City: Changing Society, Economy and Space*, 218–233.

Zhang, L. (2016). Living and working at the margin: Rural migrant workers in China's transitional cities. In *Marginalisation in China* (pp. 95–110). London: Routledge.

Zhang, S. (2011). What determines migrant workers' life chances in contemporary China? Hukou, social exclusion, and the market. *Modern China*, *37*(3), 243–285.

Zheng, S., Long, F., Fan, C. C., & Gu, Y. (2009). Urban villages in China: A 2008 survey of migrant settlements in Beijing. *Eurasian Geography and Economics*, *50*(4), 425–446.

Chapter 5

Municipal Police Department's Use of Facebook

Exploring the Potential for Differences Across Size Classifications

Bradley D. Edwards, Dustin L. Osborne, Rychelle Moses, Logan S. Ledford, and Gabriela Smith

Introduction

Police departments have long been reliant on traditional media to achieve their community outreach goals. Police often use the media to help inform the public of criminal acts, solicit information that can assist in solving crimes, and build community trust and legitimacy (Chermak & Weiss, 2005). However, this approach is limited in several ways. Traditional media outlets employ a number of gatekeepers that must prioritize which events or stories are considered newsworthy. Thus, law enforcement agencies cannot guarantee that the messages they wish to convey through these outlets reach their intended audience. In addition, those stories that are covered by traditional media might not be published in a timely manner or might not be framed in a way that promotes the preferred police narrative (Walsh & O'Connor, 2019). Perhaps most importantly, public consumption of traditional media has steadily decreased in recent years (Barthel, 2019). As a result, law enforcement agencies have increasingly sought alternative methods to interact with their communities (Dai, He, Tian, Giraldi, & Gu, 2017).

The President's Task Force on 21st Century Policing (2015) suggested that social media could be a beneficial tool for police departments to use to engage with the community, gauge public sentiment regarding agency policies, and assist in reaching various goals. Departments are increasingly adopting some type of social media presence, particularly using Facebook as a preferred platform. Despite this important trend, research on the use of social media by police has mostly been limited to large departments or those that feature the most followers (Hu, Rodgers, & Lovrich, 2018; Lieberman, Koetzle, & Sakiyama, 2013). The current chapter explores Facebook use among departments located across the population continuum to determine the types of content posted, the underlying goals of this content, and the level of interaction that posts receive.

Social Media

Social media platforms take a variety of forms, including those that focus on user-created videos (e.g., YouTube), photographs (e.g., Instagram), and written posts (e.g., Facebook). Regardless of form, however, they are distinct from traditional media in many ways. Among these differences are the speed at which information can be disseminated, the decentralization of content creation, and the potential for interaction between the content creator and consumer (Surette, 2015). Social media allows individual users—instead of news editors—to be the gatekeepers of what information is deemed important. Stories that are considered interesting to a sufficient number of social media users can spread to a large number of people at a pace much faster than that of traditional media (Budak, Agrawal, & El Abbadi, 2011).

DOI: 10.4324/9781003047117-6

The public's use of social media has become widespread in recent years. Some social media platforms (e.g., Instagram, Snapchat) are particularly popular among younger age groups, while Facebook usage is common across a range of age groups (Smith & Anderson, 2018). Despite many high-profile privacy concerns related to Facebook, it continues to be among the most frequented social media sites (Clement, 2020). In addition, nearly two-thirds of Facebook users interact with the platform daily (Perrin & Anderson, 2019), making it a particularly valuable resource for public agencies seeking to publish news and engage with the community. Many Facebook users will create extensive networks of friends with whom they can interact and share content. This content might include status updates or information that has been shared by other users or pages. Friends can "like," comment on, or share posts when this content is displayed on their news feed. Public agencies can also create pages designed to increase "brand awareness" or promote services. Individual users can follow these pages and communicate with the agency through private messages or by interacting with their posts. Posts that are made by a public agency and then shared by a user to their page can allow that agency's content to reach a large audience quickly.

Police Use of Social Media

Responding to the public's increased social media usage, police departments seeking to control their messaging and interact with the community began to utilize these platforms (Fowler, 2017; Williams et al., 2018). Police departments are often active on several social media platforms, with Facebook, Twitter, and YouTube being the most common (Kilburn & Krieger, 2014; Meijer & Thaens, 2013). A recent survey by the International Association of Chiefs of Police found that approximately 96% of all agencies in the United States regularly use at least one social media platform to interact with their community (IACP, 2016). The majority of these agencies report that they use social media to engage with the public by responding to questions. Further, many departments intentionally use humor and/or an informal tone on their social media platforms in an attempt to improve community relations (Kim, Oglesby-Neal, & Mohr, 2017). While police departments might have a presence on multiple social media platforms, Brainard and Edlins (2015) found that Facebook was most often their preferred mode of interaction.

Police departments use social media for a variety of purposes. Among the departments that use social media, the most commonly cited reasons include 1) notifying the public of safety concerns, 2) engaging with the community, 3) managing their agency's reputation, and 4) notifying the public of other (non-crime) issues in the community (Kim et al., 2017). These responses largely align with two recent content analyses, which found that the most common types of posts made by police departments related to crimes occurring in the community or public relations announcements (Hu et al., 2018; Lieberman et al., 2013).

For example, Lieberman et al. (2013) examined the Facebook posts of the largest 21 police departments in the United States that had a presence on the platform. The study found that departments that posted frequently were more likely to post crime-related messages, whereas departments with less frequent posts were more likely to focus on public relations messaging. Interestingly, neither of these content categories received the highest level of engagement from the public. Instead, posts related to officer injuries and posts sent to specific groups of people containing content irrelevant to police activities received the highest number of likes and comments. In fact, crime-related posts were among the lowest categories for citizen engagement.

Williams et al. (2018) studied the Facebook and Twitter activity for police departments serving five medium-size (population 24,000–60,000) communities in Massachusetts. These departments used social media more as a community outreach tool than a place to post crime-related news, as crime-related information accounted for less than 10% of all posts. This finding provides some indication that the type of content posted by police departments to social media might vary based on community factors and agency goals prompted by those factors.

Researchers have also examined whether law enforcement social media activity might reflect an overall departmental communication strategy. Mergel (2012) suggested that public agencies might use social media for one of four purposes. First, the agency could be motivated to disseminate information to the public. Second, some agencies might be primarily motivated to gather information, such as opinions, from the public. Alternatively, agencies might be motivated to use social media to publicize an opportunity to engage with citizens (e.g., sponsored events). Finally, a public agency might use a social media app to conduct what are referred to as transactions. Mergel (2012) suggests that this fourth motivation is difficult to observe as these transactions (e.g., offering seized property at public auction) are rare, making it nearly impossible to gather detailed data.

Two more recent studies examined the social media strategy of police departments as it relates to the overall motivation of their messaging, focusing on categories such as "push," "pull," and "interaction." The first, conducted by Meijer and Thaens (2013), explored social media strategies among three large North American police departments. They noted that the Boston Police Department utilized social media primarily for branding purposes and promoting transparency within the department. Thus, their social media usage was categorized as a push strategy due to its focus on publishing information without attempting to either interact with or obtain information from the public. The Metropolitan Police Department in Washington, DC, also used social media for some push-related purposes but primarily saw social media as a method to help solicit information from the public (pull) to assist with investigations. Alternatively, the Toronto Police Department viewed social media as a way to build useful networks between individual police officers and citizens. This is an example of an interaction approach. In sum, while each of these departments was using social media, their motivations for doing so varied.

Hu et al. (2018) extended this line of research through a content analysis of the 14 most popular law enforcement Facebook pages (as determined by the number of followers). Twelve of the departments included in the study were large departments while the remaining two were somewhat smaller but had successfully gained a large number of Facebook likes. They found that the majority (75%) of posts were designed to "push" information to the public, with soliciting information (pull) and promoting possibilities for police-community engagement (interaction) being less prevalent among these departments.

Though each of the aforementioned studies was enlightening, none sought to determine whether an agency's motivation for posting on social media—or the types of content they shared—varied based on department size. By focusing only on the Facebook activity of large or popular departments, our understanding of law enforcement use of the platform is limited. Because smaller departments may have different goals and capabilities (Williams et al., 2018), it is useful to extend this field of inquiry to include those situated across the population spectrum.

Rural Policing

Over 70% of local police departments in the United States serve a population of fewer than 10,000 residents (Reaves, 2015). Falcone, Wells, and Weisheit (2002) suggest that these smaller police departments are distinguishable from their larger counterparts in many important ways. For example, officers working in smaller police departments generally have closer relationships with their communities, are more likely to be generalists than to have a specialty, and attempt to resolve issues informally before making an arrest. It is reasonable to expect that they might also have different motivations regarding the use of social media. Due to their close informal ties with the communities that they serve, rural police departments might not feel the need to use social media to engage with the public to the same extent that is required in urban departments. Alternatively, they might not have adequate access to traditional media and thus feel a greater need to share news and events through social media platforms.

Likewise, residents living in rural communities might engage with law enforcement using social media in ways distinct from those in urban areas. Rural areas most often have lower levels of violent crime (Wells & Weisheit, 2004) and a qualitatively distinct culture compared to urban settings (DeKeseredy, 2015). Prior research suggests those living in rural areas report having overall positive perceptions of police but indicate that they would like to see more meaningful interaction between officers and the public (Benedict, Brown, & Bower, 2000; Nofziger & Williams, 2005). Given these findings, residents living in rural areas may engage with their police departments on social media more actively than those living in urban areas.

Purpose of the Chapter

Because police departments may feature unique goals and relationships with their constituency as a result of population size, it is important to explore whether size serves to influence the types of content shared, the motivations for sharing content, and the level of public responsiveness to it. The current chapter attempts to fill this knowledge gap via a content analysis of Facebook posts made by all municipal departments in the state of Tennessee that are active on the platform. Specifically, it seeks to address the following research questions:

R1: Does the size of the population served influence the frequency of Facebook posts, number of page followers/likes, and follower responsiveness (as gauged by the average proportion of followers who share, comment, or note a reaction to a post)?

R2: Does the size of the population served influence the common motivations for Facebook posts?

R3: Does the size of the population served influence the types of content commonly posted to department pages?

Methods

Data

Data were gathered from all Tennessee municipal police departments featuring a Facebook page that was active (as measured by making at least one post) between November 1, 2018, and April 30, 2019 (N=129). The six-month timeframe was selected to allow for a large sample of posts and represents an improvement over past studies on the topic, most of which have relied on a three-month span. A total of 9,154 posts were made during the timeframe and included in the analysis.

Classifying Departments by Size

As discussed, it is important to determine whether community population size influences the frequency of posting, the number of page followers/likes, post motivation, the types of content being shared, and public responsiveness (as gauged by shares, comments, and reactions). Doing so requires that departments be grouped into categories that allow for any potential variation to be observed. Four categories were selected for the current chapter based on the population size of the municipalities covered by departments: 1) those with fewer than 2,500 residents, 2) those with 2,501 to 10,000 residents, 3) those with 10,001 to 50,000 residents, and 4) those featuring over 50,000 residents (Table 5.1).

Population data was gathered from the Tennessee State Data Center (housed within the Boyd Center for Business and Economic Research at the University of Tennessee) and reflective of population estimates for 2018. Category creation was based primarily on official definitions of the rural-urban continuum provided by the US Census Bureau and White House Office of Management and Budget (OMB). For example, the Census Bureau identifies an urbanized area as featuring a population center of over 50,000 individuals, while those featuring between 2,500 and 50,000 residents are considered an urban cluster (Wilson, 2012). The OMB similarly classifies population by the size of a county's urban core (i.e., largest city), with micropolitan statistical areas defined as those featuring an urban core of more than 10,000 but less than 50,000 and metropolitan statistical areas as those with an urban core of over 50,000 residents (US Office of Management and Budget, 2010).

Though these systems differ slightly and are typically used to differentiate larger areas (e.g., counties), they allow for a rudimentary classification system to be employed. Both systems view population centers over 50,000 as meeting the requirement for an urban area (i.e., city), while the OMB definition is the only one to classify the most rural of towns (fewer than 2,500 residents). Because the Census Bureau definition suggests that micropolitan statistical areas feature an urbanized area of between 10,000 and 50,000 residents, it seems logical to use this framework to differentiate between the two remaining categories: small towns of between 2,500 and 10,000 residents and larger towns featuring between 10,001 and 50,000 residents.

Departmental Characteristics

Department-level data were collected to develop a better understanding of whether size classification serves to influence such factors as post frequency, the number of page followers/likes, and responsiveness to posts (e.g., reactions, shares, comments). Post frequency was measured as the number of posts made by each department during the timeframe under analysis. The number of followers represented the number of individuals who followed the respective departments' Facebook pages and served as a barometer of the connection between the organization and members of the community that they serve. The number of likes represented the number of Facebook users who "liked" the department's page and served as a proxy for public perception.

Because the size of the population covered by a department will serve to influence both the number of followers and the number of likes received by its page, it was essential to create a standard measure that allowed for comparisons to be made between the classifications discussed earlier. Doing so entailed dividing the number of followers and likes by the size of the municipal population covered and multiplying the resulting values by 100. This can be roughly interpreted as the percentage of residents who had either liked or followed the department's page.

Table 5.1 Population Classification

Population Category	Municipal Population	# of Departments
Rural	≤2,500	28
Small Town	2,501–10,000	57
Large Town	10,001–50,000	34
City	50,000+	10

Finally, and to gauge public interaction, information regarding the number of shares, comments, and reactions was collected for each post. Shares indicated the number of times a Facebook user shared a post with their friend group, comments measured the combined number of comments and replies received for each post, and reactions were inclusive of likes and other emotional response options provided to Facebook users (e.g., love, anger, sadness). Though these responses indicated a wide variety of emotions, aggregating them into a single category presented the opportunity to identify the degree to which users felt compelled to respond to a post and, consequently, provided some measure of the effectiveness of a post in engaging the department's target audience. Because the number of shares, likes, and reactions was expected to be dependent on the number of followers a department had (similar to likes and followers), it was important to create a standardized means of measuring each of these items. The current chapter did so by dividing the number of shares, comments, and reactions for each post by the number of followers claimed by the department making the post. In essence, the standardized values can be interpreted as the proportion of followers who shared, commented on, or logged a reaction to the post in question. These values were aggregated across posts, with mean values being compared between size classifications.

Post Characteristics

Two pieces of information were collected for each post via a coding scheme established by the research team. The first, content motivation, was based on past research and classified posts into one of three categories: 1) push, 2) pull, or 3) interaction. The push category included all posts designed to disseminate information to the public (e.g., crime blotter, severe weather notifications, sharing departmental news). The pull category was used to identify posts that sought to obtain information from the public, with examples including asking for help identifying suspects, seeking witnesses to unsolved crimes, and locating stolen property. Finally, interaction posts were defined as those promoting opportunities for citizens to connect with departments and their officers at sponsored events (e.g., community-watch meetings, coffee with a cop program).

In addition to motivation, each post was classified according to the type of content (content category) being shared. The conceptualization of these categories occurred in two stages. First, the research team relied on past studies (see Lieberman et al. (2013) for an example) to establish a list of categories common to the literature on police social media use. Second, a pilot analysis of several departments' Facebook posts identified additional categories worthy of inclusion as gauged by the frequency of their occurrence. In total, 30 content categories were selected for the coding scheme. (See Table 5.2 for a complete summary.)

Three steps were taken to ensure that the coding strategy was implemented properly and to avoid potential bias that can come from a lack of interrater reliability. First, each member of the research team was provided with a detailed coding guide, standard SPSS template, and instruction regarding how to complete the task. This was followed by a pilot assignment utilizing one of the larger departments included in the analysis. Interrater reliability was calculated in a manner similar to Lieberman et al. (2013) and involved dividing the count for total agreements by the total count of possible decisions. Results indicated an 81% agreement rate among the coders. Any discrepancies were then addressed and retraining offered where necessary. Finally, all members were advised to select the "other" category when unsure how best to code a particular post. These posts were then reviewed by two members of the team to determine whether they fit into one of the available categories or should remain classified as "other."

Table 5.2 Content Categories

Category	Description
Community Event	Advertising a community event not sponsored by the agency.
Agency Event	Advertising an event that is sponsored by the agency.
Community Interactions	Publicizing agency interactions with community groups/members.
Agency Success	Publicizing agency success (e.g., lower crime rates, anecdotal evidence).
Officer News	Posts related to officer graduations, awards, promotions, etc.
Hiring Announcements	Notifying community of agency openings and hiring instructions.
Recognizing Community	Thanking community members for donations or other assistance.
New Policies/Practices	Posts notifying the community of new policies, practices, or laws.
Animal Officers	Posts containing information related to K9 or equine officers.
Officer Death/Injury	Notifying the community of recent officer death or injury (within the last 30 days).
Remembrance	Posts remembering officers who passed away more than 30 days ago.
DUI Information	Relaying information regarding DUI stops or prevention/warnings.
Traffic Safety	General traffic safety tips and reminders.
Traffic Issue	Notification of wrecks, roadwork, or other traffic issues.
Severe Weather	Warning the public about impending severe weather.
Crime Warnings	Warning citizens of recent crime trends and emerging problems.
Suspect Identification	Seeking help from the community identifying a suspect.
Suspect Location	Asking the public for assistance locating a suspect, escapee, or individual with an active warrant (identity known).
General Help	Seeking help locating stolen property, collecting evidence, or gathering information.
Activity Blotter	Providing information on recent crimes.
Case Updates	Notifying the public of case progress or closure.
Other Services	Posts providing the public with information about other city services or departments (e.g., school closures, electricity outages).
Lost Pets	Seeking help identifying or locating lost pets.
Missing Children	Asking the public for help locating missing children.
Missing Adults	Asking the public for help locating missing adults.
Holiday Messages	Posts wishing the community a happy holiday.
Resources	Notifying the community of available resources (e.g., substance abuse support groups).
Humor	Posts designed to be humorous in nature.
Not Enough Information	Not enough information contained within the post to determine the appropriate category.
Other	Posts not falling into one of the established categories.

Results

Departmental Analysis

As previously noted, a total of 9,154 posts were logged (and coded) for the 129 included departments. This amounted to an average of less than one post per department per day ($M=0.39$). However, differences emerged when assessing post frequency by classification (Table 5.3). Post frequency increased along the size continuum, with rural departments posting the least ($M=0.18$) and city departments constituting the highest frequency category ($M=1.23$).

To assess whether these differences were statistically significant, a one-way ANOVA utilizing the Welch test (due to unequal sample sizes among the classification groups and a lack

Police Department's Use of Facebook 73

Table 5.3 Post Frequency by Department Classification

Department Classification	Mean # of Posts Per Day
Rural	0.18
Small Town	0.27
Large Town	0.52
City	1.23

Table 5.4 Games-Howell Results for Post Frequency

(I) Classification	(J) Classification	Mean Difference (I-J)	S.E.	Sig.
Rural	Small Town	−.09	.06	.479
	Large Town	−.34*	.09	.003
	City	−1.05*	.24	.007
Small Town	Rural	.09	.06	.479
	Large Town	−.25	.10	.060
	City	−.95*	.24	.013
Large Town	Rural	.34*	.09	.003
	Small Town	.25	.10	.060
	City	−.71	.25	.066
City	Rural	1.05*	.24	.007
	Small Town	.95*	.24	.013
	Large Town	.71	.25	.066

Note: *p<.05

of homogeneity of variance) was computed. Results indicated that significant differences did exist between classification groups (F =9.98; p<.00). In light of this, Games-Howell post-hoc statistics were explored to better assess these differences and develop an understanding of where they existed (Table 5.4). These revealed that rural departments averaged significantly fewer posts per day than those in large towns and cities, whereas those in cities posted significantly more than their rural and small-town counterparts.

Results for page followers and likes revealed that classification size may work differently than post frequency (Table 5.5). Recall that in order to standardize this comparison, each of these measures was divided by the total population of each respective municipality. Results indicated that across the entire sample, approximately 83% of the population followed their department's page, whereas 82% had "liked" it. Differences were observed when comparing departments by size classification, however, as rural departments featured counts for both followers and likes far exceeding their respective populations. This suggests that those outside the town's physical boundaries are also apt to interact with the department via the Facebook platform. On the other end of the spectrum, city departments featured follower and like counts of less than 25% on average, indicating that the public may be less likely to view receiving news from these departments as important.

One-way ANOVAs revealed that differences were statistically significant for both followers (F=18.35; p<.00) and likes (F=18.38; p<.00). Results of the Games-Howell post-hoc tests (Tables 5.6 and 5.7) indicated that these differences existed across all possible comparisons, providing support for the notion that population size serves to influence the level of community interest in connecting with departments via the Facebook platform.

The final department-level research question was targeted at developing a better understanding of community responsiveness, as gauged by the frequency of comments, shares, and

74 Edwards, Osborne, Moses, Ledford, and Smith

Table 5.5 Page Followers and Likes by Department Classification

Department Classification	Percentage Following Page	Percentage Liking Page
Rural	152.10%	148.70%
Small Town	78.49%	76.98%
Large Town	52.48%	51.02%
City	24.99%	24.11%

Table 5.6 Games-Howell Results for Followers

(I) Classification	(J) Classification	Mean Difference (I-J)	S.E.	Sig.
Rural	Small Town	73.61*	26.07	.040
	Large Town	99.62**	25.88	.003
	City	127.11*	26.07	.000
Small Town	Rural	−73.61*	26.07	.040
	Large Town	26.01*	7.70	.006
	City	53.50**	8.31	.000
Large Town	Rural	−99.62*	25.89	.003
	Small Town	−26.01*	7.70	.006
	City	27.49*	7.72	.008
City	Rural	−127.11**	26.07	.000
	Small Town	−53.50**	8.31	.000
	Large Town	−27.49*	7.72	.008

Note: *p<.05; **p<.000

Table 5.7 Games-Howell Results for Likes

(I) Classification	(J) Classification	Mean Difference (I-J)	S.E.	Sig.
Rural	Small Town	71.72*	25.29	.038
	Large Town	97.68*	25.09	.003
	City	124.59**	25.30	.000
Small Town	Rural	−71.72*	25.29	.038
	Large Town	25.96*	7.54	.005
	City	52.87**	8.23	.000
Large Town	Rural	−97.68*	25.09	.003
	Small Town	−25.96*	7.54	.005
	City	26.91*	7.60	.009
City	Rural	−124.59**	25.30	.000
	Small Town	−52.87**	8.23	.000
	Large Town	−26.91*	7.60	.009

Note: *p<.05; **p<.000

reactions. Across all posts, and without disaggregating differences by department size, it was revealed that the level of responsiveness was low for each of the three measures. Approximately 1% of followers noted any type of reaction for a typical post, while less than 1% posted a comment (.002%) or chose to share the information (.01%).

A series of one-way ANOVAs (again utilizing the Welch Test) indicated that significant differences did exist for comments (F=12.23; p<.000), shares (F=14.50; p<.000), and reactions

(F=18.97; p<.000) across classification groups. Results for the Games-Howell post-hoc tests (not displayed in the interest of page space) revealed that city departments were much less likely to receive comments, shares, or reactions for their posts than those in the other classifications, whereas rural departments and those located in small towns were much more likely to receive the same. Table 5.8 contains a full summary of the breakdown for responsiveness by classification type, with each value representing the mean proportion of followers who responded in each way.

Post Analysis

The initial research question related to individual posts sought to understand whether classification influenced the motivation for posting content to Facebook pages. Three categories were established in line with the previous literature: 1) push, 2) pull, and 3) interaction. Across all departments, the push motivation (disseminating information to the public) was most prevalent and accounted for approximately 81% of all posts. This was followed by posts falling within the pull category (13.9%) and those promoting interaction between the department and the public (5.3%).

Slight differences were observed when comparing motivations by classification size (Figure 5.1). For example, posts by rural departments were somewhat more likely to feature a push motivation (88.9% of all posts) than those made by departments located in small towns (84.2%), large towns (76.9%), and cities (72.4%). City departments were more apt to seek information and help (a pull motivation) from their communities (22.3% of all posts) than those located in other classifications, with rural departments (9% of posts) being least likely

Table 5.8 Post Responsiveness by Department Classification

Responsiveness	Rural	Small Town	Large Town	City
Comments	.003	.003	.001	.000
Shares	.015	.012	.006	.002
Reactions	.022	.016	.007	.003

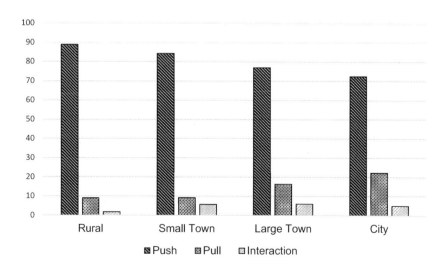

Figure 5.1 Motivations by Size Classification

to request help. Concerning the final motivation category—interaction—similarities existed between departments in small towns, large towns, and cities (ranging between 5% and 6.1% of all posts), though rural departments were less likely to seek these opportunities via Facebook (1.8% of all posts).

A chi-square test was utilized to determine whether these seemingly apparent differences were statistically significant due to the nominal nature of both measures. Results (χ^2=230.27; p<.00) indicated that significance was present. Assessment of the adjusted standardized residuals using the Bonferroni method (to reduce the likelihood of Type 1 errors) provided support for the assessment that posts by rural and small-town departments were more likely to feature a push motivation than those by their large-town and city counterparts. Conversely, they indicated that both were significantly less likely to create posts with a pull motivation than city departments. Finally, results showed that rural departments were indeed significantly less likely to create posts with an interaction motivation.

The second research question related to post characteristics sought to explore whether the forms of content (content category) shared by departments differed along the size classification continuum. Across the entire sample, notifications regarding traffic issues (8%), case updates (7.4%), publicizing community interactions (7.1%), "other" (7.1%), and recognizing community partners (6%) were the most frequently observed categories. At the other end of the spectrum, those related to missing adults (0.5%), missing children (0.6%), officer remembrance (0.7%), lost pets (0.8%), and those using humor (0.9%) all constituted less than 1% of all posts.

Exploring content categories by classification revealed some unique differences worthy of discussion. (See Table 5.9 for the five most and least common categories within each classification.) For example, departments located in cities were predominantly occupied with providing case updates (17.3% of all posts), requesting help identifying suspects (14%), publicizing community interactions (7.9%), and posting information about crimes in progress or that had recently occurred (6.8%). Their rural counterparts tended to focus on warning residents about severe weather (8.6% of posts), notifying them regarding other city services (8.6%), providing traffic safety information (6.6%), and relaying information regarding crime trends (6.6%).

In addition, rural departments were more likely to post content falling outside the established categories (16.4% of posts). This frequency was more than double that seen for small towns (6.1%) and large towns (7.4%) and far eclipsed the rate for city departments (4.1%). The topics of these posts varied but commonly included welcoming new residents, posting advertisements for community businesses, and recognizing the achievements of local sports teams. As a result, it appears that these departments were more diverse in terms of their communications with the public.

Small towns and large towns featured many similarities across both common and less common content categories. Traffic issues, publicizing community interaction, and recognizing community partners were the topic of more than 6% of posts for both groups, whereas those focused on missing children and missing adults constituted less than 1% of posts for both. Having detailed the findings of the analysis, attention is now turned to discussing their importance and what can be learned regarding social media presence among departments serving populations of various sizes.

Discussion

This chapter found that while police departments across the population continuum were active on Facebook, those serving larger populations posted content to their pages more actively than their lower-population counterparts. Perhaps ironically, there seemed to be an

Table 5.9 Content Categories by Department Classification

Rural

Most Common	% of Posts	Least Common	% of Posts
Other	16.4%	Missing Adults	0.2%
Severe Weather	8.6%	Animal Officers	0.2%
Other Services	8.6%	Missing Children	0.4%
Traffic Safety	8.1%	Remembrance	0.5%
Crime Warnings	6.6%	Crime Blotter	1.0%

Small Towns

Most Common	% of Posts	Least Common	% of Posts
Traffic Issues	8.9%	Missing Adults	0.4%
Community Interactions	6.6%	Missing Children	0.4%
Recognizing Partners	6.6%	Animal Officers	0.8%
Other	6.1%	Suspect Location	0.9%
Other Services	5.9%	DUI Information	1.2%

Large Towns

Most Common	% of Posts	Least Common	% of Posts
Traffic Issues	11.0%	Lost Pets	0.1%
Community Interactions	8.3%	Humor	0.3%
Suspect Identification	7.8%	Remembrance	0.4%
Other	7.4%	Missing Children	0.6%
Recognizing Partners	7.0%	Missing Adults	0.7%

Cities

Most Common	% of Posts	Least Common	% of Posts
Case Updates	17.3%	Humor	0.1%
Suspect Identification	14.0%	Lost Pets	0.1%
Community Interactions	7.9%	Remembrance	0.4%
Crime Blotter	6.8%	Other Services	0.7%
Officer News	5.1%	Holiday Messages	0.8%

inverse relationship between post frequency and community interaction. Rural and small-town departments saw a higher percentage of their population following or liking their Facebook page than larger departments. Further, followers of these rural and small-town departments were more responsive to the content posted (as gauged by likes, shares, and reactions) than those following larger departments. This suggests that police departments might unintentionally dilute the effect of their social media usage if they overuse the platform. Thus, it might be prudent for departments to find a way to strike a balance between being active on social media and avoiding posting excessive amounts of content.

It is important to point out that while we found that community responsiveness to Facebook posts was affected by population size, the overall level of community response was low across all size classifications. This finding is consistent with prior research (e.g., Williams et al., 2018) and not altogether surprising in light of recent developments on the platform. Facebook's algorithm does not allow every post made by a police agency to be displayed on each of its followers' news feeds but rather ranks the content based on what is most likely to be meaningful content to the user in question. The algorithm has (within the last few years) changed to prioritize posts made by friends and family over the content shared by organizations such as police departments (Nimishakavi, 2018).

Despite the overall low levels of interaction between agency posts and followers, it is clear—based on the observed data—that many residents consider their police department's social media page to be an important source of information. This appears to be particularly true in rural communities, as the analysis revealed that the typical rural agency featured a follower count well exceeding their municipality's population, even though rural residents are least likely to use any social media (Perrin, 2015). Consequently, it is apparent that many people are using the platform to like or follow rural police departments in surrounding communities. There are several reasons that this could occur. For example, it is likely that those living in remote areas (outside a defined municipality) will regularly visit nearby towns for work, shopping, and/or entertainment. As a result, they may choose to be regularly updated by the police departments serving these towns. It is also possible that traditional news sources do not adequately cover stories in their area, making it important to follow a variety of public agency Facebook pages to gather timely information about activities and crimes occurring in their community. Finally, it could be that individuals who move away from these communities continue to follow their "home town" department despite their relocation.

Police departments included in this analysis were most likely to use Facebook to disseminate information to the public. In fact, this "push" strategy accounted for approximately 81% of all posts, which is similar to the results of past studies on Facebook use among large departments. (See Hu et al., 2018, for an example.) The current chapter adds to this previous literature, however, in that it found that population size served to influence post motivation. Specifically, rural and small-town departments were most likely to use a push strategy, whereas city departments (while still mainly relying on a push strategy) also used a pull strategy more often than those in the other classifications. Across the size continuum, it appears that the push motivation increases as the population served size decreases, and vice versa for the pull motivation. Community size impacted the interaction motivation less often, though rural departments were less likely than all other classifications to utilize this strategy.

Finally, one of the current chapter's most important contributions involved examining whether the types of content posted to Facebook varied by size classification. City departments posted content (e.g., case updates, asking for suspect identification) similar in nature to that found in prior research (Hu et al., 2018; Kim et al., 2017; Lieberman et al., 2013). However, rural departments posted content that frequently fell out of established categories (with 16.4% of rural posts being classified as "other"). The topics of these posts varied greatly but included welcoming new residents, congratulating local sports teams, sharing news from local businesses, and calling attention to the natural environment (e.g., posts about recreational activities). This finding might partially reflect a lower level of serious crime in these areas and, thus, a lower need to post crime-related content on Facebook. Alternatively, it may indicate that rural departments are keener on bridging the divide between the police and the community by posting generic content of high interest to residents. Regardless, this finding reinforces the image of a rural police department as a distinct policing model (Falcone et al., 2002) and highlights the importance of including these types of departments in future examinations of law enforcement social media activity.

Limitations

Though this chapter does much to advance our understanding of Facebook use among police departments of various classifications, it is not without its limitations. First, data for page followers and likes were collected at the end of the timeframe under analysis, which rules out an accurate picture of the totals for each at the time that each post was made. Second, the counts of weather-related content might be inflated by an abnormally high amount of rainfall during the data collection timeframe, resulting in flooding for many parts of Tennessee. Next, the analysis of agency-level data relied on the assumption that all individuals residing within a community were a part of each respective agency's target population. It should be noted that not all individuals are active on the Facebook platform. Though this merits some caution when interpreting the results, they still provide a general understanding of levels of community engagement and allow for an assessment of differences across classifications (since the same reality will influence those of all sizes).

Fourth, the secondary nature of the data prevented insight into the individual(s) responsible for maintaining the Facebook page for each department. Motivations and types of content will likely differ depending upon the role of these managers. For example, pages actively managed by police chiefs (more probable in rural communities) are likely to feature a different overall tone than those managed by interns or public relations staff. Fifth, it is possible that the timeframe under analysis influenced results. As crime-related issues tend to heighten during warm weather, the lack of data for summer months may have impacted the various findings related to post content and motivation.

Finally, classifying municipalities based upon population size was an inexact science due to the lack of established methods. Most classification schemes are designed to group counties and other large geographical areas, with little attention devoted to identifying methods to situate municipalities on a rural-urban continuum. However, the reliance upon definitions provided by both the OMB and United States Census Bureau and the various ways in which they define urbanized areas within counties should allow for an exploratory understanding of how population size influences police social media strategies.

Directions for Future Research

Future researchers may seek to explore whether these findings can be replicated using a sample of municipalities from other states, as the culture of law enforcement in Tennessee (a largely rural and conservative state) may differ from that seen elsewhere. In addition, they may wish to extend the framework of this work to other social media platforms, such as Instagram or Twitter. Since each of these platforms specializes in distinct types of communication, it is unlikely that police departments would simply post identical content to each platform. Indeed, Williams et al. (2018) found some differences between the types of Facebook and Twitter posts made by five similarly sized police departments in Massachusetts. O'Conner (2017) also found that approximately 40% of tweets sent out by large police departments in Canada were designed to elicit interaction with the community. This far exceeds the percentage of interaction-motivated posts from Facebook in this chapter as well as in the prior research. It would be important to determine whether content, motivation, and community engagement varied between different-sized departments using one of these alternate social media platforms.

It may also be useful to explore potential differences in post content and motivation among municipal departments and county-level sheriff's departments, as each may be influenced by the political realities associated with each type of organization. Research has shown that residents living in rural areas have more trust in a town police department than a sheriff's office (Holmes, Painter, & Smith, 2017). As sheriff is an elected position, county-level sheriff's departments might be more motivated to connect with their communities through social media and might be more inclined to post public relations related content to improve citizens' perceptions of their departments.

Conclusion

The current chapter makes several contributions to the literature. As most prior studies of law enforcement social media usage were restricted to large departments, it was important to expand this line of research by examining every municipal police department in Tennessee that had an active presence on Facebook. This strategy allowed for the inclusion of a broad range of agency sizes within a particular geographical location. Results appeared to justify this approach, as the size was found to influence the motivation and content of Facebook posts, along with the public's level of engagement with them.

As more departments move toward using social media in their communications strategy, it is increasingly important to understand the nature and societal impact of this strategy. Police departments will likely be forced to adapt to ever-changing algorithms, which will substantially impact how and to what extent they can depend on social media to reach their intended audiences. In the future, it may become more important to target specific groups of people with sponsored content from the department's Facebook page. Police departments might also use social media in conjunction with subscription services (e.g., NIXLE), which allow residents to receive alerts from local departments directly to their mobile devices. Regardless of the specific technological advances that occur in the future, it has become clear that police departments of all sizes use social media to achieve their goals. Continued research regarding these trends will allow police departments to maximize their impact and better understand how these tactics impact the public's perception of police.

Discussion Questions

1. Why do many police departments prefer to communicate with the public using social media as opposed to traditional media?
2. What goals do police departments seek to accomplish by actively posting to Facebook and other social media platforms?
3. In what ways do the police department's motivation to use social media seem to be influenced by the community's population size?
4. In what ways does the community population size seem to influence the frequency of Facebook posts by the police departments?
5. How do rural communities differ from their city counterparts when it comes to the level of engagement with the police department on Facebook?

References

Barthel, M. (2019, July 23). *5 key takeaways about the state of the news media in 2018.* Pew Research Center. Retrieved from www.pewresearch.org/fact-tank/2019/07/23/key-takeaways-state-of-the-news-media-2018/

Benedict, W. R., Brown, B., & Bower, D. J. (2000). Perceptions of the police and fear of crime in a rural setting: Utility of a geographically focused survey for police services, planning, and assessment. *Criminal Justice Policy Review, 11*(4), 275–298. doi:10.1177/0887403400011004001

Brainard, L., & Edlins, M. (2015). Top 10 U.S. municipal police departments and their social media usage. *American Review of Public Administration, 45*(6), 728–745. doi:10.1177/0275074014524478

Budak, C., Agrawal, D., & Abbadi, A. E. (2011). Limiting the spread of misinformation in social networks. *Proceedings of the 20th International Conference on World Wide Web*, 665–674.

Chermak, S., & Weiss, A. (2005). Maintaining legitimacy using external communication strategies: An analysis of police-media relations. *Journal of Criminal Justice, 33*, 501–512. doi:10.1108/pijpsm.2006.18129 aaf.002

Clement, J. (2020). Most popular social networks worldwide as of October 20, ranked by number of active users. *Statista.* Retrieved from www.statista.com/statistics/272014/global-social-networks-ranked-by-number-of-users/

Dai, M., He, W., Tian, X., Giraldi, A., & Gu, F. (2017). Working with communities on social media: Varieties in the use of Facebook and Twitter by local police. *Online Information Review*, *41*(6), 782–796. doi:10.1108/oir-01-2016-0002

DeKeseredy, W. S. (2015). New directions in feminist understandings of rural crime. *Journal of Rural Studies*, *39*, 180–187. doi:10.1016/j.jrurstud.2014.11.002

Falcone, D. N., Wells, E., &. Weisheit, R. A. (2002). The small-town police department. *Policing: An International Journal of Police Strategies & Management*, *25*(2), 371–384. doi:10.1108/13639510210429419

Fowler, B. M. (2017). Stealing thunder and filling the silence: Twitter as a primary channel of police crisis communication. *Public Relations Review*, *43*, 718–728. doi:10.1016/j.pubrev.2017.04.007

Holmes, M. D., Painter, M. A., & Smith, B. W. (2017). Citizens' perceptions of police in rural U.S. communities: A multilevel analysis of contextual, organisational, and individual predictors. *Policing and Society*, *27*(2), 136–156. doi:10.1080/10439463.2015.1031227

Hu, X., Rodgers, K., & Lovrich, N. P. (2018). We are more than crime fighters: Social media images of police departments. *Police Quarterly*, *21*(4), 544–572. doi:10.1177/1098611118783991

International Association of Chiefs of Police. (2016). *2015 social media survey results*. Retrieved from www.iacpsocialmedia.org/wp-content/uploads/2017/01/FULL-2015-Social-Media-Survey-Results.compressed.pdf

Kilburn, M., & Krieger, L. (2014). Policing in an information age: The prevalence of state and local law enforcement agencies utilising the World Wide Web to connect with the community. *International Journal of Police Science & Management*, *16*(3), 221–227. doi:10.1350/ijps.2014.16.3.341

Kim, K., Oglesby-Neal, A., & Mohr, E. (2017). *2016 law enforcement use of social media survey*. Urban Institute. Retrieved from www.urban.org/sites/default/files/publication/88661/2016-law-enforcement-use-of-social-media-survey.pdf

Lieberman, J. D., Koetzle, D., & Sakiyama, M. (2013). Police departments' use of Facebook: Patterns and policy issues. *Police Quarterly*, *16*(4), 438–462. doi:10.1177/1098611113495049

Meijer, A., & Thaens, M. (2013). Social media strategies: Understanding the differences between North American police departments. *Government Information Quarterly*, *30*, 343–350. doi:10.1016/j.giq.2013.05.023

Mergel, I. (2012). The social media innovation challenge in the public sector. *Information Policy*, *17*, 281–292. doi:10.3233/ip-2012-000281

Nimishakavi, S. (2018, January 23). Will Facebook's latest algorithm change help or hurt nonprofits? *Nonprofit Quarterly*. Retrieved from https://nonprofitquarterly.org/will-facebooks-latest-algorithm-change-help-hurt-nonprofits/

Nofziger, S., & Williams, L. S. (2005). Perceptions of police and safety in a small town. *Police Quarterly*, *8*(2), 248–270. doi:10.1177/1098611103258959

O'Connor, C. D. (2017). The police on Twitter: Image management, community building, and implications for policing in Canada. *Policing and Society*, *27*(8), 899–912. doi:10.1080/10439463.2015.1120731

Perrin, A. (2015). *Social media usage: 2005–2015*. Pew Research Center. Retrieved from www.pewinternet.org/2015/10/08/social-networking-usage-2005-2015/

Perrin, A., & Anderson, M. (2019). *Share of U.S. adults using social media, including Facebook, is mostly unchanged since 2018*. Pew Research Center. Retrieved from www.pewresearch.org/fact-tank/2019/04/10/share-of-u-s-adults-using-social-media-including-facebook-is-mostly-unchanged-since-2018/

President's Task Force on 21st Century Policing. (2015). *Final report of the president's task force on 21st century policing*. Washington, DC: Office of Community Oriented Policing Services.

Reaves, B. (2015). *Local police departments, 2013: Personnel, policies, and practices*. Washington, DC: Department of Justice, Bureau of Justice Statistics.

Smith, A., & Anderson, M. (2018). *Social media use in 2018*. Pew Research Center. Retrieved from www.pewinternet.org/2018/03/01/social-media-use-in-2018/

Surette, R. (2015). *Media, crime, and criminal justice: Images, realities, and policies* (5th ed.). Stamford, CT: Cengage.

US Office of Management and Budget. (2010). 2010 standards for delineating metropolitan and micropolitan statistical areas; notice. *Federal Register*, *75*(123), 37246–37252.

Walsh, J. P., & O'Connor, C. (2019). Social media and policing: A review of recent research. *Sociology Compass*, *13*(1), e12648. doi:10.1111/soc4.12648

Wells, L. E., & Weisheit, R. A. (2004). Patterns of rural and urban crime: A county-level comparison. *Criminal Justice Review*, *29*(1), 1–22. doi:10.1177/073401680402900103

Williams, C. B., Fedorowicz, J., Kavanaugh, A., Mentzer, K., Thatcher, J. B., & Xu, J. (2018). Leveraging social media to achieve a community policing agenda. *Government Information Quarterly*, *35*, 210–222. doi:10.1016/j.giq.2018.03.001

Wilson, S. G. (2012). *Patterns of metropolitan and micropolitan population change: 2000 to 2010*. Washington, DC: US Department of Commerce, Economics and Statistics Administration, US Census Bureau.

Chapter 6

Consent Decrees on Police Organizations
Policies and Practices

Allan Y. Jiao

> **Acknowledgment:** This chapter is briefly updated and reprinted, with permission from Taylor and Francis, from Allan Y. Jiao, 2020, "Federal consent decrees: a review of policies, processes, and outcomes," *Police Practice and Research: An International Journal,* doi:10.1080/15614263.2020.1722664, www.tandfonline.com/

Introduction

Consent decrees, imposed by both federal and state governments (Smith, 2017), are widely viewed as a promising approach to bringing about institutional changes in police organizations in the United States, particularly in the area of police accountability. Unfortunately, agencies that have gone through consent decrees and the data accumulated in the process have rarely been carefully examined. Meanwhile, the Trump administration and attorney general's office did not initiate new consent decrees, put existing ones under review, and reduced resources for the program (Alpert, McLean, & Wolfe, 2017). The lack of support is consistent with the view that previous administrations had put too many police agencies under consent decrees and subjected them to years of costly federal oversight (MacDonald, 2016). In the absence of extensive systematic evaluations, however, no one knows for sure what impact consent decrees have on policing. The few completed studies thus far provide some preliminary evidence that reforms under the decrees may have made police agencies more accountable and effective (Alpert et al., 2017; Phillips & Jiao, 2017; Rushin, 2017). Considering the confusion and controversies surrounding consent decrees, it is important to have a review of related policies and practices to develop a better understanding of consent decrees in general and the specific areas that need to be addressed in order for them to have a positive impact on policing.

Federal consent decrees were used originally to address police use of excessive force as many unarmed civilians were shot dead or died due to police actions. Such incidents often happen to African Americans such as Michael Brown, Tamir Rice, Eric Garner, Freddie Gray, Timothy Russell, Malissa Williams, and Tanisha Anderson (Eversley, 2016; Puente, Serrano, & Pearce, 2015) and, more recently, George Floyd. After they occur, grand juries often refuse to indict the officers involved, and when officers are indicted, they are rarely convicted. In Cleveland, for example, a 2012 police chase ended with fatal shootings of Timothy Russell and Malissa Williams, and the only officer to stand trial on criminal charges related to the shootings was acquitted on two counts of voluntary manslaughter. The city also experienced the fatal shooting of Tamir Rice, a 12-year-old playing with a toy gun outside a West Side recreation center. Even with video evidence for such cases as that of Eric Garner, there was still no indictment from the grand jury. Such incidents often sparked local and national protests and led to the Black Lives Matter movement (Hustle, 2014). A core issue behind these protests

DOI: 10.4324/9781003047117-7

was the belief that local governments were unable to hold their police accountable and address unconstitutional police practices, and many citizens lost faith in their local governments and demanded federal intervention for justice (Hustle, 2014). It was in this context that police departments of cities large and small such as Cleveland; New York; and Ferguson, Missouri, became targets of US Department of Justice investigations (Hustle, 2014).

The 1994 Violent Crime Control and Law Enforcement Act gave the Civil Rights Division of the US Department of Justice (DOJ) the authority to file civil lawsuits against police agencies if they displayed a "pattern and practice" of civil rights violations and force them to adopt reforms by implementing what is known as a "consent decree" (Police Executive Research Forum, 2013). The Civil Rights Division carries out investigations of police organizations that it believes have unconstitutional policies or engage in unconstitutional practices. These investigations as well as the law are designed to address systemic issues rather than individual crimes. The alleged misconduct cannot be an isolated incident. And there is no private right of action under the statute; only the Justice Department is given authority to launch investigations and litigation (Hustle, 2014).

If the Department of Justice (DOJ) finds systemic unconstitutional practices, it usually starts negotiations with the local jurisdiction to develop strategies for implementing reforms (Police Executive Research Forum, 2013). Cities typically settle these cases before they go to trial or before a lawsuit is filed by entering into a consent decree or "memo of understanding" with the DOJ (Domanick, 2014; Police Executive Research Forum, 2013). The Justice Department has entered into consent decrees with various local police departments and agreements with many others. Police departments that agree to a consent decree can avoid serious controversies and costly litigation and maintain a positive public image. Even though the cost of complying with a consent decree can be high, it is often cheaper and easier than going to court. Most importantly, perhaps, a consent decree allows the police to move forward without admitting guilt.

While consent decrees and federal monitors have been used for correcting civil rights violations by police, some cities were put under the oversight of federal monitoring without a consent decree. The New York City Police Department (NYPD) was such a case after US District Court Judge Shira Scheindlin ruled in August 2013 that its long-standing stop-and-frisk policy amounted to racial profiling and imposed federal monitoring without a consent decree on the department (Winston, 2013). The NYPD also prevented a consent decree in 2014 by adopting police reforms preemptively when New York City saw widespread protests in response to a grand jury's decision not to indict the officer involved in the death of Eric Garner, an unarmed black man (Hustle, 2014).

Due to recent curtailing of the use of consent decrees at the federal level to push for police reform, the state of Illinois and Chicago have sought a court-enforced consent decree to implement constitutional police practices (Smith, 2017). The Chicago consent decree is a state consent decree, recommended initially by the US DOJ but pursued by the state attorney general's office. It shares the mechanism of a federal consent decree in that it is approved and enforced by a federal judge, evaluated by an independent monitor, and ends only upon compliance with the terms of the decree. The difference lies more in form than substance. Unlike in the case of a federal decree, the state is the plaintiff, and the city is the defendant. Instead of a federal lawsuit and subsequent negotiations, the state attorney general's office filed a lawsuit, and the state and the city agreed to stay the lawsuit and negotiated the decree with extensive public hearings and comments on the process (*State of Illinois v. City of Chicago*, 2019).

The requirements of a consent decree are generally based on the findings of a DOJ investigation, which are submitted in writing to the court and, once approved by a judge, become legally binding and have the power to affect police policy across the board. The exact terms and conditions of consent decrees vary in each case, but they are all lifted with the approval of a federal judge upon determination of police compliance with the terms of the agreement. Compliance is measured through auditing, which is overseen by an independent federal monitor (Hustle, 2014; Phillips & Jiao, 2017).

Consent decrees are aimed at making substantive and institutional police reforms sustainable over time. They include plans for implementing best practices and provide goals and objectives with related measurement criteria. A federal judge is given the power to ensure police compliance, and an outside monitor is appointed to watch the day-to-day progress of the reform. Since the first consent decree was issued to Pittsburgh in 1997, about 40 police departments have been issued consent decrees, including Cincinnati; Los Angeles; Washington, DC; Detroit; New Orleans; Oakland; Seattle; Portland (OR); Cleveland; New York City; Detroit; the New Jersey State Police; the Virgin Islands PD; Albuquerque (NM); and Newark (NJ) (Domanick, 2014; Police Executive Research Forum, 2013). Over the years, consent decree provisions have led to a set of best practices and well-known conditions for effective and constitutional policing, which have played a significant role in transforming police departments into more constitutionally legitimate organizations (Domanick, 2014; Walker, 2005).

Issues Addressed in Consent Decrees

The consent decrees vary in scope and substance, but they all involve unconstitutional and discriminatory policies or patterns and practices of misconduct. The types of misconduct usually include use of force, search and seizure, arrest, interrogation, management and supervision, and racial or ethnic bias. In recent years, the areas of biased policing governed by consent decrees also include gender bias in the investigation of sexual assaults; police interactions with gay, lesbian, bisexual, and transgender citizens; persons with mental illness; and bystanders' rights to observe and record officer conduct (Gomez, 2015; Police Executive Research Forum, 2013). A few police departments' consent decrees are briefly described here to provide a glimpse of the issues addressed over the years.

In Pittsburgh, where the first consent decree was signed in 1997, the Justice Department investigation uncovered a pattern and practice of police misconduct including brutality, unwarranted stops, and disrespect of citizens. The department was also criticized for its treatment of minority employees and the low number of minorities working in the department. The consent decree, which was lifted in 2002, was designed to fix a pattern of cronyism, questionable force, and strained relations between the police and minorities. The decree mandated that the department make reforms, including the establishment of an early warning system to keep track of problem officers (Benzing, 2014; Walker, 2005).

The consent decree with New Orleans was entered in 2012 and contained provisions governing use of force, use of force reporting, use of force review board, authorized firearms, conducted electrical weapons, control devices and techniques, forced interrogation, disciplinary matrix/penalty schedules, crisis intervention, sexual assault, and domestic violence. In a 110-page document, the decree encompassed a broad reform plan for constitutional and professional policing. It required appointment of a consent decree monitor by order of the United States District Court for the Eastern District of Louisiana. The role of the monitor was to evaluate and report the implementation of the decree's requirements and the results of the implementation. Within the NOPD, the Compliance Bureau was tasked with facilitating the implementation (City of New Orleans, 2017).

The DOJ and City of Cleveland reached a consent decree in 2015 to curb excessive use of force by police. The decree mandated that the police amend their use-of-force policy, establish a stronger civilian advisory committee, and guarantee full and fair investigation of misconduct (Puente et al., 2015). The decree also demanded more accountability and transparency from officers and their supervisors when justifying the use of force (Gomez, 2015), including enhanced use-of-force training; crisis-intervention training on encounters with the mentally ill; and data collection on stops, searches, and seizures and their analysis for bias. Standards were set for when an officer could use force, and each incident involving use of a weapon had to be documented. Arrests could no longer be made for simply talking back to or running away from an officer. Warnings shots and pistol whipping were specifically banned. Police were required to gather and publish data on race and gender for their encounters with the public (Gomez, 2015; Puente et al., 2015).

The city council of Ferguson, Missouri, agreed to a consent decree ordered by the Department of Justice (DOJ) in 2016 to reform the city's police department after receiving government assurances that the plan would not be financially crippling. The federal scrutiny followed a police encounter in Ferguson in which an unarmed black teenager, Michael Brown, died and found a pattern and practice of unlawful police conduct in the city. The provisions of the agreement were designed to ensure protection of the constitutional and other legal rights of the citizens, improve the city's ability to effectively prevent crime, enhance both officer and public safety, and increase public confidence in the Ferguson Police Department. The ultimate goal was to provide the framework needed to institute constitutional policing in the city (Eversley, 2016).

Baltimore's consent decree was reached in 2017 in the aftermath of Freddie Gray's death in police custody (Baltimore Police Department, 2017). The decree was based on the DOJ's findings that the Baltimore police had engaged in a pattern and practice of misconduct that violated the Constitution's First, Fourth, and Fourteenth Amendments and certain other provisions of federal statutory law. Its goal was to develop a stronger police department that fights crime while serving and protecting the civil and constitutional rights of Baltimore residents. The decree's requirements include establishing a community oversight task force to recommend reforms to the current system of civilian oversight; adopting community-oriented and problem-oriented policing principles; prohibiting unlawful stops and arrests; preventing discriminatory policing and excessive use of force; ensuring public and officer safety; enhancing officer accountability; and improving training and supervision in detainee transport, gender bias, youth involvement, and mental health issues. Under the agreement, an independent monitor would be appointed to assess whether the requirements of the agreement had been implemented and report publicly on progress of the implementation (Baltimore Police Department, 2017).

Overall, federal consent decrees cover a wide range of issues from use of force to stops and detentions, supervision of officers, and bias-free policing. Since the first decree was issued in Pittsburgh in 1997, they have grown more complex and demanding over time. The publication of the PERF report (Police Executive Research Forum, 2013) and the Michael Brown tragedy in August 2014 marked the beginning of the second generation of consent decrees. While excessive force remains front and center, community-oriented or problem-oriented policing and involvement of rank-and-file officers and their union representatives have been added to the decrees, with detailed requirements in the form of outcome measures and compliance conditions for the police to meet (Walker, 2018).

Regardless of the issues focused on or the complexity of the conditions required in different decrees over time, the goals and objectives remain the same: to reform the old policies and practices and develop a new system of constitutional and accountable policing. The process of achieving the goals usually involves identifying officers with problematic behaviors, enforcing a set of commonly recognized best practices, and instituting a new culture of accountability in policing.

Implementation and Related Challenges

A federal judge must approve a consent decree on a local government before it can be implemented (Gomez, 2015). Once the consent decree is approved, the city is legally bound to enact reform. The city begins by conducting a review of the decree and works with the DOJ in creating a plan for change (Puente et al., 2015). The process involves establishing a mandated structure for reform and addressing specific content areas that have been found deficient.

The structure of decree-driven reform requires the appointment by the court of an independent federal monitor who tracks police compliance with the consent decree. The city is responsible for paying the monitor's salary and other costs related to instituting the reform (Gomez, 2015). The specific role of the federal monitor involves assessing and reporting progress in implementing the consent decree and results and outcomes of the implementation in terms of constitutional and professional policing (Police Executive Research Forum, 2013). In New Orleans, for example, a law firm was appointed by order of the US District Court to establish the Office of the Consent Decree Monitor. The consent decree monitor conducted audits and published quarterly and/or special reports. The police department produced quarterly, biannual, and annual reports, which delineated the steps taken and progress made and plans to address any issue or concerns raised by the monitor (City of New Orleans, 2017). In Baltimore, a civilian director was hired to oversee the police department's internal affairs division, which investigates officer misconduct (Puente et al., 2015).

The content areas of the reform usually involve developing and changing the police organization through policies, procedures, and training. In Pittsburgh, for example, an early warning system was established to keep track of problem officers. The Cleveland Police Department required a new way of report writing. In the past, in writing incident reports, Cleveland officers often used boilerplate language, stating that a suspect became aggressive, for instance. Such language was no longer allowed, and details must be provided when describing incidents. Baltimore officers were required to participate in reality-based training, in which role playing was used to practice arrests and other potentially volatile actions. The goal of the training was to achieve fair and impartial policing and improve community relations (Puente et al., 2015).

Various challenges have emerged in the implementation process including costs, lack of cooperation, police subculture, and inadequate measurement criteria for evaluating compliance. Costs of implementing a consent decree are often high. Achieving compliance and paying legal fees to monitors are not only expensive but oftentimes contentious. Some police chiefs and city officials believe that it is beyond their means to implement consent decrees (Police Executive Research Forum, 2013; Salter, 2017). In New Orleans, Mayor Mitch Landrieu's administration appealed the consent decree, arguing it could not afford to pay for it as it could cost millions per year (Winston, 2013). In Seattle, Mayor Mike Bobb clashed publicly with a Los Angeles attorney and his monitoring team over expenses for which the monitoring team billed the city (Winston, 2013). Ferguson, Missouri, paid about a half-million dollars to the monitoring team in a little over a year, and city leaders questioned the value of this expense, covered entirely by city funds from a small community of 20,000 (Salter, 2017). To help offset the high cost of police reforms, some cities such as Cleveland reached out to external partners and the private sector (Gomez, 2015). While the cost of consent decrees seems exorbitant, many police and city leaders also see their benefits outweighing the costs because failing to implement reforms can be just as expensive, if not more so, and a consent decree can potentially reduce civil lawsuits and increase police effectiveness (Police Executive Research Forum, 2013).

Lack of cooperation is another challenge often manifested in resistance or opposition to the consent decree and the DOJ by local jurisdictions. The city leadership of New Orleans, for example, initially opposed the consent decree and related police reforms with a negative attitude (Winston, 2013). It was only after the superintendent was replaced that the new leadership worked closely with the monitors and the DOJ. Oakland had a decade-long struggle with the consent decree as the police and city administration resisted its implementation. The court had to appoint a compliance director, who took partial control of the police department. Meanwhile, the violent crime rate in the city was out of control, and police clearance rate dropped dramatically as more than two-thirds of the city's murders were unsolved (Winston, 2013). In Cincinnati, the monitor and the police department had a rocky relationship in the early phase of the reform, when the monitor viewed the police as uncooperative, and the police regarded the monitor as unrealistic and intrusive, causing serious delays in reforming the department (Police Executive Research Forum, 2013; Winston, 2013). In Seattle, some officers were opposed to the mandated use-of-force policies in the consent decree and took the DOJ to court. They charged that the new regulations severely limited their ability to protect themselves (Hustle, 2014), and some Seattle council members partially blamed the consent decree for a rising violent crime rate in some parts of the city (Winston, 2013).

What has really fueled the resistance to consent decrees goes far beyond negative attitudes and uncooperative behaviors and can be traced to a strong police subculture, widespread misconduct, and local political traditions. It has always been difficult to reform the police and address systemic issues (Gomez, 2015). The police subculture is difficult to change as loyalty to and solidarity with fellow officers are viewed paramount among police officers. Police leadership that focuses on rotten apples rather than institutionalized behavior only touches the tip of the iceberg (Domanick, 2014). Local politics and corresponding decentralization in American policing also make federally imposed reforms less palatable (Rushin, 2017).

Criteria used to measure police compliance with consent decrees remain inadequate although progress has been made in this area in recent years. As a general rule, consent decrees are not terminated until a police department has achieved compliance with the terms of the agreement. Defining *compliance* has proven difficult, in part because certain issues such as police use of force do not lend themselves to evaluation on a quantitative scale (Police Executive Research Forum, 2013). Some consent decree programs simply define compliance as meeting a requirement over 90% of the time over a certain period (Police Executive Research Forum, 2013), but the criteria for achieving compliance over 90% of the time over a given period may not have been clearly validated. Recent consent decrees have included outcome measures, but they have not been empirically determined or widely accepted. Related to this issue is the inadequate use of the auditing function to assess the progress of implementing the consent decree. A local office of independent police auditors charged with monitoring and auditing police conduct has not been established in most jurisdictions. Both New Orleans and New York City resisted local monitoring of their police practices (Winston, 2013).

Results and Outcomes

While rigorous evaluations of consent decrees are rare, limited evidence suggests that departments committed to institutionalizing policies and procedures in compliance with terms of the decrees are able to achieve significant improvement in their daily practice and build better community relations. An evaluation of the Pittsburgh consent decree (Davis, Henderson, and Ortiz, 2005) demonstrates that the civilian complaints review process improved with greater efficiency. An assessment of consent decrees in Pittsburgh; Washington, DC; Cincinnati; Detroit; and Prince George's County (MD) (Chanin, 2014) suggests that new training and policies had been established. and organizational change had taken place, reducing police misconduct and making the police more efficient and effective. A review of empirical evidence in several studies by Rushin (2015) also indicates that consent decrees were effective in reducing police misconduct. An earlier and a later study of the Los Angeles consent decree (Stone, Fogelsong, & Cole, 2009; Phillips & Jiao, 2017) show that the reform has led to increased public satisfaction, decreased frequency in use-of[force incidents, improved quality of stops and arrests, and significant organizational and operational changes in the LAPD.

While the studied police departments improved their operations and reduced officer misconduct, whether the benefits of implementing the consent decrees are temporary or long term cannot be ascertained without further systematic evaluations. As some researchers have noted, there is a great chance for relapse or backsliding to old ways once a decree is lifted or a reform-minded chief leaves (Chanin, 2015; Rushin, 2015; Walker, 2018). Due to various challenges described in the previous section, many question whether jurisdictions where consent decrees worked, such as Pittsburgh; Cincinnati; Washington, DC; and Los Angeles, will be able to sustain their improved conditions over time.

As results and outcomes, especially positive ones, of implementing a consent decree are examined, it is important to look deeper into the question of sustainability. Behind the successes or improvements are not only significant amounts of time and resources and dedication of local politicians and police leaders (Winston, 2013) but also institutionalization of best practices, which is rarely studied. The process of overcoming difficulties and achieving results and outcomes in compliance with a consent decree needs to be understood in light of the concept of institutionalization. The Los Angeles Police Department (LAPD) serves as an example in this regard because, unlike other police organizations in which the results of implementing a decree were presented, the process of managing and developing the police to meet the terms of the consent decree leading to organizational and cultural changes was also examined in detail (Phillips & Jiao, 2017). Although the LAPD is not typical, considering its larger size and greater complexity, its experiences in dealing with various challenges in developing the organization and institutionalizing decree-mandated practices are worth noting and should prove informative to many police organizations in the reform process.

The LAPD consent decree can be traced to the Rodney King beating and the Rampart scandal (Independent Commission on the LAPD, 1991; LAPD, 2000). The DOJ investigated the police procedures and practices and entered into a consent decree with Los Angeles on June 15, 2001. The decree was a legal document, which named the attorneys of the US DOJ as the plaintiffs and attorneys representing the City of Los Angeles as the defendants. The document provided the legal grounds of the plaintiff for bringing the lawsuit, information pertaining to rules of engagement, and the specific requirements of the consent decree (*United States of America v. City of Los Angeles*, 2001). The focus was on pattern and practice of constitutional rights violations and directed at what the LAPD was supposed to do and the timelines by which the department was expected to accomplish the mandated reform.

The implementation of the consent decree and associated federal monitoring was a long and arduous process. Bernard Parks, the chief of police when the consent decree was entered, was only able to start the process of addressing some of the issues in the decree (Police Executive Research Forum, 2013). Bill Bratton, who became chief in 2002, provided a stronger sense of direction in the reform program and made compliance with the decree a top priority for the LAPD (Winston, 2013). But due to difficulties and lack of progress in the reform process, a federal judge extended the decree for another five years after the original five.

The LAPD's audit division was formed in response to the consent decree and served as a primary channel by which reform was carried out and progress was reported to the federal judge. The audit division comprised mostly sworn officers and reported directly to the special assistant for constitutional policing, who reported to the chief of police. The audit division developed an audit charter and an audit manual for its employees. The charter set the tone for how the division should conduct its business and outlined its independence and objectivity within the LAPD. Its mission was to provide police management an independent, objective, and comprehensive review and evaluation of police operations and controls; make recommendations on how to make improvements; promote integrity and transparency; and advance accountability (LAPD, 2011).

A critical part of this process was federal monitoring, and the key mechanism used by the monitor was the audit function, carried out by LAPD audit specialists in assessing various police activities such as warrant applications, arrests, and use of force. The monitor's quarterly reports indicated that early audits were of poor quality and often incomplete. Problems arose during planning and implementation of audit procedures, including selection of samples and construction of questionnaires. Most auditors had no prior training in auditing and had only a vague understanding of randomized procedures. Some did not know how to strategize, execute, and document the audit work properly and failed to analyze collected data critically. The monitor found numerous work-paper discrepancies and a lack of supporting documentation overall (Kroll and Associates, 2002a).

The initial relationship between the audit division, the US DOJ, and the federal monitor was poor and contentious. The police did not cooperate with or trust the federal monitor. Their negative sentiment toward the consent decree and mandated reform was also evident (Kroll and Associates, 2002b). Members of the audit division felt that the decree was not so much about reform but rather about doing what the DOJ mandated and providing an opportunity for the independent monitor to take the city's money. They viewed the DOJ as intrusive and their experience with the independent monitor as confusing. While representatives of the independent monitor knew about auditing, their knowledge of policing was limited, and the nature of what was expected as an end product was unclear to the audit division.

A serious lack of knowledge pertaining to auditing police operations was obvious in the early days of the audit division. The sworn employees had no experience in conducting formal audits, and civilian auditors had no experience in policing. A steep learning curve existed for sworn employees in learning the audit process and for civilian auditors in learning police operations. The completed audits were often found to be out of compliance by the independent monitor. To address this deficiency, the audit division contacted other agencies and police associations such as the Commission on Accreditation for Police Agencies and the International Association of Chiefs of Police but was not able to find any agency with experience in conducting audits in response to a consent decree.

The audit division sought training from various professional organizations such as the Institute of Internal Auditors, Association of Local Government Auditors, MIS Training Institute, and Association of Certified Fraud Examiners. The civilian auditors held various audit certifications such as certified public accountant, certified internal auditor, and certified fraud examiner. The commanding officer and sworn members also pursued certifications. Audit staff members further attended the Association of Local Government Auditors conferences and studied generally accepted government auditing standards promulgated by the US Government Accountability Office (2011).

The quality of audits started to improve in late 2002 (Kroll and Associates, 2002c). Of 22 required audits completed, 18 were found to be in compliance (Kroll and Associates, 2005). As time passed, explicit methodologies were developed, and better relationships were established. As training from professional audit organizations was not particularly applicable to police auditing, the audit division created a training cadre and developed an auditing course with police operations in mind.

As time went on, the pressure of the consent decree was somehow transferred to the Board of Police Commissioners, which serves as the overseer of the LAPD and which the chief of police reports to. During meetings of the board, audit reports were briefed with respective commanding officers whose operations were audited. As an audit report was brought before the board, the auditee was expected to provide a plan of action for remedying the issues identified. If the board was dissatisfied with the plan of action, it would direct the auditee to return with an improved plan. The board could also direct the Office of the Inspector General to conduct further inquiries, investigations, and audits, if necessary.

Over time, a change in institutional practice and attitude toward auditing occurred in the LAPD. While the consent decree identified the risk areas, a department-wide risk assessment process was established for identifying and evaluating high risks. The role and function of the Audit Division and the audit process had taken root. In the early days, the LAPD commanders were apprehensive about audits; now they had come to see them as a way to address performance issues and improve operations. The commanders were also in a position to provide input to audit recommendations and move forward in instituting them before the reports reached the chief of police or were heard before the Board of Police Commissioners. The apprehension of audits was still there, but the fear had been mitigated, largely due to the professionalism of the audit staff and the buy-in to the audit process by many commanding officers (Phillips & Jiao, 2017).

In retrospect, auditing was clearly an effective way to measure police performance and accountability. The audit process established accountability by addressing the audit reports directly to those in charge of particular areas of police operations. Commanding officers subject to an audit were directed to report to the Board of Police Commissioners and address their action plans to the board. The audit division then kept track of the recommendations made in the audits and followed up on the status of their implementation. The division eventually reconciled the closed recommendations with the Board of Police Commissioners, and the board required a status report on all open recommendations.

The LAPD consent decree was meant to be completed in 2006, but the federal judge did not release the LAPD from federal oversight until 2013, when it was recognized that sufficient reform had been institutionalized. The decree-driven reform transcended time and politics as the department carried out the reform under three mayors and three chiefs of police (Police Executive Research Forum, 2013). The cost of the reform was significant but considered well worth it in terms of preventing future litigation and gaining credibility with the public (Police Executive Research Forum, 2013). Police-community relations, especially LAPD's relationship with black and Latino Angelenos, improved significantly as the violent crime rate dropped during Bratton's tenure. A 2009 survey of Angelenos by Harvard's Kennedy School of Government found that 83% of residents said LAPD was policing in an effective and even-handed manner (Winston, 2013).

Overall, it was recognized by both police commanders and outside investigators that the demands of the consent decree and the positive police response to them should be credited with LAPD's success (Winston, 2013). The independent monitor and the audit function contributed to the positive organizational and operational changes. As performance audits are designed to measure police efforts directly related to adhering to citizens' constitutional rights, departmental policies and procedures, and the law, it is believed that so long as the LAPD continues to conduct performance audits, the likelihood of it being targeted by the US DOJ for a pattern and practice violation of citizens' constitutional rights will be minimized.

Discussions and Conclusions

This review is meant to develop a general understanding of consent decrees as a concept for improving police accountability. Despite of the lack of research and data on the subject matter, a better understanding has been achieved in terms of the nature of consent decrees and several critical areas that need to be addressed in order for them to be successful. The nature of consent decrees is coercive. A consent decree is perhaps one of the most threatening vehicles for police reform. It poses threats to the entire police agency and the municipality because it is expensive and requires a herculean effort to resolve, and a city has no option but to comply once a decree is issued. A presiding federal judge has the power to intervene in the implementation process and determine when a decree ends. A court-appointed federal monitor provides oversight and periodic evaluation, moves reform forward, and eventually brings a decree to its end (Police Executive Research Forum, 2013). This coercive nature, as outlined in the introduction, is important to recognize also because of a lack of alternatives in making local policing more accountable.

The experiences of police organizations that have gone through a consent decree are testimony to the coercive nature of the consent decree. The police in general react negatively to the decree, the DOJ, and the independent federal monitor initially. The DOJ and the federal monitor represent the external coercive force, under which the police have to examine their policies, procedures, and overall practices and eventually develop a mechanism such as the LAPD's audit division for reform. This police experience is indicative of what is typically observed in police reforms (Simmons, 2008), which is that change does not occur unless mandated in some way. This resistance to change by police organizations and the need for strong external pressure for fundamental change to occur have been well documented in previous police studies (Bennett, 1994; Dixon & Stanko, 1993; Jiao, Lau, & Lui, 2005).

Consent decrees are not perfect and certainly have their limitations due to both the dilemmas tackled and remedies offered (Rushin, 2017; Walker, 2018; Winston, 2013). Understanding their limitations, however, should not be confused with the view that consent decrees tie the hands of the police and make them less effective in fighting crime and maintaining order. This more negative view led to the review and curtailing of federal consent decrees during the Trump administration. In light of the completed studies and reviews thus far, also considering the limitations of other reform efforts such as Supreme Court rulings, civil and criminal litigation, and internally initiated police reforms, federal and state intervention in and oversight of local policing should not only continue but also be refined and expanded (Rushin, 2017; Walker, 2018).

If federal and state intervention and oversight are to continue, consent decrees will only grow more complex and intricate. It is important to understand and address several key areas in order for a consent decree to achieve its goals and objectives. These areas include 1) terms of the consent decree, 2) functions of the independent federal monitor, 3) leadership and management, 4) institutionalization of policies and practices, 5) change and development of police culture, and 6) an audit function as an essential element of the police management system.

It is important to define clearly the terms of any agreement with the DOJ or a state attorney general's office, especially a consent decree. A consent decree itself should be based on an empirical determination of a pattern or practice of unconstitutional policing. After a consent decree is entered and approved by a federal judge, time must be spent in detailing objectives and results, including intervention strategies and activities, performance and outcome measures, and quantitative and qualitative data collection and analysis (Alpert et al., 2017). This will ensure a reform plan that is specific and practical and allow a police department to achieve compliance in a timely and cost-effective manner (Police Executive Research Forum, 2013).

The choice of a court-appointed federal monitor is essential. Police departments under consent decrees have varying experiences with federal monitors: some good, others not so good. Good federal monitors do much more than just "monitor" the implementation of a consent decree. They have substantive knowledge of policing issues, are efficient and effective in achieving goals, and serve as strong mediators and problem solvers (Police Executive Research Forum, 2013). In addition to the federal monitor, experts are often hired in the consent decree implementation process. When this happens, the experts should have knowledge in current police policies and practices as well as experience in the consent decree process in similar jurisdictions (Police Executive Research Forum, 2013).

Strong leadership with a proactive approach is critical in successfully fulfilling the mandate of a consent decree. Police chiefs without a sense of urgency, political acumen, and the conceptual skills to manage the reform will face stronger resistance within their organizations. If completing a consent decree is not made a department-wide priority or if the DOJ's role and the need for reforms are questioned, the reform process will be slowed, and cost will increase in the end (Police Executive Research Forum, 2013). If the pattern and practice issues continue, officers who commit criminal offenses are sued, criminal actions are filed, and the city and individual officers are required to pay (Hustle, 2014). Effective chiefs not only harness the energy of a competent team internally in charge of implementing the consent decree and overcoming resistance but also are keen on building strong political and public support for reforms (Domanick, 2014). In fact, they take advantage of the consent decree as an impetus to overcome political opposition to reforms, one reason some police leaders have welcomed or requested DOJ investigations. A federal investigation, whether resulting in a consent decree or not, can force otherwise reluctant local elected officials to provide funding needed for reform and possibly reduce labor union opposition to certain changes in police policies (Police Executive Research Forum, 2013).

Leaders come and go, and the short tenure of a police chief in the US does not encourage long-term planning. Departments successful in carrying out a consent decree may relapse to old ways after reform-minded chiefs leave or after a consent decree is lifted (Chanin, 2015). Developing the organization and institutionalizing good policies and practices must therefore be a vital part of the reform process. This will not only allow the police to complete the consent decree but also prevent them from future federal investigations. Institutionalized policies and practices will continue regardless of changing politics and administrations (Gomez, 2015). Such policies and practices should cover key operational areas such as use of force, search and seizure, and arrest and key managerial and supervisory measures such as training, early warning, and use of body cameras. Officers must be trained to make sure that they understand and will follow the policies. An early warning system helps ensure that police managers respond quickly to misbehavior before it develops into a serious and widespread problem (Police Executive Research Forum, 2013; Walker, 2005). Body cameras for police officers allow more accurate accounting of police compliance with use-of-force policies and have been found to reduce civilian complaints and use-of-force incidents (Ariel, Farrar, & Sutherland, 2015; Ariel et al., 2017; Hedberg, Katz, & Choate, 2017; White, Gaub, & Todak, 2017).

Institutionalized policies and practices should be accompanied by a change in police culture to ensure individual and organizational accountability in the long run. Abuses of the use of force, for example, usually have existed for decades within a department. How use-of-force incidents are investigated reflects a major part of a department's culture (Walker, 2005). The kind of questions supervisors ask, whether they probe, and whether they examine inconsistencies and contradictions demonstrate the culture of a police organization. As bad practices and attitudes have been ingrained within the police culture, it will take years to weed them out. So the endurance of police reform ultimately depends on a change in culture (Gomez, 2015).

Last but not least, a professional auditing system should be established as a vital part of the command and control mechanism. This function can be instituted as an internal police unit or an external government office. Regardless of where it is located, it plays a critical role in ensuring that reform resulting from a consent decree will continue, even after the decree has been lifted. The auditing function should be independent of the police hierarchy, professionally run, and institutionalized as an essential part of the government (Jiao, 2015). The LAPD's experience demonstrates how the use of auditing as an overarching performance management tool can help the police achieve and maintain accountability (Phillips & Jiao, 2017). The auditing system requires that performance be measured accurately and objectively. Done correctly, this process allows an empirical determination of compliance with a consent decree and helps a police department improve its overall performance.

Discussion Questions

1. What issues are usually addressed in consent decrees on police organizations in the United States?
2. What are the main challenges in implementing consent decrees?
3. How do you understand the question of sustainability or the concept of institutionalization of best practices after a consent decree is lifted?
4. How do you understand the role or function of auditing in implementing a consent decree?
5. What are the key areas that need to be addressed in order for a consent decree to achieve its goals and objectives?

References

Alpert, G. P., McLean, K., & Wolfe, S. (2017). Consent decrees: An approach to police accountability and reform. *Police Quarterly*, 1–11.

Ariel, B., Farrar, W. A., & Sutherland, A. (2015). The effect of police body-worn cameras on use of force and citizens' complaints against the police: A randomized controlled trial. *Journal of Quantitative Criminology, 31*(3), 509–535.

Ariel, B., Sutherland, A., Henstock, D., Young, J., Drover, P., Sykes, J., . . Henderson, R. (2017). 'Contagious accountability:' A global multisite randomized controlled trial on the effect of police body-worn cameras on citizens' complaints against the police. *Criminal Justice and Behavior, 44*(2), 293–316.

Baltimore Police Department. (2017). *City of Baltimore consent decree*. Retrieved September 21, 2017, from www.baltimorepolice.org/transparency/city-baltimore-consent-decree.

Bennett, T. (1994). Community policing on the ground: Developments in Britain. In D. P. Rosenbaum (Ed.), *The challenge of community policing: Testing the promises* (pp. 224–246). Thousand Oaks, CA: Sage.

Benzing, Jeffrey. (2014, July 1). Pittsburgh police could face second federal consent decree. *PublicSource*. Retrieved April 15, 2016, from http://publicsource.org/from-the-source/pittsburgh-police-could-face-second-federal-consent-decree-peduto-says#.V2gYKPkrK4Q

Chanin, J. M. (2014). On the implementation of pattern or practice police reform. *Criminology, Criminal Justice, Law & Society, 15*, 38–56.

Chanin, J. M. (2015). Examining the sustainability of pattern or practice police misconduct reform. *Police Quarterly, 18*, 163–192.

City of New Orleans. (2017). *NOPD consent decree*. Retrieved September 16, 2017, from www.nola.gov/nopd/nopd-consent-decree/

Davis, R. C., Henderson, N. J., & Ortiz, C. W. (2005). *Can federal intervention bring lasting improvement in local policing? The Pittsburgh consent decree*. New York, NY: Vera Institute of Justice.

Dixon, B., & Stanko, E. (1993). *Serving the people: Sector policing and public accountability*. Uxbridge, ON: Brunel University.

Domanick, J. (2014, July 15). Police reform's best tool: A federal consent decree. Retrieved June 15, 2016, from www.thecrimereport.org/news/articles/2014-07-police-reforms-best-tool-a-federal-consent-decree

Eversley, M. (2016, March 15). Ferguson accepts Justice Department consent decree. *USA Today*. Retrieved June 25, 2016, from www.usatoday.com/story/news/2016/03/15/ferguson-accepts-justice-department-consent-decree/81836200/

Gomez, Henry J. (2015, May 27). Cleveland consent decree provides blueprint for long-elusive police reforms: The big story. *Cleveland.com*. Retrieved June 2, 2016, from www.cleveland.com/metro/index.ssf/2015/05/cleveland_consent_decree_provi.html

Hedberg, E. C., Katz, C. M., & Choate, D. E. (2017). Body-worn cameras and citizen interactions with police officers: Estimating plausible effects given varying compliance levels. *Justice Quarterly, 34*(4), 627–651.

Hustle, Rob. (2014, December 9). Consent decrees and the federation of local police. *News, Rebel Pundit.*

Independent Commission on the Los Angeles Police Department. (1991). *Report of the independent commission on the Los Angeles police department.* Los Angeles, CA: Author.

Jiao, A.Y. (2015). *Police auditing: Standards and applications.* Springfield, IL: Charles C. Thomas.

Jiao, A. Y., Lau, R. W. K., & Lui, P. (2005). An institutional perspective of organizational change: The case of the Hong Kong Police. *International Criminal Justice Review, 15*(1), 38–57.

Kroll and Associates, Inc. (2002a). *Report of the independent monitor, first quarterly report.* New York, NY: Author.

Kroll and Associates, Inc. (2002b). *Report of the independent monitor, second quarterly report.* New York, NY: Author.

Kroll and Associates, Inc. (2002c). *Report of the independent monitor, third quarterly report.* New York, NY: Author.

Kroll and Associates, Inc. (2005). *Report of the independent monitor, third quarterly report.* New York, NY: Author.

Los Angeles Police Department (LAPD). (2000). Board of inquiry into the rampart area corruption incident. Retrieved from http://www.lapdonline.org/assets/pdf/boi_pub.pdf

Los Angeles Police Department (LAPD). (2011). *Internal audits and inspections division, audit manual* (Brochure). Los Angeles, CA: Author.

MacDonald, Heather. (2016, December 16). Trump can end the war on cops. *The Wall Street Journal.* Retrieved June 17, 2017, from www.wsj.com/articles/trump-can-end-the-war-on-cops-1481931231

Phillips, Jeffry R., & Jiao, Allan Y. (2017). Institutional isomorphism and the federal consent decree: The case of the Los Angeles Police Department. *Policing: An International Journal of Police Strategies and Management, 39*(4), 756–772.

Police Executive Research Forum. (2013). *Civil rights investigations of local police: Lessons learned.* Critical Issues in Policing Series. Washington, DC: Police Executive Research Forum.

Puente, M., Serrano, R. A., & Pearce, M. (2015, May 26). Cleveland consent decree being watched in Baltimore. *Baltimore Sun.* Retrieved July 5, 2016, www.baltimoresun.com/news/maryland/sc-dc-cleveland-police-20150526-story.html

Rushin, S. (2015). Structural reform litigation in American police departments. *Minnesota Law Review, 99*, 1343–1422.

Rushin, S. (2017). *Federal intervention in American police departments.* New York, NY: Cambridge University Press.

Salter, J. (2017, November 22). Ferguson leaders wonder if monitor worth cost. *Associated Press.* Retrieved November 24, 2017, from www.usnews.com/news/us/articles/2017-11-22/apnewsbreak-ferguson-leaders-wonder-if-monitor-worth-cost

Simmons, K. C. (2008). The politics of policing: Ensuring stakeholder collaboration in the federal reform of local law enforcement agencies. *Journal of Criminal Law & Criminology, 98*(2), 489–546.

Smith, Mitch. (2017, August 29). Illinois Attorney General Sues Chicago over Police Practices. *New York Times.* Retrieved August 31, 2017, from www.nytimes.com/2017/08/29/us/chicago-police-consent-decree.html

State of Illinois v. City of Chicago. (2019). Memorandum opinion and order approving proposed consent decree, case no. 17-cv-6260, Judge Robert M. Dow, Jr.

Stone, C., Fogelsong, T., & Cole, C. (2009). *Policing Los Angeles under a consent decree: The dynamics of change at the LAPD.* Cambridge, MA: Program in Criminal Justice Policy and Management, Harvard Kennedy School.

United States of America v. City of Los Angeles, California, Board of Police Commissioners of the City of Los Angeles, and the Los Angeles Police Department. (2001). Retrieved May 23, 2012, from www.lapdonline.org/assets/pdf/final_consent_decree.pdf

US Government Accountability Office. (2011). *Government auditing standards*. Retrieved February 19, 2013, from www.gao.gov/govaud/iv2011gagas.pdf

Walker, S. (2005). *The new world of police accountability*. Thousand Oaks, CA: Sage Publications.

Walker, S. (2018). "Not dead yet:" The national police crisis, a new conversation about policing, and the prospects for accountability-related police reforms. *University of Illinois Law Review, 2018*(5), 1777–1841.

White, M. D., Gaub, J. E., & Todak, N. (2017). Exploring the potential for body-worn cameras to reduce violence in police-citizen encounters" *Policing, 12*(1), 66–76.

Winston, Ali. (2013, August 31 Saturday). American police reform and consent decrees. *Truthout/News*. Retrieved June 8, 2016, from www.truth-out.org/news/item/18455-american-police-reform-and-consent-decrees

Chapter 7

Police Discretion

An Issue of Untestable Reasonability in a Law Enforcement Process

Jean Claude Geofrey Mahoro

Introduction

In the process of rendering justice to the needy, there is an extended network of legal and non-legal professionals. For the legislation to attain its purposes, there should be another way of making the legislation products useful through institutions preserving that power. Among those institutions, we can mention public prosecution, courts, prisons, and police. The current chapter is about the latter. It entails the police role and discretion as well as the limitations of such discretion in the critical function of law enforcement. The chapter discusses law enforcement as one of the steps of delivering justice to the needy, but it focuses on the abuse of this power by police officers. It entails police noncompliance with the three values of the law enforcement: including justice, certainty, and utility.

In the understanding of an ordinary man, the police are a political tool to threaten the citizens in order to achieve their objectives without opponents or just a public institution that uses coercive power in delivering its remits, impeding the people's liberty as a result. However, that is may not be true; the one can wonder whether the second statement is right or wrong. Should it be right or wrong, the work at hand proves it.

Background

According to Diane C. Bordner, *police* is defined as "a mechanism of social control by which law is distributed in greater or lesser quantity, in one style or another, across social space." This definition mentions the role of police concerning law enforcement. It also shows the plurality of law in its enforcement process, which raises an issue of interpretation. In this light, Bordner argues that the quantity and style of the law differ from one place to another and in different situations (Bordner, 1983). The police officers at work address conflict depending on social characteristics (Bordner, 1983). Thus, social conditions dictate police work. Besides, with their discretionary power, police officers can make crime and criminals based on *prima facie* evidence in the criminal justice system (Bordner, 1983). That is to say that police officers decide the laws to be enforced, when, where, and against whom.

Since the power of the police is rooted in different laws, police officers' work is presumed to be reasonable and beneficial to the citizens, for they aim to ensure public safety and order, which is a crucial part of the development of everyone. In this context, police work is to secure the citizens and their properties so that they enjoy their freedom and liberty. In contrast, the practice jeopardizes that role. In the course of law enforcement, police officers sometimes use offensive language, abuse their authority, and employ force that threatens the life and liberty of citizens. However, it is not easy to say that they have transgressed the law since they work under an umbrella of discretion, which gives them the leeway to act on their considerations. Also, there is a conflict between freedom and order, which implies that the

DOI: 10.4324/9781003047117-8

latter dominates the former. Therefore, police discretion needs to have control in a particular way. If police officers have responsibilities, they need to be accountable. That is problematic as it is not easy to judge what is proper and just under their discretion, which is untestable. Hence, the nature of police discretion presents a loophole in the law enforcement process.

Problem Statement

The literature presents a gap in police work in the law enforcement process that intrigued the present researcher to analyze and reveal what is behind this problem. By doing so, there is an inquiry on police discretion. The researcher needs to know whether police discretion has a specific limitation, whether it is controlled or unfettered, and the reason that gives them these two characters. The researcher also wonders about the idea that drives the police to use force that threatens the citizens' liberty since they are expected to ensure their safety. Also, what do the laws and doctrines consider reasonable or unreasonable during the law enforcement process by the police? Finally, can police accountability work, and to what extent should the police officer be accountable? The researcher will try to find replies to those questions and others that may arise during this study. He also provides a satisfactory solution to both the police and the community that is hampered by the police activities during this research.

Theoretical Framework

In this work, the Rawls theory of justice will apply. Under this theory, justice is referred to as fairness. For Rawls, no matter how efficient and well arranged, laws and institutions must be reformed or abolished if they are unjust (Rawls, 1999). This theory of justice underpins two principles that serve to evaluate the basic structure of the society (Mandle, 2009), and if they are adhered to, the inequalities will be neutralized for everyone to receive similar benefits of justice (McCartney & Parent, 2015). The first principle underlines equality in the assignment of fundamental rights and duties, and the second claims that social and economic inequalities are just when they provide benefits for everyone and particularly for the least advantaged members of the society (Lovert, 2011).

Concerning the current chapter, police officers, while on duty, are expected to do what is proper and just in rendering justice to the society. Besides, discretion is an vital leeway that helps the police reach their objectives. The current research claims that the police cannot ensure safety and order in society while infringing on the liberty and well-being of the citizens. Therefore, the police role is not to criminalize people. Instead, it is to keep order and safety in society. In doing so, the police should ensure the principle of equality for equal justice. Therefore, police agencies need to be reformed if they are unjust in order to ensure fairness in the context of the Rawls theory of justice.

Methodology

The current research is socio-legal; the researcher examines the police discretion in their complex functioning while enforcing the law. In order to ascertain their impact and provide a dependable conclusion, this chapter explores the data of secondary authority of law, including different publications—books, journals, and encyclopedias—as well as other possible sources of this kind. However, it will certainly provide an example from some legislation on particular occasions. Besides, it explores non-legal sources of data to assess the reasonability of police officers at work, whether most powers are public oriented or self-willed. Thus, the socio-legal method is the best method to find out the accurate and genuine information leading to a constructive conclusion.

Results

Theoretically, police discretion is prescribed in different state regulations, and it is said to be "controlled discretion." However, it is not because such rules do not impose constraints on the police exercise of power. They grant discretion in a general and elusive way that implies an unwarranted extent of judgements in the routine of police work. Police discretion is "unfettered" due to the police officer's considerations and a plurality of interpretation of the law when trying to fit the rule to the case.

Furthermore, the current research found that police accountability is not defined, which hinders suppression of the police threat to the people's liberty and lives. Therefore, police discretion is untested as it is rooted in reasonability, which is abstract and relative. The study findings mention the cruelty, abuse of authority, and misconduct of the police officers and highlight that police professionalism is not enough to tackle those problems. Thus, the results suggest accountability of police officers as a critical solution in the law enforcement process.

Discussion

In the current chapter, the word *power* means authority and the ability to take specific action, including the execution of legal doctrines embedded in legal texts and decisions that have legal character and transfer and exercise legal rights.[1] However, this list is not exhaustive. The power in question is not inherent but derivative as it is rooted in the laws determining the powers, responsibilities, and functioning of the police in different states. Hence, the following discussion entails the discretion of police and its self-willed and uncontrollable nature.

Police Discretion

In order to discuss the discretion of police, it is better to understand the meaning of *discretion* and its origin. In this chapter, the concepts of *discretion* and *power* will be used together as there is a connection between the two. In the current chapter, *discretion* refers to the power of the police or another public official in deciding on various issues, based on own opinion within the legal framework or general guidelines.

Etymologically, *discretion* originates from a Latin word, *discernere*, which means to distinguish an object. Generally, it is identifying what is important or true and what is not. Discretion implies "discernment," which describes a wise way of judging things. To be clear, discretion sounds stronger than deciding between the alternatives and choosing the pertinent (Heilmann, 2006). In its context, discretion refers to sifting through several solutions and getting what is correct and proper to the situation at hand. According to Groeneveld, police discretion exists when officers have some leeway or choice on how to respond to a particular situation. For example, a police officer standing in the traffic junction may ignore the traffic lights for the sake of solving a traffic jam. In this light, the officer has an ability and authority to change directions of vehicles from the busiest road to the least busy road or to manage the vehicles' movements in consideration of what is reasonable at that moment. The fewer the rules about handling incidents and situations, the more discretion officers can exercise (Heilmann, 2006). Thus, the circumstances outside the police office dictate the police officers' work performance, which refers to "street justice" (Papazoglou, 2014).

Police discretion is vaguely rooted in law. For that reason, one would understand it as controlled power. However, it is not enough to be controlled just because it is stated in the law; it should be in practice. Discretion involves both action and inaction (Walker & Hemmens, 2011). Thus, the law provides discretion to police by setting leeway in responding to a particular situation reasonably, either by taking action or by avoiding doing something due to the immediate situation. In this context, the law does not prescribe a scope of reasonability, although there are police guidelines that contribute to the daily police work. The judgement of what is correct and proper rests in the hands of the police. For that reason, the police are likely to use such discretion arbitrarily, which results in "unfettered discretion.: The latter situation takes off the people's liberty and puts the people in dominated life through arrest and detention.

> [T]he routine nature of police work tends to obscure the complexities involved with police discretion, few would argue that such decision-making is inconsequential. In fact, the point that a police officer's duties compel him to exercise personal discretion many times throughout a day is clearly evident, sometimes with catastrophic results. In a society that places tremendous value in personal liberty, the management of discretion by police officers can become a critical and difficult exercise.
>
> (Groeneveld, 2005)

The complexity of police work may result in brutality. Groeneveld has classified that complexity in two dimensions: the complexity of the situation presented to the police officer and the complexity of the police response to the situation. Emphasising the other complexity, it requires the police officer to do or undo reasonably. What makes it complicated is that there is no proper way of testing the reasonability of the officer. In this context, any response about the case at hand is justifiable. However, when it comes to the court, the judge can assess the reasonability of an act that has taken place in relation to what would have taken place from his or her appreciation.

According to John Kleinig, discretion is understood as merely making a decision based on personal judgement. He adds on that the definition does not suffice because not every personal judgement counts as discretion. Kleinig's analysis brought up another essential point in this regard: that the officer, a police officer in this case, should be *able* and have the *authority* to act. In other words, the sole ability to act is not enough in the exercise of discretion; it should be accompanied by authority, which serves as the limitation to any unlawful actions that the officer can engage in (Kleinig, 2008). In this light, Kleinig disregarded the reasonableness of such a decision. So far, his definition is incomplete as discretion compels the officer to make a reasonable and appropriate decision in terms of correctness and necessity.

Kleinig ascertains discretion in four parameters, including scope, interpretation, priority, and tactics. Under the first view, the scope of function, the police is an agency that should be involved in public matters. In this context, when policing, the police need to differentiate private matters from public matters. They should not engage in some private matters in order not to abuse their role. The police should engage in public matters for the reason of securing and ensuring the public order. Thus, police services should be limited to some extent. In the second view, the police need to interpret the law looking at its intention. With the interpretative discretion, the police officers should determine what conduct does and does not fall in their remits or whether the law reasonably intended to prohibit particular conduct. In this case, a literal or strict reading is not recommended (Kleinig, 2008). In the third view, the priority, the police need to make a priority-based decision. In this context, the police need to know how to allocate their time and resources once in the field. Also, they need to respond between two circumstances that require a choice of priority, whether it is first to assist a person in danger or chase after a wrongdoer who is trying to leave. Balancing the two is another element of discretion that the police must take into account (Kleinig, 2008). Lastly, Keinig considered tactics very important for the police in their operations. The police need to know the appropriate tactics to be employed in different cases. In this regard, the police should make sure that their tactics do not constitute any deception. The proportionality has a crucial place in police tactical work. Thus, the police patrol guides would help police officers to determine the critical means and tactics that secure their results (Kleinig, 2008).

Sources of the Discretionary Power of the Police

In law enforcement, police officers might be understood as legal professionals; nonetheless, they are not. The legal provisions serve to guide them, and there are specific codes of law stating their functions. For that reason, the police exercise their power within the limits of the law. In contrast, police officers are not necessarily compelled to delve into articles of law and legal logic. In this context, police discretion is far from judicial discretions, which is "*discernere per legem quid sit justum*": to assess what would be just under the legal provisions and premises.[2] Thus, police officers should conform to the standards set for the exercise of their functions in sifting through different solutions to consider what would be undoubtedly correct and proper in the course of handling various cases.

Police discretion takes its source from different state laws. Trying to pick one example, the Indonesian law number 2/2002 concerning the State Police of the Republic of Indonesia states, "For general interests, officials of the State Police of the Republic of Indonesia may act based on their consideration in implementing tasks and authorities."[3] By using the phrase "their consideration," the Republic of Indonesia grants discretion to the police. However, this discretion should not be for the police officers to act on their will but for general interests.

The discretionary power in question should always be under standards prescribed in the provisions of the law. This concept would be understood well because the role of enforcing and administering law does not grant any one of the officials who serve that role, now the police, to take a superior position to the law. The law reigns supreme over everyone under the principle of the rule of law.[4] Furthermore, discretion must be exercised reasonably, which serves to provide fairness in the enforcement of the law. Thus, unfettered discretion of police results in the infringement of people's liberty. However, it also leaves consequences on the side of police officials who arbitrarily use such power.

Law enforcement is critical to the principle of the rule of law in ensuring public safety and social control. Under the rule of law, everyone is accountable to the law, and the latter should be fairly applied and enforced. However, as aforementioned, law enforcement officials sometimes use coercive power to realize their duties. The problem is whether this coercive power is provided in their guiding rules or not. The earlier discussion has coped with that confusion. Nevertheless, we should keep in mind that there should be laws regulating the police, setting their primary functions and individual activities, powers, and limitations in order not to be oppressive.

Discretion of Arrest

In order to deliver a suspect to judicial institutions, there should be an arrest. Without an arrest, those institutions will not effectively carry out their duties because of the small number of suspects pleading guilty and submitting themselves to courts to face justice. This shortage would jeopardize the functioning of the courts and other judicial institutions in their role of delivering justice and eradicating the culture of impunity.

By defining arrest, Walker and Hemmens tried to retrieve some definition from different laws and case laws; however, they are not satisfactory. One of those definitions is presented here to understand the complexity of arrest.

> [Arrest] implies that a person is thereby restrained of his liberty by some officer or agency of the law, armed with the lawful process, authorizing and requiring the arrest to be

made. It is intended to serve and does serve, the end of bringing the person arrested personally within the custody and control of the law, for the purpose specified in, or contemplated by the process.

(Walker & Hemmens, 2011)

According to Kenneth, in the course of the criminal justice system, the police use arrest as a means of addressing crime and disorder. The violation of criminal law has contributed to various alternatives to arrest, including formal and informal. The police use those alternatives regardless of whether or not they are sanctioned and acknowledged to improvise in situations where criminal law is overstepped (Kathleen & Hill, n.d.). The decision of arrest needs to be controlled. It is very complex as it has severe consequences on the suspect, the arresting officer, and the organization (Groeneveld, 2005). The arrest is an aspect that needs too much attention. On the one hand, the police can mire the individual (suspect) in an unimaginable condition without reasonable grounds. On the other hand, the simple act of arresting an individual without justifiable cause and interest may result in a severe penalty to the arresting officer, and subsequent arrests that do not result in criminal prosecutions end in the police untrustworthiness in the community.

Clearly, the police have awesome power in that they have the ability to take human life, deprive citizens of their liberty by arrest and detention, and can utilize physical force to obtain compliance. What is less clear are the methods by which the police should be, and can be, held accountable to the community they serve.

(Groeneveld, 2005)

In this extract, Groeneveld brings about the accountability of the police about arrest and detention. The issue here is placed in the types of methods used, whether permitted or not, reasonable or unreasonable, and to what extent they can be found arbitrary for the arresting police officers to be held liable.

Discretion of Seizure and Detention

Imagine a situation in which a police officer accidentally meets an individual and involves him or her in questioning. Such a voluntary encounter is a strategy in policing which does not require any reasonable suspicion or probable cause. In this regard, police officers have the leeway to approach citizens and question them; they may agree or disagree and go to their businesses without any consequence, which is a consensual encounter. In contrast, when those citizens, reasonably, do not feel free to leave as they were forced to yield, those people are "seized."

Under probable cause, the officer who is executing a search warrant can conduct an arrest after finding that there is a person who is not described by that warrant. The officer can do a similar act once a person commits an offense in his or her presence. However, the officer, for his or her protection, can detain a person once there is a sufficient basis that criminal activity is afoot (Groeneveld, 2005). In the same context, luggage can also be detained for temporal investigation once it is reasonably believed that it contains contraband (Groeneveld, 2005).

The duration of detention varies from state to state, as provided for by different domestic legal systems. What is common is that those detentions serve to permit the investigatory officers to carry out their activities accumulating evidence and facts. Therefore, the police officer has the discretion of arresting, seizing, and detaining an individual in case there is reasonable suspicion or not, referring to the situation at hand. In a detention case, the police officer is likely to use unfettered discretion.

Discretion of Questioning Suspect

Questioning the suspect is another area of police discretion of in which a police officer tries to ask many questions with the intent to assess the causal link between an act that occurred in violation of the law and the suspect when there are reasonable suspicious causes. This stage is crucial in the investigation process as it is a basis of building evidence to present in the criminal courts in prosecution. To produce admissible evidence, the questioning must meet some conditions as discussed next.

THE *MIRANDA* RULE

The *Miranda* rule, also the "Free and Voluntary rule" is a test to determine the admissibility of the confession. Under this rule, for a confession to be admissible in the evidence presented against the accused, the confession must meet two conditions: being free and voluntarily. That presents the initiation and willingness of the accused to confess without any pressure, fear, and with an awareness of that confession's consequence. Also, the confession cannot be obtained through threats, promises, or psychological pressure.

Different courts of law have given approaches to the questioning of a suspect following the stringent situation of the accused. As cited by Walker and Hemmens, in *Miranda v. Arizona*, the Supreme Court decided that if the accused was taken to custody and deprived of some rights, he or she should be given warnings for it is difficult to assess the freedom and voluntariness of the confession. The *Miranda* rights include the right to remain silent,[5] the use of an accused's statement in the court, the right to have an attorney during questioning, and a prior appointment of an attorney if the accused is unable to afford the attorney. Under the *Miranda* law, police officers are bound to know any words or actions that are reasonably likely to provoke the suspect's incrimination. In order words, the questioning should comply with the *Miranda* law for the police evidence to be admissible.

Concerns About the Discretionary Power

The arbitrary police use of power is a double-edged sword. It has consequences for both the police officer and mainly the one against whom the power is exercised. It is evident in different countries that convictions for some offenses or just arrest are associated with different risks, including losing jobs, mostly in public institutions; jeopardizing professional licenses and certifications; and expulsion from office. In this respect, different states do not tolerate people being arrested, even by mistake of fact, for immoral conduct. That is the specific case of people arrested for public sexual behavior in different cities after World War II (Goluboff, 2016).

In exercising powers, the police officers have to pay much attention. They have to be well skilled and equipped proportionally to the situation at hand. Evidently, in the investigation process, a slight mistake in judgement during the contact with a suspect can restrict the process (Walker & Hemmens, 2011). For example, an illegal search may contaminate evidence obtained previously under the law and result in its inadmissibility and release of a suspect of a heinous crime.

Moreover, in the exercise of law enforcement duty, the police encounter challenges that vary from situation to situation. Some of them are even very serious: for example, arresting an armed suspect who is unwilling to put down the weapon. In this case, it will require the discretionary power to make a rational decision relating to that situation. However, in some situations, police officers are allowed to use appropriate and reasonable force to effect a lawful arrest. In this case, it might be in the protection of an arresting officer or an innocent individual in danger. The unnecessary use of force is always prohibited in all circumstances.[6]

The Use of Force and Its Limits

Due to the pressure of taking action or responding to a particular situation, police officers are likely to cause moral evil that is justifiable in the organizational bureaucratic scope. Through what is known as "street justice," discretion permits police officers to act in an extralegal way, taking into consideration what is proper and just (Papazoglou, 2014). It is in this course that the use of force occurs.

The use of force is prohibited in general, although there are circumstances in which the police officer can use force as a last resort. Once justifiable, the officer can even use deadly force, depending on the resistance encountered. According to Sheriff James Arnold, whatever the situation is, the use of force is allowed as a defensive measure that an officer takes either to protect an arresting officer or an innocent individual in immediate danger. The use of force is also permissible in the prevention of a specific violent crime during its commission (Seron, Pereira, & Kovath, 2004). Thus, the use of force is applied to effect a lawful arrest or prevention of violent crime being committed.

Other reasons that might call for the use of force include the approach of someone with a weapon or a threatening individual to the officer, an officer's injury or/and exhaustion, and information on the previous threatening character or criminal record of the suspect. Those reasons contribute to the choice of police defensive measures in an imminent danger. However, as prescribed by Hommer F. Bromme, the relevance of the value of human life should always prevail and guide the officers when deciding to use deadly force.[7]

The American Constitution, in its preamble, provides law enforcement together with the protection of criminal justice in three aims of the government; establishing justice, protecting domestic tranquility, and securing the blessings of liberty to the Americans and their posterity. The first refers to the creation of judicial and extra-judicial systems rendering justice to the citizens; the second implies the production of all means contributing to the suppression of riots, prevention of crime, and securing public order; and the last is fighting against any hindrance to the people's liberty. However, the law enforcement officials—the police, in particular—bypass the threefold aspects provided in the preamble. Various writers have highlighted this in their works at different times. For examples, Risa Goluboff, in the *Vagrant Nation: Police Power, Constitutional Change, and the Making of the 1960s*, has discussed the problem of "vagrant Laws," under which the police used to drag the citizens through the mire in different aspects particularly in employment (Goluboff, 2016). Also, Williams (2015), in *Our Enemies in Blue: Police and Power in America*, clearly stated the American police brutality in theory and practice by describing police intolerance, corruption, political repression, and violence.

Throughout the history of the United States, like any other society, there has been a tension between "freedom" and "order." The Constitution protects citizens while using the law, which is a command in nature. Freedom and order are always in a struggle; when the "order" goes up, there is a tendency for "freedom" to go down, and vice versa. This issue has been worked out by providing the freedom of speech and enactment of various acts with the intent to protect the citizens from the coercive power of the troops. Despite the work done, an equal balance between the two aspects seems to be an unrealizable ideal. For effective law enforcement and the protection of criminal justice, law enforcement agencies were compelled to develop and enforce appropriate laws and procedures that address the issues of use of force and the use of weapons and personal protection equipment in order to cope with the "order-liberty tension" and ensure the public order without putting people's liberty in danger. In reality, this is not an easy task because the direction or control of the behavior of others is more likely to imply the use of physical force, although it leaves another question of the extent to which such use of force would be.[8]

According to Hirby (2018), the use of force refers to "the right of an individual or authority figure to settle conflicts or prevent certain actions by applying measures to dissuade individuals from a course of action or to physically intervene to stop individuals." As reflected on earlier, maintaining order requires a threefold means, including weapons, personal protection equipment, and the use of force. The use of force is unavoidable for the success of police officers in two perspectives: in the protection of the police officer and the security of the innocent individual in immediate danger. In this light, the police officers are forced to use less lethal weapons, riot control agents, tear gas grenade guns, tear gas solution squirters, pistols, batons, tasers, riot control guns, stun guns, water cannons, and other kinds of weapons. However, the use of force is inadvisable and is only a last resort when other techniques of conflict resolution are not effective, and, when applied, it should be reasonable and necessary.

The circumstances in which the police officers should not use force include the elderly, disabled, unconscious, injured, and no-threat situation. Thus, those situations that present weakness and submission are not subject to the use of force to avoid victimization. However, police discretion extends that since it allows the officers to use force in some circumstances upon their necessity's considerations. In those cases, the officers should be able to detect probable threat because of deceit and pay attention to the necessary and proper use of force. For that reason, the state has the task of equipping its police officers with the required skills to handle any issues they encounter and teach its citizens the appropriate way of dealing with police without defensive means as it is not there for the taking of their rights; instead, it is for protecting them and ensuring the public order.

Origin of Use of Force

The police character of using force originates from two different perspectives, including the nature of the work and the recruitment process. To deliver efficient work in the criminal law system to the public, the police work needs to be *in optima forma*, or impeccable, which is almost impossible in the current criminal world. Police work conforms to the actual situations, which also entails discretion.

In the hands of a police officer, a law is an abstract ideal, which needs to be concrete. For that reason, the officer will use reasonable violence under given discretion to ensure its enforcement. Also, police work is under the presumption of guilt, which causes its officers to be suspicious of any movements around them, even when they might be in their ordinary course. Concisely, police work is a tainted occupation that prompts police officers to use force.

Another ground that pushes the police to use force is the recruitment baseline. In this regard, the police use of different methods during the recruitment process is problematic (Twersky-Glasner, 2005). The police use different systems when screening new candidates. MMPI-2 (Framingham, 2018) and CPI (Roufa, 2018) are the most common predictors when screening the candidates. Those psychological-based systems produce distinct results to clinicians who interpret them and later have many implications for the law enforcement candidates. For example, the MMPI-2 *K-scale* has become a single condition to disqualify a new applicant for the police (Laguna, Agliotta, & Mannon, 2013). The *K-scale* is a psychological evaluation to measure the self-control and family and interpersonal relationships of the candidate. If an applicant scores high on this scale, it implies a failure of the assessment based on being defensive, which results in his or her disqualification (Laguna, Agliotta, & Mannon, 2013).

According to Aviva Twersky-Glasner, for the weight of law enforcement, police recruitment needs too much attention not based on those multifaceted systems. That is because policing is a vital process for the effective implementation of a law that has widespread impact on the entire community (Laguna, Agliotta, & Mannon, 2013). For Laguna, Agliotta, and Mannon, the sole use of MMPI-2 in selecting police officers has bad effects on the law enforcement. Besides, those evaluations are only considered useful during recruitment since the police working environment changes the officers' psychological life from time to time. Therefore, having recruited candidates under the aforementioned screening implies having unqualified staff due to lack of other requirements that would be critical. Consequently, some police officers who probably use force are the result of unjust recruitment.

Ethics of Police

According to Seron, Pereira, and Kovath (2004), in any interactions with citizens, police officers must not use unnecessary force, abuse their authority, speak discourteously, or use offensive language. Curter has also highlighted four different types of violent police misconduct: physical abuse or excessive force, verbal or psychological abuse, violation of civil rights, and police sexual violence toward women (Papazoglou, 2014). For those authors, the four different points raise the ethics and values of the police officers, which are critical elements in their job as they present discretion. The discretion is ethical and thus untestable because it is from a personal motive.

Seron, Pereira, and Kovath (2004) have discussed discourtesy or offensive language of police as serious misconduct in community-based policing. Offensive or foul language refers to disrespectful and hurtful language. In this light, police officers should not use harsh terms when they are trying to persuade citizens. Thus, whatever the case may be, people must be treated humanely. Moreover, the officers should not abuse their authority by threatening civilians or violating the rules. Also, they should be respectful of their codes of conduct. As well, the use of force is more severe than all other misconduct as it may include pushing, punching, beating, or even shooting the civilian. In contrast, the unnecessary use of force is always prohibited. Therefore, when enforcing the law, police officers should not use any means that pose threats to the citizens.

Therefore, as highlighted by Konstantinos Papazoglou, police misconduct refers to inappropriate behavior of a police officer that discredits his/her position. It results in not only transgressing the law but also violating the moral and ethical code. Unfortunately, the distinction between the ordinary citizens' and police officers' behavior has developed an assumption of taking police ethical violations less critically, and thus, there is no punishment (Papazoglou, 2014).

Police Accountability

Despite significant efforts invested by governments in professionalizing police, there are still gaps to bridge. With their discretionary power, suspicious police officers can put the lives of citizens in danger, and mostly, they are not held accountable for their misconduct. William J. Chambliss (2001), in the following example, has defined it. That is a scenario of James Crane, a white police lieutenant with the District of Columbia Metropolitan Police, and a young black man. When Lieutenant Crane received a radio call that guns were being fired near his location, he drove to that place. Reaching it, Crane, with his patrol car, approached a young black man, who immediately walked away. The latter, after being followed by Crane and two police officers, ran away heading to his apartment, ran inside, and locked the door. The police officers, who used force, ordered him to open the door, and the young man opened the door, yelling to contest the arrest. Lieutenant Crane tried to handcuff him, but the young man resisted. "The lieutenant broke a fingernail, and the young man was bleeding from a scrape on the face." The officers did a search, although they did not find anything illegal in the house or on the young man. However, it did not preclude them from arresting him and charging him with a felony. On the following day, the prosecutor dropped the charges based on insufficient evidence, not convincing the prosecution.

Looking at the socio-legal consequences associated with this incident, as Chambliss mentions, "a young man with no prior record now has an arrest record, his fingerprints are now on file with the FBI, and his name has been entered into the National Crime Information Center's database." The suspicious police officer put the young man in danger as the arrest record may have severe effects on his future once he is applying for a job or when the police arrest him again. In contrast, this arrest values a lot to Lieutenant Crane in terms of his ability as a police officer and consequently improves his annual evaluation. Thus, Lieutenant Crane enjoys the fruits of his manufactured misfortune toward the young man.

This scenario indicates a lack of police accountability. Nonetheless, as Walker (2007) highlights in the following excerpt, individual police officers should be held accountable for their conduct for the policing to achieve its primary goals. Thus, without accountability, the police will never embrace lawfulness and legitimacy.

> Holding individual police officers accountable for their conduct is an essential element of policing. It is, directly and indirectly, related to achieving the basic goals of policing: reducing crime and disorder, enhancing the quality of neighborhood life, and providing fair, respectful and equal treatment for all people.

As long as the law governs everyone, including the police officers whose discretion is likely to infringe on the liberty and well-being of the citizens, they should be held accountable for their law encroachment associated with their misconduct. Police agencies should work within the scope of justice, certainty, and utility of law during the entire process of law enforcement. Consequently, the police would not be understood as "trouble" to society; they would be trustworthy and cooperative with the citizens and ultimately achieve their objectives in a conducive environment (Oliver, 1987).

To achieve police goals, lawfulness and legitimacy, as well as accountability procedures, are essential in policing (Walker, 2007). Under lawfulness or legality, the police should act following the law. For legitimacy, police conduct should be lawful and meet public expectations (Walker, 2007). If police keep those two goals in mind, they will not work arbitrarily, although the theory is different from the practice. Police officers sometimes act in defiance of their oath. Factually, they transgress the law and work extralegally. Consequently, they must be held to account, and the independence of the police needs to be balanced with accountability under the rule of law (Chan, 1999).

As discussed before, no one is above the law; the law always reigns supreme. Police officers, however, who work under the umbrella of discretion, should bear the consequences of their misconduct civilly and criminally, in addition to being subject to disciplinary sanctions. Such effects should not be limited to the police organizations to which an officer is related, but they should reach that very officer. Indeed, if a police organization is held civilly liable for its officers' misconduct, it is the citizens who indemnify with their taxes, which would contribute to the national development.

Bordner has stated that the factors that influence police discretion include the mood of the officer, the race of the offender, suspect legitimacy, victim legitimacy, incident severity, time of day, the attitude of the offender, and complainant preference (Bordner, 1983). Those factors, if combined with the nature of the police work, raise the particular need for behavioral management mechanisms. One of those mechanisms is holding police officers accountable for their arbitrary use of power resulting from unfettered discretion, which poses a threat to the well-being of people or takes their liberty. According to Bordner, professionalizing police has contributed to the maintenance of discretion, but there is a need for improvement in police and the way of holding its officers accountable (Bordner, 1983). Precisely, they should be financially and criminally accountable.

The accountability would impose liability on the individual police officers and their organizations. In the American context, Carol Archbold (2004) mentions that administrative control over police can reduce police use of force and other policing strategies that pose threats to the life and liberty of citizens. She also discusses the introduction of police legal advisors and risk managers in police agencies since the 1960s. Despite the effort made, police liability is still a field that needs much attention.

Conclusion

The role of the police in the context of law enforcement is incredible as a matter of order and safety in the society are concerned. It helps the development of citizens in all sectors. However, to effectively prevent and work out any difficulty in this regard, police officers, in their daily remits, should use their discretionary power consistently with the set standards. Police officers may use force only in circumstances determined by the law, although that use should be reasonable and necessary so as not to pose any threat to human life and welfare. It is concluded that police discretion should be minimized to a certain extent during legislation and setting police standards of work as well as codes of ethics. Thus, the government needs to enact and enforce specific laws that provide penalties for the police officers who trespass the provisions by imposing an aggravating circumstance on them as they would be ensuring the rights of citizens rather than hampering them.

Recommendations

As an educational psychologist Derry highlighted, there is a need for putting people of different skills and expertise together to address the issues facing the community today (Ledford, 2015). Interdisciplinarity is more critical to deal with the issues of police behavior vis-à-vis society. Thus, there should be open dialogue between the police and the police organizations and local communities to assess the characters who are immoral and improper under the standards and expectations of the local community. Moreover, although the use of deadly force is employed in life-threatening situations, police officers should lessen its application. Finally, to prevent unfettered discretion, there should be a development of emotional support and counseling for the police. On the other hand, police accountability should be imposed to prevent extralegal methods while on duty.

Discussion Questions

1. What is "police discretion", its source, and extent?
2. How does the police work help the law achieve its objectives in society?
3. What is the police position in the implementation of the law?
4. What are the principles that the police should ensure in rendering justice to society?
5. Could police officers be held accountable for their misconduct and abuse of power? If yes, how?

Notes

1. *West's Encyclopedia of American Law*, (2nd ed.). S.v. "power." Retrieved November 12, 2018, from https://legal-dictionary.thefreedictionary.com/power.
2. *Black's Law Dictionary* (2nd ed.). The four pillars of the rule of law. https://thelawdictionary.org/article/four-pillars-rule-of-law/.
3. Article 19 para. 1 of the Law of the Republic of Indonesia Number 2 Year 2002 Concerning the State Police of the Republic of Indonesia.
4. *Black's Law Dictionary* (2nd ed.). The four pillars of the rule of law. https://thelawdictionary.org/article/four-pillars-rule-of-law/.
5. Miranda rights: The who, what, where, when and why. *LawInfo*. Retrieved March 29, 2019, from https://resources.lawinfo.com/criminal-defense/miranda-rights-the-who-what-where-when-and-wh.html.
6. *Black's Law Dictionary* (2nd ed.). The four pillars of the rule of law. https://thelawdictionary.org/article/four-pillars-rule-of-law/.
7. US Department of Justice, Law Enforcement Assistance Administration, National Institute of Law Enforcement and Criminal Justice, "A community concern: police use of deadly force" (1979).
8. *Black's Law Dictionary* (2nd ed.). Law enforcement and protection. https://thelawdictionary.org/article/law-enforcement-protection/.

References

Archbold, Carol A. (2004). *Police accountability, risk management, and legal advising* (Marilyn McShane & Frank P. Williams III, Eds.). New York, NY: LFB Scholarly Publishing LLC.

Black's Law Dictionary Free Staff. (2018). The four pillars of the rule of law. In *Black's law dictionary* (2nd ed.). https://thelawdictionary.org

Black's Law Dictionary Staff. (2018). Law enforcement & protection. In *Black's law dictionary free online legal dictionary* (2nd ed.). https://thelawdictionary.org/article/law-enforcement-protection/

Bordner, Diane. (1983). Routine policing, discretion, and the definition of law, order, and justice in society. *Criminology, 21*(2), 294–304. https://doi.org/10.1111/j.1745-9125.1983.tb00263.x

Chambliss, William J. (2001). *Power, politics, and crime. Animal genetics* (Vol. 39). John Hagan. Colorado, CO: Westview Press.

Chan, Janet B. L. (1999). Governing police practice: Limits of the new accountability. *The British Journal of Sociology, 50*(2), 251–70. https://doi.org/10.1111/j.1468-4446.1999.00251.x

Framingham, Jane. (2018). Minnesota multiphasic personality inventory (MMPI). *Psych Central*, from https://psychcentral.com/lib/minnesota-multiphasic-personality-inventory- mmpi and file:///C:/Users/Guest2/OneDrive/Desktop/36C25620Q0012-005.pdf

Goluboff, Risa. (2016). *Vagrant nation : Police power, constitutional change, and the making of the 1960s*. New York, NY: Oxford University Press.

Groeneveld, Richard F. (2005). *Arrest discretion of police officers : The impact of varying organizational structures*. New York, NY: LFB Scholarly Publishing LLC.

Heilmann, Michael Raymond. (2006). *Principals' perspectives on discretion and decision-making*. Canada: University of Manitoba.

Hirby, James. (2018). *Law enforcement & protection*. Retrieved from thelawdictionary.org

Kathleen, H., & Hill Gerald, N. (n.d.). Power. In *West's encyclopedia of American law*. United States of America: The Gale Group.

Kleinig, John. (2008). *Ethics and criminal justice: An introduction*. Cambridge: Cambridge University Press.

Laguna, Louis, Agliotta, Joseph, & Mannon, Stephanie. (2013). Pre-employment screening of police officers: Limitations of the MMPI-2 K-Scale as a useful predictor of performance. *Journal of Police and Criminal Psychology, 30*(1), 1. https://doi.org/10.1007/s11896-013-9135-9

Ledford, Heidi. (2015). How to solve the world's biggest problems. *Nature*. https://doi.org/10.1038/525308a

Lovert, Frank. (2011). *Rawls's 'a theory of justice': A reader's guide*. New York, NY: Continuum International Publishing Group.

Mandle, Jon. (2009). *Rawls's a theory of justice: A animal genetics*. New York, NY: Cambridge University Press.

McCartney, S., & Parent, R. (2015). *Ethics in law enforcement*. Victoria, BC: BCcampu.

Miranda rights: The who, what, where, when and why. *LawInfo*. Retrieved March 29, 2019, from https://resources.lawinfo.com/criminal-defense/miranda-rights-the-who-what-where-when-and-wh.html

Oliver, Ian. (1987). *Police, government and accountability* (1st ed.). London: The Macmillan Press Ltd. https://doi.org/10.1007/978-1-349-18557-3

Papazoglou, Konstantinos. (2014). Police misconduct. *George Washington Law Review, 1,* 1–7. https://doi.org/10.1002/9781118517383.wbeccj029

Rawls, John. (1999). *A theory of justice* (Rev. ed.). Cambridge, MA: Harvard University Press.

Republic of Indonesia. (2002). *The law of the Republic of Indonesia number 2 year 2002 concerning the state police of the Republic of Indonesia.*

Roufa, Timothy. (2018). What to know about the psychological screening for police officers. *The Balance Careers.*

Seron, Carroll, Pereira, Joseph, and Kovath, Jean. (2004). Judging police misconduct : "Street-level" versus professional policing. *Law & Society Review, 38*(4), 665–710.

Twersky-Glasner, Aviva (2005). Police personality: What is it and why are they like that? *Journal of Police and Criminal Psychology, 20*(1), 56–67. https://doi.org/10.1007/BF02806707

Walker, Jeffery T., & Hemmens, C. (2011). *Legal guide for police constitutional issues* (Shirley Decker-Lucke & Elisabeth Ebben). United States of America: Elsevier Inc.

Walker, Samuel. (2007). Police accountability: Current issues and research needs. *National Institute of Justice Police Planning Research Workshop*, no. 218583, 1–35.

Williams, Kristian (2015). *Our enemies in Blue: Police and power in America* (3rd ed.). Oakland, CA: AK Press.

Chapter 8

The Role of Legitimacy in Police Reform and Effectiveness

A Case Study on the Bangladesh National Police

Heath Grant, Shanna O'Reilly, and Staci Strobl

Introduction

In Bangladesh since 2013, there have been religiously motivated, and often brutal, murders of approximately two dozen secular bloggers and activists (The Economist, 2016), as well as targeted killings of members of the LGBT (lesbian, gay, bisexual, and transgender) community. In addition, concerns about increasingly violent extremist attacks, including one on July 1, 2016, at the Holy Artisan Bakery, a prominent café in the upscale Gulshan-2 neighborhood, only highlight intensifying social problems and the need for more inclusive politics, community-level prevention, and effective police operations. The media spotlight on this spate of violence has drawn into question the police reform program in place in recent years, necessitating a critical review of how a well-intentioned community-policing program in the country may have failed to provide long-term increased security.

In 2007, the crime rate was 91.5 crimes per 100,000 people, with the most frequently reported being property crimes (Kashem, 2010). However, according to the US State Department's Overseas Advisory Council, common crime challenges like property theft have remained relatively constant since then and are no more frequent in Bangladesh than they might be in any major city across the US. What does continue to be signaled as a major threat, though, are the increasing levels of ethnically, socially, and especially politically motivated violence taking place across the country (Bangladesh Crime and Safety Report, 2014).

Politics and the Police in Bangladesh

The country's "criminalization of politics," as termed by ex–inspector general of police and Bangladeshi police reform expert A.S.M. Shahjahan, is evident through regular street violence and protests (called *hartals*) instigated by followers or leaders of the country's major political parties. While historically rooted in Gandhi's civil disobedience against colonial rule, these mass protests today take the form of fear-inducing national shutdowns of all transportation, shops, factories, ports, courts of law, schools, and general operations across the country for up to five business days at a time. Between 1991 and 2013, there was an average of 46 *hartals* per year (Dasgupta, 2013). During this time, *hartal* "activists," often with the assistance of the organizing political party's student wing, took to the streets to engage in a variety of violent acts, including burning buses, deployment of explosives like Molotov cocktail bombs, and other serious forms of aggression. Unfortunately, *hartal* participants are oftentimes no more than hired hands, recruited from the slums by members of the organizing party or its opposition in an effort to disrupt day-to-day operations for as little as ten *taka* (approximately USD 0.13) per day. (Ahsan & Iqbal, 2014).

This increase in violence and the overall culture of confrontation, combined with the country's corrupt party politics, affects not only the general population but also the national

DOI: 10.4324/9781003047117-9

government's ability to govern. With regard to corruption in particular, Bangladesh was ranked 139 out of 167 reviewed countries in Transparency International's (TI) Corruption Perceptions Index in 2015 (Transparency International, 2015). Evidence of this low ranking is present in the fight between political leaders for limited state resources within major institutions like the police, as well as across society more broadly in the amount of unauthorized bribes paid for public services and goods (e.g. security, health, etc.). For instance, according to TI's 2013 index, 39% of citizens surveyed reported having paid a bribe within the previous 12 months, and 72% of those who did said this was specifically during dealings with the police. According to the survey, the main reasons for paying the bribe were simply to obtain services (58%), to speed things up (33%), to express gratitude (7%), or ultimately to acquire services at a cheaper rate than normal (3%) (Transparency International, 2013). Furthermore, the 2012 index shows that citizen perceptions of key sectors most affected by corruption are the police (78% of respondents), with labor migration and land administration coming in at a close second and third (77% and 75.8%, respectively) (Transparency International, 2012). However, more broadly speaking, the lack of transparency in political party finances generally facilitates the widespread abuse of state resources, including use of police in support and coverage of illicit activities by politicians. Specifically, government corruption typically involves members of parliament (MPs), 97% of whom have been found to be actively engaged in influencing local government administration, job placements of police and those in other key posts, transfers, large public contracts, development projects, and overall procurement decisions (McDevitt, 2015).

This is compounded by a recent rise in extremist violent attacks (hacking by machete), especially on religious Hindu and Buddhist minorities, as well as secular targets such as journalists, bloggers, professors, and LGBT individuals and activities. Since September 2015, there have been over 30 such attacks, and Islamic State of Iraq and the Levant (ISIL) has claimed responsibility for 21 of them (Al Jazeera, June 2016). These attacks culminated in the largest one to date, on July 1, 2016, when five young men entered the Holy Artisan Café armed with bombs, guns, and a sword and immediately opened fired and detonated several bombs into the crowd, taking a number of people hostage. During the course of the evening, and eventually as part of the Bangladeshi government's rescue response, Operation Thunderbolt, 29 people were killed, including 20 hostages, two police, and two bakery staff, as well as the five attackers. While ISIL claimed responsibility for the incident and released photos as it was taking place, Bangladeshi Home Minister Asaduzzaman Khan argued that the perpetrators were not from ISIL, but rather part of Jamaat-ul-Mujahideen (JMB), a local militant organization outlawed in 2005 for a series of 500 bomb attacks across the country. JMB, and other extremist groups like them, are believed to be growing in popularity, developing a network of at least 10,000 members across the country (Stahl, 2007) and alleged financial assistance from international donor networks in Kuwait, Pakistan, Libya, and elsewhere (Ahsan, 2005).

While experts continue to debate the evidence regarding which of the groups is responsible for each of the attacks—and whether the source is homegrown or internationally linked— Prime Minister Sheikh Hasina's government's ongoing denial of their existence has allowed for a politicized response to the issue, often by leveraging terrorism as a pretext for her government's pursuit of political adversaries, rather than developing a comprehensive counterterrorism approach (Stark, 2016). Law enforcement is often drawn into a political game, with their time characteristically being occupied by serving the political apparatus and ongoing consolidation of power by the national ruling political party (Awami League for the past two terms), rather than the establishment of security and protection of citizens' rights.

Clearly, based on the backdrop of growing violence and an increasingly complex political response, redirecting police from protection of the ruling political party to citizen-centric policing has not been successful. Within that context, "imported" Western policing models tend to inadequately consider the social and political forces at play within the country and fail. As a post-colonial nation-state, Bangladesh suffers from a lack of internal cohesion and political instability and oftentimes still applies outdated colonial policies that exacerbate identity politics and promote exclusion. Based on field experience with police in Bangladesh, this research presents the police problem as part of a larger, post-colonial political crisis around the lack of legitimacy of the current ruling party and its police, providing a framework for understanding citizen security issues in Bangladesh. We assess the socio-political context through a discussion of political legitimacy and typical community levels of collective efficacy in the country and point to building legitimacy and collective efficacy as ingredients for more successful community policing.

The Post-Colonial Conundrum

Police legitimacy problems in Bangladesh find their origin in the colonial past. Far from being fully finished, the colonial past is palpable in the present as the basic institutional contours of the Bangladeshi government, including its police, were established under colonialism and have been maintained since without significant structural change. Modern policing in Bangladesh is a creature of the British colonial experience and, in contemporary times, an institution beholden to the modern nation-state. Colonially defined as a part of British India involved what Deleuze and Guattari (1988) have described as an abrupt and Western-imposed process of territorialization in which boundaries are drawn, placed, and named by the colonial power; deterritorialization, in which the colonial power appropriates the designated territory in order to administer it for its purposes; and reterritorialization, in which violent transformations of the social, political, and even geographical landscape occur, leading to internal resistance to these life-altering upheavals. Like many deconstructionist approaches to the colonial experience, the seeds of its unraveling are present from the beginning.

The imposition of the colonial and/or modern nation-state for Bengal is a unique path through British India, unified Pakistan, and then as an independent country in 1971. This pathway, however, started from the centralization of the "chief concentrated means of violence" (Tilly, 1985, p. 170) in Mughal and then colonial forms. These ruling powers previously maintained the authority for legitimate violence in the territory. Eclipsing traditional modes of order maintenance and violence is the necessary precursor to modern policing so that local communities become subordinate to the government rather than to their customary patrons. The imperial British agents developed modern policing, which eventually delegitimized and replaced previous forms of justice. In doing so, the locus of control shifted to the state, where it has remained—tempered only by more recent forces, such as the rise of globalization, multi-national corporations, and international laws and treaties around human rights standards, which perhaps impinge on the primacy of the state. With such a history, the style, mode, and authority of the police force can be considered alienated from the masses and their traditional cultural practices, particularly as the force continues to impose a British-style bureaucracy and mode of authority in a political and social space that is in flux.

Bangladesh is hardly unique in facing this general problem of post-colonialism. We draw broadly on post-colonialism, which challenges largely Western discourses, like police studies, to question the dominant way in which non-Western, formerly colonized spaces are characterized, hoping to avoid analysis that is ethnocentric or lacking in contextual nuance. The notion that colonial encounters ruptured local historical patterns of social, cultural, and political relations has been described vividly in the work of post-colonial theorist Gayatri Chakravorty Spivak (1999), among other post-colonial scholars of note (e.g. Bhabha, 1994; Said, 1993; Chatterjee, 1986). In Spivak's work, generally speaking, the ideal role of government is to be the vehicle of economic redistribution after divisive and fragmented historical ruptures, which concentrated social goods with particular privileged groups as defined by national, religious, ideological, or ethnic identity (2010). Spivak champions the subaltern, or the unvoiced lower class, who, if given a voice, can provide the most cutting critique of the unequal present; however, she is also careful to insist that identity-laden critiques are only pass-through spaces for societies to achieve a more universal notion of inclusion. In other words, finding resistance in the poor and dispossessed acts as a vehicle by which a more just society can be potentially constructed; power as usual must be questioned.

The imposition of imperial modes of power and control inevitably led to cultural translations, culturally hybrid histories, and new marginalities as the new eclipses the old—though never completely. Hybrid forms then "grow in pertinence when they are transposed back into specific post-colonial conditions" (Boehmer & Chaudhuri, 2011). In other words, the historical shifts in the colonial period are far from undone at independence, and the legacy of the past continues to play out in the cultural, political, and social fields within the contemporary country. As Spivak (1999) has argued, the hybridity created by colonial disruptions spawns fragile power balances after independence, involving weak national governments. Veer (1994) has argued that such modernization efforts and consolidation of power in a state create nationalism as both a unifier and as a source of exclusion. In this case, Bangladeshi policing emerges from the colonial era as a creature that is alternately Bengali, Muslim, and British colonial, among other possibilities.

British Colonial Rule: Creating Hindu-Muslim Difference

The story of understanding how fragmented political unity undermines government and thereby police legitimacy requires a *longue durée* approach. Contemporary Bangladeshi policing traces its origins to almost 200 years of British rule in the Indian sub-continent (1757–1947 CE), as well as incorporating some remaining elements of the pre-British period that was the Muslim Persianate Mughal Empire. While there was no formal police force during the Mughal period, *kotwals*, or local leaders of cities, towns, and small villages, were charged with controlling police, military, and other public service functions. *Kotwals* were appointed by the central government to support in the management of local governing units, and, to this day, some police stations still retain the name of *kotwal* as part of their administrative title.

When moving beyond the standard government constructs, order maintenance and public safety was traditionally a function of the *samaj*: a localized religious and mutual benefit association drawing from a village's extended patrilineal clans. In addition to the maintenance of a mosque and its mullah, the *samaj* featured a council of elders (*matabdars* or *sardars*) who settled village disputes. Competition between the *matabdars* formed the larger political environment of the region (Rahim, 1989). In the historical accounts of the Mughal Empire, we see that the main fault lines between groups in Bengali-Mughal society rests along Muslim-centric identity markers: *ashraf* (Muslims of the elite class of foreign origin), non-*ashraf* (indigenous Muslims), and non-Muslims (often Hindus) formed the lesser *ashraf* (Uddin, 2006).

Subsequent to the Mughal Empire, Bangladesh came under control of the British Empire starting in 1757, when the British East India Company defeated the Indian army in Bengal after a commercial dispute. By the nineteenth century, the British had perfected the Raj system, in which its power was mediated through local princes. British colonialists constructed a notion of Indian society, of which Bengal was a part, as consisting of caste and village, led by princes. Many books of the time made linkages between the British caste system and the European feudal one of the past. As a result, in arranging a bureaucracy, they privileged the less *ashraf*, or Hindu leaders, and arranged a bureaucracy that exacerbated religious differences. Distinguishing themselves from the allegedly despotic Muslim empire that came before, Cannadine (2001) describes the British obsession with the *durbar*, or elaborate ceremonial meetings between the ruler and those being ruled in Indian communities, which British officials often presided over along with the Raj princes. According to Uddin (2006), it was the construction of the Indian social system through British eyes that set the stage for the contested identities seen today in Bangladesh: Bengali ethnolinguistic nationalists, religious nationalisms, and Islamists. Van Schendel (2009) also credits the colonial period as cementing the saliency of Hindu-Muslim difference in local politics.

Despite the colonial superstructure and its influence on constructions of identity, colonial development policy largely left the people of Bengal on their own, save for matters of the economic management of resources. The administrative seat of the region was Kolkata (then Calcutta). As the imperial age progressed, the rise of an English-educated middle class ensued in the regional seat while rural Bengal remained relatively undeveloped, in terms of infrastructure and governance, due to the British policy of "permanent settlement." This policy established a land-tax system in which land owners (*zamindars*) collected taxes for the British through a series of intermediaries, with peasant labor on the bottom of the system and a "leisured class" on the top (Van Schendel, 2009). According to Chatterjee (1986), the upper class was predominantly Hindu while the lower class was predominantly Muslim. By the late nineteenth century, economic inequalities became so pronounced that the colonial planning department took on the mission of tackling rural poverty, considered pervasive and widespread in the territory. This mission often was described in paternal and infantilizing discourse (Bhuiyan, Faraizi, & McAllister, 2008), falling into the more general colonial frame of colonized (and Muslim) people being characterized as unable to take care of themselves and needing the guidance of the West (Said, 1993).

Under the Raj, police were employed as an arm of the state, meant not to serve and protect the public, but rather to amass and protect power among British colonizers. Sub-inspectors (SIs) of police were the administrative unit created and charged with overseeing law and order in each individual district in the Indian sub-continent and continue to exist with the same political charge today in Bangladesh. To support their operations, the 1861 Police Act was created in the aftermath of the Mutiny of 1857 (or the First War of Independence), as a means of squelching any further dissent or potential revolts within the colony. The power of the SIs, as well as the broader national police, was and continues to be situated within the hands of the state government, with the head, or inspector general of police (IGP) being assigned by the chief minister of national security, and the local SIs by the district commissioners (DCs). This is one of the challenges that has resulted in limited operational independence for police, who are often required to respond more to the needs of the state apparatus than to those of the community at large. To the extent to which they served the public in colonial times, locals often referred to the police as a form of *ma-bap* (mother-father) governance, in which their interests were not considered (Gould, Sherman, & Ansari, 2013). Although the basic principles of the British police at home involved being keepers of the monarch's peace, but always with an eye toward serving a local community, the colonial police jettisoned the local needs of the community ideal in other lands. Many colonial territories,

> which the British have been called upon to administer and govern, impos[e] upon [the people] an alien law until they have developed to the point of being able to legislate for themselves and manage their own affairs.
>
> (Jeffries, 1952, p. 25)

In British India, the function of the police was considered more "Roman" in nature, in which centralized forced is used in a militarized sense in order to maintain local law and order (Jeffries, 1952, p. 25), whether practiced by a British colonial police service officer or an Indian recruit. Although the hope was to create self-governing law and order as an alleged distant prospect, the day-to-day reality involved shoring up the colonial government against potential civilian acts of resistance and rebellion. According to Gwynn (1939), British colonial police systems blurred the boundaries of police and military, often using the army (the Indian Army) to maintain civil control and to put down small wars and even enforce labor provisions and taxation schemes. Meanwhile, they neglected internal crime problems (Sinclair & Williams, 2007).

The Ever-Present History of Partition

Today's Bangladesh achieved post-colonial status when, as part of India, it gained independence from British colonial rule during the Indian Independence Movement in 1947. As part of this process of decolonization, the country was partitioned into what are present-day India and Pakistan, divided between West Pakistan and East Pakistan, or present-day Bangladesh. East Pakistan was slated by the British decolonizers as the territory of the Muslim Bengali people, while Hindu Bengali people were to migrate to the Bengali state within India. Mass migrations and ethnic violence characterized Partition, making both countries fraught spaces for people caught betwixt and between the new notions of identity (defined religiously) and territory. Civil employees were allowed to choose where they wanted to land, but, as Feldman (2003) describes, the displacement's effect on institutional development was to create "uncertainty about its personnel . . . at a time when massive upheaval and dislocation called for political coherence and the securing of social order" (p. 118). As a result, policing was in a severe state of flux, and police officers chose between two countries, shifting from one side of the dividing line to the other.

Further, the lack of resources to shore up the institution once the social order began to settle made investing in new institutions difficult. Many of the resources promised Dhaka from Calcutta never materialized, leaving East Pakistan wanting in terms of administrative technology and capacity (Feldman, 2003). According to Feldman (2003) and Zafarullah (2007), with the limited resources available, the government established an elite cadre of generalist administrators, the Civil Service of Pakistan (CSP), derived directly from the colonial administrators known as the Indian Civil Service (ICS). Zafarullah's (2007) analysis described the CSP in contemporary Bangladesh as primarily serving to maintain itself, acting with great autonomy from the masses and often from politicians as well. These empowered bureaucrats are drawn from the same social backgrounds and education and enter a system of vertical integration, which only promotes from within. Coupled with frequent regime changes, the civil bureaucracy acted as a kind of institutional glue in an otherwise unstable power landscape.

Civil War (1971) and the Police

The Bangladesh Liberation War arose out of what was a Bengali nationalist push for self-determination after genocide performed by the Pakistani military on students and others involved in the liberation movement across rural and urban Bangladesh. This violent crackdown by the military, called Operation Searchlight, was in response to political discontent when the then–East Pakistani Awami League political party was ignored after winning the March 25, 1971, elections.

Before the start of the 1971 operation, all international journalists were deported from East Pakistan to ensure no internal coverage of the atrocity (Siddiqui, 1997), and, during it, all Bengali members of the military service were either disarmed or killed. While the Pakistani armed forces initially denied any pre-calculated deaths, the systematic killing of Bengalis, Hindus, and other affected refugees is estimated to have resulted in between approximately 200,000 and 3,000,000 deaths, as well as 1.5 million refugees (Van Schendel, 2009). The scale of impact was first made public when Pakistani journalist Anthony Mascarenhas was sent by the military to write the story up favorably but instead fled to the United Kingdom to publish an article in the BBC on what was actually happening. This article was the first global call for attention to the genocide taking place and paved the way for further international coverage, as well as an eventual intervention on the part of the Indian government and other countries.

Notwithstanding the bloodshed suffered by leaders of the Bengali independence movement, violence was felt by parties on all sides. In fact, one of the major criticisms has been the inability of the Bengali, Indian, and Pakistani governments to address the refugee issue that was created across the three countries' international borders as a result of Partition. In the case of Bangladesh, nationalist sentiments are strong, and, as a result, Pakistanis, Hindus, and others deemed to have been potentially unsupportive of the liberation movement were subject to persecution and torture at the time of the war and continue to bear the brunt of major discrimination efforts even today.

Interestingly, a significant number of the current Bangladesh National Police (BNP) leadership previously served as freedom fighters during the Liberation War period. At that time, they worked with law enforcement sympathetic to the Bengali movement, using police stations in East Pakistan as a frontline for arming the movement's supporters, under guidance from the Major (and eventual Bangladeshi Prime Minister) Ziaur Rahman, who oversaw refugee camp operations and fighting against Pakistani forces. Subsequently, many of the civilian freedom fighters from that period were compensated at the time of independence with integration into society and government through prime positions, especially among the national police force, as a reward for their service.

Put in the larger post-colonial context, the occurrence of the Liberation War can be explained as part of an insufficient resolution of the role of the central Pakistani government in administration of East and West Pakistan, as inherited from the vice-regal tradition of the British Raj. Because colonialism fostered a Bengal which initially privileged Hindu elites over Muslims, the government focus on an indigenous Bengali-language-and-culture-based political party was a foreseeable reaction to the social exclusion of this group from the political arena. From 1971 to 1975, the Bangladeshi government, under the Awami League, faced the challenge of disarming the civil war's freedom fighters and establishing law and order; unfortunately, corruption, nepotism, and party loyalty over parliamentary democracy prevailed. As part of this, in 1972, the Awami government seated a genocide investigation committee that engaged in the prosecutions of approximately 2,800 alleged collaborators with West Pakistan, though Majibur Rahman granted a general amnesty the following year.

To tamp down these social and political cleavages (now directed mostly at Hindu, Muslim, and ethnolinguistic communities) and to manage the demands of ordinary Bengalis, who were dissatisfied with the exclusivity of the Awami League's rule, a "bureaucratic military oligarchy" under President Zia ensued as a result of a coup d'état (Raghavan, 2013). This was similar to the fate that befell a number of post-colonial states in the 1970s, representing a general crisis in which decolonization failed to foster healthy new governments but rather saw disappointments through the reestablishment of elites instead of democracy, strident nationalism, and military rule.

The Bangladesh National Police: Strong Arm of the Ruling Party

Today, the BNP is a centralized police force, which functions under substantial supervision from the Ministry of Home Affairs. Its main operational branch is police headquarters in Dhaka, headed by the IGP with the support of additional inspector generals (AIGs) in charge of administration, key departments and deputy inspector generals (DIGs). There are several branches, which include the Central Investigation Division (CID), Special Branch (SB), and Rapid Action Battalion (RAB), responsible for investigating serious crimes and acts of terrorism; metropolitan, range, and highway police; Dhaka Metropolitan Police; and others. Range police are divided into districts (overseen by the SIs mentioned earlier), circles, and then *thanas* at local-level police stations or outposts, across which the BNP's 18 total ranks function. Approximately 123,000 make up the entire force, with at least 1,500 working in the gazette ranks, and the rest of police services occurring in one of the approximately 600 local police stations. A majority of police officials are at the subordinate level, including head constables, naiks, and constables, and perform their duties with limited training. There are currently no minimum training requirements for constables, and poor pay and work conditions can easily include up to 14-hour days with almost no weekends or time off for visiting immediate family, often located in other parts of the country due to frequent police transfers.

These numbers nationally translate to approximately one police officer or less for every 1,200 people in the districts, which is only one-third of the ratio recommended by the United Nations (2016) (1 officer: 450 citizens). In addition, the fact that subordinate and junior police make up a large portion of the police force, and many of them are assigned to administrative or political duties—e.g., serving tea, shoe shining, accompanying senior ranking party members on official duty, and other tasks—means that very few senior staff are actually available to engage in and respond to citizen needs and overall crime and violence. Of that police population, minority groups and women constitute a very small portion, the latter of which was at only 5.24% in early 2014 and situated mostly in the subordinate ranks. This limits the access to justice of vulnerable populations, such as women and minorities, who might feel uncomfortable reporting a crime, violence, or systematic abuse to members of a majority male force who are usually from the country's dominant ethnic group (International Crisis Group, 2009).

The state maintains strong control over police operations and the budget, and "politicization" of the police is considered a major problem (Kashem, 2010, p. 26), as is the case in many non-Western, British post-colonial nations. The entire force operates on a budget of approximately 400,000 *taka* and is part of the country's internal revenues system, along with other public goods, such as education and health care. Because policing plays a far second fiddle within the political arena, corrupt practices are basically perceived to be a necessary evil to make up for any resulting budgetary shortfalls that limit police salaries and institutional resources. Frequently, officers must pay "out of pocket" for basic equipment, such as fuel for vehicles; bicycle and rickshaw transportation to investigate crimes; or even office supplies such as snacks, stationary, pens, paper, and printer toner. This is difficult to do when, for example, at the bottom of the pay scale, police make as little as 5,500 *taka* (approximately 70 USD) per month, and, at the middle level, the going salary is 23,000 *taka* (approximately 300 USD), with little opportunity for promotion.

As a result, low-level corruption is present in the form of bribes or *baksheesh* of approximately 100 *taka* (a little over USD 1) and most frequently collected by police who have significant contact with the public, such as traffic or street cops. This complements some of the more high-level politically supported corruption practices, such as government contracts awarded by senior police for improving facilities or providing special protection to politicians or other elites. On top of the bribes involved in day-to-day operations, most officers must pay a political bribe to a particular party to buy their way into the system upon entering the police. This bribe can be anywhere between 60,000 and 100,000 *taka* (USD 870–1,450), but it secures them a government job in exchange for allegiance to a particular political party. Members of parliament and other senior-ranking government officials, in turn, support this process by purchasing a quota of spots to, in effect, "guarantee the loyalty" of incoming law enforcement officials. Officers who are desperate for access to a stable income, especially in rural areas, have been known to sell dowry and family assets such as land or cattle and/or even take out loans from the village loan shark (International Crisis Group, 2009) to obtain these spots.

Upon taking power, every successive incoming government since independence has made a practice of removing the majority of all top police and other government officials installed during the previous administration's time in office and promoting new ones loyal to the current political party to take their place. For example, during the 2001–2006 Bangladesh National Party administration, almost 800 police officers were dismissed on political grounds, while 1,000 were encouraged to retire, and 65 senior officers were sacked. This approach not only disrupts the natural chain of command within police hierarchy, combined with other corrupt practices; it also reduces the functionality of basic police skills and their application in daily operations.

Notwithstanding the day-to-day corrupt practicalities for covering daily work and other police-related expenses, Gould et al. (2013) advances a larger systemic explanation for the different levels of corruption that exist across the police, and throughout Bangladesh, based on the need for political allegiances. According to his theory, at Partition, the government, and in particular, the police, were highly unpopular, as the despotism of the Raj was criticized widely, and the Indian independence movement was in full swing. In India and Pakistan, hope that the new government would reform colonial institutions, including the police, was quite high. Unfortunately, the form that Partition took, as a violent and catastrophic breaking of the very social fabric across the former colonized space, led to a weak political and social foundation. Groups struggled against each other in violent contests for local power and control, often targeted for inclusion or exclusion in new government agencies based on ethnic identity. Minorities in any space were seen in a suspicious light, and civil servants who relocated during the upheaval hoped to find jobs in their new space. As a result, loyalty doubts existed across the social spectrum, and the uneven access to working in government, including jobs like policing, led to a flux in available services. Coupled with physical and economic insecurity, ordinary people turned to informal practice to secure what they needed and advance their everyday interests in accordance with a political culture supportive of such corruption. Subsequent anti-corruption, social, and political movements ultimately were ineffective and were unfortunately often used to fight vendettas against political enemies. Given that, since Partition, the country has moved through military rule and into post–civil war modes of one-party domination, the sense of trust and legitimacy in the police and other political agencies remains low and only intensifies the initial divides that existed between social groups, as well as those that exist now between government, police, and the citizens they serve.

Even before the most recent period of questionable human rights practices by the Bangladeshi police, Rafiqul and Solaiman (2003) documented the routinized nature of police torture in Bangladeshi police custody. From 1972 until 2003, the researchers reported that there were 19,000 police custody deaths in Bangladesh, with only a handful of them ever tried as crimes, despite being contrary to the Constitution of Bangladesh's provisions for the right to life and personal liberty (Article 32), equality before the law (Article 27), protection of law (Article 31), and safeguards against arrest and detention (Article 33).

Today, Bangladesh police and security forces continue to use excessive force in managing street protests, most recently killing 150 protesters and injuring at least 2,000 between February and October 2013 alone (Human Rights Watch, 2013). As part of these operations, police and the paramilitary Rapid Action Battalion (RAB) often indiscriminately fire into crowds and are known to brutally beat protesters (ibid.). Many of the protests that police have reacted to in the last couple of years are part of a public outcry (both in favor of and against) decisions from the International Criminal Tribunal regarding war crimes, such as genocide, rape, and crimes against humanity, committed during the 1971 Liberation War. These war trials are perceived by many to be directed toward punishment of opposition leaders and do not have legitimacy from any type of international buy-in, despite the name of the tribunal.

Varied Attempts at Police Reform

Since the 1971 split from then–West Pakistan, Bangladesh has been host to more than half a dozen committees created to promote police reform and modernization of the system. Included within these is the Police Reform Programme (PRP), launched in 2005 by the Ministry of Home Affairs, with financial support of over ten million pounds from the UNDP and the British Department for International Development (DFID) during two phases: Phase I from 2005 to 2009 and Phase II from 2009 to 2014. PRP has been lauded as one of the biggest efforts of its kind, with a focus on improving crime prevention, investigations, operations, prosecutions, human resource management, training, and strategic capacity and oversight. Significant results that have come out of the program, including the investigation of over 17,000 corruption cases by a recently created internal oversight unit, the first-ever strategic planning process, a considerably more structured approach to community policing, and a proposed 2007 police ordinance meant to supplement the outdated 1861 Police Act. One of the biggest successes touted by PRP is the model police station, or *thana*, effort. As the lowest, albeit most publicly visible, operating space for the police, the *thana* is one of the institution's most important units for the police, and fostering one that can effectively respond to the demands of the public is crucial for success. The PRP's model *thanas* (MTs) have been set up in various districts across the country to "showcase the best practices in policing by fostering an environment that facilitates prevention of crime, provides equitable access to justice and engages the police and public in a meaningful partnership to effectively address community concerns." The MTs are encouraged to use a pro-people, service-oriented form of policing and have standard operating procedures that encourage reform at the most basic level of the police. (See Police Reform Programme Phase II.)

Notwithstanding the positive advances made by PRP, the system of implementation has not been without its complications. For instance, the difference between MTs and regular police stations is stark, and the impact this has on both available resources and delivery has been significant. Those officers and citizens in neighborhoods that don't benefit from the resource boost are often left questioning why the next *thana* over has received an increase not only in resources but also in visibility, as a result of the change. As part of this, there are also concerns that the method for deciding in which districts MTs will be placed is opaque and even politically motivated, and recent allegations of corruption have brought under question the entire process. Specifically, a March 2015 article in the Daily Mail claimed that the DFID funding for police *thanas* was actually being "used to help corrupt regimes stamp out political opposition" in multiple countries where it operates around the world. The article cites a study by the Independent Commission on Aid Impact, which warned that many of the *thanas* that received enhanced equipment, training, and financial support were also the same locations that saw an increase in victimization (48%) and a tripling in the number of bribes paid to officers (Groves, 2015).

Beyond issues surrounding the MTs, however, there are also questions regarding why the 2007 Police Ordinance never passed. This draft ordinance was created under PRP by a reform committee led by ex-IGP A.S.M. Shahjahan and included a vision for an eleven-member national police commission, a police complaints line, a police tribunal, and separation of police operations from political intervention (BD News 24, 2008). However, after awaiting approval within the Ministry of Home Affairs for over three years, the additional secretary eventually gave a public statement "that the proposed ordinance is unrealistic and impractical" in nature and could not be implemented. Based on this public statement and closed-door discussions held among a number of district commissioners at the time, it is believed that the ordinance was tabled for fear of creating too much political independence among the police (Daily Star, 2010).

Besides the UNDP/DFID-supported PRP, a number of other organizations have also provided technical assistance to the Bangladesh National Police, especially as it relates to community-based policing practices. These include the Japanese International Cooperation Agency (JICA), the Department of Justice's International Criminal Investigative Training and Assistance Program (ICITAP), and the Asia Foundation (TAF), the latter of which has been quietly promoting a grassroots approach to community policing in 20 locations since 2008. TAF's efforts received significant recognition and an increase in funding in early 2011, when USAID backed a $3 million TAF-led community-based policing (CBP) initiative in 518 communities across northwest Bangladesh. CBP was paired by the US embassy as the citizen- or community-led arm of the ICITAP's classroom-based approach taught at the police academy to all new incoming police officers. More about these efforts to promote community policing is discussed next; however, it's important to note that these other programs receive only limited commitment from the Bangladesh National Police, being that they could not offer the significant equipment and financial incentives provided by PRP.

Community Policing: Strengths, Flaws, Implementation, and the Importance of Local Context

In 2008, the PRP introduced a national strategy for community policing. The PRP provides a framework for the community policing approach; however, it was never officially approved by the Ministry of Home Affairs because its true application would require de-politicization of, and releasing control of field operations to, the police. That said, many officers still continue to reference the national strategy as a guide for community policing. In fact, senior leaders, such as the current inspector general of police, Mr. Shahidul Hoque, who has been a strong supporter of community policing, have promoted the document as a benchmark for implementation among more junior ranks across the country.

The national strategy for community policing provides a clear definition of what it is and how it aligns with international best practices through an organizational philosophy involving citizen-police partnerships and problem solving. Still, the interpretation of this definition at the field level varies widely, often lending itself to extensive citizen involvement in police operations. In part, this has been done to fill a need created by limited internal staff and resources, but it is also based on a history of mobilization of popular support from communities to push social movements and political agendas. In essence, what it involves is a "deputization" of citizens who lead patrols, capture criminals, and basically serve as a force multiplier in police operations. This reflects a high-level misinterpretation of the meaning of community policing, which ordinarily is not a "force multiplier" meant to augment a lack of police resources.

In some cases, this has empowered citizens to go so far as to dictate how police should run operations, rather than giving them overall support by gathering information, providing testimony, or just generally following the law. In fact, there have been numerous reports of citizens who were even given firearms by police to support their efforts in street patrols. This overt involvement in and control of police operations by citizens is often done by community leaders with strong political or social agendas and has resulted in the persecution of minority groups or members of the opposing political party, in the name of rooting out terrorism. In some cases, citizens involved in the strategy have themselves asked for bribes from other citizens for services. This kind of misinterpretation of the community policing model is not uncommon and has been seen when introduced in other countries as well, such as in South

Africa and Guyana, where community policing has become a highly racially and politically charged endeavor, or Honduras, where some neighborhood security committees have transformed into self-defense groups in areas plagued by gangs and violence. In the case of Bangladesh, alternative interpretations have delegitimized community policing by making it about political party loyalty and eliminating any true representation of, or possibility to address, wider community needs.

Beyond the definition of community policing, the national strategy provides guiding principles for the implementation of community policing forums (CPFs). Approximately 20,000 of these forums were created across the country, based on orders provided by police headquarters in 2008, to encourage spaces where citizens and police could partner on problem solving key crime challenges in their communities. However, representatives from civil society and the police report the forums were created under great time and political pressure, and many of the CPF members who were identified by the police to participate at that time were chosen based on their political leadership and alliances within the community. Likewise, most of these forums have not been reactivated since their creation in 2008, and, as a result, the membership lists are outdated, with names of individuals who have either died or moved on. Furthermore, there is a lack of clarity regarding what types of crimes CPFs should address, with most covering a range from petty theft to conflicts over dowry, child marriage, gender-based violence, land disputes, and even the threat of terrorism. In the case of gender-based violence, this frequently results in CPF members promoting their own interpretation of the law among community members, often by encouraging victims of domestic violence or sexual harassment not to press charges.

Additionally, while community policing has received substantial support among senior police, implementation is still uneven across the police. In part, this is because there are no structured incentives for promoting the community-policing ethos. Community policing is not part of an internal evaluation process, institutional procedures, or daily protocols, and officers who apply it on the job are not rewarded for their efforts, but rather are perceived as working against the institutional culture of the police. Moreover, the national strategy actually designates the creation of community policing officers (CPOs) as a means of concentrating the responsibility of community-policing efforts among a few select individuals at police stations. While in theory, this would appear to prioritize community policing, in practice, many police stations don't have assigned CPOs, which provides an opportunity for sub-inspectors in charge of police stations to either deemphasize or eliminate community policing from daily operations. Furthermore, the regular rotation of police officers, oftentimes as frequent as every six months, limits law enforcement's ability to develop a real connection or partnership with the communities where they work, which is a foundational part of the community-policing approach. The result of this is that community policing is implemented on an ad hoc basis, usually because of the personal initiative of a given officer or his superiors at a specific police station, or because of targeted donor attention in a particular *thana*, instead of through national support and the provision of institutional incentives.

These ongoing challenges raise the question of whether or not importing Western models like community policing actually works. While there has been significant progress in creating a national mandate for community policing, the BNP has yet to develop a lasting organizational structure with a policy, budget, and strategic planning process supportive of best practices in citizen-police relations. This limits the incentives for sustainable implementation of a community police model that, unless truly contextualized and tied to institutional procedures, has the power to move beyond strong national and community-level politics. In this sense, exporting Western models of policing without proper understanding of or consideration for the socio-political context can lead to disastrous results, particularly in the challenging environments of post-colonial societies. The example of failures in even the well-intentioned

The Role of Legitimacy in Police Reform 123

implementation of community policing in the Bangladesh National Police points to at least two important necessary conditions prior to choosing to provide community policing training and technical assistance in a post-colonial country: 1) a moderate level of police legitimacy and 2) community-level collective efficacy as a starting point.

The Need for a Moderate Level of Police Legitimacy

As noted earlier, since its early British post-colonial origins, the BNP has become alienated from the masses and their cultural practices. In other words, there has never been even a modicum of legitimacy for citizens. Legitimacy refers to the degree to which individuals believe an institution or authority is appropriate and proper. When an institution is perceived as a legitimate authority by the people, it reflects a belief that it is to be trusted and its directives obeyed. As a result, legitimacy has a direct influence on individuals' rule violation (Tyler, 2006). Without legitimacy, the average citizen (whether law abiding or not) will not be willing to interact with the police in the meaningful way required for community-policing strategies to be successful. According to a study by Kane, a lack of police legitimacy can be associated with more crimes by citizens. The research suggested that the first indicator of compromised police legitimacy, police misconduct, was linked to more violent crime in high and extremely disadvantaged neighborhoods, controlling for factors such as residential stability, youth population, and spatial and temporal effects. The rule of law represents justice: the more society and/or citizens move away from the rule of law, the more crime prone they are. This means implementing community policing strategies in post-colonial contexts is even more dubious and challenging.

Community policing advocates might argue that this is looking at the theory of change from the wrong direction. Instead, community-policing strategies should be implemented in such societies in order to build needed legitimacy for the police in the first place.

Although it is true that the successful police-community interactions of select community-policing strategies can produce outcomes of legitimacy, the Bangladesh experience suggests that this is very unlikely in post-colonial contexts involving extreme political corruption, human rights abuses, and extensive legacies of citizen mistrust. In Bangladesh, citizens report that the types of officers they are more likely to engage with on a daily basis in the streets are not actually the few CPOs assigned to do community policing at the *thanas*, but rather the poorly trained constables who represent policing to the average citizen. These individuals make up the majority of the police force and have little power to make decisions or engage with citizens on solving general crime and violence problems and instead must wait for orders from more senior officials before taking any significant action. The constables' low capacity and the BNP's use of them as the "frontline" in the community continue to limit institutional legitimacy. In these cases, community-policing strategies may even exacerbate the problem of a lack of legitimacy if implementing authorities are not careful, given the disconnect between community challenges and external political factors affecting the ability to form meaningful police-community partnerships needed for true proactive problem-oriented activities.

Future efforts to build the legitimacy of the Bangladesh National Police may require an increasing separation from the Ministry of Home Affairs and the close control it represents to the political party in power. However, this is likely not the best place to begin. Where a lack of legitimacy is a prolonged, entrenched reality (as in the case of the BNP), it may make good sense to first lay the seeds of community-policing efforts within the community itself, through development of a sense of collective responsibility for community safety.

In Bangladesh, well-intentioned external development support such as that of USAID/ TAF, UNDP, and others ended up simply pushing the community-policing model without contributing or paying attention to the larger needed elements of police reform and professionalization that are necessary for citizen security to truly take root. In fact, this is the case of UNDP in particular; because it supports the wider Police Reform Programme, its officers were set up directly within police headquarters in Dhaka. While this provided greater access to senior police officials and allowed the UNDP to introduce a number of important initiatives—such as the 2007 Police Act and the national community policing strategy—it also impacted the neutrality of some UNDP staff, who were often overly sympathetic to police challenges of corruption and reasons to not push a reform agenda too much.

Without a sophisticated analysis of the socio-political realities in post-colonial societies, implemented Western models of policing will ultimately "take the shape" of these structures beneath the surface in a way that is counterproductive to their original intent.

Collective Efficacy as a Starting Point

The legacy of post-colonial societies is a marked shift of the locus of control to the state. Police-citizen interactions are more transactionally based in a way that can easily give way to corruption. Superimposing community-policing strategies and philosophy on top of this without first addressing the issues leading to a lack of legitimacy will not rectify the situation.

In recent years, the community-based crime prevention literature has identified the importance of collective efficacy, or a neighborhood's trust, cohesion, and shared expectations for control (Sampson, Raudenbush, & Earls, 1997), as being an important ingredient in crime reduction. Creating such shared expectations among citizens for engagement in social control may be a necessary first step for community-policing strategies in post-colonial societies to successfully move beyond the entrenched realities of corruption and abuse. By strengthening collective efficacy among minority or disadvantaged groups, citizens are more equipped to ensure police adherence to the higher standards and meaning of community-policing models.

Thus, repurposing the locus of control or collective efficacy of villages and/or neighborhoods can help ensure a police-community partnership that is capable of working through the difficult realities required to simultaneously restore police legitimacy and successful crime prevention in the long run. Community *panchayats*, or local conflict resolution councils of five or more elders, are one example of a move in this direction in South Asia: specifically, the southern Indian state of Tamil Nadu. Hoping to counter the fear and mistrust of the police that stems from the collective experience of colonial rule, *panchayats* continue to operate as local social-control and order-maintenance institutions. Some local policing efforts have worked with *panchayat*s in order to address long-standing community problems, including violence, that have thwarted the modern policing modus operandi or arrest and criminal prosecution; however, tension remains between *panchayat* elders and the police in a general sense across the region, mostly because there is no specific program or mechanism to govern the cooperation between the two different socio-legal traditions, one based on the individual rights in the modern state and the other based on community norms and values (Vincentnathan & Vincentnathan, 2009). Nonetheless, the notion that leveraging grassroots and traditional forms of order maintenance toward solving crime problems could have great potential in Tamil Nadu.

Further afield, the *sungusungu* movement in Tanzania in the 1990s is more promising as a precedent. In this case, community members organized to respond to the routine crime of stock raiding, gaining legitimacy through traditional village elders and clans. They became such an effective form of social and criminal control they were eventually absorbed into the state as an arm of community policing. Though there is some criticism that their absorption represented a co-option of their locally grounded roots, Heald (2009) argues that ultimately, they have transformed state power at the local level to be more responsive to local concerns. She writes:

> Communities have taken back power, developed their own policing capacity and, in so doing, effectively reinvented themselves. . . . In the same way, perhaps they have reformed and reclaimed the state, with the administration demonstrating an increasing responsiveness to the priorities of local communities, and allowing them a greater degree of autonomy in the management of their own affairs.
>
> (p. 78)

Summary and Recommendations Moving Forward

Prior to the implementation of community-policing models, time would be best spent on increasing the collective efficacy of citizens in places where there has been a historic lack of control or meaningful cooperation with the police. This will help ensure that community policing remains focused on partnership related to relevant and important crime considerations. Needs assessments prior to the implementation of community policing should identify existing resident groups and the socio-political context of their relationship to the police. The extent to which culturally and/or locally significant forms of legitimacy can be leveraged is a key factor in the success of any program, thereby not reinventing the wheel, but rolling with the wheel already in play and using the cultural capital and collective efficacy already in place to some degree. Meaningful collaboration between citizens and the police will not be possible where the governing powers are involved in the selection and direction of who and how police and citizens problem solve toward crime prevention. Where this is so, the citizens will simply become a "voluntary" arm of the existing state-centered power relationship and dynamics.

Police legitimacy is a necessary ingredient prior to implementing community-policing models. Without this, community-policing models are more likely to reinforce existing power or transactional politics that will counter any possible benefits of its implementation.

Discussion Questions

1. Has police reform been successful in Bangladesh?
2. Do law enforcement in Bangladesh work closely on repairing and maintaining partnerships with the community?
3. Does law enforcement in Bangladesh currently follow principles to enforce police reform efforts and effectiveness?
4. Explain the differences between police reform and effectiveness.
5. Explain the issues regarding police reform and effectiveness in Bangladesh.

References

Ahsan, R., & Iqbal, K. (2014). *Political strikes and its impact on trade: Evidence from Bangladeshi transaction-level data*. Retrieved June 27, 2016, from www.theigc.org/wp-content/uploads/2015/02/Ahsan-and-Iqbal-2014-Working-Paper.pdf

Ahsan, Zayadul. (2005, August 22). *Foreign affairs funding, local business keeps them going. The Daily Star.* Retrieved December 26, 2016, from http://archive.thedailystar.net/2005/08/22/d5082201044.htm

Al Jazeera. (2016). *ISIL claims it killed Hindu volunteer in Bangladesh.* Retrieved December 15, 2016, from www.aljazeera.com/news/2016/06/isil-claims-responsibility-bangladesh-killing-160610180627667.html

BD News 24. (2008, January 1). *Draft police ordinance waits home ministry clearance*. Retrieved September 26, 2016, from http://bdnews24.com/bangladesh/2008/01/11/draft-police-ordinance-waits-home-ministry-clearance

Bhabha, H. K. (1994). *The location of culture*. New York, NY: Routledge.

Bhuiyan, A., Faraizi, A., & McAllister, J. (2008). Planning for the deployment of development in Bangladesh. *Progress in Development Studies, 8*(3), 231–240.

Boehmer, E., & Chaudhuri, R. (2011). Introduction. In E. Boehmer & R. Chaudhuri (Eds.), *The Indian postcolonial: A critical reader* (pp. 1–14). London: Routledge.

Cannadine, D. (2001). *Ornamentalism: How the British saw their empire*. Oxford: Oxford University Press.

Chatterjee, P. (1986). *National thought and the colonial world*. London: Zed Books.

Daily Star Editorial. (2010, August 23). *Whither draft police ordinance, 2007?* Retrieved December 26, 2016, from www.thedailystar.net/news-detail-151810

Dasgupta, A (2013). *Sangbad Patrey hartal Chitra*. Dhaka: Press Institute of Bangladesh.

Deleuze, G., & Guattari, F. (1988). *A thousand plateaus: Capitalism and schizophrenia*. London: Continuum.

Feldman, S. (2003). Bengali state and nation-making: Partition and displacement revisited. *International Social Science Journal, 55*(175), 111–122. doi:10.1111/1468-2451.5501011

Gould, W., Sherman, T. C., & Ansari, S. (2013). "The flux of the matter": Loyalty, corruption and the 'everyday state' in post-partition government services in India and Pakistan. *Past & Present, 219*(1), 237–279.

Groves, Jason. (March 5, 2015). *Foreign aid "being used to stamp out political opposition": Report cities schemes being used to train security services to track mobile phones*. Retrieved December 26, 2016, from www.dailymail.co.uk/news/article-2980247/Foreign-aid-used-stamp-political-opposition-Report-cites-schemes-used-train-security-services-track-mobile-phones.html

Gwynn, C. W. (1939). *Imperial policing*. London: MacMillan & Co.

Heald, S. (2009). Reforming community, reclaiming the state: The development of Sungusungu in Northern Tanzania. In D. Wisler, & I. D. Onwudiwe (Eds.), *Community policing: International perspectives and comparative perspectives* (pp. 57–80). Boca Raton, FL: CRC Press.

Human Rights Watch. (2013). *Bangladesh security forces kill protesters*. Retrieved December 26, 2016, from www.hrw.org/news/2013/08/01/bangladesh-security-forces-kill-protesters

International Crisis Group. (2009). *Bangladesh: Getting police reform on track*. Retrieved June 27, 2016, from www.crisisgroup.org/~/media/Files/asia/south-asia/bangladesh/182%20Bangladesh%20Getting%20Police%20Reform%20on%20Track.pdf

Jeffries, C. J. (1952). *The colonial police*. London: Parrish.

Kashem, M. B. (2010). Bangladesh. In Doris Chu (Ed.), *Crime and punishment around the world, vol.3. Asia/Pacific* (pp. 24–37). Santa Barbara, CA: ABC-CLIO.

McDevitt, A. (2015). *Bangladesh: Overview of corruption and anti-corruption with a focus on the health sector*. Retrieved June 27, 2016, from www.transparency.org/files/content/corruptionqas/Country_profile_Bangladesh_2015_Focus_on_health.pdf

Police Reform Programme Phase II. *What is the project about?* Retrieved September 29, 2016, from www.bd.undp.org/content/bangladesh/en/home/operations/projects/democratic_governance/police-reform-programme-phase-ii.html

Rafiqul, M., & Solaiman, S. M. (2003). Torture under police reprimand in Bangladesh: A culture of impunity for gross violations of human rights. *Asia-Pacific Journal of Human Rights and the Law, 2*, 1–27.

Raghavan, S. (2013). *1971: A global history of Bangladesh*. Cambridge, MA: Harvard University Press.

Rahim, E. (1989). Bangladesh: The society and its environment. In J. Heitzman & R. L. Worden (Eds.), *Bangladesh: A country study* (pp. 43–96). Washington, DC: US Government, Secretary of the Army.

Said, E. (1993). *Culture and imperialism*. London: Vintage.

Sampson, R. J., Raudenbush, S. W., & Earls, F. (1997). Neighborhoods and violent crime: A multilevel study of collective efficacy. *Science, 277*(5328), 918–924.

Siddiqui, A (1997). From deterrence and coercive diplomacy to war—the 1971 crisis in South Asia. *Journal of International and Area Studies, 4*(1), 73–92.

Sinclair, G., & Williams, C. A. (2007). "Home and away": The cross-fertilization between "colonial" and "British" policing, 1921–85. *The Journal of Imperial and Commonwealth History*, 221–238.

Spivak, G. C. (1999). *A critique of postcolonial reason: Toward a history of the vanishing present*. Cambridge, MA: Harvard University Press.

Spivak, G. C. (2010). *Nationalism and the imagination*. London: Seagull Books.

Stahl, Adam E. (2007). *Challenges facing Bangladesh*. International Institute for Counter Terrorism. Retrieved December 26, 2016, from www.ict.org.il/Article/979/Challenges%20Facing%20Bangladesh

Stark, Alexander. (2016). *Dhaka attack part of the larger pattern of terrorism in Bangladesh*. Retrieved December 26, 2016, from http://thediplomat.com/2016/07/dhaka-attack-part-of-a-larger-pattern-of-terrorism-in-bangladesh/

The Economist. (2016, May 20). Despotic in Dhaka. *The Economist*, 34.

Tilly, C. (1985). War making and state making as organized crime. In P. Evans, D. Rueschmeyer, & T. Skocpol (Eds.), *Bringing the state back in* (pp. 169–187). Cambridge: Cambridge University Press.

Transparency International. (2012). *Corruption perceptions index*. Retrieved June 27, 2016, from www.transparency.org/cpi2012/results

Transparency International. (2013). *Corruption perceptions index*. Retrieved June 27, 2016, from www.transparency.org/cpi2013/results

Transparency International. (2015). *Corruption perceptions index*. Retrieved June 27, 2016, from www.transparency.org/cpi2015

Tyler, T. R. (2006). Restorative justice and procedural justice: Dealing with rule breaking. *Journal of Social Issues*, *62*(2), 307–326.

Uddin, S. (2006). *Constructing Bangladesh: Religion, ethnicity and language in an Islamic Nation*. Chapel Hill, NC: University of North Carolina Press.

United Nations Development Programme. *Beyond hartals: Towards democratic dialogue in Bangladesh*. Retrieved June 27, 2016, from www.un-bd.org/Docs/Publication/Beyond%20Hartals.pdf

United States Department of Safety, Bureau of Diplomatic Security. *Bangladesh 2014 crime and safety report*. Retrieved June 27, 2016, from www.osac.gov/pages/ContentReportDetails.aspx?cid=15389

Van Schendel, W. (2009). *A history of Bangladesh*. Cambridge: Cambridge University Press.

Veer, P. van der (1994). *Religious nationalism: Hindus and Muslims in India and Britain*. Berkeley, CA: University of California Press.

Vincentnathan, S. G., & Vincentnathan, L. (2009). The police, community, and community justice institutions in India. In D. Wisler & I. D. Onwudiwe (Eds.), *Community policing: International perspectives and comparative perspectives* (pp. 257–287). Boca Raton, FL: CRC Press.

Zafarullah, H. (2007). Bureaucratic elitism in Bangladesh: The predominance of generalist administrators. *Asian Journal of Political Science*, *15*(2), 161–173.

Chapter 9

Police Behavior and Public Understanding

Insights and Innovations

John A. Eterno

The strain on democratic policing is obvious. Watching the news, we see how the police, as a profession, are being tasked with two disparate yet critical roles. The first role is to maintain order. To do this, we hold officers to the highest of standards. They must use force, but not too much. They must restrain, but not go too far. They must uphold the law yet overlook some activities. Maintaining order is clearly a difficult task. Perhaps society expects too much.

Making matters even more arduous for police in democracy is their second critical role—protecting democratic rights. While maintaining order they must, contemporaneously, be sure to protect basic rights such as free speech, freedom to peaceably assemble, basic rights of prisoners, and so forth. This means police are charged with protecting those democratic values including, importantly, the right to protest against police.

These two key roles, maintaining order and protecting basic rights, create a tension in law enforcement that is nearly impossible to resolve. Herbert Packer (1964) discusses this dichotomy in his work on the criminal justice system. He points out two models of the system that are useful for comparison. He terms these models the crime control and due process. Packer (1964) talks about the crime control model as an assembly line. Suspects are quickly brought through the criminal justice system, convicted, and sent to prison. This model was most visible when police were heralding broken windows and CompStat or performance management methods of policing. The aim was to bring down crime numbers in any way possible. Police leaders focused heavily on stopping crime. This model was prevalent through the early twenty-first century. Police commissioners such as Raymond Kelly in New York City focused on arrests, summonses, and stop and frisks. Numbers, nearly any numbers. were the key to this system.

James Q. Wilson (1977), in his classic book *Varieties of Police Behavior*, would call this a legalistic method of policing. The law is enforced regardless of the consequences. Wilson (1977) also talks about a service and watchman style of policing. Service is a focus on community and doing what the community values most. It may mean not enforcing certain laws but taking all calls seriously. His watchman style is basically answering emergency calls but doing little else other than being present. The legalistic style was in vogue until fairly recently. The New York City Police Department (NYPD) exported its aggressive style to many other departments throughout the world. As policing expert David Bayley (1994) advises, the NYPD is a "flagship" police department. What NYPD does, other departments often follow. The sheer number of departments worldwide that came to New York City to see its well-known CompStat performance management system is a key example of this (Eterno & Silverman, 2012).

The police focus on assembly-line justice has long-term consequences. In terms of Packer, the police were myopically focused on crime control. However, the flip side of the crime control model is Packer's second model, which he terms the due process model. The due process model focuses on protecting basic rights. Packer (1964) informs us that this is more like an obstacle course than the assembly line. That is, police must ensure that rights are protected at

DOI: 10.4324/9781003047117-10

every stage of their work. Reading *Miranda* rights, getting lawyers for suspects when applicable, being sure suspects get phone calls, and so forth are examples of the due process model. Under the CompStat, performance management, or sometimes called broken-windows type of policing, the aggressiveness of police left the basic rights aspects of their job behind. Millions of people were arrested and put through the system in the name of fighting crime. Our correctional facilities swelled to unheard-of numbers. Millions upon millions were brought under the auspices of an out-of-control criminal justice system focused on assembly-line justice.

In New York City, we see the first push-back on this with the stop-and-frisk controversy. The aggressive style of policing based on numbers and crime control led to numerous stops of mostly minorities. In the late 1990s, after the shooting of an unarmed African immigrant Amadou Diallo, the NYPD was sued. In particular, the court case *Daniels v. City of New York* focused on the stop-and-frisk activities of NYPD. The Center for Constitutional Rights and the New York Civil Liberties Union spearheaded the effort against the police. At the time, the NYPD was doing about 100,000 stops. At the same time, crime was down 60% (Eterno & Silverman, 2012). The police, at this point, clearly made a case that what they were doing made some sense. By 2003, the beginning of Mayor Michael Bloomberg's and Police Commissioner Raymond Kelly's administrations, the *Daniels* case was initially settled, with the police department having to report its forcible stops, do some training, and some other relatively innocuous work.

Under Mayor Bloomberg and Commissioner Kelly, however, the aggressiveness exponentially increased. Instead of 100,000, in the span of a few years, the police reached a high point of nearly 700,000 stops per year (Eterno & Silverman, 2012). Such aggressiveness seemed out of place if not totally unwarranted and even illegal and racist. Crime in New York City was, at this point, down 80%. With crime down to record lows, the need for such aggressive tactics was questionable at best. Further, the police can only make legal stops with a level of proof known as reasonable suspicion. This is more than a gut reaction (mere suspicion) but less than the level needed for arrest, termed "probable cause." In other words, police can only stop those whom they have some articulable suspicion of being a criminal (about to commit a crime, committing a crime, or having committed a crime). Police cannot stop anyone they wish to in a free society. Ultimately, the argument by the police was untenable. That is, if crime is down so much, why are their criminal suspects so plentiful? The NYPD was able to bring down crime with far fewer stops, so why was the huge increase so necessary? Making matters more complicated, the police were stopping mostly minority youth. The NYPD claimed it was necessary to remove guns off the streets. However, it was documented that only 0.1% of the stops yielded guns (using NYPD's own figures). In fact, far more effective tactics were available (and legal) to get guns off the streets, such as intensive interrogation of arrestees to find out where they got their guns; gun tracing with the help of Alcohol, Tobacco, and Firearms agents; gun buy-back programs; and focusing more on gunrunning from other states. The NYPD argument simply had no foundation. Beyond all this, numerous whistleblowers came forward and spoke openly about heavy quotas on officers (sometimes daily) that would lead them to conduct illegal and racist stops. Research exposed these issues (e.g., Eterno, Barrow, & Silverman, 2016). Ultimately, the parties in *Daniels* returned to the courts and cried foul. With copious amounts of new evidence, the federal judge consolidated the cases into *Floy v. City of New York* (2013). The United States District Court for the Southern District of New York found the NYPD liable for unconstitutional and racist policing. With a new mayor (Bill DeBlasio), the city ultimately decided not to go forward with appeals. The NYPD at the time of this writing still has a federal monitor on them for their actions under the aggressive top-down policy of stop and frisk.

This case reverberated through police circles. It was a focal point of the two roles of police: maintaining order and protecting rights. In the early part of the twenty-first century, the myopic focus on crime control led by the NYPD ultimately had enormous repercussions that face police today. That is, protecting basic rights fell by the wayside. Police arrested, stopped, and gave summonses following a very aggressive, legalistic style of policing. Community policing of the 1980s and early 90s was simply disregarded in favor of crime control. With such an aggressive, even militaristic, model of policing exported to numerous departments and agencies, it is no wonder that there is now a movement against police agencies, especially by minorities (e.g., Black Lives Matter).

While names like Eric Garner and George Floyd are now commonplace, policing must emerge from its sometimes-racist actions as seen in *Floyd*. This does not mean that every officer or department is racist. However, there are clearly concerns. Many police departments such as Los Angeles, New Jersey State Troopers, Pittsburgh, Suffolk County, Maryland State Troopers, and many others were or are under consent decrees to monitor racist behavior. Euphemisms such as "driving while black," and "testilying" speak to a police culture that went amok. While much of this can be traced to top-down management, there are concerns that this infects policing. The well-known police culture (Drummond, 1976; Eterno, 2003) has led to difficulties in police behavior.

The police culture is based on the dangerousness of the work environment. Officers know that they need to back each other up in difficult situations. Because of this, they tend to protect one another. The idea of lying to protect other officers is not new. This is part of the culture. The Mollen Commission in New York City led to the term *testilying* (testimony in which officers lie to protect other officers). The 75th Precinct in New York City was found to be a hotbed of corruption. Former officer Michael Dowd was the ringleader of a precinct gone rogue. He knew officers would protect him and used that to conduct his illegal activities, such as stealing from drug dealers and protecting them as well.

Prior to this, the Knapp Commission in the 70s exposed major corruption in plainclothes units through the City of New York police. In this case, the commission found that there were meat-eaters and grass-eaters. The meat-eaters did the hardcore corruption activities. Again, stealing from drug dealers and protecting them were staples of corruption in this era. However, the commission found that the grass-eaters, those who looked the other way or engaged in minor corruption activities, were the root of the problem. Again, the importance of the police culture is seen.

Research on the police culture also points to the willingness of police to conduct illegal actions on suspects. Worden and Shepard (1996) and Lundman (1996) show that suspects who violate what is called the "attitude effect" will be more likely to get legal sanctions by police. That is, those suspects who do not respect the police will receive a legal sanction (arrest, summons), even though they may not have done anything illegal. Some research does suggest that police will not go so far as to violate the law but will still sanction people who violate the attitude effect (Klinger, 1996). Regardless, the police culture is seen as a mechanism for negative behavior by police.

The combination of aggressive policing from the top and the police culture from the bottom is clearly problematic. Police leaders as well as the rank and file need to be aware and address issues that lead to negative behavior. Numerous oversight agencies have been suggested. However, what we are currently seeing in New York is that police morale and even police inaction might result from too much oversight.

Oversight in New York City is complicated. After the *Floyd* case, the city council piled on with additional sanctions. One of the most important was the establishment of an inspector general. Certainly, a reasonable action. However, it was way too late. The council acted after the fact. Now, the police department is strapped with oversight from several city agencies as well as a federal monitor. City agencies include the inspector general; the Civilian Complaint Review Board; the mayor's office, including a criminal justice coordinator; and a public advocate, and those are only the main agencies. Every district attorney also has oversight responsibilities. With five boroughs, that means five separate district attorneys reviewing police actions. Of course, the federal government has oversight as well, such as the Federal Bureau of Investigation and two United States attorneys (Southern District of New York and Eastern District of New York). This is not to mention state agencies. The New York State Attorney General, Latisha James, for example, recently announced that she would be suing the city and its leaders over police behavior at Black Lives Matter rallies (Southall, 2021, January 14). Beyond this are the Center for Constitutional Rights and the New York Civil Liberties Union and other watchdog groups such as Communities United for Police Reform and the Police Reform Organizing Project. Oversight is simply not a problem in New York City. However, these agencies all have their own missions. As a result, there are countless avenues for reform but very little focus by them as a whole.

This is only part of the oversight of police officers in New York City. The pressures on officers are nearly insurmountable. A short primer on the pressures that typical officers feel is important. It will help to understand the way typical police officers feel.

Various Influences on Police Behavior

To many, police are powerful figures. They represent the face of government on the frontlines. What surprises some is that police today do not feel empowered to do their job. This can lead to low morale, police neglecting some duties, police being very non-aggressive, enormous stress, and even suicide. Typical officers are caught in a vast array of pressures. In the end, the officer is left to consider these pressures, weigh them, and ultimately determine appropriate actions. The panoply of sources of these pressures is incredible. We can divide these sources into nine basic categories: law, political, media, supervisors (bureaucracy and training), whistleblowers, unions (fraternal organizations), peers (police culture), the community where they work, and other influences.

Before explaining each of the categories, it is important to note that these categories influence each other. That is, one category can have vast consequences on another as we shall soon see. The categories are not mutually exclusive.

Law

The first category is law. The police fall under the executive branch of government, which means the executive has power over them. For example, a governor, mayor, or county executive will generally appoint police leadership. The legislative and judicial branches also check the power of the police. For example, the legislative branch may create a law that limits or expands police power. The Criminal Procedure Law of New York State, for example, includes the powers of arrest and stop and frisk. The legislative branch can also create numerous bodies to oversee the police, such as civilian complaint review boards or inspectors general. Importantly, the legislative branch also controls the powers of the purse—money. They determine the budget for police and other agencies. With many calling for "defunding of police," we can see how important this pressure can be. In New York City, for example, the police recently got their budget slashed by one billion dollars. Legally, the police get their power from this. Additionally, the courts can also circumscribe or increase the powers of police. The aforementioned *Floyd* case limited police power by placing a monitor on the police. However, the United States Supreme Court case *Terry v. Ohio* (1968) expanded police power by authorizing temporary forcible stops.

Political

The second category is political. This goes beyond the legal understanding. Let us start with political parties. Each of them has a platform that has an influence on police. Republicans have, in general, been supportive of law and order; Democrats are generally more associated with due process rights. While this is an extreme generalization, it is only for demonstration. These stereotypes may not be as clear in various situations. Nevertheless, the importance of politics should not be underestimated. On the micro level, there are some politicians who may favor a law-and-order platform more than others. For example, Mayor Rudolph Giuliani was generally associated with an aggressive policing mentality. Alternatively, Mayor David Dinkins was generally associated with a community-policing philosophy. Police, as an arm of the executive branch, are especially attuned to the ebb and flow of politics.

Media

A third influence on police is the media. Police officers, like most people, are consumers of media. Officers are well aware of movements and trends in society. The Black Lives Matter movement, for example, has been very vocal about systemic racism in policing. Police do understand that they are being accused of horrid behaviors by this group. Their reactions to that can be varied. Indeed, some may agree, and some may disagree. I do note, however, that counter-movements such as "Back the Blue" and "Blue Lives Matter" are responses. Police can be influenced by how the media reports on these political movements. Media viewpoints are also well known by police. They are aware that some outlets are more favorable to them than others. In New York City, officers are generally aware that outlets such as the *Village Voice* tend to be less favorable to them than, say, the *New York Post*. Although these stereotypes are not always the case, one must understand the key point: media images of police are clearly on the minds of officers when they do their jobs.

Supervisors

Other key influences on officer behavior are superior officers and the police bureaucracy in general. This includes the hiring and training of officers, which will be covered in more detail later in this chapter. Police have a rule book that tells them how to act in various situations. In New York City it is called the *Patrol Guide* (there are other guides as well, but this is the most suited to this discussion). It is important to recognize that this is not the law. Rather, it is police policy. As an example of the nuances of this, the Eric Garner case is instructive. Mr. Garner was placed into a chokehold by an NYPD officer (Eterno, 2019). At the time, a chokehold was not a violation of the law. However, it was a violation of NYPD policy. The NYPD *Patrol Guide* is very clear on what the chokehold is and that officers may not use the tactic: NYPD officers "shall not use a chokehold. A chokehold shall include, but is not limited to, any pressure to the throat or windpipe, which may prevent or hinder breathing or reduce the intake of air" (Eterno, 2019). Since this action was not a violation of the law, the officer's maximum penalty was being fired. In this case, the prosecutors on both the state and federal levels determined that a crime was not committed by the officer. However, the NYPD fired the officer based on the unauthorized chokehold. It should be noted that the officer can be sued civilly, and the city would not have to represent the officer. That is, an officer who is found to violate these rules would have to get his/her own attorney. Police officers, then, are keenly aware that they must obey the law, the procedures of their departments, and supervisors. Penalties for disobedience can range from a simple change of assignment (or even just a reprimand) to prison time, depending on the level of the violation. Law violations tend to be more egregious, violations of procedure less so. Disobeying an order would generally be on the same level as a procedural violation, depending on the circumstances. Also note that officers are not supposed to follow orders that are illegal. While rare, officers are supposed to know their jobs well and are deeply influenced by these regulations.

Whistleblowers and Police Departments

When dealing with whistleblowers, police agencies are supposed to listen. However, there are many examples of officers not being listened to even though they are following their training. One of the most interesting cases is that of NYPD Officer Adrian Schoolcraft. Officer Schoolcraft was assigned to the 81st Precinct. He worked during the time of heavy quotas and crime report manipulation. Studies on the NYPD indicated that higher-ups were manipulating crime reports due to enormous pressures at CompStat. A significant number of officers came forward and blew the whistle on this practice, which paralleled significant research findings coming out at the same time (Eterno & Silverman, 2012). Officer Schoolcraft tried to report these behaviors through channels but was rebuffed. Eventually, he went to the media. This was similar to the experiences of Detective Frank Serpico, who blew the whistle in the 1970s on the taking of money by plainclothes officers. In the case of Schoolcraft, the upper echelon ended up forcibly hospitalizing him for his troubles. He spent days in a hospital ward. One might think these are isolated cases; however, in Australis, the New South Wales police also forcibly hospitalized one of their own for similar whistleblowing about the crime reporting system. Officer Philip Arantz was posthumously awarded the most prestigious medal available (Eterno & Silverman, 2012). Each of the officers mentioned went through highly traumatic experiences. Other examples include Adil Polanco, who was suspended for his efforts to demonstrate how whistleblowers have been treated by police departments. Other officers are keenly aware of these experiences. In fact, in New York City, the word *Schoolcraft* is now used as a verb, as in "supervisors Schoolcrafted him." Thus, the power of the police bureaucracy is another influence on officer behavior.

Unions

As if this were not enough, officers must also contend with pressures from their fraternal organizations. Officers may not always agree with union leaders. Recently, for example, Officer Patrick Lynch supported the reelection of President Donald Trump. Certainly, there are officers who would disagree with this decision. Just as important, however, is that the union can disagree with management. For example, when NYPD was putting heavy quotas on officers to write summonses and make arrests, the police union was very vocal against this. The Patrolmen's Benevolent Association took out full page ads in local newspapers and went on a media blitz, stating, "Don't blame the beat cop, blame NYPD management." The words were emblazoned over a picture of an officer giving a seemingly docile person a summons. I can also recall times when officers were told by union representatives not to write summonses in response to not getting raises or for some other reason. Recall that officers must also obey orders. Some of this came to a head when superior officers rode with lower-ranking officers and ordered them to write summonses or even to make arrests. In those cases, the officers had to do what they were told. However, there are many fewer superior officers than rank and file, and it became obvious that most officers were not writing. Certain officers felt more pressure, such as officers whose main job was to write summonses. Usually, those officers would come to some agreement with the union and/or the commanding officer and would end up writing a certain number or lose their plum assignment.

Police Culture

The sixth influence is police culture. This was talked about previously. To quickly review, though, police culture is based on the dangerousness of the work environment. Officers often feel compelled to protect other officers, even if it means lying or looking the other way. Again, this is because officers must rely on other officers for protection. Other officers must respond when an officer is in trouble, and without that assistance, officers are helpless in the field. This is sometimes called the informal code and can be more powerful than other influences. This influence is often associated with negative behaviors by officers, such as testilying and the attitude effect.

Community

A seventh influence on police behavior is the community that the officer works in. Is the community one that supports or does not support the police? Does the officer feel comfortable with the work environment? Are they familiar with the culture they are working in? The community that the officer works in will undoubtedly have an influence on the officer just like the suspect's demeanor. Most officers appear to react to other factors more strongly, such as the legality of the situation, but the community can have an influence (Eterno, 2003). Sometimes officers can be overly influenced by a neighborhood that is obviously in trouble. The Mollen Commission's showing how the corrupt officers in that precinct took advantage of the drug dealers and the police culture is certainly an example. In the police academy, officers are carefully trained about other cultures, but that training must continue in the field. Community leaders need to be invited to precincts so that officers are not only familiar with them but also understand the culture of the community they are working in.

Other

As if this were not enough, there are other influences on officers' behavior. These may be more personal, such as an officer's religious beliefs, family, and/or friends. Depending on the officer, these can be a powerful influence. Additionally, there are organizations such as the Holy Name Society for Catholic officers, the Shomrim Society for Jewish officers, and the Guardians for black officers. These, too, on a more personal level than the union, will have an influence on officer behavior. These organizations can be very powerful, especially when core beliefs are appealed to.

Hiring and Training

There is a wide variety of training throughout the United States. A typical police agency has an academy of about five to six months. However, this varies. In Florida, for example, officers are initially trained in colleges and then get a certificate so that they can find a job. They then go through a shortened police academy. New York State has a model like that, but the police agency must agree to it. Very few agencies have. However, there is enormous cost savings to the government since the agency can have a much-shortened police academy experience. Many other professions have used this type of training: for example, nurses, doctors, and lawyers. This method of training may be preferable for police, and an open discussion is necessary. One reason this method can be preferable (other than the enormous cost savings to the government and, in turn, the taxpayers) is due to the police culture. The police culture is often transmitted to recruits beginning in the police academy.

Many police departments now recognize the benefits of a college education. New York City now requires two years of college or military experience before a potential officer can enter the police academy for training. The main concern, however, is not college education but rather the academy experience leading to negative stereotypes and developing the negative aspects of the culture before officers even graduate and work on the streets.

A study done by Eterno (2008) examines the experiences of cadets in the New York City Police. Working officers were divided into three categories according to their levels of education: high school/GED, bachelor's degree, and bachelor's with cadet experience. The Cadet Corps is similar to the ROTC in the military. Cadets get money to go to college and, in turn, must promise to work for the NYPD after they graduate. Cadets are exposed to the NYPD early on in their college careers and generally work summers for the department. Consequently, they are exposed to police culture before the other officers. The study showed that the college graduates (both with and without cadet experience) outperformed their high school–only counterparts in every category, such as felony arrests, using sick time, disciplinary action, motor vehicle accidents, and more. However, the study also showed that the cadets' performance appears to have been negatively influenced by the police culture. For example, cadets understood the sick policy and took advantage of it. So the college-educated officers without cadet experience appeared to have some inoculation from the culture, at least in the period studied. Knowing the Florida model, it may be best to have officers trained like doctors, nurses, and lawyers: that is, trained mostly by colleges and then have a shortened academy experience. This would give the benefit of college education to all officers. A liberal arts college education would have the additional benefit of exposing potential officers to various disciplines, viewpoints, and cultures. For example, sociological studies on inequality would be explained to the potential officers without the filtration of the police academy. Numerous other examples can be given. More study needs to be done on this, but it seems logical as other professions do the same.

The hiring practices of police will also influence officer behavior. Officers today generally are hired through civil service examinations. Once their score is reached on the list, they go through a battery of tests. These include psychological, physical, character background, and medical testing. An initial background check is usually done to make sure the potential officer is qualified. For example, if the person does not have a driver's license, they will be excluded until they get one. Also, if there is a felony conviction or other major issue, the person will immediately be screened out. Physical tests are generally cheaper and done fairly early in the process. These tests are of two types: agility tests and fitness tests. Agility tests have the potential officer do activities that simulate the physical stresses of policing, such as running up and down stairs, pushing and pulling, trigger-pull tests, and the like. Physical fitness tests determine whether the potential officer can be trained, such as running a mile and a half in a certain amount of time, doing a certain number of sit-ups and so forth. The idea of fitness tests is to determine the "trainability" of the potential officer. Psychological tests vary but often include a group of tests to be sure the candidate is not too aggressive or not aggressive enough, does not have some psychological problem including drinking too much alcohol, and so forth. The paper tests may be followed up with a face-to-face interview with a psychologist. The character background test will determine whether the candidate has something in their history that would prevent them from being an officer, such as a history of domestic violence. Lastly, a medical evaluation will make sure there is nothing that would prevent the officer from doing the job and includes random drug testing, whether the officer can stand for long periods, and so forth. Ultimately, all four of the qualifications will be looked at in total to determine if the candidate is qualified. Training an officer is expensive (although cheaper if the Florida model is used), so passing all these qualifications is critical.

Once the candidate is determined to be qualified, he/she will wait until an academy class is being conducted. This can take some time, depending on the department. Each department does its own screening, and this can also get expensive. Some departments will accept officers who have been trained elsewhere, which helps them to save money. Usually, however, each department will train its own. Even the officers who move from department to department will still have to go under some transition period, in which they will be indoctrinated into the new department he/she is entering. Overall, the hiring process is complicated and has been challenged by many in courts.

Once the candidate enters the police academy, he/she is sworn in. Officers must swear an oath to protect the Constitution of the United States, their relevant state constitution, and so forth. Officers are defenders of basic rights, and this is something that the police academy training will attempt to drill in. The training is complicated and fairly short for what is expected of officers. Physical training, firearms, driving, police science, law, and social science are the general topics that are covered. Some emergency medical training is also usually included. The lessons are arduous, and officers must pass examinations at every stage. Some academies have officers live in barracks, while others have officers return to their homes after each day of training. After a period of academy training, officers are then ready for field training. The initial field training can vary. However, no officer is completely ready for the streets without some field training. It takes time to understand the rigors of the job. Officers never stop learning and will generally continue some sort of lessons, albeit less strict, after the academy. Field training means officers must get used to paperwork, dealing with the public, handing all sorts of calls, and using force when necessary. New officers are carefully examined by training officers for weaknesses and strengths. Some departments will not give permanent commands to officers until some period of field training is completed. Under stressful conditions, the importance of training must not be underestimated. It is the key to doing the job correctly and needs to be scrutinized often by the department and outside oversight agencies.

Going Forward

All these pressures and influences leave officers in a complicated position. The discretion they have in many cases also complicates matters. Officers do not have to arrest or issue a summons in every situation. The job of policing is not like many others. Jobs in transportation, sanitation, and manufacturing, for example, generally do not call for split-second decisions on life or death. For police, each situation is unique. They must weigh the consequences of an action/inaction and determine the best course. In some instances, this may mean inaction; in others, shooting. Today, these pressures are even greater because there is a spotlight on policing.

More importantly, the general public is unaware of these pressures. Some will argue that officers are very brutal. However, the facts are that over 90% of officers never fire their weapons in the line of duty. The media images of police are simply and emphatically false. I have had questions of people asking why an officer did not shoot a person in the hand or the leg. Such naivete is more commonplace than one might think. This influences policy. Typical reactions about police are based on such a tortured understanding of the profession that policies based on such limited understandings are very bad, if not downright dangerous. For example, many states have now made chokeholds illegal after watching the George Floyd video. While that may seem to be a reasonable reaction, there does seem to be a lack of understanding of the life-or-death struggle in which some officers might resort to such a tactic if nothing else was available.

There needs to be a better conversation between policy makers and policing experts. Indeed, some of my recent research indicates that police agencies do a very poor job of explaining what they do and why they do it (Eterno, 2019). In a social science experiment with 95 college students, I demonstrate that people will change their minds if they understand the law and police policy in a situation. Police and the media need to carefully explain what officers are doing. Situations that seem downright horrible can actually be permissible and even suggested. A good example of this is when a woman with a baseball bat came charging at a sergeant in the Bronx. The officer shot the woman, and the mayor immediately called for the sergeant's dismissal—without due process. Everyone in our society, including police, are entitled to due process. This is bedrock. The sergeant was completely exonerated after a full investigation. Situations like this need to be carefully investigated before we jump to hasty conclusions about officer guilt.

That being said, social movements against police brutality must be heard. This is the essence of the social contract. There is an unwritten understanding in society about what is acceptable behavior and what is not. The social contract, of course, changes over time. For example, at one time, gay marriage was considered wrong but today is acceptable. Countless other examples can be shown. Police, for their part, must be especially attuned to the social contract, which can vary by community.

Tactics in policing need to change with the times as well. The downside of aggressive policing is today more obvious. Police need to develop tactics that are more community friendly but, at the same time, need to be given the power to do their jobs. This is the dilemma we talked about earlier—crime control versus due process. Modern policing experts have suggested that community partnerships, transparency, and reasonable oversight both within and outside the agency are necessary. Community partnerships mean working with local communities to determine local standards of morality and local needs. This does not mean the police must do what every local community wants but does mean they should be working together. Establishing this link is critical to the police. Instead of being an army of occupation, police need to work with communities to meet common objectives. Ultimately, reducing crime is a common objective of police and local community leaders. How to get there is a more complicated issue. Nevertheless, by working with communities, police will gain community trust, which will ultimately lead to more intelligence from within the community. Unlike the aggressive tactics of stop and frisk, which led to the alienation of minority communities, working with them and, just as important, working within legal boundaries will lead to a more harmonious and, in turn, a less crime-ridden area. This will not necessarily be easy as many police have been operating under very aggressive styles. We must work together to solve these weighty problems.

Transparency is also essential. While police cannot be completely transparent, they need to let the public know as much as possible. Freedom of Information Act (FOIA) requests, for example, should NOT routinely be denied. Rather, there should be a general tendency to release information rather than withhold information. The burden needs to be on the police to explain why they cannot release, and then there needs to be a swift process for appealing. Police have often denied the press and the public basic information that should be released—sometimes regularly. The NYPD, for example, has refused to release the number of lost property complaints for many years. For a short time, they released the information, then quickly decided not to. Such decisions need to be made with the public, not against the public. Police are public servants and must recognize that role is paramount.

Police officers must also be held accountable. Officers themselves do not want to work with corruption, brutality, and other illegal activities. Internal affairs units are critical to this. These officers need to be well trained and understand that their role is absolutely essential. The police culture, however, tends to depict these officers as "rats." The police culture needs to be dealt with. It needs to change. This may be the most difficult part of going forward. While protecting one another is understandable, it must not go to the level of illegality. There is a higher ideal—protecting the Constitution. This needs to be ingrained in every police officer in the United States. Beyond this, there does need to be a reasonable outside accountability agency for police. Right now, too many agencies have such authority. This needs to be consolidated. One focal agency needs to oversee police. I am particularly concerned with some areas of policing that never see the light of day. For example, crime reports are used to make countless policy decisions. Research clearly indicates that police are playing with those numbers (Eterno & Silverman, 2012; Eterno, Verma, & Silverman, 2016). Our corporations are held to higher accounting standards than our police. We need an agency with some teeth. That outside agency should have subpoena power and the ability to audit crime reports. An agency without teeth is useless.

Based on understanding the police, these are just some ideas on how we need to move forward. The situation is complicated but can be solved. In New York City, for example, with a federal monitor, a non-supportive political community, budgets being slashed, and communities in an uproar about their handling of large crowds and other situations, it is no wonder that inaction and poor morale have become symptomatic of police. With unions and others stating that morale has never been so low, more solutions need to be given.

As a first step, we need to let the experts determine actions. When political groups who know little to nothing about policing suggest how they should act, it is not helpful. Should the police listen? Of course. Community input is important. However, constant criticism of professional officers seems commonplace. Officers need the support of as many of these influences as possible. Officers themselves also want other officers prosecuted when they see misjustice. This includes the death of George Floyd. Nearly every officer I have spoken to thinks the way that was handled (a knee on the throat of a cuffed prisoner) is a stain on law enforcement. By working together, police experts, communities, and other interested parties can develop strategies for democratic policing to move forward. This needs to be done, however, with a better understanding of the police role and its difficulties.

Discussion Questions

1. Explain the importance of crime control versus due process.
2. Discuss the varied influences on police behavior.
3. Explain the importance of the police culture.
4. The police and minority communities seem to disagree on tactics. What are some solutions to this important issue?
5. Explain how a typical police officer might feel when he/she is working the streets. Why do you think officers feel that way? Explain your answer.

References

Bayley, D. H. (1994). *Police for the future.* Oxford: Oxford University Press.

Drummond, D. S. (1976). *Police culture.* Thousand Oaks, CA: Sage.

Eterno, J. A. (2003). *Policing within the law: A case study of the New York city police department.* Westport, CT: Praeger.

Eterno, J. A. (2008). Homeland security and the benefits of college education: An exploratory study of the New York city police department's cadet corps. *Professional Issues in Criminal Justice, 3*(2), 1–16.

Eterno, J. A. (2019, October 25). *Influence of police policy and law on public opinion.* One hour presentation at the Annual Meeting of the Criminal Justice Educators of New York State, Syracuse, NY.

Eterno, J. A., Barrow, C., & Silverman, E. (2016). Forcible stops: Police and citizens' speak out. *Public Administration Review.* Published in Early View. doi:10.1111/puar.12684

Eterno, J. A., & Silverman, E. B. (2012). *The crime numbers game: Management by manipulation.* Boca Raton, FL: CRC Press.

Eterno, J. A., Verma, A., & Silverman, E. B. (2016). Police manipulation of crime reports. *Justice Quarterly, 33*(5), 811–933. First published online in 2014. doi:10.1080/07418825.2014.98

Klinger, D. A. (1996). Bringing crime back in: Toward a better understanding of police arrest decisions. *Journal of Research in Crime and Delinquency, 33*(3), 333–336. doi:10.1177/0022427896033003004

Lundman, R. J. (1996). Demeanor and arrest: Additional evidence from previously unpublished data. *Journal of Research in Crime and Delinquency, 33*(3), 306–323. doi:10.1177/0022427896033003002

Packer, H. (1964). Two models of the criminal justice process. *University of Pennsylvania Law Review, 13*(1). Retrieved from https://scholarship.law.upenn.edu/cgi/viewcontent.cgi?article=6428&context=penn_law_review

Southall, A. (2021, January 14). New York attorney general sues NYPD over protests and demands monitor. *The New York Times*. Retrieved from www.nytimes.com/2021/01/14/nyregion/nypd-police-protest-lawsuit.html

Wilson, J. Q. (1977). *Varieties of police behavior*. Cambridge, MA: Harvard University Press.

Worden, R. E., & Shepard, R. L. (1996). Demeanor, crime, and police behavior: A reexamination of the police services study. *Criminology, 34*(1), 83–105. doi:10.1111/j.1745-9125.1996.tb01196.x

Part II

Hiring and Training

Chapter 10

Hired With Competence

An Examination of Police Hiring Standards in Canada

Scott E. Blandford

Introduction to the Study

Background of the Study

Policing rural and urban areas in Canada is an extremely costly and complex endeavor. Tax-payers spend approximately $12 billion, or nearly 1% of the Canadian GDP, on policing (Leuprecht, 2014). Human resource costs account for upward of 90% of the $5.39 billion that municipalities spend annually on policing (Blandford, 2004; Leuprecht, 2014; London Police Service, 2013). Competency-based performance management creates a direct nexus between individual and organizational performance management and directly links to improved organizational efficacy (Bonder, Bouchard, & Bellemare, 2011; Lawler, 1994; Kaiting, 2012). Police organizations generally hire for entry-level positions; therefore, there are relatively few options for influencing their human resources. By differentially selecting and retaining competent officers, organizations can shape the attitudes, values, and competencies of their workforce. Based on this premise, the recruiting and selection of entry-level officers is one of the most important functions within the organization (Coleman, 2012; Gomez-Mejia, Balkin, & Cardy, 2010; Ness, 2011; Stansfield, 1996).

Literature Review

Introduction to the Chapter and Background of the Problem

Canada is the second largest country in the world, encompassing over 3,855,103 square miles, with a population of 35.4 million dispersed across ten provinces and three territories (Statistics Canada, 2014). As a result, policing rural and urban areas in Canada is an extremely costly and complex service. Canadian taxpayers spend approximately $12 billion, or nearly 1% of the GDP of the country, on policing (Leuprecht, 2014). Human resource costs account for upward of 90% of the approximately $5.39 billion that municipalities spend annually on policing (Blandford, 2004; Leuprecht, 2014; London Police Service, 2013). It is now a fundamental prerequisite that police leaders appreciate that the policing landscape has become significantly more complex due to factors such as technological advances, financial constraints, intensified globalization, and increased societal demands (Robertson, 2012; Whitelaw & Parent, 2014). The traditional concept of police management must change for police agencies to be effective in the twenty-first century. This includes an evidence-based management approach, using modern business methods, and the exploration of new concepts in human resource management for a broad range of public and private sectors (Belcourt & McBey, 2010; Hay Group, 2007; Miller, 2011; Robertson, 2012).

DOI: 10.4324/9781003047117-12

Review of the Literature

Police Historical Perspective

The history of modern policing dates back to the efforts of Sir Robert Peel and the development of the Metropolitan Act in London, England. From its inception in 1829, Peel envisioned a police service composed of professional, trained individuals, with a paramilitary hierarchy and codes of conduct (Robertson, 2012; Stansfield, 1996). The expectation was that the new police service would respond to community and crime issues without resorting to the traditional brute force of the military. In North America, policing was not as refined, with jobs in police organizations given to individuals who demonstrated loyalty to the ruling political party of the day, resulting in hiring criteria that were exceptionally low, or even nonexistent (Ross, 2012).

The growing population in Canada of the mid-nineteenth century led to the need for police services in Upper Canada, under the authority of the Municipal Institutions of Upper Canada Act 1858 (Stansfield, 1996). This legislation permitted towns and cities to create police services under the control of their own boards of commissioners. Each individual police service determined the standards for hiring, resulting in inconsistencies in the quality of officers selected (Whitelaw & Parent, 2014). In 1867, the British North America Act (BNA) entrenched the authorities of the federal and provincial governments; in particular, the federal government delegated authority for the administration of justice, which included policing (Robertson, 2012). It is interesting to note that the BNA did not recognize the legal authority of municipalities, but rather left the delegation of any authority to those entities to the provinces. As a result, Canada has three tiers of public police jurisdiction: federal (i.e., Royal Canadian Mounted Police), provincial (e.g., Ontario Provincial Police), and municipal level police services.

Traditionally, police organizations followed a paramilitary hierarchy that was a male-dominated occupation, with officers often selected for their physical ability (Ross, 2012). Expectations from a relatively homogeneous community focused on the ability of the police to maintain the peace and apprehend criminals (Robertson, 2012). As noted by Rydberg and Terrill (2010), at one point only "two out of three police officers finished grade school and only one in ten completed high school. . . . [A]t the time of the First World War, 75% of police personnel could not pass an Army intelligence test" (pg. 94). This political era of policing ended in approximately 1920, when it was replaced by the reform era. Between 1920 and 1960 policing (particularly in the United States) the introduction of scientific methods of investigation, such as the Bertillon fingerprint system, became entrenched (Ross, 2012). Attempts were made to professionalize policing and standardize training; there were also calls for the education levels of police officers to rise (Ross, 2012). The professional era of policing extended from the 1960s until the mid-1980s, building on the efforts to standardize operations, improve efficiencies, and enforce stricter organizational controls (Cordner, 2014). In the mid-1980s, the philosophy of community policing began to emerge, resulting in a move from reactive policing to a proactive approach founded on a partnership between police and the community and creating a paradigm shift that required new skillsets and placed greater expectations on officers (More, Vito, & Walsh, 2012; Rydberg & Terrill, 2010; Whitelaw & Parent, 2014).

Modern communities within Canada are far more complex, with a heterogeneous population and conflicting expectations of what services contemporary police organizations should provide (Campbell, 1992; Oppal, 1994). Increased globalization, increasingly more diverse populations, the rapid change of technology, changes within the legal landscape, and the rise of social media and activism have all contributed to creating a challenging environment in which police officers must operate (Blandford, 2004; Grant & Terry, 2012; Leuprecht, 2014; Robertson, 2012). The various provincial legislations are unanimous in stating the core policing functions as crime prevention, law enforcement, emergency response, public order maintenance, and assistance to victims of crime (Government of Ontario, 2009; Oppal, 1994; Robertson, 2012). The duties of a police officer have evolved far beyond law enforcement, with 80% of police work involving maintaining order and social interventions (Leuprecht, 2014). In many ways, police organizations have expanded scope to become an after-hours social service agency, mental health crisis interventionists, and responders to a wide range of social ills. Police officers have adapted, utilizing critical-thinking, problem-solving, and conflict-resolution skills on a daily basis. With increased social and economic diversity, increasing community demands, and heightened legislative oversight, the skillsets required by the modern police officer eclipse those originally envisioned by Sir Robert Peel (Bowman, 2012; Grant & Terry, 2012; Robertson, 2012). Leuprecht (2014) summed up these skillsets rather succinctly as follows: "to require a mere high school diploma of people who draft court briefs, the writing requirements of which exceed those of many graduate school courses, is an anachronism" (p. 13).

Post-Secondary Education in Policing

Increased globalization of crime, the rise of social media and technology, the integration of community-based policing as a general philosophy, and higher expectations from the community have all led to an increasingly complex environment for police officers (Haberfeld, 2013; Human Resource Development Canada, 2001; Leuprecht, 2014). Traditionally modeled as paramilitary hierarchies, police organizations have a relatively strict bureaucratic structure. The current demands and the complexity of those demands on police officers have increased greatly since the early days of policing, and the need for officers to have the necessary competencies is critical to organizational success (Whitelaw & Parent, 2014). Police organizations seek to recruit the best applicants, and post-secondary education is often a deciding factor between candidates (Ontario Police College, 2013).

It was not until the early twentieth century when August Vollmer, who was chief of police in Berkeley, California, first suggested that police officers would benefit from a college education (Grant & Terry, 2012; Paterson, 2011). Since that time, the nexus between higher education for police officers and organizational effectiveness has been the subject of much research and debate. The complexity of police work requires officers to apply advanced skillsets to their current abilities; promotion through the organization based solely on experience and seniority is not sustainable (Hay Group, 2007). Through post-secondary education, police officers can develop the soft and hard skills (i.e., behavioral and technical competencies) they require to serve the public and advance their careers. Competencies such as team building, communication, critical thinking, and problem solving are all critical to individual and organizational success (Bonder et al., 2011; Bowman, 2012; Oppal, 1994; Summers, 2009).

Several researchers examined the value a post-secondary education can bring to police organizations and conceded that there are several positive aspects of an educated police officer that are considered bona fide occupational requirements (Bowman, 2012; Campbell, 1992; Hay Group, 2007; Miller, 2011; Oppal, 1994). The underlying belief is that college-educated officers are more professional in performing their duties and more efficient in providing service to the public. Further research has supported the belief that post-secondary education exposes a police applicant to broader experiences and increases exposure to cultural diversity and the ability to analyze situations in a broader context (Blakemore & Simpson, 2010; Bowman, 2012; Green & Gates, 2014; Miller, 2011; Hilal, Densley, & Zhao, 2013). Conversely, many police executives, supported by research findings, resist the movement to post-secondary education, citing the lack of definitive research that quantifies the nexus between higher education and police organization efficacy (Hensen, Reyns, Klahm IV, & Frank, 2010; Hilal et al., 2013; Paterson, 2011).

Post-secondary education will not necessarily provide all of the tools necessary for police officers to be effective; it, of itself, does not guarantee ethical actions, professionalism, or impartial service, but it can provide the foundation upon which to build a competent, professional, and effective police organization (Hay Group, 2007; Miller, 2011; Scott, Evans, & Verma, 2009). The increased challenges facing contemporary police organizations are consistent with the behavioral competencies advocated in the competency-based human resources management model for policing (Police Sector Council, 2013). As a result, there is a growing trend for police recruiters to place greater emphasis on higher levels of post-secondary education at the entry level, which can result in a latent barrier to applicants (Bowman, 2012; Hay Group, 2007; Leuprecht, 2014).

In the Province of Ontario, the minimum hiring standards for police applicants are legislated by the government. As of 2017, the Ontario Police Services Act (Government of Ontario, 2009) establishes the minimum standards for a police officer as follows:

> Section 43. (1) No person shall be appointed as a police officer unless he or she: . . .
>   (e) has successfully completed at least four years of secondary school education or its equivalent.

It is interesting to note that this legislation dates back to 1990, prior to the acceptance of community-based policing as a general philosophy, prior to the implementation of new legislation and case law that creates increased demands on police officers, and prior to the explosion of social media and technology. All these issues have greatly increased the complexity for the frontline police officer. Similarly, the Royal Canadian Mounted Police Act (Government of Canada, 2013) and the Royal Newfoundland Constabulary Regulations (Legislature of Newfoundland, 2014) set the minimum education level qualifications for a police officers as possessing a Canadian high school diploma or equivalent.

Subsequent to the initial data collection, the Ontario Police Services Act has been amended to reflect a change in the minimum hiring requirements:

(f) meets one of the following conditions:

    (i) he or she has,

        (A) a university degree, or
        (B) a degree from a college of applied arts and technology authorized to grant the degree,

    (ii) he or she has a diploma or advanced diploma granted by a college of applied arts and technology following successful completion of a program that is the equivalent in class hours of a full-time program of at least four academic semesters,

    (iii) he or she has been granted a certificate or other document by a post-secondary institution evidencing successful completion of a program that the regulations prescribe as being equivalent to a degree or diploma described in subclause (i) or (ii),

    (iv) if additional criteria have been prescribed, he or she has a secondary school diploma and meets the additional criteria.

These minimum standards are reflective of the legislated minimum education standards across Canada for entry-level hires. There are exceptions to the high school diploma minimum standard. The Province of Quebec has established a requirement for applicants to complete a diploma awarded by the École nationale de police du Québec (a post-secondary institution) or meet the standards of equivalence (École nationale de police du Québec, 2013). British Columbia has established a Grade 12 diploma or equivalent, with most police organizations also requiring a minimum 30 credits (one year) of academic post-secondary education from an accredited university or college.

In the current employment climate, many high school students have recognized the need for further education. Over the past decade, two out of every three new jobs required post-secondary education, with the majority requiring a university degree (Council of Ontario Universities, 2011). According to Statistics Canada, the proportion of adults aged 25 to 64 who had completed post-secondary education was 60.7% (Statistics Canada, 2013). Given the expectations of police organizations to be reflective of the citizens they serve and the increased interactions between police officers and professionals (often university educated) within the community, the need for post-secondary education becomes that much more relevant. There is research that supports a post-secondary education requirement for entry-level police officers (Bowman, 2012; Miller, 2011) and research that discounts the perceived benefits of post-secondary education (Blakemore & Simpson, 2010; Hensen et al., 2010). Of the number of studies conducted examining the nexus between police officer education levels and organization benefits, none (that can be located) have specifically examined the minimum level of education required as a police applicant relevant to CBM.

Competency-Based Performance Management

There have been a number of fundamental shifts in the traditional paradigms of police organizations and expectations by the public they serve over the past several decades. These shifts have challenged police administrators and elected officials to reassess their methods and adapt to the changing demands of the populations they serve (Blandford, 2004; Campbell, 1992; Coleman, 2012; Oppal, 1994). Modern police organizations continue to subscribe to the Peelian model, measuring efficiency and effectiveness of police service by relying on statistics such as crime rates, clearance rates, number of charges, and so on (Leuprecht, 2014).

These performance metrics attempt to demonstrate the efficiency of the organization; however, they are evidence of efficiency after the fact. The difficulty with these traditional methods is that they cannot measure how many crimes were prevented (Cordner, 2014; Grant & Terry, 2012; Leuprecht, 2014). This highlights the difficulty of establishing a linkage between police effort and community outcomes. For example, if reported crime decreases or increases, it may be the result of a reduction in, or an increase in, community confidence that the police cannot, or can, do something about crime. Additionally, police leaders discontinue many programs if specific police strategies do not yield immediate results. Normally, policing costs are calculated on a per-capita basis, but using costs as a simple comparator among police services may be misleading and does not account for several important considerations, including range and variance of demands on a police service, differing geographical considerations, relevant and distinctive social and economic conditions, and locally defined priorities (Hutchins, 2014; Leuprecht, 2014). In the end, however, efficiency and effectiveness inextricably link to strategic human resource management strategies.

As a public service, police organizations devote anywhere from 80% to 90% of their operating budgets to employee salaries (Blandford, 2004; Leuprecht, 2014; London Police Service, 2013) and therefore have a substantial investment in their personnel. Historically, Canadian police services, with respect to police officers, have operated as closed personnel systems, with recruiting and hiring efforts directed at entry-level positions (e.g., constables). Due to the closed personnel systems, human resource strategies in police organizations must ensure selection of highly qualified persons.

It is essential that the capacity of police organizations improve through human resource strategies that include the development of competency profiles and training standards for all jobs in policing (Aguinis, 2013; Belcourt & McBey, 2010; Hay Group, 2007; Heneman, Judge, Smith, & Summers, 2010). Competency-based human resource management is an approach to managing people and supporting organizational goals and objectives. Organizations must consider how to balance the needs of the organization and hiring of persons who already have the necessary competencies. Making appropriate hiring and placement decisions at all levels is critical for future success (Belcourt & McBey, 2010; Bonder et al., 2011; Campbell, 1992; Heneman et al., 2010). As stated very succinctly by Coleman (2012), "the effective and efficient management of police organizations and the accountability of police leaders is thus dependent, through strategic human resource management, on hiring the 'right' employees, and placing the 'right' employees into the 'right' positions at the 'right' time" (p. 5). In Canada, police officers have the benefit of security of tenure; once an officer is appointed and has completed a probationary period, they may only be dismissed for just cause and upon the decision of the chief (subject to an independent review) (Robertson, 2012). This underscores the need to ensure the correct decision at entry-level hiring.

A competency model is a collection of competencies that are relevant to successful performance in a particular job position. These competencies are classified as core or behavioral competencies and functional or technical competencies (Hay Group, 2007; Police Sector Council, 2013). Behavioral competencies are foundational and form a component of an applicant's personality. Through development, such as higher levels of education, honing and shaping of these skills can occur; for example, communication skills are a core competency for police officers. The writing of critical essays, scholarly debate, and exposure to opposing points of view contribute to the development of strong communication skills (Green & Gates, 2014; Ness, 2011; Paterson, 2011). Researchers suggest that assessment by competencies provides greater reliability and validity in predicting future performance (Ferguson & Ramsay, 2010; Haberfeld, 2013; Lawler, 1994).

Behavioral competencies, the traits and characteristics that differentiate superior from average performers, are significantly more predictive of performance than aptitude, skills, or experience (Zwell, 2000). Clearly defined indicators within each behavioral competency provide a strong base for an effective management performance system; by reviewing the competencies required by a particular job and those possessed by the person performing the job, integration by linking competencies with the hiring process, performance appraisals, career development, and the promotional process occurs. One survey of 134 persons across diverse organizations found that the primary reason for using a competency-based system was to provide a linkage between the mission, vision, values, and culture of an organization through the selection, appraisal, and learning of the persons in the organization (Zwell, 2000). Therefore, a strong and effective organizational plan that has an integrated competency model that clearly identifies competencies for each specific position can assist in identifying and developing personnel for middle and senior management positions within a police organization. This means identifying and developing the talent pool early and utilizing techniques such as coaching and mentoring people to assume positions of leadership in executive positions (Cordner, 2014; Haberfeld, 2013; Thibault, Lynch, & McBride, 2011). It also has implications with respect to developing and implementing an effective performance assessment tool that will identify personnel for these positions at an early enough stage so that development for senior management positions can occur.

Traditional approaches to determining competencies involve observing superior performers and then identifying the traits and characteristics that differentiate them from average performers. The difficulty with this methodology is the relative subjectivity involved. A second common approach is to perform interviews and organize focus groups with key stakeholders (e.g., supervisors, incumbents, HR specialists) in which the competencies and descriptive behavioral indicators are developed through a consultative, inclusive process. The resulting competencies should then reflect the uniqueness of the organization and its jobs (Catano, Wiesner, & Hackett, 2013; Coleman, 2012; Police Sector Council, 2013).

The competencies and related behavioral indicators then form the framework for a competency model, which is a cluster of individual competencies relative to a specific job or family of jobs within the organization. Current research suggests that competency models should contain between 7 and 16 competencies, and there should be specific competency models for each job function (Coleman, 2012; Gomez-Mejia et al., 2010; Lawler, 1994; Zwell, 2000). Within police services, perhaps with the exception of the larger national and provincial organizations, there is a tendency to promote individuals to a specific rank (e.g., sergeant, inspector), as opposed to promoting individuals to specific positions (e.g., investigators, branch commanders). Therefore, in keeping with accepted methodologies, police services might consider developing competency models relative to rank. However, there are core competencies that must retain a level of commonality between the ranks as promotions are generally extensions and expansions of job scope, but the foundation remains fundamentally rooted in the core competencies (Bonder et al., 2011). This building block approach ensures that officers develop for progression throughout the organization, congruent with the organizational value system.

The Police Sector Council is the research and development section of the Canadian federal government regarding policing issues. A series of studies, starting in 2001, have culminated in the development of a competency-based human resources management framework for Canadian police services (Hay Group, 2007; Human Resource Development Canada, 2001; Police Sector Council, 2013). This framework provides competency models for the ranks of constable, sergeant, staff sergeant, and inspector; the ranks of superintendent, deputy chief, and chief are under development. The requisite competencies and corresponding descriptors within each rank competency model are identified as behavioral or technical. A rating scale guides an assessment of the degree to which the officer demonstrates the competency and links to an assessment of a police officer's overall ability. At the hiring stage, the behavioral competencies form the basis for an evaluation of the applicant's suitability and future performance. Founded on community expectations and legislation, the role of a police officer in Canada is consistent across the country. As a result, there is consensus regarding the desired characteristics, behaviors, and attributes for a police officer (Campbell, 1992; Hay Group, 2007; Police Sector Council, 2013; Summers, 2009). There are, however, no clear, consistent criteria for the selection of a new police officer. Police organizations can establish any selection criteria above the minimum legislated standards and can compromise on the attributes of the ideal candidate.

Once developed, these competency models form the foundation for the HR process—selection, performance management, career development, and promotion—to ensure a truly integrated systems approach. Increasingly, competencies and competency models are being used to communicate organizational values and standards, create awareness and understanding of the need for organizational change, develop leaders, identify training strategies, and evaluate individual performance (Aguinis, 2013; Heneman et al., 2010; Police Sector Council, 2013).

Competency-based management (CBM) is an approach that standardizes and integrates human resource activities based on competencies that support organizational goals, with the competencies required for a position clearly defined in terms of behaviors necessary for successful job performance. Research indicates that when selection, hiring, promotion, and employee development programs are aligned with competencies, there are improvements in performance throughout the organization (Catano et al., 2013; Hay Group, 2007; Kai-ting, 2012; Police Sector Council, 2013).

Competency-based management, therefore, is not a static process. Methods of appraisal and systems for personnel selection and development must adapt to changing demands and organizational directions; otherwise, the systems do not contribute in a productive manner to the needs of the organization or the public it serves.

Current Hiring Practices

The Police Sector Council is the research and development section of the Canadian federal government in regards to policing issues. A series of studies, starting in 2001, have culminated in the development of a competency-based human resources management framework for Canadian police services (Hay Group, 2007; Human Resource Development Canada, 2001; Police Sector Council, 2013). This framework provides competency models for the ranks of constable, sergeant, staff sergeant, and inspector; the ranks of superintendent, deputy chief, and chief are still under development. Identified within each rank competency model are the requisite competencies, identified as behavioral or technical, with corresponding descriptors. A rating scale guides an assessment of the degree to which the officer demonstrates the competency and links to an assessment of a police officer's overall ability. All police organizations in Canada received the resulting manual as a guide to implementing a competency-based performance management system; it remains a voluntary process.

At the hiring stage, the behavioral competencies form the basis for an evaluation of the applicant's suitability and future performance. The role of a police officer in Canada is consistent across the country; not only is it founded on community expectations, but it is enshrined in legislation. There is also reasonable consensus regarding the desired characteristics, behaviors, and attributes for a police officer (Campbell, 1992; Hay Group, 2007; Oppal, 1994; Police Sector Council, 2013). Many police organizations have competency-based human resources management processes in place, but consistent, objective application of the competencies during the hiring process is absent (Coleman, 2012; Hay Group, 2007; Summers, 2009). Police organizations can establish any selection criteria above the minimum legislated standards or can compromise on the attributes of the ideal candidate. This inconsistency is one of the subjects of this chapter.

Methodology

Statement of the Problem

In Canada, provincial (and, in the case of the Royal Canadian Mounted Police, federal) legislation governs policing within the provinces and territories of Canada and sets the minimum standards required to become a police officer. Leaders of police organizations declare that policing is a profession (Bowman, 2012; Green & Gates, 2014; Rydberg & Terrill, 2010), yet the minimal entry levels are not consistent with that premise. In reality, researchers suggest that the majority of police organizations hire new police officers with some form of post-secondary education and qualifications exceeding the minimum, thereby presenting a latent barrier to a potential recruit who meets only the minimum standard (Hay Group, 2007; Rydberg & Terrill, 2010). Police organizations, by adoption of this standard practice, suggest post-secondary education is a bona fide occupational requirement, with the expectation that many job competencies are developed through education (Bowman, 2012; Carlan &

Lewis, 2009; Sniderman, Bulmash, Nelson, & Quick, 2010; Summers, 2009). The overall problem is the lack of an understanding of the extent of the integration between competency-based hiring and competency-based performance management processes in relation to hiring entry-level police recruits. This chapter examines those issues within the policing industry in Canada and provides recommendations to guide police leaders and key stakeholders in making positive changes in the management of police human resources.

Research Questions and Hypotheses

The following research questions and hypotheses guided this quantitative study:

R1 To what extent, if any, is there a statistically significant deviation of preferences to hire police recruits from what would be expected given the minimum legislated education requirement of high school education?

$H1_0$ There is no statistically significant deviation of preferences to hire police recruits from what would be expected given the minimum legislated education requirement of high school education.

H1a There is a statistically significant deviation of preferences to hire police recruits from what would be expected given the minimum legislated education requirement of high school education.

R2 Is there a correlation between the size of a police service and the use of a competency-based hiring process?

$H2_0$ There is no statistically significant correlation between the number of sworn police officers of a police service and the use a behavioral competency model for hiring.

H2a There is a statistically significant correlation between the number of sworn police officers of a police service, and the use a behavioral competency model for hiring.

R3 To what extent, if any, is there a statistically significant correlation between the use of a behavioral-competency model for entry-level hiring and the use of a competency-based performance management system.

$H3_0$ There is no statistically significant correlation between the use of a behavioral-competency model for entry-level hiring and the use of a competency-based performance management system.

H3a There is a statistically significant correlation between the use of behavioral-competency model for entry-level hiring and the use of a competency-based performance management system.

For R1, the dependent variable is the minimum legislated level of education; the independent variable is the level of education beyond the minimum level. For R2, the independent variable is the size of the police service. The dependent variable is the use of a behavioral competency-based performance-management process in the recruitment, selection, and hiring of entry-level police constables. For R3, the independent variable is the use of a behavioral competency-based performance-management process in the recruitment, selection, and hiring of entry-level police constables. The dependent variable is the probability of post-secondary education being a requirement of a behavioral competency-based performance-management process.

Research Methodology

This research project used a quantitative, correlational methodology research design to collect new quantitative data through a self-administered survey sent to the police chiefs of selected police services (*N*=145) in Canada. There are currently 69,539 police officers in Canada, distributed across approximately 200 law enforcement organizations (Statistics Canada, 2014). Excluded from the survey were the many law enforcement services that do not deliver front-line, community policing; rather, they are specialty or private enforcement organizations. Also excluded from the survey were First Nations (i.e., Aboriginal) police organizations, as they have a unique governance structure that differs in many ways from other Canadian police services. Proper protocol required that the chief of police receive the surveys, but the recruiting officers were the targeted respondents. The chosen methodology allowed for the identification of the characteristics and possible correlations between the existing minimum educational requirements for police applicants and the actual practices of police organizations across the province. This cross-sectional research collected data about a broad range of police organizations and hiring practices.

The researcher adopted an existing survey (Coleman, 2012) to administer an internet-based survey to collect data from Canadian police organization recruiting staff. This survey consists of 30 questions utilizing a variety of designs and was used with permission from the author. This survey had been previously used in a doctoral dissertation research project and was found to have validity and reliability.

The data analysis tested research question one (R1) by examining the fixed variable of a legislated minimum educational level for police recruits relative to the actual levels of education recruits preferred by Canadian police organizations' HR personnel.

Research question two (R2) examined the correlation between the number of sworn police officers of a police service and the use a behavioral competency model for hiring. In this case, the size of the police service (i.e., number of sworn police officers) was the independent variable, while the use of a behavioral competency–based performance-management process was a dependent variable.

The final research question (R3) examined the correlation between the use of a behavioral competency model for constables and the education level of a police recruit in Canada. Given that a police organization either uses a behavioral competency–based performance-management process or they do not, the independent variable was the use of a behavioral competency–based performance-management process (Carver & Gradwohl-Nash, 2012; Hair Jr., Black, Babin, & Anderson, 2010). The dependent variable in this case was the probability of post-secondary education being a requirement of a behavioral competency–based performance management process. Additionally, given the various levels of post-secondary education, this was an interval dependent variable.

For H_2 and H_3, demographic information of each respondent provided data to identify police service size, while several survey questions probed the integration of a competency-based performance management into the organizational recruiting process.

Data collected from the web-based survey were coded and imported into SPSS (Statistical Package for the Social Sciences) from the online survey service provider. Analyses through a variety of statistical tools were used to identify the current practices relative to recruitment and hiring of new police officers and provided insight about why there might be a disconnect between the current legislated requirements and the actual practices of police recruiters.

Instrumentation

The data-gathering methodology for this research project consisted of the adaptation and administration of an internet-based survey instrument to solicit responses to a series of questions focused on the hiring processes of Canadian police services. The actual components of the survey instrument included a letter, addressed to the chief of police, explaining the purpose of the research and requesting their assistance and a 30-question online survey. The letter explaining the purpose of the research followed the recommendations of the Columbia Southern University Institutional Research Board. The survey questions consisted of a variety of scales, including yes or no responses, multiple choice, and a series of subjective questions utilizing a five-point Likert scale. Provided to each respondent was the opportunity to provide additional qualitative comments for specific questions.

Administration of the survey instrument was through an online survey provider. Many Canadian public sector and private sector organizations are reluctant to respond to online surveys in which data stored in the United States is subject to the Patriot Act legislation; utilizing this process addressed concerns regarding confidentiality and ethical concerns (Hagan, 2014; Leedy & Ormrod, 2010). Automatic coding of collected data by the online survey provider allowed for downloading into an Excel spreadsheet for exportation in SPSS.

Limitations

The major limitation of this research project is a small population size of Canadian police organizations. Dependence on federal and provincial police services to service rural and smaller communities, combined with the use of regional police services for large urban areas, has greatly reduced the number of "small town" police services. In contrast, the United States Department of Justice found there were 17,985 state and local law enforcement agencies across the United States (US Department of Justice, 2011). In order to minimize any negative impacts to the study results, the entire population ($N=145$) of police services were surveyed.

As a self-report survey, the responses were based on perception as well as fact (e.g., current practices, policies, and procedures) and may therefore contain some inherent biases. Several questions called for a subjective reflection by the respondent. Additionally, survey research has strong reliability but has an inherent validity weakness, as the artificial nature of the survey format may affect the validity (Leedy & Ormrod, 2010). Given the relatively small population size and the proficient use of computers within the policing industry (e.g., proficiency in completing web-based surveys), sample bias was limited, but the researcher remained cognizant of the potential. Time constraints required that the survey was distributed during the traditional summer holiday period, which may have affected the response rate. Additionally, the response rate might have been higher if the survey instrument had fewer but more targeted questions.

Another limitation identified after examining the data was the potential biases by respondents as the majority had post-secondary education; there existed a possibility that the respondents self-identified more highly with recruits that had post-secondary education.

Summary, Conclusions, and Recommendations

Summary of Findings and Conclusions

Responses were received from representatives of a broad range of Canadian police services, varied in size from less than 50 to over 1,000 officers. The majority of respondents had 20 years or more of service and were sworn police officers, as opposed to civilian members. In addition, a large majority had some form of human resource management credential, either professional or academic. This suggests that police organizations recognize the value of personnel specifically trained and qualified in human resource management issues.

Education

The initial research question and hypothesis examined the current recruiting and hiring practices of Canadian police services. The first null hypothesis ($H1_0$) stated that there is no statistically significant difference between the current legislated minimum educational requirements and the hiring practices for police recruits by a Canadian police service. With the exceptions of the provinces of Quebec and British Columbia, the minimum education required by legislation to be a police officer in Canada is a high school diploma. Notwithstanding, when questioned what level of education was actually preferred for recruits, respondents overwhelmingly indicated post-secondary education. This suggests that there is a gap between the legislated education level and the reality of what is preferred, presenting a latent barrier to an applicant with only a high school diploma.

Respondents were asked to force rank nine core competencies for the entry-level rank of constable in order of importance and then asked to identify, in their opinion, the most effective method to develop each competency. Ethical accountability and responsibility, the first ranked competency, presented an anomaly as many of the respondents identified "other." This option accounted for competency development through any number of external factors other than the other presented options. This competency could be considered as a moral construct and developed through an applicant's upbringing and includes influences founded in family, faith, and community.

Respondents identified post-secondary education as the primary indicator of competency development for five of the nine competencies; further probing questioned respondents as to the appropriate level respondents to identify the appropriate level of education for each competency. A completed university degree ranked as the highest indicator of competency development, followed by college diploma, some university education, high school education, then some college education as the lowest ranking. The preference for a university degree over a college diploma was minimal; conversely, the preference for a post-secondary credential compared to a high school education was very pronounced. A common perception of police recruiters (based on this researcher's experience) is that an applicant who failed to complete post-secondary education, whether college or university, may be an indicator of reduced dedication to policing as a career, possibly explaining the lower ranking.

The responses support the belief that post-secondary education is a prime indicator of competency development and is highly valued by police recruiters. Lacking are clearly defined standards that link that education to the desired competencies. The college diploma pathway provides an applicant with a focused, career-specific education, but the learning outcomes for these programs do not align directly with the competency model for an entry-level police officer. Conversely, the preference at the university level is very nonspecific, suggesting that the broader critical thinking and analytical reasoning skills are the desired outcome. There appears to be a disconnect between the expectations from the college level and the university level relative to competency development

Many of the respondents believed that the current legislated minimum level of education was insufficient for police applicants. For currently serving police officers, just over half the respondents were of the opinion that officers did not have a sufficient level of post-secondary education; this is consistent with all police organizations providing some form of support for ongoing post-secondary education for serving officers.

Whether officers receive direct financial support or accommodation of work schedules, there is a budgetary impact to the organization, which raises the question of why organizations do not download this cost to the pre-hire level (i.e., increased entry-level education requirements). With increasing pressures to remain fiscally responsible, realigning the resulting financial savings to operational budgets would be prudent. This presents opportunities for police organizations to collaborate with colleges and universities and push competency development downstream to these post-secondary institutions. From a human resource management perspective, the hiring of employees with the necessary competencies is financially desirable, compared to hiring employees and then educating/training them to the desired entry-level competencies.

This null hypothesis (H1$_0$) was rejected. There is clear evidence that the preference for a recruit with post-secondary education is significantly greater than the minimum legislated standard. From a human resource perspective, there was inconsistency across the policing sector in the application of minimum versus preferred standards. In order to ensure predictive validity for new recruits, to enhance the image of police organizations, and to increase the level of public trust, consistent application of entry-level education requirements by police organizations across the country is required.

Competencies

The second null hypothesis (H2$_0$) stated that there is no statistically significant correlation between the number of sworn police officers of a police service and the use a behavioral competency model for hiring. The third null hypothesis (H3$_0$) stated that there is no statistically significant correlation between the use of a behavioral competency model for entry-level hiring and the use of a competency-based performance-management system.

From an organizational perspective, most of respondents indicated their organization had a formalized human resource strategy and utilized both competency-based performance management and competency-based hiring processes. Analysis of the data indicated that many HR staff directly involved in the hiring of police recruits are not trained or qualified to do so, which is very concerning. Given that policing in Canada is relatively homogenous, the expectations of community stakeholders—whether they are in Vancouver, British Columbia, or Halifax, Nova Scotia—demand a high level of reliability and predictive validity in the selection of police recruits. Training and qualifying human resource staff (i.e., recruiters) to a consistent level would accomplish this. There was insufficient evidence to reject the null hypothesis (H2$_0$), but there was sufficient evidence to reject the null hypothesis (H3$_0$).

It appears that Canadian police services have reached some level of maturity regarding the adaptation and integration of competency-based performance management into the recruiting and selection process, as well as the ongoing performance management of existing officers. Notwithstanding, there are gaps in the selection process and in a consistent, valid approach to competency assessment of police applicants. A disconnect exists between the minimum legislated educational requirements and the realities of what is happening in police organizations. There is some reluctance to increase the minimum educational standards through legislation. Many police executives anecdotally comment that raising the education standard would eliminate many potential candidates. This is flawed logic; the increased standard may contribute to a reduction in applicants, but police services need to consider the new complexities of contemporary policing and develop strategies to attract and retain a new breed of applicants. Ironically, police executives remain adamant that policing is a profession even when it lacks one of the basic tenants that define a profession—post-secondary education. Rather than keeping the standards artificially low for the exception, raising the bar to be reflective of the actual expectations would better serve police applicants and the communities, essentially ensuring that police recruits are "hired with competence."

Although not statistically significant, there is some indication that smaller police services struggle with implementing a competency-based hiring process with properly trained personnel. The establishment of nationwide standards would define the core competencies that a recruit must possess and the standards by which an applicant meets those competencies and recruiters evaluate them. There is opportunity for smaller services to collaborate with larger services in their HR processes. These economies of scale would serve to standardize the process, increase the validity, and address the potential concerns of smaller communities that their officers may be less qualified to serve. Similarly, the creation of a national standard and the appropriate assessment tools to ensure competent officers are hired would also serve to increase transferability and portability of credentials from one police organization to another.

Recommendations for Practice

Policing in the twenty-first century is far more complex than in previous generations and must include a balance between police training and education. Expectations placed on officers require a shift from the traditional vocational level of training to include post-secondary education that can develop the critical thinking, analytical reasoning, and sociological skillsets that are required to be an effective police officer. This chapter has identified the preference for police applicants to have post-secondary education, along with work experience, prior to hiring. In order to enhance the image of police organizations and the level of public trust, police leaders must support processes and legislation to ensure a common minimal level of competence for officers. Upon reflection, and thoughtful consideration of the data analysis and literature review, I make the following recommendations to assist police executives and HR personnel.

Recommendation 1

Raising the legislated standards for becoming a police officer in Canada to a minimum of a university degree is recommended. This is perhaps the most contentious recommendation offered, but it cuts directly to the heart of this research project. Implementation of this new standard would provide a level of confidence to police recruiters that applicants have developed the desired competencies. This would also increase public confidence and enhance the image of professionalism for police organizations. Education levels in Canada are on the rise, and police applicants reflect this with an increased number having post-secondary education. By supporting an increase in the minimum education standard for recruits, police organizations demonstrate commitment to being reflective of the community demographics and validation for police officers with increased intellectual capacity and potential. This research project identifies support for the minimum level of education to be a university degree, suggesting police organizations value the broader liberal education at the university level, rather than the vocational-type education at the college level. Indeed, many college-level vocational programs (e.g., police foundations diploma) duplicate many of the education/training components that recruits receive post-hire (e.g., police colleges or academies), thereby making such college programs redundant.

This recommendation moves beyond simply raising the bar and leaving potential applicants to chart their own course. It provides police organizations with the opportunity to shape their future through focused recruiting, raise their public image, and advance toward becoming a true profession. Removal of the latent barrier (i.e., minimum of high school versus the preference for post-secondary education) would also serve to raise the transparency and credibility of the application process.

Recommendation 2

The creation of police studies university degree program is recommended. Police organizations need to lead from the front and work to establish policing as a true profession with a specialized post-secondary credential that aligns learning outcomes to desired competencies. Police leaders must work collaboratively with post-secondary institutions to develop a professional degree, with learning outcomes that align with the desired competencies for police recruits. There are many similarities between nursing and policing, yet the profession of nursing has transitioned to a university-level professional degree (i.e., Bachelor of Nursing or Bachelor of Science in Nursing) as the post-secondary education requirement in order to practice. Why policing hesitates to make a similar transition is due, perhaps, to a deep-seated tradition of paramilitary structure and dependence upon on-the-job training. The creation of a professional degree that incorporates theoretical and applied (i.e., education and training) would parallel the nursing model.

As a minimum requirement for entry into the field, formal education is only one factor to consider for the ideal police recruit. It is essentially a screening criterion and does not diminish the ability of police recruiters to select the most qualified candidates. It does, however, move policing one step closer to profession status, increase public perception of professionalism, and ensure police organizations hire competent officers.

Recommendation 3

The creation of a national professional policing organization/body that would oversee admission-to-practice requirements and competency-based management standards and establish and enforce adherence to a code of ethics is recommended. This oversight organization would function similarly to other existing profession bodies, such as the Upper Canada Law Society (for lawyers), the Ontario Teachers College, the Canadian Institute of Chartered Accountants, and the Canadian Nursing Association. The creation of such a police organization would require collaboration among the key stakeholders (e.g., police unions, police leaders, government officials), but the initial framework could be developed within the mandate of the Canadian Police College (CPC). Located in Ottawa, the CPC holds itself out to be the leader in advanced/specialized training and executive development for Canadian police services. Additionally, it is tasked with establishing and advancing, in partnership with stakeholders and communities, national standards of excellence in police education and leadership training. A logical progression to this mandate would be to become the oversight authority for Canadian police services relative to competency-based and ethical standards and certification of qualified police officers to practice. This national standardization, combined with a post-secondary education entrance requirement, would significantly enhance the transition to recognition of policing as a true profession.

Recommendation 4

Police organizations continue to transition to competency-based management systems and develop standardized recruiting practices across Canada to ensure reliability and validity in the process. A key component is ensuring use of the appropriate assessment methods to determine competency development. As noted in the data analysis, 38.9% (N=21) of HR staff directly involved in the hiring of police recruits are not trained or qualified to do so. As part of a standardized recruiting process, training of all staff directly involved in the hiring process would ensure consistency and transparency.

Recommendation 5

The Police Sector Council (PSC) has laid a strong foundation for the transition to competency-based management for Canadian police organizations; I recommended that this foundation becomes the standard for Canadian police organizations. The competency-based management manual produced by the PSC, developed after extensive consultation with key stakeholders across the Canadian policing industry, is a highly credible document. This study identified that many police services have already adopted the PSC competency models or some variation thereof, but mandatory adoption of this standard would reduce inconsistency of use across the Canadian policing industry and contribute to competent police recruits entering the field.

Discussion Questions

1. Given geographic and demographic differences, can the various competencies be standardized across police organizations on a national level?
2. Can the evaluation of competencies required for serving police officers adequately assess a police recruit, given they would lack full context and experience as an officer?
3. Should academic programs be specific to policing or criminal justice, or could post-secondary education in unrelated disciplines provide the same competency development?
4. How would a national oversight body (e.g., College of Policing) be structured and implemented? Would such a body develop standards and best practices, or would it act as a professional body for the purposes of censure and discipline?
5. Should the hiring of police officers be conducted solely by police officers, or should hiring decisions include human resource specialists to ensure consistency and transparency in the hiring process?

References

Aguinis, H. (2013). *Performance management*. Upper Saddle River, NJ: Pearson Prentice Hall.

Belcourt, M., & McBey, K. J. (2010). *Strategic human resources planning*. Toronto, ON: Nelson Education Inc.

Blakemore, B., & Simpson, K. (2010). A comparison of the effectiveness of pre- and post-employment modes of higher education for student police officers. *The Police Journal, 83*(1), 29–41. doi:10.1358/pojo.2010.83.1.481

Blandford, S. (2004). The impact of adequacy standards on Ontario police services. *The Canadian Review of Police Research, 1*(1), 118–129.

Bonder, A., Bouchard, C. D., & Bellemare, G. (2011). Competency-based management—an integrated approach to human resource management in the Canadian public sector. *Public Personnel Management, 40*(1), 1–10.

Bowman, T. L. (2012, January). *Is policing a job or a profession? The case for a four year degree*. Retrieved from www.calea.org/calea-update-magazine/issue-108/policing-job-or-profession-case-four-year-degree

Campbell, D. S. (1992). *Police learning system for Ontario: Final report and recommendations*. Toronto, ON: Government of Ontario.

Carlan, P. E., & Lewis, J. A. (2009). Dissecting police professionalism: A comparison of predictors within five professionalism subsets. *Police Quarterly, 12*(4), 370–387.

Carver, R. H., & Gradwohl-Nash, J. (2012). *Doing data analysis with SPSS*. Boston, MA: Cengage Learning.

Catano, V. M., Wiesner, W. H., & Hackett, R. D. (2013). *Recruitment and selection in Canada*. Toronto, ON: Nelson Education Ltd.

Coleman, T. (2012). *A model for improving the strategic measurement and management of policing: The police organizational performance index University of Regina*. Moose Jaw, SK: University of Regina.

Cordner, G. W. (2014). *Police administration*. Waltham, MA: Anderson Publishing.

Council of Ontario Universities (2011). *Council of Ontario universities*. Largest First Year Class Enters Ontario Universities. Retrieved October 22, 2011, from www.cou.on.ca/news/media-releases/cou/largest-first-year-class-enters-ontario-universiti.aspx

École nationale de police du Québec. (2013, January). *How to become a police officer?*. Retrieved from www.enpq.qc.ca/en/les-incontournables/how-to-become-a-police-officer.html

Ferguson, L. H., & Ramsay, J. D. (2010, October). Development of a profession. *Professional Safety*, 24–30.

Gomez-Mejia, L. R., Balkin, D. B., & Cardy, R. L. (2010). *Managing human resources*. Upper Saddle River, NJ: Prentice Hall.

Government of Canada (2013). *Royal Canadian mounted police act*. Ottawa, ON: Minister of Justice.

Government of Ontario (2009). *Police services act*. Toronto, ON: Government of Ontario.

Grant, H. B., & Terry, K. J. (2012). *Law enforcement in the 21st century*. Upper Saddle River, NJ: Pearson Education.

Green, T., & Gates, A. (2014). Understanding the process of professionalisation in the police organisation. *Police Journal, 83*(2), 75–91. doi:10.1350/pojo.2014.87.2.662

Haberfeld, M. R. (2013). *Police leadership: Organizational and managerial decision making process*. Upper Saddle River, NJ: Pearson Education.

Hagan, F. E. (2014). *Research methods in criminal justice and criminology*. Upper Saddle River, NJ: Prentice Hall.

Hair Jr., J. F., Black, W. C., Babin, B. J., & Anderson, R. E. (2010). *Multivariate data analysis*. Upper Saddle River, NJ: Pearson Prentice Hall.

Hay Group (2007). *A national diagnostic on human resources in policing*. Ottawa, ON: Hay Group.

Heneman, H. G., Judge, T. A., Smith, V., & Summers, R. (2010). *Staffing organizations*. Whitby, ON: McGraw-Hill Ryerson.

Hensen, B., Reyns, B. W., Klahm IV, C. F., & Frank, J. (2010). Do good recruits make good cops? Problems predicting and measuring academy and street-level success. *Police Quarterly, 13*(1), 5–26.

Hilal, S., Densley, J., & Zhao, R. (2013). Cops in college: Police officers' perceptions of formal education. *Journal of Criminal Justice Education, 24*(4), 461–477. doi:10.1080/10511253.791332

Human Resource Development Canada (2001). *Strategic human resources analysis of public policing in Canada*. Ottawa, ON: Police Sector Council.

Hutchins, H. (2014). *Police resources in Canada*. Statistics Canada, Canadian Centre for Justice Studies. Ottawa: Statistics Canada. Retrieved from www.statcan.gc.ca/pub/85-002-x/2014001/article/11914-eng.pdf

Kai-ting, M. C. (2012). Development and impacts of a new performance management system in the Hong Kong police force. *Policing: An International Journal of Police Strategies & Management, 35*(3), 468–490. doi:10.1108/13639511211250758

Lawler, E. E. (1994). From job-based to competency-based organizations. *Journal of Organizational Behaviour, 15*(1), 3–15. Retrieved from ttp://ezproxy.library.dal.ca/login?url=http://search.proquest.com/docview/228837970?accountid=10406

Leedy, P. D., & Ormrod, J. E. (2010). *Practical research: Planning and design*. Boston, MA: Pearson Education.

Legislature of Newfoundland. (2014, August 29). *Royal newfoundland constabulary regulations*. Consolidated Newfoundland and Labrador Regulation 802/96. Retrieved from www.assembly.nl.ca/legislation/sr/regulations/rc960802.htm#3_

Leuprecht, C. (2014). *The blue line or the bottom line of police services in Canada*. MacDonald-Laurier Institute. Ottawa, ON: MacDonald-Laurier Institute.

London Police Service. (2013). *Operating expenses*. London: London Police Service.

Miller, A. (2011, March–April). The case for college: Why higher education enhances law enforcement. *FBI National Academy Associate, 13*(2), 26–31.

More, H. W., Vito, G. F., & Walsh, W. F. (2012). *Organizational behavior and management in law enforcement*. Upper Saddle River, NJ: Pearson Education Inc.

Ness, J. J. (2011, March–April). The importance of higher education for law enforcement. *National Academy Associate, 13*(2), 14–30.

Ontario Police College (2013, September 29). *Basic constable training program: Educational demographics 1996–2012*. Aylmer, ON: Ontario Police College.

Oppal, W. T. (1994). *Closing the gap: Policing and the community*. Vancouver, BC: Attorney General of British Columbia.

Paterson, C. (2011). Adding value? A review of the international literature on the role of higher education in police training and education. *Police Practice and Research, 12*(4), 286–297. doi:10.1080/15614263.2011.563969

Police Sector Council (2013). *A guide to competency-based management in police services*. Ottawa, ON: Police Sector Council.

Robertson, N. (2012, September). Policing: Fundamental principles in a Canadian context. *Canadian Public Administration, 55*(3), 343–363.

Ross, J. I. (2012). *Policing issues*. Sudbury, MA: Jones & Bartlett.

Rydberg, J., & Terrill, W. (2010). The effect of higher education on police behavior. *Police Quarterly*, *13*(1), 92–120. doi:10.1177/1098611109357325

Scott, J., Evans, D., & Verma, A. (2009). Does higher education affect perceptions among police personnel?: A response from India. *Journal of Contemporary Criminal Justice*, *25*(2), 214–236. doi:10.1177/1043986209333592

Sniderman, P. R., Bulmash, J., Nelson, D. L., & Quick, J. C. (2010). *Managing organizational behaviour in Canada*. Toronto, ON: Nelson Education Ltd.

Stansfield, R. T. (1996). *Issues in policing: A Canadian perspective*. Toronto, ON: Thompson Educational Publishing Inc.

Statistics Canada (2013, October 6). *Education in Canada: Attainment, field of study and location of study*. Ottawa: Statistics Canada. Retrieved from www.statcan.gc.ca/tables-tableaux/sum-som/l01/cst01/educ42-eng.htm

Statistics Canada (2014). *Statistics Canada*. Retrieved from www.statcan.gc.ca/start-debut-eng.html

Summers, M. (2009). *The role of education plays in police performance: Perceptions of law enforcement administrators*. New York, NY: Western Illinois University, School of Law Enforcement and Justice Studies.

Thibault, E. A., Lynch, L. M., & McBride, R. B. (2011). *Proactive police management*. Upper Saddle River, NJ: Prentice Hall.

US Department of Justice (2011). *Census of state and local law enforcement agencies, 2008*. Washington, DC: Bureau of Justice Statistics.

Whitelaw, B., & Parent, R. B. (2014). *Community-based strategic policing in Canada*. Toronto, ON: Nelson Education.

Zwell, M. (2000). *Creating a culture of competence*. New York, NY: John Wiley & Sons Inc.

Disclosure statement. This is to acknowledge that no financial interest or benefit has arisen from the direct applications of this research.

Chapter 11

An Examination of Police Corruption Utilizing the Theory of Planned Behavior

Ben Stickle

Introduction

The integrity of law enforcement officers is essential to an impartial and effective justice system. However, on occasion, law enforcement officers betray the principles they swear to uphold, resulting in what is commonly referred to as police corruption. The results may include corrosion of trust with the officer, the agency, a community, and the justice system as a whole.

Police corruption may come in many forms: excessive use of force, theft, misappropriation of public funds, false testimony, and more. Addressing the concerns related to police corruption is especially important as worldwide crime rates are dramatically changing as a result of the COVID-19 pandemic (Boman & Gallupe, 2020; Jennings & Perez, 2020; Stickle & Felson, 2020), and policing has become the focus of United States politics after several high-profile deaths leading many to call for defunding police agencies (Robinson, 2020). This chapter will examine the problem of police corruption and available data sources on the topic. Next, it will utilize the theory of planned behavior to examine how three components—behavioral beliefs, normative beliefs, and control beliefs—merge and form an intention to commit a corrupt act. Once a thorough application has been completed, this chapter examines the policy implications, guiding police employers to detect corrupt intentions before and during employment. Lastly, methods to alter the subjective norms of corruption within an agency and strengthen the perceived behavioral controls are discussed as a means to change corruption within an agency.

Problem

Law enforcement in the United States is unlike any other profession when examining the opportunity for corruption. Officers across the United States are given a wide swath of discretion to act and enforce laws as necessary and often receive little supervision while carrying out these duties. What amplifies the potential for police corruption primarily is an individual officer's ability to affect personal liberty to an alarming degree. Officers are entrusted with the authority and power to arrest, levy legal charges, remove children from parents, use force—including lethal force—and seize evidence and other items. This broad channel of power can cause significant issues within a society if improperly wielded (Stickle, 2020; Weitzer, 2002) and to a greater extent to an individual's life if theft, physical injury, or even death occur as a result of officer corruption.

In the United States, over 697,195 sworn law enforcement officers, working in over 17,000 individual police agencies, are authorized to carry weapons and impose criminal charges (FBI, 2019). Every week, many law enforcement officers encounter the opportunity to falsify statements, steal property, falsely arrest persons, seize money and drugs for personal use, apply

DOI: 10.4324/9781003047117-13

unnecessary force, threaten citizens into compliance, and commit many other crimes. While most of them do not participate in such corrupt actions (Cato, 2012; Stickle, 2016, 2017), it is difficult to quantify the exact number of law enforcement officers involved in some form of corruption for two primary reasons.

First, it is challenging to define police corruption. There is what many people would consider apparent violations of ethics that law enforcement officers may partake in, however; a cursory review of police corruption cases show, just as in other types of crime, there is no end to the creatively illegal or unethical acts that are possible (Cato, 2012). Even scholars researching corruption rarely agree on a single definition (Meyer, 1976). It is out of this chapter's scope to list all possible crimes or lapses of ethical judgement considered corruption. Therefore, a broad, easily understood, and commonly utilized definition will be employed for this study: "police corruption is the abuse of police authority for gain" (Klockars, Ivkovich, Harver, & Haberfeld, 2000, p. 1). This definition provides an excellent foundation to examine police corruption without being unnecessarily strict or broad.

The second difficulty in studying and preventing police corruption is the challenge to identify police corruption when it does occur. This may be for various reasons, such as departmental hesitancy to investigate itself and a desire not to "air its dirty laundry" to the public. Perhaps victims do not report unethical behavior by law enforcement (Klockars et al., 2000), or they are bribed or coerced into not reporting. Further, law enforcement officers may be less likely to report fellow officers' corrupt activities, often referred to as "the Blue Code of Silence" (Kutnjak Ivković, Morgan, Cajner Mraović, & Borovec, 2020; Skolnick, 2002; Westmarland & Conway, 2020). Finally, no organization is known to collect and publish consistent data on the prevalence of police corruption (Ivkovic, 2003). What is typically known of police corruption is based on localized investigations of an agency. Examples of this include studies of the Los Angeles, New York, Oakland, and Chicago Police Departments (Sherman, 1978).

Due to these challenges, a majority of corruption incidents are likely either not reported (Martin, 2001), handled internally, or not violations of a specific statute and therefore not reported to national clearinghouses on crime statistics. Thus, there is a potential for an unknown level or a "dark figure of crime" to be a factor that affects how police corruption is understood and studied (Lawrence & Langworthy, 1979). These factors make it nearly impossible to determine the extent to which police corruption occurs.

Available Data Sources

Because of this lack of data, the Cato Institute (a private reach institute) launched an aggressive effort to capture known instances of police corruption. CATO's goal was to "determine the extent of police misconduct in the United States, identify trends affecting police misconduct, and report on issues about police misconduct in order to enhance public awareness on issues regarding police misconduct across the country" (CATO, 2018, paragraph 1). The primary method for collecting data was by an automated computer search through a considerable volume of digitally published news stories available on the internet. Through a series of keyword searches, all possible related instances of police corruption reported in the news were captured and stored in a database. Then, researchers categorized and analyzed each news story to produce accurate and quarterly reports on police corruption nationwide as reported by the news media. This was a potentially vast wealth of data on the topic of police corruption. However, after several years of collecting data, the process was abandoned in 2017 (CATO, 2018) and is now only available for download by reaching out to the organization.

Another potential source of data conducted by Klockars (1999) is titled "Police Corruption in 30 Agencies in the United States" and utilizes a questionnaire distributed to over

6,000 police officers (with a nearly 50% response rate). It examines police officers' perceptions and tolerance for corruption. This survey described 11 hypothetical scenarios of police corruption and then asked the officers to rate on a Likert-type scale the seriousness of the corruption, the extent to which they would support agency discipline, and their willingness to report said behavior (Klockars, 1999). To some degree, this study is instructive of normative beliefs and subjective norms within law enforcement and, to a lesser degree, may indicate perceived behavioral control. However, it alone does not provide any indication of an officer's *intent* to commit corrupt activity, which is what leads to and is necessary for the behavior to occur. Thus, this study is instructive in its development and design as an example of loosely combining several aspects of the theory of planned behavior, albeit unintentional; however, it falls short of usability for the current chapter.

Theory of Planned Behavior

The challenges surrounding studying police corruption are many. It is difficult to define, sporadically reported (if at all), and even more difficult to prevent. Nevertheless, society's costs are steep when corruption occurs, both at an individual level and across the community. Even more concerning is that when corruption is identified, it is often too late—the illegal or unethical act has already been committed, and departments are left trying to salvage the community relationship while juggling actions to take against the officer. What is needed is a process for identifying officers who may engage in corrupt behavior before the incident occurs and the procedure for what to do with those officers. This chapter argues that adapting the theory of planned behavior may be a step toward achieving those needs.

The theory of planned behavior (TPB) is a widely tested psychological theory with over 200 empirical studies and several meta-analyses, which confirm the theory's ability to predict individuals' behavior based on the determinate measures of intentions (Fishbein & Ajzen, 2010). A primary assumption of the theory is that "human beings usually behave in a sensible manner; that they take account of available information and implicitly or explicitly consider the implication of their actions" (Ajzen, 2005, p. 117). This does not mean that all behavior will be seen as rational by others or that every time a behavior is committed, it proceeded from a long rational evaluation process by an individual. Instead, individuals are usually rational (in their minds), even if they are wrong in fact, and thus will act according to their perceived options and rationality. When social influences and perceived behavioral controls are changed, a different rational action may occur (Ajzen & Fishbein, 2000). Thus, the theory of planned behavior can be applied within the general concepts of crime, such as rational choice (Cornish & Clarke, 2017, 2014) and routine activities theories (Clarke & Felson, 1993; Cohen & Felson, 1979).

The theory of planned behavior by Ajzen (1985, 1991) states that a person's intention to perform or refrain from performing a behavior is the most critical and proximal determinant of that action. The theory postulates that this intention is formed by the combined interaction of three components: 1) attitude, 2) subjective norm, and 3) perceived behavioral controls (Ajzen, 2005) (see Figure 11.1).

Generally, people intend to perform a behavior when they have a favorable attitude toward the behavior, others have a positive attitude toward the behavior (subjective norm), and controls are limited. In some cases, only one or two of these determinate factors are needed to explain the intention, while in other cases, all three play a role to varying degrees. These factors change according to individuals, circumstances, roles, and social settings. Figure 11.2 displays the logic model of the theory of planned behavior presented by Icek Ajzen (1985, 1991). What follows is an explanation of each concept and how they combine to form a measurable intention.

Figure 11.1 Three Primary Determinants

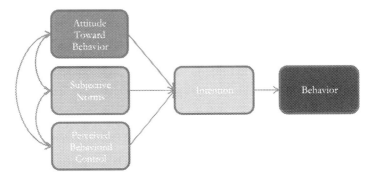

Figure 11.2 Theory of Planned Behavior (Modified Logic Model)

It should first be noted that attitude toward behavior, subjective norms, and perceived behavioral controls are interlinked. Each one may affect the others to varying degrees in different situations. The fluidity and interaction of the concept are vital to understanding and applying the theory. Many studies of behavior focus only on one determinate indicator, lack fluidity, and are poorly equipped to predict behavior accurately (Ajzen, 2005). As a result, studies have often failed to predict behavior with any accuracy (Fishbein & Ajzen, 2010). However, studies utilizing the theory of planned behavior provide strong support for the proposition that intentions to perform a behavior can be predicted from attitudes toward the behavior, subjective norms, and perceptions of behavioral control. Many studies utilizing this technique use multiple linear regressions to estimate the three determinate indicators' predictive power. The range of the recent meta-analyses that tested the theory of planned behavior utilizing the multiple correlations of all three determent intentions range from 0.63 to 0.71 (Albarracin, Johnson, Fishbein, & Muellerleile, 2001; Armitage & Conner, 2001; Godin & Kok, 1996; Sheeran & Taylor, 1999).

The theory of planned behavior draws its power by utilizing three determent intentions to identify attitudes toward the behavior. TPD posits that beliefs determine attitudes toward behavior about the consequences of behavior or behavioral beliefs. For example, a police officer may believe that accepting even small gratuities (the behavior) leads to other illegal, corrupt behavior later and therefore refuses to accept any gratuity no matter the amount (the outcome).

> The attitude toward the behavior is determined by the person's evaluation of the outcomes associated with the behavior and by the strength of these associations. By multiplying

belief strength and outcome evaluation and summing the resulting products, we obtain an estimate of the attitude toward the behavior, an estimate based on the person's accessible beliefs about the behavior.

(Ajzen, 2005, p. 123)

Therefore, a person who believes that performing a behavior will lead to positive results will hold a favorable attitude toward that behavior and vice versa. There are various useful evaluation techniques to identify and rank attitudes toward various behaviors (see Albarracin et al., 2001; Armitage & Conner, 2001).

However, a person's attitude is not the only determinate indicator utilized in the theory of planned behavior. Subjective norms are another primary factor that measures an individual's beliefs that other individuals or groups disapprove of the behavior. The individuals and groups that may influence a person's behavior are limitless; however, the most influential are close family members, peers, church, colleagues, and other social organizations. For example, if a police officer transfers onto a different shift at a local police department, and his fellow officers are lax with their ethics, preferring to "work outside" the law to "get things done," these subjective norms will influence the officer's attitude and ultimately his intention to engage in corrupt behavior. While the officer will undoubtedly be subjected to such views, it is still the officer's choice to submit to such actions. Thus, a person with a lower intent to commit corruption will be less likely to be pressured into such acts. Subjective norms can be assessed by asking respondents to judge the likelihood that influential people would approve or disapprove of specific behavior.

The last predictor in the theory of planned behavior is the perceived behavioral controls. These controls are an individual's beliefs of what factors will facilitate or impede a behavior. Past experiences influence these beliefs in committing future behavior, as does secondhand information from others about the risks involved and other physical factors (i.e., body-worn cameras) that may increase or decrease the likelihood that the action can be carried forth with perceived positive results. "In totality, these control beliefs lead to the perception that one can or cannot carry out the behavior, i.e., perceived behavioral control" (Ajzen, 2005, p. 125). An example might be the different actions an officer takes when he knows he is being recorded during public interaction by a camera that is occasionally reviewed by department supervisors. The officer may choose to limit his corrupt behaviors due to the perceived controls.

On the other hand, in public interaction where the use of a camera or some other control is absent, an officer may evaluate the perceived controls to be lower and may be more likely to engage in corruption. Perceived behavioral controls can be measured by asking subjects to relate the likelihood they believe an action would result in being discovered and the perceived level of punishment.

It is the interplay between these three determents that indicates intention. The intention is of primary importance because behavior can often be predicted with high accuracy from intentions. Ajzen (2005, p. 100) states, "barring unforeseen events, people are expected to do what they intend to do. . . . [T]his discussion implies that we should be able to predict specific behaviors with considerable accuracy from intentions to engage in the behaviors under consideration." It also implies that by strengthening, lessening, or removing one determinate, corrupt behavior may be reduced.

Application to Law Enforcement

It cannot be overstated that the identification of intention is where this theory's power is located. Suppose a law enforcement department could devise adequate tests for officers to determine an intention to commit an act of corruption. In that case, the department could decline to employ a candidate or relocate a current officer to an area where a difference in behavior controls and subjective norms would influence the officer *not* to commit corruption. In other words, it would be possible to prevent corruption in a law enforcement agency using TPB effectively.

The theory of planned behavior is also valuable as it coincides with many legal concepts with which law enforcement administrators are comfortable and familiar. The idea of investigating a person to uncover intent is prevalent at all levels of law enforcement and, thus, a natural and appropriate idea in the context of police corruption. Further, just as law enforcement officers understand the legal difference between the *mens rea* (guilty mind or intention) and *actus resus* (guilty act), they should not be too quick to jump to conclusions when discovering that an officer is displaying an *intent* to commit corruption. Instead, they may be inclined to observe for possible corrupt acts and utilize the findings to support a change in an assignment in an attempt to intervene. In essence, the police may actually be encouraged to police themselves.

Application of the Theory of Planned Behavior to Police Corruption

For decades, law enforcement agencies have been circling the issue of effectively identifying and controlling for corrupt behavior and may not have known many of the necessary resources were already within their grasp. What is needed is a scientifically based integration of data and an easy-to-understand guide for interpreting and applying the findings. Utilizing the theory of planned behavior to predict individual intention and thus behavior and then analyzing the aggregated individual results at a department and unit level may be the method law enforcement has been waiting for.

The theory of planned behavior posits that a fluctuating combination of a person's attitude, subjective norms, and perceived behavioral control will indicate that person's intention to commit or abstain from corruption (Ajzen, 2005). Additionally, through statistical analysis, it may be possible to predict the likelihood that a person will or will not partake in corrupt acts as a law enforcement officer (Schifter & Ajzen, 1985). It then follows that agencies can determine through pre-employment testing and continued testing after initial employment the probability an officer will commit an act of corruption.

However, law enforcement's significant challenges are quantifying the departmental subjective norms and the ability or inclination of law enforcement agencies to control for corruption, thus affecting the perceived behavioral controls (Punch, 2000). In other words, law enforcement presents a unique challenge for the application of the theory of planned behavior because the subjective norm is either unknown, varies by shift and unit, or is very difficult to control. The behavioral controls are also challenging to quantify and control due to law enforcement's nature, limited supervision, powers of discretion, and non-structured calls for service.

Therefore, law enforcement should seek to measure and understand an individual's attitude, subjective norm, and perceived control and an agency's subject norm and behavioral control. When combining these aspects, a clearer picture will be developed of overall departmental ethics. Figure 11.3 presents a modified theory of planned behavior, which includes measures for the collective agency or unit for subjective norms and behavioral control. It should be noted that a police department's collective subjective norms and departmental controls operate in a reciprocal relationship; both determinants affect the officers and are affected by the officers. These norms and controls function to push and pull each other. It is the sum of these interactions that, when combined with individual attitude, indicate intention.

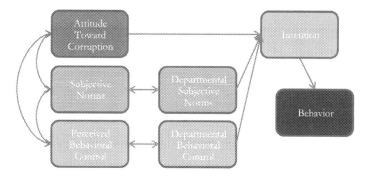

Figure 11.3 Theory of Planned Behavior (Modified Logic Model)

Attitude Toward the Behavior

As mentioned previously, law enforcement has been conducting tests for years to determine a potential officer's attitudes toward various issues, including corruption. The logic model in TPB is that understanding a person's behavioral beliefs (or attitude), when combined with the other determinants (norms and controls), will indicate the intention to abstain from or commit corruption (Ajzen, 2005). The current pre-employment tests at many law enforcement agencies already include various psychological tests such as intelligence tests, aptitude tests, neuropsychological tests, occupational tests, and personality tests such as the Minnesota Multiphasic Personality Inventory (Richmond, 2013). These tests can be used to establish a potential officer's attitude toward corrupt behavior.

However, these psychological tests may not meet all the requirements, and it would be necessary to develop a complete battery of tests to examine an officer's attitudes toward specific corruption instances. A good starting point for developing this testing tool is the Klockars, Ivković, Harver, and Haberfeld (1997) case scenario, which utilizes questionnaires to examine police corruption in 30 police departments across the country. However, the tool would need to be further developed to measure attitude. Currently, only a few of the 11 questions would satisfy the intention component.

SUBJECTIVE NORM

Subjective norm measurements and evaluation in law enforcement are where the logic model for the TPB is slightly adapted from the traditional format. After individual responses, every department and unit (e.g., traffic, narcotics, investigations, night shift) would then be examined collectively (combining all assigned personal scores) to observe differences in each group's subjective norms. For example, a researcher may find that the night shift's subjective norms differ from the day shift's subjective norms, and even more differences exist among leadership groups. This shift and assignment difference can be used when determining where to place officers, whether to hire them, and if they should be promoted to specific positions.

PERCEIVED BEHAVIORAL CONTROL

Similarly, perceived behavioral controls should be measured with a specially developed tool that seeks information regarding the chance of discovery, likely punishment, other officers' perceived ability to discover wrongdoing, identification of current policy, and other factors.

Once again, the department's score will be averaged and broken into categories according to the assigned unit. Another critical aspect of this measure will involve analyzing the department itself and the written policy in place for corruption issues.

For example, the examination would involve thoroughness and clarity of the policy regarding corruption and ethics, policy distribution to and understanding of said policy by officers, and other factors. Additionally, each department and unit would be evaluated to determine the supervisor-to-officer ratio and use of body cameras. All four components (the officer has perceived behavioral controls, policy, use of body cameras, and supervision ratios) would be combined to develop an index of perceived and actual behavioral control.

Bringing It All Together

The resulting examination will yield variables that will be utilized to predict and control future corruption. For an officer who is already a department member and is considering an assignment transfer or promotion, the following equation may be utilized, in which an officer's probability of committing corruption in the opportunity for advancement (OA) is indicated by the sum of his attitudes toward corruption (A), his subjective norms (SN), and his perceived behavioral control (PBC). This individual score is then multiplied by the departmental behavior control (DBC), which is developed according to department guidelines based on supervision density and policy and the average intention score for the other members of the unit he will be transferred to (DSN).

$$OA = \sum(A + SN + PBC) \times (DBC + DSN)$$

This formula will result in a quantifiable method to ensure that members of the department who have a high tendency toward corruption are not transferred with or allowed to supervise others who have similar tendencies. This formula may also justify placing, or not placing, an officer within certain groups of other officers.

Similarly, during the pre-employment hiring process, candidates can be tested for corruption intention and their scores compared to those of the department as a whole. The only factor that would change would be the decision to hire (DH) as opposed to an opportunity for advancement (OA).

$$DH = \sum(A + SN + PBC) \times (DBC + DSN)$$

Policy Implications

The policy implications for this theory are powerful and broad. The outcomes can primarily be divided into two categories: 1) pre-employment hiring decisions and 2) post-hiring internal assignment decisions. The first category will help reduce the likelihood of hiring an officer who will likely give in to corruption if influenced by subjective norms. The latter will help identify weak and robust officers, providing insight for assignment and promotions within a law enforcement agency to reduce overall corruption.

Pre-Employment Screen

The first line of defense within an agency to prevent corruption is to tightly control who enters the ranks as a law enforcement officer. One retired police chief expressed his view this way: "We hire for character and train for skills" (Waltrip, 2013), indicating his belief that selecting candidates who have high morals and low intentions of partaking in corrupt activates will enhance the department's image and function. The impact of corruption within a department may negatively affect potential applicants and result in a barrier to hiring (Vermeer, Stickle, Frame, & Hein, 2020), impact the level of stress that is growing within all types of policing (Ledford, Osborne, Edwards, & Stickle, 2020). It may drive even more corruption as those who have less intention to be corrupt are kept from hiring, perpetuating the cycle of corruption. Further, if a department is filled with people who are likely to commit corrupt acts, then the combined subjective norms and low behavioral controls will lead to higher intentions, resulting in corrupt behavior. These factors are why hiring decisions are vital and why TPB is a significant advancement to the process.

An officer's score of intention toward corrupt behaviors should be considered when making a job offer. This is not the only factor that should be considered if the results indicate a high likelihood of intention to commit corruption. The department should carefully consider the aspects of the applicant. This consideration can be done at two levels. First, the applicant's score should be considered with all other information, such as criminal and personal background investigations, polygraph results, and other standard hiring practices.

Secondly, an officer's intention score should be considered in light of the department's overall score. A department that scores low (unlikely to commit corruption) may be able to employ a candidate who scored a little higher (slightly more likely to commit corruption) than the department's average. This is because the theory of planned behavior postulates that these three determinates operate on a sliding scale. For example, if a department's subjective norms and behavior controls are low, it can be concluded that the department as a whole would have a positive effect on the applicant who scored higher and would be likely bring that person up to their standards.

However, the reverse is also true. If the department scores high on the tests, a candidate who scores high should not be hired, and a candidate who scored lower should be offered the position. This is the part of the TPB that will affect the overarching trends in a department and work to self-correct corruption over time by attrition. If a department can identify the probability of its current officers committing corruption and then measure an applicant's probability of committing corruption, the administration can begin to move from being a corrupt department to a less corrupt department. This can be accomplished by hiring officers with intentions to maintain ethics (low scores). Hiring highly ethical rookie officers who have strong beliefs in ethical behavior means they will eventually permeate the department, but this effect will take time. It should be cautioned that this effort takes appropriate testing and consistent selective hiring to locate candidates who score high enough to succumb to a low level of subjective norms of a department and perceived behavioral controls.

Departmental Subjective Norms

Internal Assignments

During an officer's tenure at a law enforcement agency, the developed corruption survey should be administered regularly. This will provide constant analysis of an individual officer's attitude toward corruption and the department's prevailing subject norms and perceived behavioral controls. An individual officer's score should be considered in his assignment and promotion. For example, a police department knows that the drug task force unit members have higher scores (indicating the likelihood to commit corrupt acts). Based on the TPB, officers who maintain higher ethics levels in all determinate intention categories are far less likely to commit corruption. Therefore, the officers who apply for the position should have their scores compared to the unit's, and only officers who score very low (indicating a strong commitment to ethical behavior) should be given this position.

Supervision

Supervision is a vital aspect of policing and also crucial to controlling corruption. Unfortunately, police leaders are not always free to remove supervisors from their duties, especially if no crime has been recorded or punishment stipulated when corruption has occurred in the past. Thus, police leaders are often stuck with the supervision they have within their ranks. However, leadership is often free to move supervision to different areas within the department.

Supervisors should be assigned, at least partially, based on the system described here. The supervisors who score high on this scale should never supervise officers who also score high. It is possible that high-scoring supervisors and low-scoring officers, or the reverse, will be a stabilizing factor. Considering these factors when placing officers on different shifts and into different assignments will allow an astute administrator to breed out corruption from within by identifying units with high scores and only assigning officers with low scores. Officers who test low would be assigned to areas with higher-scoring officers and higher perceived behavioral controls.

Departmental Behavioral Controls

This chapter has emphasized the ability of agencies to use the TPB and officer scores to identify those who have an intention to commit corruption. Thus far, the focus has been on changing a department's subjective norms by controlling hiring, supervision, and unit assignment. However, departments also can change policy and practice that will impact behavioral controls.

Efforts to change behavioral controls may be straightforward to establish and implement. For example, if an agency has a unit or shift with a higher score, implementing body-worn cameras and regular review of those videos by superiors with low scores may be a priority. Conversely, units with the lowest scores may receive cameras after other units. This concept can be widely applied with many of the techniques used to prevent corruption, such as the officer-to-supervisor ratio, requiring review of search warrants, required reporting, and more. Finally, any deficiencies in perceived behavioral controls (e.g., poorly written policy, poorly enforced policies) that the department can address should be changed. While a department's efforts to reduce corruption may be applicable across the entire department, police leadership should focus on the areas where there is the most risk first.

Conclusion

Officer corruption within police departments in the United States is an issue that society has been attempting to address since law enforcement departments' inception. There is always an opportunity for corruption with the authority, autonomy, and limited supervision inherent in police work. While police departments' corruption in the United States may be reasonably low compared to that of other countries (Ward & McCormack, 1987), it is still a concern, and rightfully so.

Until recently, police agencies have piecemealed various techniques, attempting to identify candidates and current officers who are likely to commit acts of corruption. However, most of these efforts have failed because they relied only on one measure of corruption, often attitude, and failed to consider how control factors and social norms influence intentional behavior. However, it is vital to include subjective norms and perceived behavioral controls at the individual, unit, and department levels to obtain a clear picture of who is likely to violate ethical principles. It is even more critical to have an early intervention (Gullion & King, 2020) with officers who may show signs of an intention to commit corruption. The theory of planned behavior can combine all the appropriate determinate factors to create an intention quotient. This ability means that agencies can now determine each officer's probability of committing some form of corruption.

The TPB application presented in this chapter can provide a department the tools needed to bridge the gap between theory and practice that are often needed and asked for by police leaders (Stickle, 2020), equipping departments to address corruption. With this information, a department will have the tools to address the problem of corruption proactively. Equipped with scientific and testable data, a department can obtain a more precise snapshot of the agency and will be able to control it more efficiently. Eventually, through better hiring practices and a change in promotion and assignment procedures that align with the theory of planned behavior as applied in this chapter, the department will be able to "weed out" officers from within an organization and prohibit candidates from entering the agency who have a high tendency toward corruption.

Discussion Questions

1. Describe the theory of planned behavior.
2. What is police corruption, and how frequent is it?
3. How do attitudes toward behavior, subjective norms, and perceived behavioral controls interact to indicate a person's intention?
4. How can the intention quotient be used to prevent corruption within police departments?
5. Why is it important to measure a small group of officers' (e.g., shift, unit) intention quotient, and what can a police leader do with this information?

References

Ajzen, I. (1985). From intentions to actions: A theory of planned behavior. In J. Kuhl & J. Beckmann (Eds.), *Action control: From cognition to behavior* (pp. 11–39). Berlin: Springer.

Ajzen, I. (1991). The theory of planned behavior. *Organizational Behavior and Human Decision Process*, *50*(2),179–211.

Ajzen, I. (2005). *Attitudes, personality, and behavior*. Berkshire: Open University.

Ajzen, I., & Fishbein, M. (2000). Attitudes and the attitude-behavior relation: Reasoned and automatic processes. *European Review of Social Psychology*, *11*(1), 1–33.

Albarracin, D., Johnson, B. T., Fishbein, M., & Muellerleile, P. A. (2001). Theories of reasoned action and planned behavior as models of condom use: A meta-analysis. *Psychological Bulletin*, *127*(1), 142–161.

Armitage, C. J., & Conner, M. (2001). Efficacy of the theory of planned behavior: A meta-analytic review. *British Journal of Social Psychology*, *40*(4), 471–499.

Boman, J. H., & Gallupe, O. (2020). Has COVID-19 changed crime? Crime rates in the United States during the pandemic. *American Journal of Criminal Justice*, *45*(4), 537–545.

Cato (2012). *Policemisconduct.net*. Retrieved from www.policemisconduct.net/

Cato (2018, July). *What happened to PoliceMisconduct.net?* Retrieved from www.unlawfulshield.com/2018/07/what-happened-to-policemisconduct-net/

Clarke, R. V. G., & Felson, M. (Eds.). (1993). *Routine activity and rational choice* (Vol. 5). Piscataway, NJ: Transaction Publishers.

Cohen, L. E., & Felson, M. (1979). Social change and crime rate trends: A routine activity approach. *American Sociological Review*, *44*, 588–608.

Cornish, D. B., & Clarke, R. V. (Eds.). (2014). *The reasoning criminal: Rational choice perspectives on offending.* Piscataway, NJ: Transaction Publishers.

Cornish, D. B., & Clarke, R. V. (2017). Understanding crime displacement: An application of rational choice theory. In *Crime Opportunity Theories* (pp. 197–211). Abington, UK: Routledge.

Federal Bureau of Investigation (2019). *Crime in the United States 2009.* Police Employee Data. Retrieved April 2, 2013, from https://ucr.fbi.gov/crime-in-the-u.s/2019/crime-in-the-u.s.-2019/topic-pages/police-employee-data

Fishbein, M., & Ajzen, I. (2010). *Predicting and changing behavior the reasoned action approach.* New York, NY: Psychology Press.

Godin, G., & Kok, G. (1996). The theory of planned behavior: A review of its applications to health-related behaviors. *American Journal of Health Promotion, 11*(2), 87–98.

Gullion, C. L., & King, W. R. (2020). Early intervention systems for police: A state-of-the-art review. *Policing: An International Journal, 43*(4), 643–658. doi:10.1108/PIJPSM-02-2020-0027

Ivkovic, S. K. (2003). To serve and collect: Measuring police corruption. *Criminology, 93*(2–3), 593.

Jennings, W. G., & Perez, N. M. (2020). The immediate impact of COVID-19 on law enforcement in the United States. *American Journal of Criminal Justice, 45,* 690–701.

Klockars, C. B. (1999). *Police corruption in thirty agencies in the United States.* Washington, DC: US Department of Justice, National Institute of Justice.

Klockars, C. B., Ivković, S. K., Harver, W. E., & Haberfeld, M. R. (1997). *The measurement of police integrity* (pp. 65–70). Washington, DC: National Institute of Justice.

Klockars, C. B., Ivkovich, S. K., Harver, W. E., & Haberfeld, M. R. (2000). *The measures of police integrity.* Washington, DC: US Department of Justice, Office of Justice Programs, National Institue of Justice.

Kutnjak Ivković, S., Morgan, S. J., Cajner Mraović, I., & Borovec, K. (2020). Does the police code of silence vary with police assignment? An empirical exploration of the relation between the code and assignment. *Police Practice and Research, 21*(2), 101–116.

Lawrence, S. W., & Langworthy, R. H. (1979). Measuring homicide by police officers. *The Journal of Criminal Law & Criminology, 70*(4).

Ledford, L. S., Osborne, D. L., Edwards, B. D., & Stickle, B. (2020). Not just a walk in the woods? Exploring the impact of individual characteristics and changing job roles on stress among conservation officers. *Police Practice and Research,* 1–16. doi:10.1080/15614263.2020.1821682

Martin, R. (2001). *Law enforcement bulletin: Police corruption an analytical look into police ethics.* Washington, DC: Federal Bureau of Investigation.

Meyer, J. C. (1976). Definitional and etiological issues in police corruption: Assessment and synthesis of competing perspectives. *Journal of Police Science and Administration, 4*(1), 46–55.

Punch, M. (2000). Police corruption and its prevention. *European Journal on Criminal Policy and Research, 8*(3), 301–324.

Richmond, R. L. (2013). A guide to psychology and its practice. *Psychological Testing.* Retrieved April 3, 2013, from www.guidetopsychology.com/testing.htm#8

Robinson, P. H. (2020, June 21). Don't abolish the police: It didn't work for 1960s communes and it won't work for us. *USA Today.*

Schifter, D. E., & Ajzen, I. (1985). Intention, perceived control, and weight loss: An application of the theory of planned behavior. *Journal of Personality and Social Psychology, 49*(3), 843–851.

Sheeran, P., & Taylor, S. (1999). Predicting intentions to use condoms: A meta-analysis and comparison of the theories of reasoned action and planned behavior. *Journal of Applied Social Psychology, 29*(8), 1624–1675.

Sherman, L. W. (1978). *Scandal and reform: Controlling police corruption.* Los Angeles, CA: University of California Press.

Skolnick, J. (2002). Corruption and the blue code of silence. *Police Practice and Research, 3*(1), 7–19.

Stickle, B. (2016). A national examination of the effect of education, training, and pre-employment screening on law enforcement use of force. *Justice Policy Journal, 13*(1), 1–15.

Stickle, B. (2017). Does the use of physical force during contact with the police affect one's perception of procedural justice? *Journal of Behavioral and Social Sciences, 14*(2), 87–97.

Stickle, B. (2020). Steve Conrad: Chief, Louisville metro police department, Kentucky, USA. In B. F. Baker & D. K. Das (Eds.), *Trends in policing: Interviews with police leaders across the globe* (Vol. 6). London: Routledge.

Stickle, B., & Felson, M. (2020). Crime rates in a pandemic: The largest criminological experiment in history. *American Journal of Criminal Justice, 45*(4), 525–536.

Vermeer, S. J., Stickle, B., Frame, M., & Hein, M. (2020). Reasons and barriers for choosing police careers. *Policing: An International Journal, 43*(5), 817–830.

Waltrip, B. (2013, April 9). *Retired chief of police Bowling Green Police Department, Bowling Green, Kentucky* (B. Stickle, Interviewer).

Ward, R. H., & McCormack, R. (1987). *Managing police corruption: International perspectives.* Chicago, IL: University of Illinois.

Weitzer, R. (2002). Incidents of police misconduct and public opinion. *Journal of Criminal Justice, 30*(5), 397–408.

Westmarland, L., & Conway, S. (2020). Police ethics and integrity: Keeping the "blue code" of silence. *International Journal of Police Science & Management, 22*(4), 378–392.

Chapter 12

Relationship of Police Stress With Coping, Moral Reasoning, and Burnout

Priya Xavier

Introduction

Although job stress is a concern for many industries and occupational groups, some professions appear to be more vulnerable to experiencing high levels of stress at work than others (Kop et al., 1999). Stress and burnout can be detrimental to police officers and their respective departments in a variety of ways. There is a need for policing services to have an in-depth understanding of the origins of stress and to use this information to help the officer use effective stress prevention strategies.

Though the officers have the freedom to use great discretion when performing their duties, they are not involved in policy-making—a condition that has led to an increase in officer tension and distress (Coman & Evans, 1991; He, Zhao, & Archbold, 2002). Moreover, while officers are asked to protect society from violence and disorder by putting themselves at risk of injury and death, their actions are simultaneously subjected to heightened scrutiny by media, interest groups, and the public they are sworn to serve (Roberg, Novak, & Cordner, 2005). Because of these demands on law enforcement, stress and burnout in policing are not uncommon (McCarty, Zhao, & Garland, 2007; Patterson, 2002; Stinchcomb, 2004).

A better understanding of the sources of stress among police officers and its deleterious effect due to maladaptive coping mechanisms is essential to maintain a psychologically and physically healthy law enforcement machinery. Additional efforts should be made to address the issue of ethical decision-making among police officers. Among the many stressors and other complications that police encounter in their work, it seems that the issue of moral dilemmas and the challenges and frustrations associated with them has so far not received the amount of attention that it rightly deserves.

Review of the Literature

Research on police occupational stress has gathered momentum since the 1970s in concert with US government–sponsored symposia and studies reporting that police officers had higher rates of stress-related illnesses. There was an increase in studies describing the nature of police stressors and exploring stress-reduction techniques (Davidson & Veno, 1978; Kroes, 1976; Kroes & Hurrell, 1977), as well as research focused on officer burnout (Maslach & Jackson, 1979; Roberg, Hayhurst, & Allen, 1988; Wallace, Roberg, & Allen, 1985).

Studies exploring police stress focus on determining specific stressors and their effects on stress (Lawrence, 1984; Malloy & Mays, 1984). Several stressors, such as organizational characteristics, jurisdiction characteristics, and personal differences, are identified as specific causes of occupational stress in policing. These studies generally examine police organizations in the USA. Most of these studies focus on local organizations and have thus far omitted state

DOI: 10.4324/9781003047117-14

and federal law enforcement agencies (Newman & Rucker-Reed, 2004). Only a limited number of studies published in English examine the variety of contributors to police stress in countries outside the USA (Berg, Hem, Lau, Haseth, & Ekeberg, 2005; Davidson & Veno, 1979; Coman & Evans, 1991; Lee, 2002; Stansfield, 1996; Zukauskas, Dapsys, Jasmontatite, & Susinskas, 2001).

Yet there is a lack of information addressing whether generally accepted stressors have the same effects in other nations' police organizations as they do in local police organizations in the USA. This gap has been taken for study in this research. Brown and Campbell (1990, 1994); Alexander, Walker, Innes, and Irving (1993); and Biggam, Power, MacDonald, Carcary and Moodie (1997) conducted empirical studies on work stressors in policing. All concluded that there are two important categories of potential stressors in police work. First is the nature of police work, such as physical threat, force, exposure to danger, facing the unknown, and shift work. Second is the organizational aspect of police work, such as a lack of confidence in management, lack of internal communication, and continuous organizational changes. The most salient stressors identified by these researchers were organizational factors rather than specific police tasks.

Continuous work stress can result in burnout. Human service professionals report burnout relatively frequently (Maslach, 1993). Contact with demanding clients has been identified as a major factor for burnout in many of these studies. Three dimensions of burnout are usually distinguished: emotional exhaustion, which refers to the draining of emotional response; depersonalization, a callous and cynical attitude toward civilians; and a decrease in personal accomplishment (Maslach, 1993).

The use of excessive force is frowned upon by the general public and the media. Police officers are expected to use social skills with minimal use of force as they fulfill their task.

Positive coping mechanisms are viewed by researchers as the most appropriate way to decrease stress and feelings of burnout. Officers using negative coping strategies face the likelihood of experiencing chronic stress that may result in loss of motivation, burnout, and an eventual withdrawal from police work (Hurrell, 1986; Maslach, 1976; Zhao, He, Lovrich, & Cancino, 2003).

Burnout results from ill-managed stress (Garland, 2002). Police officers interact mostly with people in extremely stressful situations (Jespersen, 1988), which, over a period of time, leads them to experience symptoms of burnout. Viewed as a psychological syndrome, burnout occurs in response to chronic work-related stressors (Maslach, Schaufeli, & Leiter, 2001). Burnout was defined by Maslach as a crisis in one's relationship with work, which might vary from engagement to burnout (Maslach, Jackson, & Leiter, 1996). Engagement is an energetic state in which one is confident in one's effectiveness, whereas burnout is a state of exhaustion in which one is cynical about the value of one's work and ability to cope.

Robert Loo (1994) inferred burnout among 135 Canadian police managers and found that few police managers had burnout as measured by Maslach Burnout Inventory (MBI) because only 3.7% of the sample fell into phase VIII of Golembiewski and Munzenrider's phase model of burnout. Many researchers (Loo, 1994, 1986a, 1986b; Reiser,1982; Stratton, Parker, & Snibbe, 1985) have studied numerous stressors in police work and the kind of stress reactions exhibited by police officers, especially the more problematic (e.g., alcohol and drug abuse) or dramatic reactions (suicide or post-traumatic stress disorder).

Schaible and Gecas (2010) examined 109 police officers in the Pacific Northwest to find out the impact of emotional labor and value dissonance on burnout. It has been widely recognized that inherent in the police role are numerous tensions that emerge because of the wide discretion officers possess to apply force (Bittner, 1967; Manning, 1977; Wilson, 1968). As theirs is a "tainted occupation," the public has tasked police with resolving problems considered unsavory that they are unwilling or unable to deal with themselves (Bittner, 1967).

Drawing on this mandate, police have traditionally favored minimal interference in the exercise of police discretion in pursuit of the "public good" (Dubber, 2005).

Research interest is growing for examining issues relevant to police stress in theory-driven analyses (Hart, Wearing, & Headey, 1993). In a series of studies, Hart and colleagues (1993, 1994, 1995) examined officers' appraisals of their daily work experiences, levels of psychological distress and well-being, and the potential mediating effects of coping style and personality. Findings suggested unique roles for these various components of stress, thereby highlighting the need for their inclusion in future assessments of psychological outcomes among officers.

Kohan and Mazmanian (2003) carried out their study on 199 police officers in Ontario in a theory-driven approach to stress but incorporated burnout as an index of psychological distress/well-being because it is a specific work-related stress outcome measure. Kohan and Mazmanian (2003) inferred that police officers appraised operational hassles more negatively than organizational ones, differing from previous studies. Coping refers to a person's cognitive and behavioral efforts to manage environmental demands that have been appraised as threatening or exceeding personal capabilities (Folkman & Lazarus, 1986; Lazarus & Folkman, 1984a). Such efforts include any responses that prevent, avoid, or control personal distress (Pearlin & Schooler, 1978). Two specific categories of coping—problem-solving and emotion-focused coping—have been found to exist. Problem-focused coping may include aggressive interpersonal efforts to alter the stressful situation as well as efforts to solve problems related to stressors. Emotion-focused coping is aimed more at reducing stress and regulating emotion and includes distancing, self-control, escape, accepting responsibility, and positive reappraisal of stressors.

Coping style is reported to be a mediating factor between job stress and job satisfaction in management-level police personnel (Cooper, Kirkcaldy, & Brown, 1994; Kirkcaldy, Cooper & Brown, 1995). On facing demands, individuals engage in a two-stage process: first assessing the demands being placed on them by the situation and then assessing their resources to meet these demands. When the demands outweigh the perceived resources, the result is stress (Kemeny, 2003). Spielberger, Westberry, Grier, & Greenfield (1981) pointed out that administrative and professional pressure and lack of support are also major police stressors besides physical and psychological danger. Many important factors in the police stress survey (e.g., disagreeable regulations, support, or supervision) are under the control of senior administrators and police organizations. Other factors, such as the ineffectiveness of the judicial system and court decisions restricting police, can be changed too. The main effects of police stress on illness and absenteeism are both significant Thomas Li-Ping Tang and Monty L. Hammontree (1992).

Suggestions by Thomas and Hammontree (1992) included that special plans be formulated for the prevention or remediation of stress: stress audits, stress management, time management, employee participation, quality circles (e.g., Tang, Tollison & Whiteside, 1987, 1989, 1991), work design, and wage and salary programs. The ultimate goal is to achieve a better person-environment (P-E) fit so that police officers and society will benefit from these programs (cf. Caplan, Cobb, French, Van Harrison, & Pinneau, 1975; Kulik, Oldham, & Hackman, 1987; Muchinsky & Monahan, 1987).

Moral reasoning refers to interpreting the effects of individual actions on the self and others, judging the moral righteousness of an action, prioritizing the actions that are judged to be morally right, and following through on the intention to behave morally (Rest, 1986). It forms the cornerstone of ethical behavior (Piaget, 1932; Kohlberg, 1969; Treviño, 1992; Weber & Wasieleski, 2001; Treviño & Weaver, 2003; Cohen, 2004).

The ethical dilemmas police officers face are both complex and consequential. In the context of policing, moral reasoning goes beyond simple legalistic interpretation of statutes.

Police work is a high-risk occupation. The work is inherently discretionary, usually takes place out of sight of direct supervision, and requires extralegal resolutions to problems that frequently are not covered by regulations manuals (Bittner, 1967; Delattre, 2002; Hall, 2000; Wilson, 1968, 2000).

Ethics researchers and police reformers point to developing a healthy organizational climate and a degree of self-regulation among police officers as imperatives for the future of policing (Cordner, Scarborough, & Sheehan, 2004; Crank & Caldero, 2010; DeLord, Burpo, Shannon, & Spearing, 2008; Marks & Sklansky, 2008; Ortmeier & Meese, 2010; Sklansky, 2007; Toch & Grant, 2005). A study of the relation between stress, coping, moral reasoning, and burnout is necessary. This has been conducted among Indian police officers, specifically from the southern state of Tamil Nadu.

Methodology

Population for Study

The population for this study comprises full-time police officers from the ranks of sub inspectors and above falling in the North Zone of the Tamil Nadu Police, including the districts of Villupuram, Cuddalore, Thiruvanamalai, Vellore, Kancheepuram, and Thiruvallur. The study includes a group of 600 special sub inspectors attending a promotional training at the Tamil Nadu Police Academy, Vandalore, from all four zones of the Tamil Nadu Police. Most police officers come from North Zone. Each subject in this population (N=1,100) was sent a packet containing the questionnaire and instructions to complete and return.

This research study involves the voluntary participation of police officers. The North Zone police officers were circulated the questionnaire by the office of the North Zone inspector general of police. Permission to conduct the survey was obtained from the director general of police at police headquarters. Each subject was asked to read the instructions carefully and to be as honest as possible in responding to the data items. Upon completion of their research materials, participants were asked to submit them to their officer in charge.

Out of 1,100 questionnaires sent to respondents, 299 completed responses were returned. The final sample size was 296, as three responses could not be considered for lack of internal consistency. The police officers' role was to maintain law and order in the state of Tamil Nadu, India. Once the data were collected and checked for completeness, the data were coded and entered onto an Excel spreadsheet for statistical analysis.

Subjects

The subjects of this study were 296 police officers, of whom 102 officers were from the North Zone of Tamil Nadu and were direct recruits. The remaining 194 were special sub inspectors from all four zones of the Tamil Nadu Police, which include the North, South, West, and Central Zones, who were well-experienced police personnel. A brief demographic questionnaire was utilized, followed by the Police Stress Survey (PSS), the Maslach Burnout Inventory-Human Service Survey (MBI-HSS), the Coping Response Inventory (CRI), and the Defining Issues Test 2 (DIT 2). Correlation, mediation analysis, and SEM were used to analyze the relationship of police stress to coping, moral reasoning, and burnout. Primary data were collected via questionnaire during the period from June 2014 to April 2015. Secondary data were also collected from various sources like textbooks, peer-reviewed journals, newspapers, and the police training academy library.

Measures

The police officers were asked to complete the following information: a demographic questionnaire, the Police Stress Survey, Maslach Burnout Inventory-Human Services Survey, the Coping Response Inventory, and the Defining Issues Test 2. A PSS instrument was used for collecting data regarding measurement of police stress in this study. Spielberger et al. (1981) developed the instrument as part of the research conducted in the Florida Police Stress Project (FPSP). Reliability for the data collected showed Cronbach's alpha for the total PSS as 0.953. For the administrative/organizational pressure, the reliability was 0.928, and for the physical/psychological threat, the reliability was 0.890.

The MBI is now recognized as the leading measure of burnout. Although the initial research on the MBI was based on data from the United States and Canada, subsequent studies have been done in many countries around the world. Psychometric studies of the MBI in these different settings have continued to validate the three-dimensional structure of the measure. The MBI-HSS assesses three aspects of burnout syndrome: emotional exhaustion, depersonalization, and lack of personal accomplishment. Each aspect is measured by a separate subscale. The emotional exhaustion (EE) subscale assesses feelings of being emotionally overextended and exhausted by one's work. The depersonalization (Dp) subscale measures an unfeeling and impersonal response toward recipients of one's service, care, or instruction. The personal accomplishment (PA) subscale assesses feelings of competence and successful achievement in one's work with people.

For this research on police officers, the reliability for the complete MBI was 0.743. For the emotional exhaustion subscale, Cronbach's alpha = 0.757. For the depersonalization subscale, Cronbach's alpha = 0.617, and for the personal accomplishment subscale, Cronbach's alpha = 0.676.

The Coping Responses Inventory-Adult Form (CRI-Adult) is a measure of eight different types of coping responses to stressful life circumstances. These responses are measured by eight scales—logical analysis (LA), positive reappraisal (PR), seeking guidance and support (SG), problem-solving (PS), cognitive avoidance (CA), acceptance or resignation (AR), seeking alternative rewards (SR), and emotional discharge (ED). The first set of four scales measures approach coping; the second set of four scales measures avoidance coping. The first two scales in each set measure cognitive coping strategies; the third and fourth scales in each set measure behavioral coping strategies. For the entire CRI, the Cronbach's alpha was found to be 0.883.

This study used the Rest, Narvaez, Thoma, and Bebeau's (1999) DIT-2. The DIT-2, based on Kohlberg's six-stage theory of CMD, is an objective test that assesses how people use different considerations in making sense of a moral situation. The DIT-2 is an improved version of the older DIT but has clearer instructions and is shorter (five versus six dilemmas). The P score is the simple sum of the scores from Stages 5A, 5B, and 6, converted to a percentage. The P% score can range from 0 to 95. It is interpreted as the extent to which a person prefers postconventional moral thinking. The N2 score is a new index that outperforms the P score on six criteria for construct validity. N2 scores are adjusted to have the same mean and standard deviation as the P score so that comparisons between P and N2 can be made.

Conceptual Framework

The conceptual framework for this study is shown in Figure 12.1.

Relationship Between Police Stress and Coping Styles

H_{2a}: There is a significant relationship between moral reasoning and police stress, coping styles, and burnout.

H_{3a}: There is a significant relationship between police stress and burnout.

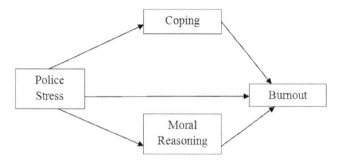

Figure 12.1 Conceptual Framework

Results

Correlation was used to find whether there was any significant relation between police stress and coping, moral reasoning, and burnout.

H_1: There is a significant relationship between police stress and coping styles.
H_{01}: There is no significant relationship between police Stress and coping styles.

Table 12.1 explains the relationship between police stress, administrative/organizational pressure, physical/psychological threat, and coping styles.

Police stress: All the constructs are positively related; the constructs seeking guidance and emotional discharge are statistically significant at the 1% level while acceptance or resignation and avoidance are statistically significant at the 5% level.

Administrative/organizational pressure: Mostly, all the constructs are positively related while the construct problem-solving is negatively related. The constructs seeking guidance, acceptance or resignation, and emotional discharge are statistically significant at the 1% level, and the construct avoidance is statistically significant at the 5% level.

Physical/psychological threat: All the constructs are positively related. The constructs seeking guidance and emotional discharge are statistically significant at the 1% level.

H_2: There is a significant relationship between moral reasoning and police stress, coping styles, and burnout.
H_{02}: There is no significant relationship between moral reasoning and police stress, coping styles, and burnout.

Table 12.2 explains the relationship between police stress and moral reasoning. Most of the constructs are positively related, while the constructs police stress, administrative/organizational pressure, logical analysis, emotional exhaustion, depersonalization, personal accomplishment, and burnout are negatively related. The construct emotional discharge is statistically significant at the 1% level, while seeking alternative rewards and avoidance are statistically significant at the 5% level.

Table 12.3 explains the relationship between police stress and emotional exhaustion, depersonalization, personal accomplishment, and burnout.

Emotional Exhaustion: All the constructs are positively related and statistically significant at the 1% level.

Depersonalization: All the constructs are positively related, and the constructs police stress and administrative/organizational pressure are statistically significant at the 1% level.

180 Priya Xavier

Table 12.1 Correlation of Police Stress with Coping Styles

Correlation

Statistics=Pearson Correlation

	Police Stress	Administrative/ Organizational Pressure	Physical/ Psychological Threat
Logical Analysis	045	.061	.060
Positive Reappraisal	031	.038	.022
Seeking guidance	.152**	.145**	.141**
Problem-solving	026	−.008	.017
Cognitive Avoidance	039	.031	.030
Acceptance or Resignation	099*	.143**	.065
Seeking alternative rewards	043	.058	.026
Emotional Discharge	148**	.171**	.148**
Approach	077	.072	.073
Avoidance	115*	.139*	.095

** Correlation is significant at the 0.01 level (1-tailed).
* Correlation is significant at the 0.05 level (1-tailed).

Table 12.2 Correlation of Moral Reasoning with Police Stress, Coping, and Burnout

Correlation

Statistics=Pearson Correlation

	N2. Moral reasoning
Police Stress	−.019
Administrative/Organizational Pressure	−.040
Physical/Psychological Threat	.058
Logical Analysis	−.023
Positive Reappraisal	.061
Seeking Guidance	.060
Problem-Solving	.005
Cognitive Avoidance	.025
Acceptance or Resignation	.089
Seeking Alternative Rewards	.108*
Emotional Discharge	.173**
Approach	.030
Avoidance	.137*
Emotional Exhaustion	−.038
Depersonalization	−.006
Personal Accomplishment	−.074
Maslach Burnout Inventory	−.062

* Correlation is significant at the 0.05 level (1-tailed).
** Correlation is significant at the 0.01 level (1-tailed).

Personal Accomplishment: All the constructs are positively related and statistically significant at the 1% level.

Burnout: All the constructs are positively related and statistically significant at the 1% level.

Police stress and burnout are moderately related (.301), which is significant at the 1% level. Within police stress, administrative pressure is better related to burnout, which is .339, than to physical or psychological dimensions.

Coping, Moral Reasoning, and Burnout 181

Table 12.3 Correlation of Police Stress with Burnout

Correlation				
Statistics=Pearson Correlation				
	Emotional Exhaustion	*Depersonalization*	*Personal Accomplishment*	*Maslach Burnout Inventory*
Police Stress	256**	165**	.167**	301**
Administrative/ Organizational Pressure	310**	218**	.152**	347**
Physical/Psychological Threat	164**	072	.160**	207**

** Correlation is significant at the 0.01 level (1-tailed).

Structural Equation Model

To explain the conceptual model, SEM was done, and the following results achieved.

Model Specification

Model specification is the first step in order to test the path in the SEM approach. In the model, the study attempted to find the causality relation between police stress and coping style, moral reasoning, and burnout. Coping style and moral reasoning can lead to burnout. The path analysis has the following hypothesis to be tested:

H_1: Coping style leads to burnout.
H_2: Moral reasoning leads to burnout.
H_3: Police stress is directly related to burnout.
H_4: Police stress leads to coping style and moral reasoning.

Model Identification

When the sample covariance matrix (S) is greater than the estimated covariance matrix (E), the model is over-identified. If model is under-identified or just identified, it fails to move to the next step of the model estimates. From Table 12.4, it is understood that degrees of freedom are more than 0, so the model is over-identified.

Model Estimation

Model estimation includes model testing. Though there are different methods to estimate the model, the default model estimates in AMOS or any SEM software is ML—maximum likelihood estimation.

The only two paths that are statistically significant at <.05 and <.001 are coping leading to burnout and police stress leading to burnout, respectively. The critical ratio (CR), which is equivalent to t-test value, is more than 1.96, indicating the paths are significant: at least the 5% level. One unit increase in police stress leads to an increase in burnout at 3.2. There are nine coping styles; all are significant.

The standardized regression weights are correlation loadings that are ranged between –1 and +1. Coping influences burnout, which is .142. Police stress leads to coping (.085) and burnout (.252). Therefore, hypotheses H1, H3, and H4 are retained. Hypothesis H2 does not hold and is rejected.

182   Priya Xavier

Table 12.4 Model Identification

Number of Distinct Sample Moments	10
Number of Distinct Parameters to Be Estimated	9
Degrees of Freedom (10–9)	1

Table 12.5 Regression Weights

			Estimate	S.E.	C.R.	P
P SCORE	<---	PSS	−.455	.584	−.779	.436
COPING	<---	PSS	.215	.157	1.370	.171
BURNOUT	<---	COPING	.736	.331	2.225	.026*
BURNOUT	<---	P SCORE	−.105	.076	−1.367	.172
BURNOUT	<---	PSS	3.280	.774	4.236	***
A	<---	COPING	1.000			
R	<---	COPING	1.343	.113	11.918	***
G	<---	COPING	1.091	.101	10.787	***
S	<---	COPING	1.136	.106	10.721	***
A	<---	COPING	.861	.102	8.412	***
R	<---	COPING	.779	.106	7.373	***
R	<---	COPING	1.083	.111	9.792	***
D	<---	COPING	.851	.106	8.060	***
E	<---	BURNOUT	1.000			
P	<---	BURNOUT	.410	.085	4.830	***
A	<---	BURNOUT	−.036	.051	−.709	.478

Table 12.6 Standardized Regression Weights

			Estimate
P SCORE	<---	PSS	−.045
COPING	<---	PSS	.085
BURNOUT	<---	COPING	.142
BURNOUT	<---	P SCORE	−.081
BURNOUT	<---	PSS	.252
LA	<---	COPING	.667
PR	<---	COPING	.831
SG	<---	COPING	.729
PS	<---	COPING	.724
CA	<---	COPING	.548
AR	<---	COPING	.475
SR	<---	COPING	.651
ED	<---	COPING	.523
EE	<---	BURNOUT	.939
DP	<---	BURNOUT	.690
PA	<---	BURNOUT	−.044

Model Fit Summary

The model shows the selected indices to assess the fit. CMIN is 256.2, and DF is 62. CMIN/DF ratio is 4.1, which is less than 5, which indicates the model is quite good.

Good indices, such as CFI, AGFI, and TLI, should be greater than .90; all the indices are greater than threshold value.

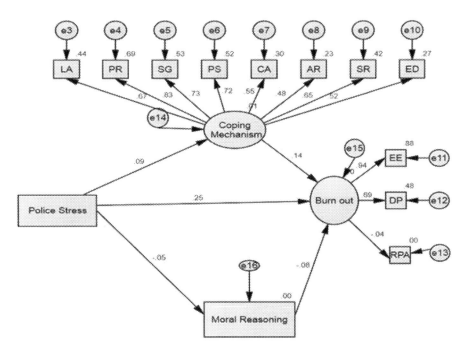

Figure 12.2 SEM Model Output

Table 12.7 Chi Square MIN

Model	NPAR	CMIN	DF	P	CMIN/DF
Default model	29	256.213	62	.000	4.132

Table 12.8 Good Indices

Model	CFI	AGFI	TLIrho2
Default model	.900	.903	.920

Table 12.9 Poor Indices

Model	RMR	RMSEA	SRMR
Default model	.772	.103	.65

Poor indices should be close to 0. RMR, RMSEA, and SRMR all are close to 0, indicating the model fits the data well.

Mediation Analysis

From Figure 12.3 and Table 12.10, it is understood that the direct and indirect effects are statistically significant. The indirect effect (ab) is .1067, the direct effect is 2.14, and the total

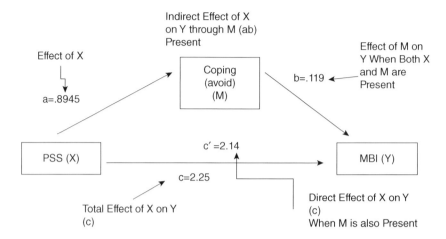

Figure 12.3 Mediation Model

Table 12.10 Mediation Model—Paths-Total-Direct-Indirect Effect

Independent variable (X)	Police Stress
Dependent variable (Y)	Burnout
a	0.89
b	0.119
ab=indirect	0.1067
Direct	2.14
Total	2.25
BootLLCI	.009
BootULCI	.3151
Indirect Sig	Sig @ 5%
Direct Sig	0.000
Total Sig	0.00
Ratio (indirect/direct)	5%

effect is .905; the indirect effect is contributing more than the direct effect for the model. Since both LCL and UCL are the same sign, it ensures that the indirect effect is statistically significant at the 5% level. Hence, avoidance is enacting in an indirect role between police stress and burnout.

Discussion and Conclusion

The current study is based on the research question "How is police stress related to moral reasoning, burnout, and coping styles?" This question was answered by these hypotheses:

H_{1a}: There is a significant relationship between police stress and coping styles.
H_{2a}: There is a significant relationship between moral reasoning and police stress, coping styles, and burnout.
H_{3a}: There is a significant relationship between police stress and burnout.

Hypothesis H_1

There is a significant relationship between police stress and coping styles. Correlation analysis supports hypothesis H_{1a} that there is a significant relationship between police stress and coping styles. Seeking guidance and emotional discharge are significantly related to police stress. Acceptance or resignation and comprehensive avoidance coping are significantly related to police stress. Within police stress, administrative/organizational pressure is significantly related to seeking guidance, acceptance or resignation, and emotional discharge while avoidance coping is significant at 5% to administrative/organizational pressure. Physical/psychological threat is related to seeking guidance and emotional discharge. It may be discerned that one approach coping style and two avoidance coping styles are related to police stress and organizational pressure while one approach and one avoidance coping style are related to physical/psychological threat.

Hypothesis H_2

There is a significant relationship between moral reasoning and police stress, coping styles, and burnout. It is found that moral reasoning is not related to police stress and burnout. The research study found no significant correlation between administrative/organizational pressure and moral reasoning. This result suggests that administrative/organizational pressure does not seem to influence an officer's degree of moral reasoning. Moral reasoning is a continuous developmental process that is based on one's level of cognitive development (Rest, 1979). A fundamental tenet of this process is that a person's perceptions of reality are cognitively constructed and tend to develop in complexity as a person's experiences accumulate. Since police stress is based on an officer's cognitively constructed perceptions of occupational experiences (Lauferweiler, 1995; Violanti, 1981), it was reasonable to assume that these constructs would affect moral reasoning.

Further, individuals who enter policing begin a process of assimilation into the police role, in which adhering to an established hierarchy and following orders are standard operating procedures. Throughout the assimilation process, police organizations use a strong mixture of militaristic and bureaucratic control methods to coerce officers to behave and reason in a manner consistent with the police role (Violanti, 1999). As a result, a common trait of the police role is the use of a dichotomized decision-making process (the situation is either right or wrong) to resolve problems (Blau, 1994). Thus, it was assumed that officers who tend to incorporate a high level of moral reasoning would have difficulty adjusting to the organizational structure and police role. These officers would perceive organizational stress as high. Based on these assumptions, it was hypothesized that police stress was related to moral reasoning. The present study's findings did not support this hypothesis.

One explanation for this is that organizational stress and moral reasoning are two constructs that may not be related conceptually, even though they share some aspects related to cognitive development. Another explanation is that the paramilitary structure of law enforcement agencies and the police role may have contributed to the present findings.

Law enforcement organizations select and train officers who are more likely to adhere to an established hierarchy and assimilate into the police role. This process begins early in police training and is often supported by the police subculture (Violanti, 1999). Officers who have difficulty adapting to this structure and role are usually weeded out during the initial academy training or probationary process. It was found that the police officers in the present study fall into the maintaining norms stage of moral reasoning, which substantiates the explanation of rigid organizational norms in the police profession. Thus, officers do not have higher levels of moral reasoning, as their N2 scores are low.

Regarding physical/psychological pressure and moral reasoning, it was found that there was no significant relationship between the two. The conceptual framework developed for this research posited a relationship between police stress and moral reasoning. This was due to several assumptions. Researchers such as Violanti, Vena, Marshall, and Petralia (1996), Violanti (1999) and Williams (1987) have suggested that while police officers are not engaged in military combat, they do tend to experience similar conditions and outcomes. This includes a continued sense of danger from an unknown enemy, witnessing violence and death, depersonalization of emotion, lack of public support, increased risk of suicide, substance abuse, and disrupted family life (Violanti et al., 1996, Violanti, 1999).

A second assumption was based on research involving wartime soldiers. Several studies have indicated that post-traumatic stress disorder (PTSD) is related to a soldier's level of moral development, depending on the amount of combat exposure (Berg et al., 1994; Jackson, 1982; Wilson, 1978). Based on these assumptions, it was hypothesized that the physical and psychological threats would be related to an officer's level of moral reasoning. Specifically, it was hypothesized that officers with high levels of physical/psychological threat would exhibit a high level of moral reasoning. But the research findings did not support this hypothesis. But moral reasoning is related to avoidance coping styles like seeking alternative rewards and emotional discharge. Thus, this hypothesis is supported as far as coping is concerned.

Hypothesis H_3

There is a significant relationship between police stress and burnout. It is found that police stress is related significantly (at the 1% level) to burnout and its three dimensions. Within police stress, administrative/organizational pressure is related to all three dimensions of burnout—namely, emotional exhaustion, depersonalization, and personal accomplishment—while physical/ psychological threat is related to emotional exhaustion and personal accomplishment. It is inferred that administrative/organizational pressure is contributing more to burnout than physical/psychological threat.

Mediation analysis revealed that the seeking guidance and support, acceptance or resignation, and emotional discharge coping styles act as mediators between police stress and burnout. Though it's partial mediation, it still contributes toward burnout. Police officers use one approach coping style (seeking guidance and support) and two avoidance coping styles (acceptance or resignation and emotional discharge style) when facing stress that is leading them to experience burnout. Also, moral reasoning does not act as a mediator between police stress and burnout. The structural equation model shows that increases in police stress lead to burnout. Police stress further influences coping styles, and that leads to burnout.

Implications for Policy-Makers

Police administrators can take steps to reduce the organizational sources of stress. Communications channels can be made more effective, and work atmosphere made congenial. Grants of leave can be given, considering the needs of the police officer. There is a need to empower the police officer. It is known that motivational workshops are being conducted. Steps can be taken to introduce organization-wide interventions that will uproot the sources of stress and make the officer feel confident and happy to work. The administration can implement a stress management program targeted at solving the stress experienced by the officers due to the nature of the work and the department. The police administration should periodically review and update departmental policies, procedures, and practices that contribute significantly to organizational stress.

It is important to give training and counseling to officers to use more approach coping styles and reduce the use of avoidance coping styles. An officer using emotional discharge as a coping style tends to show negative emotions and to be an alcoholic. This leads him or her to use more force on criminals and, in turn, leads to more aggression. This is detrimental to the health of the officer. It is recommended to introduce psychologists who are trained to specifically address the stress-related needs, problems, and concerns of the law enforcement population. It is recommended that psychologists develop stress management techniques and conduct stress training workshops for the officers. Officers need to be trained to withstand conflicting situations and increase their mental strength.

Future Research

Further studies need to be undertaken to establish the relation between police stress and burnout in the Indian context. Moral reasoning can be taken as a separate area for research. A training program can be conducted on moral issues, and officers can be tested on their moral reasoning prior to training and post training. A larger sample of officers can be taken to establish the relationship of police stress to coping, moral reasoning, and burnout.

Discussion Questions

1. Discuss the kinds of coping styles that are related to police stress in this research.
2. Why is there no relation between moral reasoning and police stress?
3. Explain the relation between moral reasoning and coping mechanisms among police officers.
4. Elaborate on the concept of police stress and burnout.
5. Why is there a partial mediation of coping with police stress and burnout?

References

Alexander, D. A., Walker, L. G., Innes, G., & Irving, B. L. (1993). *Police stress at work*. London: Police Foundation.

Berg, A. M., Hem, E., Lau, B., Haseth, K., & Ekeberg, O. (2005). Stress in the Norwegian police service. *Occupational Medicine, 55*, 113–120.

Berg, G. E., Watson, C. G., Nugent, B., Gearhart, L. P., Juba, M., & Anderson, D. (1994). A comparison of combat's effects on PTSD scores in veterans with high and low moral development. *Journal of Clinical Psychology, 50*(5), 669–676.

Biggam, F. H., Power, K. G., MacDonald, R. R., Carcary, W. B., & Moodie, E. (1997). Self-perceived occupational stress distress in a Scottish police force. *Work & Stress, 11*, 118–133.

Bittner, E. (1967). The police on skid-row: A study in peacekeeping. *American Sociological Review, 32*(5), 699–715.

Blau, T. H. (1994). *Psychological services for law enforcement*. New York, NY: Wiley Publications.

Brown, J. M., & Campbell, E. A. (1990). Sources of occupational stress in the police. *Work & Stress, 4*, 305–318.

Brown, J. M., & Campbell, E. A. (1994). *Stress and policing: Sources and strategies*. Chichester, UK: Wiley Publications.

Caplan, R., Cobb, S., French, J., Van Harrison, R., & Pinneau, S. (1975). *Job demands and worker health: Main effects and occupational differences*. Washington, DC: US Department of Health, Education, and Welfare.

Cohen, S. (2004). *The nature of moral reasoning: The framework and activities of ethical deliberation, argument and decision making*. Oxford: Oxford University Press.

Coman, G., & Evans, B. (1991). Stressors facing Australian police in the 1990s. *Police Studies, 14*(4), 153–165.

Cooper, L., Kirkcaldy, B. D., & Brown, J. (1994). A model of job stress and physical health: The role of individual differences. *Personality and Individual Differences, 16*, 653–655.

Cordner, G., Scarborough, K., & Sheehan, R. (2004). *Police administration*. Cincinnati, OH: Anderson Publishing.

Crank, J. P., & Caldero, M. (2010). *Police ethics: The corruption of noble cause*. New Providence, NJ: Mathew Bender & Company.

Davidson, M. J., & Veno, A. (1978). Police stress: A multicultural, interdisciplinary review and Perspective. *Abstracts on Police Science, 6*, 187–199.

Davidson, M. J., & Veno, A. (1979). Police stress in Australia: A current perspective. *Australian and New Zealand Journal of Criminology, 12*, 153–1561.

Delattre, E. (2002). *Character and cops: Ethics in policing*. Washington, DC: The AEI Press.

DeLord, R., Burpo, J., Shannon, M., & Spearing, J. (2008). *Police union power, politics, and confrontation in the 21st century*. Springfield, IL: Charles C. Thomas.

Dubber, M. D. (2005). *The police power: Patriarchy and the foundations of American government*. New York, NY: Columbia University Press.

Folkman, S., & Lazarus, R. (1986). Stress process and depressive symptomatology. *Journal of Abnormal Psychology, 95*, 107–113.

Garland, B. (2002). Prison treatment staff burnout: Consequences, causes, and prevention. *Corrections Today, 64*(7), 116–121.

Hall, R. (2000). *The ethical foundations of criminal justice*. Boca Raton, FL: CRC Press.

Hart, P., Wearing, A., & Headey, B. (1993). Assessing police work experiences: Development of the police daily hassles and uplifts scales. *Journal of Criminal Justice, 21*, 553–572.

Hart, P., Wearing, A., & Headey, B. (1994). Perceived quality of life, personality, and work experiences: Construct validity of the police daily hassles and uplifts Scales. *Criminal Justice and Behavior, 21*, 283–311.

Hart, P., Wearing, A., & Headey, B. (1995). Police stress and well-being: Integrating personality, coping and daily work experiences. *Journal of Occupational and Organizational Policy, 68*, 133–156.

He, N., Zhao, J., & Archbold, C. (2002). Gender and police stress: The convergent and divergent impact of work environment, work-family conflict, and stress coping mechanisms of female and male police officers. *Policing: An International Journal of Police Strategies & Management, 25*, 678–708.

Hurrell, J. (1986). Some organizational stressors in police work and means for their amelioration. In J. T. Reese & H. A. Goldstein (Eds.), *Psychological services for law enforcement, national symposium on police psychological services*. Quantico, VA: FBI Academy.

Jackson, H. C. (1982). *The impact of combat stress on adolescent moral development in Vietnam veterans* (Unpublished doctoral dissertation). Smith College, Northampton, MA.

Jespersen, A. (1988). New approaches to stress. *Police Review*, 436–437.

Kemeny, M. E. (2003). The psychobiology of stress. *Current Directions in Psychological Science, 12*, 124–129.

Kirkcaldy, B. D., Cooper, C. L., & Brown, J. M. (1995). The role of coping in the stress-strain relationship among senior police officers. *International Journal of Stress Management, 2*, 69–78.

Kohan, A., & Mazmanian, D. (2003). Police work, burnout, and pro-organizational behavior: A consideration of daily work experiences. *Criminal Justice and Behavior, 30*, 559. doi:10.1177/0093854803254432

Kohlberg, L. (1969). Stage and sequence: The cognitive developmental approach to socialization. In D. A. Goslin (Ed.), *Handbook of socialization theory and research* (pp. 347–380). Chicago, IL: Rand McNally.

Kop, N., Euwema, M., & Schaufeli, W. (1999). Burnout, job stress, and violent behavior among Dutch police officers. *Work & Stress, 13*(4), 326–340.

Kroes, W. (1976). *Society's victim—the policeman: An analysis of job stress in policing*. Springfield, IL: Charles C. Thomas.

Kroes, W., & Hurrell, J. (1977). *Job stress and the police officer: Identifying stress reduction. techniques*. Washington, DC: US Government Printing Office.

Kulik, C., Oldham, G., & Hackman, J. (1987). Work design as an approach to person-environment fit. *Journal of Vocational Behavior, 31*, 278–296.

Lauferweiler, D. L. (1995). *Organizational stress: A tri-level analysis of the factors which affect perceived stress* (Unpublished doctoral dissertation). Virginia Commonwealth University, Richmond, VA.

Lawrence, R. A. (1984). Police stress and personality factors: A conceptual model. *Journal of Criminal Justice, 12*, 247–263.

Lazarus, R., & Folkman, S. (1984). *Stress, appraisal, and coping*. New York, NY: Springer.

Lee, S. (2002). A study of Korean police sergeants' stress. *International Journal of Comparative and Applied Criminal Justice* (26), 85–99.

Loo, R. (1986a). Post-shooting stress reactions among police officers. *Journal of Human Stress, 12*, 27–31.

Loo, R. (1986b). Suicide among police in a federal force. *Suicide and Life-Threatening Behavior, 16*, 379–388.

Loo, R. (1994). Burnout among Canadian police managers. *The International Journal of Organizational Analysis, 2*(4), 406–417.

Malloy, T. E., & Mays, G. L. (1984). The police stress hypothesis: A critical evaluation. *Criminal Justice and Behavior, 11*, 197–224.

Manning, P. (1977). *Police work: The social organization of policing*. Cambridge, MA: MIT Press.

Marks, M., & Sklansky, D. (2008). Voices from below: Unions and participatory arrangements in the police workforce. *Police Practice & Research, 9*(2), 85–94. doi:10.1080/15614260802081238

Maslach, C. (1976). Burned-out. *Human Behavior, 5*, 16–22.

Maslach, C. (1993). Burnout: A multidimensional perspective. In W. Schaufeli, C. Maslach, & T. Marek (Eds.), *Professional burnout: Recent developments in theory and research* (pp. 19–32). Washington, DC: Taylor & Francis.

Maslach, C., & Jackson, S. (1979, January–February). Burned out cops and their families. *Psychology Today*, 20–21.

Maslach, C., Jackson, S., & Leiter, M. (1996). *Maslach burnout inventory manual* (3rd ed.). Palo Alto, CA: Consulting Psychologists Press.

Maslach, C., Schaufeli, W., & Leiter, M. (2001). Job burnout. *Annual Review of Psychology, 52*, 397–422.

McCarty, W. P., Zhao, J. S., & Garland, B. E. (2007). Occupational stress and burnout between male and female police officers: Are there any gender differences? *Policing: An International Journal of Police Strategies & Management, 30*, 672–691.

Muchinsky, P., & Monahan, C. J. (1987). What is person-environment congruence? Supplementary versus complementary models of fit. *Journal of Vocational Behavior, 31*, 268–277.

National Institutes of Mental Health. (1967). *The functions of police in modern society*. Bethesda, MD: United States Government.

Newman, D., & Rucker-Reed, M. (2004). Police stress, state-trait anxiety, and stressors among US Marshals. *Journal of Criminal Justice, 32*, 631–641.

Ortmeier, P., & Meese, E. (2010). *Leadership, ethics, and policing: Challenges for the 21st century*. New York, NY: Prentice Hall.

Patterson, G. T. (2002). Predicting the effects of military service experience on stressful occupational events in police officers. *Policing: An International Journal of Police Strategies & Management, 25*, 602–618.

Pearlin, L., & Schooler, C. (1978). The structure of coping. *Journal of Health and Social Behavior, 19*, 2–21.

Piaget, J. (1932). *The moral judgment of the child*. Harcourt, Brace.

Reiser, M. (Ed.). (1982). *Police psychology*. Los Angeles, CA: Lehi Publications.

Rest, J. (1979). *Development in judging moral issue*. Minneapolis, MN: University of Minnesota Press.

Rest, J. (1986). *Moral development: Advances in research and theory*. New York, NY: Praeger.

Rest, J., Narvaez, D., Thoma, S., & Bebeau, M. (1999). Dit2: Devising and testing a revised instrument of moral judgment. *Journal of Educational Psychology, 91*, 644–659. doi: 10.1037/0022-0663.91.4.644

Roberg, R., Hayhurst, D., & Allen, H. (1988). Job burnout in law enforcement dispatchers: A comparative analysis. *Journal of Criminal Justice, 16*, 385–393.

Roberg, R., Novak, K., & Cordner, G. (2005). *Police and society* (3rd ed.). Los Angeles, CA: Roxbury.

Schaible, L., & Gecas, V. (2010). The impact of emotional labor and value dissonance on burnout among police officers. *Police Quarterly, 13*, 316. doi:10.1177/1098611110373997

Sklansky, D. (2007). Seeing blue: Police reform, occupational culture, and cognitive burn-in. In M. O'Neill & M. Marks (Eds.), *Police occupational culture: New debates and directions*. Oxford: Elsevier Science.

Spielberger, C., Westberry, L. G., Grier, K., & Greenfield, G. (1981). *The police stress survey: Sources of stress in law enforcement*. Monograph Series Three (No. 6), College of Social and Behavioral Sciences, University of South Florida.

Stansfield, R. (1996). *Issues in policing: A Canadian perspective*. Toronto, ON: Thompson Educational Publishing.

Stinchcomb, J. (2004). Searching for stress in all the wrong places: Combating chronic organizational stressors in policing. *Police Practice and Research, 5*(3), 259–277.

Stratton, J., Parker, D., & Snibbe, J. (1985). Post-traumatic stress: Study of police officers involved in shootings. *Psychological Reports, 55*, 127–131.

Tang, T., Tollison, P., & Whiteside, D. (1987). The effect of quality circle initiation on motivation to attend quality circle meetings and on task performance. *Personnel Psychology, 40*, 799–814.

Tang, T., Tollison, P., & Whiteside, D. (1989). Quality circle productivity as related to upper-management attendance, circle initiation, and collar color. *Journal of Management, 15*(1), 101–113.

Tang, T., Tollison, P., & Whiteside, D. (1991). Managers' attendance and the effectiveness of small work groups: The case of quality circles. *Journal of Social Psychology, 131*(3), 335–344.

Thomas, L., & Hammontree, H. (1992). The effects of hardiness, police stress, and life stress on police officers' illness and absenteeism. *Public Personnel Management, 21*(4).

Toch, H., & Grant, J. (2005). *Police as problem solvers: How frontline workers can promote organizational and community change.* Washington, DC: American Psychological Association.

Treviño, L. (1992). Moral reasoning and business ethics: Implications for research, education, and management. *Journal of Business Ethics, 11*(5–6), 445–459.

Treviño, L., & Weaver, G. (2003). *Managing ethics in business organizations.* Stanford, CA: Stanford University Press.

Violanti, J. M. (1981). *Police stress and coping: An organizational analysis* (Unpublished doctoral dissertation). State University of New York at Buffalo, New York.

Violanti, J. M. (1999). Trauma in police work: A psychosocial model. In J. Villati & D. Paton (Eds.), *Police trauma* (pp. 88–96). Springfield, IL: Charles C. Thomas.

Violanti, J. M., Vena, J. E., Marshall, J. R., & Petralia, S. (1996). A comparative evaluation of police suicide rate validity. *Suicide and Life-Threatening Behavior, 26*(1), 79–85. doi:10.1111/j.1943-278X.1996.tb00259.x

Wallace, P., Roberg, R., & Allen, H. (1985). Job burnout among narcotics investigators: An exploratory study. *Journal of Criminal Justice, 13*, 549–559.

Weber, J., & Wasieleski, D. (2001). Investigating influences on managers' moral reasoning: The impact of context, personal and organizational factors. *Business & Society, 40*(1), 79–111.

Williams, C. (1987). Peacetime combat: Treating and preventing delayed stress reactions in police officers. In T. Williams (Ed.), *Post-traumatic stress disorders: A handbook for clinicians* (pp. 267–292). Cincinnati, OH: Disabled American Veterans.

Wilson, J. (1968). *Varieties of police behavior: The management of law and order in eight communities.* Cambridge, MA: Harvard University Press.

Wilson, J. (1978). *Identity, ideology, and crisis: The Vietnam veteran in transition* (Unpublished Paper). Cleveland State University, Cleveland, OH.

Wilson, J. (2000). *Bureaucracy: What government agencies do and why they do it.* New York, NY: Basic Books.

Zhao, J., He, N., Lovrich, N., & Cancino, J. (2003). Marital status and police occupational stress. *Journal of Crime and Justice, 26*(2), 23–46.

Zukauskas, G., Dapsys, K., Jasmontatite, E., & Susinskas, J. (2001). Some psychological problems of police officers in Lithuania. *Policing: An International Journal of Police Strategies & Management, 24*, 301–309.

Chapter 13

An Evaluation of Safety and Security
A South African Perspective

Doraval Govender

Introduction

The year 1994 will be remembered in policing circles as a year of great changes for safety and security in South Africa. This period will always be remembered as a political watershed for South Africa. A shift was being made from a repressive police state to a democracy, which required the application of democratic policing principles and values. Since policing is and remains one of the most important mechanisms in social control, a meaningful balance needed to be found between persuasive and enforced control in the new South Africa. When police officials are confronted with situations that require sensitivity, they on occasion use maximum force or more force than is necessary. Situations often leads to allegations of police brutality or to public violence and criminal charges being preferred against the police (Afrika & Hofstatter, 2015). Policing in South Africa should be rapidly transformed because modern, democratic, multicultural societies are oriented toward individual rights, demanding "policing by consent" rather than mere enforcement of laws. It is clear that the criminal justice system is failing its citizens by not providing adequate community policing, social services interventions, and sufficient restorative justice and dispute resolution platforms to resolve different types of social problems (Hargovan, 2009). Gender-based violence, police brutality, corruption, protests, and noncompliance with COVID-19 regulations is the talk of the day, with very little focus on the overall crime problems. Since 1994, different National Commissioners came with different leadership styles and changed the South African Police to what we have today (Govender, 2010).

Robert Peel's dream of "a truly preventative police force" being "substantially accomplished" through private security rather than through public policing thus holds true. This is evident in the fact that private security, while still retaining "traditional" private security tasks, engages in more and more law enforcement duties (Shearing & Stenning, 1982, p. 100).

Safety and security in communities, businesses, and private and public entities and at learning institutions are becoming problematic for the police to handle. They have to rely on private security to support them at these places. Protecting the well-being of communities, employees, students, and visitors and being proactive will help reduce risk and exposure to threats. In-house security at learning institutions, businesses, and private and public entities are now dealing with a greater variety of safety and security incidents including occupational, health, and safety issues such as COVID-19. At the same time, costs associated with incidents have driven the costs of responding to issues to extremely high levels. These costs are now so high that the only sustainable, viable model for mitigating risks is preventing them before they can occur, and that requires new proactive ways to approach them (Parent, 2018).

During this technological age of the fourth Industrial Revolution (4IR), many entities still rely on the traditional physical protection systems, such as access control registers, boom gates,

DOI: 10.4324/9781003047117-15

security guards, and analogue electronic surveillance. Computerized identification (computer analytics) of objects and events without human assistance and reaction to diffuse dangerous situations is often ignored due to budgetary constraints (Hi-Tech Solutions, 2010). An earlier article published on incorporating new technology to the traditional security function of guarding in South Africa also argues for advanced surveillance systems (Sewpersad & van Jaarsveld, 2012). It is therefore important to show the convergence of security measures with technology, making reference to the risk analysis model ISO 31000–2009 and the extent to which this internationally recognized risk management model is implemented to satisfy the scientific process of risk identification, assessment, evaluation, and treatment as a basis for decision-making on risks (Govender, 2019; Liuksiala, 2012). The probability theory provides the element of probability for the ISO31000 risk management model to evaluate the risk so that a most fitting solution to mitigate risk can be found (Bernstein, 1996, p. 48). A security risk analysis plan should be developed to incorporate strategies to reduce both the cost of risk management relative to identified threats and to assign the most appropriate risk treatment to each identified risk. A key element of the design of the security risk analysis process involves the application of treatments that (in priority order) involve the objectives to deter, deny, delay, detect, and respond with regard to a potential attack (Talbot & Jakeman, 2008, pp. 188–189).

According to Fay (2006, p. 111), risk identification normally arises from the defined context, which is informed by *threat, vulnerability, and criticality assessments* as well as historical information management systems and program activities. During the assessment, we need to ask the questions what, when, where, how, and who for clarity. Prevention is the most effective form of mitigation of risks. Stopping an incident before it can take place is always better, for all parties involved, than responding after the fact. The most effective way to prevent incidents of all kinds—accidents, crime, and natural disasters, etc., that threaten the personal safety and well-being of everyone—is for safety and security officials to receive advanced intelligence of a potential problem and act before the situation can develop. Receiving this intelligence requires open and anonymous lines of communication between security officials and the employees, students, and visitors they are protecting. Upon notification of a threat or an ongoing incident, private security should begin implementing an emergency response plan as appropriate to meet the nature of the threat and the situation. Private security should notify management that the emergency response plan is being implemented (Parent, 2018).

Safety and security of communities, businesses, private and public entities, and learning institutions is a continuous process that requires detail analysis and planning. The geographic location of the assets to be protected—the social and economic pressures experienced by personnel and visitors and the surrounding environment—cannot be ignored when designing and developing a plan to protect the assets (Hi-Tech Security Solutions, 1999). The findings of a quantitative study in the United kingdom show that the management of security services at entities ought to consider adopting a strategic approach to security as part of its responsibility to manage all identified risks and obtaining value for money from limited resources. This approach will need to be supported by other security risk control measures such as training and developing effective procedures and ensuring the dissemination of management information to all levels of the entity (Wallace & Lauwerys, 2002).

Businesses and public and private entities have a legal duty to make the workplace a safe working environment for their employees and visitors. It is the employer's responsibility to regularly conduct a workplace risk analysis and put in place measures to make the workplace as safe as is reasonably practicable to try and minimize the risk to employees and visitors from contracting COVID-19. Employees and visitors also have responsibility to comply with safe working practices (Scottish Government, 2020). First and foremost, *good infection prevention* and control practice is key to minimizing the risk of employees contracting COVID-19 in the workplace. This includes symptom vigilance, hand hygiene, increased environmental cleaning, and physical distancing, as much as is reasonably practical. Where an employee has symptoms of COVID-19, they are expected to self-isolate, book a test immediately and self-isolate as per national guidance (Scottish Government, 2020).

This study became more important during the Covid-19 pandemic in 2020, because of the number of police officers engaging in unethical behavior, as this type of behavior often originates in the norms of organizational culture (Kingshott & Prinsloo, 2004). This article is located within the routine activity theory, which identifies a potential offender with a premeditated motive to commit a crime, a suitable victim to whom the crime is directed, and the absence of a capable guardian such as security official or the SAPS police official (Hsieh & Wang, 2018, p. 335). This article will discuss the status quo of safety and security since the advent of democracy in South Africa.

Methodology

The study followed a case study design to collect qualitative data on safety and security issues. The researcher used media reports, academic literature, and his experience as a former police officer to look at the evolution of safety and security in South Africa. All data was analyzed using the descriptive analysis process.

Status Quo of Safety and Security Since the Advent of Democracy

Most common types of safety and security incidents confronting people and property in communities, businesses, public and private entities, and learning institutions in South Africa start with incidents that have happened in which the culprits are known. In most cases, private security attends to these incidents, be it in communities, businesses, private and public entities, or learning institutions; the security officer responding to such an incident gives priority to safeguard all the available evidence as quickly as possible in order to prevent it from being tampered with, overlooked, or lost, intentionally or otherwise. Under these circumstances the scene of the incident (crime) is secured. All loopholes need to be identified and closed. Searches should be conducted lawfully and with due regard to decency. A decision has to be made as soon as possible to call SAPS. If the police do attend and commence with the investigation, then all operational decisions will pass through them. If it is decided that an internal inquiry should be conducted, it may be necessary to call upon the internal investigation unit or external specialists servicing the business or private or public entity to assist with the investigation or to review particular systems or processes (Stelfox, 2009, p. 95).

In some incidents that happen, the perpetrator is unknown and information comes from a reliable source of a likely incident taking place on the premises that is bound to negatively affect the assets of the entity. Under these circumstances, an investigation is immediately instituted by private security. Unconventional methods are used to collect evidence for the investigation of these types of incidents, which includes the covert intelligence collection method using undercover investigations, surveillance, etc. This is commonly known as intelligence gathering (Stelfox, 2009, p. 95). Many people who may be in a position to provide open source information on such incidents are complainants, witnesses to incidents, victims of crimes, suspects, journalists and representatives from agencies/institutions, students and personnel (Van Rooyen, 2008, p. 218).According to Altbeker (1998, p. 34), in order to move against the leader of an organized criminal group or syndicate, it is necessary to have intelligence on criminal activities in which the syndicate members are involved. Intelligence can be obtained through closed means, namely electronic interception of communication from informers and agents.

Victim surveys conducted from 1994 show that the poor are more at risk of being victims of murders caused through interpersonal violence, and the wealthy living in the suburbs are most at risk of residential robberies and burglary (Mc Cafferty, 2003). In 2005, the World Health Organisation found that South Africa is no different from the rest of the world; domestic violence in South Africa is committed across geographical, religious, racial, and gender boundaries. It is prevalent in both urban and rural areas (World Health Organisation Report, 2005).

To date, recidivists reoffend due to a variety of personal reasons and circumstantial factors. These include the individual's social environment of peers, family, and community, as well as a lack of support systems and appropriate policies to assist in the reintegration of offenders into their families and communities. It is sometimes suggested that recidivism is an indication that prison is somehow attractive or "not too bad" (South African Catholics Bishops Conference on Recidivism, 2012). According to Montesh and Berning, an estimated 20% of criminals are usually responsible for 80% of all violent crimes in South Africa (Montesh & Berning, 2014). Although there are no accurate statistics of the rate of recidivism, it is estimated by the Department of Corrections in South Africa to be about 47% (South African Catholics Bishops Conference on Recidivism, 2012).

There is still a huge problem with the relationship between the use of drugs/alcohol and the commission of crimes in general. This does not mean that drug/alcohol users are criminals; however, there is a perception that perpetrators under the influence of drugs and alcohol are more likely to be aggressive and out of control. The most common drugs seized in South Africa are mandrax, cat, cocaine powder, dagga, and a mixture of other drugs known as nyaope. According to Montesh and Berning, there is a strong relationship between age and crime. People who are arrested are mostly youth and the homeless (Montesh & Berning, 2014). They would commit any crime to obtain cash to buy drugs (Naik & Serumula, 2015).

About 3.5 million South Africans legally possess some 4.2 million firearms, of which slightly more than half are handguns. A similar number of illegal firearms are circulating in South Africa. South Africa's porous borders allow arms smugglers to bring large quantities of firearms into the country. Because of an oversupply of small arms in the continent, these sell cheaply, making them accessible to petty criminals and juveniles in South Africa, who frequently use them to commit violent crimes or resolve personal disputes (Schönteich & Louw, 2001).

According to Landman and Liebermann (2005, pp. 21–26), businesses in South Africa have reacted to crime by increasing security measures to protect their property. They make use of methods that range from changes to the interior of buildings, for example using electronic surveillance (closed-circuit television) cameras to bulletproof glasses in banks and in 24-hour garage shops. Exterior changes include burglar bars in front of windows, security gates on doors, and shutters covering entire shop windows. High fences or walls are constructed around properties. Access-control entrances are common in many businesses and organizations.

Residents have also responded with increased security measures. These vary from the installation of electronic devices for electronic surveillance such as closed-circuit surveillance cameras, alarm systems, panic buttons, electronic gates, and intercom systems, to physical modifications such as burglar bars, security gates, and fences and walls around properties. The extent and nature of the changes depend, among other things, on the location of people's homes, their financial abilities, the measure of security perceived to be necessary, and the perceptions about the risk of victimization (Landman & Liebermann, 2005, pp. 21–26). In the absence of visible physical protection systems, a residence may be perceived as a relatively easy target and therefore more vulnerable to burglary than residences that are well protected through a range of security measures. Physical protection systems may include all the means that could be used to protect the household and its residents—for example, access control, fences with spikes, electrified barbed wire fences, entry phones, burglar-proofing at windows and doors, locks, security guards, armed response services, security lights, dogs, and CCTV surveillance systems. Physical protection systems, as a measure, are implemented for the protection of assets or facilities against criminals, terrorists, commercial or industrial competitors, malicious people, or unlawful attacks (Van Zyl, Wilson, & Pretorius, 2003; Govender, 2013).

From 1995 to 2007, demonstrations, strikes, marches and a show of force by unions were common. The Area Crime Combating Units (ACCU), in terms of the Gathering Regulations, peacefully policed these activities. The Gathering Regulations were enforced in an integrated fashion including all role-players, from the organizers, local government, and SAPS Area Commissioners to the local station commissioner and the ACCU. A magistrate approved the gathering to take place within a specific time frame on a specific date and venue. Organizers and the SAPS officers worked together to police the event. This approach guaranteed the *principle* use of minimum force as opposed to maximum force. This worked well until 2007, when the Area Commissioners' and the ACCU's offices were closed and the personnel moved to police stations.

The Farlam Commission of Inquiry, which was commissioned by the President of South Africa, was tasked with examining the events and the role of the police in the Marikana strike. This is not the first such commission to examine the role of the police involvement in violent protests. After the shooting of rioters in Soweto by the police in 1976, the Cillié Commission was instituted. This Commission made recommendations on the role of the police. The Goldstone Commission of Inquiry also made recommendations, which gave rise to the Regulation of Gatherings Act. The Ngoepe Commission examined the events at Ellis Park stadium, in which 43 people died after a stampede by supporters of the two biggest football clubs. The stampede occurred when the supporters wanted to get into the stadium. There were recommendations for policing from all four commissions of inquiry. The author examined the policy and legislative framework, current literature, and the recommendations of all four South African Commissions of Inquiry for public order policing in South Africa (Govender, 2016). Despite the recommendations by these commissions, we are still confronted with allegations of police brutality and poor crowd management practices. Violent crowds seeking attention for poor service delivery, strikes and protests, and turf wars between gangs in any society impact negatively on businesses and personnel, while profits and productivity go down. Investor confidence becomes eroded. Violence experienced at home affects the ability of victims to work and increases fear. Children are affected in their ability to do well at school, and their health becomes affected in the long term.

Corruption Watch's Analysis of Corruption Trends (ACT) report paints a picture of heavy-handedness and bribery on the part of police officers. Researchers said:

> These reports speak to SAPS' lack of humanity and consideration for the members of the public whom it serves, and a blatant disregard for law and order on the part of officers and officials. Perhaps, predictably, bribery features in 31% of reports of police corruption, highlighting how police officers solicit bribes from suspects and victims alike, as well as residents.

The report continues: "during the lockdown period, officers seemed to act with impunity in both their behaviour and extraction of favours; patterns that also featured in the 29% of allegations relating to abuse of power" (Williams, 2020).

According to the Canadian Occupational Health and Safety Act, there is a need for emergency plans because, besides the benefit of providing guidance during an emergency, hazardous conditions or threats of criminal activity that would aggravate an emergency may be discovered. The planning process may also bring to light a lack of resources such as equipment and trained personnel. The lack of an emergency plan could lead to severe losses and casualties in the event of an emergency and possibly the financial collapse of the organization. An emergency plan specifies procedures for handling sudden situations. The objective is to reduce the possible consequences of an emergency by preventing fatalities and injuries and reducing damage to buildings, stock, and equipment as well as accelerating the resumption of normal operations (Canadian Centre for Occupational Health and Safety, 2005). The South African legislative framework for emergency response can be found in the Occupational Health and Safety Act 85 of 1994 in South Africa.

According to Reid, in Seldon (2019, p. 38), members from the community policing forum (CPF), businesses, private and public entities, or learning institutions should have a social media monitoring and management system in place to keep an electronic ear to the ground. This enables entities to become more proactive and will potentially even prevent unpleasant experiences. It is suggested that a policy on media and human relations be developed and implemented. This policy should educate and help people understand what is acceptable social media reporting. The policy and training should be made available to all.

Changes Initiated by Police Leadership Since 1995

Before 1995, we had geopolitical policing (KwaZulu-Natal and Lebowa police agencies; homeland policing in the Transkei, Bophuthatswana, Venda, and Ciskei). These different policing agencies were amalgamated into one single police service. Today we still have differentiated policing (traffic and military policing) and parallel policing (private security) (Govender, 2010).

The following operational strategies were implemented but not monitored or evaluated; instead, they were displaced through more emphasis being placed on something new, without conducting any form of impact analysis on what had been implemented (Pruitt, 2010):

- National Crime Prevention Strategy (NCPS) 1996
- National Crime Combating Strategy (NCCS) 2000
- Community Policing
- Sector Policing
- Intelligence-led Policing

On January 1, 2000, a new National Commissioner, Mr. Jackie Selebi, was appointed to provide strategic leadership to the SAPS. He was the former Director General from the Department of Foreign Affairs and a long-standing senior member of the African National Congress (ANC). He started in the SAPS by monitoring all the persons wanted for syndicate crime in South Africa, transnationally and internationally. He became chairperson of the South African Regional Police Chiefs Committee (SARPCCO) and later became President of Interpol in Lyon, France. His strategic direction was already chartered by the policies developed by his predecessor George Fivaz, the first National Commissioner of the South African Police Service. During the Fivaz era, many of the policies were in the infancy of implementation. The NCCS operational strategy was already drafted for implementation from 2000. Selebi became the driver of this policy.

Selebi compared Provincial crime statistics at his national meetings and demanded changes to the crime picture with feedback and guidance. He provided strict leadership and dictated the things he wanted done by his management. His management felt intimidated by his threats of being fired (discharged from employment). His Provincial management used him as a role model to intimidate their subordinates to achieve targets or be fired. He held quarterly "Compare Statistics" meetings with Provincial Commissioners and his National Management team. This strategic action played a vital role in making a difference in the violent crime statistics and building confidence between the SAPS and the community. Being the first black civilian National Commissioner made him a popular figure among the majority in the country. He was also known as a person who could provide resources to police stations, as he used his political influence to improve resources and the budget in the SAPS and the salaries of SAPS members. He also used his charm in controlling union activities within the SAPS. He closed down the Transformation Committee of SAPS and restructured the SAPS twice. He closed the Area structures, the specialized units, and increased the appointment of senior officers. He used his power to compel senior officers to deliver on performance targets. He was a leader who made decisions on his own and told his subordinates what to do. He sometimes called consultative meetings with his Provincial Commissioners and management personnel to discuss his decisions with them.

The South African transition brought about a restructuring of the criminal justice system by the abolishment of a number of laws and the promulgation of new ones. Reform of the apartheid-era policing was one of the major challenges for the new government in 1994 (De Vries, 2008). The effects of apartheid, in addition to years of political violence and the continued exposure to violence in the home and in the neighborhoods, have produced a destructive culture that manifests itself in violence as a means of solving conflicts domestically and socially.

The Resolution Seven restructuring process of the SAPS during 2003, carried out under the leadership of the National Commissioner and his top management, inhibited service delivery through the centralization of specific policing functions, inter alia, local criminal record centers. The biggest mistake in this restructuring process was the closing down of specialized units; inter alia, the South African narcotics units, vehicle theft units, child and family violence units, and the Area Commissioners' offices. This action was tantamount to taking away policing from the people, thus leaving more and more demotivated personnel at different levels of the organization and an increase in violent crime levels (Burger & Boshoff, 2012). During 2006, further restructuring under the same leadership resulted in the closing down of remaining specialized units and the area structures (Govender, 2010). South African Police brought in lateral appointments with no police training, police experience, or related qualifications and gave them senior management positions with police ranks to manage experienced police officials performing the core business of policing. Instead of giving them civilian support service appointments with applicable salaries, they were given strategic tasks, for example, to restructure the police service and to support policing with operational plans, etc. According to De Vries (2008, p. 135), the President of the Republic suspended National Commissioner Selebi in 2007, and he was charged soon after on charges of corruption. He was privy to all the top criminals being investigated for syndicate crime by the SAPS Organised Crime Unit. Many of the lateral entries left the service prematurely on discovering that their strategic decisions had impeded service delivery and demotivated police officials in the policing environment (Govender, 2010). According to the vision of police leadership during 2009–2012, they were intent on ending violent crime by applying the maximum force allowed by law. This era showed an increase in incidents of police brutality. Against this brutality is the increase in the killing of police officials (Khobane, 2010).

In 2015, the then Acting National Commissioner emphasized the need for a "Back to Basics" approach focussing on, *inter alia*, the wellness of police officers and aims at ensuring that the morale of the men and women in blue is lifted, so that their primary preoccupation remains fighting crime. The 'Back to Basics' approach includes emphasis on police visibility in all public spaces (South African Police, Department of Police, 2015). An important aspect to note was the most obvious change in the South African Police Service (SAPS) from "force" to "service" in the South African Police Service Act. This crucial back to basics change which was implemented in the South African Police Service (SAPS) in 1994 was reversed in 1998 by management to make the SAPS once again a quasi-military organization. This shows that going back to basics is a fallacy. In reality, changing policing back to basics will not succeed if the policing style of front-line managers and top management is not aligned to the vision of the SAPS.

In response to rising levels of violent crimes, many desperate communities started their own street policing activities, operating under the Community Policing Forums (CPFs) or sector policing without any reference to local police structures or talk of partnerships with the South African Police Services (SAPS) (Minnaar, 2009, p. 51). Different types of street policing began to grow within communities, resulting in pluralistic street policing. Pluralistic street policing has since grown with no coordination, management, and control.

The 2018/2019 annual report of the Independent Police Investigative Directorate (IPID) showed there has been an upsurge in cases of police brutality. Almost 2,000 dockets involving police brutality have been sent to the NPA by IPID. Cases investigated by IPID included 1,794 for assault, 337 for discharging official firearms, 157 of death as a result of police action, 154 of death in police custody, 81 of torture, 60 of corruption, 57 of criminal misconduct, and 12 of rape while in police custody. Dr. Johan Burger, a senior researcher at the Institute for Security Studies, blamed police brutality on the training of officers and their understanding of human rights. "Police brutality is a question of the poor quality of some of our officers, in particular our detectives. Good detectives will never feel the need to assault or torture a suspect to get the truth" (Rampedi & Manaya, 2020).

Challenges Confronting Safety and Security

Police are challenged with political volatility, criminal justice policy changes, and rapid technological change that introduces new complexities and uncertainties into the policing environment (Manning, 2003, pp. 164–170). According to Ayling, Grabosky, and Shearing (2009, p. 11), the translation of private sector plans and activities into public sector plans and activities over the last decade or so has driven changes in a way in which police strategize and implement resource decisions. These are only few of the plans and activities that were implemented in the criminal justice environment. The intensity and magnitude of crime in South Africa generally extends beyond the parameters of normal law enforcement, whereby civil society has a major role to fulfil in crime prevention and the investigation of crime and to a limited extent on human resources. There are considerable demands on and expectations of policing in South Africa. Most demands come from the taxpayers and of those who allocate funds for policing. These investors are concerned with their return on investment in policing. The most frequently asked question is "Are we getting a return on our investment?" The art of police management in the twenty-first century is to meet the public's needs efficiently, in part by involving the public in policing and in part by targeting policing resources to the most important issues. The first and major expectation that the public has of its police is that the police should always be available. Community policing requires officers to be available to the community consistently and over a sufficient period of time. This expectation is certainly addressed, as the police do indeed provide 24-hour service, seven days a week, all year round (Edwards, 2011, p. 142).

Three core policing functions were identified for the twenty-first century by Les Johnston in Patterson and Pollock (2011, p. 33). They include crime-oriented policing, community policing, and order maintenance. The three core policing functions are central to policing in South Africa. However, the private security companies seem to conduct street policing together with citizens as an initiative arising from CPF structures with minimum guidance from the local police station. Community policing comes at a high price, as its fundamental principle is to develop improved communication and a relationship of trust among the police, private security, and the public, which means that a police officer must build a professional rapport with individuals and groups within the community. Policing is in need of major change to meet the needs of modern society. According to Burger (2007, p. 102), the role of community policing, and more specifically sector policing, is more focused on the monitoring of public complaints than on solving community problems.

The introduction of the CPFs led to a shift in focus from crime and offenders (looking at the causes of crime) to crime prevention and community safety networks (finding solution to community problems). This restructuring of response to crime involved a modern pluralization of policing in which the police's previous monopoly of control of policing services was being fragmented and was increasingly undertaken by a multitude of policing providers from the statutory, voluntary, and commercial sectors (Patterson and Pollock, 2011, p. 15). In South Africa, we have pluralized policing to a large extent. Some of the forms of pluralized policing includes bicycle patrols, private security street patrols, business watch, neighborhood watch, sector policing, street committees, car guards, and of course public policing by the SAPS, the Metro Police, Traffic, Special Investigation Units (SIUs), government departments such as municipalities, Home Affairs, the Receiver of Revenue, etc.

Constitutionally, "community policing" is the core of transformed policing in South Africa. Community policing was institutionalized by the policy-makers in order to police in a more humane and sensitive way according to the needs of the communities. It is a legally recognized entity that represents the policing interests of the local community. The CPFs are also intended to exert civilian oversight over the police at various levels, in particular at the local police station level (Minnaar, 2009, pp. 20–25).

In 2000, sector policing was introduced as an intensive policing and patrol strategy in specific high crime identified areas in order to increase police visibility, improve community involvement, build trust, and get the public to report crime and any suspicious activities in their neighborhood and to try to address the causes of crime and the fear of crime. It was established to bring about operational improvement, increase police effectiveness, and grow community policing (Minnaar, 2009, p. 39).

> Street Committees initiated by Government in 2007, needed the involvement of the community in a particular area. It serves as a formalised communication structure for information to and from the community. It creates a platform for teamwork and cooperation within the community with a structured protocol to lodge concerns, obtain information and create accountability when dealing with challenges that require solutions.
> (Vukukhanye Community Upliftment Initiatives, 2009)

Pluralistic street policing is related to the service style of policing, where policing is directed toward the maintenance of an orderly state of affairs rather than the absolute enforcement of the laws. According to Van Heerden (1982, p. 107), police action is to a great extent led and directed by public opinion. The power of the police to fulfil their functions and duties is dependent on public approval of their existence, actions, and behavior and their ability to secure and maintain public respect (Pike, 1985, p. 37).

Police leadership since 1994 has also been characterized by different leadership styles, the most popular being the autocratic leadership style, which seem to have helped in improving the crime statistics. However, the doctrine of minimum force remains a key behavioral element of professional policing, A strict adherence to this important doctrine by the police is vital. It must be accepted that the rule of law remains supreme. There is still work that needs to be done regarding the use of minimum force, police ethics, police discretion/ decision-making, and police sense and sensitivity. New police leadership should give attention to these important principles of policing.

It is evident from our recent experiences that public order policing in South Africa is unique and different from the international world, since we come from a culture of violence generated during the apartheid era. We need to consider different epistemologies to design and develop a curriculum to satisfy our tactical options. The training program should generally consist of Platoon Members Training and Platoon Commander Training (PCT), which is a course for commanders, and more advanced operational courses for First-line Operational Managers and Operational Commanders (Ministry of Police, 2011).

Recommendation

Pluralistic street policing activities take place daily in our communities. The South African Police Service is the legislative organ to maintain social order, and therefore the question arises, "Who coordinates and manages the pluralistic street policing initiatives in our communities?" There are different agencies performing street policing in the police station precinct. The CPF as a legislative structure should coordinate quality interaction with the SAPS and the public with the aim of influencing variations in the levels of reported crimes. Community policing structures need to take responsibility together with SAPS for the formalization of street policing and not to allow entities to act on their own under the guise of community policing, conducting arbitrary policing activities that can result in injury, loss of life, and civil claims. This will also help to bring the implementation of street committees to fruition.

Information and intelligence are the greatest tools for use by investigators in the investigation of crime. It helps them in making arrests and solving crimes. The collection of crime information is important to assessing the nature and distribution of crime, in order to efficiently allocate resources and personnel.

In order to give impetus and ensure compliance with the human rights culture, the Constitution, legislative framework, policies, and international standards, the SAPS must urgently review its current dispensation and operational approach in public order policing. Smarter and more accountable public order policing is the answer for the reduction of violence in the management and control of crowds.

An effective service will not only help to prevent crime, but it also contributes to a positive image of the entities being protected by creating a safe and secure environment for all. This role needs to be recognized, supported, and integrated with the services provided by SAPS. The security emergency response plan at entities should operate together with the support of SAPS and all other stakeholders (Wallace & Lauwerys, 2002).

Communities, businesses, public and private entities, and learning institutions should develop a strategy that takes into account an assessment of risks of the entity's activities, personnel, and visitors; the need to balance technology and other resources and IT; and the implementation of operational plans and activity based budgets and good governance. There should be a clear line of communication and coordinating mechanism within and outside the entities. Management should be part of the security strategy, thus defining management responsibility for security, introducing service standards for internal and external providers, providing continuous personnel training, and collecting and disseminating information/intelligence to inform decision-making. (Wallace & Lauwerys, 2002).

A national police commission (NPC) should be established to examine the policing system in South Africa and recommend rapid transformation to decolonize the police.

Conclusion

Safety and security is important for everyone, as security risks in the form of accidents, crime, and natural disasters threaten the personal safety and well-being of everyone. The issue of pluralistic street policing may be the answer, since the police cannot be everywhere at the same time. Therefore, it is important that there is proper coordination, management, and control over these entities that are involved in pluralistic policing, empowered by statutory provisions. The Community Police Forums are the legislative structures responsible for supporting SAPS and making SAPS more accountable to communities. Sector policing structures and street committees have since strengthened them. The status quo of these structures and other pluralistic street policing activities and their contribution to the maintenance of law and order need to be evaluated. They should be monitored in the short, medium, and long term to see if the expectations outlined in this strategy are being achieved by police management.

Discussion Questions

1. Discuss your understanding of the concept of safety and security in society.
2. How has safety and security evolved?
3. Explain the challenges that have been faced following changes to the safety and security protocol.
4. Has law enforcement successfully maintained social order following these changes?

References

Afrika, M. W., & Hofstatter, S. (2015, November 15). When cops stoop to criminal tactics, *Sunday Times*, p. 8.

Altbeker, A. (1998). *Solving crime: The state of the SAPS detective service*. ISS Monograph No. 31. The State of the Detective Service. Pretoria: Institute for security studies.

Ayling, J., Grabosky, P., & Shearing, C. (2009). *Lengthening the arm of the law: Enhancing policing resources in the twenty-first century*. New York: Cambridge University Press.

Bernstein, P. L. (1996). *Against the Gods: The remarkable story of risk*. New York: John Wiley and Sons.

Burger, J. (2007). *Strategic perspectives on crime and policing in South Africa*. Pretoria: Van Schaik Publishers.

Burger, J., & Boshoff, H. (2008). *The states' response to crime and public security in South Africa*. Retrieved October 22, 2012, from www.afriforum.co.za/wp-content/uploads/2008/12/states-response-to-crime-etc.pdf

Canadian Centre for Occupational Health and Safety. (2005). *Emergency planning*. Retrieved from March 2020, www.ccohs.ca/oshanswers/hsprograms/planning.html

De Vries, I. D. (2008). Strategic issues in the South African police service (SAPS) in the first decade of democracy. *Acta Criminologica: Southern African Journal of Criminology*, 21(2), 125–138.

Edwards, C. (2011). *Changing policing theories for the 21st century societies* (3rd ed.). Sydney: The Federation Press.

Fay, J. J. (2006). *Contemporary security management*. Oxford: Elsevier Butterworth-Heinemann.

Govender, D. (2010). Policing a changing society in South Africa: Challenges for the police officer. *Acta Criminologica: Southern African Journal of Criminology*, 72–87. CRIMSA Special Edition No. 2.

Govender, D. (2013, June). Designing physical protection systems for the prevention of house robberies. *Servamus Police Journal*, 56–69.

Govender, D. (2016).Operational strategies for public order policing: A South African case study. *Acta Criminologica: Southern African Journal of Criminology*, *29*(2), 107–122.

Govender, D. (2019). The use of the risk management model ISO 31000 by private security companies in South Africa. *Security Journal*, *32*(3), 218–235.

Hargovan, H. (2009). Doing justice differently: Is restorative justice appropriate for domestic violence? *Acta Criminologica*, *2*, 25–41.

Hi-Tech Security Solutions. (1999). *Considerations and thought on the security of tertiary institutions*. Retrieved July 23, 2020, from www.securitysa.com/article.aspx?pklarticleid=197

Hi-Tech Security Solutions. (2010). *Technology secures campuses*. Retrieved July 21, 2020, from www.securitysa.com/news.aspx?pklnewsid=35680

Hsieh, M., & Wang, S. K. (2018). Routine activities in a virtual spree: A Taiwanese case of an ATM hacking space. *International Journal of Cyber Criminology*, *12*(1), 333–352.

Khobane, F. (2010, July 10). Zuma must reign in our cowboy police. *Sunday Times*, p. 1.

Kingshott, B. F., & Prinsloo, J. H. (2004). The universality of the "police canteen culture". *Acta Criminologica*, *16*(1), xx.

Landman, K., & Liebermann, S. (2005). Planning against crime: Preventing crime with people not barriers. *SACrime Quarterly, 11*, 21–26.

Liuksiala, A. (2012). *The use of the risk management standard ISO 31000 in Finnish organisations* (Unpublished master's thesis), Insurance Science, University of Tampere, School of Management, Tampere.

Manning, P. K. (2003). *Policing contingencies*. Chicago: University of Chicago Press.

Mc Cafferty, R. (2003). *Murder in South Africa: A comparison of the past and present* (1st ed.). Retrieved August 28, 2015, from www.frontline.org.za/Files/PDF/murder_southafrica%20(5)Pdf

Ministry of Police. (2011, August 29). *Policy and guidelines: Policing of public protests, gatherings and major events*. Retrieved from http://www.policesecretariat.gov.za/downloads/policies/policing_public_protests_2013.pdf

Minnaar, A. (2009). Community policing in a high crime transitional state: The case of South Africa since democratisation in 1994. In D. Wisler & I. D. Onwudiwe (Eds.), *Community policing international patterns and comparative perspectives* (pp. 19–53). Boca Raton: CRC.

Montesh, M., & Berning, J. (2014). Need for a youth crime prevention strategy for South Africa. In F. Lemieux, G. D. Heyesre, & D. K. Das (Eds.), *Economic development, crime and policing: Global perspectives* (pp. 224–256). International Police Executive Symposium Co-Publication. Boca Raton: CRC Press.

Naik, S., & Serumula, R. (2015, August 29). Nyaope that sends futures up in smoke. *Saturday Star,* p. 29.

Parent, C. (2018). *A 21st century approach to campus safety and security*. Retrieved December 28, 2020, from https://campuslifesecurity.com/Articles/2018/12/01/A-21st-Century-Approach-to-Campus-Safety-and-Security.aspx

Patterson, C., & Pollock, E. (2011). *Policing and criminology: Policing matters*. Devon: Learning Matters Ltd.

Pike, M. S. (1985). *The principles of policing*. Hong Kong: Macmillan.

Pruitt, W. D. (2010, June 4). The progress of democratic policing in post-apartheid South Africa, North Eastern University: *African Journal of Criminology and Justice AJCJS*, *1*, 119–137.

Rampedi, P., & Manaya, M. (2020). *Rise in police brutality linked to poor training—experts*. Retrieved December 25, 2020, from http://thesundayindependent.newspaperdirect.com/epaper/showarticle.aspx?article=65c8aed5-f686-4634-92b03c69a2c498d0&key=h0UCeppz78AZ0XWmlHNLng%3d%3d&issue=7035202002160000000001001

Schönteich, M., & Louw, A. (2001). *Crime in South Africa: A country and cities profile*. Occasional Paper No 49. Pretoria: Institute for Security Studies.

Scottish Government. (2020). *Coronavirus (COVID-19): Guidance on individual risk assessment for the workplace*. Retrieved December 28, 2020, from www.gov.scot/publications/coronavirus-covid-19-guidance-on-individual-risk-assessment-for-the-workplace/

Seldon, A. (2019). Surviving the new norm: The 2018 Camprosa conferences took a hard look at some of the most important issues tertiary institutions and the security teams will face in 2019. *Hi-Tech Security Solutions*, *25*(1), 34–41.

Sewpersad, S., & van Jaarsveld, L. (2012). Campus Security and safety: Incorporating new technology to an old paradigm of guarding. *Acta Criminologica: Southern African Journal of Criminology, Crimsa 2011 Conference Special Edition, 1*, 46–55.

Shearing, C. D., & Stenning, P. C. (1982). Snowflakes or good pinches?—Private security's contribution to modern policing. In R. Donelan (Ed.), *The maintenance of order in society* (pp. 96–105). Ottawa: Canadian Police College.

South African Catholics Bishops Conference on Recidivism. (2012). *Parliamentary Liaison office.* Retrieved August 28, 2015, from www.cplo.org.za/?wpdmdl=2&&ind=13

South African Police, Department of Police. (2015). Retrieved from G:\ARTCLES PRESENTED, PUBLISHED 2016\BACK TO BASICS NATIONAL COMMISSIONER

Stelfox, P. (2009). *Criminal investigation: An introduction to principles and practice.* Devon: Willan.

Talbot, J., & Jakeman, M. (2008). *Srmbok: Security risk management body of knowledge.* Australia: Ligare.

Van Heerden, T. J. (1982). *Introduction to police science.* Pretoria: UNISA.

Van Rooyen, H. J. N. (2008). *The practitioner's guide to forensic investigations in South Africa.* Pretoria: Henmar.

Van Zyl, G. S., Wilson, G. D. H., & Pretorius, R. (2003). Residential Burglary in South Africa: Why individual households adopt reactive strategies? *Acta Criminologica, Southern African Journal of Criminology, 16*(3), 107–123.

Vukukhanye Community Upliftment Initiatives. (2009). *Street committees.* Retrieved August 1, 2012, from www.vukukhanye.org/site/street-committees

Wallace, D., & Lauwerys, J. (2002). *Management of security services in higher education.* Retrieved December 28, 2020, from https://dera.ioe.ac.uk/11542/1/02_30.pdf

Williams, M. (2020). *SA's rotten cops among most crooked during Covid-19, finds corruption Watch report.* Retrieved December 25, 2020, from www.news24.com/news24/southafrica/news/sas-rotten-cops-among-most-crooked-during-covid-19-finds-corruption-watch-report-20200922

World Health Organization report. (2005). *WHO multi-country study on women's health and domestic violence against women, Initial results on prevalence, health outcomes and women's responses.* Retrieved November 15, 2015, from www.who.int/en/

Chapter 14

The Effects of Medical and Recreational Marijuana Policies on Hiring in US Municipal Police Departments

A Case Study of Mesa Police Department, Mesa, AZ

Diana Scharff Peterson and Carlos Avalos

> Police integrity is the normative inclination among police to resist temptations to abuse the rights and privileges of their occupation.
>
> (Klokars, Ivkovik, & Haberfeld, 2006)

> The country is facing a looming crisis in the hiring of police officers. Agencies continue to rely on hiring standards that were created decades ago, for a different philosophy of policing and a different generation of police officer candidates—even while many cities are having trouble finding enough suitable candidates to keep up with requirements and fill vacant positions.
>
> (Ronald L. Davis, Director, Office of COPS, 2017)

Introduction

In a climate where marijuana usage, whether for medical or recreational purposes, is becoming more acceptable in American society, it may be "nearly impossible to find completely drug-free job applicants. Scores of police applicants have been turned away from careers in policing due to the realities that countless people have experimented with some form of illicit drug" (Bruns, 2010, p. 1). According to Rosenbloom, Kravchuk, and Clerkin (2019), public administrators are held to higher standards than their counterparts in the private sector. This is because they serve the public. Klokars et al. (2006) contend, as do many other police scholars, that integrity is the rationale behind many no-tolerances or (low-level tolerance) drug policies for new police applicants. A key hiring criterion must focus on "identifying individually corrupt police officers-those who take illicit drugs, accept bribes, and otherwise exploit their police position for gain" (p. 7–8).

Morison (2017) further complicates the matter by stipulating that of all hiring situations and concerns, the most difficult to manage or even confront is prior drug usage among police applicants. Among these substances, the most relevant and controversial is prior marijuana usage. The differences between chronic, regular, and experimental prior usage also confuse this situation. The matter is further muddled by public attitudinal shifts pertaining to the medical and recreational use of marijuana, as in America, over 60% of states and the District of Columbia have laws that have legalized marijuana configurations, with 15 states (and DC) allowing marijuana usage on a recreational basis (Brenan, 2020; Governing Data, 2019), and 36 states allowing marijuana usage on a medical basis. The Center for Behavioral Health Statistics and Quality (2016) indicates over 22 million Americans over the age of 12 are current users of marijuana, with over 94 million experimenters reporting at least a one-time use (Foundation for a Drug-Free World International, 2021).

DOI: 10.4324/9781003047117-16

Police departments have reported difficulties finding applicants without prior drug experimentation, which has significantly reduced applicant pools (Bruns, 2010). Even with the advent of allowing limited prior marijuana usage for police applicants, the Supreme Court held in *Coats v. Dish Network* (2013) that the use of medical marijuana in a legal state in a work-related environment is a violation of federal law: "Employees who engage in an activity such as medical marijuana use that is permitted by state law but unlawful under federal law are not protected by the statute" (*Coats v. Dish Network*, 2013). This is where new policies become somewhat vague and slippery. This results from the fact that navigating federal and state marijuana laws is often challenging and confusing. However, a decade ago, there was little to no tolerance for prior illegal drug use for federal policing applicants. Municipal departments across the United States vary regarding prior drug use policies for new hires. Most departments have fairly clear language, including no marijuana use in the past one to five years (depending on locality) and, for example, no more usage than 10 to 20 (varies by locality) times in an applicant's lifetime (Bruns, 2010).

Although in 2007, the Federal Bureau of Investigation (FBI) made efforts to ease hiring protocols concerning prior drug usage, essentially, the number of times drugs were used in the past is not the critical issue. Instead, it is whether the candidate is honest about the past indiscretion on a polygraph examination (Johnson, 2007). Police departments across America (although not in huge numbers) are calling for relaxing the former standards on prior marijuana usage for new hires, as in the past it had been the predominant reason for disqualifying a candidate from employment (Bruns, 2010). The main reason lies with integrity, as mentioned in the introductory quote: "Police integrity is the normative inclination among police to resist temptations to abuse the rights and privileges of their occupations" (Klokars et al., 2006, p. 7).

Arguments for Barring Marijuana Use (Prior and Current, Off Duty for Medical Purposes)

- According to Violanti et al. (2016), "a sense of hopelessness may occur among officers given the negative aspect and perceived futility of their work and work-related stress" (p. 409). With traumatic work and stress-related occupational hazards, many police officers feel both hopeless and uncontrollably stressed.
- Rosenberg and Mazzett (2016) report, "for all the aspiring spies, diplomats, and FBI agents living in states that have liberalized marijuana laws, the federal government has a stern warning: Put down the bong, throw out the vaporizer and lose the rolling papers" (p. 1). Many police officers at municipal levels aspire to move into a federal law enforcement position. Loosening regulations for state-level hiring indeed muddles federal recruitment efforts as it is clear marijuana use is indefensible at the federal level.

Policy and Background

The Mesa Police Department in Mesa, Arizona, (as of 2017) made alterations to its drug policy hiring protocols where, formerly, candidates were held to much tighter standards than in other local/neighboring jurisdictions. Prior to 2017, marijuana use was limited to fewer than ten times, but not less than five years prior to hire (for example). Therefore, the policy being examined herein is the relaxation of the former hiring protocols on prior marijuana use for police applicants. It must be stated with care that only prior use of marijuana is specifically identified as being acceptable, under certain conditions (Mesa, AZ, 2021). No other substances, such as steroids, opium, barbiturates, or amphetamines, are included. The limitations and rules for employees are specified in the City of Mesa Personnel Manual, Resolution 2012–11 City of Mesa (2011–2012) stipulating that, additionally,

> the presence of trace amounts of alcohol, cannabis and/or over-the-counter drugs as evidenced by a drug or alcohol test, shall not be grounds for disciplinary action to the extent that job performance and/or the ability to perform safety if not lessened to any appreciable degree.
>
> (p. 20)

Disqualifiers for police applicants (Mesa Police Department):

1. Marijuana use in past three years, more than 20 times in lifetime; use more than 5 times after age 21 *without* a prescription (medical marijuana card); and/or
2. Any illicit drug uses other than marijuana (and if the marijuana was used *without* medical prescription) in the past seven years; and/or
3. Any illegal narcotics or dangerous drugs more than 5 times (*exception* marijuana); and/or
4. Use of illegal narcotics or substance (*excluding marijuana*) more than once after age 21.

What the Policy Change Addresses

This policy change addresses hiring shortages while attempting to mitigate that fact that millions of American citizens over age 12 have experimented with marijuana. In the past, marijuana use tended to be an automatic disqualifier for police hires (Bruns, 2010). Hernandez (2019) provides that currently, if a medical card was formerly obtained and if the past usage of marijuana was under the order of a prescription by a medical doctor, the rules/protocols *may* be relaxed in several states (California, Utah, Arizona, Connecticut, and Washington, for example), but this is new and controversial, and the timeframe for prior usage specified in job descriptions vastly vary.

This means that the net for new police applicants has widened—those who were once facing automatic disqualification from employment in policing positions due to prior marijuana use (even medical marijuana use) are no longer absolutely denied the right to be hired. However, there are limitations. It is a very slippery slope and a very fine line, with the purpose of opening job opportunities for those once denied due to teenage decisions that were formerly impactful on future occupational choices and directions.

Impetus for Introduction of the Policy Change

The main impetus for the change was the sheer number of Americans over the age of 12 who have experimented with marijuana. Furthermore, there is a growing public sentiment surrounding the belief that Americans should not be prevented from trying to find/hold a job due former marijuana experimentation or medical use (Geiger & Gramlich, 2019). This includes being a police officer. As Bruns (2010) illustrated,

> [S]cores of applicants are turned away from careers in policing due to the realities that countless people have experimented with some form of illicit drug. Although most police departments would not consider hiring an applicant with prior experimental drug use it is challenging to recruit police candidates who have never experimented with illegal substances.
>
> (p. 1)

The landscape is rapidly changing, however, with 36 states in America currently legalizing marijuana for medical use and four more (Kansas, Kentucky, South Carolina, and Alabama) potentially doing so in 2021 (Smith, 2021). According to Jaeger (2020), "Every single marijuana provision placed on state ballots passed in 2020" (p. 1). Fifteen states have passed recreational provisions, indicating that marijuana is completely legalized (Williams, 2020). It may one day be impossible to find applicants who have not experimented with marijuana. Therefore, unless policy changes evolve to reflect societal changes, there will continue be a rapidly shrinking pool of applicants for policing positions. This pertains to limited and experimental use, however, not chronic, heavy, or regular use. What is being explored in this analysis is those who have experimented with marijuana more times than allowed for in job descriptions. This argument does not apply to regular or chronic users.

Previous Steps Taken to Address Issue

This issue has been discussed in the media for many years, dating back to the late 1990s.

Little action was taken until the federal government's decision in 2007 to lighten former drug use standards due to shrinking applicant pools. The Mesa PD has been quite progressive in its hiring change initiatives. Although scholars are reluctant to review this "hot" topic, many media outlets are giving this issue coverage. Prior marijuana use must be distinguished from medical marijuana use, other forms of illicit drug and marijuana use, and whether medical or non-medical use occurs on or off duty. It would appear the courts are not protecting medical marijuana users at work. Yet prior use is not as great an issue for entering law enforcement as it once was. More important, after previously addressing the federal government's stance on prior marijuana use and hiring, protocols continue to vary by greatly city, county, and state. It is a very gray area and will likely remain enigmatic for some time.

Important Actors

The specific stakeholders and actors involved in the debate around both the policy and its adoption include any citizen interested in pursuing a law enforcement position in the future. Other actors include citizens currently holding a law enforcement position; the public at large, as they are the beneficiaries of police services; and those who are in key positions of power, making decision about public safety—essential policies to protect the public and being accountable to the public concerning policy decisions. Motivations for the actors (the future recruits) include the newfound availability of positions once closed to them and a belief that citizen participation is important in light of the government's acknowledging that people make mistakes and may later be allowed to apply for law enforcement positions. This is important because it brings a human element to the hiring process. It shows that the employers doing the hiring realize that marijuana use is in no way a direct indicator of a person becoming a bad police officer. The belief in a more responsive and forgiving government would also be apparent, as well as one that is more trusting of its citizens.

Additional resources may need to be allocated for education regarding marijuana misuse and abuse due the increased legalization and its impact on the work environment. As the courts have demonstrated, it not recommended that officers consume marijuana after the hiring process. However, the City of Mesa Resolution 2012–11 did address this issue, making trace amounts insufficient grounds for disciplinary actions. Not all jurisdictions agree. This is a very debatable issue, which needs further and careful exploration.

Applying Approaches to the Field of Public Administration to the Relaxing of Drug Hiring Protocols

As Rosenbloom et al. (2019) reveal, there are three unique and fundamental lenses through which to examine the field of public administration, no one of which is superior to another. These include the managerial approach (both traditional and new public management, or NPM), the political approach, and the legal approach. Before analyzing the fit of each approach to the drug policy changes in the Mesa Police Department, it is essential to discuss the predominant focus of public administration, which Rosenbloom et al. (2019) clearly identifies as the public. In this sense, the public can be future employers or employees or those whom the police may protect, interact with, or coexist with in the present or future. When the public is the focus, this furthers the trust of the public in the police, demonstrating that the public is truly the focal point of public safety. Now potentially more than ever, the respect both of and for the police is at a heightened need in America and beyond its borders. Typically, the "old-guard" or former way of thinking is still prevalent. This is often labeled an "archaic" way of thinking and is at direct odds with the new way of thinking, which purports that prior experimental marijuana usage should not disqualify an officer from employment. This is also the sentiment of many Americans, for whom it soon could be easier to use medical or recreation marijuana than for a woman in a Southern state to obtain an abortion, even in the event of rape or incest.

All three approaches can be applied to the policy change in some fashion. Following a discussion of each variant of approaches, future needed policy actions for police officer hiring are explored.

The Traditional Managerial Approach: Implications for Drug Policy Changes for New Hires in Municipal Police Departments

This approach emphasizes three predominant characteristics that should be maximized: effectiveness, economy, and efficiency (Rosenbloom et al., 2019). Before policy changes were effected, clients (or potential police officer candidates) were thought of as numbers or cases. When one is reduced to a number, empathy and care about that individual is reduced. An atmosphere of depersonalization or impersonality would promote drug policy standards that would not allow for human error or experimentation. For example, as mentioned previously, the Federal Bureau of Investigation relaxed prior drug use standards for applicants for two main reasons: it was difficult to find applicants who had not experimented with illegal substances at some point in their lives, and a rigid requirement of no tolerance did not allow for past indiscretions or mistakes people made in their youth. It was no longer economical to adopt a no-tolerance policy as hiring pools dwindled, and more resources had to be spent on recruiting and hiring. This raises the question: Does experimenting with medical marijuana make one less effective later in life regarding decision-making and efficiency than a person who did not experiment?

Other methods that may be applied to the policy change are cognitive or scientific approaches (Rosenbloom et al., 2019). In this manner, scientific studies could be conducted on officers who have previously utilized medical marijuana, controlling for all other factors on police behavior, such as citizen complaints, arrest rates, and even job satisfaction and performance evaluation. This approach enhances accountability to citizens, both by safeguarding their rights to be protected by the police (who are drug-free but have experimented with drugs) and by allowing them a chance to apply for positions after using marijuana, which had formerly banned them from employment. Relaxing former substance use protocols is a more efficient and less stringent practice in general as it pertains to evolving with societal attitudes, beliefs, and behaviors regarding former experimentation, rather than to prior regular (chronic) or heavy usage.

The NPM Variant of the Managerial Approach: Implications for Drug Policy Changes for New Hires in Municipal Police Departments

The NPM variant may be applicable to this policy change if police applicants (or future police applicants) could be viewed as customers, rather than numbers or cases, as well as anyone who meets the police. The emphasis remains on effectiveness, efficiency, and cost reduction and may be applied, as previously mentioned, similarly to the traditional managerial approach. Outputs can be analogized to increased job applicant pools as the net is widened by allowing those who have experimented with medical marijuana to apply for a policing role.

This philosophy is that the government should steer, not row. (Rosenbloom et al., 2019) further indicates that the government should be responsive to citizen needs and opinions, including those regarding drug policies and former drug use. Other characteristics of the NPM variant that could be applied to the utility of the drug policy changes in Mesa include employee empowerment and flexibility, meaning that employees may feel more empowered to work for the City of Mesa due to its responsiveness to the public needs and desires. Flexibility is demonstrated in that policies were changed, while other departments remain in the infancy stage of adopting similar policies or are at a standstill.

The Political Approach: Implications for Changes for New Hires in Municipal Police Departments

Rosenbloom et al. (2019) emphasize that the political approach focuses on policy-making. This approach is the most useful in adopting and applying this new policy, as one of the strong arguments embedded in this approach concerns public representation and represents both responsive and accountable government. While a recent Gallup Poll suggests that nearly 70% of the American population are in favor of legalizing marijuana on a medical basis (Brenan, 2020), a responsive government would allow for prior usage by its own (police officers), but within certain parameters. Holding limits on prior drug use, such as only allowing a certain number of usages under the direction of a physician, makes the government more accountable to the people and forgiving. As mentioned previously, the fact the additional states are legalizing medical marijuana demonstrates that the public has a proper means of participating in public administrative activities.

The representative value of the political approach further signals that the public supports the increasing number of individuals in the populations who hold medical marijuana cards. However, it again must be noted, this discussion only pertains to hiring and not to marijuana usage after employment. Where the managerial approach is more scientific in nature, the political approach focuses on building consensus and coalitions (or political support) to determine the proper course of action (Rosenbloom et al., 2019). Consensus across the United States clearly demonstrates an approval of medical marijuana. A responsive government should listen. A responsive Mesa Police Department has acted and made policy changes in its hiring protocols. Many departments across the country have not acted as representatively. Lastly, Rosenbloom et al. (2019) emphasizes that a predominant goal of the political approach is to have a government that represent diversity in its citizenry. This also entails diversity of opinion about medical and recreational marijuana.

Furthermore, the political approach is predominantly concerned with representation and responsiveness, looking for broad coalitions to determine what is correct, relying on scientific evidence to establish facts. Public opinion, interest groups, and the media have a significant impact on consensus development. As mentioned previously, scholars could play a crucial role in furthering the consensus on acceptable marijuana usage for police officers or the public in general. However, they need to have the courage to do this by paying attention to statistics through public sentiment.

The Legal Approach: Implications for Drug Policy Changes for New Hires in Municipal Police Departments

The legal approach in a broad sense views the public administrator as the agency that both applies and enforces the law (Rosenbloom et al., 2019). This approach focuses more on the citizens who are impacted by the policy, ensuring that police do not violate citizen rights (constitutional or statutory). The public is further protected against the arbitrary and capricious actions of the government and police. If police officers were hired with any types of former drug usage or without drug provisions, the government would indeed be viewed as a highly unaccountable organization in which citizens' due process rights could be ignored. As mentioned previously, drug protocols are in place for police officer recruits, with the principles of integrity at the heart of the ethos of policing. If former drug dealers could be police officers, integrity would vanish, as would accountability. Rosenbloom et al. (2019) further identify police as street-level administrators, or those who come into the contact with the public on a regular basis. The police are liable for their actions, as the court records are demonstrating across America. In this regard, prior drug usage becomes an issue if liability concerns persist. As the legal approach adheres to treating individuals as unique, it would be rational that drug policy changes would apply to police applicants. Uniqueness indicates humanness and equity. As mentioned previously, this issue becomes legally problematic once the medical marijuana user entertains using the substance in his or her work environment. The courts have addressed this, and it is an issue that is likely to persist as more states legalize marijuana.

Suggestions From the Literature: What Is Needed for Policy Action Plans (Regardless of Approach)

1. If a hiring requirement is a barrier, the validity of that requirement should be examined to ensure that it is a strong predictor of future job performance and that there are no alternative tools that are equally valid but show less adverse impact. If the problem is identified at the recruitment stage, the agency can experiment with changes in the type and/or targeting of recruiting (Matthies, Kellar, & Lim, 2012, p. 6).
2. Police leaders are not solely responsible for fighting crime and providing a service to the community, but the scrutiny of its own organizational performance in times of heightened accountability is paramount for transparency and trust. Therefore, police leaders must be committed to inquiring all tenets of their organizations, guaranteeing "the answers provided are objective and supported by facts. Are we effective? Are we accountable? Are the results that we are seeking what the community expects? Are we doing the right things?" (Brann, 2012, p. 41).
3. Effective police administrators must "understand and examine the challenge of screening out "candidates whose performance would be impacted by past drug use, without pushing out otherwise strong candidates who may have used marijuana recreationally in the past but whose performance would not be affected" (Morison, 2017, p. 14).
4. "Disqualifying applicants for past marijuana use is fundamentally inconsistent with where we are as a society" (Rector, 2016, p. 1).

5. According to Magers (2013), "police organizations must hire people of character. Flawed hiring practices make having an ethical organizational environment difficult. There can be little expectation that police recruits of questionable character will improve when they become police officers, when working independently, with considerable discretion and power, and when tempted by the many influences that provide opportunity for misconduct" (p. 124).

Concluding Remarks

Regardless of the approach utilized, all three approaches are beneficial to understanding the policy change of 2017 at the Mesa Police Department as it relates to the drug policy for new hires. Overall, this decision reflects a broader societal attitude. This issue has not been readily addressed by the scientific community as very few studies have been conducted on this issue. One must question why this topic is not being addressed by the scholarly community. Is it because it could harm the academic field and reputation? Scholars have the potential to help this topic to not stay enigmatic. They also need to respond to larger polarizing issue that are at the forefront of one of the biggest public policy debates in American history, the federal legalization of marijuana. When news outlets report on this topic and scholars do not, this is a problem. With the array of information that is at the fingertips of scholars, one could reasonably assume that if they got involved in this debate, they would help police officers, the public, and public officials with scientific and reliable answers to questions that plague the marijuana issue surrounding police recruitment.

Modern research highlighting the effects of marijuana adds credence to the idea that such past light usage, as opposed to regular or even chronic use, does not decrease current mental functions (Gabrys & Porath, 2019). When referring to regular use over long time periods, there is a difference in associations in levels of cognitive functioning. "Regular cannabis use is associated with mild cognitive difficulties, which are typically not apparent following about one month of abstinence" (Gabrys & Porath, 2019, p. 1). Shen (2020) adds strong, compelling scientific evidence that provides insight into many prior inconclusive findings in the research:

> Different methods are likely at the root of some of the mixed results. Studies often sample different age groups, or people with varying levels of drug use, and them examine them for different durations, ranging from weeks to decades.
>
> (p. 10)

Former Baltimore Police Commissioner Kevin Davis held that police departments are "disqualifying otherwise perfectly qualified applicants based on a hiring standard that is inconsistent with where we are as a profession and a society" (Calvert, 2017). It is a hot topic that will remain for years to come and will continue as more states legalize marijuana.

The Arizona Peace Officers Standards and Training Board (AZPOST) recently modernized state hiring policy regarding regulations on police applicants' prior marijuana usage. The new policy will go into effect on April 1, 2021 (Kingston, 2020). The new rules will be applicable to all local departments across the state of Arizona; however, the standards can be altered the at discretion of city leaders.

> Applicant cannot have used cannabis in the two years prior to applying; applicant's amount of cannabis use is irrelevant, and applicants' cannabis use after the age of 21 is irrelevant.
>
> (Kingston, 2020, p. 2)

Continued research is needed on the legalities of the use of medical marijuana's effects upon employment. It is apparent that this is only the beginning of a new era, and the real issue under consideration is not upon former rigorous or daily usage of marijuana, but for those who have experimented with it in the past but used beyond the limits of current hiring protocols over their lifetime. The balance should be further reviewed as public sentiment toward marijuana use evolves with its changing legality both recreationally and medically across North America.

Discussion Questions

1. Should a police officer's potential to succeed be based on past actions during his/her early years, which might not accurately be indicative of future potential to succeed? Why or why not? Discuss the advantages and disadvantages of allowing for prior minimal marijuana use among police applicants and expand arguments into other types of behaviors that could be viewed as acceptable or unacceptable past behaviors.
2. Should the issue of updating policy manuals and hiring requirements on former drug use be examined through the lens of prior officer behavior or as a new line of thinking toward progressing as a society toward public sentiments regarding the evolving acceptance and legalization of marijuana?
3. Discuss rationales as to why scientific literature has been sparce on the topic of changing substance use policies for police officers. How might recent political and societal uprisings in the United States have made this a greater issue?
4. If marijuana legislation passes on a federal level in the United States, how should police agencies and administrators manage further evolutions of policy for new hires as well as marijuana use by existing officers while off duty?
5. If prior marijuana usage has significantly diminished police officer applicant pools, the recruitment process will either stay the same or continue to dwindle. With more Americans both in favor of the use of marijuana and in support of legislation to further legalize it, how can police administrators think outside the box to address this issue?

References

Brann, J. (2012). Asking the tough questions. In D. McCullogh & D. Spence, D. (Eds.), *American policing in 2022: Essays on the future of a profession*. Washington, DC: US Department of Justice, Office of Community Oriented Policing Services.

Brenan, M. (2020). Support for legal marijuana inches up to new high of 68%. *Gallup*. Retrieved from https://news.gallup.com/poll/323582/support-legal-marijuana-inches-new-high.aspx

Bruns, D. (2010). Exploring change in drug policy standards among local law enforcement agencies. *Western Journal of Criminal Justice*, 2. Retrieved from https://docsbay.net/exploring-change-in-drug-policy-standards-among-local-law-enforcement-agencies

Calvert, S. (2017). How much marijuana is too much for a police recruit? *The Wall Street Journal*. Retrieved from www.wsj.com/articles/how-much-marijuana-is-too-much-for-a-police-recruit-1493118001

Center for Behavioral Health Statistics and Quality. (2016). Key substance use and mental health indicators in the United States: Results from the 2015 national survey on drug use and health (HHS Publication No. SMA 16–4984, NSDUH Series H-51). Retrieved from www.samhsa.gov/data/

City of Mesa. (2011–2012). *City of Mesa personnel manual: Resolution 2012–11*. Retrieved from http://mrsc.org/getmedia/4d6db12c-7ebe-406d-a5cb-b163fd54b8e3/M47PersPol.pdf.aspx

Coats *v. Dish Network*, LLC, 303 P. 3d 147—Colorado Court of Appeals, Div. A 2013.

Foundation for a Drug-Free World. (2021). *The truth about marijuana: International statistics*. Retrieved from https://www.drugfreeworld.org/drugfacts/marijuana/international-statistics.html

Gabrys, R., & Porath, A. (2019). *Clearing the smoke on cannabis: Regular use and cognitive functioning*. Retrieved from www.ccsa.ca/sites/default/files/2019-04/CCSACannabis-Use-Cognitive-Effects-Report-2019-en.pdf

Geiger, W., & Gramlich, J. (2019). Six facts about marijuana. *Pew Research Center*. Retrieved from www.pewresearch.org/fact-tank/2019/11/22/facts-about-marijuana/

Governing Data. (2019). *State marijuana laws—US map: Governing the states and localities*. Retrieved from www.governing.com/archive/state-marijuana-laws-map-medical-recreational.html

Hernandez, F. (2019). Can police officers use medical marijuana? *Leafbuyer*. Retrieved from www.leafbuyer.com/blog/cops-medical-marijuana/

Jaeger, K. (2020). Every single marijuana and drug policy ballot measure passing on election day bolsters Federal reform push. *Marijuana Moment*. Retrieved from marijuanamoment.net/every-single-marijuana-and-drug-policy-ballot-measure-passing on-election-day-bolsters-federal-reform-push/

Johnson, K. (2007). FBI drug policy eased for hiring: Changed amid push to add agents. *USA Today*. Retrieved from www.lexisnexis.com/hottopics/lnacademic

Kingston, D. (2020). Prior marijuana use rules relaxed for Arizona police. *Arizona Cannabis News*. Retrieved from https://azmarijuana.com/arizona-medical-marijuana-news/prior-marijuana-use-rules-relaxed-for-arizona-police-applicants/

Klokars, C., Ivkovik, S., & Haberfeld, M. (2006). *Enhancing police integrity*. The Netherlands: Springer Publications.

Magers, J. (2013). From followers to leaders: Principled decision making in policing. In C. D'Argenio, D. Owens, & J. Chin (Eds.), *Contemporary issues in criminal justice: Research based introduction* (pp. 111–128). Flushing, NY: Looseleaf Law Publications, Inc.

Matthies, C. F., Keller, K. M., & Lim, N. (2012). *Identifying barriers to diversity in law enforcement agencies*. Santa Monica, CA: Rand Corporation. Retrieved from www.rand.org/pubs/occasional_papers/OP370.html.

Mesa, A. Z. (2021). *City of Mesa invites applications for the position of police officer-recruit*. Retrieved from www.mesaaz.gov/Home/ShowDocument?id=3548

Morison, K. (2017). *Hiring for the 21st century law enforcement officer: Challenges, opportunities, and strategies for success*. Washington, DC: Office of Community Oriented Policing Services. Retrieved from https://ric-zai-inc.com/Publications/cops-w0831-pub.pdf

Rector, K. (2016). Davis wants to relax restrictions on past marijuana use for police recruits in Maryland. *The Baltimore Sun*. Retrieved from www.baltimoresun.com/ . . . /bs-md-ci-police-marijuana-standard-20160721-story.html

Rosenberg, M., & Mazzett, M. (2016). State marijuana laws complicate federal job recruitment. *The New York Times*. Retrieved from www.nytimes.com/2015/06/30/us/state-marijuana-laws-complicate-federal-job-recruitment.html

Rosenbloom, D., Kravchuk, R., & Clerkin, R. (2019). *Public administration: Understanding management, politics and law in the public sector*, 8e. New York, NY: McGraw Hill Publications.

Shen, H. (2020). Cannabis and the adolescent brain. *Proceedings of the National Academy of Sciences, 111*(7), 7–11. doi:10.1073/pnas.1920325116. Retrieved from www.pnas.org/content/117/1/7

Smith, J. (2021). States that could legalize medical marijuana in 2021. *Marijuana Business Daily*. Retrieved from https://mjbizdaily.com/these-four-states-could-legalize-medical-marijuana-through-legislation-in-2021/

Violanti, J. M., Andrew, M. E., Mnatsakanova, A., Hartley, T. A., Fekedulegn, D., & Burchfiel, C. M. (2016). Correlates of hopelessness in the high suicide risk police occupation. *Police Practice and Research, 17*(5), 408–419.

Williams, S. (2020). A state-by-state look at where marijuana is legal. *The Motley Fool*. Retrieved from www.fool.com/investing/2020/11/07/a-state-by-state-look-at-where-marijuana-is-legal/

Part III

Crime Control

Chapter 15

Policing Cybercrime

Is There a Role for the Private Sector?

Rick Sarre

Introduction

Societies today are now well entrenched in the digital edge. Global technological innovations are ubiquitous; they are used everywhere and at any time. The nature and quality of data are changing too. The amount of digital information stored and available to us expands exponentially, and the consequences for each one of us are significant.

> [Collections of data are] no longer mainly stocks of digital information—databases of names and other well-defined personal data, such as age, sex and income. The new economy is more about analysing rapid real-time flows of unstructured data: the streams of photos and videos generated by users of social networks, the reams of information produced by commuters on their way to work, the flood of data from hundreds of sensors in a jet engine. . . . The world will bristle with connected sensors so that people will leave a digital trail wherever they go.
>
> (Economist, 2017, p. 24)

The digital world and the data it produces expand exponentially year by year (Kirkpatrick, 2018). In 2016, Amazon, Alphabet (Google), and Microsoft together spent nearly US$32 billion in capital expenditure and capital leases, up 22% from the previous year. According to IDC, a market research firm, the digital universe (the data created and copied each year) will reach 180 zettabytes (180 followed by 21 zeros) in 2025 (Economist, 2017).

However, there is a significant downside of this revolution: the willingness and aptitude of those who share our cyberspace to engage in criminality (Sarre, Brooks, Smith, & Draper, 2014). Cybercrime is now a serious worldwide problem (Broadhurst & Chang, 2013). Recent estimates suggest the total cost of cybercrime in Australia alone to be well above $AU1 billion per year (Australian Crime Commission, 2015). It costs the global economy countless billions of dollars annually. How best can this new crime landscape be monitored and policed? What role can and should the private sector adopt? Before we deal with these questions, it is important to examine more closely the nature of the phenomenon.

What Is Cybercrime?

There is no precise and clear definition of cybercrime. It has been referred to as "computer crime," "computer-related crime," "high-tech crime," "technology-enabled crime," "e-crime," and "cyberspace crime" (Chang, 2012). Grabosky (2007) helpfully classified three general forms, including crimes in which the computer is used as the instrument of crime, crimes in which the computer is incidental to the offense, and crimes in which the computer is the target of crime. McGuire and Dowling (2013) developed a similar idea, classifying cybercrime into

DOI: 10.4324/9781003047117-18

"cyber-enabled" crime and "cyber-dependent" crime. Cyber-enabled crimes are traditional crimes facilitated by the use of computers. Cyber-dependent crimes are those crimes that would not exist without the technology. Another useful classification is the one devised by Gordon and Ford (2006), who divided activities into Type I and Type II offenses. Type I cybercrimes are crimes that are more technical in nature (for example, hacking). Type II cybercrime is crime that relies on human contact rather than technology (for example, illegal online gambling).

Regardless of how cybercrime is classified, there is little doubt that its range is broad—it includes fraudulent financial transactions, identity theft, romance scams, theft of electronic information for commercial gain, drug trafficking, money laundering, aberrant voyeuristic activities, image-based sexual abuse, harassment, stalking, and other threatening behaviors (Sarre, Lau, & Chang, 2018). While these sorts of activities have always been classified as criminal, they are now so much easier to pursue with a computer and a modem, and from anywhere in the world.

Cybercrime includes terrorist recruitment and terrorist financing. It includes implementing malware attacks designed to disrupt a business by destroying its database. It includes the activities of the "hacktivist," someone who protests against an organization's actions or policies by orchestrating a denial of service (Sarre et al., 2018). Today's criminals can commit cybercrime without the need for high-level technical skills. In fact, the internet itself can assist with "do-it-yourself" malware kits, for example, available in online forums.

The borderless nature of the internet means that potential victims of cybercrime can be targeted from thousands of miles away, making law enforcement not only challenging but, in some instances, impossible (Sarre, 2008).

The most recent threat report by the Australian Cyber Security Centre, for example, notes that "malicious cyber activity against Australia's national and economic interests is increasing in frequency, scale, sophistication and severity" (Australian Cyber Security Centre, 2017, p. 16). Cybercrime is thus an escalating problem for national and international police and security agencies.

The Role of Police

The police role in tackling cybercrime is an important yet difficult one. There are a number of factors that militate against effective prevention in this domain.

The first is the difficulty associated with jurisdictional boundaries. It is exceedingly problematic for police in one nation to assume control over an investigation in another nation, especially if the other nation denies that the crime emanated from within their country. It is clear that no other field of criminality finds international borders more permeable than they are in cyber criminality (Holt, 2018, p. 141).

The second is the lack of expertise of law enforcement when pitted against some of the best information-technology minds in the (ill-gotten gains) business (Holt, 2018, p. 144). Moreover, just when the police-resourced teams catch up capacity-wise, the cybercrime operatives shift into opaque and lawless territory again.

The third factor is the rising cost in dollar terms. Resourcing high-tech crime abatement is an expensive task, especially when there are other, more highly visible calls upon the law enforcement budget (Holt, 2018). Politicians do, it must be said, continue to pay lip service to make appropriate funding available.

> To help combat terrorism at home and deter Australians from committing terrorist acts abroad, we need to ensure our security agencies are resourced properly and have the powers to respond to evolving threats and technological change.
>
> (Former Australian Prime Minister Tony Abbott, cited in Grattan, 2015)

However, there is no guarantee that the funding will ever be adequate to meet the growing demand for prophylactic measures, especially given the highly versatile and transitory nature of cyber criminality.

When one considers these factors, it should come as no surprise that, in a time of fiscal restraint, there is a general reluctance of governments to do all the heavy lifting. Other resourcing is needed, and the demand is being met enthusiastically by a resource that is very amenable to the task at hand: the private sector.

Embracing the Private Sector in the Cybercrime Prevention Task

A great deal of the responsibility of policing the world of cybercrime has been shifted to the private sector, not only in terms of the discrete roles it can play in industry regulation, but also in challenging the sector to keep vigilant in order not to fall prey to the hustlers of cyberspace (Sarre & Prenzler, 2021). Former Australian Prime Minister Malcolm Turnbull offered the following by way of explanation:

> If we are to fully realise the social, economic and strategic benefits of being online, we must ensure the internet continues to be governed by those who use it—not dominated by governments. Equally, however, we cannot allow cyberspace to become a lawless domain. The private sector and government sector both have vital roles to play.
>
> (Australian Government, 2016, p. 2)

There are two particular fields of endeavor in which public and private cooperation has a vital role to play in meeting the task of preventing or forestalling cybercrime: the fields of metadata retention (in telecommunications) and digital imaging (CCTV).

Metadata Retention in Telecommunications

A key way in which governments have sought to target cybercrime is by the accessing of digital data through what is referred to as "metadata retention," which relies heavily on the cooperation of the private telecommunications sector (Australian Parliament, 2017), which is well assisted by taxpayer dollars (Sarre, 2017a). In order to frustrate and block those who would orchestrate organized crime, or who would perpetrate violence in the name of some particular ideology, governments now have the capacity to keep track of metadata by enlisting the compliance of private sector telecommunications companies (Kowalick, Connery, & Sarre, 2018).

Branch (2014) defines *metadata* as data that puts other data into context. It is an electronic "building block" that can be used in investigations into any form of cybercrime, such as terrorism, organized crime, and crimes that are carried out online (such as a person viewing or dealing with child sexual exploitation materials). Metadata records can now be accessed by national, state, and local government departments under recent Australian legislation (Sarre, 2017a).

Metadata does not contain content. It is simply information about the telephone numbers or message links involved in the communication, the location of the caller and receiver, the date and time of the calls, and the length of the conversation. It includes data pertaining to short message service (SMS) text messages sent and received. Uniform resource locators (URLs) and World Wide Web (www) browsing histories are said to be specifically excluded from the Australian metadata retention law, although the internet protocol (IP) addresses of users' devices are accessible (Fernandes & Sivaraman, 2015). What this means is that the locations of the devices that are sending messages can be tracked. Getting a warrant to access telecommunications (conversation) data is much more difficult than accessing metadata: hence, the great interest shown by law enforcement agencies in the gathering and analyzing of the latter. In 2015, new laws came into force in Australia requiring telecommunications service providers to retain and store their metadata so that it remains available for analysis by anti-terrorism strategists and organized crime fighters (Gal, 2017). The new laws were not universally welcomed, however.

> Access to private communications records is already out of control in Australia, with telecommunications regulator the ACMA [the Australian Communications and Media Authority] reporting 580,000 warrantless demands in the last financial year. . . . But in the few years I've been working up close to government, I've learned one important lesson: Governments cannot be trusted. This government, the one before it, the one that will come after it.
>
> (Ludlam, 2015)

The vehicle for the change in Australian policy was the Telecommunications (Interception and Access) Amendment (Data Retention) Act 2015. This Act came into effect in October 2015. Under the Act, all telecommunications providers were given 18 months (until April 13, 2017) to put in place a capacity to retain their customers' metadata for two years, making it available to government agencies (principally police agencies) without complaint and upon request. Until this legislation was in place, metadata was kept for various periods by communications providers on an ad hoc basis, simply for the purpose of billing their customers and made available on an ad hoc basis to law enforcement agencies if they made demands. The new legislation regularized this process, circumventing any objection by the public that, contractually, their metadata was private between them and their telecommunications provider (Sarre, 2018).

The jury is still "out" on whether this legislation has had the effect its designers intended (Sarre, 2017b).

CCTV

Visual imaging has played an important role in reducing criminal offending generally and has linked the public and private sectors associated with it inextricably. The most pervasive of electronic surveillance is the digital camera, linked to a closed-circuit television (CCTV) system. These cameras are now widespread throughout the world. CCTV can accommodate overt and covert cameras, traffic flow cameras, speed infringement cameras, and red light intersection cameras. Casinos, department stores, convenience and fuel shops, streets and car parks, reserves and nature parks, railway and bus stations, universities, and sports arenas are all likely candidates for CCTV surveillance. These cameras can be and have been deployed by national, regional, and local governments in "public" areas and by the private sector on and around private property. The vast majority are operated and monitored by private security personnel to whom such responsibilities have been outsourced by contractual arrangements.

The main application of CCTV is the monitoring and reviewing of recorded scenes, principally as a crime prevention tool. In retail shops and market precincts, CCTV has become seemingly indispensable, with widespread business support for its potential value as a means of crime reduction (Prenzler & Sarre, 2012). Another innovation is the ability of cameras, loaded with "search" software, to allow police, building owners, sportsground managers, and retail proprietors (to name a few) to watch and count people moving past a certain point. Such systems can track children or people wearing certain distinctive clothing, which is very help-ful in search-and-rescue situations and in following up matters pertaining to the commission of a crime. Having accurate time and date stamps on digital video can contribute significantly to supporting a police investigation.

In the not-too-distant past, the market for CCTV was limited by the size of the investment required to install and use the technology. The high cost of cameras, housings, switching and control equipment, video recorders, and the physical infrastructure and cabling required to support the operation of the CCTV system was frequently too great for a user to jus-tify choosing CCTV above other available security options. Over the last decade, however, advances in camera technology and "drone" capability have been phenomenal (Sarre, 2015). There is now a massive capacity to store and process data in even the simplest of CCTV models. This growth has occurred in parallel with a greatly improved and converging com-munications infrastructure and significant reductions in the costs of the technology. CCTV systems no longer need to be purchased from specialty security contractors. Sophisticated systems can now be purchased from retail outlets such as hardware stores, and the prices are rapidly becoming more affordable (Sarre et al., 2014).

There has been some academic interest in the potential for abuse of CCTV, principally by virtue of the public intrusiveness exercised by those who operate and monitor the cam-eras (Prenzler & Sarre, 2017) and the potential misuse of the images collected and stored by CCTV hardware. In days gone by, this was not a problem; access to recorded video was rela-tively easy to control due to the inherent technical limitations found in CCTV systems and the fact that very few people knew how to install and monitor them. However, these technical limitations no longer apply. YouTube, Vimeo, Instagram, Twitter, Facebook, and other social media platforms now provide mechanisms for the almost immediate worldwide distribution of recorded video and images. These advances bring with them opportunities to use images and video in innovative ways to manage and respond effectively to crises and crime risks, but they also raise privacy concerns. An Australian casino in 2011, for example, was exposed as an employer that allowed its security staff to collect and copy CCTV footage of patrons and other staff for their own prurient interests and in clear defiance of privacy courtesies (if not rights) and company policy (Sarre, 2014).

Private Corporate Activity as a Tool of Cybercrime Crime Prevention

So the foundations have been laid for a strong level of cooperation between governments and private telecommunication companies. This trend continues to go hand in hand with private sector policing and security cooperation, which has operated under the aegis of government agencies for years and across most nations of the world (Prenzler & Sarre, 2012). In current trends, the public/private nexus in telecommunications and CCTV is set to continue well into the future (Prenzler & Sarre, 2017). It can be safely assumed that modern Western socie-ties currently trust both sides of the police and security equation (public and private) to meet their expectations. In the fight against cybercrime, should we have any fears?

Yes, there is good reason for apprehension. Concerns about dubious ethical practices and the regularity of instances of "overreach" by private companies were heightened by the March 2018 revelations that the information company Cambridge Analytica had manipulated and exploited the data of more than 80 million Facebook profiles. This was done, apparently, to facilitate the targeting of American voters with strategic electronic interruptions ahead of the 2016 United States election. Just 46 days later, Cambridge Analytica announced it would close its doors. So, too, did its parent company, SCL Elections.

Facebook admitted that it was (unwillingly and unwittingly) complicit in this privacy breach.

> It might seem inherently incompatible with democracy for that knowledge to be vested in a private body. Yet the retention of such data is the essence of Facebook's ability to make money and run a viable business. . . . Maybe the internet should be rewired from the grassroots, rather than be led by digital oligarchs' business needs.
>
> (Joseph, 2018)

Mark Zuckerberg, Facebook CEO, later admitted to the United States Congress that Facebook routinely gathers data on non-members, and the only way for a person to remove or correct that data is to join Facebook (Manokha, 2018). According to Manokha, there is a new era of "surveillance capitalism" brewing.

> The outcry against Cambridge Analytica has not attempted to sanction, nor even to question, the existence of digital platforms and other actors which depend on the ever more extensive acquisition and monetisation of personal data. If anything, the Cambridge Analytica story has unintentionally contributed to the further normalisation of surveillance and the lack of privacy that comes with being an internet user nowadays. Even the web pages of the sites that broke the story (*The Observer* and *New York Times*) allow dozens of third-party sites to obtain data from the browser of the user accessing the articles. It was 75 and 61 sites, respectively, last time I checked.
>
> (Manokha, 2018)

The case of Cambridge Analytica provides a sobering reminder of why the relationship between government policing agencies and the private sector needs to be kept under constant scrutiny (Holt, 2018, p. 153). We have struggled to determine how best any society finds an acceptable balance between the rights of its citizens to enjoy freedom from the prying eyes of government and the legitimate interests that the state might have in monitoring them. In July 2015, then–Australian Communications Minister (and later Prime Minister) Malcolm Turnbull expressed the challenge in this way.

> [W]e need to recognise that getting the balance right is not easy (not least because the balance may shift over time) and we are more likely to do so if there is a thoughtful and well informed public debate—weighing up the reality of the national security threat, the effectiveness of particular proposed measures and then asking whether those measures do infringe on our traditional freedoms and if so whether the infringement is justifiable.
>
> (Turnbull, 2015)

But now there is an added complication. When those prying eyes are not subjected to the scrutiny of parliamentary inquiries and governmental oversight, but are found in "outsourced" private corporations, how is that balance to be determined and maintained, consistent with democratic principles? It is to that question that we now turn.

Getting the Balance Right

An appropriate equilibrium must be struck between forestalling crime and terrorism using all available electronic means (public and private) and not unduly curtailing the legitimate rights to privacy that citizens in modern democracies currently expect to enjoy. What controls should society employ over the private sector to monitor its engagement in cyber surveillance? What degree of intrusion is acceptable? There are no easy answers, especially given that modern society appears uncertain about what levels of privacy its citizens wish to demand and the extent to which its citizens trust private operators to manage their data.

On the one hand, there is the view that we should safeguard strictly the privacy of the personal data held by private companies, given that digital data can spread worldwide in a matter of seconds or can be hacked or used to target our potential voting preferences. In this view, we should be very cautious of any covert surveillance that allows an emboldening of private agencies to spy on the legitimate activities of those whom they (or any other authorities) deem "undesirable." The case of *Schrems v. The Data Protection Commissioner and Digital Rights Ireland Ltd* (Case C-362/2014) illustrates that we have good reason to be cautious.

In this case, the European Court of Justice was asked to determine a challenge to what is referred to as the "Safe Harbor" agreement. This agreement between the European Union and the United States was formed in 2000 and was designed to protect private data collected by internet companies. Specifically, it protects data collected in Europe when that data is shared with US providers. The court found that US legislators fell short of providing the sort of privacy guarantees that their European subsidiaries were bound by; hence, the agreement was unsustainable. In other words, the "Safe Harbor" agreement could not proceed because it did not comply with European human rights law. The case provides us with a reminder that data security cannot be trifled with. We should not always trust those who tell us that their databases are secure.

On the other hand, there is a strong sense that lives can be enhanced by having a ready supply of data available to anyone who wishes to access it. The new generations of digital users appear to be ambivalent about how much privacy they are willing to sacrifice in the rush to maintain contemporaneous contact with the world (Sarre, 2014). Access to Instagram, Facebook, FaceTime, WhatsApp, Viber, and Tango, for example, has enhanced the communication channels across the globe. They provide instantaneous and useful information. They can act as a safety and protection tool, too, when, say, a user is lost or becomes a victim of crime.

It is becoming clear that police need private sector communication networks to combat cybercrime. Private companies, however, cannot be trusted unequivocally to deal with our data in a manner that befits our privacy and meets our expectations (Gal, 2017).

Is There a Way Through the Maze?

There is a way through this dilemma, and a preferred path is available if we allow for the adoption of the following five requirements.

Requirement 1: Start with first principles regarding human rights.

This is best done with a reaffirmation of Article 12 of the Universal Declaration of Human Rights (1948):

> No one shall be subjected to arbitrary interference with his privacy, family, home or correspondence, nor to attacks upon his honor and reputation. Everyone has the right to the protection of the law against such interference or attacks.

Requirement 2: Determine what we as a society want and expect from cyberspace technology.

This requirement means that we need to decide what we can and cannot abide with the innovations that arise from technology and how much we are prepared to sacrifice in the privacy/connectedness dichotomy.

> [This] means more innovative forms of public debate. And it means that the most influential institutions in this space— . . . governments, technology firms and national champions—need to listen and experiment with the goal of social, as well as economic and technological, progress in mind.
>
> (Davis & Subic, 2018)

Requirement 3: Put appropriate rules in place.

These rules need to ensure that we can enjoy the benefits of the digital age without bringing us closer to a "surveillance society" in which our every move is monitored, tracked, recorded, and scrutinized by the government and private interests (Rodrick, 2009). We must build in more safeguards as the technology becomes more widespread.

Requirement 4: Encourage and adopt governmental guidelines.

The Australian experience on this front is one worth emulating. On May 8, 2017, the Australian government tabled the Productivity Commission's Data Availability and Use Inquiry (Australian Government, 2018). The inquiry made 41 recommendations designed to shift from policies based on risk avoidance toward policies based on value, choice, transparency, and confidence. A year later, on May 1, 2018, the Australian government committed to establishing an office of the national data commissioner, introducing legislation to improve the sharing, use and, reuse of public sector data while maintaining the strong security and privacy protections the community expects and a consumer data right to allow consumers of data to share their usage with private service competitors and comparison services. The bill that flowed from the inquiry (but has not yet been debated) sets out that the role of the commissioner will be enshrined in legislation, and data sharing and release will be authorized for specified purposes (such as informing and assessing government policy and research and development with public benefits), provided data safeguards are met (Flannery, 2019).

Requirement 5: Engage the private sector, but be suitably wary of its power and motive.

Policy-makers must be on guard to ensure that the private sector is thoroughly accountable for its cybercrime-prevention efforts (Chang, Zhong, & Grabosky, 2018, pp. 108–110). Can private corporations be trusted with sensitive personal data that may be generated as they "police" the internet?

> There are . . . serious unintended consequences that may result from the various extralegal measures employed by industry and corporate entities. Specifically they have no legal or constitutional remit to enforce national laws or the interests of any one country. Industrial involvement in transnational investigations . . . may lead some to question whether they have overstepped their role as service providers into order maintenance based on their economic interests only.
>
> (Holt, 2018, p. 152)

Moreover, the public might think less of the law enforcement agencies because it appears that the "real" work is driven by private interests. Indeed,

> [I]ndustry efforts to limit cybercrimes . . . may have negative consequences for the general public that could damage industries' reputation and potentially create legal challenges as to the legitimacy of their activities. Such efforts may also inadvertently

diminish the perceived legitimacy and competency of law enforcement agencies in the eye of the public.

(Holt, 2018, p. 152)

It becomes, in the end, a matter of balance. As Chang et al. (2018) point out, while some private actors may become overzealous in the protection of their own interests, "where state capacity to control cybercrime is limited, the socially and economically marginalized may suffer, directly or indirectly, no less than the privileged among us. A degree of citizen involvement in securing cyberspace can, thus, be useful" (Chang et al., 2018, p. 111).

Conclusion

The focus of policing is, and has always been, on responding to crime. Police have a role in policing cyberspace, but their resources devoted to crime prevention are limited. Police cannot go it alone against cybercrime. That being the case, the private sector has been and will continue to be co-opted. In two significant ways, its assistance has been successful. There is great trust between public and private agencies in relation to the collection and storage of metadata and the monitoring of visual digital data. However, given the excesses of some corporate entities, particularly in the processing of digital data records, governments cannot adopt a "hands-off" approach and allow the private sector free rein in their quest to defeat cybercrime. Instead, they must develop a clear overarching framework to require compliance of private owners of surveillance tools and data managers in the same way as controls are in place to protect the private nature of government-collected data. We must applaud the creation of a privacy commissioner and national data commissioner in Australia to monitor breaches of all forms of privacy in the manner set out in the Productivity Commission's Data Availability and Use Inquiry report. It is imperative that we regulate and monitor the interventions (in relation to surveillance and data management) by the private sector into our daily lives, even if it is done in the name of cyber security, lest it leave us more vulnerable to cyber incursion.

Discussion Questions

1. Distinguish between 'cyber-enabled' and 'cyber-dependent' cybercrime. Why is this distinction important in combatting their manifestations?
2. Discuss the trade-off between offering an opportunity in global cyberspace to all those who wish to access it, against the heightened possibility that easily accessible cyberspace will become a lawless domain.
3. What role do police play in the prevention of cybercrime? Why is it that increasingly the private sector is being asked to contribute to that fight? Are there any concerns attached to private sector involvement?
4. Critique the five suggested requirements for a successful crime prevention strategy in cyberspace. Should any others be added?

References

Australian Crime Commission. (2015). *Organized crime in Australia report*. Canberra: Commonwealth of Australia.

Australian Cyber Security Centre. (2017). *Australian cyber security centre 2017 threat report*. Retrieved from www.acsc.gov.au/publications/ACSC_Threat_Report_2017.pdf

Australian Government. (2016). *Australia's cyber security strategy*. Retrieved February 20, 2019, from www.pmc.gov.au/sites/default/files/publications/australias-cyber-security-strategy.pdf

Australian Government. (2018). *New Australian government data sharing and release legislation*. Issues Paper for Consultation. Canberra: Department of Prime Minister and Cabinet.

Australian Parliament. (2017, April 13). *Review of the implementation period of the telecommunications (interception and access) amendment (data retention) act 2014*. Canberra: Joint Parliamentary Committee on Intelligence and Security.

Branch, P. (2014, December). Surveillance by metadata. *Issues, 109,* 10–13.

Broadhurst, R., & Chang, L. Y. C. (2013). Cybercrime in Asia: Trends and challenges. In J. Liu, B. Hebenton, & S. Jou (Eds.), *Handbook of Asian criminology* (pp. 49–63). New York, NY: Springer.

Chang, L. Y. C. (2012). *Cybercrime in the greater China region: Regulatory responses, and crime prevention across the Taiwan strait*. Cheltenham: Edward Elgar Publishing.

Chang, L. Y. C., Zhong, L., & Grabosky, P. (2018). Citizen co-production of cyber security: Self-help, vigilantes, and cybercrime. *Regulation & Governance, 12*(1), 101–114.

Davis, N., & Subic, A. (2018, May 18). Hope and fear surround emerging technologies, but all of us must contribute to stronger governance. *The Conversation*. Retrieved February 1, 2019, from https://theconversation.com/hope-and-fear-surround-emerging-technologies-but-all-of-us-must-contribute-to-stronger-governance-96122

Economist. (2017, May 6–7). Data is the new oil. *Weekend Australian*, 24.

Fernandes, C., & Sivaraman, V. (2015). It's only the beginning: Metadata retention laws and the internet of things. *Australian Journal of Telecommunications and the Digital Economy, 3*(3). Retrieved February 1, 2019, from http://telsoc.org/ajtde/index.php/ajtde/article/view/21

Flannery, A. (2019). *Public sector data: The proposed data sharing and release act and implications for governments*. Retrieved February 1, 2019, from www.mondaq.com/article.asp?article_id=772966&signup=true

Gal, U. (2017, June 16). The new data retention law seriously invades our privacy—and it's time we took action. *The Conversation*. Retrieved February 1, 2019, from https://theconversation.com/the-new-data-retention-law-seriously-invades-our-privacy-and-its-time-we-took-action-78991?sa=pg2&sq=metadata&sr=1

Gordon, S., & Ford, R. (2006). On the definition and classification of cybercrime. *Journal of Computer Virology, 2,* 13–20.

Grabosky, P. (2007). *Electronic crime*. Upper Saddle River, NJ: Prentice Hall.

Grattan, M. (2015, May 12). $131 million for companies' metadata retention in budget boost to counter terrorism. *The Conversation*. Retrieved February 1, 2019, from https://theconversation.com/131-million-for-companies-metadata-retention-in-budget-boost-to-counter-terrorism-41637

Holt, T. J. (2018). Regulating cybercrime through law enforcement and industry mechanisms. *The Annals of the American Academy of Political and Social Science, 679*(1), 140–157.

Joseph, S. (2018, April 3). Why the business model of social media giants like Facebook is incompatible with human rights. *The Conversation*. Retrieved February 1, 2019, from https://theconversation.com/why-the-business-model-of-social-media-giants-like-facebook-is-incompatible-with-human-rights-94016

Kirkpatrick, D. (2018, April 23). Technology. *TIME Magazine*, 38–41.

Kowalick, P., Connery, D., & Sarre, R. (2018). Intelligence-sharing in the context of policing transnational serious and organized crime: A note on policy and practice in an Australian setting. *Police Practice and Research: An International Journal, 19*(6), 596–608.

Ludlam, S. (2015, February 27). Data retention: We need this opposition to oppose. *ABC, The Drum*. Retrieved February 1, 2019, from www.abc.net.au/news/2015-02-27/ludlam-we-need-this-opposition-to-oppose/6269504

Manokha, I. (2018, May 3). Cambridge Analytica's closure is a pyrrhic victory for data privacy. *The Conversation*. Retrieved February 1, 2019, from https://theconversation.com/cambridge-analyticas-closure-is-a-pyrrhic-victory-for-data-privacy-96034

McGuire, M., & Dowling, S. (2013, October). *Cyber crime: A review of the evidence: Summary of key findings and implications*. Home Office Research Report 75. London: Home Office.

Prenzler, T., & Sarre, R. (2012). Public-private crime prevention partnerships. In T. Prenzler (Ed.), *Policing and security in practice: Challenges and achievements* (pp. 149–167). Basingstoke: Palgrave Macmillan.

Prenzler, T., & Sarre, R. (2017). The security industry and crime prevention. In T. Prenzler (Ed.), *Understanding crime prevention: The case study approach* (pp. 165–81). Samford Valley: Australian Academic Press.

Rodrick, S. (2009). Accessing telecommunications data for national security and law enforcement purposes. *Federal Law Review, 37*(3), 375–415.

Sarre, R. (2008). Privacy and cyber forensics: An Australian perspective. In A. Marcella & D. Menendez (Eds.), *Cyber forensics: A field manual for collecting, examining, and preserving evidence of computer crimes* (2nd ed, pp. 231–240). Boca Raton, FL: Auerbach Publications.

Sarre, R. (2014). The use of surveillance technologies by law enforcement agencies: What are the trends, opportunities and threats? In E. Płacwaczewski (Ed.), *Current problems of the penal law and criminology* (pp. 755–767). Białystok, Poland: Temida Publishing House.

Sarre, R. (2015). Eyes in the sky. *Drone Magazine, 1*, 48–51.

Sarre, R. (2017a). Metadata retention as a means of combatting terrorism and organized crime: A perspective from Australia. *Asian Journal of Criminology, 12*, 167–179.

Sarre, R. (2017b). The surveillance society: A criminological perspective. In E. Viano (Ed.), *Cybercrime, organized crime, and societal responses: International approaches* (pp. 291–300). New York, NY: Springer.

Sarre, R. (2018, June 8). Revisiting metadata retention in light of the government's push for new powers. *The Conversation*. Retrieved March 1, 2019, from https://theconversation.com/revisiting-metadata-retention-in-light-of-the-governments-push-for-new-powers-97931

Sarre, R., Brooks, D., Smith, C., & Draper, R. (2014). Current and emerging technologies employed to abate crime and to promote security. In B. Arrigo & H. Bersot (Eds.), *The Routledge handbook of international crime and justice studies* (pp. 327–349). London: Routledge.

Sarre, R., Lau, L., & Chang, L. (2018). Responding to cybercrime: Current trends. *Police Practice and Research: An International Journal, 19*(6), 515–518.

Sarre, R., & Prenzler, T. (2021). Policing and security: Critiquing the privatisation agenda. In P. Birch, M. Kennedy, & E. Kruger (Eds.), *Australian policing: Critical issues in 21st century police practice*. Melbourne: Oxford University Press.

Turnbull, M. (2015, July 7). *Magna Carta and the rule of law in the digital age*. Speech to the Sydney Institute, Sydney. Retrieved February 27, 2019, from www.malcolmturnbull.com.au/media/speech-to-the-sydney-institute-magna-carta-and-the-rule-of-law-in-the-digit

Universal Declaration of Human Rights. (1948). General Assembly Resolution 217A, December 10, 1948. Retrieved June 10, 2021, from https://www.un.org/en/about-us/universal-declaration-of-human-rights

Chapter 16

Gunrunning 101

A How-To Guide About What to Look For

Gregg W. Etter Sr. and Jeffery M. Johnson

Introduction

Guns are an integral part of American culture. Gun violence is a problem in the United States, especially in the cities and with gangs. The Supreme Court of the United States has ruled that the Second Amendment of the United States Constitution allows a person an individual right to own a firearm (*District of Columbia v. Heller*, 554 U.S. 570, 2008; *McDonald v. City of Chicago*, 561 U.S. 742, 2010).

However, the Supreme Court further ruled that governments (federal, state, and local) have the right to regulate the sale, manufacture, transport, and possession of firearms. Jacobs and Potter (1995) observed:

> Keeping firearms out of the hands of dangerous and irresponsible persons is one of, if not the primary goal of United States gun control policy. The logic of restricting gun ownership to responsible, law abiding citizens is immediately apparent and uncontroversial, even to the National Rifle Association. It reflects a widely shared belief that members of certain social categories pose an unacceptably high risk of misusing firearms. As in the case of denying a driver's license to people who are legally blind, there is a strong consensus that people who have demonstrated certain kinds of irresponsible and unstable behavior should not possess weapons which are capable of injuring or killing the possessor or others. Federal gun control law attempts to strike a balance between permitting law-abiding citizens to obtain firearms with relative ease and preventing certain categories of presumptively irresponsible people from purchasing and possessing firearms. Those that are conclusively presumed irresponsible include ex-felons, former mental patients, drug addicts, juveniles, and illegal aliens.
>
> (pp. 93–94)

Major Laws Governing Firearms

The Sullivan Act of 1911

One of the earliest attempts to regulate firearms in the hands of gangsters and criminals occurred in the state of New York. In New York City, many different street gangs had battled over turf and control of crime since the 1820s (Asbury, 1928, p. 21). In 1911, The New York Legislature passed the Sullivan Act of 1911. (Patterson & Eakins, 1998, p. 48). The Sullivan Act required that firearms small enough to be concealed would have to be licensed. Failure to license a firearm covered by the act was a misdemeanor. The concealed carry of a handgun without a license was a felony. In addition to handguns, the Sullivan Act prohibited the possession or carrying of weapons that were commonly used by gang members, such as brass

DOI: 10.4324/9781003047117-19

knuckles, sandbags, blackjacks, bludgeons, or bombs, as well as possessing or carrying a dagger, "dangerous knife," or razor "with intent to use the same unlawfully."

Interestingly, one of the backers of this law was former United States Congressman Timothy Daniel Sullivan (D-NY, 1903–1906), who was known as "Big Tim" Sullivan. Sullivan was a corrupt Tammany Hall politician and, furthermore, was also one of the leaders of the Five Points district gang in New York City (Asbury, 1928, p. 319). Some of the more cynical noted that many gang members who had patronage from Tammany Hall were arrested and the charges dismissed by Tammany Hall lawyers.

The first person to be convicted under the Sullivan Act was an Italian immigrant named Marino Rossi, who, in 1911, was sentenced to one year in prison for carrying a pistol. Rossi argued that it was his people's habit to do so in defense against gangsters such as the Black Hand (NYT, 1911). Reflecting the disparity in who was changed under this act, the *New York Times* (1911) observed:

> Now that the police have suitably impressed the minds of aliens that the Sullivan law forbids their bearing arms of any kind, would it not be well "to get after" the notorious characters who are not aliens? Hundreds of men in this city with criminal records, whose haunts are known to the police, habitually carry concealed weapons. The process of "frisking" such persons is less common, perhaps than it ought to be, now that their offense has been made a felony and its penalty increased. In fact, it has always been the duty of the police to search them, yet we hear of no arrests or convictions.

The Sullivan Act included a provision that local police departments "may issue" a concealed weapon permit, without specifying any criteria for doing so. There was initially a three-dollar fee that was paid to the NYPD for this permit. This is opposed to the "shall issue" concealed weapon statutes in many states.

The National Firearms Act of 1934, 26 USC Ch. 53

The 18th Amendment was ratified in 1919 and took effect on January 16, 1920. This amendment forbade the production, transport, or sale of alcohol in the United States. A law known as the National Prohibition Act or "Volstead Act" was passed to enforce this amendment. This set off a series of gang wars in many major American cities to control the illegal alcohol trade. Wilson (2007) found:

> Gangster violence carried out by organized crime groups during the early 1930's, was the major impetus behind the National Firearm's Act of 1934 (NFA). The NFA was an attempt to regulate the marketplace through taxes that made certain types of firearms, including sawed-off shotguns and machineguns quite expensive. Each weapon transfer carried a $200 tax, and importers, manufacturers, and dealers were taxed in addition to the transfer tax. All such weapons had to be registered with the national government. Congress chose to enact heavy taxes rather than ban the firearms outright due to concerns regarding the legislature's authority and the Second Amendment.
>
> (p. 87)

The NFA was enacted on June 26, 1934. It required registration of and a tax on machine guns, sawed-off shotguns, short-barreled rifles, and other weapons. The NFA also prohibited the altering or removal of serial numbers on weapons. In addition, it prohibited possession of weapons with altered numbers. However, flaws emerged with the enforcement of the NFA.

Enforcement of the NFA was initially held as being constitutional as a tax (*Sonzinsky v. United States*, 300 US 506, 1937). ATF (2017) noted:

> As structured in 1934, the NFA imposed a duty on persons transferring NFA firearms, as well as mere possessors of unregistered firearms, to register them with the Secretary of the Treasury. If the possessor of an unregistered firearm applied to register the firearm as required by the NFA, the Treasury Department could supply information to State authorities about the registrant's possession of the firearm. State authorities could then use the information to prosecute the person whose possession violated State laws. For these reasons, the Supreme Court in 1968 held in the Haynes case that a person prosecuted for possessing an unregistered NFA firearm had a valid defense to the prosecution—the registration requirement imposed on the possessor of an unregistered firearm violated the possessor's privilege from self-incrimination under the Fifth Amendment of the U.S. Constitution. The Haynes decision made the 1934 Act virtually unenforceable.
> (*Haynes v. US*, 390 U.S. 85, 1968)

Federal Firearms Act of 1938

The Federal Firearms Act of 1938 was designed to regulate interstate commerce in firearms. The act required the licensing by the federal government of firearms dealers. The FFA also prohibited the purchase of firearms by persons with legal disabilities, such as convicted felons, those under indictment, or fugitives from justice. (Public Laws-CH. 850, 1938) In describing the act, Wilson (2007) found:

> The FFA applied to all firearms, but the controls it mandated were relatively modest. It required any interstate dealers to be licensed (the cost of a license was $1), and there were some additional restrictions on the interstate shipment of firearms. Manufacturers and importers were required to purchase licenses. Selling to a restricted class of persons was criminalized, but the enforcement mechanism was weak. Dealers were required to keep records of sales, but penalties for violation of this law were minimal. Dealers were defined as "any person engaged in the business of selling firearms or ammunition . . . at wholesale or retail" as well as gunsmiths and manufacturers. Thus obtaining a license was neither difficult nor expensive. Over the years many average citizens became dealers to facilitate purchasing firearms for themselves.

The Gun Control Act of 1968, Public Law 90–618

There was great social turbulence in the United States during the 1960s, including frequent demonstrations and even riots (civil rights, anti-war, women's rights, etc.). Patterson and Eakins (1998) noted:

> After three decades of relative quiet on the gun control front, a new wave of demand for a stronger federal role swelled in the 1960s. This demand was fueled by the assassination of President John F. Kennedy in Dallas on November 22, 1963; the urban riots beginning in 1964; and the murders of Martin Luther King in Memphis on April 4 and Robert F. Kennedy in San Francisco on June 6, 1968. The House of Representatives passed an omnibus crime bill containing gun control provisions the day after Robert Kennedy was assassinated, and a few weeks later, with the tide in favor of stricter federal firearms regulations, Congress enacted the Gun Control Act of 1968.
> (p. 49)

The Gun Control Act of 1968 repealed the FFA of 1938 but kept many of the provisions contained in it, such as the licensing of federal firearms dealers and the requirement to keep records of gun sales. The Gun Control Act of 1968 stopped mail-order gun sales. The act regulated imports and manufacture of certain weapons. The act also expanded firearm prohibition by certain persons. It prohibited gun possession by felons, fugitives, persons under indictment, the mentally ill, addicts (drugs or alcohol), dishonorably discharged individuals, illegal aliens, persons who had renounced their US citizenship, and persons under a restraining order by the courts.

To correct the constitutional flaws exposed in the NFA of 1934 by *Haynes v. US* (1968), the ATF (2017) observed that in the Gun Control Act of 1968, certain changes were made to the law:

> Title II amended the NFA to cure the constitutional flaw pointed out in Haynes. First, the requirement for possessors of unregistered firearms to register was removed. Indeed, under the amended law, there is no mechanism for a possessor to register an unregistered NFA firearm already possessed by the person. Second, a provision was added to the law prohibiting the use of any information from an NFA application or registration as evidence against the person in a criminal proceeding with respect to a violation of law occurring prior to or concurrently with the filing of the application or registration. In 1971, the Supreme Court reexamined the NFA in the Freed case and found that the 1968 amendments cured the constitutional defect in the original NFA. Title II also amended the NFA definitions of "firearm" by adding "destructive devices" and expanding the definition of "machine gun."

The Brady Handgun Violence Prevention Act of 1993, Public Law 103–159, 107 Stat. 1536

After the attempted assassination of President Ronald Reagan in 1981 and the resulting wounding of his press secretary, James Brady, there was a renewed push for increased handgun control. The result was the Brady Handgun Violence Prevention Act of 1993. Wilson (2007) observed:

> The law created a five-day waiting period for handgun purchases from federally licensed dealer. The dealer was also required to submit information about the buyer to local authorities to confirm the buyer was indeed eligible to purchase the handgun. Authorities could not retain purchase records. Within five years, the Brady Bill mandated that a National Instant Criminal Background System (NICS) be created to replace the local authorities' check and the waiting period. Those states that already had background checks or handgun licensing were exempted. The bill also increased fees for FFLs.
>
> (p. 94–95)

In 1997, the requirement that local authorities perform records checks of prospective handgun buyers was challenged by local sheriffs as a violation of the Tenth Amendment to the Constitution in *Printz v. United States* (521 U.S. 898, 1997). The court ruled that the requirement that local authorities check the background of prospective handgun buyers was unconstitutional but upheld the other parts of the act. The provision for a background check using NICS remained.

In addition, the Brady Act prohibits transfer of a firearm to a person who is under indictment for, or has been convicted of, a crime punishable by imprisonment for more than one year; is a fugitive from justice; is an unlawful user of, or addicted to, a controlled substance;

has been adjudicated as a mental defective or committed to a mental institution; is an illegal alien or has been admitted to the US under a nonimmigrant visa; or dishonorably discharged from the US Armed Forces; has renounced US citizenship; is subject to a court order restraining him or her from harassing, stalking, or threatening an intimate partner or child; has been convicted of a misdemeanor crime of domestic violence; or is under age 18 for long guns or under age 21 for handguns.

Are unqualified potential firearms purchasers being stopped by the Brady Act? The NICS is the predominant screening tool for handgun purchases. BJS (2016) found:

> About 1.3% of the nearly 15 million applications for firearm transfers or permits in 2014 were denied—about 91,000 by the FBI and about 102,000 by state and local agencies. An estimated 193,000 applications for firearm transfers or permits in 2013 were denied—about 88,000 by the FBI and about 104,000 by state and local agencies.
>
> (p. 1)

Of the potential firearms purchasers that were denied by NICS, the BJS (2016) found that "a felony conviction (42%) was the most common reason for the FBI to deny an application in 2014, followed by a fugitive from justice status (19%)" (p. 1).

State and Local Firearms Laws

Each of the 50 states within the United States has its own firearms laws that regulate the commerce in and possession of firearms. Some states have very restrictive laws and require the licensing of each individual firearm, have strict rules on the transfer of firearms, and limit the type of firearms that may be possessed legally by citizens. Pierce, Braga, and Wintemute (2015) found that "California has firearm-related laws that are more stringent than many other states and regulates its retail firearms dealers to a unique degree" (p. 179).

Illinois has chosen to license firearm owners rather than the weapons themselves. Other states do not have laws as restrictive relating to firearms. Some municipalities have enacted their own firearms rules or even attempted to enact complete bans on the sale or possession of handguns within their jurisdictions. Two major cities, Chicago and Washington, DC, attempted to ban or severely restrict the possession of handguns within their jurisdictions. These bans were challenged on constitutional grounds and overturned by the United States Supreme Court as violations of the Second Amendment. (*District of Columbia v. Heller*, 554 U.S. 570, 2008; *McDonald v. City of Chicago*, 561 U.S. 742, 2010) Kraft (2002) notes, "Firearms trafficking is profitable because of the disparity in firearm laws in different jurisdictions" (p. 6).

Gunrunning in Theory and Practice

What Is Gunrunning or Illegal Firearms Trafficking?

While millions of Americans legally own firearms, some people are prohibited by law from possessing or purchasing a firearm. BATF Special Agent Mark Kraft (2002) observed:

> ATF defines firearms trafficking as the illegal diversion of firearms out of lawful commerce and into the hands of criminals, prohibited persons and unsupervised juveniles. Firearms traffickers are motivated by the profit, prestige and power they obtain by supplying guns to criminals and juveniles who cannot legally obtain them. Firearms trafficking

is how drug dealers, gang members and violent criminals get the guns they need to commit violent crimes.

(p. 6)

What Is a Straw Man Purchase?

According to the Law Center to Prevent Gun Violence (2012):

> A "straw purchase" occurs when the actual buyer of a firearm uses another person, a "straw purchaser," to execute the paperwork necessary to purchase a firearm from a federally licensed firearms dealer (FFL). A straw purchaser is a person with a clean background who purchases firearms specifically on behalf of a person prohibited from purchasing a firearm because he or she is a convicted felon, domestic violence misdemeanant, juvenile, mentally ill individual or other federally or state-defined prohibited person. The straw purchaser violates federal law by making a false statement to the FFL about a material fact by lying on ATF Form 4473 (the firearm transaction record) or presenting false identification in connection with the purchase.

In a successful straw purchase, the actual buyer is never specifically linked to the gun, but both the prohibited purchaser and the straw purchaser have committed a federal felony. The straw purchaser violates 18 U.S.C. § 922(a)(6) or 18 U.S.C. § 924(a)(1)(A) by falsely stating or falsely providing evidence that he or she is the actual gun buyer, while the prohibited purchaser—usually the actual buyer—is criminally liable for aiding and abetting the straw purchaser in such violations or in causing the making of the false statements.

The United States Department of Justice, Office of the Inspector General (2017) found:

> ATF has identified circumstances that it considers indicative of straw purchasing and gun trafficking. These include the following:
>
> - multiple sales to a purchaser who appears on past gun traces;
> - sales of five or more firearms to a single buyer;
> - sales of multiple firearms at the same FFL on the same day;
> - trace requests for firearms purchased as part of a multiple sale;
> - trace requests with a "short time-to-crime" (the time that passes between the purchase of a gun and its recovery in connection with a crime);
> - sales paid for in cash; and
> - multiple sales of guns considered "weapons of choice" for drug trafficking organizations.

(OIG, 2017)

Who Participates in a Straw Man Purchase?

In his study of illegal firearms traffickers, Kraft (2002) observed:

> Frequently firearms traffickers will travel from a market area to a source area and recruit a network of straw purchasers who are residents of the state and who need a few extra dollars. Straw purchasers are not traffickers. They are pawns of the traffickers. They are frequently people desperate for money or drugs. Gun traffickers typically pay straw purchasers $50 to $100 per gun or provide them with a $20 to $50 rock of cocaine in exchange for their services.

(p. 7)

The Chicago-Mississippi Delta Pipeline of Firearms Trafficking

The inconsistency in gun laws among the states and the willingness of criminals in Chicago to travel to attain firearms provided them an opportunity to purchase those firearms in the Mississippi Delta. An investigation in 2004 showed that over 300 guns that were being used by Chicago street gangs and were seized by the Chicago police were coming from four specific gun shops in the Mississippi Delta near Clarksdale, Mississippi (Hizemann, 2004). Why Clarksdale, Mississippi?

Clarksdale is a town of 20,645 residents located in Coahoma County, Mississippi. It is considered by many to be the home of blues music. Many residents of the area moved to the Chicago area seeking work after the International Harvester Corporation invented a mechanical cotton picker in 1946, and GIs returning from WWII did not wish to work in the fields. (The Illinois Central Railroad provided direct passenger service at the time.) Thus, many Clarksdale residents had relatives in Chicago and vice versa.

According to Joyner (2007), Chicago-based youth street gangs have been a problem in the Mississippi Delta since the 1980s, thanks to family connections between the regions dating back to the Great Migration of the 1940s and 1950s. He noted that federal authorities have cracked down on gangs to shut down a pipeline that sends guns to the North and drugs back South, according to Randall Samborn, an assistant US attorney in Chicago.

As a result of this traffic and other family connections, Gangsta Disciples and Vice Lords are abundant in the Mississippi Delta now. The Chicago-based gangs that received these weapons were the Gangsta Disciples, New Breeds, Conservative Vice Lords, Insane Imperial Vice Lords, Four Corner Hustler Vice Lords, and the Unknown Vice Lords. The guns seized by the Chicago Police Department came from four specific gun shops. Between 2004 and 2008, 76 weapons were recovered by CPD that were traced to Krosstown Trade & Pawn, Clarksdale, Mississippi. At least one of the 9mm handguns used in a gunfight between the New Breeds and CPD in November, 2006, on Chicago's West Side came from North Delta Gun Shop in Clarksdale. Both handguns and assault-type weapons were among the weapons acquired from Mega Pawn in Clarksdale to ship to Chicago. More guns came from Route 61 Trade & Pawn in Tunica, Mississippi, which is about 30 miles from Clarksdale (Kirk, 2008; Hinezmann, 2004).

Who were the players in this gunrunning operation? Eddie Nesby, who was 25 and from Chicago (a convicted felon), recruited straw men and transported weapons from Mississippi to Illinois. Julius Statham, who was 37 and from Chicago (a convicted felon), purchased firearms acquired by R. Brunt and distributed to his gang. Antonio Brunt who was 30 and from Chicago (a convicted felon) sold R. Brunt's guns to gangs. Roy Christopher Brunt (29) and Sylvester Rice (29) from Jonestown, Mississippi, recruited straw men and transported guns. Fourteen others in Mississippi were also charged with acting as straw man purchasers in this case (Kirk, 2008; Joyner, 2007; Hinezmann, 2004).

What Can Happen as a Result of a Straw Man Purchase?

When a straw purchaser buys a firearm for a prohibited person, there can be very negative consequences. On December 2, 2015, Syed Rizwan Farook and his wife, Tashfeen Malik, killed 14 people and wounded 22 in San Bernardino, California. The shooters were killed.

Enrique Marquez Jr. (an Islamic convert) was indicted on federal charges of supporting terrorism, firearms violations, and immigration fraud. He allegedly supplied the two AR-15 rifles to the shooters in a straw man–type purchase. Marquez confessed to buying the rifles for Farook because Farook thought he would not pass a background check

(Lovett, Healy, Schmidt, & Turkewitz, 2015). On February 14, 2017, in a plea agreement with federal prosecutors, Marquez pled guilty in federal court to providing material support to terrorists and lying about the acquisition of weapons to investigators (Balsamo, 2017).

Gun Shows

Gun shows are another way that firearms are sold. The vast majority of sellers are licensed FFL dealers, and all federal, state, and local laws are observed during firearms purchases, including background checks. The so-called "gun show exception" occurs when an individual who is not an FFL decides to sell their individually owned firearm to another individual. There is no requirement for a background check for these firearms purchases. However, ATF (1999) states:

> More than 4,000 shows dedicated primarily to the sale or exchange of firearms are held annually in the United States. There are also countless other public markets at which firearms are freely sold or traded, such as flea markets. Under current law, large numbers of firearms at these public markets are sold anonymously; the seller has no idea and is under no obligation to find out whether he or she is selling a firearm to a felon or other prohibited person. If any of these firearms are later recovered at a crime scene, there is virtually no way to trace them back to the purchaser.

ATF (2017c) notes that all state and local laws still apply. Also, there is a limit to how many guns an individual may sell in this fashion each year before they are required to obtain an FFL license. Individuals selling their weapons this way at gun shows often are seen carrying them through the gun show with signs that advertise the weapons for sale, or they have rented tables, and the contents are labeled "private collection." These type of transactions are usually conducted in cash. This individual exception also allows for a firearm to be bequeathed to another individual as a part of an inheritance without going through an FFL.

Auctions

Auctions are another way that firearms are sold. Sometimes stolen goods are moved through auctions. The federal firearms regulations on auctions are less stringent. ATF noted that there are basically two types of auctions: estate sales and consignment sales. In describing regulations for auctions (ATF Ruling 96–2), ATF (2017b) stated:

> In estate-type auctions, the articles to be auctioned (including firearms) are being sold by the executor of the estate of an individual. The firearms belong to and are possessed by the executor. The firearms are controlled by the estate, and the sales of firearms are being made by the estate. The auctioneer is acting as an agent of the executor and assisting the executor in finding buyers for the firearms. In these cases, the auctioneer does not meet the definition of engaging in business as a dealer in firearms and would not need a license. An auctioneer who does have a license may perform this function away from his or her licensed premises.

Because estate auctions come under the individual property rule, it is possible that the firearms could be sold to a person who is not eligible to own one. Few records are kept of sales to individuals, and no background checks are performed at this type of sale.

ATF (2017b) acknowledged that consignment auctions were slightly different but basically came under the same ruling, stating:

> In consignment-type auctions, an auctioneer often takes possession of firearms in advance of the auction. These firearms are generally inventoried, evaluated, and tagged for identification. The firearms belong to individuals who have entered into a consignment agreement with the auctioneer giving that auctioneer authority to sell the firearms. The auctioneer therefore has possession and control of the firearms. Under these circumstances, an auctioneer would generally need a license.

Because the auctioneer would need an FFL license at a consignment sale, the normal background checks on prospective firearm purchasers would be performed.

Theft of Legal Firearms

Sometimes legally owned firearms are stolen in burglaries or thefts. The arms then enter the illegal market. BATF Agent Mark Kraft (2002) observed:

> Stolen firearms represent a huge problem, although no one can accurately establish the percentage of trafficked firearms market they account for, as there is no way to determine how many guns are stolen. Numerous factors contribute to the inability to accurately determine the number of firearms stolen each year. Private citizens are generally not required to keep records regarding their firearms and many do not even maintain a record of the serial number of their firearms. When firearms are stolen from individual's residences, owners often cannot properly identify them to law enforcement. As a result, many stolen firearms enter illicit markets as stolen, undocumented, and undetectable.

In addition to there being no federal law requiring private citizens to report stolen firearms, most states do not require the reporting of the theft of firearms by private citizens. In a report for the Connecticut State Legislature, Coppolo (2007) reported that only Massachusetts, Michigan, New York, Ohio, and Rhode Island had laws that require gun owners to report lost or stolen firearms to the police, although he noted that several other states were considering such legislation.

Attempting to determine the scope of the problem, in 2013, the BATF conducted a study to determine how many firearms had been lost or stolen in the United States during 2012. ATF (2013) found:

> In 2012, NCIC received reports reflecting 190,342 lost and stolen firearms nationwide. Of those 190,342 lost and stolen firearms reported, 16,667 (9% of the total reported) were the result of thefts/losses from FFLs. Of the 16,667 firearms reported as lost or stolen from a FFL, a total of 10,915 firearms were reported as lost. The remaining 5,762 were reported as stolen.
>
> (p. 4)

In an earlier study of firearms theft during household burglaries over a five-year period (2005–2010), Langton (2012) found that "overall, about 1.4 million guns, or an annual average of 232,400, were stolen during burglaries and other property crimes in the six-year period from 2005–2010" (p. 1). In addition, Langton (2012) noted that multiple guns were often stolen in a single incident and that at least one handgun was stolen in at least 63% of the reported burglaries in which a gun was taken. He also discovered that

> burglaries accounted for 58% of the 153,900 victimizations each year in which a gun was stolen, and robberies accounted for about 7% of the victimizations involving a gun theft.
> (Langton, 2012, pp. 2–3)

Although the burglaries included in these studies were largely residential burglaries, sometimes federally licensed firearms dealers (FFL) get burglarized as well. KWCH TV 12 (2017) reported that on February 10, 2017, the P-4 Gun Store in Wichita, Kansas, was burglarized. In the burglary, 37 guns were taken, including 33 handguns. The Wichita Police Department was notified and is still investigating the burglary. FFLs are required by federal law to report the loss or theft of firearms. The owners of the P-4 Gun Store complied with this requirement and also provided a list of stolen firearms and their serial numbers to the media in order to assist in their recovery.

Another source of illegal firearms is the theft from law enforcement or military sources. For example, Fox News (2017) cited the theft of a Heckler & Koch MP5 submachine gun from the car of an FBI agent in Contra Costa County, California, near San Francisco. The firearm itself was legally possessed by the FBI agent, and it was the property of the United States government. However, it is currently on the illegal firearms market until and if it is recovered by law enforcement authorities.

The problem is not limited to just one law enforcement agency or area. In an investigative report, Peele (2016) reported that California law enforcement agencies in the San Francisco Bay area reported 600 pistols or revolvers, 251 shotguns, 27 assault rifles, 16 rifles, 15 sniper rifles, 12 tear gas grenade launchers, a submachine gun, and 22 other firearms as stolen, lost, or unaccounted for in the period from 2010 to 2016. He stated:

> [I]n all, since 2010, at least 944 guns have disappeared from police in the Bay Area and state and federal agents across California—an average of one almost every other day—and fewer than 20 percent have been recovered.
> (2016)

In addition, there have been firearms thefts from military sources. For example, CBS (2016) reported the arrest of a 34-year-old former army reservist who was involved in the theft of weapons from the Lincoln Stoddard Army Reserve Center in Worcester, Massachusetts. Among the weapons stolen were six M-4 rifles (fully automatic) and ten Sig Sauer M11 9mm pistols. The former reservist, James Walker Morales, was discharged from the army as a result of being convicted of aggravated assault and battery. He was awaiting trial on a child rape charge at the time of the break-in. Some but not all of the weapons were recovered.

In another case, thieves were stealing handguns from shipments from the firearms' manufacturer. Witkin (1997) reported that in 1994, agents from the Bureau of Alcohol, Tobacco, and Firearms arrested two employees of the Lorcin Engineering Company of Mira Loma, California, who had stolen over 2,000 handguns from shipments leaving the factory (p. 34).

Thefts of legal firearms in interstate transport while being shipped from the manufacturer to a retail outlet are a major problem. Tarm (2017) reported that there are frequent cargo thefts from the railyards in Chicago. Some of the boxes taken were shipments of firearms that were in transit from manufacturers to retail outlets. In reporting this theft, Tarm (2017) noted:

> The guns had been en route from New Hampshire weapon maker Sturm, Ruger & Co. to Spokane, Washington. Instead, the .45-caliber Ruger revolvers and other firearms

spread quickly into surrounding high-crime neighborhoods. Along with two other major gun thefts within three years, the robbery helped fuel a wave of violence on Chicago's streets.

Tarm also reported that in a 2015 rail yard theft, 111 guns were taken. He also found that a major cargo theft of guns had also taken place in 2014 in the same rail yards. How are these guns used by Chicago gang members, and are they ever recovered? Tarm (2017) found:

Only 16 of the stolen Rugers have been recovered since the 2015 break-in, according to hundreds of recent court records reviewed by the Associated Press (2007). One was used in a Jan. 22, 2016, shooting. Police woke an attempted-murder suspect and found one by his bed. Another was in a dealer's home amid 429 bags of heroin. Police recovered another during a traffic stop; the driver said his friend had just been shot 10 times and he had to protect himself. "*It's a war going on over here*," he told police.

Regarding the Chicago rail yard thefts, CBS (2017) observed that "Chicago's biggest rail yards are on the gang-and homicide-plagued South and West sides where most of the city's 762 killings happened last year." CBS (2017) also found:

Such boxcar thefts have happened elsewhere, including 100 assault rifles from an Atlanta train in 2012. But the frequency in Chicago stands out, and it has a lot to do with the city's role as the nation's largest freight hub.

Our Neighbors' Firearms Laws and Smuggling Problems (Mexico and Canada)

Mexico and Firearms

The right of a Mexican citizen to own a firearm is guaranteed in Article 10 of the Mexican Constitution:

Article 10. The inhabitants of the United Mexican States have a right to arms in their homes, for security and legitimate defense, with the exception of arms prohibited by federal law and those reserved for exclusive use of the Army, Navy, Air Force, and National Guard. Federal law will determine the cases, conditions, requirements, and places in which carrying of arms will be authorized by the inhabitants.

(Kopel, 2013, p. 29)

Kopel (2013) found that this provision in the Mexican Constitution was very similar to provisions in the constitutions of Guatemala (Article 38) and of Haiti (Article 268–1). However, the possession of arms and ammunition by civilians in Mexico is strictly regulated by the Mexican government.

Where do guns illegally coming into Mexico come from? Chappel (2016) reports:

[F]rom 2009 to 2014, more than 73,000 guns that were seized in Mexico were traced to the U.S., according to a new update on the effort to fight weapons trafficking along the U.S.-Mexico border. The figure, based on data from the Bureau of Alcohol, Tobacco, Firearms and Explosives, represents about 70 percent of the 104,850 firearms seized by Mexican authorities that were also submitted to U.S. authorities for tracing.

Seizures have included not only rifles and pistols, but also hand grenades and rocket launchers. Cross-border gun trafficking is known as "the *hormiga* [ant] trade" Serrano (2008) found:

> [M]ore than 90% of guns seized at the border or after raids and shootings in Mexico have been traced to the United States, according to the U.S. Bureau of Alcohol, Tobacco, Firearms and Explosives. Last year, 2,455 weapons traces requested by Mexico showed that guns had been purchased in the United States, according to the ATF. Texas, Arizona, and California accounted for 1,805 of those traced weapons.

Canada and Guns

Guns are strictly regulated in Canada by law. Guns must be registered, and both ownership and possession of handguns are severely restricted. There is a problem of handguns and other weapons being smuggled into Canada from the United States. In 2009, US and Canadian authorities convicted Ricardo Tolliver of smuggling over 500 handguns into Canada. In addition to smuggling, Tolliver had gun parts shipped to Canada and assembled them here. He even tried unsuccessfully to mail three of the guns to Canada. But most of the guns were smuggled across the Windsor border after being acquired in Ohio and Kentucky through straw purchases, in which convicted felons and others who can't legally buy firearms get a third party to purchase the weapons for them. The criminals brought the guns to Canada, traded them for marijuana, and smuggled the drugs back to the US. Windsor often played a central role (Wilhelm, 2009). Some of the guns smuggled by Tolliver were used in a murder of eight Banditos bikers in 2006; others were used in a shootout with the London Police (Wilhelm, 2009).

In 2013, Pearson and Wilhelm found:

> Most of the weapons are carried up Highway 401 to the Greater Toronto Area—and to Toronto's gang-ridden neighborhoods like Dixon Road. But Windsor isn't just a pipeline. The trickle of guns left behind have lethal consequences here, too, most notably and harrowingly the 2006 slaying of John Atkinson, a Windsor police officer.

Pearson and Wilhelm (2013) also found that many of the smuggled guns from the United States were no longer being acquired through straw purchases but were privately purchased weapons acquired on the secondary market, and these were harder to trace for both Canadian authorities and the ATF. They reported:

> Provincial Weapons Enforcement Unit statistics show that between 2005 and September of this year, the joint-force operation seized 7,793 guns, and laid 10,765 charges against 2,174 people in Ontario. The stats reflect all 13 police agencies involved in PWEU.

Conclusion

The gunrunning trade is alive and well in America. Where access to firearms is limited, there is cash to be made in an illicit firearms trade. Illicit firearms are acquired through thefts, smuggling, and straw man purchases. They are often used in other illegal enterprises, such as the drug trade, and by gangs. BATF and local law enforcement are attempting to stem the tide of illegal arms traffic in the United States. This is a growing concern for the United States government. More research is needed to better understand gunrunning, as well as gun control laws in the United States. Gun violence continues to be a major issue; further research is

Discussion Questions

1. Do you believe that gun control laws are effective? Why or why not?
2. Gun rights advocates argue that there are plenty of gun laws on the books. The problem is that the federal government is uneven in its enforcement of existing laws, particularly regarding felons in possession of a firearm. Do you think that stricter enforcement of the laws about felons and firearms possession would lessen the problem of gun violence? Why or why not?
3. What is a "straw man purchase"? How does it circumvent the existing gun laws?
4. Gun violence is a problem in the United States. However, most gun owners are law abiding. To stem gun violence, do you think that there should be mandatory federal prosecution with a mandatory minimum sentence for any crime committed with a firearm? Why or why not?
5. How has the smuggling of guns from the United States contributed to civil unrest, particularly in places such as Mexico?

References

Alcohol, Tobacco, and Firearms, United States Department of Justice. (1999). *Gun shows: Brady checks and crime gun traces.* Retrieved from www.atf.gov/file/57506/download

Alcohol, Tobacco and Firearms, United States Department of Justice. (2013). *2012 summary: Firearms reported lost or stolen.* Retrieved from www.atf.gov/file/11846/download

Alcohol, Tobacco, and Firearms, United States Department of Justice. (2017a). *National Firearms Act.* Retrieved from www.atf.gov/rules-and-regulations/national-firearms-act

Alcohol, Tobacco, and Firearms, United States Department of Justice. (2017b). *Does an auctioneer who is involved in firearms sales need a dealer's license?* Retrieved from www.atf.gov/firearms/qa/does-auctioneer-who-involved-firearms-sales-need-dealer%E2%80%99s-license

Alcohol, Tobacco, and Firearms, United States Department of Justice. (2017c). *To whom may an unlicensed person transfer firearm under the GCA?* Retrieved from www.atf.gov/firearms/qa/whom-may-unlicensed-person-transfer-firearms-under-gca

Asbury, H. (1928). *The gangs of New York: An informal history of the New York underworld.* New York, NY: Alfred A. Knopf, Inc.

Associated Press. (2007). *U S guns Bolster Mexican traffickers.* Retrieved September 8, 2010, from http://archive.newsmax.com/archives/articles/2007/8/16/141559.shtml

Balsamo, M. (2017). Friend of Syed Farook pleads guilty to aiding in San Bernardino terror attack. *The Washington Times.* Retrieved from www.washingtontimes.com/news/2017/feb/14/enrique-marquez-pleads-guilty-helping-syed-farook-/

Bureau of Justice Statistics, Unites State Department of Justice. (2016). *Background checks for firearm transfers, 2013–2014-statistical tables* (NCJ 249849). Retrieved from www.bjs.gov/content/pub/pdf/bcft1314st.pdf

CBS. (2017, March 3). Gang thieves use rail yards as shopping malls, steal scores of guns. *CBS Chicago 2.* Retrieved from http://chicago.cbslocal.com/2017/03/03/gang-thieves-use-rail-yards-as-shopping-malls-steal-scores-of-guns/

CBS. (2016, November 19). Former army reservist charged in weapons theft from Worchester Armory. *CBS Boston.* Retrieved from http://boston.cbslocal.com/2015/11/19/worcester-armory-weapons-theft-fbi-arrest/

Chappell, B. (2016, January 12). In Mexico, tens of thousands of illegal guns come from the U.S. *The Two Way, National Public Radio.* Retrieved from March 25, 2017, from www.npr.org/sections/thetwo-way/2016/01/12/462781469/in-mexico-tens-of-thousands-of-illegal-guns-come-from-the-u-s

Coppolo, G. (2007). *Lost or stolen firearms.* OLR Research Report. 2007-R-0211. Retrieved from www.cga.ct.gov/2007/rpt/2007-R-0211.htm

District of Columbia v. Heller, 554 U.S. 570 (2008).

Fox News. (2017). *FBI sub-machine gun stolen from California agent's car.* Retrieved from www.foxnews.com/us/2017/01/21/fbi-sub-machine-gun-stolen-from-california-agents-car.html

Haynes v. US, 390 U.S. 85 (1968).

Hinezmann, D. (2004). Gangs run gun pipeline from Delta to Chicago. *Chicago Tribune.* Retrieved from www.chicagotribune.com/news/local/chi-040205guns-traced-graphic,0,4685518.graphic

Jacobs, J., & Potter, K. (1995). Keeping guns out of the "wrong" hands: The Brady Law and the limits of regulation. *The Journal of Criminal Law & Criminology, 86*(1), 93–120.

Joyner, C. (2007). Law cracks down on Chicago–Miss. Delta pipeline of crime. *USA Today.* Retrieved from www.usatoday.com/news/nation/2007-10-28-Missgangs_N.htm

Kirk, M. (2008). *Kirk, federal and local officials target illegal guns.* Retrieved from www.house.gov/apps/list/press/ill_kirk/Kirk_targets_illegal_guns.html

Kopel, D. (2013). Mexico's gun-control laws: A model for the United States? *Texas Review of Law & Politics,* 28–95.

Kraft, M. (2002, January). Firearms trafficking 101 or where do crime guns come from? *United States Attorney's Bulletin, 50*(1), 6–10.

KWCH TV 12. (2017). P4 firearms store in Wichita burglarized. *KWCH TV 12.* Retrieved from www.kwch.com/content/news/P4-Firearms-in-Wichita-burglarized-413510613.html

Langton, L. (2012). *Firearms stolen during household burglaries and other property crimes, 2005–2010* (NCJ 239236). Washington, DC: Bureau of Justice Statistics.

Law Center to Prevent Gun Violence. (2012). *Straw purchases policy summary.* Retrieved from http://smartgunlaws.org/straw-purchases-policy-summary/

Lovett, I., Healy, J., Schmidt, M., & Turkewitz, J. (2015, December 11). San Bernardino attackers' friend spoke of "sleeper cells" before rampage. *The New York Times.* Retrieved from www.nytimes.com/2015/12/12/us/enrique-marquez-san-bernardino-attacks.html?_r=0

McDonald v. City of Chicago, 561 U.S. 742 (2010).

New York Times. (1911, September 29). The Rossi pistol case. *The New York Times.* Retrieved from http://query.nytimes.com/mem/archivefree/pdf?res=9C07EED81531E233A2575AC2A96F9C946096D6CF

Office of the Inspector General. (2017). *A review of investigations of the Osorio and Barba firearms trafficking rings.* Washington, DC: United States Department of Justice, Office of the Inspector General. Retrieved from https://oig.justice.gov/reports/2017/o1701.pdf

Patterson, S., & Eakins, K. (1998). Congress and gun control. In J. Bruce & C. Wilcox (Eds.), *The changing politics of gun control.* Lanham, MD: Rowman & Littlefield Publishers, Inc.

Pearson, C., & Wilhelm, T. (2013, December 13). The pipeline: "A lot of people in Canada want guns." *The Windsor Star.* Retrieved from http://windsorstar.com/news/local-news/gunrunners-a-grim-gateway

Peele, T. (2016, June 26). Disarmed and dangerous: 944 lost guns. *The Mercury News.* Retrieved from http://extras.mercurynews.com/policeguns/

Pierce, G., Braga, A., & Wintemute, G. (2015, June). Impact of California's firearms sales laws and dealer regulations in illegal diversion of guns. *Injury Prevention, 21*(3), 179–184.

Printz v. United States, 521 U.S. 898 (1997).

Public Laws-CH. 850. (1938, June 30). *The Federal Firearms Act of 1938.* Washington, DC: GPO.

Serrano, R. (2008, August 10) Guns from U.S. equip drug cartels. *Los Angeles Times.* Retrieved from http://articles.latimes.com/2008/aug/10/nation/na-guns10

Sonzinsky v. United States, 300 U.S. 506 (1937).

Tarm, M. (2017, March 3). Railroad thefts and guns: A deadly mix in Chicago. *Chicago Tribune.* Retrieved from www.chicagotribune.com/news/ct-chicago-railroad-thefts-20170303-story.html

Wilhelm, T. (2009, April 25). Gun smuggling ring foiled. *The Windsor Star.* Retrieved from http://www2.canada.com/windsorstar/news/story.html?id=99dc04c8-856e-4420-9615-6e9e295662dd&p=1

Wilson, H. (2007). *Guns, gun control, and elections.* Lanham, MD: Rowman & Littlefield Publishers, Inc.

Witkin, G. (1997, June 9). Handgun stealing made real easy. *US News &World Report, 122*(22), 34–35.

Disclosure Statement:

This is to acknowledge that neither author has any financial interest or benefit that has arisen from the direct applications of their research.

Chapter 17

United We Stand

Collaborations to Combat Human Trafficking in Central Florida

Ketty Fernández, Madelyn Diaz, Jolene Vincent, Lin Huff-Corzine, Jay Corzine, and Tomas J. Lares

Introduction

It was 1999 in Immokalee, an area in the Southwest region of the state of Florida, when a young woman who had been kidnapped from her home in Guatemala was discovered. She had been forced to work in the tomato fields by day and cook, clean, and care for a couple's children by night while receiving no pay and also being sexually abused by the husband of the family. Ana Rodriguez, a victim advocate, became aware of her situation, and the case proceeded into the criminal justice system, citing slavery laws that dated back to the nineteenth century, the only applicable statutes available to prosecutors at the time. The result of this case, *US v. Tecum*, not only led to the husband being convicted under the dated slavery statutes and receiving a sentence of 33 months in prison, but the case was also a major turning point with legal and policy implications in 2000 to better address other similar situations. Following this case and others, there was a prompt increase in acknowledgment of and opposition to human trafficking in the United States (US) and internationally.

On the international level, the Protocol to Prevent, Suppress, and Punish Trafficking in Persons was passed by the United Nations to supplement that body's previously enacted Convention Against Transnational Organized Crime in 2000. In the US, the Trafficking Victims Protection Act (TVPA) (Public Law 106–386) was enacted as an amendment to the Violence Against Women Act in 2000 and subsequently renewed several times, most recently in 2013. The intent by supporters of both measures was to pass legislation that would enable a more focused and successful campaign against human trafficking operations.

Recently, Google's CEO, Sundar Pichai, announced the company's efforts to assist in combating human trafficking by aiding in the development of opportunities for collaborations across agencies and nations. They will award $1 billion in grants over five years to assist in combating human trafficking by the development of opportunities (Google, n.d.). An important precursor of these efforts was Google awarding the Polaris Project the Global Impact Award in 2013 to support their creation of a Global Safety Net for survivors of human trafficking. Through research, this award allows the Polaris Project to collaborate with several other international organizations to combat human trafficking on a large scale. As initial efforts to identify victims, develop relationships across various social service and governmental agencies, and locate areas that need resources, the Polaris Project created the National Human Trafficking Hotline and the BeFree Textline. Thus far, with assistance from Google, the Polaris Project has made significant improvements in international efforts by working to create human trafficking hotlines in Canada and Mexico. In addition to the nations directly bordering the US, the Polaris Project has connected with countries in Southeast Asia, Eastern Europe, and the Middle East to provide training on the hotlines and the use and sharing of data systems housing information from hotlines and even hosted a discussion between Thailand and Vietnam (Global Safety Net, 2018).

DOI: 10.4324/9781003047117-20

Collaborations among various organizations to aid in international efforts against human trafficking are still developing with some success that is likely to continue in the future. For example, the Polaris Project, the Freedom Fund, and the Global Fund to End Slavery created the Global Modern Slavery Directory, which allows for victims and at-risk populations to be connected and for the ability to have multiple agencies around the world working together. As of 2018, the Global Modern Slavery Directory contained information from thousands of organizations among more than 180 countries (Global Safety Net, 2018).

Arrests and Prosecutions of Human Traffickers

Thus far, there have been notable successes in the campaign to combat human trafficking across national boundaries. In the US, the level of public awareness of human trafficking has dramatically increased, leading to expansion and improvement of the training of persons in law enforcement, transportation, and other related fields (Farrell & Cronin, 2015). In addition, the recent shutdown of Backpages' personal ads section, which had become the primary avenue for marketing sex trafficking in the US, has been heralded as a significant success, but there are legitimate concerns that similar ads will now appear on other websites, including the dark web. In the US, the passage of TVPA and similar laws in each of the 50 states has not produced the expected increase in the volume of arrests and prosecutions for human trafficking violations (Farrell, Owens, & McDevitt, 2014; Spohn, 2014), suggesting that much more needs to be done to help reduce this complex issue. Underscoring the scarcity of human trafficking cases in the criminal justice system, a well-known and often-cited study is titled "New laws but few cases: Understanding the challenges to the investigation and prosecution of human trafficking cases" (Farrell et al., 2014).

The terminology of TVPA is very similar to most state statutes and provides insight into the legal difficulties of prosecuting cases of human trafficking in the US. The US Department of State, the US Department of Homeland Security, and Immigration and Customs Enforcement share the same definition of a "severe form in trafficking in persons" as described by the US Department of Homeland Security (2014) as:

> sex trafficking in which a commercial sex act is induced by force, fraud, or coercion, or in which the person induced to perform such act has not attained 18 years of age; or the recruitment, harboring, transportation, provision, or obtaining of a person for labor or services, through the use of force, fraud, or coercion for the purpose of subjection to involuntary servitude, peonage, debt bondage, or slavery.
>
> (p. 9)

The prosecution of perpetrators for trafficking persons under 18 years of age is straightforward in the US because minors are now defined as victims solely based on their age. However, for adults, proving the element of "force, fraud, or coercion" is difficult if there is not a survivor who is willing to participate as a witness in the criminal case (Cocchiarella, 2017; Nichols & Heil, 2015). Without a participating survivor, criminal charges against the trafficker are often dismissed or reduced to prostitution-related offenses with lesser penalties, such as pimping or pandering. The human trafficking survivor may be charged with an offense in some jurisdictions to provide the prosecution with leverage to ensure cooperation, but this is a form of re-victimization that may be counterproductive to securing witness cooperation.

The slow advancement in the prosecution of human traffickers also reflects the two major and sometimes competing goals in the anti–human trafficking movement. The first is the successful criminal prosecution of human traffickers and the dismantling of their organizations, often referred to as the "criminalization approach." This goal has been the primary focus of actors and agencies in the criminal justice system. The second is the transition of rescued victims into survivors and members of society with a moderate-to-high level of self-efficacy, often referred to as the "victim-centered" approach. This second goal is the primary focus of actors and agencies in the social service field and non-governmental organizations (NGOs). Proponents of these overlapping but not antithetical approaches have often disagreed about how to move forward with particular human trafficking cases.

The need for strong interagency collaboration in the human trafficking field to meet the goals of both the criminal justice system and the victim-centered services has been recognized for well over a decade (US Government Accountability Office (GAO), 2007). The umbrella organizational structure that has emerged in the US to achieve concerted cooperation is the human trafficking task force (HTTF). The original impetus for the development of HTTFs was federal funding from the Bureau of Justice Assistance (BJA), which began in 2004 and continues today (GAO, 2007). HTTFs typically coordinate the efforts of law enforcement organizations, social service agencies, and NGOs that operate in the same or an overlapping geographical area that varies from a single county to several spatially adjacent counties within the same US state. Representatives of the member agencies meet periodically to exchange information, plan training and other activities, and disseminate updates related to human trafficking at the local and state levels. Although a small number of HTTFs obtained federal dollars at their inception or for improving their services, most HTTFs rely on both private contributions and public funds from different levels of government.

There has been minimal research on the effectiveness of HTTFs, or the task force approach, for achieving a coordinated response to human trafficking. A study recently published by Huff-Corzine, Sacra, Corzine, and Rados (2017) found that Florida counties that were members of task forces had a higher number of state-level prosecutions for human trafficking offenses than counties that were not affiliated with a task force. It is unclear whether the cooperation among law enforcement and other organizations within a task force was primarily responsible for the higher level of activity by prosecutors; however, to our knowledge, no studies have examined the effect of task forces on the number of human trafficking victims recovered through law enforcement operations.

It is important to consider that not all HTTFs are created equal or have access to the same resources. Because of their geographical proximity and the authors' involvement in anti–human trafficking efforts, we are most familiar with the HTTFs active in the state of Florida. There were 14 HTTFs at the beginning of 2017; a subset of these task forces has been stable for a decade or more, while others have experienced periods of inactivity or reorganization or are defunct. This chapter focuses on one of the stable HTTFs, the Greater Orlando Human Trafficking Task Force (GOHTTF), which has been in continuous existence since 2007. During this period, ongoing collaborative relationships have been formed in Central Florida between law enforcement, social service agencies, and NGOs, including those in the faith-based community. The outcomes of the GOHTTF and its long-term collaborations may serve as a model for best practices within the US and also internationally, where efforts are underway to reduce the scope of human trafficking.

Scope and Prosecution of Human Trafficking

The estimates of the number of human trafficking victims in the US and worldwide vary widely and are generally considered unreliable (Bales & Soodalter, 2009; Zhang, 2009). Nevertheless, there is an agreement that the number of prosecutions for human trafficking is small compared to the victim estimates (Farrell et al., 2014; McDonald, 2014). The most widely known data source on human trafficking in the US is the annual number of victims identified through calls to the National Human Trafficking Hotline and texts to the BeFree Textline, both operated by the Polaris Project.

In 2017, Polaris Project sources reported 10,615 victims. Internationally, the number of estimated prosecutions for human trafficking was 9,460 in 2013, with 44,758 official victims (US Department of State, 2014). The consensus is that all such projections underestimate the true scope of the problem (Bales & Soodalter, 2009).

Although there has been some discussion of a perceived overemphasis on prosecutions in combating human trafficking (Fouladvand, 2018), most law enforcement officials, victim advocates, and policy-makers see this as an indispensable part of a systemic or systemwide approach to addressing modern-day slavery (Goltz, Potter, Cocchiarella, & Gibson, 2017). After all, the TVPA and the Palermo Protocol exist to enable the prosecution of persons who profit from the trafficking of human beings. But there is no denying that the low number of prosecutions for trafficking offenses has been a surprise and disappointment for advocates in the human trafficking field in the US.

Amy Farrell and her associates at Northeastern University in Boston have completed some of the most systematic research on human trafficking prosecutions (Farrell et al., 2014; Farrell & Cronin, 2015). Their work shows that many criminal offenses that could be charged as trafficking cases are instead taken to court as lesser charges, such as pimping and pandering. Additionally, adult trafficking victims have been found to be charged for prostitution offenses. Farrell et al. (2014) attribute this pattern to prosecutors' unfamiliarity with the new human trafficking statutes and the lack of a relevant body of prior case law. As noted earlier, another problem is the difficulty that a prosecutor has proving "force, fraud, or coercion," in trafficking cases with only adult victims. As will be discussed further later in this chapter, this can be a difficult legal hurdle in the absence of one or more cooperative victims who are willing to stay with the case as it winds its way through the criminal justice system, a process that is often slow and labyrinthine.

The Human Trafficking Victim

The survivors of sex trafficking have had their autonomy eroded, and their self-esteem and self-efficacy, including the ability to make decisions, are significantly compromised (Aboul-hosn, Koszalka, & Ortiz, 2017). Trafficked individuals may fear violence at the hands of their traffickers toward themselves and their family members. The trafficker controls the profits from forced sex, so victims do not have the finances to become self-supporting when they are rescued or escape their trafficker on their own. The dilemma of not knowing what decision to make can also be a potent force preventing attempted escapes from their slavery status. Compounding these psychological and financial issues is the trauma bond, also known as the Stockholm syndrome, that victims often experience with their trafficker (Aboul-hosn et al., 2017). Because of this bond, they may not even see themselves as victims. A likely scenario is one in which the trafficker develops a relationship with the victim, who may be experiencing difficulties at home or is in the foster care system, homeless, or a runaway. The vulnerability of the victim makes them an easy target for the trafficker to romance, and he then gradually moves them toward performing sex acts for money that primarily benefits the trafficker. The victim may question the appropriateness of the situation but remembers the better days shared with the trafficker and knows that the consequences of not performing as required may end in violence. A less likely scenario, but one that occurs with some regularity, involves kidnapping or a fast, romantic date that ends in the victim being drugged, raped, and beaten into compliance.

In the US and other nations, it is known that a significant number of sex trafficking victims are often fearful and bewildered by law enforcement officials. Although its adoption is uneven across the US and even within the state of Florida, a "victim-centered" approach to intervening on behalf of victims has been developing over the past several years. The key to this strategy is the collaboration of law enforcement, prosecutors, and social service providers from the beginning of a human trafficking investigation. The survivors often need medical care and basic necessities, including toiletries and cosmetics, legal assistance, and a safe house, immediately, suggesting that some aspects of interventions may be better handled by social services than law enforcement, but also the need for these agencies to work in collaboration.

This shift from defining adults engaged in sex acts for money as prostitutes—that is, criminals—to victims is a major change in the zeitgeist for stakeholders in the criminal justice system. Similarly, working closely with law enforcement is a new experience for many persons working in social services and the helping professions. As stated earlier, the development of an organizational structure to facilitate this new type of relationship is the primary goal of HTTFs. As Sergeant James McBride, founder of the HTTF in Clearwater, Florida, and a pioneer in human trafficking investigations, stated in an interview with one of the co-authors, "You have to provide help to the victims right away, not the next morning" (J. McBride, personal communication, 2015). The need to help victims on several fronts with urgency is imperative.

Serendipitously, the shift toward a victim-centered approach to combat sex trafficking in Central Florida has aided law enforcement and prosecution efforts to bring cases to a successful closure: that is, a conviction. Many trafficking victims do not trust law enforcement because of past encounters with the police, stories told by their traffickers, or the fear of deportation. In some communities, corrupt public officials may support trafficking organizations, either directly or indirectly. The injection of social services and NGOs at the earliest stage of a trafficking case provides some assurance to recovered victims that there are people who are willing to help them and agencies that are capable of supporting them. Some of the first services, such as shelter and food, reduce the need for victims to rely on their traffickers, who were previously the source of this assistance. In the Orlando area of Central Florida, services for victims are provided at the time of rescue. The Metropolitan Bureau of Investigation (MBI), an interagency task force specializing in middle-level organized crime, has joined with Florida Abolitionist (FA), an NGO. When feasible, an employee from FA accompanies law enforcement officers on raids of suspected trafficking operations. Once the scene is secure and law enforcement officials arrest the suspects, an FA employee accompanies the victims/survivors to a secure setting, such as a short-term shelter. Contacts with social service providers able to help the victim(s) will ensue the next day.

Navigating the criminal justice system in the US is stressful for witnesses in many cases, but even more so for trafficking survivors. MBI personnel includes two victim advocates, who work exclusively with trafficking survivors who are assisting the prosecution, and the State Attorney's Office for the Florida Ninth Judicial District, which has specialized attorneys that handle human trafficking cases. The connected responses from law enforcement and social services are summarized by Aboul-hosn et al. (2017):

> In central Florida, a collaborative effort has been developed between law enforcement agencies and non-governmental organizations who come together during prostitution stings. Once victims are identified by victim advocates and law enforcement officials, social services are immediately offered.

(p. 60)

Of course, the strategy for tackling human trafficking in Central Florida has developed over the last decade with great efforts from various groups. In the next section of this chapter,

Tomas J. Lares, the founder of FA, details some of the important steps that have occurred to implement the current collaborations.

The Emergence of Human Trafficking Organizations in Central Florida

Tomas J. Lares, founder and executive director of Florida Abolitionist (FA), advocates that services for survivors must be ready as soon as individuals are rescued from their life of slavery. This intervention is routinely tied to law enforcement beginning the rescue process as they escort the survivor to safety, typically during the immediate aftermath of a raid. Mr. Lares, who is also the co-founder and current chair of the GOHTTF, has made it his mission since 2007 to educate the public and be a source for survivors who need care from advocates and other available resources in Florida targeted to assist their immediate needs.

In a recent interview, Mr. Lares explained how he got involved in fighting human trafficking in the Central Florida region. A synopsis of his career before his leadership in human trafficking indicates the type of background and employment that equipped him with the skills necessary to be an excellent service provider to those in need and lead the efforts to establish FA and GOHTTF. Mr. Lares came to Central Florida to attend Southeastern University, where he also worked with Big Brothers/Big Sisters. After graduation, Mr. Lares began working at Circles of Care near Melbourne, Florida. There he worked with victims of incest and rape to offer high-quality health care focused on alcohol and drug abuse and related services. From there, Mr. Lares moved to a hospital setting, where he gained experience working with adults, the elderly, and children who had been Baker Acted. He left the hospital to start working in the faith-based part of the Yellow Umbrella, a nationally accredited family support and child abuse center in Brevard County, Florida. After his time at Yellow Umbrella, Tomas assisted in the development of Links of Hope, a family counseling and child safety center.

In 2004, he and Rita Atkins, the faith-based director of Links of Hope, wrote a grant to offer parenting classes in conjunction with the Division of Child and Families, which were generally court ordered. If the participants came early to the classes, they would also get help with résumé preparation and seeking employment. Due to the popularity of the program, they had about 20 centers in Brevard County offering these services, which were recognized by the Department of Labor as a model to use in other states. That honor earned them a trip to Washington, DC, in 2004, where they met Senator Sam Brownback of Kansas, who invited them to a meeting on human trafficking where he concluded, "I need to do something about this" (T. Lares, personal communication, 2018).

With assistance from the key stakeholders in Central Florida's anti-trafficking organizations, Florida's response to human trafficking developed rapidly in the following decade. Polaris (2014) ranks states based on their human trafficking efforts according to the presence of the following ten key human trafficking policies that are seen as essential for a comprehensive anti-trafficking legal framework:

- Sex and labor trafficking provisions
- Asset forfeiture and/or investigative tools
- Training requirement and/or human trafficking task force
- Posting of a human trafficking hotline phone number
- Safe harbor
- Protection for sex-trafficked minors
- Lower burden of proof for sex-trafficked minors
- Victim assistance

- Access to civil damages
- Vacating convictions for sex trafficking victims

These conditions were met, and FA has evolved into the leading human trafficking volunteer organization in the state, known for assisting survivors and offering resources.

Local anti-trafficking efforts in Florida benefit from high levels of support from state leaders, notably the previous attorney general, Pam Bondi, who helped bring together local, state, and national figures through an annual statewide council meeting on human trafficking. Through this conference, members of law enforcement, governmental leaders, trafficked survivors, educators, prosecutors, health-care professionals, and community leaders attend presentations that offer insight into tactics that identify, assist, and bring justice to trafficking survivors. Collaborative efforts encouraged by meetings with a wide array of professionals working together to combat this issue not only assist law enforcement officers and prosecutors but also educate members of the community about what they can do to help.

A multi-agency task force or working group has been the preferred structure in the state of Florida to ensure the most holistic approach in providing services to victims and increasing arrests of traffickers (Huff-Corzine et al., 2017). Florida's task forces are supported by federal funding or nonprofit organizations and include three types of agencies: law enforcement, social service agencies, and NGOs (Huff-Corzine et al., 2017). Given that the significant challenges of human trafficking cases involves the constant mobility of victims and traffickers, the cost of the investigation, and lack of known services available, adopting a multi-agency task force can help mediate these difficulties. With more agencies working together, each professional can use their expertise to lower the costs of investigation through sharing resources and support in order to work toward the common goal of combating human trafficking. Moreover, the use of multi-agency task forces tackles the problem of arresting traffickers whose activities cross jurisdictional boundaries. Most human trafficking cases in Central Florida begin with direct calls to the FA hotline or those routed from the Polaris Project, the National Center for Missing and Exploited Children, the National Human Trafficking Resource Center, community crime lines, or the Florida Department of Children and Families (DCF) Abuse Hotline. However, as law enforcement continues to become more educated about the likelihood of human trafficking occurring in their communities, future cases may increasingly be initiated by law enforcement officers (Mapp, Hornung, D'Almeida, & Juhnke, 2016).

Task forces are responsible for organizing meetings to discuss current practices and conduct training, as well as brainstorming for future operations. Ideally, representatives from each of the three entities will be present to learn how their organization can keep improving its primary responsibilities. Law enforcement officers are commonly regarded as the frontline and the most likely professional to come in contact with a human trafficking victim; thus, their focus is on arresting traffickers and recovering victims (De Baca & Tisi, 2002; Wilson, Walsh & Kleuber, 2006; Huff-Corzine et al., 2017). Law enforcement is critical in the fight against human trafficking; accordingly, continuing education for police officers is mandatory (Grubb & Bennett, 2012).

Service providers are essential for providing the immediate needs of victims, such as food, clothing, and medical care, especially to minor, or juvenile, victims. The Department of Children and Families (DCF) and the Department of Juvenile Justice (DJJ), two agencies serving children in Florida, consistently contact and respond to the commercial sexual exploitation of children. In Florida's extensive efforts to identify juvenile victims, access to the Florida Abuse Hotline is publicly available. DCF has confirmed 170 victims of commercial sexual exploitation from investigations sparked by calls to the hotline and have identified victims who have come in direct contact with DJJ (Office of Program Analysis and Government Accountability, 2015; Florida Department of Juvenile Justice and Department of Children and Families Data

Analysts, 2016). Juvenile victims identified through the DJJ were most often charged with misdemeanor battery, burglary, or petty theft, with a smaller percentage of minors involved in commercial sexual exploitation charged under a prostitution-related offense. Although, as of 2016, juveniles can no longer be arrested for prostitution-related offenses, given their age and lack of ability to give consent to this activity due to the passage of the Florida House Bill 545 (Carroll, Daly, Dudek, Stewart, & Phillip, 2016).

Given that fewer governmental organizations focus on trafficking victims over the age of 18, NGOs are responsible for assisting adult victims in receiving necessary services but can also aid juvenile victims as well if needed (Huff-Corzine et al., 2017). This sector of the task force gathers information on services throughout the state and manages agreements ensuring that the participating agency will provide support to all human trafficking victims. Assistance from NGOs includes short- and long-term housing, employment assistance, education (including English training for international victims), mental health care, and pro bono legal assistance.

Visions for the Future of GOHTTF

The current collaborative success of FA and GOHTTF achieved over the past decade has been significant, but there are plans to expand the efforts and programs within the state and outside its boundaries. According to Mr. Lares, the future holds several new directions for those working with the FA, which will expand beyond Florida as United Abolitionist (UA) when training in other states and/or the GOHTTF. There are three organizations now, with the addition of the Central Florida Alliance on Human Trafficking (CFAHT). GOHTTF has taken the lead in the founding of CFAHT, a coalition of 15 task forces whose area encompasses Central Florida. CFAHT meets quarterly at the Orlando Police Department and is charting its future course.

Within the state of Florida, FA will retain its original name, but operations by the organization in other areas of the US will be referred to as UA The reason for Florida keeping the FA affiliation is that they have been asked to train others in the US, and more donations are expected if the trainers are more appropriately known as UA. The benefits of donations will not be viewed as only assisting human trafficking efforts in Florida. Increased contributions will allow UA to maintain and expand its programs in an era when public funding is likely to decrease. With the name change to UA in 2018, Mr. Lares envisions investigating the corporate model to benefit FA by creating a for-profit social enterprise entity, much like when a church starts child care that helps fund their ministry. The plan is to expand the training currently done in Florida by forming a national-level training center.

As an example, with a national-level training center, companies such as Chick-Fil-A, a fast-food restaurant, that are asking FA/UA for training, can be more appropriately served. They have asked UA to pilot training on human trafficking in a few restaurants so their employees can identify potential traffickers. Parents think that because it is a "Christian" restaurant and has Christian music playing, their children are safe at these restaurants. On the contrary, predators, sex offenders, and traffickers have targeted some Chick-Fil-A restaurants. Thus, they want to train the staff on spotting the red flags and how to report suspicious activity to law enforcement. Training for that organization would be provided under the UA name because the company is based in Atlanta, Georgia.

Other organizations, such as hotels and airlines, that are requesting training could also be served. These corporations normally have training money, so Mr. Lares and other UA leaders believe training programs can provide an important revenue source, especially with grant money being scarce. Corporations have a social responsibility to those they serve, so when the UA Training Center is in place, it will benefit the corporations, and UA will be able to charge an annual fee that, by law, has to go back to the nonprofit. In this way, the nonprofits are funded. The UA Training Center is expected to be viable, in part, because there will be programs designed specifically for various groups: first responders, judges, prosecutors, defense attorneys, and so on. The relationship between FA/UA and the University of Central Florida, for example, is critical because research is necessary to show how this model can become a best practice for the nation (Corzine et al., 2017).

Implications for Other Jurisdictions

Even with the success of the collaborative model continuing to develop in Central Florida, other states aiming to develop a similar task force model may have varied results. Within the US, the success of other task forces (HTTFs) has not been consistent, and there is some evidence that without a commitment from law enforcement, progress in reducing sex trafficking will not be impressive. Adopting a victim-centered approach requires a partial ideological shift by law enforcement: specifically, the long-standing view that prostitution-related offenses are vice crimes, and persons selling sex for money are criminals. The federal government advocates a victim-centered approach, but its acceptance at the state and, especially, local levels is not universal. Part of the difficulty is the fragmented nature of law enforcement within the US, where there are approximately 15,000 federal, state, and local agencies with law enforcement responsibilities. Once law enforcement collectively commits to a victim-centered approach, its implementation will be easier to accomplish, as in nations with a single national police agency.

As discussed earlier, the problem of the small number of prosecutions of human trafficking cases is not limited to the US, and considering the differences between areas within the US suggests that the underlying reasons will vary greatly between nations. Researchers and practitioners in the US point to the requirement to show "force, fraud, or coercion" as difficult for prosecutors to overcome. A review of nations' legal definitions of human trafficking is beyond the scope of this chapter, but there have been recent criticisms of legislation in some nations, notably Australia (Davy, 2017), and the legal framework of the European Union (Fouladvand, 2018). These critiques center on the argument that their interventions emphasize a criminalization model with little attention given to the needs of the victims. The primary advantage of the victim-centered approach is that it aims to strike a balance between a legal response to modern-day slavery focused on arresting traffickers and assisting victims in re-entering society.

The advantages of the victim-centered approach for law enforcement are not restricted to securing an increased number of cooperative witnesses for successful prosecutions. If embedded in a task force model, law enforcement establishes contacts with a network of organizations from the social services field and with NGOs. Collectively, the agencies can leverage their respective resources to combat human trafficking. A recent study by Heiss and Kelley (2017) suggests this is a pressing need. Their survey of 500 anti-trafficking organizations in 133 nations reports a high level of collaboration between NGOs but a much lower level of contacts between NGOs and governmental organizations. In the US, Jones and Lutze (2016) found a low level of collaboration among agencies in the anti-human trafficking field in Michigan. What we need is collaboration and cooperation among NGOs, social services, law enforcement, and governmental agencies at the local, regional, state, and international levels if we are to see a future reduction in human trafficking worldwide.

Discussion Questions

1. Describe the difference between the criminalization approach and victim-centered approach of the anti-human trafficking movement.

2. In this chapter, we discussed a number of challenges that prosecutors face when attempting to put together a case that will lead to the prosecution of a suspected human trafficking offender. What are some of these prosecutorial challenges?
3. Trace the development of the present legal system for addressing the problem of human trafficking in the United States. How has it been influenced by international efforts?
4. Why do you think that the number of arrests and prosecutions for human trafficking in the US has not met the expectations of human trafficking advocates? What additional steps could be taken to increase arrests and prosecutions?
5. Describe the characteristics of a human trafficking task force (HTTF).
6. What organization is primarily responsible for estimates of the number of human trafficking victims in the US? How do they calculate their estimates? How accurate are the estimates?
7. What are barriers that impede cooperation between law enforcement and human trafficking victims? Is there a way to resolve them?
8. What types of collaboration between law enforcement, nonprofit organizations, and social services have developed in Central Florida?
9. Discuss the goals of United Abolitionist and how have they built on prior efforts in Central Florida by Florida Abolitionist.
10. What advantages do the authors see in adopting a victim-centered approach to human trafficking in the US? Do you agree with their assessment? Why or why not?

References

Aboul-hosn, S., Koszalka, S., & Ortiz, Y. (2017). Social services role and fostering victims of human trafficking. In J. W. Goltz, R. H. Potter, J. A. Cocchiarella, & M. T. Gibson (Eds.), *Human trafficking: A systemwide public safety and community approach* (pp. 59–97). St. Paul, MN: West Academic Publishing.

Bales, K., & Soodalter, R. (2009). *The slave next door*. Berkeley, CA: University of California Press.

Carroll, M., Daly, C., Dudek, E., Stewart, P., & Phillip, C. (2016). *Human trafficking response in Florida*. 2016 Report to the Council.

Cocchiarella, J. A. (2017). Prosecution of human trafficking. In J. W. Goltz, R. H. Potter, J. A. Cocchiarella, & M. T. Gisson (Eds.), *Human trafficking: A systemwide public safety and community approach* (pp. 115–154). St. Paul, MN: West Academic Publishing.

Corzine, J., Huff-Corzine, L., Strohacker, E., Vincent, J., Francis, B., & Sacra, S. A. (2017). The dark side of the Sunshine State: Past and future policies to identify and resist human trafficking. In R. H. Potter, J. W. Goltz, & M. T. Gibson (Eds.), *Human trafficking: A system wide public safety and community approach* (pp. 243–268). St. Paul, MN: West Academic Publishing.

Davy, D. (2017). Justice for victims of human trafficking in Australia? Issues associated with Australia's criminal justice response to trafficking in persons. *Contemporary Justice Review, 20*(1), 115–131.

De Baca, L., & Tisi, A. (2002). Working together to stop modern-day slavery. *Police Chief, 69*(8), 78–80.

Farrell, A., & Cronin, S. (2015). Policing prostitution in an era of human trafficking enforcement. *Crime, Law, and Social Change, 64*, 211–228.

Farrell, A., Owens, C., & McDevitt, J. (2014). New laws but few cases: Understanding the challenges to the investigation and prosecution of human trafficking cases. *Crime, Law, and Social Change, 61*(2), 139–168.

Florida Department of Juvenile Justice and Department of Children and Families' Data Analysts. (2016). Internal communication.

Fouladvand, S. (2018). Decentering the prosecution-oriented approach: Tackling both supply and demand in the struggle against human trafficking. *International Journal of Crime, Law and Justice, 52*, 129–143.

Global Safety Net. (2018). Retrieved from https://polarisproject.org/initiatives/global-safety-net

Goltz, J. W., Potter, R. H., Cocchiarella, J. A., & Gibson, M. T. (Eds.). (2017). *Human trafficking: A systemwide public safety and community approach*. St. Paul, MN: West Academic Publishing.

Google. (n.d.). Our $1 billion commitment to create more opportunity for everyone. Retrieved from www.google.org/billion-commitment-to-create-more-opportunity/

Grubb, D., & Bennett, K. (2012). The readiness of local law enforcement to engage in U.S. anti-trafficking efforts: An assessment of human trafficking training and awareness of local, county, and state law enforcement in the State of Georgia. *Police Practice and Research*, *13*(6), 487–500.

Heiss, A., & Kelley, J. G. (2017). From the trenches: A global survey of anti-TIP NGOs and their views of U.S. efforts. *Journal of Human Trafficking*, *3*(3), 231–254. Retrieved from https://doi.org/10.1080/23322705.2016.1199241

Huff-Corzine, L., Sacra, S. A., Corzine, J., & Rados, R. (2017). Florida's task force approach to combat human trafficking: An analysis of county-level data. *Police Practice and Research*, *18*(3), 245–258.

Jones, T. R., & Lutze, F. E. (2016). Anti-human trafficking interagency collaboration in the State of Michigan: An exploratory study. *Journal of Human Trafficking*, *2*(2), 156–174.

Mapp, S., Hornung, E., D'Almeida, M., & Juhnke, J. (2016). Local law enforcement officers' knowledge of human trafficking: Ability to define, identify, and assist. *Journal of Human Trafficking*, *2*(4), 329–342.

McDonald, W. F. (2014). Explaining the under-performance of the anti-human-trafficking campaign: Experience from the United States and Europe. *Crime, Law, and Social Change*, *61*(2), 125–138.

Nichols, A. J., & Heil, E. C. (2015). Challenges to identifying and prosecuting sex trafficking cases in the Midwest United States. *Feminist Criminology*, *10*(1), 7–35.

Office of Program Analysis and Governmental Accountability. (2015, June). *State and local agencies are in initial stages of addressing child victims of sexual exploitation*, No. 15–6. Report.

Polaris Project. (2014). *A look back: Building a human trafficking legal framework*. Retrieved from www.polaris-project. org/storage/2014SRM-capstone-report.pdf

Spohn, C. (2014). The non-prosecution of human trafficking cases: An illustration of the challenges of implementing legal reforms. *Crime, Law, and Social Change*, *61*(2), 169–178.

US Department of Homeland Security. (2014). *Immigration and customs enforcement*. Retrieved from www.ice.gov/

US Department of State. (2014b). *Trafficking in persons report: Global law enforcement Data*. Retrieved from https://2009-2017.state.gov/documents/organization/226844.pdf

US Government Accountability Office (GAO). (2007). *Human trafficking: A strategic framework could help enhance the interagency collaboration needed to effectively combat trafficking crimes*. Washington, DC: Government Printing Office.

Wilson, D., Walsh, W., & Kleuber, S. (2006). Trafficking in human beings: Training and services among U.S. law enforcement agencies. *Police Practice and Research*, *7*(2), 149–160.

Zhang, S. X. (2009). Beyond the 'Natasha' story—A review and critique of current research on sex trafficking. *Global Crime*, *10*(3), 178–195.

Chapter 18

Are Attacks Against Abortion Providers Acts of Domestic Terrorism?

A Three-Box Operational Sub-Theory of Merton's Anomie

Gregg W. Etter Sr. and Hannah Collison (nee Socha)

Author Note

An earlier version of this chapter was presented at the American Society of Criminology meeting in San Francisco, California, in November 2010.

Introduction

The abortion issue and the violence associated with it continue to be brought into national focus by attacks on abortion providers and abortion facilities in the United States. The 2009 murder of abortion provider George Tiller in Wichita, Kansas, has once again brought this issue into the limelight. Abortion is an emotional issue with political, religious, and feminist implications. Law enforcement officers are tasked with enforcing the law, maintaining the peace, and attempting to ensure the safety of all involved parties. Since the 1973 US Supreme Court decision in *Roe v. Wade* (410 U.S. 113, 1973) that allowed legal abortions in the United States, there has been much controversy about the legality and morality of abortion. Many of the arguments are political. Efforts to control or limit abortion at the ballot box have met with mixed success when reviewed by the courts. Many of the arguments are religious. Some of the actions taken by the protesters have been violent and illegal.

Although views on abortion are controversial, the fact is it is a legal activity in the United States. Opponents of abortion have reacted in a wide variety of ways including legislation, protests, and violence. The manner in which many abortion opponents have reacted is perfectly legal; other reactions are not, and violence has resulted. The issue has caused many strange alliances to form between legitimate religious groups and extremist groups such as the Army of God. This chapter does not seek to answer questions about the morality or legality of abortion in the United States. Nor does it make the argument that peaceful protesters cannot exercise their constitutional rights of protest and petition of redress to their government.

This chapter examines illegal attacks on abortion providers and the law enforcement response to them. The number and types of attacks are examined using a database provided by the National Abortion Federation. The assassinations of several abortion providers are explored for associations between the murders and extremist groups. The methods of the three-box theory will be utilized to look at the 2009 case of Wichita, Kansas, abortion provider George Tiller. The "necessity defense" being used by some of the accused killers is examined and discussed. In investigating a crime, law enforcement searches for motive (anti–abortion views), method (three-box theory), and opportunity (the individual attacks against abortion providers). This chapter attempts to compare these attacks, FBI definitions of terrorism, and

DOI: 10.4324/9781003047117-21

anti–abortion political violence using the methods of the three-box theory to determine whether attacks on abortion providers should be considered acts of domestic terrorism.

Merton, Strain, and Anomie

In his studies of anti-social behavior, Merton (1938) described a theory that he called anomie. In this theory, those individuals who could achieve power or success using legitimate means usually did so. He also observed that if an individual could not achieve success through legitimate means, they would often turn to the usage of illegitimate means to achieve success. However, Merton (1938) noted that those individuals who could not achieve success using either legitimate or illegitimate means often attempted to adapt to compensate for the failure to achieve their cultural goals by using one of five methods: conformity, innovation, ritualism, retreatism, or rebellion (p. 676). In observing the adaptation of rebellion, Merton (1968) later found:

> It is the conflict between culturally accepted values and socially structured difficulties in living up to these values which exerts pressure towards deviant behavior and disruption of the normative system. This outcome of anomie, however, may be only a prelude to the development of new norms, and it is this response which we have described as "rebellion" in the typology of adaptation. When rebellion is confined to relatively small and relatively powerless elements in a community, it provides a potential for the formation of subgroups, alienated from the rest of the community but unified within themselves.
>
> (p. 245)

In their reexamination of Merton's anomie theories, Cloward and Ohlin (1960) found that those individuals who experienced what they called a "double failure" and were unable to achieve their goals by either legitimate or illegitimate means often would turn to violence in their rebellion to achieve their goals (pp. 182–184).

In his examination of anomie, Menard (1995) observed:

> [O]ne element in the test of anomie theory, then, should be a test of whether there appears to be a universally prescribed success goal. Although the goal need not be universally accepted, universal or near universal acceptance would strengthen the argument for the existence of a universal prescription for success that might lead to anomie at the social-structural level.
>
> (p. 137)

Definition of Terrorism

As with most controversial issues, one person's terrorist is another person's freedom fighter. Wilson and Lynxwiler (1988) observed:

> The pro-choice movement has defined violence against abortion clinics and other activities directed against patients and staff of abortion facilities as terrorism. While the Federal Bureau of Investigation (FBI) has maintained that these actions are not terrorism.
>
> (p. 263)

To focus the argument to the question posed by the study, the authors elected to use the Federal Bureau of Investigation's definition of terrorism. Riley and Hoffman (1995) observed that the Federal Bureau of Investigation defined terrorism as the unlawful use of force or violence against persons or property to intimidate or coerce a government, the civilian population, or any segment thereof in furtherance of political or social objectives.

The Nature of Extremists and Extremism

Extremist individuals feel that their world is falling apart—they are looking for a place to stand. Most extremists are upset about or obsessed with one issue (abortion, race, anti-gay, etc.) and are willing to do literally anything for the "cause" or to do anything against those who do not believe the same way that they do. Lipset and Rabb (1978) called extremism "the politics of despair."

Many extremists adhere to fringe religious or anti-religious beliefs. Conspiracy theories are integral to extremist folklore and beliefs. Distrust of the establishment is also inherent (distrust of business on the left, distrust of government on the right). Alternate views of history, politics, or religion often provide a theoretical basis for extremist beliefs. However, in the anti-abortion movement, many are members of "mainline" Christian religions.

Extremist group members are often pressured into acceptance of "group norms" or ideas by their leaders. There is a perception that there can be no affective address of grievances through normal legitimate channels. Violence is often seen as an effective means of affecting social change. It is this last perception that has caused vandalism, bombings, and killings across the United States against those who the extremists view as the "enemy" of their movement. In this context, the targets of violence conducted by extremists or extremist groups are often symbolic. The vandalism, destruction, or killing of the target not only punishes the target for engaging in conduct that is considered offensive to the group; it also brings publicity to the extremist group. (They often claim responsibility for the violent act.) The violence acts as a terroristic warning to others to conform to the ideas of the extremist group or face violent actions by the extremist group against them. Thus, fear becomes a controlling factor used by the extremist group to dissuade others from committing or continuing actions objected to by the extremist group.

The Three-Box Operational Sub-Theory of Extremist Groups

In 1927, Andrew Kehoe bombed a school in Bath, Michigan, to protest taxes. Over a period of several years, Kehoe had attempted to use legitimate means to achieve his goals through elections and court actions, and he finally resorted to illegitimate means in a suicide bombing to protest school taxes. As a result of this, many extremist groups in the United States have adopted a three-box operational sub-theory as a method to deal with perceived problems: the ballot box, the jury box, and the cartridge box are all seen as solutions. As Merton (1968) observed:

> When the institutional system is regarded as the barrier to the satisfaction of legitimized goals, the stage is set for rebellion as an adaptive response. To pass into organized political action, allegiance must not only be withdrawn from the prevailing social structure but must be transferred to new groups possessed of the new myth.
>
> (p. 210)

The way that this sub-theory works is that the group attempts to champion their issue at the ballot box, either by electing politicians who are sympathetic to their cause or through voter referendums that mandate that government act in the desired way or prohibit the action that the group does not want to occur.

If the ballot box fails, the next step is the jury box. The group attempts to either obtain their way or block the opposition through actions in the court system. This may take the form of civil lawsuits or criminal prosecutions. The criminal prosecutions may be from indictments obtained from grand juries raised by citizen's petitions, which is allowed in some states, such as Kansas. (KSA 22–3301, 2005), or from citizen complaints against the group's perceived enemies to the local authorities. In either case, a specific violation of an existing law or statute must be cited in the complaint. The interpretation of what constitutes a violation in these cases may be somewhat vague, and therefore, these types of prosecutions are seldom successful in the long run. Nice (1988) observed:

> When people are receiving what they want from public officials, such as a state call for banning abortion, resorting to violence is likely to seem unnecessary and to risk antagonizing the officials as well.

(p. 180)

If the jury box fails and the usage of legitimate means is exhausted, the cartridge box remains. This is either actual or threatened armed criminal action against the group's perceived foes. Arson, assaults, bombings, shootings, and vandalism are common tactics. The group attempts to obtain the desired results by fear or terror that they cannot obtain by legitimate means. As a last resort, some of these groups even advocate armed revolution against the existing government so their ideas can dominate society.

The Ballot Box: Prior to Roe v. Wade

The anti-abortion position prior to *Roe v. Wade* was well represented in who was sent to the state legislatures and the anti-abortion laws that they passed. Prior to *Roe v. Wade*, most state legislatures had adopted laws that either severely restricted abortion or banned it entirely. However, the winds of political change were blowing during the 1960s, and the state of Colorado was one of the first states to ease its abortion laws, making abortions more accessible in 1967 (Hull & Hoffer, 2001). Referenda to legalize abortion on demand were tried in two states (North Dakota and Michigan) during the 1972 elections. Both propositions were soundly defeated by the voters in those states (McAdam, 2011).

The Ballot Box: After Roe v. Wade

The ruling of the Supreme Court in *Roe v. Wade* was a game changer for anti-abortion opponents. Abortion could no longer be completely banned. This left anti-abortion forces two options: protest abortion and the ruling of the Supreme Court or attempt to limit the effects of the ruling by severely limiting the availability of abortion by state statute or administrative regulation. The anti-abortion forces did both.

Hospitals with a religious affiliation were often directed by their religious board of directors not to perform abortions on their premises. This often left abortions to be performed in health-care clinics. The clinics providing such services were picketed. Protests were organized by both religious groups and other opponents. Of course, these legitimate protests were protected by the First Amendment of the United States Constitution and were a perfectly legal expression of political and religious beliefs in their opposition to abortion.

The second area was the national and state political arenas. The abortion issue became a sort of litmus test for those aspiring to run for political office in many states. Congress and many state legislatures attempted to pass restrictions on who could receive abortion services, when, and how. These restrictions were vigorously fought in the legislatures by the pro-choice forces. Political and religious lobbying efforts were intense on both sides of the issue. If the pro-choice forces failed in the legislatures, then the battle began anew in the courts. This was especially true in Kansas. Again, these efforts were legitimate, protected expressions of political or religious beliefs to elected officials and, as such, were fully protected under the First Amendment of the United States Constitution (Hull & Hoffer, 2001).

Extremist Group: The Army of God

The Army of God is a Christian anti-abortion group that advocates violent action against abortionists that was founded around 1982. The AOG is believed to have around 30 active members (Jefferis, 2011). However, many other anti-abortion radicals have claimed to be AOG affiliates or sympathizers. The AOG produced a manual on how to attack abortion providers (now in its third edition). The AOG is active in the United States and Canada. The followers of AOG believe in a leaderless resistance. Several followers of AOG have been involved in attacks on abortion providers. AOG has claimed credit for bombings and shootings of abortion providers.

The AOG has threatened to carry out an "embryonic jihad" against abortion providers.

AOG member Reverend Michael Bray has been called the "chaplain" of the group. Bray authored a book titled *A Time to Kill*, which cited biblical scripture as a justification for violence against abortion doctors (Bray, 1994). A link to Bray is on AOG's website. In 1985, Bray was convicted of conspiracy and possession of an unregistered explosive device in a series of bombings of abortion facilities and an ACLU office in the Washington, DC, and Maryland areas, which the Army of God claimed credit for. He served a prison sentence resulting from that conviction from 1985 to 1989 (Zalman, 2011).

The Army of God maintains a website, as do many extremist groups. The website is hosted by Reverend Donald Spitz and lists an address in Chesapeake, Virginia. That website touts that the killing of Dr. George Tiller was justifiable homicide and shows a picture of Tiller's body being wheeled out of the crime scene on a gurney next to an artist's depiction of a fiery hell. The website praises Scott Roeder and Paul Hill as being "heroes" of the anti-abortion movement. Links are given to pages for Eric Rudolph and Shelley Shannon as well.

The AOG website lists individuals they call "Prisoners of Christ." These are people who have been convicted of murder, arson, and bombings against abortion providers. This section of their website solicits material and moral support for those incarcerated. Speaking about one inmate, Stephen Jordi (who was convicted of plotting to bomb abortion clinics and is currently in federal custody), the AOG website warns members:

> Stephen's own brother and his church sold him out to the authorities. Another example not to tell ANYONE; before, during or after, if you are planning to act. Your family, pro-lifers, and your church "friends" will sell you out in a heartbeat, thinking they are doing God's will.
>
> (AOG, 2011)

The Cartridge Box: The Attempted Shooting of Justice Blackmun (1985)

Justice Harry A. Blackmun is generally acknowledged as the author of the *Roe v. Wade* (1973) Supreme Court decision that made abortion legal in the United States. As a result, he was often the subject of threats to his person. On February 29, 1985, an unknown person fired a 9mm bullet through the third-story window of his apartment, which was in a 12-story high rise in Arlington, Virginia. The justice was not injured, although his wife was hit by flying glass. Although the FBI recovered the bullet, no arrests were ever made, and some law enforcement officials speculated that the incident "might" have occurred from a random shot. However, the justice was unconvinced (Yarbrough, 2007; Franklin, 1985).

The Cartridge Box: Michael F. Griffin and the Murder of David Gunn

On March 10, 1993, Michael F. Griffin shot and killed Dr. David Gunn at a Pensacola, Florida, abortion clinic (Pensacola Women's Medical Services). Prior to the shooting, Griffin had confronted Dr. Gunn on March 5 and asked him if he planned to kill children next week (Risen & Thomas, 1998). Griffin claimed that God had motivated him to kill the abortion doctor to prevent him from killing any more unborn children. During his trial, Griffin's attorneys argued that he had been unduly influenced by the urgings of anti-abortion activist and former Ku Klux Klan member John Burt and brainwashed into thinking that killing Dr. Gunn was the right thing to do. Griffin was sentenced to life imprisonment for his crime. Among those attending the trial of Michael Griffin was Paul J. Hill (Singular, 2011; Risen & Thomas, 1998). Griffin is listed as a "Prisoner of Christ" on the Army of God's website (AOG, 2011).

The Situation in Wichita, Kansas

Prior to *Roe v. Wade*, Kansas was one of the first states to legalize abortion in 1969 (Risen & Thomas, 1998). After *Roe v. Wade*, Kansas was one of the few states that permitted late-term abortions. The unintended result of this was a type of medial tourism that saw patients seeking this type of medical service coming to Kansas, as well as people who opposed the offering of this type of medical service coming to Kansas to protest. According to Lefler (2009), in 2008 (the year before the assassination of George Tiller), Kansas Department of Health and Environment (KDHE) figures show that 10,642 abortions were performed in the state of Kansas. Of these abortions, 5,131 were performed on pregnant women who were from out of state and had come to Kansas for the procedure. Many these abortions were performed in Wichita.

Dr. George Tiller, M.D., was a respected medical doctor in Wichita, Kansas. He ran Women's Health Care Services, a clinic located on East Kellogg that provided abortion services. Therefore, he was an abortionist by most definitions of the term. His father was also a physician and had provided abortion services in Wichita prior to the procedure being legal in Kansas (Singular, 2011: Gruver, 2009). Tiller's clinic was the scene of frequent anti-abortion protests, beginning about 1975. Threats to Dr. Tiller's family, his staff, and his personal safety became commonplace. Tiller was constantly taunted with chants of "Tiller, Tiller, baby killer" by protesters. Protesters drove by the clinic with graphic images of aborted fetuses on the sides of panel trucks as they slowly circled the block around the clinic. Tiller practiced with several other physicians who performed abortion procedures at the clinic. The fact that late-term abortions were performed at the clinic was perhaps the most controversial aspect of the operations that took place there (Singular, 2011).

The Cartridge Box: The Bombing of Tiller's Clinic (1986)

On June 9, 1986, a pipe bomb was planted at the front of the Women's Health Care Services clinic. The explosion damaged the building and contents causing extensive damage (estimated at $70,000 to $100,000), but no one was injured. An extensive investigation was conducted by the Bureau of Alcohol, Tobacco, and Firearms and the Wichita Police Department but resulted in no arrests. As a result of the bombing, Tiller installed gates and put up fences around the clinic. Floodlights were installed, and metal detectors were added. Bulletproof glass was placed in many of the windows of the clinic. Armed guards were hired to protect staff and patients while at the clinic (Singular, 2011).

The Summer of Mercy (1991)

Beginning on July 15 in the summer of 1991, and for the next 45 days, thousands of protesters from both sides of the argument came to Wichita and held protests in front of abortion clinics in the "Summer of Mercy." Many of the protesters were from Operation Rescue, an anti-abortion group that had begun in 1988 under their leader, Randall Terry, in Binghamton, New York. Operation Rescue's tactics included civil disobedience during their protests at abortion clinics and at the 1988 Democratic Convention. Arrests of Operation Rescue members by law enforcement authorities were frequent. Tiller shut down the WHCS clinic for a week to allow the protests to run their course. But when the clinic reopened, the protests became more and more confrontational. Over 2,600 arrests were made by WPD and United States Marshals enforcing court orders. Kansas governor Joan Finney traveled to Wichita and made statements that appeared to back the anti-abortion protestors. The orders of US Federal Judge Patrick F. Kelly that sent US Marshals to keep the abortion clinics open were appealed in an amicus brief by the office of then–US Attorney General Richard Thornburgh and the United States Department of Justice. The Tenth US Circuit Court of Appeals overturned Kelly's injunction against the protestors. Judge Kelly soon began to receive death threats and was physically attacked by an anti-abortion protestor (Singular, 2011; Risen & Thomas, 1998). Despite much threatening rhetoric on both sides, most of the arrestees were given very lenient treatment by the local judiciary in both district and federal courts.

The Cartridge Box: The Shooting of George Tiller (1993)

On August 19, 1993, Dr. George Tiller was shot through both arms by Rachelle "Shelley" Shannon. Shannon shot Tiller with a .32 caliber handgun while he was driving his vehicle out of the WHCS clinic parking lot. Risen (1994) stated that Shannon admitted shooting Tiller in an article in the *Los Angeles Times*. Within hours of the shooting, Shannon was arrested, had confessed to police, and had written a jailhouse letter to her daughter detailing her crime. As she was led away by police in the early morning hours, she turned to the waiting media and asked, on camera, "Did I get him?" She added to a police officer, "If ever there was a justifiable homicide, this was it."

Shannon was convicted of this crime in 1994. An Army of God manual had been found by law enforcement authorities buried in the backyard of her home in Oregon. Some sources say that she was one of the editors of the manual. She was also convicted of being involved in arson attacks on abortion clinics in California, Nevada, and Oregon (Thomas, Rodriguez, & Finger, 2009). Reaction to her crime was mixed. Many cheered her efforts, while many anti-abortion leaders attempted to distance themselves from them. Among those leaders was Paul Hill. Risen (1994) noted:

> Even those who openly support anti-abortion violence stress that they have had no involvement in any of it. "Violence is not my calling; I use the weapon of the spirit and pray for people like Shelley Shannon," said Paul Hill, founder of Defensive Action, a group that endorses anti-abortion violence.

Scott Roeder came to visit Shannon while she was in custody in Topeka, Kansas (Thomas, 2009). Singular cites Shannon's shooting of Tiller as an inspiration for the Clinton administration to begin to investigate anti-abortion organizations for evidence of conspiracy to murder abortion providers. As a result of this investigation, the Clinton administration introduced the Freedom of Access to Clinic Entrances Act of 1994, or FACE, and it was passed by Congress in 1994 (FACE, 1994). Among those attending Shannon's trial was Paul J. Hill (Singular, 2011). While incarcerated, Shannon signed the Army of God's statement in support of the actions of Paul Jennings Hill. Shannon is still listed as a link on the Army of God's home page and is considered a hero by the group. AOG categorizes her as a "Prisoner of Christ" (AOG, 2011).

Freedom of Access to Clinic Entrances Act of 1994 (FACE, 18 U.S.C. 248)

The Freedom of Access to Clinic Entrances Act of 1994 was passed by Congress in response to anti-abortion protesters' tactics of physically blocking the entrances to abortion clinics, thus preventing patients from entering. (These tactics were known as "rescues.") It was signed into law in 1994. Under the provisions of the FACE Act, or 18 U.S.C. 248, prohibited activities are described as follows:

whoever—

(1) by force or threat of force or by physical obstruction, intentionally injures, intimidates, or interferes with or attempts to injure, intimidate, or interfere with any person because that person is or has been, or to intimidate such person or any other person or any class of persons from, obtaining or providing reproductive health services.

(2) by force or threat of force or by physical obstruction, intentionally injures, intimidates, or interferes with or attempts to injure, intimidate, or interfere with any person lawfully exercising or seeking to exercise the First Amendment right of religious freedom at a place of religious worship; or

(3) intentionally damages or destroys the property of a facility, or attempts to do so, because such facility provides reproductive health services, or intentionally damages or destroys the property of a place of religious worship.

(FACE, 1994)

First-time offenders can receive fines of $100,000 and jail sentences of up to one year.

The FACE Act, which directs that US Marshals will enforce access to clinics, had a sudden dampening effect on the number of blockades and the number of arrests at blockades. Anti-abortion protestors seem to change tactics and engaged in hate letters, harassing phone calls, bomb threats, picketing, etc. Federal prosecutors also changed tactics, and the RICO Act began to be applied to anti-abortion groups. Federal court rulings in 2003 limited this.

Cartridge Box: Paul J. Hill (1994)

On July 29, 1994, a former Presbyterian minister named Paul J. Hill assassinated an abortion physician (Dr. John Britton) and his bodyguard (James Barrett) outside an abortion clinic, the Ladies Clinic in Pensacola, Florida. In the shotgun attack, he also wounded Britton's wife. After shooting the individuals he had targeted, Hill laid down his weapon and calmly waited

Attacks Against Abortion Providers 261

to be arrested. Hill had been defrocked and excommunicated by the church in 1993 for his extremist anti-abortion views. Hill believed that violence was justified in preventing abortions (Kennedy, 1994). He was an anti-abortion activist with Army of God connections.

Hill was the first person tried in federal court under the FACE ACT, and unsuccessfully attempted to use the necessity defense. He was convicted and given two life sentences.

Hill was then tried in Florida state court for murder. He was convicted and given a death sentence. The judge in the state trial and several other Florida officials received threatening mail with envelopes containing live bullets after Hill was convicted and his execution approached (Campo-Flores & Rosenberg, 1994).

While in prison, Hill continued to advocate violence against abortion providers. He signed the Defensive Action Statement while in prison. Paul Hill wrote a book titled *Blood of the Unborn* while he was in prison awaiting his execution. Paul Hill was executed by the Florida Department of Corrections on September 3, 2003. Paul Hill is lionized as a martyr to the anti-abortion cause on the Army of God website (AOG, 2011).

The Cartridge Box: Eric R. Rudolph

Eric R. Rudolph was a notable exception to the one-issue politics that dominate the anti-abortion movement. On July 27, 1996, in a symbolic gesture against "one world government" and Washington's allowing abortions, Rudolph set off a bomb at the Olympics in Centennial Park in Atlanta, Georgia, killing 1 and injuring 111. He was also responsible for the bombings of an abortion clinic (Sandy Springs Professional Building) in Sandy Springs, Georgia, on January 16, 1997, which damaged the building but caused no injuries; a homosexual bar (Otherside Lounge) in Atlanta, Georgia, on February 21, 1997, which injured five; and an abortion clinic in Birmingham, Alabama (Northside Family Planning Services), on January 29, 1998, which killed a police officer and injured a nurse (Conklin, 2016). He successfully evaded capture by law enforcement (with the aid of many religious sympathizers who provided food and other supplies) for many years. Rudolph was finally captured by a local police officer in Murphy, North Carolina, on May 31, 2003 (Schuster & Stone, 2005).

In his manifesto, which Rudolph demanded be published as a part of his agreement to plead guilty to the government's charges, Rudolph outlines his perceived "logic" and the motive behind some of his actions:

> Because I believe that abortion is murder, I also believe that force is justified and, in an attempt, to stop it. Because this government is committed to the policy of maintaining the policy of abortion and protecting it, the agents of this government are the agents of mass murder, whether knowingly or unknowingly. And whether these agents of the government are armed or otherwise they are legitimate targets in the war to end this holocaust, especially those agents who carry arms in defense of this regime and the enforcement of its laws. This is the reason and the only reason for the targeting of so-called law enforcement personnel.
>
> (AP, 2005)

In his manifesto, Rudolph also provided his perceived logic as to why the government was willing to plea bargain in his case and why he accepted that plea bargain:

> But Washington had a problem, and therefore they entered this deal. The problem that they had was that a significant minority of the population, especially here in Northern Alabama, regarded what happened there at the abortion facility on that day of January 29,

1998, as morally justified. It is my opinion some of these people were likely to vote not guilty no matter what evidence was presented to them. Their jury questionnaire centered on efforts to discover and exclude those potential jurors who held strong anti-abortion beliefs. Therefore, they approached us—they were afraid that in at least one jurisdiction they were going to run into this recalcitrant pro-life juror who would hand the jury and deliver a political defeat and embarrassment to Washington's effort to make an example out of person who assaulted their specially protected policy of child murder. The evidence was sufficiently weak enough for us to talk to this juror, and they were afraid of this, so they offered the deal. The fact that I have entered an agreement with the government is purely a tactical choice on my part and in no way legitimates [sic] the moral authority of the government to judge this matter or impute guilt.

(AP, 2005)

Rudolph openly admitted that his religious beliefs influenced his actions. However, he denied any racist connections or beliefs. Sentenced to life imprisonment, Eric Rudolph is listed as a "Prisoner of Christ" on the Army of God website (AOG, 2011).

Jury Box: The Grand Jury Investigation of the WHCS (2006)

In the state of Kansas, grand juries may be summoned by a petition of the people. KSA 22-3301(2) states:

A grand jury shall be summoned in any county within 60 days after a petition praying therefore is presented to the district court, bearing the signatures of several electors equal to 100 plus 2% of the total number of votes cast for governor in the county in the last preceding election.

Using this section of the Kansas statutes, Operation Rescue and Kansans for Life started a petition drive to call for a grand jury investigation into the death of Christin Gilbert, who had died of complications resulting from an abortion performed at WHCS in 2006, according to the autopsy report. Dr. Tiller had not performed the abortion himself, but another physician working at the clinic had. On April 19, 2006, a petition was presented to the county clerk in Sedgwick County calling for the empanelment of a grand jury. After the certification of the 7,700 signatures on the petition, the grand jury was empaneled according to Kansas law. In July 2006, the grand jury was unable to return an indictment and was dismissed by District Attorney Nola Fulston in accordance with Kansas law. This infuriated the anti-abortion forces (Singular, 2011; Thomas et al., 2009).

Jury Box

Later that same year, on December 21, 2006, Kansas Attorney General Phillip D. Kline (a Republican) charged Tiller with 30 misdemeanors counts involving abortions performed on minors. These charges were dismissed at the request of Sedgwick County District Attorney Nola Fulston (a Democrat). However, there was considerable pressure by anti-abortion forces to prosecute Tiller for something, and a general feeling by all that politics was being played with the Kansas judicial system. The following year, on June 28, 2007, Kansas Attorney General Paul J. Morrison (a Democrat) charged Tiller with 19 misdemeanor counts involving basically the same charges. Morrison resigned as Kansas attorney general on January 31, 2008, amid charges of a sex scandal involving an alleged affair with a staffer in his former district attorney's office. The prosecution of Tiller was continued by the new Kansas attorney general, Stephan N. Six (a Democrat). The trial was extensively covered by the press because abortion issues are "big news" in Kansas. Scott Roeder was one of the persons who viewed the trial in the courtroom in Wichita (Singular, 2011; Thomas, 2009). Tiller was acquitted of all charges in a jury trial on May 27, 2009. However, the doctor who had provided the second medical opinions that were required by law for late-term abortions, Dr. Ann Kristin Neuhaus, was stripped of her medical license by the Kansas State Board of Healing Arts on June 22, 2012, after accusations of "performing inadequate mental health exams on young patients she then referred to the late Dr. George Tiller for late-term abortions" (Hanna, 2012).

The Necessity Defense

The necessity defense is based on a belief that a criminal action can be undertaken by a defendant in defense of an innocent third party. This was applied to attacks on abortion providers in a thesis by a Regent University law student, Michael Hirsh (1993), who argued that Michael Griffin's murder of abortion doctor David Gunn should be considered an act of justifiable homicide because of Gunn's ongoing murder of unborn fetuses during abortions. Hirsh based his arguments on Florida law, which allows the use of deadly force to prevent an attempted murder or a felony assault on one's person or an innocent third party. In the preface to his thesis, Hirsh lionizes AOG member Michael Bray as a "Defender of the Unborn, Soldier of the Cross, and Hero of the Faith" (Jefferis, 2011).

The Cartridge Box: The Murder of George Tiller (2009)

Tiller's movements and residence had been tracked and published online by Operation Rescue on a website called Tiller Watch (Singular, 2011). On May 18, 2009, Scott Roeder purchased a handgun from a gun dealer in Lawrence, Kansas. Since his previous mental treatment had been privately arranged (as opposed to ordered by a probate court), the record was unavailable to law enforcement, and his conviction on his previous arrest had been set aside on a technicality by the courts, so there was no statutory reason to deny him permission to buy the handgun. Therefore, he passed the BATF check. Roeder bought ammunition at another store and picked up his new handgun back in Lawrence a few days later (Singular, 2011).

On May 23, 2009, Roeder was observed on video surveillance camera gluing the locks shut at a Kansas City, Kansas, abortion clinic. A report was filed with the Kansas City Police Department. On May 24, 2009, Roeder attended the Sunday service at the Reformation Lutheran Church in Wichita. He was carrying a concealed handgun and was hunting George Tiller. Tiller did not attend that service, and Roeder left a note in the collection plate that read "Do you believe in taxes?" After the church service, Roeder returned to Kansas City.

On the morning of May 30, 2009, Roeder again approached the same abortion clinic in Kansas City, Kansas. He was spotted by a female employee as he prepared to glue the door locks. The employee shouted at Roeder, and he left, calling her a "baby killer." However, she not only observed Roeder, but also got a good look at his car. She called her boss at the clinic, and they were able not only to identify the vehicle (a powder-blue Ford Taurus) but also to obtain the automobile's license tag number (Kansas, 225 BAB). The FBI was notified. Roeder then went to the pawn shop where he had purchased his handgun and bought some more ammunition. He told the pawn shop employee that he had been practicing with his newly purchased weapon. Roeder then went to Topeka and practiced shooting for a while with his brother David. Roeder was showing off his new handgun to his brother while they shot. Completing his day, Roeder traveled to Wichita and attended the Saturday evening service at

Reformation Lutheran Church, again looking for Tiller. Tiller was not present at that service either (Singular, 2011; Thomas, 2010a, Bauer & Thomas, 2009).

On Sunday morning, May 31, 2009, Scott Roeder was once again sitting in the pews of the Reformation Lutheran Church, awaiting his intended victim, George Tiller. Tiller was scheduled to be an usher at the 10:00 AM service, and that fact was indicated in the church bulletin. Roeder spotted Tiller in the foyer of the church, performing his duties as an usher. Roeder approached Tiller and drew a handgun from his pocket. Roeder was heard to say, "Lord forgive me!" He then shot George Tiller in the head at very close range. Roeder then left the church. He was pursued into the parking lot by two ushers. Roeder threatened the ushers with the handgun, and they withdrew. Roeder and his automobile tag number were observed by the ushers as he drove out of the church parking lot. These details were provided to the police as 911 was called and help summoned. Attempts by bystanders to revive Tiller were unsuccessful (Singular, 2011).

As the Wichita Police Department arrived and began to investigate the shooting, a description of both the shooter and the automobile that he was driving was broadcast to law enforcement authorities. Roeder attempted to escape by driving along lesser-used highways and avoided the Kansas Turnpike while driving home toward Kansas City, although many have said that he habitually avoided the turnpike to avoid paying the toll for using the road. Roeder was stopped and arrested by a unit of the Johnson County Sheriff's Office on I-35 near Gardner, Kansas (Singular, 2011; Thomas et al., 2009).

When interviewed by Singular (2011):

> Scott Roeder did not deny killing Tiller. When asked about the murder, Roeder stated: "My only regret is that I didn't do this sooner." When asked if he (Roeder) knew that Kansas had reinstated the death penalty in the 1990s, Roeder replied, "That never crossed my mind. What Tiller was doing was wrong, even if it is legal, it violates God's law. God's law is always more important than man's law. I stopped abortion in Wichita. . . . Wichita is no longer the abortion capital of the world."
>
> (6–7)

Who Is Scott Roeder?

In the 1970s, while in high school, Roeder had experimented with drugs and received residential treatment for a mental illness that has been described as the early signs of schizophrenia. Upon release from mental treatment, Roeder stopped taking his prescribed medication as he felt it was unnecessary (Singular, 2011, p. 22). Roeder drifted from job to job. He married Lindsey Roberts in 1986, and they had a child together. Roeder became fascinated with evangelists on television, such as Pat Robertson and Robert Tilton. He also became interested in the Sovereign Citizen movement after attending an anti-tax seminar in Kansas City in 1991. Roeder became obsessed with religion and anti-government politics (Singular, 2011, pp. 23–27). By 1994, Roeder was associating with members of local militia movements, including the Unorganized Kansas Militia. After increasingly arguing with his wife, Roeder moved out in 1994. He was committed to a mental hospital in Topeka for a short time by his sister Denise after an episode that seemed to his estranged wife as manic. Roeder left the hospital the next day. Roeder began to be fascinated with the freeman movement. His wife, Lindsey, divorced him in 1996.

In April 1996, he was stopped by Shawnee County sheriff's deputies in Topeka for driving with an illegal tag (a homemade freeman-type tag was on the vehicle) and arrested for illegal possession of bomb-making materials (fuse cord, a blasting cap, ammunition, one pound of gunpowder, and nine-volt batteries with wiring and switches). Roeder told the deputies that he intended to blow up an abortion clinic. Roeder was convicted and sentenced to 24 months of intensive probation. However, the conviction was overturned in 1997 when the appeals court ruled that the deputies' search of Roeder's car had been illegal (Bauer & Klepper, 2009).

Roeder began to be more and more involved in anti-abortion activities, including those in Wichita. He donated over $1,000 to Operation Rescue—a considerable sum, when you consider that he only worked sporadically and often did not have the money to pay his ex-wife child support for his son. Lindsey Roeder told reporters that her ex-husband, Scott, thought that doctors who performed abortions were murderers (Bauer & Klepper, 2009). Roeder had been observed gluing the door locks shut in an abortion clinic in Kansas City, Kansas, on two occasions in 2000. But the FBI had told clinic authorities that the surveillance video camera images were too blurry to make a positive identification (Singular, 2011).

Roeder fathered a daughter in 2001 with a different woman. Their relationship quickly ended as well. Roeder began to be obsessed with Tiller. Roeder stalked Tiller and attended Tiller's church, at least once (by his own admission) with a concealed pistol in August 2008, intending to kill Tiller. Tiller was not there that Sunday. Roeder later was forced to pawn the pistol, and it was not the weapon that he shot Tiller with.

In April 2009, the FBI's Kansas City office received a tip that had been sent anonymously via a letter that warned that Scott Roeder had targeted George Tiller and possibly other abortion providers for physical harm. The letter turned out to have been written by Mark Archer, who was the husband of the women Roeder had had a child with in 2001. Singular (2011) found that the purpose of the letter was to get Roeder placed on a terrorist no-fly list so that he could not fly to Pennsylvania to see his daughter. The Archers were engaged in a custody battle with Roeder at the time (Singular, 2011).

The Jury Box: The Trial of Scott Roeder

The aftermath of the murder of George Tiller caused a national sensation, with both sides of the abortion question fueling the argument. Pro-choice advocates mourned his loss and warned of more possible violence to come against abortion providers. Anti-abortion advocates attempted to distance themselves from the violent act, fearing federal retribution, describing what Tiller did as murder. In other words, he had it coming, but do not look at us. We did not do it!) Some religious leaders still voiced their objections to abortion but were publicly appalled at the act of violence.

Roeder often spoke to the press while awaiting his trial for the murder of Dr. Tiller. He called the Associated Press on Sunday, June 7, 2009, and told the reporters, "I know there are many similar events planned around the country as long as abortion remains legal." When asked to elaborate, Roeder declined. In response to the shooting, the United States Department of Justice opened an investigation to see if Roeder had acted alone or had accomplices in his actions (Hegeman, 2009). Another, more immediate judicial response to Roeder's statement was that his bail was raised from $5,000,000 to $20,000,000 by Judge Warren Wilbert. Roeder received correspondence from Donald Spitz, the sponsor of the Army of God website, while he was awaiting trial in the Sedgwick County Jail. The correspondence consisted of anti-abortion pamphlets (Singular, 2011).

Roeder continued to speak to the press despite advice from his legal counsel not to. He freely admitted killing Tiller, often stating that it had been necessary to protect unborn children. Roeder told the AP that he intended to use the necessity defense in his trial. On

September 9, 2009, a revised third edition of Paul Hill's Defensive Action Statement was issued and signed by 21 noted anti-abortionists. The proclamation stated:

> We, the undersigned, declare the justice of taking all godly action necessary to defend innocent human life including the use of force. We proclaim that whatever force is legitimate to defend the life of a born child is legitimate to defend the life of an unborn child. We assert that if Scott Roeder did in fact kill George Tiller, his use of lethal force was justifiable provided it was carried out for the purpose of defending the lives of unborn children. Therefore, he ought to be acquitted of the charges against him.

Among those who signed the third edition of the Defensive Action Statement were Eric Rudolph, Shelly Shannon, and Roeder himself (Singular, 2011; Stone, 2009; Saltshaker, 2009).

Both prosecution and defense attorneys filed motions with the courts, arguing whether the necessity defense should be allowed in Roeder's upcoming trial. Judge Wilbert ruled that the necessity defense was not recognized under Kansas law. However, he stated that he would leave the door open for Roeder's attorneys to argue that Roeder was acting on an unreasonable but honest belief that deadly force was necessary to save lives (Singular, 2011; Thomas, 2010b). Judge Wilbert refused to let the trial become an argument about the legality of abortion or the abortion issue, despite efforts of the defense to do so. The defense had even subpoenaed former Kansas attorney general Phil Kline to testify on behalf of Roeder. Army of God members announced that they were coming to Wichita for the trial (Singular, 2011). After a contentious trial in which Roeder testified that he had killed Tiller to save unborn children, Roeder was convicted on all charges. On April 10, 2010, Judge Wilbert sentenced Roeder to 50 years without the possibility of parole for the murder and an additional 2 years for each of the aggravated assault convictions.

Roeder had openly stated that he was motivated by his religious convictions to commit the crime. While he may have been influenced by association with various religious or anti-government groups, Roeder acted as a lone wolf in his actions. He views himself as a martyr in the anti-abortion movement. This is a view shared by the Army of God, which lists him as a hero on their website (AOG, 2011).

Terrorists: Lone Wolves Versus Organized Plots

Terrorist actions may be the result of an organized plot by a specific terrorist group acting as a team. The group usually proclaims its action in some type of statement. Sometimes the group that takes credit for the terrorist incident is not the group that performed the terrorist act. The difficulty of properly identifying suspects is a barrier to investigating these crimes, just as it is in any other crime. Other terrorist incidents are the result of a single terrorist acting alone. These terrorists are called lone wolves. Stewart and Burton of Stratfor Global Intelligence (2009) discussed the threat posed by lone-wolf militants and the unique challenges that they pose to law enforcement and security personnel:

> Of course, the primary challenge is that, by definition, lone wolves are solitary actors, and it can be very difficult to determine their intentions before they act because they do not work with others. When militants are operating in a cell consisting of more than one person, there is a larger chance that one of them will get cold feet and reveal the plot to authorities, that law enforcement and intelligence personnel will intercept a communication between conspirators, or that law enforcement authorities will be able to introduce

an informant into the group. Obviously, lone wolves do not need to communicate with others or include them in the planning or execution of their plots.

Elaborating on the problems posed by this type of offender, Stewart and Burton (2009) further observed:

> Lone wolves also pose problems because they can come from a variety of backgrounds with a wide range of motivations. While some lone wolves are politically motivated, others are religiously motivated, and some are mentally unstable.

Stewart and Burton specifically cited Eric Rudolph and Scott Roeder as offenders who had acted as lone wolves.

Colorado Springs, November 27, 2015

On November 27, 2015, a lone gunman entered a Planned Parenthood clinic before noon, holding four SKS rifles and wearing a homemade bulletproof vest made of silver coins and duct tape. The gunman, Robert Lewis Dear, approached a woman outside the clinic and shot her multiple times. Once inside the clinic, Dear held authorities back for almost six hours. Dear killed one officer and two civilians before being apprehended by police (Grinberg, 2016).

The gunman was a 57-year-old man from South Carolina. After the shooting, Dear said, "No more baby parts," referring to the Planned Parenthood shooting (Fieldstadt, 2015). The remarks were considered rants that were like statements about politics and one remark about President Obama being the antichrist. Dear told detectives working the shooting that he dreamed of being met in heaven by aborted babies who were grateful for his actions, and he called himself "a warrior for the babies" (Grinberg, 2016).

One police officer, Garrett Swansey, and two civilians, Jennifer Markovsky and Ke'Arre Marcell, were killed when the gunman opened fire at the Planned Parenthood; he also wounded four civilians and five police officers (Fieldstadt, 2015). Dear was charged with 179 felony charges, including murder and attempted murder. In court, Dear was deemed incompetent to stand trial and to converse with his attorney due to a delusional disorder (Grinberg, 2016).

Conclusion

The issue of abortion and abortion rights has political, religious, and legal implications.

Anyone has the right to lawfully protest. Both sides of the argument have extensively exercised their rights to protest on this issue. Abortion has been a hot political topic in elections and court actions for decades. These are legitimate means to achieve the institutional goals of the groups. However, when the protests turn violent, they become a matter for law enforcement authorities. In investigating a crime, law enforcement looks for motive (anti-abortion views), method (three-box operational sub-theory) and opportunity (individual attacks against abortion providers).

Anti-abortion groups abandoning legitimate means have turned to rebellion as an adaptation as predicted by Merton (1968, p. 245). Violence has occurred against abortion clinics and abortion providers. The violence was largely for political and religious reasons (Nice, 1988). As acts of political violence, do the bombing and killings of abortion providers meet the FBI's definition of terrorism? From a law enforcement perspective, the answer would have to be yes. No matter how well meaning the perpetrators, when the line of perfectly legal protests is crossed and turns into violence or crimes against persons or places with the intent to terrorize or prevent a person from exercising their right to take part in a legal activity (moral or not), then that is legally an act of terrorism.

Discussion Questions

1. Discuss the significance of the US Supreme Court decision in *Roe v. Wade* (410 U.S. 113, 1973), which allowed legal abortions in the United States. Do you think that the US Supreme Court decided that case correctly? Explain your position.
2. Describe the necessity defense as used by anti-abortion extremists. Has it been an effective defense in these types of cases?
3. Bomber Eric Rudolph issued a manifesto to justify his crimes. Explain the major points in Rudolph's manifesto.
4. Describe the difference between a lone wolf and an organized plot. Which type of terrorist action is more effective and why?
5. Extremist groups such as the Army of God are a composite of radicals and people with sincere religious beliefs. How does this make it more difficult for law enforcement of identify and prosecute members for criminal actions?

References

AOG. (2011). *Army of God website*. Retrieved from www.armyofgod.com/index.html

AP. (2005, April 18). Eric Rudolph's manifesto. *The Decatur Daily News*. Monday. Retrieved from http://archive.decaturdaily.com/decaturdaily/news/050418/manifesto.shtml

Bauer, L., & Klepper, D. (2009, June 2). Alleged killer was troubled, his family says. *The Kansas City Star*. Tuesday. A1.

Bauer, L., & Thomas, J. (2009, June 3). Roeder's anti-abortion activism scrutinized. *The Kansas City Star*. Wednesday. Al.

Bray, M. (1994). *A time to kill*. Portland, OR: Advocates for Life Publications.

Campo-Flores, A., & Rosenberg, D. (1994, September 3). An abortion foe's end. *Newsweek, 142*(10).

Cloward, R., & Ohlin, L. (1960). *Delinquency and opportunity: A theory of delinquent gangs*. New York, NY: The Free Press.

Conklin, G. (2016, Winter). Terrorism in the United States: A case study of Eric Rudolph, a homegrown terrorist. *Torch Magazine*, 10–14.

Fieldstadt, E. (2015, November 30). Who is Robert Dear? Planned Parenthood shooting suspect seemed strange, not dangerous, neighbors say. *The Associated Press*. Retrieved from www.nbcnews.com/news/us-news/who-robert-dear-planned-parenthood-shooting-suspect-seemed-strange-not-n470896

Franklin, B. (1985, March 5). Shot fired through window of Blackmun home. *The New York Times*. Tuesday. Retrieved from www.nytimes.com/1985/03/05/nyregion/shot-fired-through-window-of-blackmun-ho

Freedom of Access to Clinic Entrances Act of 1994. (1994). 18 U.S.C. 248.

Grinberg, E. (2016). *Planned Parenthood shooting suspect ruled incompetent*. Retrieved from www.cnn.com/2016/05/11/us/planned-parenthood-shooting-robert-lewis-dear-hearing/

Gruver, D. (2009, June 1). Tiller studied medicine at KU. *The Kansas City Star*. Monday, A6.

Hanna, J. (2012, June 22). Kansas revokes doctor's license in abortion case. *Associated Press*. Friday. Retrieved from http://news.yahoo.com/kansas-revokes-doctors-license-abortion-case-152745500.html

Hegeman, R. (2009, June 9). Statement from Roeder fuels unease. *The Wichita Eagle*. Tuesday. A1.

Hirsh, M. (1993). *Use of force in defense of another: An argument for Michael Griffin* (Master's thesis). Regent University, Virginia Beach, VA, vii.

Hull, N., & Hoffer, P. (2001). *Roe v. Wade: The abortion rights controversy in American history*. Lawrence, KS: University of Kansas Press.

Jefferis, J. (2011). *Armed for life: The Army of God and anti-abortion terror in the United States*. Santa Barbara, CA: Praeger.

Kennedy, J. (1994, September 12). Killings distort pro-life message. *Christianity Today, 38*(10), 56.

KSA 22–3301. (2005). Grand juries: Summoning, membership, quorum. Retrieved from http://kansasstatutes.lesterama.org/Chapter_22/Article_30/

Lefler, D. (2009, June 9). Access to abortion now farther away: George Tiller's death leaves KC the closest. *The Wichita Eagle*. Tuesday. A1.

Lipset, S., & Rabb, E. (1978). *The politics of unreason: Right-wing extremism in America, 1790–1977* (2nd ed.). Chicago, IL: The University of Chicago Press.

McAdam, T. (2011). Legal history of abortion in America. *The McAdam Report*. Retrieved from www.mcadamreport.org/Abortion.html

Menard, S. (1995). A developmental test of Mertonian anomie theory. *Journal of Research in Crime and Delinquency, 32*(2), 136–174.

Merton, R. (1938). Social structure and anomie. *American Sociological Review, 3*(5), 672–682.

Merton, R. (1968). *Social theory and social structure*. New York, NY: The Free Press.

Nice, D. (1988). Abortion clinic bombings as political violence. *American Journal of Political Science, 32*(1), 178–195.

Riley, K. J., & Hoffman, B. (1995). *Domestic terrorism: A national assessment of state and local preparedness*. Santa Monica, CA: Rand Publications.

Risen, J. (1994). Anti-abortion zealot's gun may have wounded allies: Protest: Shelley Shannon shot a doctor, then she shot off her mouth. Her case helped spur racketeering probes. *Los Angeles Times*. Retrieved from http://articles.latimes.com/1994-04-18/news/mn-47337_1_shelly-shannon

Risen, J., & Thomas, J. (1998). *Wrath of angels: The American abortion war*. New York, NY: Basic Books.

Roe v. Wade, 410 U.S. 113 (1973).

Saltshaker, D. (2009). *Defensive action statement*. Retrieved from www.saltshaker.us/Scott-Roeder Resources/DefensiveActionStatement3rdEdition.pdf

Schuster, H., & Stone, C. (2005). *Hunting Eric Rudolph: An insider's account of the five-year search for the Olympic bomber*. New York, NY: Berkley Books.

Singular, S. (2011). *The Wichita divide: The murder of Dr. George Tiller and the battle over abortion*. New York, NY: St. Martin's Press.

Stewart, S., & Burton, F. (2009, June 3). Security weekly: Lone wolf lessons. *Stratfor Global Security & Intelligence Report*. Retrieved from www.stratfor.com

Stone, M. (2009, November 9). Christian terrorists release Defensive Action Statement, justify political assassination. *Portland Humanist Examiner*. Retrieved from www.examiner.com/humanist-in-portland/christian-terrorists-release-defensive-action-statement-justify-political-assassination

Thomas, J. (2009, July 26). Roeder foresees a long time in prison. *The Kansas City Star*. Sunday. A1 & A8.

Thomas, J. (2010b, January 10). All eyes will be on the trial of Roeder. *The Kansas City Star*. Sunday. A1 & A18.

Thomas, J. (2010a, January 23). Practice with gun preceded killing. *The Kansas City Star*. Saturday. A1.

Thomas, J., Rodriguez, J., & Finger, S. (2009, June 1). Abortion doctor slain: George Tiller shot in church. *The Kansas City Star*. Monday. A1.

Wilson, M., & Lynxwiler, J. (1988). Abortion clinic violence as terrorism. *Terrorism, 11*(4), 263–273.

Yarbrough, T. (2007). *Harry A. Blackmun: The outsider justice*. New York, NY: Oxford University Press.

Zalman, A. (2011). *Michael Bray (Army of God)*. Retrieved from http://terrorism.about.com/od/groupsleader1/p/MichaelBray.htm

Chapter 19

Freedom Versus Safety on the Roadways in Mesa, AZ

Analysis of Distracted Driving Incidents

Diana Scharff Peterson

> Everyone has the right to life, liberty, and the security of persons.
> (General Assembly of the United Nations, Universal Declaration
> of Human Rights, 1948)

> When drivers are distracted, their reaction time slows way down. That is bad because every millisecond counts behind the wheel. *Car and Driver Magazine* tested a 22-year-old driver's reaction time as he drove under different conditions. In one test, he read a short text message while driving 35 miles per hour. He was so distracted that he traveled an extra 21 feet—more than a car length—before hitting the brakes. Overall, his reaction times were slower when he was sending and reading text messages than when he was legally drunk.
> (Weir, 2011, p. 1)

Introduction and Rationale for Project

> Human beings are a distractible bunch, and their propensity to be elsewhere, mentally speaking, is particularly dangerous when they are motoring.
> (*Economist*, 2015, p. 1)

The impetus for this project arose from Freudenberg (2014): "with such rewarding and often subconscious payoffs, it is hardly surprising that many people choose to consume, even in ways that cause illness, death, pain, and suffering" (p. 144)—consuming while celebrating personal freedoms to do what they wish, such as Snapchatting, FaceTiming, or texting while driving the largest vehicle they can afford to purchase. Whereas Freudenberg (2014) indicated that "in a modern, democratic society, the prerequisites for health—clean air, healthy food, safe consumer products—should be rights, not privileges" (p. 222), I would specifically add safe roadways. "A primary goal of governments is to protect public health. Only government has the resources and mandate to fulfill this function effectively" (Freudenberg, 2014, p. 222).

With her eyes on her phone, Harden did not see a patch of ice on the road ahead. She lost control of the vehicle, and it slammed into a parked car and then a rock wall. She fractured her pelvis, seven ribs, and two disks in her neck. Both legs were badly broken. Sections of muscle, skin, and bone from her lower right leg were lost. In the hospital, Harden suffered a stroke—brain damage caused by the interruption of blood supply to the brain. It left her unable to control her muscles on the right side of her body. "I didn't fully understand what happened to me until a month after the accident." As the shattered

DOI: 10.4324/9781003047117-22

pieces of memory reassembled, it became clear to her that her decision to text behind the wheel was a devastating mistake.

(Weir, 2011, p. 1)

Although one could not imagine life on the road without access to a cell phone or smartphone as the advantages are plentiful, so, too, are the risks. Gliklich, Guo, and Bergmark (2016) demonstrate the magnitude of the safety crisis on American roadways, with over 60% of drivers reporting one or more distracted cellphone-related driving incidents (locating the phone, touching the phone, looking at the phone, looking up a contact, dialing the phone, texting, emailing, checking Facebook, FaceTiming, videoconferencing, playing a video game, watching a movie) within the past 30 days, with 48% admitting to reading and sending texts or emails and 33% writing texts within that same period. For young drivers, that percentage rises to 50% (Gliklich et al., 2016). Most recently, nearly three-quarters, or 70.4%, of Apple iOS users confess to driving while video chatting (Covington, 2021). Shockingly, Raja and Hansen-Bundy (2013) report that the number one cause of death among teens of driving age is not drinking but texting and driving. This statistic runs parallel with findings from the US Department of Health Services, Centers for Disease Control (2019): a report that unintentional injuries (accidents) are the leading cause of death among teens.

Regarding crashes, for drivers who commonly check texts or emails at intersections or stoplights, the following statistic may provide an interesting warning. As most traffic crashes (41%) occur at intersections, Ale, Varma, and Gage (2014) argue a strong need to grasp and improve comprehension of the risk factors and causation of crashes as paramount in understanding of the causes, as well as the risks, of the crashes.

The most common crash type in all crashes was found to be the rear-end (RE) type (42%), followed by the right-angle (RA) type (38%). In case of right-turn (RT) crashes, the most common crash type was the rear-end type (39%), followed by the same-direction sideswipe (SS) 29%. These four crash types constituted 96% of the crashes caused by right-turning vehicles, with driver error or inattention identified as contributing to crashes.

(p. 5)

Responsibilities of Government to Keep Citizens Safe from Harm

In 2003, the Montreal Declaration: People's Right to Safety recognized the enormity and significance of violent injuries on an international scale (Mohan, 2003). Furthermore, the conception of engagement in "universal criteria that extend beyond safety as it is embodied implicitly in civil liberties—the right to bodily integrity and the right to social stability—to generate a minimum gold standard for safety in and of itself" (Stevens, 2003, p. 168). Furthermore, at the Sixth World Conference on Injury Prevention and Control held in Montreal, Canada, in May 2002, the People's Right to Safety was established, concurring with findings from the Fifth World Conference in New Delhi, India (Mohan, 2003). In this declaration:

The relationship between the state and its citizens is enshrined in each country's constitution, most of which ensure that its citizens have a right to life. It is this right to life that is translated into a right to live free from debilitating injury. This endorses the notion of safety as a human right and as an important policy tool for injury control and safety promotion.

(Mohan, 2003, p. 165)

272 Diana Scharff Peterson

Mohan (2003) further stipulates the right to live in a world free of harm—in a safe world, free from the injurious behaviors of others—as an essential human right.

Harm Done by Distracted Driving in the United States: Review of the Relevant Literature

According to Cismaru and Nimegeers (2017), driving while utilizing a handheld mobile cell phone or smartphone, including texting, dialing, reaching for the device, and reading emails, is as likely to result in an accident as drunk driving and speeding. More frightening, a study conducted by the Virginia Tech Transportation Institute (2019) reveals that those who text behind the wheel are at a 23 times greater risk of being involved in an accident than those who are not texting behind the wheel (Fitch et al., 2013). These finding may be explained partially by the theory of the inherent limited capacity of human inattention (Kahneman, 1973), whereby humans are known to best allocate their resources to one activity at the expense of the other (Rosenbloom, 2005).

Distracted driving can include many behaviors while inside a vehicle, including handheld cell phone/smartphone use (answering calls, dialing) and other computer use, including texting, emailing, Snapchatting, FaceTiming, other use of social media, playing video games, etc.); watching movies or television; taking photos; grooming; eating, applying makeup; disciplining children; changing clothing; adjusting a GPS, etc. However, the US National Highway Traffic Safety Administration (2015) provides a dire warning: 10% of all fatal crashes involve distracted driving, with 16% resulting in serious injuries. The number of deaths resulting from distracted driving in 2012 was 3,330, and distracted driving caused 421,000 injuries on roadways in the US (US Department of Transportation National Highway Traffic Safety Administration, 2015).

In 2015, the US National Highway Traffic Safety Administration (NHTSA) provided data that distracted drivers caused 3,154 deaths and 424,000 injuries while using roadways. Even in states with bans on cell or smartphone activity while driving, enforcing such bans against distracted driving incidents has had mixed success (Economist, 2015), meaning that many drivers continue to utilize cell phones while driving, regardless of the respective state bans.

The US Department of Health and Human Services, Centers for Disease Control and Prevention (2019) claims texting is incredibly dangerous, as texting while driving conglomerates three types of distractions: visual, cognitive, and manual (Cismaru & Nimegeers, 2017). Although Rozario, Lewis, and White (2010) indicate that gender and age are non-predictive of a driver's willingness to utilize a cell phone, under high urgency scenarios while driving, using a phone is more likely with peers present in the vehicle. However, Gliklich et al. (2016) acknowledge thousands of cell phone use–related crashes per year; the "specific cell phone activities of drivers are limited" (p. 486). This indicates that cases are difficult to document and record by police officers and are then often notated/categorized into vague or unknown categories of "unspecified types of distracted driving." Cismaru and Nimegeers (2017) acknowledge that enforcing a cell phone ban is a difficult task for police.

Findings From Relevant Studies

- The age group most affected by texting and driving is teenagers (Sherin et al., 2014).
- Driving with Bluetooth (hands-free) devices continues to be associated with distracted driving situations (Sherin et al., 2014); however, the Virginia Tech Transportation Institute (2019) finds that, although utilizing hands-free devices remains a safety hazard, drivers are less inclined to be involved in an accident when using them.

- Using a cell phone (dialing, talking, texting, listening) hampers driving performance at the sensory level (Rosenbloom, 2005).
- "The longer a driver is absorbed in conversation, the more automatic his or her driving becomes, which in turn may lead to the increase in driving speed" (Rosenbloom, 2005, p. 210).
- Drivers in states with cell phone bans continue to evade the bans (Highway Loss Data Institute, HLDI, 2010). "Previous research from the Highway Loss Data Institute has found that cell-phone and texting bans have no beneficial effect on crashes" (HLDI, 2010).

In 2014, the American College of Preventative Medicine (a group of clinicians and decision-makers in the public health arena) addressed concerns about texting while driving statistics and provided the following recommendations to all 50 states:

> Encourage state legislatures to develop and pass legislation banning texting while driving, while simultaneously implementing comprehensive and dedicated law enforcement strategies including penalties for these violations. Legislatures should establish a public awareness campaign regarding the dangers of texting while driving as an integral part of this legislation.
>
> (Sherin et al., 2014, p. 681)

The Distracted Driving Education Act of 2017 (HR 4542), sponsored by Representative Kathleen M. Rice (D-NY-4), was introduced on December 4, 2017, in the US House of Representatives' Transportation and Infrastructure Subcommittee (GovTrack.us, 2021a, 2021b). The following day, the bill was referred to the Subcommittee on Highways and Transit. After being held for two years in the subcommittee, it was cleared from the books. HR 4542 was reintroduced as HR 3002 on May 23, 2019, but not acted upon and was finally removed from all consideration on January 23, 2021 (GovTrack.us, 2021a, 2021b).

Summary of Bans on Cell Phones, Handheld Devices, and Texting in the United States

Legislation surrounding bans on cell phones, handheld devices, and/or texting while driving is complicated. By 2017, only three states remained in America without some type of texting and driving ban (Arizona, Missouri, and Montana). The only state continuing to allow all texting, cell phone use, and handheld device use is Montana. The National Conference of State Legislatures (NCSL) (2021) confirms that 48 states in the US have banned texting and driving in some form, such as while driving in school zones or by type of drivers (school bus drivers, young/teen, or novice drivers who only hold learner's permits).

Currently, states with handheld bans allow users to utilize phones while driving only if drivers utilize hands-free technology, such as Bluetooth. Cell phones that do not contain hands-free technology cannot be utilized, touched, or held in states with "all cell phone" bans; this includes all drivers in automobiles that are not Bluetooth enabled. According to the National Conference of State Legislatures (2021), ban types have three categories: handheld bans in 25 states; cell phone bans that only pertain to teens or novice drivers in 36 states; and texting bans, which have been enacted in 48 states.

In Missouri, drivers under the age of 21 have not been permitted to text while driving since 2013, but all other age groups can do so. Arizona remained one of the final three states to allow for cell phone/smartphone use while driving until January 1, 2021, when a cell phone ban was implemented by Arizona HB 2381 (Legiscan, 2019). However, there was a one-year period (January 1, 2020–December 31, 2020) during which only warnings, not fines, were permitted as drivers adjusted to the new legislation. (See the examples of fines associated with statewide bans later in this chapter.)

Summary of Distracted Driving Laws by State (2021)

Handheld bans: 24 states and Washington, DC
AZ, A.K, CA, CT, DE, GA, HI, IL, LA, ME, MD, MA, MN, NV, NY, OK, RI, TN, TX, VA, WV
All cell phone bans (novice drivers): 38 States and Washington, DC
AZ, AK, CA, CO, CT, DE, HI, IL, IN, KS, KY, LA. ME, MD, MI, MN, NE, NJ, NM, NC, ND, OH, OR, RI, SD, TN, TX, UT, VT, VA, WA, WV, WI
All cell phone bans (bus drivers): 20 states plus Washington, DC
AZ, AK, CA, CT, DE, HI, IL, IN, IA, KS, KY, ME, MD, MA, MI, MN, MS, NE, NV, NC, RI, TN, TX, UT, VA
Text messaging bans: 48 states plus Washington, DC
All states except MT and MO (only drivers under age 21)
(*Source*: GHSA, 2021, www.ghsa.org/sites/default/files/202101/DistractedDrivingLaw-Chart-Jan21.pdf)

Examples of Statewide Bans on/Fees for Texting and Driving (First Offense)

Illinois: $75.00
Washington: $124.00
Oregon: $500.00
Louisiana: $125.00
Indiana: $500.00
Missouri: Only bus drivers fined
West Virginia: $150.00
California: $20.00
Alaska: $10,000.00
Arizona: $75.00–150.00
Montana: No ban
Texas: New and bus drivers only
Florida: $30.00
Nebraska: $200.00
South Dakota: No ban
New Jersey: $400.00
New York: $243.00

(Source: Raja and Hansen-Bundy, 2013)

Texas was one of the more recent states in America to pass a texting-while-driving-ban in late 2017. According to Dutton (2017), banning texting while driving was proclaimed a needed strategy and solution to the alarming rising death statistics on the Texan streets, roads, freeways, and highways. Those in opposition to the 2017 legislation complained that the ban would be

> "a cure that would be worse than the disease," assuming some ideas in the Texas Legislature needed wind, while others needed landing gear. The latter should be the fate of the "texting while driving bill."
>
> (p. 1)

However, Texas banned texting and driving after overwhelming evidence provided by the Texas Department of Transportation associating a 50% increase in traffic fatalities to forms of cell phone use between 2006 and 2010 (Swartswell, 2012).

Similarly, in Arizona, after 11 attempts and failures (see the text box that follows) over a span of a decade (Cassidy, 2018), Arizona made progress and good strides in early 2017, banning teens (ages 15 through 19) from utilizing cell phones for the duration of new driver training and six months following; therefore, it was only applicable to new teen drivers. With SB 1080, the Arizona House joined the Senate in banning texting and cell phone use by teens with a learner's permit or within the first six months after license procurement (Arizona State Legislature, 2021). According to Christie (2017):

> [T]he legislation marks the first time in years the Legislature has approved a bill addressing cell-phone use and distracted driving. Many Republican lawmakers contend distracted driving is already covered by existing laws and passing even a small cell-phone ban will look to broaden efforts to ban phone use behind the wheel.
>
> (p. 1)

AZ House and Senate: Bills Regarding Distracted Driving That Failed

HB 2397, HB 2396, HB 2398, SB 1443, SB 1111, SB 1538, HB 2426, SB 1334, SB 1538, HB 2125, HB 2512, HB 2311, SB 1218, SB 1241, SB 1268, SB 1393, SB 1056, SB 2125

(Source: D'Andrea, N. (2014) www.phoenixmag.com/2014/03/01/fatal-distraction/)

On February 20, 2018, Arizona lawmakers proposed a new prohibition against texting and driving (SB 1261), with a recommended fine of between $25 and $99 for the first offense and between $100.00 and $200.00 for the second offense (Cassidy, 2018). Furthermore, the bill included language stating that if the texting caused death or injury to another, the perpetrator's charge would be a misdemeanor (Class 2), with a resulting fine of potentially $4,000 (Cassidy, 2018). Suffering the same fate as other attempts, SB 1168 was not passed by the Arizona Senate majority caucus, which made the bill the 12th failure in legislation on texting-and-driving bans.

After 12 failed bills over a decade, all handheld cell phone use while driving was finally banned in the state of Arizona after a local patrol officer was struck and killed by a texting driver (Lugo, 2019). HB 2318 (Texting while driving; prohibition; enforcement) was passed on April 22, 2019 (GovTrack.us, 2021a, 2021b). HB 2318, effective January 1, 2021 (warning timeframe January 1, 2020 through December 31, 2020), bans all drivers from using cell phones, all handheld devices, and all text messaging.

Opposing Arguments: Distracted Driving

In arguments between those in favor of distracted driving legislation and those opposed, succinctly, this is an issue of safety versus freedom. Former Texas governor and US Secretary of Energy Rick Perry contended that cell phone use while driving should not be banned as it would be another governmental attempt to micromanage adults (Dutton, 2017); in Arizona, similar arguments included loss of freedoms, government overreach, and unenforceable and impractical laws (Hands-Free Info, 2008). Arguments from proponents of cell phone and texting bans included issues of safety, dangerousness, statistics, and clear evidence of risks associated with cell phone use while operating a motor vehicle (Hands-Free Info, 2008). Those who oppose driving with handheld devices (without Bluetooth technology) find it difficult to understand why anyone would oppose banning cell phone use for drivers with the knowledge available.

To better understand the arguments regarding freedom to use handheld devices while driving, opinions from one of the country's most conservative areas, Texas, were explored. Findings from legislative proceedings on proposed cell phone bans provide an understanding as to why the issue may continue to remain a problem on American roadways: government overreach.

- How can a police officer determine what an individual is doing with his cell-phone in his car? Are drivers just holding it? Is a call being made? And even worse, will the cell-phone have to be confiscated as evidence by law enforcement?

  (Dutton, 2017, p. 1)

- I don't think we need greater gun regulation because of the number of deaths and injuries caused by guns. Cell-phone usages should be viewed in the same way.

  (Dutton, 2017, p. 1)

- There is also the problem of expanding probable cause after enacting a texting ban. Passing such a bill means that law enforcement would have another tool in its arsenal to routinely stop individuals.

  (Dutton, 2017, p. 1)

Understanding Distracted Driving Incidents: Data from a Case Study in Mesa, AZ

To better understand distracted driving incidents in Mesa, Arizona, it is necessary to describe the terrain and population characteristics of the area. According to Citydata.com (2018), Mesa is the second-largest city in Arizona, with a population of 484,622. All the vital statistics for Mesa that follow were gathered from Citydata.com (2018):

- Median household income = $52,393
- Median home value = $209, 000
- Median gross rent = $960.00
- Unemployment rate = 5.4%
- Mean age = 37.5
- Race/Ethnicity: White: 61%; Black: 3.6%; Hispanic: 27%; American Indian: 3.0%; Two+ Races: 2.3%; Hawaiian/Native Pacific Islander: .06%; Other: 0.7%

- Education Level: High school: 88.5%; 4-year college degree or higher: 26.6%; graduate or professional degree: 9.2%
- Land area of Mesa: 125.0 square miles
- Population density: 3,877 per square mile
- Workers who live and work within city limits: 84,979 (37.6%)
- Daytime population change due to commuting: -52,909
- Average commute time to work: 23.3 minutes per worker

Methodology

Distracted Driving Incidents (Mesa, Arizona)

The World Population Review (2021) ranks Arizona as the seventh-worst state for drivers in the United States. Data from the police department of Arizona's second-largest city, Mesa, sheds light on distracted driving incidents from January 1, 2013 through March 31, 2018. The department classifies distracted driving into the following seven categories:

- Unknown distractions
- Another inside vehicle
- Outside vehicle
- Manually operating electronic devices
- Other activity electronic devices

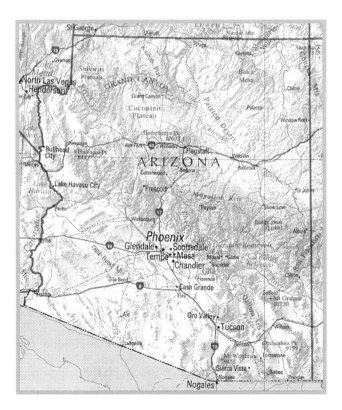

Figure 19.1 City of Mesa

(Source: Maps of Mesa (2018) http://travelsmaps.coRm/map-mesa-arizona.html)

Figure 19.2 Map of Mesa (Streets and Roadways)

(*Source:* Maps of Mesa (2018) http://travelsmaps.com/map-mesa-arizona.html. A color version of this figure is downloadable as Support Material from www.routledge.com/9780367491000.)

- Talking on a handheld
- Passenger

For the five-year period from January 1, 2013 through March 31, 2018, the Mesa Police Department provided data for all distracted driving cases (N=11,149), including the date, time, day of the week, street location, city, and category of distraction. Utilizing geographic information systems software (ArcGIS-10), the distracted driving incidents were geocoded and mapped into visual representations as data points respective to each distracted driving incident's location and timeframe. Geographic information is helpful in this endeavor, as it identifies the parameters of the physical environment and its associated data, providing the ability to map and analyze dangerous hazards while envisioning their hypothetical effects (ESRI, 2008). As with any hazard, to reduce the loss of life and property damage, public safety officials, policy decision-makers, and the public must be aware of potentially hazardous conditions well in advance. In many past disasters, the public would have been able to respond in a crisis if they had knowledge of existing conditions. Geographic information science in its research and education initiatives appears to be able to offer concrete support here (Radke et al., 2000, p. 3).

Data Analysis

Table 19.1 contains all the data points recorded for distracted driving incidents (N=11,149) during the five-year data collection period (January 1, 2013–March 31, 2018) by the Mesa Police Department. The greatest concern is that 85% (N=9432) of the distracted driving incidents recorded by the Mesa Police Department were categorized as unknown distractions; therefore, they cannot be accurately measured. As noted from the data, by utilizing ArcGIS-10, there are no general patterns in the data. It is clear that distracted drivers continue to persist day and night, on all roads, in all parts of the city, on all days of the week. This is consistent with both national and international trends—these activities are occurring whether protocols or laws are in place or not (HLDI, 2010; Gliklich et al., 2016).

Table 19.2 provides a summary of seven distraction identifiers and the percentage of their occurrences. Table 19.3 contains visual information regarding distracted driving incidents in Mesa (N =11,149) per time of day. Table 19.4 contains visual information regarding distracted driving incidents as they occurred per day of the week (DOW), with Table 19.5 offering a summary of the Table 19.4 findings that most days (Monday–Saturday) are nearly identical in the number of incidents, with the lowest number of occurrences being on Sunday. Table 19.5 contains the distracted driving incidents in Mesa (N =11,149) according to when the incident occurred per day of the week (DOW). Table 19.6 describes a summary of distracted driving incidents per time of day, with the largest number of distracted driving incidents falling between noon and 6:00 PM. Essentially, the data show that real patterns do not reveal themselves, as distracted drivers seem to fall everywhere on the spectrum of the roadways, and always, on all days, in all areas—they are everywhere.

Utilizing Political Theory to Understand Arizona's Hesitance to Pass Legislation

The rational choice theory, as Kraft and Furlong (2018) stipulate, is one that

> tries to explain public policy in terms of the actions of self-interested individual policy actors, whether they are voters, corporate lobbyists, agency officials, or legislators . . . [w] hich forces people to think about the core motivation of individual actors and its consequences for the larger political system and for public policy.
>
> (p. 86)

Stemming from ideals of retaining individual freedoms, the rational choice theory (RCT) explains why some states were reluctant to pass bans on cell phone use while driving. Although Arizona recently imposed a ban, ideologies involving individual freedoms prevailed over safety throughout the past decade, shown through many failed legislative attempts.

Although this is only conjecture due to the scant research conducted, the RCT may be a good choice because, in other states, when higher fines are sought, texting rates could

Table 19.1 All Distracted Driving Incidents (N=11,149), Mesa, AZ (1/1/2013–3/31/2018)

Note: A color version of this table is downloadable as Support Material from www.routledge.com/9780367491000

drastically decrease. For example, the first texting and driving offense in Alaska is $10,000.00 and up to one year in jail, but in California, the fine for the same offense is only $20.00 (Raja & Hansen-Bundy, 2013). Therefore, higher fines may be an incentive to encourage drivers to keep their smartphones out of sight while driving. On the other hand, many bills have favored a fine of $25 for the first offense of texting and driving.

By utilizing the rational choice theory, the low costs of fines for the first offense (as in Florida) may not be a viable option to curb the offenses. If the fines were raised to $500 (as in Oregon), or $10,000 (as in Alaska), drivers might be increasingly deterred from using smart phone devices while driving. More research is needed on whether higher fines can curb distracted driving incidents, as is data as to where street signs are posted about distracted driving

Table 19.2 Summary of Distracted Driving Identifiers

Summary Distracted Driving Identifiers (7) per Total N=11,149 Incidents

Description of Distraction	n	%
Manually operating an electronic device	122	1.0%
Other activity electronic device	237	2.1%
Other inside the vehicle (eating/drinking/etc.)	536	4.8%
Outside the vehicle (includes unspecified distractions)	540	4.8%
Passenger	169	1.5%
Talking on handheld	96	.01%
Talking on hands free device	16	.001%
Unknown distractions	**9432**	**85%**

Note: N=11,149

Table 19.3 Time of Day of Distracted Driving Incidents (N=11,149)].

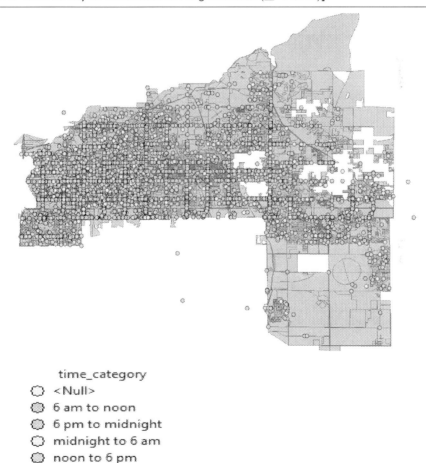

Note: A color version of this table is downloadable as Support Material from www.routledge.com/9780367491000

and the content of the messages. Hadrick and DeSanto (2014) and Strider (2015) suggest that new issues will emerge as theories of liability continue to evolve, including potential liability claims against employers who encourage their employees to respond to calls, emails, or texts when driving. This includes drivers using cell phones as well as sender liability, if the senders

Table 19.4 Distracted Driving Incident by Day of Week

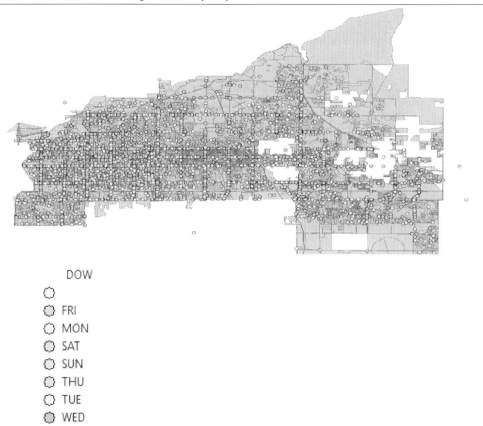

Note: A color version of this table is downloadable as Support Material from www.routledge.com/9780367491000.

Table 19.5 Summary of Distracted Driving Incidents by Day of Week (DOW)

Day of Week	n	%
Monday	1720	15.0%
Tuesday	1724	15.0%
Wednesday	1610	14.0%
Thursday	1590	14.0%
Friday	1761	15.0%
Saturday	1563	14.0%
Sunday	1155	10.0%

Note: N=11,149

of text messages have knowledge that recipients of the messages were driving at the time of messaging.

In *Kubert v. Best*, a case before a New Jersey state court, the plaintiffs were riders on a motorcycle who were both injured when a teenage driver steered his truck into their lane of travel and struck them head on. As the first court to consider this issue, the New Jersey court determined that "the sender of a text message can potentially be liable if an

Table 19.6 Summary of Statistics of Distracted Driving Incidents by Time of Day

N	11149.00
Mean	1370.52
Median	1431.00
Mode	1500.00
Std. Deviation	528.216
Variance	279012.470
Range	2359
Minimum	0
Maximum	2359

Note: N=11,149

accident is caused by texting, but only if the sender knew or had special reason to know that the recipient would view the text while driving and thus be distracted." In doing so, the court started with the reasonable and obvious premise that a vehicle passenger who actively encourages the vehicle driver to engage in illegal or reckless behavior should and can be held liable and responsible for his/her distracting conduct.

(Hadrick & DeSanto, 2014, p. 1)

Conclusion, Discussion, and Implications for Future Research

Geographic information was very helpful in this endeavor, as it identifies the parameters of the physical environment and its associated data, providing the ability to map and analyze dangerous hazards while envisioning their hypothetical effects (ESRI, 2008). As with any hazard, to reduce the loss of life and property damage, public safety officials, policy decision-makers, and the public must be aware of potentially hazardous conditions well in advance. In many past disasters, the public would have been able to respond in a crisis if they had knowledge of existing conditions.

In the five years studied (January 1, 2013 through March 31, 2018), there were 11,149 distracted-driving accidents in Mesa, Arizona. However, in that data, no demographic variables, such as age, gender, ethnicity/race, whether drivers were insured, etc., were provided, nor were related demographics pertaining to the victims. More care is needed in reporting the driver's age and other important demographics so that we have a better overall picture of who is most impacted in these senseless acts. More alarming, of those cases (N=11,149), most (85%) were notated as unspecified, leaving holes in research attempts to make needed changes. More care is needed by police officers taking notes in distracted driving cases, as the notion of safety is an implied human right. What was further missing in the Mesa Police Department data was the type of collision.

From the literature, it is very relevant that most accidents occur during right turns (RT) at intersections (Ale et al., 2014). Therefore, it would be very helpful in distracted-driving cases to know if the accident was a rear-end collision (RE), a right-turn (RT), sideswipe/angle crash, or at a stoplight. According to Ale et al. (2014), "better understanding the causes and risks of the crashes is vital in reducing these crashes, which is a major societal need" (p. 1). If the police strived to report more accurate/detailed information, it would help better understand distracted-driving behaviors.

The Insurance Institute for Highway Safety, Highway Loss and Data Institute (2021) promotes technologies involving crash avoidance for two reasons: evidence that banning cell phones while driving will not eliminate crashes involving other types of distracted driving and because crash-risk associations and handheld device use remain unclear.

It is vital to determine which areas, locations, counties, states, and jurisdictions (both rural and urban) are making better strides in enforcing such legislation. Additional research is needed to explore all types of distracted driving incidents, as well as better documentation of the types of incidents, such as eating or applying cosmetics while driving. More research is needed into where street signs are placed informing drivers of the dangers of and laws against distracted driving, as well as the content of the messages.

Individuals around the world, young and old, continue to text while driving, knowing how dangerous it is. Campaigns against texting and driving, as well as other smartphone-related activities, should be used in tandem with cell phone bans in order to save lives. Suggested campaigns include:

- Make efforts at red lights: No texting (Canada).
- If you know people are driving, do not text them or respond to their texts (Canada).
- When idling in traffic: Resist the urge to text (Canada).
- If there is a distraction, stop in a safe area any time something needs your attention. Simply stop your vehicle (US).
- Ensure before starting the car all reading material is out of reach of the driver (US).
- Let it be heard and spread the word: distracted driving is the #1 killer of teens in America (California).

(Cismaru & Nimegeers, 2017)

Campaigns against texting and driving, combined with strategically placed road signs warning drivers to put away their devices, must be pursued, studied, and measured to determine their value against fighting this epidemic. Not enough is known regarding each smartphone-related activity and its propensity to cause a crash (Highway Loss Data Institute, HLDI, 2010) and what is most dangerous (talking versus texting or emailing versus playing a video game while driving, all of which are deemed highly inappropriate and dangerous). In closing, Freudenberg (2014) calls for real change with the following thoughts:

For some, the threats in the survival of our children and grandchildren as well to human civilization and the environment that supports life may be too distant or dire to motivate action. For those, the more immediate consequences of continuing our current patterns of corporate consumption—high rates of diabetes, heart disease, and cancer, as well as automobile and firearm injuries and deaths—may be what inspire action.

(p. 151)

Discussion Questions

1. Considering research indicates that handheld bans while driving are not as effective as planned, what other ideas or bans could be instituted to curb cell phone use while behind the wheel? What does current research support? Does the rational choice theory appropriately apply to imposing greater fines for utilizing handheld devices while driving? What other types of criminological theories might also apply?
2. What are suggestions for additional campaigns aimed at teen drivers to halt texting while driving? Review current statistics on the prevalence and incidence of distracted driving in your country or region to support arguments for additional campaigns of your choosing.

3. Describe several benefits of utilizing GIS technologies, including ARC-GIS, in criminal justice programs and/or criminology programs in higher education. What would be the advantages and disadvantages of requiring criminal justice/criminology students to learn about mapping criminal justice issues, such as distracted driving incidents?
4. Discuss several political and legal arguments utilizing opposing viewpoints on a driver's right to freely use a smartphone while driving. Why do you think the state of Montana continues to support no bans on handheld devices, including cell phone or smartphone use while driving?
5. Based on the reading, how can being safe on American roadways be viewed as an essential human right?
6. After reviewing the variables involved in reporting distracted driving incidents by the Mesa Police Department, what other types of other variables should be reported on?

References

Ale, G., Varma, A., & Gage, B. (2014). Safety impacts of right-turn lanes at unsignalized intersections and driveways on two-lane roadways: Crash analysis. *Journal of Transportation Engineering*. Retrieved from www.cmfclearinghouse.org/study_detail.cfm?stid=38

Arizona State Legislature. (2021). *Bill history for SB1080*. Retrieved from https://apps.azleg.gov/BillStatus/BillOverview/68707

Cassidy, M. (2018). After 11 attempts, will Arizona ban texting and driving? *The Republic*. Retrieved from www.azcentral.com/story/news/politics/legislature/2018/02/06/after-11-attempts-arizona-ban-texting-while-driving/311636002/

Centers for Disease Control and Prevention (CDC). (2019). *Distracted driving*. Retrieved from www.cdc.gov/motorvehiclesafety/distracted_driving/index.html

Christie, B. (2017). *Arizona bans new teen drivers from using cell-phones*. Retrieved from www.usnews.com/news/best-states/arizona/articles/2017-04-27/ducey-signs-bill-banning-teen-drivers-from-using-cell-phones

Cismaru, M., & Nimegeers, K. (2017). Keep your eyes up, don't text and drive: A review of anti-texting while driving campaigns' recommendations. *International Review on Public and Non-Profit Marketing, 14*(1), 113–135. doi:http://dx.doi.org.ezproxy1.lib.asu.edu/10.1007/s12208-016-0166-7

Citydata.com. (2018). *Mesa, Arizona*. Retrieved from www.city-data.com/city/Mesa-Arizona.html

Covington, T. (2021). Distracted driving statistics: Research and facts in 2021. *Insurance Zebra*. Retrieved from www.thezebra.com/resources/research/distracted-driving-statistics/

D'Andrea, N. (2014). *Fatal distraction*. Retrieved from www.phoenixmag.com/2014/03/01/fatal-distraction/

Dutton, H. (2017). No texting-while-driving ban: Opposing view. *USA Today*. Retrieved from https://usa-today.com/story/opinion/2017/02/27/Texas-texting-while-driving-editorials-debates/98503644/

Economist. (2015). Driven from distraction. *Road Safety, 415*(8935), 74. Retrieved from www.economist.com/science-and-technology/2015/04/25/driven-from-distraction

ESRI. (2008). *Geographic information systems providing the platform for comprehensive emergency management*. Report prepared for the Environment System Research Institute, Inc., Redlands, CA.

Fitch, G., Soccolich, S., Gou, F., McClauffertry, J., Fang, Y., Olsen, R., . . . Dingus, T. (2013). *The impact of handheld and hands-free cell phone use on driving performance and safety-critical event risk*. Report prepared for the National Highway Traffic Safety Commission, Washington, DC.

Freudenberg, N. (2014). *Lethal but legal: Corporations, consumption, and protecting public health*. New York, NY: Oxford University Press.

Gliklich, E., Guo, R., & Bergmark, R. (2016). Texting while driving: A study of 1211 US Adults with the distracted driving survey. *Preventive Medicine Reports, 4*, 486–489.

GovTrack.us. (2021a). *HR 4542–115th congress: Distracted driving education act of 2017*. Retrieved from www.govtrack.us/congress/bills/115/hr4542

GovTrack.us. (2021b). *HR 3009–116th congress: Distracted driving education act of 2019*. Retrieved from www.govtrack.us/congress/bills/116/hr3009

Hadrick, R., & DeSanto, J. (2014). Can sending a text message make you liable for a car accident? *Litigation News*. Retrieved from www.mcneeslaw.com/litigation-news-2/

Hands-Free Information (Ed.). (2008). *Arizona: Cell phone laws, legislation*. Retrieved from http://handsfree-info.com/arizona-cell-phone-laws-legislation/

Highway Loss Data Institute. (2010). *Highway loss data bulletin: Texting laws and collision claims frequencies*. Retrieved from www.iihs.org/iihs/topics/t/distracted-driving/hldi-research

Insurance Institute for Highway Safety, Highway Loss & Data Institute. (2021). *Distracted driving*. Retrieved from www.iihs.org/topics/distracted-driving

Kahneman, D. (1973). *Attention and effort*. Englewood Cliffs, NJ: Prentice-Hall.

Kraft, M., & Furlong, S. (2018). *Public policy: Politics, analysis, and alternatives*. Thousand Oaks, CA: Sage.

Kubert v. Best, No. A-1128–12T4, 2013 WL 4512313, 1 (NJ Super. Ct. App. Div. Aug. 27, 2013).

Legiscan. (2019). *AZ HB 2318, Texting while driving; prohibition: Enforcement*. Retrieved from https://legiscan.com/AZ/bill/HB2318/2019

Lugo, J. (2019). Enough is enough: State considers cell-phone ban for drivers' weeks after officer's death. *Cronkite News*. Retrieved from https://cronkitenews.azpbs.org/2019/01/24/arizona-cellphone-ban-proposed/

Mesa, Arizona. (2018). *City of Mesa, AZ*. Retrieved from www.city-data.com/city/Mesa-Arizona.html

Mohan, D. (2003). Introduction: Safety as a human right. *Violence, Health and Human Rights, 6*(2), 161–167.

National Conference of State Legislatures. (2021). *Distracted driving, cell phone use*. Retrieved from www.ncsl.org/research/transportation/cellular-phone-use-and-texting-while-driving-laws.asp

National Highway Traffic Safety Administration (NHTSA). (2015). *Research: Distracted driving 2013*. Retrieved from http://distraction.gov/stats-research-laws-research.html

Radke, D., Cova, M., Sheridan, F., Troy, A., Lan, M., & Johnson, R. (2000). *Challenges for GIS in emergency preparedness and response*. Report prepared for the Environment System Research Institute, Inc., Redlands, CA.

Raja, T., & Hansen-Bundy, B. (2013). How much does your state fine for texting and driving? *Mother Jones*. Retrieved from www.motherjones.com/media/2013/10/numbers-texting-and-driving/

Rosenbloom, T. (2005). Driving performance while using cell-phones: Observational Study. *Journal of Safety Research, 37*, 207–212.

Rozario, M., Lewis, I., & White, K. (2010). An examination of the factors that influence drivers' willingness to use handheld mobile phones. *Transportation Research, 13*(6), 365–376.

Sherin, K., Lowe, A., Harvey, B., Leiva, D., Malik, A., Matthews, S., Suh, R., & the American College of Preventative Medicine Prevention Practice Committee. (2014). Preventing texting while driving: A statement of the American College of Preventive. *American Journal of Preventive Medicine, 47*(5), 681–688.

Stevens, G. (2003). Advancing safety as a fundamental human right. *Health and Human Rights, 6*(2), 168–170.

Strider, E. (2015). Don't text a driver: Civil liability of remote third-party texters after *Kubert v. Best. William & Mary Law Review, 56*(3), 1004–1028.

Swartswell, N. (2012). Cities disagree on texting-driving ban. *The Texas Tribune*. Retrieved from www.nytimes.com/2012/10/28/us/texans-disagree-on-texting-driving-ban.html

United Nations. (1948). *Universal declaration of human rights: Report to the general assembly*. Retrieved from www.un.org/en/universal-declaration-human-rights

US Department of Health and Human Services, Center for Disease Control and Prevention. (2019). *Underlying causes of death 1999–2019*. Retrieved from http://wonder.cde.gov/ucd-icd10.html

US Department of Health and Human Services, Centers for Disease Prevention. (2018). *Distracted driving, types of distraction*. Retrieved from www.cdc.gov/transportationsafety/distracted_driving/index.html

US Department of Transportation National Highway Traffic Safety Administration. (2015). *Traffic safety facts research note: Distracted driving 2012*. Retrieved from https://crashstats.nhtsa.dot.gov/Api/Public/ViewPublication/812012#

Virginia Tech. (2019, February 7). Safe to use hands-free devices in the car? Yes, suggests new research. *ScienceDaily*. Retrieved from www.sciencedaily.com/releases/2019/02/190207173255.htm

Weir, K. (2011). Driven to distraction: Why is texting while driving so dangerous? *HEALTH: Current Science, a Weekly Reader Publication, 96*(13), 4.

World Population Review. (2021). *Worst drivers by state*. Retrieved from https://worldpopulationreview.com/state-rankings/worst-drivers-by-state

Chapter 20

An Overview of Wildlife Enforcement Cooperation in Canada and North America

Samantha de Vries

Introduction to Wildlife Enforcement and Trade

This chapter will serve as an introductory overview of the wildlife enforcement structure within Canada and North America, identifying relevant treaties and national legislation in place to facilitate cooperation. The author has conducted research in the region with Canadian and American officials (wildlife investigators and prosecutors) and therefore will focus more on Canada and the USA, given the author's experience with authorities from these two countries. Two case study reviews will identify the illicit wildlife trade (IWT) as a transnational and transboundary problem negatively affecting North American species. Wildlife enforcement in North America covers vast territories, rough terrain, and numerous species of endangered and at-risk wildlife. Canada, Mexico, and the United States employ different sustainability approaches to conservation to maintain a legal "extraction" of wildlife and other "natural resources." North America is a source, transit, and destination region for the IWT due to the multiple ports and airports, diverse landscape, and wildlife populations. Given the transnational nature of the IWT and the multiple border crossings and ports in the region, cooperation between agencies within each country and between authorities bilaterally and multilaterally is integral to stopping wildlife traffickers. There is an overall lack of harmonization in the region, particularly regarding species-at-risk listings and trade, and a general lack of resources to support larger-scale IWT detection.

Common Challenges

Wildlife crime is generally managed as a regulatory crime that in some countries and spaces incorporates non-government organizations (NGOs) as partners and allies (Nurse, 2016; Jernigan, 2006), more so than with other, "traditional" crime types. This is often the result of advocacy and resources obtained by NGO and inter-governmental organization (IGO) groups, rather than resource-strained wildlife authorities. The involvement of NGO and IGO groups is also present at high-level enforcement meetings on wildlife crime. Wildlife enforcement is unique in this regard, as it is not necessarily built on a foundation of criminal law and rehabilitation with only law enforcement involved, but rather on regulations, fines, and provisions that allow some legal exploitation and use of wildlife body parts (hunting, harvesting, trophies, trade, subsistence) with diverse non–criminal justice advocates. Despite the regulatory system and potential lack of will to criminally prosecute wildlife offenders (Nurse, 2016), individuals continue to source wildlife for multiple reasons, feeding and fueling demands at the individual, community, regional, and global levels. Eco-enforcement (environmental and wildlife enforcement) faces multiple challenges in investigating crimes, given the offenses' locations, the regulatory nature of eco-crimes, and their subsequent perceived lack of importance in the criminal justice system. According to Nurse (2016), environmental enforcement

DOI: 10.4324/9781003047117-23

challenges include resource scarcity, inconsistent legislation, sentencing, police tactics, and low priority. These challenges are further compounded as eco-issues are categorized and divided among different bodies (Nurse, 2016), likely resulting in jurisdictional overlap and potential mandate differences.

Canada in particular has multiple enforcement agencies at the federal and provincial/territorial levels; at the federal level for endangered species, the Environment and Climate Change Canada's Wildlife Enforcement Directorate is the main enforcement body, and at the provincial/territorial level, there are conservation agencies responsible for offenses committed against species within their jurisdictions. Wildlife agencies often have overlapping mandates given that species are transboundary. There are also capacity challenges, as wildlife enforcement must rely on policing bodies and customs officials to detect wildlife at border points, and depending on the breadth of offenses committed by the individual suspect(s), some crimes may be outside the authority and responsibility of wildlife officials.

Wildlife killing and importing/exporting are all regulated acts and therefore not always illegal, resulting in the identification of a crime and identification of a species being complex. Wildlife forensics are a key component to determining illegality and producing sufficient evidence with proper forensic testing (Linacre, 2009). Wildlife crime deterrence (specific and general) and recidivism rates of wildlife offenders are not well known. North America has largely been ignored in wildlife crime literature (aside from the USA), despite the biological diversity within the region and the prevalence of the IWT and wildlife crime in North America.

International and Regional Mechanisms

Canada, Mexico, and the USA are all signatories to the Convention for International Trade in Endangered Species of Wild Fauna and Flora (CITES, 1973), which regulates sustainable trade in wildlife. All member states of CITES (1973) report their national legal trade data for species listed under the convention. The convention controls and regulates sustainable trade in wild fauna and flora that are at risk without such regulation (through three appendices based on species health) (CITES, 1973). The CITES trade database (CITES, n.d.) is accessible on the web and can be used as a tool to identify legal wildlife trade trends per species and country; however, the data is voluntarily reported by countries and may not accurately reflect true trade volumes.

Wildlife protection and regulation enforcement are particularly important in North America, given the biodiversity in the region. For example, Canada and the USA are home to some of the most iconic Arctic species facing imminent habitat loss due to global warming impacts (Marine Mammal Commission, 2020). Threats to the polar bear (mainly habitat loss, but also hunting and human-wildlife conflict deaths, among others) have landed them in a "special concern" status with the Committee on the Status of Endangered Wildlife in Canada (COSEWIC, 2018, p. vii). According to the CITES trade database (CITES, n.d.), in 2019, Canada legally exported 11 polar bear parts internationally, indicating a "special concern" species still has an international legal market for its parts (often hides). As with any legal market, there are avenues open to exploitation.

Mexico is extremely biodiverse, and is home to over 10% of all of the world's known species (Tajbakhsh, 2012). This biodiversity may be viewed by wildlife traffickers as a potential source for in-demand "product." Traffickers illegally poach and export wildlife parts while the legal trade aids the movement of illicit wildlife as the demand outweighs sustainable use numbers (CEC, 2005). This is driven by financial gains (Nurse, 2015a). This facilitation in the North American context might be further compounded by free trade in the region and the difficulty for border control agents to locate and identify wildlife products and determine their (il)legality.

All three countries are members of the International Criminal Police Organization (INTERPOL) and the Wildlife Crime Working Group (WCWG), and all three countries cooperate trinationally through the Commission for Environmental Cooperation (CEC) and its North American Wildlife Enforcement Group (NAWEG). Currently, there is no regional mechanism in North America that provides jurisdictional powers to wildlife enforcement across all three countries. Cooperation is usually engaged in through regional groups, such as the CEC or NAWEG, or through agreements such as mutual legal assistance treaties (MLATs)—for example, the MLAT between Canada and the USA on mutual legal assistance in criminal matters (Treaty E101638, 1990)—or memoranda of understanding (MOUs) for joint enforcement operations. An in-depth analysis of North American cooperation mechanisms to combat the IWT shows a current gap in green criminological literature on wildlife crime relevant to Canada and North America. International and regional agreements exist for North American countries; however, implementation is often where challenges lie.

Cites and Wildlife Enforcement Networks (WENS)

Species are considered a natural resource, and when global natural resources began to deplete in the 1970s, CITES was born (CITES, 1973; CEC, 2005). CITES "was developed to safeguard species vulnerable to trade from *over*-exploitation" (CEC, 2005, p. 13, emphasis added). "Beyond economic incentive, strong cultural elements are also driving some wildlife trade" (CEC, 2005, p. 9). Not only does the IWT threaten species and shared ecosystems, but it can also affect other wildlife and humans through the transmission of disease—"Illegal wildlife trade is a means of dispersing infectious-contagious diseases" (CEC, 2005, p. 12)—such as viruses like COVID-19 and its apparent transmission through the poaching of pangolins in China for human consumption (UNODC, 2020a). There has been an identified potential threat for bear bile (and other wildlife derivatives) to potentially be used as a traditional Chinese medicine (TCM) treatment for COVID-19 (UNODC, 2020b: Introduction). This is concerning, given that black bears have been poached in Canada for their gall bladders to fulfill TCM remedies/cures (*R v. Kim*, 2016).

At the Conference of the Parties (CoP) to CITES, animal and plant committees meet, including operations and enforcement-based networks (called wildlife enforcement networks, or WENs). The second meeting of global WENs, including the NAWEG, took place in 2016 and was organized by the International Consortium on Combating Wildlife Crime (ICCWC) initiative (an international partnership comprising of INTERPOL, the United Nations Office on Drugs and Crime, the World Bank Group, the World Customs Organization, and CITES), with the meeting being funded by the USA (ICCWC, 2016). After the second meeting, the report outlined three main objectives: creating best-practice guidelines for WENs, enhancing cooperation, and operational objectives, and major challenges raised included the lack of forensic wildlife labs, species identification, and wildlife management for frontline officers (ICCWC, 2016). The US Fish and Wildlife Service presented its attaché program of wildlife officers who would be posted worldwide (ICCWC, 2016). Currently, the Environment and Climate Change Canada's Wildlife Enforcement Directorate does not have an attaché program like that of the US Fish and Wildlife Service. The only law enforcement program in Canada with a global operational reach is the Royal Canadian Mounted Police (RCMP) liaison officer (LO) program. This may indicate a lack of political will in Canada to address the IWT on an international scale and failure to identify the threat of global biodiversity loss. By the third meeting of WENs, the guidelines were not yet finalized but had been reviewed by participating WENs (CITES, 2019a); however, no meeting report was publicly available as of September 2020. Promotion of the WENs appears to have faded slightly in

Regional Harmonization

recent years, with international efforts such as the INTERPOL WCWG emerging more prominently with their multiple global operations series.

Regional Harmonization

Cooperation between wildlife agencies in Canada and the USA has been described by many wildlife officials as symbiotic (ongoing interviews with wildlife officials from Canada and the USA, 2019–2020). Jernigan (2006) also documented this successful partnership but identified that conservation efforts might be more effective in transboundary areas if the collaboration was expanded, potentially through the North American Agreement on Environmental Cooperation or other MOUs and agreements. Existing agreements do not always translate into actual conservation practice (Jernigan, 2006) or sufficient ongoing enforcement measures aside from one-off cases (personal observation, de Vries). The North American Free Trade Agreement (NAFTA) (North American Free Trade Agreement Implementation Act, 1993); its environmental agreement, the North American Agreement on Environmental Cooperation (International Trade and Investment Agreements Implementation Act, 2000, Part 3 NAAEC); and the Canada-United States-Mexico Agreement (CUSMA) (Canada-United States-Mexico Agreement Implementation Act, 2020) facilitate trade in North America. Free trade and conservation of transboundary species at times are conflicting (Jernigan, 2006).

Within the NAAEC and CEC are special groups dedicated to wildlife capacities and enforcement; however, such wildlife groups' reach and scope are unknown. Free trade agreements make the import and export of countries' natural resources easier but also place added pressure on wildlife and border enforcement of inspection and monitoring (CEC, 2005). The wide mandate of wildlife enforcement agencies and the global reach of the IWT result in wildlife and police bodies working together (CEC, 2005). Cooperation is a requirement for effective wildlife enforcement and regulation domestically, regionally, and internationally, given that conservation mandates span multiple agencies in which enforcement may be a small unit within the larger environmental body (as in Canada). This further entrenches the notion that wildlife crime is an environmental regulation issue, not a criminal justice issue.

Historically, Environment Canada and the US Fish and Wildlife Service have cooperated on operations that have resulted in successful convictions of wildlife traffickers (CEC, 2005), as have Mexican and American authorities (see Case Study 1 later in this chapter). Protection legislation exists in all three countries in North America, although species listings differ based on species' country of habitat and national views on the sustainable use of certain species: Canada has the Species at Risk Act (2002), Mexico has the Law for Endangered Species Protection (1994) (Tajbakhsh, 2012), and the USA has the Endangered Species Act (1973). Both Canada and the USA have environmental funds, but they have different systems. In Canada, the Environmental Damages Fund is fulfilled by wildlife and environmental offenders' fine penalties, which help support restoration and environmental projects (Government of Canada, 2020). In the USA, the Lacey Act Reward Fund functions to reward credible intel provided by citizens about potential wildlife crimes (US Fish and Wildlife Service, 2017).

Specific wildlife legislation exists in Canada through many federal and provincial/territorial acts, with the Wild Animal and Plant Protection and Regulation of International and Interprovincial Trade Act (WAPPRIITA, 1992) being the most prominent piece of legislation for trafficking in endangered species. Mexico has specific wildlife legislation, mainly through its General Law of Ecological Equilibrium and Environmental Protection (LGEEPA) and General Wildlife Law (LGVS) (CEC, 2005). The USA's Lacey Act (as amended in 2008) is particularly strong and criminalizes all wildlife that is illegal under national and foreign law (specifically section 3372, which has also been identified by Nurse (2015b) as a key section in the act for wildlife trafficking cases).

These pieces of legislation criminalize trade in endangered species (unless proper permits are obtained from CITES) and regulate wildlife trade to ideally maintain sustainable use (CEC, 2005). Each country has different wildlife agencies to enforce their national legislations. The USA appears to have the largest capacity as they have national agencies as well as a high-level presidential task force combating wildlife trafficking, involving senior-level representatives from multiple government agencies, which was founded by President Barack Obama (see The White House, 2013, Executive Order Combating Wildlife Trafficking), as well the US Fish and Wildlife Service Law Enforcement Management Information System (LEMIS), which maintains import/export trade data (CEC, 2017a). The US Fish and Wildlife Service also has international reach through its attaché program (mentioned earlier in the chapter), including one posting in Mexico City (US Fish and Wildlife Service, 2018), ideally providing increased bilateral cooperation between the USA and Mexico on criminal wildlife matters. One practical barrier to effective regional cooperation (or regional capacity buildings between wildlife agencies in all three countries) is language. (Canada has two official languages—English and French—Mexico's official language is Spanish, and the USA's official language is English; all three countries' Indigenous Peoples also have their respective languages.) Differences among legal systems, evidence thresholds, and processes are also common barriers to formal cooperation between countries.

There is also the difference of what governing body oversees wildlife agencies in the respective country; differences have been identified between Canada (and the Canadian Wildlife Service) operating under the Environment Ministry and the US (and US Fish and Wildlife Service) being principally enforcement based (Nurse, 2015b). Typically, enforcement is founded under the government's public safety arms, but wildlife enforcement (given the legal facilitation of wildlife exploitation) is managed differently in some countries. Unlike criminal laws enforced by national and state/provincial policing bodies in most countries, there are multiple legislations and agencies with the responsibility of protecting wildlife and enforcing regulations, which often differ by country.

Implementing CITES alongside national considerations (such as rural Inuit livelihoods in the Canadian Arctic) can conflict with other countries' interpretations of CITES and national protection levels. CITES and similar regulatory frameworks for the use of wildlife protect animals to some extent while simultaneously providing the legal foundations for humans to "use" animals (Nurse, 2015c). In the USA, it is illegal to import polar bear hides and narwhal tusks (Marine Mammal Protection Act, 1972), despite CITES permits being available for both species and a legal harvest operating in Canada. CITES provisions are essentially voluntary guidelines and can be followed and implemented by member states or can be used merely as a baseline, allowing member states to implement more stringent national provisions (as the USA has done with trade in some Arctic species). Sustainability is threatened with the IWT.

Other regions, such as the European Union (EU), have a stronger harmonization and regional response (Nurse, 2015c). Wildlife traffickers have exploited the lack of harmonization by acquiring wildlife parts legally in one country, then illegally smuggling them across borders. This makes it easier for individuals to acquire the wildlife parts as the countries have different regulations on the same species. One is example is ex-RCMP officer Mr. Logan, who legally purchased narwhal tusks from Canadian Arctic cooperatives for over a decade and illegally smuggled them into the USA, filling a regional and international market (*USA v. Logan*, 2014; *Logan v. The Attorney General of Canada*, 2015). Another individual implicated in the illicit narwhal network was an American, Mr. Boone, who purchased narwhal tusks illegally imported from Canada (a fact he would have known, given that he operated a trading company), then resold the tusks for profit (US Fish and Wildlife Service, 2017). The lack of harmonization between Canada and the USA on species' apparent sustainability in trade (such as polar bears and narwhals) signifies the economic component of wildlife regulations.

The Commission for Environmental Cooperation (CEC) and the North American Wildlife Enforcement Group (NAWEG)

The IWT is a problem for North America where shared borders, demand markets, and transit routes converge (CEC, 2005). The IWT is consistently estimated to be somewhere in the billions of dollars annually (CEC, 2005), although exact amount of the IWT cannot be calculated and estimates fluctuate, depending on which species and trades are included in the estimate (CEC, 2005). "If these ecosystems are to continue to be a source of life and prosperity, they must be protected. Doing so is a responsibility shared by Canada, Mexico and the United States" (CEC, 2005, Preface, p. 2). Some species are transboundary, making them targets for poaching if legislation is not harmonized in the region. International attention on species conservation and combating wildlife crime is typically focused on charismatic species residing on the continent of Africa, such as elephants and rhinos, with a large demand market in Asia (usually identified as China, Viet Nam, and Laos, among others). However, species of concern exist in North America, such as the polar bear, the narwhal, the American black bear (poached for their gall bladders for TCM; UNODC, 2016), as well as other large mammals killed for their meat, hides, or other body parts; parrots (for the pet trade); and turtles and tortoises, among others. North America is also used as a transit region where foreign species are smuggled in from other regions.

The CEC promotes sustainable use, trade, and captive breeding of some species involved in the IWT (for example, promotion for sustainable use of turtles and tortoises, parrots, and sharks, among others) through sustainable trade action plans (see CEC, 2017a, 2017b, 2017c). The CEC promotes sustainable trade while simultaneously acknowledging that priority shark populations have declined due to overexploitation (CEC, 2017c, p. 7). The CEC has recommended staff exchanges between Canada, Mexico, and the USA; trinational and national trainings on shark identification and combating parrot trafficking (CEC, 2017b, 2017c); and legislation changes to allow parrot trade importation from Mexico (CEC, 2017b). Actual enforcement or joint operation initiatives to dismantle IWT networks stemming from such species-specific research and subsequent action plans are unknown, beyond enforcement measures that directly coincide with sustainable legal trade efforts. Sustainability cannot be maintained if overexploitation and the IWT flourish without proper criminal justice research and responses.

The CEC Secretariat has a citizen submission function (SEM), which allows citizens to report a perceived lack of enforcement of environmental laws (Environment and Climate Change Canada, 2020), and has been successful in at least soliciting responsive action by government agencies in Canada in one case (Jernigan, 2006). Tremblay, Tice, Boisvert, and Fitzpatrick (2007) evaluated Canada's participation in the CEC and found that the federal governments of all three countries need to understand the importance of the CEC and implement the CEC's recommendations. The SEM submissions need to be processed efficiently with a real impact on enforcement and policy. Tremblay et al. (2007) found overall that the CEC has made the most impact in compliance and enforcement through public awareness, with the CEC's support mostly coming from academics and some NGOs (Tremblay et al., 2007). The enforcement support and citizen submissions are only a portion of the CEC's mandate, which covers a breadth of environmental matters affecting the region (such as pollution, waterways, emergency preparedness for disasters, and so on).

The North American Agreement on Environmental Cooperation led to the creation of the CEC and the CEC's Enforcement Working Group, which includes the North American Wildlife Enforcement Group (NAWEG) (CEC, 2005). Through NAWEG, the CEC builds networks between wildlife enforcement in the region and builds capacity through training initiatives and by forming a regional forensic DNA database (NAWEG, n.d.). NAWEG is represented by Canada through the Environment and Climate Change Canada, by Mexico through the Procuraduria Federal de Proteccion al Ambiente (PROFEPA), and by the USA through the US Fish and Wildlife Service (NAWEG, 2016). There has not been a CEC/NAWEG report on the IWT in North America since 2005 (see CEC, 2005), despite the detection and prosecution of numerous transnational wildlife trafficking cases in the region since 2005. Increased transparency on the IWT, capacity-building efforts, and NAWEG initiatives to dismantle illicit wildlife networks should be more accessible and potentially evaluated to increase and harmonize regional impact. NAWEG, through the CEC, does not appear to be as active as it could be and may be an underused resource. The USA appears to be the most equipped, or politically driven and supported, to carry out larger-scale investigations (aside from INTERPOL operations involving North America). For example, Operation Crash in the USA resulted in restitution and fines in the millions of dollars for rhino horn traffickers in the US (Eisele, 2017).

Interpol Wildlife Crime Working Group (WCWG)

INTERPOL facilitates informal police-to-police cooperation in wildlife enforcement matters and coordinates global operations. The INTERPOL WCWG and other partners from the International Consortium on Combating Wildlife Crime (ICCWC), alongside INTERPOL member states, have engaged in key global wildlife operations that have targeted specific species and specific regions. Global operations to combat wildlife crime are led by INTERPOL and are conducted by member states' law enforcement agencies within an operation series. Three key operations relevant to North America that have been carried out(to date under the "Thunder series" consisted of 1) Operation Thunderbird in 2017, consisting of agencies from 49 countries resulting in 1,300 illicit wildlife and forestry seizures (INTERPOL, 2018); 2) Operation Thunderstorm in 2018, which resulted in 1,974 illicit seizures including the carcasses of two polar bears and 18 tons of eel confiscated in Canada (CITES, 2018); and 3) Operation Thunderball in 2019, consisting of 109 countries and 582 suspects arrested with 1,828 illicit seizures including 23 live primates and close to 10,000 marine wildlife "products" (CITES, 2019b). Operation Blizzard was also implemented in 2019, aimed at the illegal trade in reptiles and involving Canada and the USA (INTERPOL, 2019a). INTERPOL is a powerful organization for wildlife enforcement as it can connect agencies and officers with other ICCWC partner organizations. Police agencies worldwide can issue global border alert notifications, and national police agencies can communicate through the I247 chat communication tool (of which INTERPOL is the caretaker).

Participant observation data from the INTERPOL WCWG 30th annual meeting held in Singapore in 2019 (collected by the author with the permission of one of the hosts and with ethics approval from Simon Fraser University study #2019s0350) informed an article (in preparation) by the author. Preliminary data suggest four main themes relevant to North America: Theme 1: Partnership. The workshop includes a unique involvement of NGOs and academics with different involvement levels (more concrete involvement such as panel positions were provided for NGOs); Theme 2: Organized wildlife crime. There was a debate between some academics and some private organizations and wildlife enforcement representatives about the term *organized wildlife crime* and whether this should be referred to as organized wildlife networks or traditional crime syndicates; Theme 3: Follow the money. There was an overall push for financial investigations into wildlife networks and for countries to identify wildlife crime on the internet; and Theme 4: Risk modeling. One country promoted risk modeling for wildlife enforcement to better use limited resources and target problem areas, which would be useful in North America, where enforcement agencies are responsible for large territories (INTERPOL WCWG Meeting, 2019). According to the INTERPOL press release (INTERPOL, 2019b) regarding the meeting:

> During the 30th meeting of the INTERPOL Wildlife Crime Working Group, some 160 participants from police, government agencies, international organizations, the transport and financial sectors, academia and social media companies gathered to review the latest environmental threats, trafficking trends and challenges to tackling the criminal networks behind such crime.
>
> (INTERPOL, 2019b, 3rd para.)

It was evident that participants felt the workshop was useful as the fringes of the workshop provided space for officials across the globe to interact informally and exchange information, which may indicate new species at risk, new trafficking routes, or new offender networks. This forum is operationally based and seemingly effective, with tangible investigative operation results and clear support from representatives in attendance. Further involvement of academics, potentially as panel experts, would be a welcome addition to future meetings. Other academics, such as Wyatt (2013), have identified INTERPOL WCWG meetings as useful, concluding that these global operations (specifically Operations Predator and Prey, focused on the IWT in Asian big cats) are "Seemingly, the results of the operation were good and will enhance the capacity of those involved to be able to carry out further such operations" (Wyatt, 2013, p. 157). INTERPOL is the only international policing body with the expertise, reach, and capacity to conduct global operations in wildlife crime across multiple regions and species.

Willemsen and Watson (2018) advocated for a transdisciplinary approach to tackling wildlife crime, with one component being the fostering of concrete collaborations between academics, NGOs, and practitioners. The transdisciplinary approach (TD), according to Willemsen and Watson (2018), is more holistic than other approaches (such as the interdisciplinary approach, in which agency-to-agency cooperation occurs without a unified mandate, or the multidisciplinary approach, in which organizations tackle the same issue without harmonization). Willemsen and Watson (2018) believe that the TD approach deals with the context of wildlife crime first by engaging all stakeholders, as opposed to working forward from the extinction/threat perspective in silos, and that utilizing this TD approach seems common sense but is not commonplace.

The INTERPOL WCWG has started to employ a TD approach. At the 30th annual meeting, academics, NGOs, and enforcement provided space to express suggestions for future work or collaborations. Whether an inter-, multi-, or transdisciplinary approach is adopted, there is one common element among them, in that all three require political will and engaged cooperation across agencies and political borders. Ideally, INTERPOL will continue its progressive collaborations with academia and civil society. Jernigan (2006) identified NGO initiatives in the North American region (particularly the Yellowstone to Yukon Y2Y initiative) as being particularly useful in identifying conservation needs and gaps. North American NGOs may benefit from involvement at the INTERPOL WCWG (or NAWEG meetings) to foster stronger collaboration. Wildlife crime and wildlife conservation are so intertwined that a TD approach would streamline efforts.

In White's (2008) discussion on corporations, states, and organized crime in illegal waste disposal, White stated, "A distinction can be made between organised criminal activity and organised criminals" (White, 2008, p. 131), which is further explained as legitimate companies committing waste crimes and traditional syndicates that may engage in waste crimes, facilitating the merging of legal/illegal operations (White, 2008). This can be seen in the

An Overview of Wildlife Enforcement   295

IWT, where the legal market has been identified as facilitating in some ways the illegal market or movement of wildlife "product," but the direct involvement of "traditional" organized criminal groups has been only on a case-by-case basis. The possibility of organized crime involvement in the IWT was also identified during a trinational meeting between Canada, Mexico, and the USA on sustainable trade in turtles and tortoises (CEC, 2017c). It may be that what is implied by the term *organized crime* needs to be redefined in the wildlife context. This might include adopting different terms that clearly identify the specific criminality involved in different wildlife crimes. Potential terms might include *organized wildlife crime* for illegal wildlife-trafficking groups; *organized wildlife networks* for individuals with legitimate organizations that then exploit and use their positions, knowledge, and access to move illegal product; and *organized wildlife syndicates* for illegal groups involved in trafficking wildlife and other illicit goods such as drugs.

Shelley and Kinnard (2018) made such a distinction in their work on rhino horn and elephant ivory trafficking and referred to the infamous corrupt rhino hunts in Africa as "run more by criminal networks than criminal organizations" (Shelley & Kinnard, 2018, p. 119). Shelley and Kinnard (2018) further discussed the involvement of Asian organized crime groups in wildlife trafficking in different African countries, often through Asian diaspora communities. Such communities were also identified by the Elephant Action League (2018, discussed further later in this chapter) as having community members involved in the facilitation, transportation, or trafficking of totoaba bladders from coastal Mexico. Preliminary data (from an article in preparation on Canadian wildlife enforcement) highlight a possible increase in the number of Asian hunters obtaining hunting licenses in one Canadian province thought by one interview participant to potentially be a way of internalizing bear poaching within the Asian community. It may be that some diaspora communities produce a localized demand market, and some individuals within some diaspora communities may act as travel nodes for illicit wildlife goods destined for other demand markets. (See Case Study 1.)

Two Key Regional Cases

Despite the lack of formal jurisdictional power within the region, the cooperation between wildlife agencies appears to be strong in North America and well supported by wildlife enforcement officials. A key component in the below two transnational case studies is the apparent political will and capacity of US agencies to pursue wildlife offenders. Given the unknown extent of wildlife crime, particularly within North America's vast rural habitats, identifying such large-scale illicit networks (discussed next) is alarming and may indicate further criminal wildlife activity is going undetected. The first case discussed here involves Mexico (as a source country) and the USA (as a transit country) and highlights impact of illegal wildlife crime on other species within an ecosystem. The second case involves a guide outfitter operating in the USA (Alaska) but in close proximity to the Canadian border (in the Yukon) and hunters/poachers from both countries.

Case Study 1: Trafficking of Totoaba Bladders and the Unintended Deadly Consequences for the Vaquita

The case of the totoaba and totoaba conservation–dependent vaquita is a prime example of the interconnectedness of NGOs and law enforcement in combating wildlife crime and the transnational nature of illicit markets in North America. The totoaba is a large fish in demand for its swim bladders, and the vaquita, an endangered porpoise, is being unintentionally killed in the fishing nets (Elephant Action League, 2018). The vaquita is close to extinction, and both the totoaba and vaquita live only off the coast of Mexico, where totoaba are being killed for the economic value of their swim bladders (as well as issues such as overfishing and poor fishing tactics, negatively affecting both species) (Elephant Action League, 2018). The Elephant Action League, an advocacy NGO, conducted a 14-month investigation into the illicit totoaba bladder trade and identified a supply chain in which a few Mexican individuals funded poachers who sourced Chinese buyers in Mexico to fulfill the demand market in China for the bladders (Elephant Action League, 2018). According to the Elephant Action League (2018), the NGO Sea Shepherd has successfully protected the vaquita by removing fishing nets and through their partnership with Mexican authorities. NGOs' involvement in tackling wildlife exploitation is integral to protecting species, but their reports must always be reviewed through a critical lens, given their advocacy position. The Elephant Action League identified mostly Asian countries as transit points out of Mexico (2018); however, US cases indicated the USA was also a transit intermediary for the bladders ultimately destined for China. According to the Elephant Action League (2018), traditional drug cartels in Mexico were paid off by organized totoaba groups and may have assisted with the movement of product. The reported tactics observed by the Elephant Action League (2018) mirrored those of drug cartels.

The organized nature of the totoaba networks appears to be vast. Mr. Zhen was caught crossing the border at Calexico with 27 totoaba bladders, and through undercover surveillance, it was identified that Zhen's Calexico home was a totoaba bladder–drying facility worth an estimated $3.6 million (United States Department of Justice, 2013b). Another totoaba trafficking player, California resident Mr. Xie, pleaded guilty in 2013 for their role in the illicit network and conspiracy to traffic totoaba bladders between Mexico and the USA and on to Asian markets (United States Department of Justice, 2013a). Mr. Xie was identified through undercover surveillance and operations from border seizures of totoaba bladders (United States Department of Justice, 2013a). Due to the corruption of wealthy drug cartels in Mexico and a difficult environment for enforcement, there have been reports in the media of the involvement of the Sinaloa drug cartel in the totoaba bladder trade (AP News, 2018) and individuals involved in the totoaba trade who have connections with the Sinaloa drug cartel (Alcántara, 2017). Wildlife trafficking of one species has the potential to negatively impact other species, such as the effect of the trafficking of totoaba on the vaquita, driving them close to extinction. The transnational nature of wildlife crime (different sources, transit, and demand countries in the chain) and globalization results in cross-border operations being pivotal in identifying new networks and species at risk and dismantling traffickers' supply chains.

Case Study 2: Operation Bruin—Exposing a Northern Poaching Network

Operation Bruin was a joint undercover operation carried out by wildlife officers from Canada and the USA. Given that the focal point of the operation was Alaskan/Kluane guide outfitter Mr. Martin, it is likely that the US initiated the investigation and brought in Canadian authorities when it was discovered that Mr. Martin had Canadian clients engaging in hunting and importing violations. Mr. Martin and his clients engaged in numerous offenses of illegally baiting animals and unregistered sites, falsifying records, not accompanying clients on kills, and trafficking (*USA v. Martin*, 2013). In 2002, Martin and his colleague illegally baited a site used by a client to kill a brown bear and then falsified the trophy certificate, which was eventually brought to the client's home in Alberta, Canada (*USA v. Martin*, 2013). In 2010, in an illegally baited area, a client of Mr. Martin shot a bear but did not kill it (*USA v. Martin*, 2013). According to Mr. Martin's plea agreement, "The next day, MARTIN and CLEMETT tracked the wounded bear by following the blood trail. The bear was never recovered" (*USA v. Martin*, 2013, p. 20). In the Yukon in 2011, Mr. Martin killed a Dall sheep under First Nations rights; however, it was not registered with the Yukon, and he did not obtain an export permit for the sheep's horns (*USA v. Martin*, 2013). Mr. Martin pleaded guilty and received a substantively light sentence, given his blatant disregard for wildlife regulations and the numerous offenses he committed. Mr. Martin was sentenced in 2013 to three years' probation, which stipulated he could not guide, outfit, or hunt during the three years and could not hunt worldwide for two years; a $40,000 fine; and forfeiture of his listed trophies (*USA v. Martin*, 2013).

This is where the legal market or activity of hunting and transporting trophies can facilitate the illegal trade as permits and paperwork can be forged, and individuals can hide illegal actions behind their legal hunts in the wilderness with few witnesses. Mr. Martin's guiding status, and an apparent lack of regulatory inspections and controls, allowed Martin and clients to hunt in any location, at any time, regardless of tags, as Mr. Martin would falsify records to balance the regulation paperwork. This case raises the question of whether Martin's actions are an indication that the trophy-hunting culture in North America is largely unregulated. Mr. Martin may have engaged in numerous other violations that were never identified due to the clandestine nature of wildlife offenses occurring in vast rural areas where carcasses and other evidence are eaten, where resource-consuming undercover operations are likely rare, and where those involved in the hunting trips may maintain discretion in order not to implicate themselves.

Discussion

Key regional cases reviewed in this chapter identify the transboundary nature of the IWT. Several species in the North American region are in demand in both the licit and illicit markets. For example, the United Nations Office on Drugs and Crime (UNODC) world wildlife crime report published in 2016 identified the illicit demand for North American bear gall bladders used in TCM. Despite this illicit demand, bear parts are still legally exported out of Canada following international convention regulations (CITES, n.d.), and hunting permits are still granted for hunting and harvesting different species of bears.

Wildlife enforcement in North America must navigate complex regulatory frameworks and multiple species involved in legal and illegal trade and attempt to identify wildlife offenses occurring in different jurisdictions and in vast wilderness areas, on a budget. Transnational wildlife networks allow for wildlife offenses to go undetected unless cooperation and joint operations are funded and pursued. Enforcement cooperation appears to be successful in North America in some cases but may require further resources and capacity. International and regional mechanisms exist (such as CITES and CEC/NAWEG in North America); however, there is a lack of harmonization within the region regarding certain species protections and enforcement structures. WENs and the INTERPOL WCWG are key in promoting collaboration among wildlife practitioners and building networks for future cooperation in criminal cases and intelligence sharing. Regional operations might need to be undertaken between Canada, Mexico, and the USA, potentially through NAWEG, to further investigate INTERPOL WCWG operational findings in the region. Key operations of INTERPOL and key regional cases highlight the transboundary nature of the IWT. Enforcement operations should be actively supported, potentially through a regional enforcement network with jurisdictional authority between Canada, Mexico, and the USA to carry out (undercover) operations in IWT networks identified by national agencies, and NGOs and through already-established networks like the CEC, NAWEG, and INTERPOL WCWG.

Conclusion

Cooperation structures are in place in the region, and North American enforcement has cooperated successfully in transnational wildlife cases. However, the last assessment report of the IWT in the region by CEC/NAWEG available to the public was in 2005 (CEC, 2005), and the last evaluation of Canada's cooperation in the CEC was in 2007 (Tremblay et al., 2007). This indicates a lack of available knowledge and transparency on IWT figures and cooperation engagement in wildlife matters in North America. Overall, the IWT in North America should be assessed from a regional perspective, and cooperation structures and their implementation should be re-evaluated.

Discussion Questions

1. What similarities and differences can be identified between the two regional case studies discussed in the chapter?
2. How would you define the "organized crime" involved in Case Study 1 and Case Study 2?
3. How might wildlife crime with a transnational component (individuals/product crossing borders) complicate wildlife enforcement efforts?
4. Why is cooperation within the region important in the fight against wildlife crime?
5. How does the Commission for Environmental Cooperation (CEC) support cooperation in wildlife matters in North America?

References

Alcántara, A. (2017). *Vaquita: The business of extinction*. Retrieved from https://money.cnn.com/interactive/news/vaquita-business-of-extinction/index.html

AP News. (2018). *Mexican judge frees suspect of poaching in vaquita habitat*. Retrieved from https://apnews.com/article/20f5a2520b054e9f94bace21967f647e

Canada-United States-Mexico Agreement Implementation Act, c 1, SC, CanLII (CUSMA, 2020).

CEC. (2005). *Illegal trade in wildlife: A North American perspective*. Montreal, ON. Retrieved from http://www3.cec.org/islandora/en/item/2226-illegal-trade-in-wildlife-north-american-perspective

CEC. (2017a). *Action plan for North America: Sustainable trade in turtles and tortoises*. Montreal, ON. Retrieved from http://www3.cec.org/islandora/en/item/11699-sustainable-trade-in-turtles-and-tortoises-action-plan-north-america

CEC. (2017b). *Action plan for North America: Sustainable trade in parrots*. Montreal, ON. Retrieved from http://www3.cec.org/islandora/en/item/11696-sustainable-trade-in-parrots-action-plan-north-america

CEC. (2017c). *Action plan for North America: Sustainable trade in sharks*. Montreal, ON: Retrieved from http://www3.cec.org/islandora/en/item/11714-sustainable-trade-in-sharks-action-plan-north-america

CITES. (2018). *Month-long transcontinental operation hit wildlife criminal hard*. (Press release.) Retrieved from www.cites.org/eng/news/month-long-trans-continental-operation-hit-wildlife-criminals-hard_20062018

CITES. (2019a). *Wildlife enforcement networks from around the world meet to further strengthen collaborative efforts against wildlife crime*. Retrieved from https://cites.org/eng/Wildlife_enforcement_networks_from_around_the_world_meet_to_further_strengthen_collaborative_efforts_against_wildlife_crime_2608 2019#:~:text=The%20Third%20Global%20meeting%20of%20the%20WENs%20followed%20the%20first,funded%20by%20the%20United%20States

CITES. (2019b). *Wildlife trafficking: Organized crime hit hard by joint INTERPOL-WCO global enforcement operation*. (Press release.) Retrieved from https://cites.org/eng/news/wildlife-trafficking-organized-crime-hit-hard-by-joint-interpol-wco-global-enforcement-operation_10072019

CITES. (n.d.). Retrieved from https://trade.cites.org/

CITES Trade Database. Retrieved September 2020 from https://trade.cites.org/

Convention on International Trade in Endangered Species of Wild Fauna and Flora (CITES) (1973) (Amended April 30, 1983).

COSEWIC. (2018). *COSEWIC assessment and status report on the polar bear Ursus maritimus in Canada: Executive summary*. Retrieved from www.registrelep-sararegistry.gc.ca/default.asp?lang=en&n=24F7211B-1

Eisele, T. (2017). *Operation crash: Stopping a network of illegal wildlife traffickers in United States*. (Press release.) Retrieved from www.naclec.org/press-pages/2017/10/11/operation-crash-stopping-a-network-of-illegal-wildlife-traffickers-in-united-states

Elephant Action League. (2018). *Operation Fake Gold, the totoaba supply chain—from Mexico's totoaba cartels to China's totoaba maw wholesalers—an illegal trade killing the vaquita*. Retrieved from https://earthleagueinternational.org/operation-fake-gold/

Endangered Species Act Department of the Interior, US Fish and Wildlife Service. (1973).

Environment and Climate Change Canada. (2020). *Compendium of Canada's engagement in international environmental agreements and instruments, environment and climate change Canada: North American agreement on environmental cooperation (NAAEC)*. Retrieved from www.canada.ca/content/dam/eccc/documents/pdf/international-affairs/compendium/2020/batch-11/north-american-agreement-environmental-cooperation.pdf

Government of Canada. (2020). *Environmental damages fund*. Retrieved from www.canada.ca/en/environment-climate-change/services/environmental-funding/programs/environmental-damages-fund.html#toc2

ICCWC. (2016). *Second global meeting of the wildlife enforcement networks*. Retrieved from https://cites.org/sites/default/files/eng/prog/iccwc/WENs/Report_2nd_Global_WEN_meeting-final.pdf

International Trade and Investment Agreements Implementation Act, RSA, c 1–7, CanLII (Part 3, NAAEC, 2000).

INTERPOL. (2018). *Global wildlife enforcement: Strengthening law enforcement cooperation against wildlife crime*. Retrieved from www.interpol.int/en/Crimes/Environmental-crime/Wildlife-crime

INTERPOL. (2019a). *Illicit trade in reptiles: Hundreds of seizures and arrests in global operation*. (Press release.) Retrieved from www.interpol.int/en/News-and-Events/News/2019/Illicit-trade-in-reptiles-hundreds-of-seizures-and-arrests-in-global-operation

INTERPOL. (2019b). *INTERPOL wildlife crime working group looks at threats, challenges*. (Press release.) Retrieved from www.interpol.int/en/News-and-Events/News/2019/A-multi-sector-approach-to-tackling-wildlife-crime

INTERPOL WCWG Meeting. (2019, November 18–22). 30th INTERPOL Wildlife Crime Working Group Meeting, Singapore.

Jernigan, C. (2006). The howling of lat. forty-nine: Assessing collaborative wildlife management efforts along Western Canada-US Border. *Journal of International Wildlife Law and Policy, 9*(1), 55–89. doi:10.1080/13880290500536466

Lacey Act, 18 USC 42–43, 16 USC 3371–3378 (2008 as amended).

Linacre, A. (2009). Nature of wildlife crimes, their investigations and scientific processes. In *Forensic science in wildlife investigations* (1st ed., p. 10). Boca Raton, FL: CRC Press.

Logan v. The Attorney General of Canada (on behalf of the United States of America), 59, CanLII (NBCA 2015).

Marine Mammal Commission. (2020). *Climate change and the Arctic*. Retrieved from www.mmc.gov/priority-topics/arctic/climate-change/

Marine Mammal Protection Act, 16 USC 1361–1407 (1972).

NAWEG. (2016). *North American Wildlife Enforcement Group (NAWEG)*. Retrieved from https://cites.org/sites/default/files/eng/prog/iccwc/WENs/NAWEG-info_sheet_Sept16.pdf

NAWEG. (n.d.). NAWEG, Making a difference for wildlife, Une action positive pour les espèces sauvages, Una oportunidad para la vida silvestre. Retrieved from http://www3.cec.org/islandora/en/item/1716-naweg-making-difference-wildlife

North American Free Trade Agreement Implementation Act, c44, SC, CanLII (NAFTA, 1993).

Nurse, A. (2015a). Theoretical perspectives on wildlife law enforcement. In *Policing wildlife: Perspectives on the enforcement of wildlife legislation* (pp. 83–100). London: Palgrave Macmillan.

Nurse, A. (2015b). National wildlife legislation and law enforcement policies. In *Policing wildlife: Perspectives on the enforcement of wildlife legislation* (pp. 63–82). London: Palgrave Macmillan.

Nurse, A. (2015c). International and Regional Wildlife Legislation. In *Policing wildlife: Perspectives on the enforcement of wildlife legislation* (Vol. 3, pp. 41–62). London: Palgrave Macmillan.

Nurse, A. (2016). Investigating environmental crime. In *An introduction to green criminology and environmental justice* (1st ed., pp. 145–158). London: Sage.

Regina v. Kim, No. 0113 CanLII (BCPC 2016).

Shelley, L., & Kinnard, K. (2018). The convergence of trade in illicit rhino horn and elephant ivory with other forms of criminality. In W. D. Moreto (Ed.), *Wildlife crime: From theory to practice* (pp. 109–134). Philadelphia, PA: Temple University Press.

Species at Risk Act (SARA), s.s. C. 29 (2002).

Tajbakhsh, M. (2012). *Two nations, one goal.* (Press release.) Retrieved from www.fws.gov/endangered/news/bulletin-spring2010/two-nations-one-goal.html#:~:text=Again%20in%201994%2C%20Mexico%20enacted,established%20Mexico's%20national%20wildlife%20agency.&text=Then%2C%20in%202000%2C%20Mexico%20enacted,country's%20most%20comprehensive%20wildlife%20legislation

Treaty E101638, CTS No. 19, Treaty Between the Government of Canada and the Government of the United States of America on Mutual Legal Assistance in Criminal Matters (1990).

Tremblay, M. C., Tice, S., Boisvert, S., & Fitzpatrick, L. (2007). *Evaluation of Canada's participation in the Commission for Environmental Cooperation (CEC).* Retrieved from 4.2 Canada-Specific Findings www.ec.gc.ca/doc/ae-ve/CEC-CCE/toc_eng.htm

United States of America v. Logan, No. 133 CanLII (NBQB 2014).

United States of America vs. Ronald L. Martin, No. 1:13-cr-006-TMB-LCL (District of Alaska 2013).

United States Department of Justice. (2013a). *Trafficker of endangered wildlife pleads guilty.* (Press release.) Retrieved from www.justice.gov/usao-sdca/pr/trafficker-endangered-wildlife-pleads-guilty

United States Department of Justice. (2013b). *Massive trade in endangered species uncovered; U.S. Attorney charges 7 with smuggling swim bladders of endangered fish worth millions on black market; Officials see trend.* (Press release.) Retrieved from www.justice.gov/usao-sdca/pr/massive-trade-endangered-species-uncovered-us-attorney-charges-7-smuggling-swim

UNODC. (2016). *World wildlife crime report: Trafficking in protected species.* Retrieved from www.unodc.org/unodc/en/data-and-analysis/wildlife.html

UNODC. (2020a). *Wildlife crime: Pangolin scales.* Retrieved from www.unodc.org/documents/wwcr/2020/Wildlife_crime_Pangolin_UNODC.pdf

UNODC. (2020b). *World wildlife crime report: Trafficking in protected species.* Retrieved from www.unodc.org/documents/data-and-analysis/wildlife/2020/World_Wildlife_Report_2020_9July.pdf

US Fish and Wildlife Service. (2017). *Brinnon resident sentenced to prison for trafficking protected narwhal tusks: Defendant trafficked marine mammal parts worth as much as $400,000.* (Press release.) Retrieved from www.fws.gov/news/ShowNews.cfm?ref=brinnon-resident-sentenced-to-prison-for-trafficking-protected-narwhal-&_ID=36144#:~:text=Narwhals%20are%20Arctic%20whales%20often,tusks%20into%20the%20United%20States

US Fish and Wildlife Service. (2018). *U.S. government bolsters overseas law enforcement capacity to combat illegal trade in wildlife.* (Press release.) Retrieved from www.fws.gov/news/ShowNews.cfm?ref=u.s.-government-bolsters-overseas-law-enforcement-capacity-to-combat-&_ID=36326

The White House. (2013). *Executive order combating wildlife trafficking.* (Press release.) Retrieved from https://obamawhitehouse.archives.gov/the-press-office/2013/07/01/executive-order-combating-wildlife-trafficking

White, R. (2008). Transnational environmental crime. In *Crimes against nature* (pp. 115–143). New York, NY: Routledge.

Wild Animal and Plant Protection and Regulation of International and Interprovincial Trade Act (WAPPRIITA), c. 52, S.C. (1992).

Willemsen, M., & Watson, R. (2018). A transdisciplinary approach to wildlife crime prevention. In W. D. Moreto (Ed.), *Wildlife crime: From theory to practice* (pp. 256–278). Philadelphia, PA: Temple University Press.

Wyatt, T. (2013). *Wildlife trafficking: A deconstruction of the crime, the victims, and the offenders* (1st ed.). London: Palgrave Macmillan.

Chapter 21

A National Perspective on Retail Theft

Melody Hicks and Ben Stickle

The Threat of Theft: The Scope of the Problem

Contrary to what most people might think, in the United States, property crimes are far more prevalent than violent crimes. According to the Federal Burau of Investigation (2018) Uniform Crime Report, the ratio of property offenses to violent offenses was roughly 6:1 as of 2018. When talking about specific types of property offenses (e.g., larceny-theft, motor vehicle theft, burglary, vandalism, and arson), larceny-theft is, by far, the most common offense. With more than seven million instances of theft occurring each year, it accounts for almost two-thirds of reported crime in the United States.

Larceny-theft is an umbrella term used to cover many constituent offenses, including retail theft broadly. The term *retail theft* generally refers to the act of removing a product or item from a retail establishment without presenting the proper payment. Retail theft can be accomplished in various ways, ranging from merely concealing products when exiting a store to elaborately switching or altering barcodes on items so that lower prices are rung up when the thief goes to pay for the items.

Examining the crime even further, retail theft can be categorized into external theft, internal theft, and organized retail theft. External theft, colloquially known as shoplifting, occurs when someone who is not an employee intentionally takes a product from a business without paying for it. At the same time, internal theft occurs when an employee steals merchandise from his or her employer. Although some thieves show a tremendous amount of ingenuity in how they steal items, retail theft does not necessarily require a high degree of skill, and because of the potential financial reward for the crime, quite a few people commit retail theft. In 2010 alone, retailers in the US caught 6.2 million shoplifters and apprehended just under a million employees who stole from their workplaces (Retail Theft Goes Global, 2011). However, this may be only a small portion of the theft actually committed, as the British Retail Consortium claims that British retailers are only aware of about 18.9% of retail crimes (as cited in Bamfield, 2004, p. 236).

The final form of theft is organized retail crime, which involves several persons working together to steal or defraud retail establishments (Finklea, 2010). While this type of crime is less common than the first two and requires more skill, it is very costly. Cumulatively, all three types of theft result in profound financial damage to retail establishments.

Researchers and industry leaders attempt to gauge the financial damage retail theft causes by measuring "shrinkage." Retail shrinkage is defined as "financial loss attributable to a combination of employee theft, vendor fraud, shoplifting, and administrative process error" (Bailey, 2006, p. 802). The vast majority of retail shrinkage comprises employee theft and shoplifting (Bamfield, 2004; National Retail Federation, 2016). Some of the items that are frequently targeted by employees and shoplifters include the following:

> [G]oods with certain characteristics are the most vulnerable to theft. These are: high value; relatively small size; "designer" brand, or manufactured by well-known company;

DOI: 10.4324/9781003047117-24

in great or regular demand by the public . . . particularly where the supply is less than demand. Products meeting this specification can be easily slipped into the pocket or concealed about one's person and can be readily sold direct to "customers" or to an intermediary.

(Bamfield, 2003, p. 52)

In 2009, global retail shrinkage amounted to an astounding $114.8 billion (Bamfield, 2010). North America possesses the highest shrinkage rate globally at 1.85% of sales, with Europe following closely behind at 1.83% and Latin America with 1.81% shrink; Asia-Pacific is the lowest at 1.75% (Planet Retail RNG, 2018). While these may seem like small percentages of sales, the value lost is exceptionally high. For example, the USA lost $42 billion to shrink, Europe $29 billion, Asia-Pacific $24 billion, and Latin America $4 billion (Planet Retail RNG, 2018). Globally, retailers lose by theft, fraud, spoilage, damaged goods, shoplifting, return fraud, and other means nearly 2% of their inventory, or nearly $1 trillion in value.

Such a high shrinkage rate is attributed to two factors. One is that North America boasts more retail stores than any other nation. Secondly, North America's high shrink rate is partially the result of its loss prevention expenditures—North America spends less on loss prevention than any other region in the world (Deyle, 2015). The global average for loss prevention expenditures as a percentage of retail sales is about .80%, whereas the United States spends about half of that—0.42%, or $12.02 billion per year (Deyle, 2015; Bamfield, 2010).

On average, shoplifters take approximately $300 worth of merchandise per incident of theft, while the average amount an employee steals is much higher—about $1,200 (Jack L. Hayes International, Inc., 2019). Losses attributable to shoplifting and employee theft are estimated to exceed $44 billion per year in the United States (Hayes, 2007) and just shy of $1 trillion globally (Planet Retail RNG, 2018). This figure is an estimate, of course; retail theft is a notoriously difficult offense to quantify in concrete terms of financial losses, and researchers have posited several reasons for this. The primary explanation is that many losses are not reported to law enforcement entities in the first place; in fact, most retail crimes go undetected at the time of their commission, even to the company, which may partially contribute to underreporting (Beck & Bilby, 2001). The National Association for Shoplifting Prevention (2019) estimated that shoplifters in the US are apprehended, on average, during their 49th theft commission, indicating a great deal of crime unaccounted for in official crime statistics and unrecorded by the retail industry. Shoplifting, as well as employee theft and fraud, may also be underreported because of a perceived lack of evidence, because of perceptions that the police would not be of assistance, and because some proprietors may believe that the crime is considered not to be severe enough to warrant contacting the law enforcement (Mirrlees-Black & Ross, 1995; Walker, 1994).

In some jurisdictions, even if police are alerted to an instance of shoplifting, the police department's standard operating procedure may dictate that officers will only respond if the value of the stolen goods is over a predetermined amount, such as the particular state's felony theft threshold; jurisdictions often have this policy in order to devote more resources and time to crimes that are perceived to be more serious. Furthermore, some retailers may be hesitant to contact the police and prosecute shoplifters because of the negative media attention the incident would draw (Smith, 1999). Though the reasons for underreporting and non-cooperation with police are diverse, the consequences are the same; the true scope of retail theft is difficult to calculate and challenging to prevent.

As long as retail theft remains a prevalent but underreported crime, the quantity and quality of resources to aid in crime prevention efforts will be insufficient to address the problem, although retailers have made some strides toward combating internal and external theft. This

A National Perspective on Retail Theft   303

chapter will provide an overview of the three main types of retail theft that occur and describe methods to prevent the thefts and cooperate with police to develop solutions to this global problem.

Internal Theft: Employee

Employees are an integral part of any business operation. They are entrusted with the protection and stewardship of valuable company assets; however, when they betray that trust, it can cause a real headache for the employer, entailing expenditures for increased site security and the launching of internal investigations, as well as the hiring of additional employees, among other considerations. In 2013, employee theft was the largest component of retail shrinkage in North America (Taylor, 2016), costing US retailers around $18 billion in damages (Deyle, 2015).

Worldwide, internal theft accounts for around 23% of shrink (Planet Retail RNG, 2018). Employee theft is a versatile crime, which makes it challenging to prevent. Employees may act alone or in collusion with others—either another employee or an outsider. Thefts range from simple, garden-variety theft (in which the employee removes merchandise from the store by concealing it) to more complicated operations, such as product substitution and embezzlement. Product substitution, commonly referred to as sweet-hearting, occurs when the employee places an expensive product inside another, less expensive box so that when he or she goes to buy the item, the less expensive purchase is rung up. With embezzlement, employees may under-record sales and then pocket the funds that were not put into the system; similarly, they may also deliberately short-count inventory and remove the products that were not officially logged (Kimiecik & Thomas, 2006).

Several theories attempt to explain why employees steal from their employers. The social sciences generally view employee theft through from an individualist perspective, a socio-cultural perspective, or both. The individualist philosophy maintains that theft from the workplace is merely an expression of an already-existing proclivity for criminal endeavors (Canter & Alison, 2000). Some scholars theorize that employees steal because they want or need the item, are unwilling or unable to pay for it, and have the opportunity to do so because of shoddy or nonexistent safeguards. In the opposite school of thought, the socio-cultural view alleges that the workplace environment itself allows criminal activity to thrive: that workplace culture and inadequate controls over inventory may contribute to thefts. For example, workplace intimidation has been correlated to employee theft. Sometimes, when inaccurate counts of products are made, accidental shortages can occur, and employees may overcharge customers to cover up their mistakes (see Ditton, 1977). Thus, employee wariness of the wrath of upper management may contribute to incidents of internal theft.

In marrying the two theories, other scholars have suggested that a person's attitude toward the criminal behavior and the subjective norms in the environment produce an intention to commit the crime. For example, even if the opportunity to steal a product is removed, the intention to commit the theft may still be present. Therefore, some criminologists contend that the most pragmatic way to diminish thefts is to generate more commitment to the organization itself, appropriately adjust or augment the environment's moral norms, and implement internal controls (see Bailey, 2006).

Internal Theft Prevention

Since retail theft is such a versatile crime, retailers are forced to utilize a diverse range of internal control methods to counter it. Internal controls are designed to diminish the opportunity for thefts to occur, such as "pre-employment screening programs; human resources programs, including decent retail wages and employee incentives, as well as various detection procedures" (Bailey, 2006, p. 804). Pre-employment screenings are perhaps the most valuable internal control tool that retailers have at their disposal; these screenings utilize various integrity tests in the hiring process to filter out candidates with low levels of integrity and are also used to identify desirable candidates. These screenings' premise is to save the employer time, money, and resources by hiring honest and trustworthy employees instead of employees who pose more risk. These screenings have been shown to reduce financial losses and employee terminations attributed to theft by up to 50% (see Brown, Jones, Terris, & Steffy, 1987).

Internal control systems can utilize programs to track register operations, price changes on items and bar codes that are scanned, among other functions (Mishra & Prasad, 2006). Many internal control systems also have "cutoff" limits for shrinkage, which sets an acceptable percentage of loss due to shrinkage (Radner, 1985). If the cutoff is surpassed, the business is alerted so that an investigation can be launched quickly. Randomized inspections are also useful as part of an internal control system. Randomized inspections utilize "honesty shoppers" who are employed by the retail company to "shop" at different locations to ensure that company policy and the quality of customer service are held to company standards (Mishra & Prasad, 2006). However, researchers have determined randomized inspections are cost prohibitive and irritate employees (Mishra & Prasad, 2006). Consequently, it seems that these inspections should be done infrequently or reserved for situations in which it is definitive that someone is stealing from a company. Other aspects of internal control systems include restricting employee access to particular products or areas, conducting regular inventory checks, spot-checking employee belongings, and prohibiting parking in close proximity to where shipments are received (see Kimiecik & Thomas, 2006).

External Theft: Shoplifting

External theft or shoplifting constitutes the second-largest portion of retail shrinkage in North America and is responsible for about $16 billion worth of damages each year (Deyle, 2015). Worldwide external theft accounts for around 34% of shrink (Planet Retail RNG, 2018). It has been estimated that close to a million shoplifters are apprehended every year in the United States, but many more go undetected (Kimiecik & Thomas, 2006). Several attempts have been made at classifying shoplifters by their demographics, skillsets, and criminal motivation to discern patterns in offending so that law enforcement and retailers can be more cognizant of who is most likely to shoplift.

Demographically, most shoplifters are between 18 and 30, and approximately 50% to 75% of shoplifters are women (Deyle, 2015). Regarding the skillset of shoplifters, there are at least four types of shoplifters—juveniles, amateurs, thrill-seekers, and professionals (Greggo & Kresevich, 2010). Juveniles reportedly do not pose as much of a financial threat because they generally take items of less value, usually as a means of supplementing their allowances or succumbing to peer pressure. Amateurs are more difficult to apprehend because they do not enter a store with the intention of stealing; they decide on a whim and are generally impulsive. Thrill-seeking shoplifters, on the other hand, steal because of the adrenaline rush the theft produces, whereas professional shoplifters often steal as a primary means of income. Greggo and Kresevich (2010) argued that shoplifters often influence the type of merchandise they target. For example, amateur shoplifters are frequently drawn to items that are expensive and beyond their means to pay for, such as in-style clothing items; conversely, professional shoplifters tend to steal concealable items that are of high value and easy to resell.

When discussing various motivations for shoplifting, scholars have categorized shoplifters as having rational and nonrational motivations. Rational shoplifters steal for reasons such as monetary gain because they think they can get away with the theft; because they see theft as a challenge; because they are in a hurry and do not want to pay for the item(s); or because they are angry at the retail establishment, and the theft is a form of retribution (Schlueter, O'Neal, Hickey, & Seiler, 1989). On the other hand, nonrational shoplifters are not characterized as having a particular motivation. Nonrational shoplifters commit thefts because they are anxious, unwell, depressed, angry, or emotionally unstable and seem to disregard the potential for apprehension, arrest, and prosecution (Schlueter et al., 1989). Therefore, of the two categories, nonrational offenders appear to be the most troublesome for retailers because they are more difficult to deter. More overt methods of store security may be helpful in making nonrational shoplifters rethink their criminal inclinations; however, there has not been much research that further explores this dynamic (Schlueter et al., 1989).

Regarding the methods of shoplifters, shoplifting is primarily executed via sleight of hand, with the help of a device, or by distraction. Sleight of hand simply refers to the thief hastily taking an item and concealing it. This is the most frequent method of shoplifting (Kimiecik & Thomas, 2006). On the other hand, professional shoplifters are the ones who use devices to aid in the commission of their crimes. One example of such a device is "booster boxes." Kimiecik and Thomas (2006) described them—they are:

> devices disguised to look like ordinary garment boxes, boxes ready for mailing, or gift boxes. Their unique feature is at the bottom, or one end is false or spring-operated. The shoplifter places the box on or near the targeted item, pushes it against the box, and like magic, it disappears.
>
> (p. 65)

In addition to booster boxes, some shoplifters have been known to wear "booster coats," coats or outer garments that have been altered to have many pockets and hooks designed to hold a surprising number of stolen products (Kimiecik & Thomas, 2006).

Shoplifters who distract sales staff members often work in pairs or groups. One common ruse involves a shoplifter faking a medical emergency, and while the sales staff is not paying attention, the shoplifter's cohorts steal whatever items they please. Another example of theft by distraction involves a shoplifter asking the salesperson to check the stockroom for a specific item, and while the salesperson is gone, other shoplifters pocket merchandise (Kimiecik & Thomas, 2006).

A rarer but particularly insidious method of shoplifting is called "clean" shoplifting. The clean shoplifter makes the retail establishment employees think that they are stealing by intentionally acting shady and obviously taking merchandise. In actuality, the person covertly leaves the products they took in specific places in the store for an accomplice to pick up later. When the "clean" shoplifter is confronted by security, they "initiate civil lawsuits for false arrest, malicious prosecution, or defamation of character" (Kimiecik & Thomas, 2006, p. 66). The goal in this instance is setting the groundwork for a lawsuit and reaping the benefits of a legal settlement, which would typically be more damaging than a single incident of shoplifting.

Due to the variety of characteristics, skillsets, and motivations of shoplifters, some researchers disagree on whether a generalized profile can be created (see Taylor, 2016). Because shoplifting is such a prevalent crime, because so many different people commit it, and because many shoplifters are never apprehended, a profile of the "typical" shoplifter has not emerged. To put it succinctly, criminologists do tend to see vague patterns and trends with shoplifters; however, there is not currently a universal consensus on an empirically validated shoplifter typology.

External Theft Prevention

Techniques to prevent external theft (shoplifting and fraud) are as varied as are the types of shoplifters and their techniques. No "one" technique or process universally reduces shrink. This is true not only because the types of items commonly stolen vary but also because each country has different shopping experiences that place products at higher or lower risks.

Standard techniques include methods visible to offenders, such as cameras, public-view monitors, signs, electronic article surveillance (EAS) tags, alarms, and security personnel. These efforts may provide some level of deterrence but are unlikely to deter professional shoplifters, organized retail crime groups, and employees. Other retailers use unobtrusive methods such as RFID tags and facial recognition to identify shoplifters.

An entire industry has developed around these and other prevention devices and techniques, offering potential solutions. While these efforts can be costly, they may be the best solution for preventing theft. Regardless of which effort a retailer uses, layering these efforts is vital to preventing the most types of thefts and deterring the broadest array of offenders (Hayes, 2007).

Organized Retail Crime

Organized retail theft can involve employees (internal theft), shoplifting (external theft), or a combination of both. For that reason, it needs to be considered separately from the internal and external theft discussion. Concomitant with run-of-the-mill shoplifting is organized retail theft. Scholars and criminal justice professionals have had difficulty studying and understanding organized crimes, such as organized retail theft, because of a lack of universal terminology regarding what an organized crime entails (Sergi, 2015). From a law enforcement perspective, police typically look at three elements to determine whether a crime is organized: the characteristics (gang affiliations) of the offender, the offender's modus operandi, and the motivation for the crime (Crocker et al., 2017). Organized retail theft is referred to as being "organized" because executing the theft requires a modicum of planning, because there are several criminals involved in the process, and because this offense involves multiple offenders shoplifting from multiple locations. Organized retail theft is a challenging scheme to detect because law enforcement entities rarely link separate shoplifting incidents together on either a macro or a micro level, which is another reason the crime is not well understood (Greggo & Kresevich, 2010).

According to a government subcommittee on criminal justice, drug policy, and human resources, there are four problems that are intrinsic to an organized retail theft. The first problem is the financial impact of organized retail theft. It is not unheard of for organized retail theft rings to accumulate hundreds of thousands of dollars in stolen goods (US Congress, Committee on Government Reform, 2004). For example, in 2018, retailers in China reported an average loss of $3,613 during each incident of organized retail crime (Planet Retail RNG, 2018). Further, it is estimated that every minute, retail businesses lose about $64,600 to organized retail crime (Greggo & Kresevich, 2010). The second point is that organized retail theft interrupts the retailer's supply chain to the consumer, and products that are stolen are often not kept in ideal conditions for preserving their quality, which puts the consumer at a disadvantage when products they desire are not in stock or damaged (US Congress, Committee on Government Reform, 2004). Thirdly, stolen goods are frequently resold in areas where consumers do not know they are purchasing ill-gotten gains, such as flea markets, on the street, online, etc., thereby camouflaging the crime.

Lastly, it is not uncommon for gangs or other criminals to do the initial theft by having groups of individuals shoplift and then hide the numerous stolen goods in a rented storage facility, which makes the crime all of the more difficult to detect (US Congress, Committee on Government Reform, 2004). Thieves can then resell the stolen goods to individuals who have legitimate businesses. These individuals, known as "fences," can, in turn, sell the products to consumers. The result of this cycle is money laundering on a large scale, and some of the revenue goes on to finance terrorism and other illegal activities. In summation, organized retail theft has a cascading effect on crime in multiple dimensions.

Organized Retail Theft Prevention

Accordingly, companies have resorted to using several strategies to deter and detect organized retail theft. One tactic is to place magnetized tags on valuable merchandise (Rafacz, Boyce, & Williams, 2011). Recently, the retail establishment has been implementing RFID chips in clothing and other goods. However, a 2017 report examined 50 studies of RFID technology to reduce theft and found mixed results (Sidebottom et al., 2017). Another type of intervention, as Rafacz et al. noted, is that businesses place expensive merchandise "within the line of sight of employees, behind counters, or attaching magnetized tags to items that are demagnetized or removed upon purchase" (2011, p. 151). As Kimiecik and Thomas (2006) observed, convex mirrors are also useful for assisting employees to see around tall objects to watch potential shoplifters.

Nonetheless, all these suggestions have drawbacks. Magnetized tags can be removed, and not all items' shapes are conducive to that method (Rafacz et al., 2011). Shoplifters can use convex mirrors to monitor when employees are not in the vicinity so that they know when to steal without being observed (Kimiecik & Thomas, 2006). CCTV systems are useful, but they can be expensive and have to be monitored (Kimiecik & Thomas, 2006). RFID is not widely used in retail, and its effectiveness is impacted by tagging's complexity (Sidebottom et al., 2017). Unfortunately, there is little research that strenuously examines the deterrence capability of most of these measures on organized criminals. However, as Ratcliffe, Taniguchi, and Taylor (2009) found, the installation of CCTVs in certain areas in Pennsylvania resulted in a 13% reduction in overall crime. Some offenders may desist their criminal activities if they know they are being monitored, but more research is needed in this area.

A few pieces of legislation have helped law enforcement agencies better tackle organized theft rings. For example, section 1105 of the 2006 Department of Justice Reauthorization Bill requires the Federal Bureau of Investigation to establish and maintain a task force whose mission it is to rapidly detect, apprehend, and prosecute individuals involved in organized retail theft rings; the bill allotted $5 million per year to the FBI for those endeavors (Greggo & Kresevich, 2010). Laws have also become more punitive for those who commit major retail crimes. In 2006, President George W. Bush signed the Cargo Theft Prevention Act in response to organized retail theft; the act mandated stricter sentences for those convicted of stealing cargo (Greggo & Kresevich, 2010). For thefts of less than $1,000, the act increased the sentence to a minimum 3-year prison term; for thefts greater than $1,000, it increased the sentence up to a 15-year prison term (Greggo & Kresevich, 2010). Since the nature of the crime entails the transport of massive amounts of stolen products, the act also established cargo theft as its category in the Uniform Crime Report (UCR); this was done in order to better inform law enforcement agencies of the whereabouts of stolen goods (Greggo & Kresevich, 2010).

Information sharing between retailers and police may be an important effort to disrupt organized retail crime. ALERT (www.usalert.org) is one such effort that provides collaboration efforts between retailers and law enforcement entities. It is a network designed to pursue cases of organized retail theft and other financial crimes, such as fraud and counterfeiting. It was developed in Tennessee by the Shelby County Sheriff's Office, and it is responsible for distributing information on offenders and offenses to local, state, and federal law enforcement entities and retailers who wish to use it (Greggo & Kresevich, 2010).

Police and Loss Prevention Partnerships

Retail theft is difficult to combat from a law enforcement perspective because the crime often goes undetected and underreported. Additionally, because of the sheer volume of thefts, it is cost prohibitive and immensely challenging for police departments to respond adequately to the crime. This is made even more complicated by recent US trends to increase the amount necessary to qualify as a misdemeanor or felony charge. For example, a recent California bill, commonly known as Proposition 47, increases the threshold of felony shoplifting to $950 (Turner, 2018). When combined with other directives and policies not to arrest on charges of misdemeanor shoplifting, some are saying the law provides a "virtual get-out-of-jail-free card" (Saslow, 2015). California is not alone, as Texas requires shoplifting of $1,500 and South Carolina $2,000 before the theft becomes a felony (Turner, 2018). These legal changes place retailers in a difficult position as the justice system provides fewer protections and remedies for a private business that falls victim to theft.

The solution to this situation is unclear. As retail theft increases, the justice system seems less eager to assist businesses with thefts that are impacting business and private persons. Retailers are increasingly left to respond without the police's assistance and must increase the focus on prevention rather than prosecution. While this shift may not necessarily be wholly negative, retailers should engage politicians to encourage appropriate use of the justice system and collaborate with police to pursue serious offenders legally. Without this collaboration, it will be difficult for retailers to stem the rise in retail theft.

The Future of Retail Theft

As the world adjusts to the arrival of COVID-19, retail will look different. Already, brick-and-mortar stores are experiencing a sharp decline in foot traffic, which may translate into reduced shoplifting. Some early research bears this concept out. However, the shift in crime in 2020 resulted in uneven changes in the type, location, and other circumstances (Stickle & Felson, 2020). In other words, as the world emerges from the pandemic of 2020 and beyond, crime will be different, and so will retail theft.

It is possible that shoplifting may remain at a lower level while internal theft or even organized retail crime may increase. Looking beyond the storefront, the recent trend of home delivery of products creates another opportunity for crime. Package theft, "taking possession of a package or its contents, outside of a residence or business, where it has been commercially delivered or has been left for commercial pick-up, with intent to deprive the rightful over of the contents" (Hicks et al., 2020, p. 4), has risen dramatically—nearly 40% during the 2020 crisis—and is impacting one in five US customers (Hurst, 2020). With limited information on this emerging crime type (Stickle et al., 2020), police, consumers, and retailers must work together to prevent shrink even after a product leaves the store.

The Path Forward

Retail theft, in all its forms, is a lucrative crime—to the detriment of businesses and consumers. To counter shrink, businesses employ loss prevention personnel and techniques, spending a worldwide average of 1.25% of sales to prevent loss (Planet Retail RNG, 2018). This effort impacts the business and consumers as occasionally retailers mark up their inventory prices to compensate (Rafacz et al., 2011) or implement theft prevention techniques that impact the customer experience. Therefore, shoplifting, employee theft, organized retail crime, and even package theft negatively affect the entire retail system. To fully address this crime, consumers, retailers, suppliers, police, and solutions providers must work together to address retail theft. Without this collaboration, efforts to curb these costly trends will be less effective.

Discussion Questions

1. Describe organized retail theft.
2. What future trends could develop within retail theft, and how can police and private industry collaborate to address these challenges?
3. Explain the importance of collaboration between retailers and police to address the issues of retail theft.
4. What is retail shrink, and how does it impact retailers and consumers?
5. After reading this chapter, describe some of the retail theft prevention techniques or products you have observed and explain how the methods/products work and whom they are targeted toward (internal, external, organized).

References

Bailey, A. A. (2006). Retail employee theft: A theory of planned behavior perspective. *International Journal of Retail & Distribution Management, 34*(11), 802–816.

Bamfield, J. (2003). What is happening to shrinkage and theft amongst Europe's retailers? *European Retail Digest*, 50–53.

Bamfield, J. (2004). Shrinkage, shoplifting and the cost of retail crime in Europe: A cross-sectional analysis of major retailers in 16 European countries. *International Journal of Retail & Distribution Management, 32*(5), 235–241.

Bamfield, J. (2010). *Shrinkage and loss prevention: Evidence from the global retail theft barometer*. Retrieved from https://www.asmag.com/showpost/8799.aspx

Beck, A., & Bilby, C. (2001). *Shrinkage in Europe: A survey of stock loss in the fast moving consumer goods sector*. Brussels: ECR Europe.

Brown, T. S., Jones, J. W., Terris, W., & Steffy, B. D. (1987). The impact of pre-employment integrity testing on employee turnover and inventory shrinkage losses. *Journal of Business and Psychology, 2*(2), 136–149.

Canter, D., & Alison, L. (2000). *Profiling property crimes*. Aldershot: Ashgate.

Crocker, R., Skidmore, M., Webb, S., Garner, S., Gill, M., & Graham, J. (2017). Uncovering organized shoplifting and theft networks. *Policing: A Journal of Policy and Practice, 13*(4), 377–385.

Deyle, E. (2015). The global retail theft barometer: 2013–2014 shrink trends and performance results. *Loss Prevention Magazine*, 39–46.

Ditton, J. (1977). *Part-time crime: An ethnography of fiddling and pilferage*. London: Macmillan.

Federal Bureau of Investigation. (2018). *Larceny-theft*. Washington, DC. Retrieved from https://ucr.fbi.gov/crime-in-the-u.s/2018/crime-in-the-u.s.-2018/topic-pages/larceny-theft

Finklea, K. M. (2010). *Organized retail crime*. Darby, PA: DIANE Publishing.

Greggo, A., & Kresevich, M. (2010). *Retail security and loss prevention solutions* (1st ed.). Boca Raton, FL: CRC Press.

Hayes, R. (2007). *Retail security and loss prevention*. New York, NY: Springer.

Hicks, M., Stickle, B., & Harms, J. (2020). Assessing the fear of package theft. *American Journal of Criminal Justice*, 1–20. Retrieved from https://doi.org/10.1007/s12103-020-09600-x

Hurst, A. (2020). Nearly 1 in 5 consumers experienced package theft since the start of the quarantine. *Value Penguin*. Retrieved from www.valuepenguin.com/nearly-one-in-five-consumers-experienced-package-theft-since-start-of-quarantine

Jack L. Hayes International, Inc. (2019). *32nd annual retail theft survey*. Retrieved from https://hayesinternational.com/news/annual-retail-theft-survey/

Kimiecik, R. C., & Thomas, C. (2006). *Loss prevention in the retail business*. Hoboken, NJ: Wiley.

Mirrlees-Black, C., & Ross, A. (1995). *Crime against retail premises in 1993.* Great Britain: Home Office, Research and Statistics Department.

Mishra, B. K., & Prasad, A. (2006). Minimizing retail shrinkage due to employee theft. *International Journal of Retail & Distribution Management, 34*(11), 817–832.

National Association for Shoplifting Prevention. (2019). *The shoplifting problem in the nation.* Retrieved from www.shopliftingprevention.org/the-shoplifting-problem/

National Retail Federation. (2016). *2016 national retail security survey (Publication).* National Retail Federation. Retrieved April 5, 2018, from https://nrf.com/system/tdf/Documents/retail%20library/NRF_2016_NRSS_restricted-rev.pdf?file=1&title=National%20Retail%20Security%20Survey%202016

Planet Retail RNG. (2018). *The Sensormatic Global Shrink Index: Results & executive summary.* Boston, MA: Johnson Controls.

Radner, R. (1985). Repeated principal-agent games with discounting. *Econometrica, 53*(5), 1173–1198.

Rafacz, S. D., Boyce, T. E., & Williams, W. L. (2011). Examining the effects of a low-cost prompt to reduce retail theft. *Journal of Organizational Behavior Management, 31*(2), 150–160.

Ratcliffe, J., Taniguchi, T., & Taylor, R. (2009). The crime reduction effects of public CCTV cameras: A multi-method special approach. *Justice Quarterly* (4), 746.

Retail Theft Goes Global. (2011). Security: Solutions for enterprise security leaders, *48*(2), 14.

Saslow, E. (2015). A "virtual get-out-of-jail-free card." *The Washington Post.* Retrieved from www.washingtonpost.com/sf/national/2015/10/10/prop47/?utm_term=.ed3f2bbc08a1

Schlueter, G. R., O'Neal, F. C., Hickey, J., & Seiler, G. (1989). Rational vs. nonrational shoplifting types: The implications for loss prevention strategies. *International Journal of Offender Therapy and Comparative Criminology, 33*(3), 227–239. Retrieved January 31, 2018, from http://journals.sagepub.com/doi/abs/10.1177/0306624X8903300307

Sergi, A. (2015). "Divergent mind-sets," convergent policies: Policing models against organized crime in Italy and in England within international framework. *European Journal of Criminology, 12*(6), 658–680.

Sidebottom, A., Thornton, A., Tompson, L., Belur, J., Tilley, N., & Bowers, K. (2017). A systematic review of tagging as a method to reduce theft in retail environments. *Crime Science, 6*(1), 1–17.

Smith, R. (1999). Organizations as victims of fraud, and how they deal with it. In *Trends & issues in crime and justice* (p. 127). Canberra: Australian Institute of Criminology.

Stickle, B., & Felson, M. (2020). Crime rates in a pandemic: The largest criminological experiment in history. *American Journal of Criminal Justice, 45*(4), 525–536.

Stickle, B., Hicks, M., Stickle, A., & Hutchinson, Z. (2020). Porch pirates: Examining unattended package theft through crime script analysis. *Criminal Justice Studies, 33*(2), 79–95.

Taylor, E. (2016). Supermarket self-checkouts and retail theft: The curious case of the SWIPERS. *Criminology & Criminal Justice: An International Journal, 16*(5), 552–567.

Turner, B. (2018). Welcome to California: Still a shoplifter's paradise? *Loss Prevention Magazine.* Retrieved from https://losspreventionmedia.com/welcome-to-california-a-shoplifters-paradise/#:~:text=Retailers%20and%20law%20enforcement%20officials,no%20pursuit%20and%20no%20punishment

US Congress, Committee on Government Reform. (2004). Organized retail theft: Conduit of money laundering: Hearing before the Subcommittee on Criminal Justice, Drug Policy and Human Resources of the Committee on Government Reform, House of Representatives, One Hundred Eighth Congress, second session, November 10, 2003 (Cong. Doc. from 108th Cong., first sess.). Washington, DC: US GPO. Retrieved from www.gpo.gov/fdsys/pkg/CHRG-108hhrg94005/pdf/CHRG-108hhrg94005.pdf

Walker, J. (1994). *The first Australian national survey of crimes against businesses.* Canberra: Elect Printing.

Chapter 22

Sustained Footwear Characteristics Across Athletic Footwear Over Several Years

A Case Study of Impression Wear Patterns for Investigative Value

Lee M. Wade

Introduction

In recent years, crime scene investigation techniques that are published, researched, and featured are primarily focused on DNA and/or fingerprinting methods. Unfortunately, there have been fewer studies and features on footwear identification processes in the media or academia. This could be attributed to the differences in these methods due to investigative efficiency, validity, and the probability of producing a suspect's identification. Furthermore, there seem to be more resources allocated toward non-footwear-type evidence and using database systems at federal, state, and local levels with these methods. These techniques related to DNA and fingerprint methods have had much investment by stakeholders to increase their use further and remain at the forefront of investigative goals.

Despite these methods' popularity, footwear evidence left at a crime scene remains one of the oldest and most abundant pieces of evidence (Bodziak, 1990). Although this is often an overlooked piece of evidence, footwear investigative techniques still have value in producing leads or confirming suspect identification in many criminal cases.

Due to the decentralization of police services in the United States, the resources available for law enforcement investigative methods vary across approximately 18,000 jurisdictions. In some areas, the need for investigative leads varies depending on the case facts, crime scene, and resources throughout the investigation. The use of footwear impression evidence left at the crime scene can be useful with cases that have possible suspects connected via testimonial evidence. Identification of suspects is possible through individual characteristics related to specific factors throughout the life and usage of footwear (Bodziak, 1990). However, with athletic footwear, some brands are ubiquitous and used by various persons within any jurisdiction population (Tonkin, Bond, & Woodhams, 2009). In some serial crimes, impression patterns can be found frequently with both class and random characteristics. Class characteristics of footwear are the features associated with the manufacturing of a brand of shoes, which are shared with other shoes of the same brand. Random characteristics are the result of a random or accidental removal of features of the original outsole structure (Hilderbrand, 1999). Some wear patterns are consistent and can be left on substrates throughout a crime scene (Smith, 2009). Careful documentation and collection of evidence related to these patterns at a crime scene can be of investigative value, especially when footwear is used consistently by suspects. This chapter evaluates a case in which wear patterns from similar footwear were found to be consistent throughout the life of the shoe, and it presents the argument that documenting the growth of the wear patterns from suspects' footwear can have important value in an investigation and create investigative leads.

DOI: 10.4324/9781003047117-25

Literature Review

For investigative purposes, footwear evidence can be impacted by many factors, including manufactured design, manufactured materials, the suspects' weight, the suspects' gait, and the substrate the footwear impacts with at a crime scene. Identifications can be based on random characteristics, and class characteristics are possible if a suspect's shoes are obtained for comparison (Richetelli, Bodziak, & Speir, 2019). Certain class characteristics, like the pattern of the outsole, the size of the shoe, and the shape of the outsole are in line with a logo or fashion from a manufacturer (Bodziak, 1990).

There can be some distortion in impression evidence, depending on the individual's gait and their foot injuries (Ramsey, Lamb, Kaur, Baxter, & Ribeiro, 2019). Furthermore, how an individual's weight and gait impact the footwear dynamics can result in outsole pattern wear. This can range from normal wear to overloaded metatarsal conditions that exist for the individual (Lucock, 1979).

According to Hilderbrand (1999) and Bodziak (1990), there are three critical areas of investigative value concerning footwear impressions. The first is evaluating the physical characteristics of the outsoles of the footwear. The second is knowing the manufacturing brand, design, and process of the footwear. Thirdly, which is the focus of this inquiry, the wearing of the footwear by the individual is also critical. Moreover, any detail, including wear characteristics, may be important to the comparison process, and wear characteristics can change due to the use of footwear over time. Hilderbrand (1999) stated, "The more extensive the wear, the more original the appearance will appear when compared to another outsole of the same design" (p. 52).

Tang, Srihari, Kasiviswanathan, and Corso (2010) argued that clustering of footwear patterns could aid in comparing footwear evidence by the examiner. Clustering is the organization of geometric shapes with comparable patterns on the outsoles of footwear. Furthermore, by selecting geometric shapes to cluster outsole design patterns, actual databases of recorded impressions can be searched and retrieved using specific algorithms.

Therefore, certain wear patterns can be categorized and documented to the point of database inclusion. Consequently, the London Metropolitan Police normally take a scan of a suspect taken into custody to record their specific footwear; moreover, if individual characteristics emerge from wear patterns, the probability of including the footwear evidence in an individualization increases. "A database of outsole patterns may not only provide the pattern prevalence but also more specific and minute characteristics such as type, size, common wear patterns and individual damages, which could be used in different comparison procedures" (Johansson & Stattin, 2008, p. 63).

In terms of establishing a database or even just documenting patterns related to footwear, the British have identified profiles associated with athletic shoes in serial crimes. One study indicated a correlation between the high frequency of athletic shoe wear among burglars to approximately 94% of all residential burglaries over a few years (Tonkin et al., 2009).

Case Study and Results

The footwear in this case study are from two potential suspects, and color, medium-resolution photographs were taken of the outer soles of this footwear. The focus of the footwear impression to compare was of one particular brand of athletic shoes. Various sets of shoes were obtained from two potential suspects. Photographs were taken of both sets of the suspects' footwear, including some casual shoes as well. The photographs' resolution was a challenge due to the date of investigation and obtaining the exemplar footwear from suspects.

For this evaluation, there are six photographs from multiple brands of shoes for the first potential suspect (PS1), and there are two photographs from a second potential suspect (PS2). These are older photographs, which is why the resolution is approximately 300 to 400 dpi. The height and weight of the potential suspects were similar at approximately 5 feet 10 inches and approximately 180 pounds. The type of shoes primarily of interest was a similar-brand athletic running shoe. Other shoes obtained from PS1 were a different brand of running shoes and casual shoes for wear comparison. All outer sole documentation originated from the left footwear of PS1 and PS2.

For footwear associated with PS1, athletic running shoes 1 and 2 were worn for over four years (Photo 22.1) and two to three years (Photo 22.2), respectively. Running shoe 1 showed a larger area of wear characteristics, primarily in the forefoot zone. In the midfoot zone, there was crushed damage to the outer sole that was significant. Running shoe 2, which was the younger of this shoe brand in terms of wear, had more random characteristics associated with dirt and grass. Again, in terms of wear characteristics, the wear pattern was located primarily in the forefoot region and slightly to the right, just like in running shoe 1, but it was less spread out. There was minor crush damage to the outer sole, located in the midfoot region. Running shoes 1 and 2 were the same brand and style for PS1. From this comparison of running shoes 1 and 2, the wear pattern from PS1 appeared to originate in the middle right and began to spread over time and a wider area after year three of use.

Running shoes 3 and 4 were of the same brand that PS1 wore after running shoes 1 and 2. Running shoe 3 had been worn by PS1 for approximately six months to one year, and running shoe 4 had been worn for approximately two years. The outer sole pattern and composition were different across these shoes, where one could infer the materials were sturdier in design. Running shoe 3 had wear characteristics originating in the same middle-right area of the forefoot, but it was less pronounced than in running shoes 1 and 2. There were degradation and wear damage in the midfoot area consistent with running shoes 1 and 2.

Running shoe 4 had been worn for approximately two years or more. Although a different shoe, the brand and model were the same as running shoe 3. The wear pattern characteristics appeared to originate in the same area as on running shoe 3 but had more wear from forefoot to midfoot. The midfoot wear pattern that was consistent with the first three footwear samples appeared to be larger as well in the area where the brand name is located. From the comparison of these two shoes, one could infer that the wear patterns were consistent across all four footwear samples, but the outsole materials impacted the spread of wear characteristics.

Running shoe 5 and casual shoe 1 were evaluated to see if sustained wear characteristics were consistent across other brands of athletic shoes and materials. Running shoe 5 had been worn for approximately six months, and casual shoe one had been worn by PS1 for approximately one to two years. Running shoe 5 had significant wear pattern characteristics in the middle-right section of the forefoot that were consistent with the other running shoes from PS1. The wear pattern, however, was more concentrated in the middle and wide across the forefoot than on the other running footwear.

Furthermore, running shoe 5 had a wear pattern in the midfoot consistent with running shoes 1 through 4. Casual shoe 1 had wear characteristics similar to running shoe 5, which were more in the middle of the forefoot but also showed wear to the right of the middle. Please note the Schallamach pattern in the center area. A Schallamach pattern is defined as an abrasive wear feature on the outsole, and it occurs early in the wear process (Johannsson & Stattin, 2008). The preceding examples show wear that has occurred over significant time. The forefoot region appears to be consistent with the preceding five footwear samples for comparison. One important difference is that there was no midfoot wear or damage to the outsole present in the athletic footwear. This could be attributed to the angle at which the casual shoe strikes the surface, wear, and the outsole design materials.

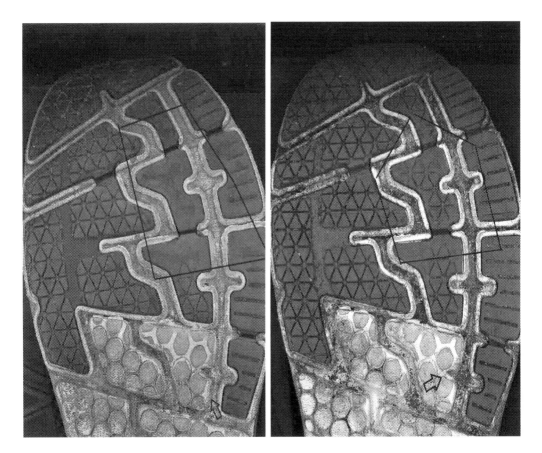

Photo 22.1 Sustained Wear Patterns from Running Shoe 1 (left) After 4 Years and Running Shoe 2 (right) After 2.5 Years. A color version of this photo is downloadable as Support Material from www.routledge.com/9780367491000.

From the comparison of these two footwear samples from PS1 with each other and the other athletic running shoes, one can observe a sustained set of wear pattern characteristics that appear to be mitigated by the shoe outsole design and brand. PS1 seemed to wear out their footwear in the middle-right forefoot area of each shoe and would also have some impact wear damage or wear in the center-right of the midfoot zone.

As a control, possible suspect 2's (PS2) footwear was evaluated. Unfortunately, we were only able to obtain two sets of footwear from PS2. These footwear are also athletic running shoes, and PS2 was selected because of the brand of athletic shoe used for comparisons to PS1's footwear. In this comparison of sustained wear characteristics, the brand is the same for footwear, but two different models/designs were evaluated for PS2.

Running shoe 7 from PS2 was the same brand of athletic shoe as running shoes 1 and 2 from PS1, and it was assumed the same design and material for the outsole. Running shoe 7 was worn for approximately two years by PS2. From running shoe 7, one can observe that the wear characteristics for PS2 originate on the extreme right side of the shoe, and the pattern extends from the forefoot across the midfoot, ending in the rearfoot. The wear pattern from PS2 causes some of the material to be worn completely off, in addition to a smoothing effect. Running shoe 8 from PS2 was an athletic shoe of the same brand, but

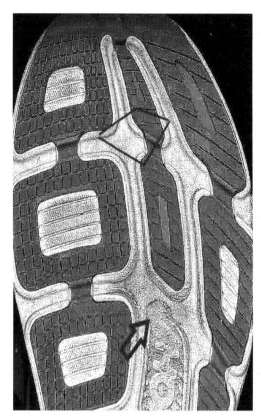 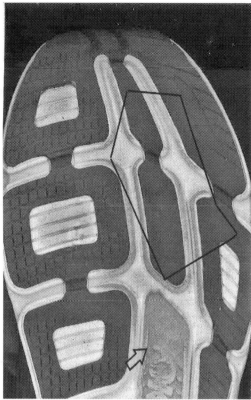

Photo 22.2 Sustained Wear Patterns from Running Shoe 3 (left) After Six Months and Running Shoe 4 (right) After Two Years. A color version of this photo is downloadable as Support Material from www.routledge.com/9780367491000.

a different model and outsole design than running shoe 7. PS2 had worn running shoe 8 for approximately five years. As a result, the wear pattern characteristics were similar to running shoe 7, where the wear began on the extreme right side of the shoe, and the pattern extended from the forefoot through to the rearfoot. The pattern, after several more years of wear, was more pronounced than in running shoe 7. The wear characteristics in the midfoot zone extended from the right to the middle of the footwear. The wear pattern was also substantial to the point of wearing out the outsole design completely and creating a smoothing effect.

Considerations

For traditional investigative value, the individual characteristics found from a footwear impression at a crime scene can create a lead associated with a potential suspect, provided an exemplar footwear is found connected to the suspect. The purpose here is to evaluate constant and attributed characteristics to an individual through similar footwear and tread manufactured materials. Wear patterns can be used in association with random characteristics to lead to an identification (Bodziak, 1990). However, as Bodziak (1990) clearly has shown in his research, the wear pattern, sans random characteristics, might not be an exact wear

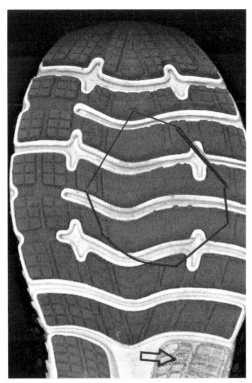 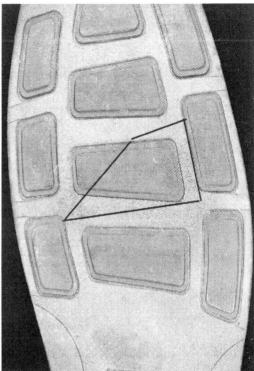

Photo 22.3 Sustained Wear Patterns from Running Shoe 5 (left) After 6 Months and Casual Shoe 1 (right) After 1.5 years. A color version of this photo is downloadable as Support Material from www.routledge.com/9780367491000.

pattern on another shoe. Moreover, Bodziak (1990) attributed this to the micro-cellular material and more wear.

Given the foundation here for research, we can consider that after significant wear (same shoe + time worn) for athletic shoes, a growth wear pattern will emerge that can be consistent across footwear with similar materials in the outsole pattern. What makes this slightly significant is the trend of athletic footwear usage in the commission of crimes. Furthermore, we argue that if local databases are developed to store footwear impressions, agencies should document and include an estimated time of wear on each scan of the impression, also remarking on location of wear of the outsole and Schallamach patterns, if present.

There are limitations to classifying footwear impression evidence, especially where footwear characteristics are concerned. Concerning evaluating patterns from exemplars to impression evidence, some examiners may have differing classifications of comparisons, some may have different laboratory definitions, and some may have differing interpretations of wear patterns (Taylor, Krosch, & Chaseling, 2020). Shor and Weisner's study (1999) of ten laboratories across seven countries showed variation in interpreting two sets of footwear impressions as evidence. There were variations not only in definitions but also in the probability that the impression matched the exemplar.

Anecdotally, any lead in an investigation is a lead of value, especially in cases in which there are no tangible leads from a crime scene. If one has worked criminal cases in which the only evidence is a footwear impression, the application of any method to confirm leads may be

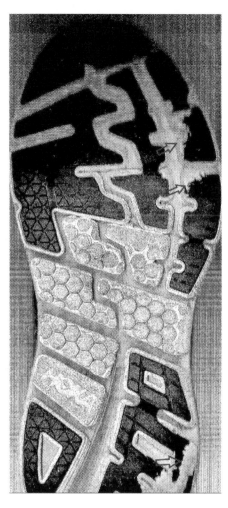 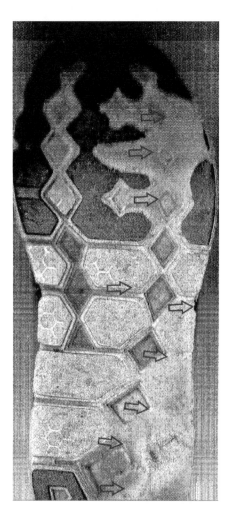

Photo 22.4 Sustained Wear Patterns from Running Shoe 7 (left) After Two Years and Running Shoe 8 (right) After 5 Years. A color version of this photo is downloadable as Support Material from www.routledge.com/9780367491000.

important to emphasize for the investigator and/or examiner. This case study has indicated that geometric patterns of wear in athletic footwear are sustained over time. Therefore, in terms of profiling or evaluating suspects, the void left in an impression where the wear pattern can be inferred may have some value. If so, then this could be documented by investigators or agencies in a local database. Furthermore, the documentation could have value for footwear examiners in looking at probable cases of identification.

Discussion Questions

1. Compared to DNA and fingerprint evidence, what priority is given to footwear impression evidence at a crime scene?
2. Considering footwear that is favored consistently, how can athletic footwear impression evidence have investigative value?

3. Can suspects have sustained wear characteristics with athletic footwear over time?
4. Based on this case study, is it important to examine how long a suspect might have worn their shoes in documenting footwear?
5. If two possible suspects wear a similar brand of shoes, can random and sustained wear characteristics create possible leads or identifications of suspects?
6. Based on the research, should law enforcement agencies create a database of characteristics from repeated offenders' footwear?

References

Bodziak, W. (1990). *Footwear impression evidence*. New York, NY: Elsevier.

Hilderbrand, D. (1999). Four basic components of a successful footwear examination. *Journal of Forensic Identification, 49*(1), 37–59.

Johansson, Å., & Stattin, T. (2008). *Footwear impression as forensic evidence – Prevalence, characteristics and evidence value* (Dissertation). Matematiska institutionen. Retrieved from http://urn.kb.se/resolve?urn=urn:nbn:se:liu:diva-11805

Lucock, L. (1979). Identification from footwear. *Medical Science Law, 19*(4), 225–229.

Ramsey, C. A., Lamb, P., Kaur, M., Baxter, G. D., & Ribeiro, D. C. (2019). How are running shoes assessed? A systematic review of characteristics and measurement tools used to describe running footwear. *Journal of Sports Sciences, 37*(14), 1617–1629.

Richetelli, N., Bodziak, W. J., & Speir, J. A. (2019). Empirically observed and predicted estimates of chance association: Estimating the chance association of randomly acquired characteristics in footwear comparisons. *Forensic Science International, 302*, 109833.

Shor, Y., & Weisner, S. (1999). A survey on the conclusions drawn on the same footwear marks obtained in actual cases by several experts throughout the World. *Journal of Forensic Science, 44*(2), 380–384.

Smith, M. B. (2009). The forensic analysis of footwear impression evidence. *Forensic Science Communications, 11*(3).

Tang, Y., Srihari, S. N., Kasiviswanathan, H., & Corso, J. J. (2010, November). Footwear print retrieval system for real crime scene marks. In *International workshop on computational forensics* (pp. 88–100). Berlin, Heidelberg: Springer.

Taylor, K. M., Krosch, M. N., Chaseling, J., & Wright, K. (2020). A comparison of three shoe sole impression lifting methods at high substrate temperatures. *Journal of Forensic Sciences. 66*(1), 303–314.

Tonkin, M., Bond, J. W., & Woodhams, J. (2009). Fashion conscious burglars? Testing the principles of offender profiling with footwear impressions recovered at domestic burglaries. *Psychology, Crime & Law, 15*(4), 327–345.

Index

Note: **Boldface** page references indicate tables. *Italic* references indicate figures and boxed text.

abortion 253, 258, 267
abortion provider attacks: anomie theory and 254; Army of God and 253, 257, 266; background information 253–254; ballot box concept and 256–257; Blackmun attempted shooting and 257–258; cartridge box concept and 256, 257–262; conclusions 267–268; extremism and 253, 255–257; Freedom of Access to Clinic Entrances Act (FACE) and 260; grand jury investigation of WHCS and 262; Gunn murder and 258, 263; Hill and 257–261; investigations of 253; jury box concept and 256, 262–263, 265–266; Kansas for Life and 262; lone wolves versus organized plots 266–267; necessity defense and 253, 263; Operation Rescue and 259, 262; on Planned Parenthood clinic (Colorado Springs) 267; RICO Act and 260; Roeder and 257, 260, 263–266; *Roe v. Wade* and 253, 256–257; Rudolph and 257, 261–262; Shannon and 257, 259–260; "Summer of Mercy" and 259; as terrorism 253–255, 266–267; three-box operational sub-theory of extremist groups and 255–256; on Tiller and his clinic 253, 257–260, 262–266
Aboul-hosn, S. 246
academy training of police officers 136
accountability of police 83, 86, 90–91, 98–99, 102, 106–108, 148, 208, 210
Ackroyd, P. 44
actus resus (guilty act) 166
Agliotta, Joseph 106
Ajzen, Icek 163, 165
Alcohol, Tobacco, and Firearms (ATF) 235–236
Alc, G. 271, 283
ALERT system 307–308
Alexander, D. A. 175
Altbeker, A. 193
American College of Preventative Medicine 273
An Garda Siochana ("guardians of the peace") 45–46
Anglo-Irish Treaty 45
animal trafficking *see* wildlife enforcement
anomie theory 254

ANOVAs 72–74
anti-abortion movement 257; *see also* abortion provider attacks
Arantz, Philip 133
ArcGIS-10 278–279
Area Crime Combating Units (ACCU) 195
Arizona 273–275, 277; *see also* Mesa distracted driving case study; Mesa Police Department hiring protocols
Arizona Peace Officers Standards and Training Board (AZPOST) 211
armed/arming police 39–40, 47–50
Army of God (AOG) 253, 257, 266
Arnold, James 104
arrest and discretionary power of police 101–102
Atkins, Rita 247
auctions, gun 235–236
auditing police 85, 87–94
Australia 218–220, 222, 224–225
Australian Cyber Security Centre report 218
Awami League 116–117
Ayling, J. 198

Back to Basics approach 198
Back the Blue counter-movement 132
ballot box concept 255–257
Baltimore 86
Bangladesh: British colonial rule and 114–116; Civil Service of Pakistan in 116; civil war (Liberation War) (1971) in 116–117, 119; Hindu-Muslim difference in 114–116; Independence Movement in 116; model police station (*thana*) efforts in 120; Mutiny of 1857 (First War of Independence) in 115; Operation Searchlight in 116; Operation Thunderbolt in 112; partition in 116; Police Act (1861) in 115; Police Act (2007) in 124; Police Reform Programme in 120–121, 124; political corruption in 111–112; Rapid Action Battalion in 119
Bangladesh National Police (BNP): background information 111; bribes (*baksheesh*) and 118–119; civil war and 117; colonial history and 113–114;

community policing and 121–125; crime rate and 111; criminalization of politics and 111–112; force and, use of 111–113, 119; *hartals* and 111; Hindu-Muslim difference and 114–116; *kotwals* and 114; legitimacy and 113–114, 123–125; *matabdars* and 114; partition and 116; politicalization of 118; politics and 111–113; post-colonial conundrum and 113–114; recommendations 125; reform and 120–121; ruling party and 117–120; *samaj* and 114; *thana* effort and 120; violence by 111–113, 119

BATF study 236
Bayley, David H. 42–44, 128
BeFree Textline 242
Belgium 48
Bergmark, R. 271
Berning, J. 194
Beto, D. R. 56
Biggam, F. H. 175
Bittner, Egon 41–42
Black Hand gangsters 239
Black Lives Matter movement 44, 46, 83, 131
Blackmun, Harry A. 257–258
Blake, Jacob 47
Bloomberg, Michael 129
Blue Lives Matter counter-movement 132
Bobb, Mike 87
body worn cameras 165, 170
Bodziak, W. 312, 315
Boisvert, S. 292
booster boxes 305
booster coats 305
Bordner, Diane C. 97, 107–108
Boston Police Department 68
Brady Handgun Violence Prevention Act (1993) 231–232
Brady, James 231
Braga, A. 232
Brainard, L. 67
Branch, P. 219
Bratton, William (Bill) 41, 89
Braun, V. 3
Bray, Michael 257, 263
British East India Company 114
British North American Act (BNA) (1867) 144
Britton, John 260
Brodeur, J. P. 42
Brogden, M. 56
broken windows 128–129
Bronitt, S. 43
Brownback, Sam 247
Brown, J. M. 175
Brown, Michael 86
Bruns, D. 206
Brunt, Antonio 234
Brunt, R. 234
Brunt, Roy Christopher 234
brutality of police 104, 137, 191, 195, 197–198
Bureau of Justice Assistance (BJA) 244
Bureau of Justice Statistics (BJS) 232

Burger, J. 199
burnout 175, 179–180, *179*, **181**
Burt, John 258
Burton, F. 266–267

Cambridge Analytica 221–222
cameras, body worn 165, 170
Camerer, C. F. 36n26
Campbell, E. A. 175
Canada 68, 143, 146, 149, 239, 288–291, 293; *see also* Canadian police hiring standards
Canadian Occupational Health and Safety Act 196
Canadian Police College (CPC) 157
Canadian police hiring standards: background of problem 143; background of study 143; competencies 155–156; competency-based performance management 143, 147–150; conclusions 153–155; current practices 150; education and 145–147, 153–155; historical perspective of police 144–145; hypotheses 151; instrumentation 152–153; limitations of study 153; literature review 143–150; post-secondary education in policing 145–147, 154; recommendations 156–158; research methodology 151–152; research questions 151; statement of problem 150–151
Cannadine, D. 114–115
Cano, I. 48
Carcary, W. B. 175
cartridge box concept: Blackmun, attempted shooting of 257–258; describing 256; Gunn's murder 258; Hill 260–261; Rudolph 261–262; Tiller clinic attack 258–260; Tiller's murder 263–264
Cassidy, Tyler 46
Cato Institute 162
CBS 237–238
cell phone bans 273–274
Center for Behavioral Health Statistics and Quality 204
Center for Constitutional Rights 129, 131
Centers for Disease Control and Prevention 272
Central Florida 242, 246–250
Central Florida Alliance of Human Trafficking (CFAHT) 249
Chaires, R. H. 40–41
Chambliss, William J. 106–107
Chandler, George Fletcher 47
Chang, L. Y. C. 225
Chappel, B. 238
character background test for police officers 135
Chatterjee, P. 115
Chicago 234
Chick-Fil-A restaurants 249
China *see* community justice initiatives in China
chokeholds 136
Christie, B. 275
Cillié Commission 195
Cismaru, M. 272
citizen-citizen encounters 23

Index 321

citizen-police encounters *see* police-citizen encounters
civil rights and consent decrees 84
Civil Rights Division of DOJ 84
civil service examinations 135
Civil Service of Pakistan (CSP) 116
Clarke, V. 3
Clark, J. P. 23
Clarksdale (Mississippi) 234
clean shoplifting 308
Clear, T. R. 63
Clerkin, R. 204
Cleveland 83, 85–87
Cleveland Police Department 87
closed-circuit television (CCTV) 219–221
Cloward, R. 254
Coats v. Dish Network (2013) 205
college education and policing 35, 145–147, 154
Commission for Environmental Cooperation (CEC) 289–290, 292
communication of police 12, 16–20, 48, 68, 76, 186, 192, 199, 201, 223; *see also* social media use by police
community-based policing (CBP) 121–125, 132
community corrections 56
community justice, defining 56
community justice initiatives in China: background information 56–57; composition of floating population as perceived by police 60; crimes committed by and against floating population 61; criminal justice and floating population and 57–59; impact of 62–63; interviews of police and 59; police assessment of community perception of floating population 60–61; police perception of floating population 61; police programs for floating population 62; public order offenses and floating population 61
community partnerships 137
community and police behavior 134
community police forums (CPFs) 122, 196, 199, 201
community police officers (CPOs) 122
community policing 121–125
Compare Statistics meetings 197
competency-based management (CBM) 148–150
competency-based performance management 143, 147–150
compliance with consent decrees 88
CompStat 128, 133
Conference of the Parties (CoP) 289
consent decrees: assessments/evaluations of 88–91; auditing system and 93–94; background information 83–85; in Baltimore 86; challenges of 87–88; civil rights and 84; in Cleveland 83, 85–87; coercive nature of 91–92; compliance with 88; conclusions 91–94; curtailing use of 84; federal 83–84, 86; in Ferguson (Missouri) 86–87; first 85; in future 92; implementation of 87–88; issues addressed in 85–86; limitations of 92; in Los Angeles 89–91; in New Orleans

85, 87; in New York City 84; in Oakland 88; in Pittsburgh 85; police departments issuing 85–86; reform of police and 83, 85, 91–92; requirements of 84–85; in Seattle 87; success in fulfilling 93; Trump administration and 83; view of 83
Convention for International Trade in Endangered Species of Wild Fauna and Flora (CITES) 288–291, 297
Coping Response Inventory 178
Coping Responses Inventory-Adult Form (CRI-Adult) 178
coping styles 175–176, 179–180, *179*, **180**
Coppolo, G. 236
corruption of police: background information 161; conclusions 170–171; COVID-19 pandemic and 161; data sources 162–163; defining 162; identifying 162; intent to commit corruption and 163, 166; problem 161–162; in South Africa 195; supervision in controlling 170; in United States 161–162; *see also* theory of planned behavior (TPB)
Corruption Watch's Analysis of Corruption Trends (ACT) report 195
Corso, J. J. 312
Corzine, J. 244
COVID-19 pandemic 161, 191–193, 308
Crane, James 106–107
Crang, M. A. 57
crime *see specific type*
crime control model in criminal justice system 128
criminalization approach 243–244
criminal justice and floating population in China 57–59
Criminal Procedure Law of New York State 131
Critchley, T. A. 44
culture of police 79, 87–88, 93, 122, 130, 134–135, 137–138, 185
cybercrime: in Australia 218–220, 222, 224–225; challenges to fighting 218–219; closed-circuit television and 219–221; conclusions 225; defining 217–218; equilibrium in, finding 222–223; governmental guidelines and 224; growth of 217; human rights and 222–223; metadata retention in telecommunications and 219–220; police role in 218–219; privacy issues and 222–223; private sector's help with 219–222, 224–225; Productivity Commission's Data Availability and Use Inquiry report and 224–225; range of 218; requirements for moving forward and 223–225; rules in preventing surveillance society and 224; technology/innovation and, determining desired 223–224

Daniels v. City of New York 129
Davis, Kevin 211
Dear, Robert Lewis 267
De Camargo, C. R. 49
Defining Issues Test 2 178
defunding of police 131, 138, 161
Deleuze, G. 113

322 Index

democratic rights and policing 128
Democrats 132
Department of Children and Families (DCF)
   (Florida) 248
Department of Juvenile Justice (DJJ) (Florida)
   248–249
DeSanto, J. 281
detention and discretionary power of police 102
De Vries, I. D. 197
Diallo, Amadou 129
Diamond, Justine 46
Dick, G. P. 5
Dinkins, David 132
discretionary power of police: accountability
   of police and 99, 106–108; arrest 101–102;
   background information 97–98; concerns about
   103; conclusions 108; consistency standards
   for 108; controlled 99; ethics of police and
   106; force and, use of 104–106, 108; Kleinig's
   understanding of 100–101; law and 99–100;
   methodology 98; *Miranda* rule and 103; overview
   97; parameters of 100; power and 99; problem
   statement 98; questioning suspect 103; Rawls
   theory of justice and 98; reasonability and
   99, 108; recommendations 108; seizure and
   detention 102; sources of 101–103; surveillance
   of police officers and 8; theoretical framework
   98–99
distracted driving: in Arizona 273–274; cell phone
   bans and 273–274; conclusions from case study
   in Mesa 283–284; data analysis from case study
   in Mesa 279–283, *280*, *281*, **281**, **282**, **283**;
   data from case study in Mesa 276–277; by day
   of the week 279, *282*, **282**; Distracted Driving
   Education Act and 273; failed bills in Arizona
   275; fines and *274*, 280–281; future research
   on 284; government's responsibility in keeping
   citizens safe and 271–272; handheld devices
   ban and 273–274; harm from 271, 272–273;
   identifiers 279, **281**; incidents 277–279, *280*;
   Kubert v. Best and 282–283; literature review
   272–273; in Missouri 273; opposing arguments
   276; rationale for studying 270–277; state laws
   274; texting ban and 273–275, *274*; by time of
   day 279, *281*, **283**
Distracted Driving Education Act (2017) 273
DNA evidence 311
domestic terrorism *see* abortion provider
   attacks
Dowling, S. 217–218
driving while black 130
drug use policy in hiring police *see* marijuana
   policies on hiring municipal police; Mesa Police
   Department hiring protocols
dualities/dualisms in police workplace:
   communication in distress 16–18; conclusions
   18; defining 12; support, accessing and
   perceptions of 12–16
due process model in criminal justice system 128

due process rights 132
Dutton, H. 274

Eakins, K. 230
East Pakistan Awami League 116–117
Edlins, M. 67
education and policing 35, 145–147, 153–155
Elephant Action League 296
emotion-focused coping style 176
employee retail theft 303–304
Employment Assistance Program (EAP) 13
endangered species 288; *see also* wildlife
   enforcement
Endangered Species Act (1973) 290
Environment Canada 290
Eterno, J. A. 135
ethics of police 106, 176–177; *see also* moral
   reasoning
Europe/European Union 223, 291
European Court of Justice 223
Evans, R. *39*, 48
evidence of crime 9, 97, 102–103, 193, 311; *see also*
   footwear impression evidence
evidence-based management approach 143
extremism 253, 255–257

Facebook 67, 222; *see also* social media use by
   police
fairness equilibria of Rabin 26–31, *29*, 33–34
Falcone, D. N. 68
Farlam Commission of Inquiry 195
Farmer, C. *39*, 48
Farook, Syed Rizwan 234
Farrell, Amy 245
FA/UA 249–250
Fay, J. J. 192
Federal Bureau of Investigation (FBI) 205,
   253–254, 258, 265, 301, 307
Federal Firearms Act (FFA) (1938) 230–231
Feldman, S. 116
Ferguson (Missouri) 86–87
field training of police officers 136
Fifth World Conference (2003) 271
fingerprint evidence 311
Finney, Joan 259
firearm laws: Brady Handgun Violence Prevention
   Act 231–232; in Canada 239; Federal Firearms
   Act 230–231; Gun Control Act 230–231; local
   232; in Mexico 238–239; National Firearms Act
   229–230; National Prohibition Act (Volstead
   Act) 229; state 232; Sullivan Act 228–229; *see
   also* gunrunning
firearms trafficking, illegal *see* gunrunning
Fitzpatrick, L. 292
Fivaz, George 196
floating population (*Liudongrenkou*) in China:
   community justice initiatives and 56–57, 62–63;
   composition of as perceived by police 60; crimes
   committed by and against 61; criminal justice

and 57–59; defining 57; impact of community justice initiatives and 62–63; police assessment of community perception of 60–61; police perception of 61; police programs for 62; public order offenses and 61
Florida 134
Florida Abolitionist (FA) 246–249
Florida Police Stress Project (FPSP) 178
Floyd case 130–131
Floyd, George 43–44, 47, 130, 138
Floy v. City of New York (2013) 129–130
footprints *see* footwear impression evidence
footwear impression evidence: background information 311; case study 312–315, *314*, 316, 317, *318*; considerations 315–317; database 312; literature review 312
force, use of 104–106, 108, 111–113, 119; *see also* minimum force doctrine
forcible stops 128–129, 131, 137
Ford, R. 218
fourth Industrial Revolution (4IR) 191–192
Fox News 237
Freedom of Access to Clinic Entrances Act (1994) 260
Freedom Fund 243
Freedom of Information Act (FOIA) 137
Freudenberg, N. 270, 284
Fulston, Nola 262
Furlong, S. 279
Fyfe, J. J. 43

Gage, B. 271
Games-Howell posthoc statistics 73, **73**, **74**, 75
gangster violence 229, 234
Garner, Eric 130, 132
Gathering Regulations 195
Gecas, V. 175
General Law of Ecological Equilibrium and Environmental Protection (LGEEPA) 290
General Wildlife Law (LGVS) 290
Geographic Information Systems (GIS) 278–279, 283
Gerber, J. 56
Gilbert, Christin 262
Giuliani, Rudolph 132
Gliklich, E. 271–272
Global Fund to End Slavery 243
Goldstone Commission 195
Golembiewski, ? 175
Goluboff, Risa 104
Google 242
Gordon, S. 218
Gould, W. 119
Grabosky, P. 198, 217
grand jury investigation of WHCS (2006) 262
Gray, Freddie 86
Great Britain *see* United Kingdom
Greater Orlando Human Trafficking Task Force (GOHTTF) 244, 247, 249–250

Greenfield, G. 176
Greggo, A. 304
Grier, K. 176
Griffin, Michael F. 258, 263
Groeneveld, Richard F. 99–100
Guattari, F. 113
gun auctions 235–236
Gun Control Act (1968) 230–231
Gunn, David 258, 263
gunrunning: auctions and 235–236; background information 228; Canada's situation and 239; Chicago-Mississippi Delta pipeline 234; conclusions 239–240; crossborder 239; defining 232–233; gun shows and 235; laws governing firearms and 228–232; Mexico's situation and 238–239; seizure and 239; straw man purchase and 233–235; theft of legal firearms and 236–238
gun show exception 235
gun shows 235
Guo, R. 271
Gwynn, C. W. 116

Haberfeld, M. R. 167
Hadrick, R. 281
Hammontree, Monty L. 176
Hansen-Bundy, B. 271
Hart, P. 176
Harvard Kennedy School of Government survey of Angelenos 91
Harver, W. E. 167
Hasina, Sheikh 112
Haynes v. US (1968) 231
Heald, S. 125
Heiss, A. 250
Hemmens, C. 101, 103
Hendy, R. 48–50
Hernandez, F. 206
Hilderbrand, D. 312
Hill, Paul Jennings 257–261
Hindu-Muslim difference 114–116
Hirby, James 105
hiring police officers 35, 134–135, 204; *see also* Canadian police hiring standards; Mesa Police Department hiring protocols
Hirschfield, P. J. 43
Hirsh, Michael 263
Hoffman, B. 254–255
Hoque, Shahidul 121
Huff-Corzine, L. 244
Hukou system in China 57–59
human resource management 143, 146–151, 153–155; *see also* hiring police officers
human rights 222–223
human trafficking: arrests of human traffickers and 243–244; background information 242–243; in Central Florida 242, 246–250; Central Florida organizations fighting, emergence of 247–249; criminalization approach to 243–244; Greater Orlando Human Trafficking Task Force and

244, 247, 249–250; human trafficking task force and 244, 246, 250; implications of Central Florida model and 250; international laws against 242; Polaris Project and 242–243, 245, 247; prosecution of human traffickers 243–245; scope of 244–245; Stockholm syndrome and 245; *US v. Tecum* and 242; victim-centered approach to 244, 246; victims 245–247
human trafficking task force (HTTF) 244, 246, 250
Hu, X. 68

I247 chat communication tool 293
illicit wildlife trade (IWT) 287; *see also* wildlife enforcement
Independence Movement 116
Independent Police Investigative Directorate (IPID) report (2018/19) 198
India 115
Indian Civil Service (ICS) 116
Indonesia 101
Innes, G. 175
Insurance Institute for Highway Safety, Highway Loss and Data Institute 283–284
integrity of police 90, 161, 204
interdisciplinary approach 294
inter-governmental organizations (IGOs) 287; *see also specific name*
International Association of Chiefs of Police survey (2016) 67
International Consortium on Combating Wildlife Crime (ICCWC) 293
International Criminal Police Organization (INTERPOL) 289, 293–295, 297
International Criminal Tribunal 119–120
Ireland 45–46
Irish Free State 45
Irving, B. L. 175
ISO31000 risk management model 192
Ivković, S. K. 167

Jacobs, J. 228
Jaeger, K. 207
Jamaat-ul-Mujahideen (JMB) party 112
James, Latisha 131
Jefferson, Burtell 3
Jernigan, C. 290
Jiao, Allan Y. *83*
Johnston, Les 199
Jones, T. R. 250
Jordi, Stephen 257
Joyner, C. 234
jury box concept 256, 262–263, 265–266

Kane 123
Kansas Department of Health and Environment (KDHE) 258
Kansas for Life 262
Kasiviswanathan, H. 312
Kehoe, Andrew 255

Kelley, J. G. 250
Kelley, Patrick F. 259
Kelly, Raymond 128–129
Kennison, P. 49
Khan, Asaduzzaman 112
Kim, B. 56
Kimiecik, R. C. 305, 307
King, Rodney 89
Kleinig, John 100–101
Kline, Phillip D. (Phil) 262, 266
Klockars, C. B. 162–163, 167
Klokars, C. 204
Knapp Commission 130
Knutsson, J. 48
Kohan, A. 176
Kopel, D. 238
Kovath, Jean 106
Kraft, Mark 232–233, 236, 279
Kravchuk, R. 204
Kresevich, M. 304
Kubert v. Best 282–283

Lacey Act 290
Laguna, Louis 106
Landman, K. 194
Landrieu, Mitch 87
Langton, L. 236–237
Lares, Tomas 247, 249
Law Center to Prevent Gun Violence 233
Law for Endangered Species Protection (1994) 290
Law Enforcement Management Information System (LEMIS) 291
law and police behavior 131
Lefler, D. 258
legal approach 208, 210
legitimacy of police: accountability of police and 107; Bangladesh National Police and 113–114, 123–125; community-based policing and 125; effective policing and 43, 50; minimum force doctrine and 44, 46, 50; police-citizen encounters and 24
Lentz, S. A. 40–41
Leuprecht, C. 145
Lewis, I. 272
Li, B. 59
Liberation War 116–117, 119
Lieberman, J. D. 67, 71
Liebermann, S. 194
Lipset, S. 255
litigaphobia 8
Liu, J. 60–61
local areas of command (LACs) 3, 15
London Metropolitan Police 41, 312
Loo, Robert 175
Los Angeles 89–91
Los Angeles Police Department (LAPD) 89–91
Lutze, F. E. 250
Lynch, Patrick 133
Lynxwiler, J. 254

MacDonald, R. R. 175
Magers, J. 211
Malik, Tashfeen 234
managerial approach 208–209
Mannon, Stephanie 106
Manokha, I. 222
mapping with GIS 278–279, *278*, 283
Marcell, Ke'Arre 267
marijuana policies on hiring municipal police: arguments for barring marijuana use 205; background information 204–205; conclusions 211–212; policy 205–211; *see also* Mesa Police Department hiring protocols
Marikana strike 195
Markovsky, Jennifer 267
Marquez, Enrique Jr. 234–235
Marshall, J. R. 186
Mascarenhas, Anthony 117
Maslach Burnout Inventory (MBI) 175, 178
material payoff 27–28, 33, 35n16, 36n26
Mayne, Richard 40–42
Mazmanian, D. 176
Mazzett, M. 205
McBride, James 246
McGuire, M. 217–218
McNiffe, L. 45
media and police 66, 132; *see also* social media use by police
medical evaluation for police officers 135
Meijer, A. 68
Menard, S. 254
Menezes, Jean Charles de 46
mens rea (guilty mind/intention) 166
Mergel, I. 68
Merton, R. 254, 255, 267
Mesa distracted driving case study: conclusions 283–284; data analysis 279–283, *280*, *281*, **281**, **282**, **283**; data from 276–277; day of week and 279, *282*, **282**; failed bills regarding distracted driving and *275*; incidents 277–279; texting ban and 275–276; time of day and 279, *281*, **283**
Mesa Police Department hiring protocols: actors in drug use policy change 207; conclusions about drug use policy change 211–212; impetus for drug use policy change 206–207; issues addressed by drug use policy changes 206–207; legal approach to drug use policy 208, 210; managerial approach to drug use policy 208–209; New Public Management and 208–209; policy on marijuana use and 205–211; political approach to drug use policy 208–210; previous efforts in addressing drug use 207; recommendations from literature 210–211
metadata retention in telecommunications 219–220
Metropolitan Act in London (1829) 144
Metropolitan Bureau of Investigation (MBI) 246
Mexican Constitution 238
Mexico 238–239, 288–291, 293

minimum force doctrine: arming police and 47–50; background information 39; development of 41–44; effects of, need to quantify and monitor 50; framing 41–44; legitimacy of police and 44, 46, 50; operationalization of 46–47; overview 39–40; peace and, question about 44–46; Peel's Principles and 40–46, 50; in South Africa 195
Minnesota Multiphasic Personality inventory 167
Miranda rule (Free and Voluntary rule) 103, 129
Miranda v. Arizona 103
Missouri 273
MMPI-2 K-scale 105–106
Mohan, D. 271–272
Mollen Commission 130, 134
Montesh, M. 194
Montreal Declaration (2003) 271
Moodie, E. 175
Morales, James Walker 237
moral reasoning 176–177, 179–180, *179*, **180**; *see also* ethics of police
Morison, K. 204
Morrison, Paul J. 262
Mummolo, J. 50
Munzenrider, ? 175
Mutiny of 1857 (First War of Independence) 115
mutual legal assistance treaties (MLATs) 289

Nash equilibrium 26, 29–30, 35n10
National Abortion Federation 253
National Association for Shoplifting Prevention 302
National Conference of State Legislatures (NCSL) 273
National Crime Information Center 107
National Firearms Act (NFA) (1934) 229–230
National Human Trafficking Hotline 242
National Instant Criminal Background System (NICS) 231–232
National Prohibition Act (Volstead Act) 229
necessity defense 253, 263
Nelson, W. R. 33
Nesby, Eddie 234
Neuhaus, Ann Kristin 263
New Orleans 85, 87
New Orleans Police Department (NOPD) 85, 128–129, 131, 133, 137
New Police 40–41, 43–45
New Public Management (NPM) 3, 208–209
New South Wales Police Force (NSWPF) study: conclusions 18–20; dualities/dualisms in workplace and 12–18; Employment Assistance Program and 13; general public and 11–12; local area commands and 3, 15; Ombudsman and 9–11; overview 3; Police Services Act and 9, 11; PTSD diagnosis and 13–14; Review of Injury Management Practices and 12; sample in 3, **4**; staff turnover 6–8; surveillance of officers and 3, 8–12, 18–19; trust and 3–8, 18

New York City Police Department (NYPD):
aggressive style of 128; CompStat and 133;
consent decrees and 84; lost property complaints
and, refusal to release number of 137; *Patrol
Guide* and 132
New York Civil Liberties Union 129
New Zealand 49
Ngoepe Commission 195
Nice, D. 256
Nijhar, P. 56
Nimegeers, K. 272
non-governmental organizations (NGOs) 244, 249,
287; *see also specific name*
nonrational shoplifters 304–305
Noor, Mohammed 46
North American Agreement on Environmental
Cooperation 290, 292
North American Wildlife Enforcement Group
(NAWEG) 289, 292–293
Northern Ireland 45
Nurse, A. 287–288, 290
NZ Police Association (NZPA) 49

Oakland 88
Obama, Barack 267, 291
O'Connor, C. D. 79
Office of Management and Budget (OMB) 70
Ohlin, L. 254
Olympics bombing (1996) 261
Ombudsman 9–11
Ontario Police Services Act (2017) 146
open-up policy of China 57
Operation Bruin 296–297
Operation Rescue 259, 262
Operation Searchlight 116
Operation Thunderbolt 112
organized crime: retail theft 306–308; wildlife
293–295
Orlando Police Department 249
Osse, A. 48
outsole patterns *see* footwear impression evidence

Packer, Herbert 128–129
Papazoglou, Konstantinos 106
Parks, Bernard 89
Patriot Act legislation (US) 153
Patrol Guide 132
Patrolmen's Benevolent Association 133
Patterson, C. 199, 230
Pearson, C. 239
Peele, T. 237
Peel, Sir Robert 40–41, 144–145, 191
Peel's Principles 40–46, 50
Pereira, Joseph 106
PERF (Police Executive Research Forum) report
(2013) 86
performance management 93–94, 128–129, 143,
147–152, 155
Perry, Rick 276

Petralia, S. 186
physical protection systems 194–195
physical tests for police officers 135
physical training of police officers 136
Pichai, Sundar 242
Pierce, G. 232
Pittsburgh 85
Planned Parenthood clinic (Colorado Springs)
shooting 267
poaching 296–297; *see also* wildlife enforcement
Polanco, Adil 133
Polaris Project 242–243, 245, 247
Police Act (1861) 115
Police Act (2007) 124
police-citizen encounters: aggression in 22–23;
background information 22–23; citizen-
citizen encounters versus 23; conclusions
33–34; dilemma in 24–26, 31; expectations
of, coordination of 30, 31, 33–34; fairness
equilibria of Rabin and 26–31, *29*, 33–34; game
theoretical construction of 24–26, *26*, 34, 35n6;
German police officer's stabbing and 22, 32,
35nn1–3, 35n5; implications for improvement
30–32; legitimacy of police and 24; limitations in
improving 32–33; material payoff and 27–28, 33,
35n8, 35n16, 36n26; nature of 23–24
Police Reform Programme (PRP) 120–121, 124
Police Sector Council 149
Police Services Act (2003) 9, 11
police shootings of civilians 46–47, 83
Police Stress Survey 178
political approach 208–210
politics and police behavior/policing 111–113, 132
Pollock, E. 199
post-secondary education and policing 35,
145–147, 154
post-traumatic stress disorder (PTSD) 13–14, 186
Potter, K. 228
power 99; *see also* discretionary power of police
Power, K. G. 175
precise, notion of 27
President's Task Force on 21st Century Policing
(2015) 66
pressures on police 6, 9, 104, 131, 133, 136, 176,
179–180, **180**, **181**, 185–186
prima facie evidence 97
principles, policing 40–46, 50
Printz v. United States (1997) 231
prisoner's dilemma 31, 35n11, 36n26
privacy issues and cybercrime 222–223
private sector's help with cybercrime 219–222,
224–225
problem-solving coping styles 176
pro-choice movement 265
Productivity Commission's Data Availability and
Use Inquiry Report 224–225
Proposition 47 308
prostitution 246; *see also* human trafficking
psychological contract 4

psychological tests for police officers 135
public understanding of police behavior: background information 128–131; community and 134; conversations to improve 136–137; culture of police and 134; hiring police and 134–135; influences on behavior and 131–134; law and 131; media and 132; moving forward and 136–138; politics and 132; pressures of policing and 136; supervisors and 132–133; training police and 136; transparency and 137; unions and 133; whistleblowers and 133

questioning suspect and discretionary power of police 103

Rabb, E. 255
Rabin, M. 26–31, 33–34
Rados, R. 244
Rafacz, S. D. 307
Rafiqul, M. 119
Rahman, Ziaur 117
Raja, T. 271
Rampart scandal 89
Rapid Action Battalion (RAB) 119
rational choice theory (RCT) 279–280
rational shoplifters 304–305
Rawls, John 98
Rawls theory of justice 98
Reagan, Ronald 231
reasonability 99, 108
recidivism/recidivist offenders 194, 288
reform of police 83, 85, 91–92, 120–121, 124
Reid, ? 196
Reith, Charles 40, 42, 44–45, 47, 50
religion and police behavior 134
Republicans 132
Resolution Seven 197
retail shrinkage 301–302
retail theft: ALERT system and 307–308; booster boxes and 305; booster coats and 305; clean shoplifting 308; defining 301; by distraction 305; external (shoplifting) 301, 304–306; future of 308; goods targeted in 301–302; internal (employee) 301, 303–304; legislation 307; loss prevention partnerships and 308; moving forward 308–309; nonrational shoplifters and 305; organized 301, 306–308; police and 302, 308; preventing 303–304, 306–308; Proposition 47 and 308; rational shoplifters and 304–305; scope of 301–303
Review of Injury Management Practices 12
Rice, Kathleen M. 273
Rice, Sylvester 234
Rice, Tamir 83
RICO Act 260
Riley, K. J. 254–255
Risen, J. 259
Rodriguez, Ana 242
Roeder, Lindsey 265

Roeder, Scott 257, 260, 263–266
Roe v. Wade (1973) 253, 256–257
Rosenberg, M. 205
Rosenbloom, D. 204, 208–210
Rowan, Charles 40–42
Royal Canadian Mounted Police (RCMP) 289
Royal Irish Constabulary (RIC) 45
Rozario, M. 272
Rudolph, Eric R. 257, 261–262
rural migrant workers (*nongmingong*) in China 57
rural policing 68–69
Rushin, S. 88
Russell, Timothy 83
Rydberg, J. 144

Sacra, S. A. 244
Safe Harbor agreement 223
safety/security in South Africa: apartheid-era policing reform and 197; Area Crime Combating Units and 195; Back to Basics approach and 198; background information 191–193; challenges confronting 198–200; Cillié Commission and 195; Compare Statistics meetings and 197; conclusions 201; COVID-19 pandemic and 191–193; design of study 193; Farlam Commission of Inquiry and 195; Gathering Regulations and 195; Goldstone Commission and 195; individual security measures and 194–195; Ngoepe Commission and 195; physical protection systems and 194–195; police leadership since 1995 and 196–198; recidivist offenders and 194; recommendations 200–201; Resolution Seven and 197; South African Police Service and 193, 195–201; status quo of 193–196; victim surveys and 194
Samborn, Randall 234
Sarre, R. 48
Schaible, L. 175
Scheindlin, Shira 84
Schelling, T. C. 30–31
Schoolcraft, Adrian 133
Schrems v. The Data Protection Commissioner and Digital Rights Ireland Ltd. (2014) 223
Seattle 87
Second Amendment 228, 232
seizure and discretionary power of police 102
Seldon, A. 196
Selebi, Jackie 196–197
Seron, Carroll 106
Serpico, Frank 133
Serrano, R. 239
sex trafficking *see* human trafficking
Shahjahan, A.S.M. 120
Shannon, Rachelle (Shelley) 257, 259–260
Shearing, C. 198
Shen, H. 211
Shepard, R. L. 130
shoplifting 304–306
Shor, Y. 316

328   Index

Simon, D. 43
Singular, S. 264–265
Six, Stephen N. 263
Sixth World Conference on Injury Prevention and Control (2002) 271
Skogan, W. G. 23
Skolnick, J. H. 43
smart phone bans 273–274
social media use by police: background information 210; conclusions 79–80; data 69; departmental analysis 72–75, **73**, **74**; departmental characteristics 70–71; department classification by size 69–70, **70**; findings 76–78; forms of 66; future research 79; Games-Howell posthoc statistics 73, **73**, **74**, 75; limitations in understanding 78–79; post analysis 75–76, **77**; post characteristics 71, **72**; public use of social media and 67; purposes for 67–68; research questions 69; rural policing and 68–69
social movements against police brutality 137; *see also specific movement*
Solaiman, S. M. 119
South Africa 191–193, 195, 197; *see also* safety/security in South Africa
South African Police Service (SAPS) 193, 195–201
Species at Risk Act (2002) 290
Spielberger, C. 176
Spitz, Donald 257, 266
Spivak, Gayatri Chakravorty 113–114
Squires, P. 49
Srihari, S. N. 312
staff turnover 6–8
State Police of the Republic of Indonesia 101
Statham, Julius 234
Statistics Canada 147
stealing *see* retail theft
Stenning, P. 43
Stewart, S. 266–267
Stockholm syndrome 245
stop and frisk 128–129, 131, 137
stop, question and frisk 128–129, 131, 137
straw man purchase 233–235
stress of police: background information 174; burnout and 175, 179–180, *179*, **181**; conceptual framework/model 178, *179*, 181–183, **182**, *183*, **183**; conclusions 184–186; coping styles and 175–176, 179–180, *179*, **180**; future research 187; Hart's study on 176; hypotheses 178–179, 184–186; implications for policymakers 186–187; literature review 174–177; measures 178; mediation analysis 183–184; moral reasoning and 176–177, 179–180, *179*, **180**; Tamil Nadu Police as population for study 177; post-traumatic stress disorder and 186; subjects of study 177
Strider, E. 281
structural equation model (SEM) 181–183, **182**, *183*, **183**
Strype, J. 48

subculture of police 87–88, 185
Sugden, R. 31
Sullivan Act (1911) 228–229
Sullivan, Daniel ("Big Tim") 229
"Summer of Mercy" 259
sungusungu movement in Tanzania 124–125
supervision and policing 132–133, 170
support for police, accessing and perceptions of 12–16
surveillance capitalism 222
surveillance of police officers: conclusions 18–19; discretionary power of police and 8; general public and 11–12; issue of 8; Ombudsman and 9–11; other police officers and 8–9
surveillance society 224
Swansey, Garrett 267
Sweden 50
Sykes, R. E. 23

tactics of police, changing 137
Tamil Nadu Police *see* stress of police
Tang, Thomas Li-Ping 176
Tang, Y. 312
Tanzania 124–125
Tarm, M. 237–238
Taylor, Breonna 46–47
Taylor, D. N. 44
Telecommunications (Interception and Access) Amendment (Data Retention) Act (2015) 220
telecommunications, metadata retention in 219–220
Tennessee State Data Center 70
Tenth Amendment 231
Terrill, W. 144
terrorism 253–255, 266–267; *see also* abortion provider attacks
Terry, Randall 259
Terry v. Ohio (1968) 131
testilying 130
Texas 274–275
texting bans 273–275, *274*
Thaens, M. 68
theft, legal firearms 236; *see also* retail theft
theory of planned behavior (TPB): attitude toward behavior and 164–165, *164*, 167, *167*; behavioral controls and *164*, 165, 167–168, *167*; corruption of police and, application to 166–168, *167*, 171; departmental behavioral controls and 170; departmental subjective norms and 169–170; describing 163, *164*; determinants in 164–165, *164*; law enforcement and, application to 165–166; policy implications of 168; pre-employment screen and 168–169; subjective norms and *164*, 165, 167, *167*; value of 166, 171
Thomas, C. 305, 307
Thomas, L. 176
three-box operational sub-theory of extremist groups: ballot box 255–257; cartridge box

256–264; describing 255–256; jury box 256, 262–263, 265–266
Thunder series wildlife operations 293
Tice, S. 292
Tiller, George 253, 257–260, 262–266
Tolliver, Ricardo 239
Toronto Police Department 68
totoaba fish bladders, trafficking 295–296
trafficking *see* human trafficking; wildlife enforcement
Trafficking Victims Protection Act (TVPA) 242–243
training police officers 136
transdisciplinary approach 294
Transparency International (TI) Corruption Perceptions Index 112
transparency of police 68, 86, 90, 137, 210, 293, 298
Tremblay, M. C. 289
Trump administration 83
Trump, Donald 133
trust and policing 3–6, 12–13, 18–19, 24, 107, 137, 156, 208
Turnbull, Malcolm 219, 222
turnover of police officers 6–8
Twersky-Glasner, Aviva 105–106

UA Training Center 250
Uddin, S. 115
unarmed police 44–46
unions and police behavior 133
United Kingdom: arming police and 49; Bangladesh colonial rule by 114–116; footwear impression database in 312; London Metropolitan Police 41, 312; Metropolitan Act in 144; New Police 40–41, 43–45
United Nations 118
United Nations Office on Drugs and Crime (UNODC) report 297
United States: abortion in 253, 258, 267; corruption of police in 161–162; human trafficking task force in 244; law enforcement officers in 161; Patriot Act legislation in 153; Second Amendment and 228, 232; tension between freedom and order in 104; Tenth Amendment 231; wildlife enforcement in 288–291, 293; *see also specific name of agency, city, state, police department*
Universal Declaration of Human Rights (1948) 223
University of Central Florida 250
USA v. Martin (2013) 296–297
US Census Bureau 70
US Constitution 104, 136, 138, 228, 231–232
US Department of Health and Human Services 272
US Department of Homeland Security 243
US Department of Justice (DOJ) 84–88, 90–92, 153, 233, 307
US District Court for Eastern District of Louisiana 85
US Fish and Wildlife Service 289–290, 291

US National Highway Traffic Safety Administration (NHTSA) 272
US State Department's Overseas Advisory Council 111
US v. Tecum 242

vagrant laws 104
Van Heerden, T. J. 200
Van Maanen, J. 24, 32
Van Schendel, W. 115
vaquita fish 295–296
Varma, A. 271
Veer, P. van der 114
Vena, J. E. 186
victim-centered approach 244, 246
victim surveys 194
Violanti, J. M. 186, 205
Violence Against Women Act (2000) 242
Violent Crime Control and Law Enforcement Act (1994) 84
Virginia Tech Transportation Institute 272
Vollmer, August 145
Volstead Act (National Prohibition Act) 229

Waldren, M. 49
Walker, Jeffrey T. 101, 103
Walker, L. G. 175
Walker, Samuel 107
Washington, DC Metropolitan Police Department 68
Watson, R. 294
Wei, Jinsheng 57
Weisheit, R. A. 68
Weisner, S 316
Welch test 72–74
well-being among police: background information 3; conclusions 18–20; dualities/dualisms in workplace and 12–18; general public and 11–12; New South Wales Police Force study and 3; psychological contract and 4; staff turnover and 6–8; surveillance and 8–12; trust and 3–6
Wells, E. 68
Westberry, L. G. 176
whistleblowers 133
White, K. 272
White, R. 294
Wichita Police Department 237
Wilbert, Warren 265
Wild Animal and Plant Protection and Regulation of International and Interprovincial Trade Act (WAPPRIITA) (1992) 290
Wildlife Crime Working Group (WCWG) 289, 293–295, 297
wildlife enforcement: background information 287; in Canada 288–291, 293; challenges, common 287–288, 297; citizen submission function 292; Commission for Environmental Cooperation and 289–290, 292; conclusions 298; Convention for International Trade in

Endangered Species of Wild Fauna and Flora and 288–291, 297; cooperation among Canada, Mexico, and US 290–291, 298; in European Union 291; interdisciplinary approach to 294; International Criminal Police Organization (INTERPOL) 289, 293–295, 297; mechanisms, international and regional 288–289; in Mexico 288–290, 293; mutual legal assistance treaties 289; North American Agreement on Environmental Cooperation 290, 292; North American Wildlife Enforcement Group and 289, 292–293; Operation Bruin and 296–297; organized wildlife crime and 293–295; poaching 296–297; regional cases 295–297; Thunder series and 293; trafficking of totoaba fish bladders and 295–296; transdisciplinary approach to 294; United Nations Office on Drugs and Crime world wildlife crime report and 297; in United States 288–291, 293; Wildlife Crime Working Group 289, 293–295, 297; wildlife enforcement networks and 289–290, 297

wildlife enforcement networks (WENS) 289–290, 297

Wilhelm, T. 239

Willemsen, M. 294

Williams, C. 186

Williams, C. B. 67–68, 79

Williams, Kristian 104

Williams, Malissa 83

Wilson, H. 229–231

Wilson, James Q. 128

Wilson, M. 254

Wintemute, G. 232

Witkin, G. 237

Women's Health Care Services clinic 258–259

Woods, J. B. 47

Worden, R. E. 130

workplace dualities/dualisms *see* dualities/dualisms in workplace

World Health Organisation 194

World Population Review 277

Wyatt, T. 294

Zafarullah, H. 116

Zamarrón, I. Z. 31

Zhang, J. 57

Zhang, K. H. 58

Zhang, S. 58

Zuckerberg, Mark 222

Printed in the United States
by Baker & Taylor Publisher Services